ORDER OF BATTLE OF THE UNITED STATES LAND FORCES IN THE WORLD WAR

Zone of the Interior: Directory of Troops

Volume 3, Part 3

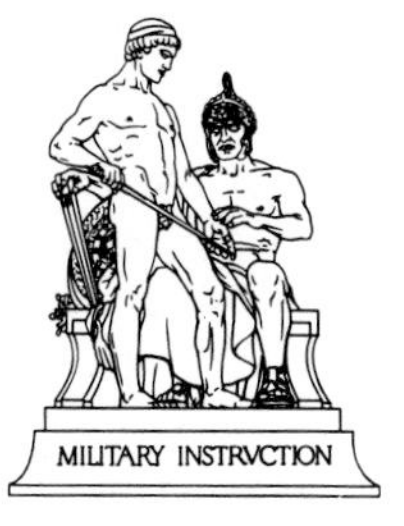

CENTER OF MILITARY HISTORY
UNITED STATES ARMY
WASHINGTON, D.C., 1988

Library of Congress Cataloging-in-Publication Data

Order of battle of the United States land forces in the World War.

Reprint. Originally published: Washington: U.S. G.P.O., 1931-1949.
Contents: v. 1. American Expeditionary Forces: General Headquarters, armies, Army Corps, services of supply, and separate forces—v. 2. American Expeditionary Forces: divisions—v. 3. Zone of the interior. pt. 1. Organization and activities of the War Department. pt. 2. Territorial departments, tactical divisions organized in 1918, and posts, camps, and stations. pt. 3. Directory of troops.
Supt. of Docs. no.: D114.2:B32
1. United States. Army—History—World War, 1914-1918. I. Center of Military History.
D570.073 1987 940.4′12′73 87-600306

Facsimile Reprint

First Printed 1949—CMH Pub 23-5

For sale by the Superintendent of Documents, U.S. Government Printing Office
Washington, D.C. 20402

Foreword

The United States entered "the war to end all wars" seventy years ago, but much may still be learned from a study of that vast military and diplomatic experience. Accordingly, the Center of Military History is now bringing back into print a series of volumes on the World War I period. The facsimile reprint of the *Order of Battle of the United States Land Forces in the World War,* in five volumes, provides a logical introduction to the series. It will be followed shortly by a newly formatted edition of the *United States Army in the World War (1917-1919),* a major collection of documents pertaining to the conflict.

The concise and unique data in the *Order of Battle* is central to any serious examination of the Army's involvement in World War I. The Center's predecessors—the Army War College's Historical Section, and the Special Staff's Historical Division—originally published this work in three volumes. The first two concentrated on the American Expeditionary Forces (AEF). Volume 1 covers the AEF's general headquarters; the American Services of Supply; armies; army corps; and separate forces, including the three French army corps under American command in 1918 as well as American units in North Russia and Siberia. Volume 2 provides outline histories of the AEF's divisions. The essays in these two volumes combine information about the command and composition of units with tables that offer the reader a broad survey of operations in both major and minor theaters and the rear areas. Volume 3, consisting of five chapters organized in two parts, presents an array of useful information on the zone of the interior. Part 1 includes the organization and activities of the War Department, the territorial departments, the divisions that did not deploy overseas, and data about posts, camps, and stations. Part 2 consists of a directory of troops, covering all organizations that made up the Army between 1917 and 1919. Each volume begins with a guide to the use of the material.

In publishing this facsimile reprint, the Center has made some formatting changes to assist the modern reader, but the original text is unchanged. Volumes 1 and 2 are reprinted intact. Volume 3, first published in two parts, is now divided into three, in three separate volumes. For the reader's convenience, a new appendix, "Posts, Camps, and Stations

Index," has been added to the new Part 2. The original Part 2, the directory of troops, is now Part 3. The volume's consecutive pagination remains the same. To all volumes the Center has added its own front matter and, after the half-title, incorporated relevant pages of the original introductory material (indicated by brackets around original folios).

Any work that attempts to describe such a vast and complex subject inevitably includes errors of both omission and commission. The *Order of Battle* is no exception. No attempt has been made to correct any errors in the work. For those students who wish to pursue these matters, they will find most of the original source material in the custody of the National Archives and Records Administration. What remains of the original manuscript for the volumes is in the custody of the Center and is available for examination.

In increasing numbers, military historians are coming to realize that the Army's experiences in World War I offer students of the profession of arms a vast classroom in which they might study the many facets of their subject. The *Order of Battle* is not a definitive guide, but it is a fine place to begin any in-depth study of that mighty war.

WILLIAM A. STOFFT
Brigadier General, USA
Chief of Military History

Washington, D.C.
7 August 1987

Contents

Zone of the Interior: Directory of Troops

CHAPTER V

DIRECTORY OF TROOPS

SHOWING

MOBILIZATION, CHANGES IN STATUS, MOVEMENTS, DEMOBILIZATION, AND OTHER DISPOSITION, OF UNITS IN THE ZONE OF THE INTERIOR

INTRODUCTION

The Directory has been prepared with the object of accounting for all troops forming part of the Army in 1917, 1918, and 1919. Included therein are the troop units stationed in the Zone of the Interior, i.e., within the continental limits of the United States and its possessions; and those serving in the American Expeditionary Forces abroad.

ARRANGEMENT OF CHAPTER

Two methods have been employed to treat the several units, viz: (a) All tactical, special, and technical units down to and including independent battalions, as well as independent tactical units of company or similar size are traced through all posts, camps, or stations, from outbreak of war or organization to demobilization or reversion to peace status. Stations occupied for a very brief period only have generally been omitted. Exceptions to this rule are the units of the American Expeditionary Forces, for which no stations are recorded for service overseas; but the period of such service is shown. (b) Special and technical units of company or lesser size are shown in special tables with period of active service, but without indication of posts, camps, or stations where such service was rendered.

Replacement units of a temporary nature, whether tactical or technical, have been omitted.

All troop units have been arranged by categories and subcategories according to the order shown in Unit Index, p. 996.

TREATMENT OF SPECIAL CASES

In some branches, cases will be found where two or more units have the same numerical designation. In order to avoid confusion and properly to identify each of these units, a Roman figure in parentheses has been placed immediately in rear of the numerical designation, thus: 5th (I) Aero Squadron; 5th (II) Aero Squadron.

A good many changes in unit designation occurred within the Air Service and within other categories. All such changes have been carefully accounted for by cross references under column of remarks with a view to following the life of any unit, from the beginning to the end of the war, under its various names. In order to mark successive changes in the designation of a squadron, for instance, there have been entered the letters *a, b,* etc., under each squadron concerned, opposite which is related the history of that particular unit in all its transformations.

To illustrate, in the case of the 2d Reserve Aero Squadron, "*a.* 45th (II) Aero Squadron" denotes that the 2d Reserve Aero Squadron was redesignated as the 45th Aero Squadron, the Roman figure in parentheses indicating that it was the second squadron of this numerical designation, which may be verified by consulting page 1005 where the 45th (1) Aero Squadron is accounted for. The letter *b.* under 2d Reserve Aero Squadron preceding "Squadron A" means that the 45th (II) Aero Squadron was transformed into Squadron A, Gerstner Field, La.

The numerical designation of school squadrons at the various flying fields in the United States was discontinued in the summer of 1918, and replaced by letter designation. Thus, 2d (I) Aero Squadron became Squadron A, Kelly Field. In Nov. 1918, the personnel of the lettered squadrons of each flying field was merged into a so-called Flying School Detachment at such station.

As far as practicable, the next higher tactical organization of which a particular unit formed a part at any time during the war is shown in the column of remarks.

INSTRUCTIONS FOR USE OF TABLES

In order to obtain an outline of the history of any unit, it will be necessary to consult first of all the Unit Index on page 996. Having found the proper page number appearing opposite the particular category in the Index, look for the proper tables in which the unit in question appears in its numerical order.

For instance, in the case of the 91st Aero Squadron (observation), by perusing the various columns from left to right, it will be found that it was organized in Aug. 1917 at Kelly Field, Tex. From there it moved to Garden City, N. Y., in Oct. 1917; left for overseas from the Port of Embarkation of Hoboken during the same month; returned from overseas in June 1919 and took station at Mitchel Field, N. Y.; moved to Park Field, Tenn., in July 1919, and to Rockwell Field, Calif., in Sept 1919; and was stationed at Mather

Field in Oct. 1919. From the column of remarks it will be learned that this squadron was a component of the First Army Observation Group. All such entries in column of remarks, opposite each unit, must be regarded as having general application only and not as referring to any particular date appearing in other columns pertaining to the unit.

In the example of the 74th (I) Aero Squadron, we find that it was organized in Aug. 1917 at Kelly Field, Tex.; that its designation was changed in Sept. 1917 at Kelly Field, Tex., to 74th Aero Squadron (construction); that it moved in Dec. 1917 to Camp Morrison, Va., where its designation was changed, a second time, in Feb. 1918 to 486th Aero Squadron (construction); that it moved to the Port of Embarkation of Hoboken in Mar. 1918, went overseas during the same month, and returned from overseas in June 1919; and that it was demobilized in June 1919 at Mitchel Field, N. Y.

If it be desired to trace the history of any unit while overseas, it will be necessary to consult Volume I or II, or both of the Order of Battle Series, after ascertaining the particular division or higher tactical organization, of which the unit in question formed a part. Inasmuch as only major tactical organizations are described in Volumes I and II, it will generally not be possible to find any individual unit history below brigade organization, but a record of battle participation of any tactical unit can, as a rule, be deduced from the information presented in these volumes.

UNIT INDEX

AIR SERVICE

AERO SQUADRONS

Unit designation and redesignation	Organization		Stations in United States		Overseas		Demobilization		Remarks
	Month and year	Place	Month and year	Place	From—	To—	Month and year	Place	
1st Aero Squadron (observation).	Organized 1913		April 1917	Columbus, N. Mex.					Cmpnt. of I Corps Obsn. Gp.
			August 1917	Ft. Hamilton, N. Y.					
			do	P. of E., Hoboken	August 1917.				
			August 1919	Park Field, Tenn.		August 1919.			
			October 1919	Mitchel Field, N. Y.					Corps troops. Active through 1919.
1st Reserve Aero Squadron.	May 1917	Hazelhurst Field, N. Y.	August 1917	P. of E., Hoboken	August 1917.				
a. 26th Aero Squadron (instruction).	September 1917	A. E. F.				May 1919	June 1919	Mitchel Field, N. Y.	S.O.S. troops.
2d (I) Aero Squadron	July 1917	Ft. Mills, P. I.	November 1917	Kelly Field, Tex.					
a. Squadron "A"	July 1918	Kelly Field, Tex.					November 1918	Kelly Field, Tex.	
2d (II) Aero Squadron	June 1919	Rockwell Field, Calif.	December 1919	Ft. Mills, P. I.					Active through 1919.
2d Reserve Aero Squadron.	July 1917	Chandler Field, Pa.							
a. 45th (II) Aero Squadron.	August 1917	do	November 1917	Gerstner Field, La.					
b. Squadron "A"	July 1918	Gerstner Field, La.					November 1918	Gerstner Field, La.	
3d (I) Aero Squadron	April 1917	Ft. Sam Houston, Tex.	May 1917	Kelly Field, Tex.					
			August 1917	Post Field, Okla.					
a. Squadron "A"	July 1918	Post Field, Okla.					January 1919	Post Field, Okla.	
3d (II) Aero Squadron (observation).	May 1919	Mitchel Field, N. Y.	August 1919	Cp. Stotsenburg, P. I.					Do.
4th (I) Aero Squadron	May 1917	Ft. Sam Houston, Tex.	September 1917	Post Field, Okla.					
a. Squadron "B"	July 1918	Post Field, Okla.					January 1919	Post Field, Okla.	

4th (II) Aero Squadron	June 1919	Hazelhurst Field, N. Y.	November 1919	Mitchel Field, N. Y.					Do.
5th (I) Aero Squadron	May 1917	Kelly Field, Tex	April 1918	Souther Field, Ga.					
a. Squadron "A"	July 1918	Souther Field, Ga.					November 1918	Souther Field, Ga.	
5th (II) Aero Squadron	October 1919	Hazelhurst Field, N. Y.	November 1919	Mitchel Field, N. Y.					Do.
6th Aero Squadron	March 1917	Ft. Kamehameha, T. H.	September 1918	Luke Field, T. H.					
a. 6th Aero Squadron (observation).	October 1919	Luke Field, T. H.							Do.
7th Aero Squadron	March 1917	Corozal, C. Z.	May 1917	Cp. Empire, C. Z.					
			August 1917	Ft. Sherman, C. Z.					
			March 1918	Cristobal, C. Z.					
			May 1918	Coco-Walk, C. Z.					
			August 1918	France Field, C. Z.					Do.
8th Aero Squadron (observation).	June 1917	Kelly Field, Tex	July 1917	Selfridge Field, Mich.					Cmpnt. of IV Corps Obsn. Gp.
			October 1917	Garden City, N. Y.					
			November 1917	P. of E., Hoboken	November 1917.				
			May 1919	Mitchel Field, N. Y.		May 1919.			
			May 1919	Kelly Field, Tex.					
			August 1919	Airdrome, McAllen, Tex.					Corps troops. Active through 1919.
9th Aero Squadron (night observation).	do	do	July 1917	Selfridge Field, Mich.					Cmpnt. of First Army Obsn. Gp.
			October 1917	Mineola Field, N. Y.					
			November 1917	P. of E., Hoboken	November 1917.				
			June 1919	Mitchel Field, N. Y.		June 1919.			
			July 1919	March Field, Calif.					
			August 1919	Rockwell Field, Calif.					
			November 1919	March Field, Calif.					
			December 1919	Rockwell Field, Calif.					Army troops. Active through 1919.

AERO SQUADRONS—Continued

Unit designation and redesignation	Organization		Stations in United States		Overseas		Demobilization		Remarks
	Month and year	Place	Month and year	Place	From—	To—	Month and year	Place	
10th Aero Squadron	June 1917	Kelly Field, Tex.	July 1917	Chanute Field, Ill.					
			November 1917	Garden City, N. Y.					
			December 1917	P. of E., Philadelphia.	December 1917	May 1919	June 1919	Mitchel Field, N. Y.	S.O.S. troops. Erroneously demobilized; reconstituted at Bolling Field, D. C. Active through 1919.
	July 1919	Bolling Field, D. C.							
11th Aero Squadron (day bombardment).	July 1917	Kelly Field, Tex.	August 1917	Scott Field, Ill.					Cmpnt. of 1st Day Bombardment Gp. Army troops.
			December 1917	Garden City, N. Y.					
			do	P. of E., Hoboken.	December 1917	May 1919	May 1919	Haselhurst Field, N. Y.	Demblsd. Haselhurst Field, N. Y. Reconstituted Ft. Bliss, Tex. Active through 1919.
	June 1919	Ft. Bliss, Tex.	November 1919	Kelly Field, Tex.					
12th Aero Squadron (observation).	June 1917	Kelly Field, Tex.	July 1917	Wilbur Wright Field, Ohio					Cmpnt. of I Corps Obsn. Gp.
			November 1917	Garden City, N. Y.					
			December 1917	P. of E., Philadelphia.	December 1917.				
			June 1919	Mitchel Field, N. Y.		June 1919.			
			July 1919	Scott Field, Ill.					
			October 1919	Kelly Field, Tex.					Corps troops. Active through 1919.

13th Aero Squadron (pursuit).	do	do	July 1917	Wilbur Wright Field, Ohio.					Cmpnt. of 2d Pur. Gp.
			November 1917	Garden City, N. Y.					
			December 1917	P. of E., Philadelphia.	December 1917	March 1919	March 1919	Garden City, N. Y.	Army troops.
14th (I) Aero Squadron (training).	August 1917	Rockwell Field, Calif.							
a. Squadron "A"	July 1918	do					November 1918	Rockwell Field, Calif.	
14th (II) Aero Squadron	June 1917	Kelly Field, Tex.							
a. 19th Aero Squadron (service).	do	do	July 1917	Wilbur Wright Field, Ohio.					
			November 1917	Garden City, N. Y.					
			December 1917	P. of E., Philadelphia.	December 1917	April 1919	April 1919	Mitchel Field, N. Y.	S.O.S. troops.
15th Aero Squadron	August 1917	Hazelhurst Field, N. Y.					September 1919	Hazelhurst Field, N. Y.	
16th (I) Aero Squadron (construction and repair).	do	Chanute Field, Ill.	November 1917	Garden City, N. Y.					
			December 1917	P. of E., Philadelphia.	December 1917	May 1919	May 1919	Mitchel Field, N. Y.	Do.
16th (II) Aero Squadron	May 1917	Kelly Field, Tex.							
a. 21st Aero Squadron (pursuit).	June 1917	do	August 1917	Scott Field, Ill.					
			December 1917	Garden City, N. Y.					
			January 1918	P. of E., Hoboken	January 1918	April 1919	April 1919	Hazelhurst Field, N. Y.	Do.
17th Aero Squadron (pursuit).	July 1917	do	August 1917	Cp. Borden, Canada.					Cmpnt. of 4th Pur. Gp.
			October 1917	Taliaferro Field #1, Tex.					
			December 1917	Garden City, N. Y.					
			January 1918	P. of E., Hoboken	January 1918	March 1919	April 1919	Garden City, N. Y.	Army troops.
17th Provisional Aero Squadron.	June 1917	Do.							
a. 22d Aero Squadron (pursuit).	do	do	August 1917	Royal Flying Corps School, Toronto, Can.					Cmpnt. of 2d Pur. Gp.
			October 1917	Taliaferro Field #1, Tex.					
			January 1918	Garden City, N. Y.					
			do	P. of E., Hoboken	January 1918	May 1919	June 1919	Mitchel Field, N. Y.	Army troops.

AERO SQUADRONS—Continued

Unit designation and redesignation	Organization		Stations in United States		Overseas		Demobilization		Remarks
	Month and year	Place	Month and year	Place	From—	To—	Month and year	Place	
18th (I) Aero Squadron (training).	August 1917	Rockwell Field, Calif.							
a. Squadron "B"	July 1918	do					November 1918	Rockwell Field, Calif.	
18th (II) Aero Squadron.	June 1917	Kelly Field, Tex.							
a. 23d Aero Squadron (repair).	do	do	September 1917	Hazelhurst Field, N. Y.					
			July 1918	P. of E., Hoboken	July 1918	March 1919	March 1919	Garden City, N. Y.	S.O.S. troops.
19th Aero Squadron (service).									See 14th (II) Aer. Sq.
20th (I) Aero Squadron (day bombardment).	June 1917	Kelly Field, Tex.	July 1917	Wilbur Wright Field, Ohio.					Cmpnt. of 1st Day Bombardment Gp.
			November 1917	Garden City, N. Y.					
			December 1917	P. of E., Hoboken	December1917	May 1919	May 1919	Mitchel Field, N.Y.	Demblzd. Mitchel Field, N. Y.
	July 1919	Ellington Field, Tex.	September 1919	Kelly Field, Tex.					Reconstituted Ellington Field, Tex. Active through 1919.
20th (II) Aero Squadron	June 1917	Kelly Field, Tex.							Army troops.
a. 25th Aero Squadron (pursuit).	do	do	December 1917	Garden City, N. Y.					
			January 1918	P. of E., Hoboken	January 1918	June 1919	June 1919	Mitchel Field, N.Y.	Army troops.
21st (I) Aero Squadron (pursuit).									See 16th (II) Aer. Sq.
21st (II) Aero Squadron	June 1917	Kelly Field, Tex.							
a. 27th Aero Squadron (pursuit).	do	do	August 1917	Cp. Leaside, Can.					Cmpnt. of 1st Pur. Gp.

			October 1917	Taliaferro Field #1, Tex.					
			January 1918	Garden City, N. Y.					
			February 1918	P. of E., Hoboken	February 1918				
			March 1919	Mitchel Field, N. Y.		March 1919.			
			April 1919	Selfridge Field, Mich.					
			August 1919	Kelly Field, Tex.					Army troops. Active through 1919.
22d Aero Squadron (pursuit).									See 17th Prov. Aer. Sq.
23d Aero Squadron (repair).									See 18th (II) Aer. Sq.
24th Aero Squadron (observation).	July 1917	Kelly Field, Tex.	January 1918	Garden City, N. Y.					Cmpnt. of First Army Obsn. Gp.
			do	P. of E. Hoboken	January 1918.				
			August 1919	Mitchel Field, N. Y.		August 1919.			
			do	Park Field, Tenn.			October 1919	Park Field, Tenn.	Army troops.
25th Aero Squadron (pursuit).									See 20 (II) Aer. Sq.
26th Aero Squadron (instruction).									See 1st Res. Aer. Sq.
27th Aero Squadron (pursuit).									See 21st (II) Aer. Sq.
28th Aero Squadron (pursuit).	July 1917	Kelly Field, Tex.	August 1917	Cp. Leaside, Canada.					Cmpnt. of 3d Pur. Gp.
			November 1917	Taliaferro Field #1, Tex.					
			January 1918	Garden City, N. Y.					
			February 1918	P. of E., Hoboken	February 1918	May 1919	June 1919	Mitchel Field, N. Y.	Army troops.
29th Provisional Aero Squadron.	do	Ft. Wood, N. Y.	July 1917	P. of E., Hoboken	July 1917.				
a. 400th Aero Squadron (construction).	February 1918	A. E. F.				July 1919	July 1919	Cp. Devens, Mass.	S.O.S. troops.
29th (I) Aero Squadron (service).									See 502d (II) Aer. Sq. (cons.)
29th (II) Aero Squadron	October 1918	Cp. Knox, Ky.	January 1919	Godman Field, Ky.			September 1919	Godman Field, Ky.	

AERO SQUADRONS—Continued

Unit designation and redesignation	Organization		Stations in United States		Overseas		Demobilization		Remarks
	Month and year	Place	Month and year	Place	From—	To—	Month and year	Place	
30th Aero Squadron (service).	July 1917	Kelly Field, Tex.	August 1917	Ft. Totten, N. Y.					
			do	P. of E., Hoboken.	August 1917	April 1919	April 1919	Mitchel Field, N. Y.	S.O.S. troops.
31st Aero Squadron (training).	do	do	do	Ft. Totten, N. Y.					
			do	P. of E., Hoboken.	do	do	do	do	Do.
32d Aero Squadron (training).	do	do	do	Ft. Totten, N. Y.					
			do	P. of E., Hoboken.	August 1917	do	do	do	Do.
33d Aero Squadron (training).	do	do	do	Ft. Totten, N. Y.					
			do	P. of E., Hoboken.	August 1917	April 1919	April 1919	do	Do.
34th Aero Squadron (construction).	do	do	do	Ft. Totten, N. Y.					
			do	P. of E., Hoboken.	do	May 1919	June 1919	do	Do.
35th Aero Squadron (construction).	do	do	do	Ft. Totten, N. Y.					
			do	P. of E., Hoboken.	do	March 1919	March 1919	Garden City, N. Y.	Do.
36th Aero Squadron (construction).	do	do	do	Ft. Totten, N. Y.					
			do	P. of E., Hoboken.	do	March 1919	April 1919	do	Do.
37th Aero Squadron (training).	do	do	do	Ft. Totten, N. Y.					
			do	P. of E., Hoboken.	do	April 1919	April 1919	Mitchel Field, N. Y.	Do.
38th Aero Squadron	do	do	do	Chanute Field, Ill.					
a. Squadron "A"	July 1918	Chanute Field, Ill.					December 1918	Chanute Field, Ill.	
39th Aero Squadron	July 1917	Kelly Field, Tex.	August 1917	Chanute Field, Ill.					
			December 1917	Rich Field, Tex.					
a. Squadron "A"	July 1918	Rich Field, Tex.					November 1918	Rich Field, Tex.	
40th Aero Squadron	July 1917	Kelly Field, Tex.	August 1917	Selfridge Field, Mich.					

a. Squadron "A"	July 1918	Selfridge Field, Mich.					do	Selfridge Field, Mich.	
41st Aero Squadron (pursuit).	August 1917	Kelly Field, Tex.	August 1917	Selfridge Field, Mich.					
			February 1918	Garden City, N. Y.					
			February 1918	P. of E., Hoboken	February 1918	June 1919	July 1919	Cp. Lee, Va.	Army troops.
42d Aero Squadron	July 1917	do	August 1917	Wilbur Wright Field, Ohio.					
a. Squadron "I"	October 1918	Wilbur Wright Field, Ohio.					February 1919	Wilbur Wright Field, Ohio.	
43d Aero Squadron (pursuit).	July 1917	Kelly Field, Tex.	August 1917	Wilbur Wright Field, Ohio.					
			December 1917	Ellington Field, Tex.					
			February 1918	Garden City, N. Y.					
			do	P. of E., Hoboken	February 1918	April 1919	April 1919	Haselhurst Field, N. Y.	S.O.S. troops.
44th Aero Squadron	do	do	August 1917	Wilbur Wright Field, Ohio.					
a. Squadron "K"	October 1918	Wilbur Wright Field, Ohio.							
b. Squadron "P"	November 1918	do					April 1919	Wilbur Wright Field, Ohio.	
45th (I) Aero Squadron	July 1917	Kelly Field, Tex.							
a. 81st Aero Squadron.	August 1917	do							
b. 81st Aero Squadron (construction).	September, 1917	do	November 1917	Garden City, N. Y.					
c. 493d Aero Squadron (construction).	February 1918	A. E. F	do	P. of E., Hoboken	November 1917	January 1919	January 1919	Cp. Devens, Mass.	S.O.S. troops.
45th (II) Aero Squadron									See 2d Res. Aer. Sq.
46th (I) Aero Squadron	July 1917	Kelly Field, Tex.	September 1917	Garden City, N. Y.					
a. 631st Aero Squadron (supply).	February 1918	Garden City, N. Y.					October 1919	Garden City, N. Y.	

AERO SQUADRONS—Continued

Unit designation and redesignation	Organization		Stations in United States		Overseas		Demobilization		Remarks
	Month and year	Place	Month and year	Place	From—	To—	Month and year	Place	
46th (II) Aero Squadron	April 1918	Kelly Field, Tex.	April 1918	Ellington Field, Tex.					
			July 1918	Hazelhurst Field, N. Y.					
			September 1918	Roosevelt Field, N. Y.			January 1919	Garden City, N. Y.	
47th Aero Squadron (observation).	July 1917	do	August 1917	Wilbur Wright Field, Ohio.					
			February 1918	Garden City, N. Y.					
			March 1918	P. of E. Halifax	March 1918	July 1919	July 1919	Cp. Devens, Mass.	S.O.S. troops.
48th (I) Aero Squadron (construction).	August 1917	do	September 1917	Mineola, N. Y.					
			October 1917	P. of E., Hoboken	October 1917				
a. 435th Aero Squadron (construction).	February 1918	A. E. F.							
b. 462d Aero Squadron (construction and repair).	March 1918	do				do	August 1919	Mitchel Field, N. Y.	Do.
48th (II) Aero Squadron.	April 1918	Kelly Field, Tex.	April 1918	Ellington, Field, Tex.					
			July 1918	Hazelhurst Field, N. Y.					
			August 1918	Mitchel Field, N. Y.			January 1919	Garden City, N. Y.	
49th Aero Squadron (pursuit).	August 1917	do	January 1918	Garden City, N. Y.					Cmpnt. of 2d Pur. Gp.
			do	P. of E., Hoboken	January 1918	March 1919	March 1919	Garden City, N. Y.	Army troops.
50th Aero Squadron (observation).	do	do	do	Garden City, N. Y.					Cmpnt. of I Corps Obsn. Gp.
			January 1918	P. of E., Hoboken	January 1918				

			May 1919	Mitchel Field, N. Y.		May 1919			
			do	Scott Field, Ill.			August 1919	Langley Field, Va.	Demblzd. Langley Field, Va. Reconstituted Langley Field, Va. Active through 1919. S.O.S. troops.
	September 1919	Langley Field, Va.							
51st (I) Aero Squadron (construction).	August 1917	Kelly Field, Tex.	September 1917	Mineola, N. Y.					
			October 1917	P. of E., Hoboken	October 1917.				
a. 463d Aero Squadron (construction and repair).	February 1918	A. E. F.				July 1919	July 1919	Mitchel Field, N. Y.	
51st (II) Aero Squadron	April 1918	Kelly Field, Tex.	April 1918	Ellington Field, Tex.					
			July 1918	Mitchel Field, N. Y.					
			November 1918	Henry J. Damm Field, N. Y.			January 1919	Garden City, N. Y.	
52d (I) Aero Squadron (construction).	August 1917	do	September 1917	Mineola, N. Y.					
			October 1917	P. of E., Hoboken	October 1917				
a. 464th (I) Aero Squadron (construction and repair).	February 1918	A. E. F.				May 1919	May 1919	Hazelhurst Field, N. Y.	
52d (II) Aero Squadron	April 1918	Kelly Field, Tex.	April 1918	Ellington Field, Tex.					
			July 1918	Mitchel Field, N. Y.					
			November 1918	Hazelhurst Field, N. Y.					
			December 1918	Mitchel Field, N. Y			January 1919	Garden City, N. Y.	
53d Aero Squadron (construction).	August 1917	do	September 1917	Mineola, N. Y.					
			October 1917	P. of E., Hoboken	October 1917.				
a. 465th Aero Squadron (construction and repair).	February 1918	A. E. F.				March 1919	March 1919	do	S.O.S. troops.

AERO SQUADRONS—Continued

Unit designation and redesignation	Organization		Stations in United States		Overseas		Demobilization		Remarks
	Month and year	Place	Month and year	Place	From—	To—	Month and year	Place	
54th Aero Squadron (construction).	August 1917	Kelly Field, Tex.	September 1917	Mineola, N. Y.					
			October 1917	P. of E., Hoboken	October 1917.				
a. 466th Aero Squadron (construction).	February 1918	A. E. F.				January 1919	February 1919	Garden City, N. Y.	S.O.S. troops.
55th Aero Squadron (construction).	August 1917	Kelly Field, Tex.	September 1917	Mineola, N. Y.					
			October 1917	P. of E., Hoboken	October 1917.				
a. 467th Aero Squadron (construction).	February 1918	A. E. F.				March 1919	March 1919	do	Do.
56th Aero Squadron (construction).	August 1917	Kelly Field, Tex.	September 1917	Mineola, N. Y.					
			October 1917	P. of E., Hoboken	October 1917.				
a. 468th Aero Squadron (construction).	February 1918	A. E. F.				June 1919	July 1919	Mitchel Field, N.Y.	
57th Aero Squadron (construction).	August 1917	Kelly Field, Tex.	September 1917	Mineola, N. Y.					
			October 1917	P. of E., Hoboken	October 1917.				
a. 469th Aero Squadron (construction).	February 1918	A. E. F.				March 1919	March 1919	Garden City, N. Y.	Do.
58th Aero Squadron	August 1917	Kelly Field, Tex.							
a. 58th Aero Squadron (construction).	September 1917	do	October 1917	Cp. Morrison, Va.					
			January 1918	P. of E., Newport News.	January 1918.				
b. 470th Aero Squadron (construction).	February 1918	A. E. F.				December 1918	December 1918	do	Do.

59th Aero Squadron	August 1917	Kelly Field, Tex.							
a. 59th Aero Squadron (construction).	September 1917	do	October 1917	Cp. Alfred Vail, N. J.					
b. 471st Aero Squadron (construction).	February 1918	A. E. F	November 1917 January 1918	Cp. Morrison, Va. P. of E., Newport News.	January 1918	do	do	Cp. Mills, N. Y	Do.
60th Aero Squadron	August 1917	Kelly Field, Tex.							
a. 60th Aero Squadron (construction).	September 1917	do	October 1917 January 1918	Cp. Morrison, Va. P. of E., Newport News.	January 1918.				
b. 472d Aero Squadron (construction).	February 1918	A. E. F				do	do	Garden City, N. Y.	Do.
61st Aero Squadron	August 1917	Kelly Field, Tex.							
a. 61st Aero Squadron (construction).	September 1917	do	December 1917 January 1918	Cp. Morrison, Va. P. of E., Newport News.	January 1918.				
b. 473d Aero Squadron (construction).	February 1918	A. E. F				do	do	do	Do.
62d Aero Squadron	August 1917	Kelly Field, Tex.							
a. 62d Aero Squadron (construction).	September 1917	do	January 1918	Cp. Morrison, Va.					
b. 474th Aero Squadron (construction).	February 1918	Cp. Morrison, Va.	March 1918	P. of E., Newport News.	March 1918	January 1919	January 1919	do	Do.
63d (I) Aero Squadron	August 1917	Kelly Field, Tex.							
a. 63d Aero Squadron (construction).	September 1917	do	December 1917 January 1918	Cp. Morrison, Va. P. of E., Newport News.	January 1918.				
b. 475th Aero Squadron (construction).	February 1918	A. E. F				December 1918	December 1918	do	Do.
63d (II) Aero Squadron	August 1918	Kelly Field, Tex.	April 1918	Gerstner Field, La.					
a. Squadron "B"	July 1918	Gerstner Field, La.					September 1918	Gerstner Field, La.	
	October 1918	do					November 1918	do	Reconstituted.

AERO SQUADRONS—Continued

Unit designation and redesignation	Organization		Stations in United States		Overseas		Demobilization		Remarks
	Month and year	Place	Month and year	Place	From—	To—	Month and year	Place	
64th (I) Aero Squadron	August 1917	Kelly Field, Tex.							
a. 64th Aero Squadron (construction).	September 1917	do	December 1917	Cp. Morrison, Va.					
			January 1918	P. of E., Newport News.	January 1918.				
b. 476th Aero Squadron (construction).	February 1918	A. E. F				December 1918	December 1918	Garden City, N. Y.	S.O.S. troops.
64th (II) Aero Squadron	April 1918	Kelly Field, Tex	April 1918	Gerstner Field, La.					
a. Squadron "C"	July 1918	Gerstner Field, La.					September 1918	Gerstner Field, La.	
	October 1918	do					November 1918	do	Reconstituted.
65th (I) Aero Squadron	August 1917	Kelly Field, Tex.							
a. 65th Aero Squadron (construction).	September 1917	do	January 1918	Cp. Morrison, Va.					
b. 477th Aero Squadron (construction).	February 1918	Cp. Morrison, Va.	March 1918	P. of E., Newport News.	March 1918	January 1919	January 1919	Garden City, N. Y.	S.O.S. troops.
65th (II) Aero Squadron	April 1918	Kelly Field, Tex	April 1918	Park Field, Tenn.					
a. Squadron "A"	July 1918	Park Field, Tenn.					December 1918	Park Field, Tenn.	
66th (I) Aero Squadron	August 1917	Kelly Field, Tex.							
a. 66th Aero Squadron (construction).	September 1917	do	December 1917	Cp. Morrison, Va.					
			January 1918	P. of E., Newport News.	January 1918.				
b. 478th Aero Squadron (construction).	February 1918	A. E. F				December 1918	do	Garden City, N. Y.	Do
66th (II) Aero Squadron	April 1918	Kelly Field, Tex	May 1918	Eberts Field, Ark.					
a. Squadron "A"	July 1918	Eberts Field, Ark.					November 1918	Eberts Field, Ark.	

67th (I) Aero Squadron	August 1917	Kelly Field, Tex.							
a. 67th Aero Squadron (construction).	September 1917	do	December 1917	Cp. Morrison, Va.					
			January 1918	P. of E., Newport News.	January 1918.				
b. 479th Aero Squadron (construction).	February 1918	A. E. F				December 1918	December 1918	Garden City, N. Y.	Do.
67th (II) Aero Squadron	April 1918	Kelly Field, Tex	April 1918	Brooks Field, Tex.					
a. Squadron "B"	July 1918	Brooks Field, Tex.					November 1918	Brooks Field, Tex.	
68th (I) Aero Squadron	August 1917	Kelly Field, Tex.							
a. 68th Aero Squadron (construction).	September 1917	do	December 1917	Cp. Morrison, Va.					
b. 480th Aero Squadron (construction).	February 1918	Cp. Morrison, Va	March 1918	P. of E., Newport News.	March 1918	February 1919	February 1919	Cp. Meade, Md	Do.
68th (II) Aero Squadron	March 1918	Rockwell Field, Calif.	June 1918	March Field, Calif					
a. Squadron "A"	July 1918	March Field, Calif.					November 1918	March Field, Calif.	
69th (I) Aero Squadron	August 1917	Kelly Field, Tex.							
a. 69th Aero Squadron (construction).	September 1917	do	February 1918	Cp. Morrison, Va.					
b. 481st Aero Squadron (construction).	February 1918	Cp. Morrison, Va	March 1918	P. of E., Newport News.	March 1918	February 1919	February 1919	Garden City, N. Y.	Do.
69th (I) Aero Squadron.	February 1918	Ellington Field, Tex.							
a. Squadron "A"	July 1918	do					December 1918	Ellington Field, Tex.	
70th (I) Aero Squadron	August 1917	Kelly Field, Tex							
a. 70th Aero Squadron (construction).	September 1917	do	December 1917	Cp. Morrison, Va					
b. 482d Aero Squadron (construction).	February 1918	Cp. Morrison Va	March 1918	P. of E., Newport News.	March 1918	March 1919	March 1919	Garden City, N. Y.	Do.

AERO SQUADRONS—Continued

Unit designation and redesignation	Organization		Stations in United States		Overseas		Demobilization		Remarks
	Month and year	Place	Month and year	Place	From—	To—	Month and year	Place	
70th (II) Aero Squadron	March 1918	Ellington Field, Tex.							
a. Squadron "B"	July 1918	do					December 1918	Ellington Field, Tex.	
71st (I) Aero Squadron	August 1917	Kelly Field, Tex							
a. 71st Aero Squadron (construction).	September 1917	do	December 1917	Cp. Morrison, Va.					
b. 483d Aero Squadron (construction).	February 1918	Cp. Morrison, Va.	March 1918	P. of E., Newport News.	March 1918	February 1919	February 1919	Cp. Lee, Va	S.O.S. troops.
71st (II) Aero Squadron	do	Waco, Tex	February 1918	Love Field, Tex.					
a. Squadron "A"	July 1918	Love Field, Tex					November 1918	Love Field, Tex.	
72d (I) Aero Squadron	August 1917	Kelly Field, Tex							
a. 72d Aero Squadron (construction).	September 1917	do	February 1918	Cp. Morrison, Va.					
b. 484th Aero Squadron (construction).	February 1918	Cp. Morrison, Va.	March 1918	P. of E., Newport News.	March 1918	January 1919	February 1919	East Potomac Park Washington, D. C.	Do.
72d (II) Aero Squadron (service).	do	Waco, Tex	February 1918 July 1918 August 1918	Rich Field, Tex. Garden City, N. Y. P. of E., Hoboken	August 1918	June 1919	July 1919	Mitchel Field, N. Y.	Do.
73d (I) Aero Squadron	August 1917	Kelly Field, Tex.							
a. 73d Aero Squadron (construction).	September 1917	do	December 1917	Cp. Morrison. Va.					
b. 485th Aero Squadron (construction).	February 1918	Cp. Morrison, Va	March 1918	P. of E., Newport News.	March 1918	May 1919	May 1919	do	Do.

73d (II) Aero Squadron (service).	do	Waco, Tex.	March 1918	Call Field, Tex.					
			July 1918	Garden City, N. Y.					
			August 1918	P. of E., Hoboken	August 1918	June 1919	July 1919	Hazelhurst Field, N. Y.	Army troops.
74th (I) Aero Squadron	August 1917	Kelly Field, Tex.							
a. 74th Aero Squadron (construction).	September 1917	do	December 1917	Cp. Morrison, Va.					
b. 486th Aero Squadron (construction).	February 1918	Cp. Morrison, Va.	March 1918	P. of E., Hoboken	March 1918	June 1919	June 1919	Mitchel Field, N.Y.	S.O.S. troops.
74th (II) Aero Squadron (service).	do	Waco, Tex.	do	Call Field, Tex.					
			August 1918	Hazelhurst Field, N. Y.					
			September 1918	Roosevelt Field, N. Y.			January 1919	Garden City, N.Y.	
74th (III) Aero Squadron.	June 1919	Langley Field, Va.					September 1919	Langley Field, Va.	
75th (I) Aero Squadron	August 1917	Kelly Field, Tex.							
a. 75th Aero Squadron (construction).	September 1917	do	November 1917	Garden City, N.Y.					
			December 1917	P. of E., Philadelphia.	December 1917				
b. 487th Aero Squadron (construction).	February 1918	A. E. F.				May 1919	May 1919	Mitchel Field, N.Y.	Do.
75th (II) Aero Squadron (service).	do	Waco, Tex.	March 1918	Gerstner Field, La.					
a. Squadron "D"	July 1918	Gerstner Field, La.					November 1918	Gerstner Field, La.	
76th (I) Aero Squadron	August 1917	Kelly Field, Tex.							
a. 76th Aero Squadron (construction).	September 1917	do	November 1917	Garden City, N.Y.					
			December 1917	P. of E., Philadelphia.	December 1917.				
b. 488th Aero Squadron (construction).	February 1918	A. E. F.	February 1919	Cp. Stuart, Va.		February 1919	March 1919	Langley Field, Va.	Do.
76th (II) Aero Squadron (service).	do	Waco, Tex.	March 1918	Carlstrom Field, Fla.					
			April 1918	Dorr Field, Fla.					
a. Squadron "A"	July 1918	Dorr Field, Fla.					November 1918	Dorr Field, Fla.	

AERO SQUADRONS—Continued

Unit designation and redesignation	Organization		Stations in United States		Overseas		Demobilization		Remarks
	Month and year	Place	Month and year	Place	From—	To—	Month and year	Place	
77th (I) Aero Squadron	August 1917	Kelly Field, Tex.							
a. 77th Aero Squadron (construction).	September 1917	do	November 1917	Garden City, N.Y.					
			December 1917	P. of E., Philadelphia.	December 1917.				
b. 489th Aero Squadron (construction).	February 1918	A. E. F	February 1919	Cp. Stuart, Va		February 1919.			
			do	Cp. Lee, Va			March 1919	Cp. Lee, Va	S.O.S. troops.
77th (II) Aero Squadron (service).	do	Waco, Tex	February 1918	Taliaferro Field #1 Tex.					
			March 1918	Taliaferro Field #2 Tex.					
			May 1918	Barron Field, Tex					Taliaferro Field #2 redesignated Barron Field May 1, 1918.
a. Squadron "A"	July 1918	Barron Field, Tex					November 1918	Barron Field, Tex.	
78th (I) Aero Squadron	August 1917	Kelly Field, Tex.							
a. 78th Aero Squadron (construction).	September 1917	do	November 1917	Garden City, N.Y.					
			do	P. of E., Hoboken	November 1917.				
b. 490th Aero Squadron (construction).	February 1918	A. E. F				February 1919	February 1919	Garden City, N. Y	S.O.S. troops.
78th (II) Aero Squadron	February 1918	Waco, Tex	February 1918	Taliaferro Field #1, Tex.					
a. Squadron "A"	July 1918	Taliaferro Field, Tex.					November 1918	Taliaferro Field, Tex.	
79th (I) Aero Squadron	August 1917	Kelly Field, Tex							
a. 79th Aero Squadron (construction).	September 1917	do	November 1917	Garden City, N. Y.					
			do	P. of E., Hoboken	November 1917.				

b. 491st Aero Squadron (construction).	February 1918	A.E.F				January 1919	January 1919	Garden City, N. Y.	Do.
79th (II) Aero Squadron (service).	do	Waco, Tex	February 1918	Taliaferro Field #1, Tex.					
a. Squadron "B"	July 1918	Taliaferro Field, Tex.					November 1918	Taliaferro Field, Tex.	
80th (I) Aero Squadron	August 1917	Kelly Field, Tex.							
a. 80th Aero Squadron (construction).	September 1917	do	November 1917	Garden City, N. Y.					
			do	P. of E., Hoboken	November 1917.				
b. 492d Aero Squadron (construction).	February 1918	A. E. F				January 1919	February 1919	Garden City, N. Y.	Do.
80th (II) Aero Squadron (service).	March 1918	Waco, Tex	March 1918	Post Field, Okla.					
a. Squadron "C"	July 1918	Post Field, Okla					January 1919	Post Field, Okla.	
81st (I) Aero Squadron									See 45th (I) Aer. Sq.
81st (II) Aero Squadron (service).	March 1918	Waco, Tex	March 1918	Post Field, Okla.					
a. Squadron "D"	July 1918	Post Field, Okla					January 1919	Post Field, Okla.	
82d (I) Aero Squadron	August 1917	Kelly Field, Tex.							
a. 82d Aero Squadron (construc-(rion).	September 1917	do	November 1917	Garden City, N. Y.					
			do	P. of E., Hoboken	November 1917.				
b. 494th Aero Squadron (construction).	February 1918	A. E. F				May 1919	May 1919	Mitchel Field, N.Y.	S.O.S. troops.
82d (II) Aero Squadron (service).	March 1918	Waco, Tex	March 1918	Taliaferro Field #1, Tex.					
a. Squadron "C"	July 1918	Taliaferro Field, Tex.					November 1918	Taliaferro Field, Tex.	
83d (I) Aero Squadron	August 1917	Kelly Field, Tex.							
a. 83d Aero Squadron (construction).	September 1917	do	February 1918	Cp. Morrison, Va.					
b. 495th Aero Squadron (construction).	February 1918	Cp. Morrison, Va.	March 1918	P. of E., Newport News.	March 1918	January 1919	January 1919	Garden City, N. Y.	S.O.S. troops.

AERO SQUADRONS—Continued

Unit designation and redesignation	Organization		Stations in United States		Overseas		Demobilization		Remarks
	Month and year	Place	Month and year	Place	From—	To—	Month and year	Place	
83d (II) Aero Squadron (service).	February 1918	Chanute Field, Ill.	March 1918	Langley Field, Va.					
a. Squadron "A"	July 1918	Langley Field, Va.					November 1918	Langley Field, Va.	
84th Aero Squadron	August 1917	Kelly Field, Tex.					August 1919	Kelly Field, Tex.	
85th Aero Squadron (observation).	do	do	September 1917	Scott Field, Ill.					
			February 1918	Garden City, N. Y.					
			do	P. of E., Hoboken	February 1918	July 1919	July 1919	Mitchel Field, N. Y.	Army troops.
86th Aero Squadron (supply).	do	do	September 1917	Scott Field, Ill.					
			February 1918	Garden City, N. Y					
			March 1918	P. of E., Halifax	March 1918	May 1919	May 1919	Cp. Lee, Va	S.O.S. troops.
87th Aero Squadron	do	do	September 1917	Selfridge Field, Mich.					
			December 1917	Park Field, Tenn.					
a. Squadron "B"	July 1918	Park Field, Tenn.					December 1918	Park Field, Tenn.	
88th (I) Aero Squadron (observation).	August 1917	Kelly Field, Tex.	October 1917	Garden City, N. Y.					Cmpnt. of III Corps. Obsn. Gp.
			do	P. of E., Hoboken	October 1917.				
			June 1919	Mitchel Field, N. Y.		June 1919.			
			July 1919	Scott Field, Ill.			August 1919	Scott Field, Ill.	Army troops.
88th (II) Aero Squadron	September 1919	Langley Field, Va.							Active through 1919.
89th Aero Squadron (service).	August 1917	Kelly Field, Tex.	October 1917	Garden City, N. Y.					
			do	P. of E., Hoboken	October 1917	March 1919	April 1919	Garden City, N. Y.	S.O.S. troops.
90th Aero Squadron (observation).	September 1917	do	do	Garden City, N. Y.					Cmpnt. of III Corps Obsn. Gp.
			do	P. of E., Hoboken	October 1917.				
			May 1919	Haselhurst Field, N. Y.		May 1919.			
			do	Kelly Field, Tex.					

			November 1919	Airdrome, Sanderson, Tex.					Active through 1919. Army troops.
91st Aero Squadron (observation).	August 1917	do	October 1917	Garden City, N. Y.					Cmpnt. of First Army Obsn. Gp.
			do	P. of E., Hoboken	October 1917.				
			June 1919	Mitchel Field, N. Y.		June 1919.			
			July 1919	Park Field, Tenn.					
			September 1919	Rockwell Field, Calif.					
			October 1919	Mather Field, Calif.					Army troops. Active through 1919.
92d Aero Squadron (service).	do	do	October 1917	Garden City, N. Y.					
			do	P. of E., Hoboken	October 1917	December 1918	December 1918	Hempstead Field, N. Y.	S.O.S. troops.
93d Aero Squadron (pursuit).	do	do	do	Garden City, N. Y.					Cmpnt. of 3d Pur. Gp.
			do	P. of E., Hoboken	October 1917	March 1919	March 1919	Garden City, N. Y.	Army troops.
94th Aero Squadron (pursuit).	do	do	do	Hazelhurst Field, N. Y.					Cmpnt. of 1st Pur. Gp.
			do	P. of E., Hoboken	October 1917.				
			May 1919	Mitchel Field, N. Y.		May 1919.			
			June 1919	Selfridge Field, Mich.					
			August 1919	Kelly Field, Tex.					Army troops. Active through 1919.
95th Aero Squadron (pursuit).	do	do	October 1917	Hazelhurst Field, N. Y.					Cmpnt. of 1st Pur. Gp.
			do	P. of E., Hoboken	October 1917	March 1919	March 1919	Garden City, N. Y.	
	August 1919	Selfridge Field, Mich.	August 1919	Kelly Field, Tex.					Demblzd. Garden City, N. Y. Reconstituted Selfridge Field Mich. Active through 1919. Army troops.

AERO SQUADRONS—Continued

Unit designation and redesignation	Organization		Stations in United States		Overseas		Demobilization		Remarks
	Month and year	Place	Month and year	Place	From—	To—	Month and year	Place	
96th Aero Squadron (day bombardment).	August 1917	Kelly Field, Tex.	October 1917	Mineola, N. Y.					Cmpnt. of 1st Day Bombardment Gp.
			do	P. of E., Hoboken	October 1917.				
			May 1919	Mitchel Field, N. Y.		May 1919.			
			do	Ellington Field, Tex.					
			June 1919	Columbus, N. Mex.					
			July 1919	Ft. Bliss, Tex.					Army troops. Active through 1919.
97th Aero Squadron (service).	do	do	October 1917	Garden City, N. Y.					
			do	P. of E., Hoboken	October 1917	January 1919	February 1919	Garden City, N. Y.	S.O.S. troops.
98th Aero Squadron (service).	do	do	November 1917	Garden City, N. Y.					
			do	P. of E., Hoboken	November 1917	April 1919	May 1919	Hazelhurst Field, N. Y.	Do.
99th Aero Squadron (observation).	do	do	do	Garden City, N. Y.					Cmpnt. of V Corps Obsn. Gp.
			do	P. of E., Hoboken	November 1917.				
			May 1919	Hazelhurst Field, N. Y.		May 1919.			
			July 1919	Cp. Alfred Vail, N. J.					
			August 1919	Bolling Field, D. C.					Active through 1919. Army troops.
100th Aero Squadron (bombardment).	do	do	October 1917	Hazelhurst Field, N. Y.					
			January 1918	P. of E., Hoboken	January 1918	May 1919	June 1919	Mitchel Field, N. Y.	Army troops.

101st Aero Squadron (service).	do	do	November 1917	Garden City, N. Y.					
			December 1917	P. of E., Philadelphia.	December 1917	April 1919	April 1919	Mitchel Field, N. Y.	S.O.S. troops.
102d Aero Squadron (service).	do	do	November 1917	Garden City, N. Y.					
			do	P. of E., Hoboken	November 1917	April 1919	May 1919	Garden City, N. Y.	Do.
103d Aero Squadron (pursuit).	do	do	do	Garden City, N. Y.					Cmpnt. of 3d Pur. Gp.
104th Aero Squadron (observation).	do	do	do	P. of E., Hoboken	November 1917	March 1919	August 1919	Garden City, N. Y.	Army troops.
			do	Garden City, N. Y.					Cmpnt. of V Corps Obsn. Gp.
			do	P. of E., Hoboken	November 1917.	April 1919.			
			April 1919	Roosevelt Field, N. Y.					
			May 1919	Mitchel Field, N. Y.					
			do	Airdrome, El Paso, Tex.					
			June 1919	Kelly Field, Tex.					
			November 1919	Airdrome, El Paso, Tex.					Active through 1919. Army troops.
105th Aero Squadron (service).	do	do	November 1917	Garden City, N. Y.					
			do	P. of E., Hoboken	November 1917	April 1919	May 1919	Mitchel Field, N. Y.	S.O.S. troops.
106th (I) Aero Squadron.	do	Do.							
a. 106th Aero Squadron (repair).	September 1917	do	November 1917	Garden City, N. Y.					
b. 800th Aero Squadron (repair).	February 1918	A. E. F	December 1917	P. of E., St. Johns	December 1917	do	do	do	Flights "A" "B," 800th Aer. Sq.
						June 1919	July 1919	do	Flight "C," 800th Aer. Sq. Sq returned in two det. S.O.S. troops.
106th (II) Aero Squadron (service).	March 1918	Waco, Tex	March 1918	Taliaferro Field #2, Tex.					
			May 1918	Barron Field, Tex.					
a. Squadron "B"	July 1918	Barron Field, Tex					November 1918	Barron Field, Tex	Taliaferro Field #2 redesignated Barron Field May 1, 1918.

AERO SQUADRONS—Continued

Unit designation and redesignation	Organization		Stations in United States		Overseas		Demobilization		Remarks
	Month and year	Place	Month and year	Place	From—	To—	Month and year	Place	
107th (I) Aero Squadron	August 1917	Kelly Field, Tex.							
a. 107th Aero Squadron (repair).	September 1917	do	October 1917 December 1917	Garden City, N. Y. P. of E., St. Johns	December 1917.				
b. 801st Aero Squadron (repair).	February 1918	A. E. F				March 1919	March 1919	Garden City, N. Y.	S.O.S. troops.
107th (II) Aero Squadron (service).	March 1918	Waco, Tex	March 1918	Carlstrom Field, Fla.					
a. Squadron "A"	July 1918	Carlstrom Field, Fla.					November 1918	Carlstrom Field, Fla.	
108th (I) Aero Squadron	August 1917	Kelly Field, Tex.							
a. 108th Aero Squadron (repair).	September 1917	do	November 1917 December 1917	Garden City, N. Y. P. of E., St. Johns	December 1917.				
b. 802d Aero Squadron (repair).	February 1918	A. E. F				May 1919	June 1919	Mitchel Field, N. Y.	S.O.S. troops.
108th (II) Aero Squadron (service).	March 1918	Waco, Tex	March 1918	Carlstrom Field, Fla.					
a. Squadron "B"	July 1918	Carlstrom Field, Fla.					November 1918	Carlstrom Field, Fla.	
109th (I) Aero Squadron	August 1917	Kelly Field, Tex.							
a. 109th Aero Squadron (repair).	September 1917	do	November 1917 December 1917	Garden City, N. Y. P. of E., St. Johns	December 1917.				
b. 803d Aero Squadron (repair).	February 1918	A. E. F				June 1919	June 1919	Mitchel Field, N. Y.	Do.
109th (II) Aero Squadron (service).	March 1918	Waco, Tex	April 1918 do	Carlstrom Field, Fla. Dorr Field, Fla.					
a. Squadron "B"	July 1918	Dorr Field, Fla					November 1918	Dorr Field, Fla.	

110th (I) Aero Squadron	August 1917	Kelly Field, Tex.							
a. 110th Aero Squadron (repair).	September 1917	Do.							
b. 804th Aero Squadron (repair).	February 1918	Do.							
c. Squadron "K"	July 1918	do					do	Kelly Field, Tex.	
110th (II) Aero Squadron (service).	April 1918	Waco, Tex	May 1918	Dorr Field, Fla.					
a. Squadron "C"	July 1918	Dorr Field, Fla					do	Dorr Field, Fla.	
111th (I) Aero Squadron	August 1917	Kelly Field, Tex.							
a. 111th Aero Squadron (supply).	September 1917	Do.							
b. 632d Aero Squadron (supply).	February 1918	do					August 1919	Kelly Field, Tex.	
111th (II) Aero Squadron (service).	April 1918	Waco, Tex	May 1918	Dorr Field, Fla.					
			do	Carlstrom Field, Fla.					
a. Squadron "C"	July 1918	Carlstrom Field, Fla.					November 1918	Carlstrom Field, Fla.	
112th (I) Aero Squadron	August 1917	Kelly Field, Tex.							
a. 112th Aero Squadron (supply).	September 1917	Do.							
b. 633d Aero Squadron (supply).	February 1918	do					August 1919	Kelly Field, Tex.	
112th (II) Aero Squadron (service).	April 1918	Waco, Tex	May 1918	Chanute Field, Ill.					
a. Squadron "B"	July 1918	Chanute Field, Ill.							
b. 112th Aero Squadron.	December 1918	do	December 1918	Avn. Gen. Sup. Dep., Americus, Ga.			December 1918	Avn. Gen. Sup. Dep., Americus, Ga.	112th and 287th Aer. Sq. were consolidated into Avn. Sup. Dep. Det. Jan. 1, 1919, at Americus, Ga.

AERO SQUADRONS—Continued

Unit designation and redesignation	Organization		Stations in United States		Overseas		Demobilization		Remarks
	Month and year	Place	Month and year	Place	From—	To—	Month and year	Place	
113th (I) Aero Squadron	August 1917	Kelly Field, Tex.							
a. 113th Aero Squadron (supply).	September 1917	do	September 1917	Avn. Gen. Sup. Dep., Middletown, Pa.					
b. 634th Aero Squadron (supply).	February 1918	Avn. Gen. Sup. Dep., Middletown, Pa.					March 1919	Avn. Gen. Sup. Dep., Middletown, Pa.	
113th (II) Aero Squadron (service).	March 1918	Ellington Field, Tex.							
a. Squadron "C"	July 1918	do					December 1918	Ellington Field, Tex.	
114th (I) Aero Squadron	August 1917	Kelly Field, Tex.							
a. 114th Aero Squadron (supply).	September 1917	do	September 1917	Avn. Gen. Sup. Dep., Richmond, Va.					
b. 635th Aero Squadron (supply).	February 1918	Avn. Gen. Sup. Dep., Richmond, Va.					July 1919	Avn. Gen. Sup. Dep., Richmond, Va.	
114th (II) Aero Squadron (service).	do	Scott Field, Ill.							
a. Squadron "A"	July 1918	do					November 1918	Scott Field, Ill.	
115th (I) Aero Squadron	August 1917	Kelly Field, Tex.							
a. 115th Aero Squadron (supply).	September 1917	do	October 1917	Garden City, N. Y					
			December 1917	P. of E., Hoboken	December 1917.				
b. 636th Aero Squadron (supply).	February 1918	A. E. F				March 1919	April 1919	Garden City, N. Y.	S.O.S. troops.
115th (II) Aero Squadron.	March 1918	Kelly Field, Tex.							
a. Squadron "B"	July 1918	do					November 1918	Kelly Field, Tex.	

116th (I) Aero Squadron	August 1917	Do.							
a. 116th Aero Squadron (service).	September 1917	do	October 1917	Garden City, N. Y.					
			December 1917	P. of E., St. Johns	December 1917.				
b. 637th Aero Squadron (supply).	February 1918	A. E. F				May 1919	May 1919	Mitchel Field, N. Y.	Do.
116th (II) Aero Squadron (service).	March 1918	Kelly Field, Tex	May 1918	Souther Field, Ga.					
a. Squadron "B"	July 1918	Souther Field, Ga					November 1918	Souther Field, Ga.	
117th (I) Aero Squadron	August 1917	Kelly Field, Tex.							
a. 117th Aero Squadron (service).	September 1917	do	October 1917	Garden City, N. Y.					
			December 1917	P. of E., Hoboken	December 1917.				
b. 638th Aero Squadron (pursuit).	February 1918	A. E. F				June 1919	July 1919	Mitchel Field, N. Y.	Army troops.
117th (II) Aero Squadron.	March 1918	Kelly Field, Tex.							
a. Squadron "C"	July 1918	do					November 1918	Kelly Field, Tex.	
118th (I) Aero Squadron	August 1917	Do.							
a. 118th Aero Squadron (supply).	September 1917	do	January 1918	Garden City, N. Y.					
			do	P. of E., Hoboken	January 1918.				
b. 639th Aero Squadron (supply).	February 1918	A. E. F				May 1919	June 1919	Mitchel Field, N. Y.	S.O.S. troops.
118th (II) Aero Squadron.	April 1918	Kelly Field, Tex	April 1918	Brooks Field, Tex.					
a. Squadron "C"	July 1918	Brooks Field, Tex					November 1918	Brooks Field, Tex.	
119th Aero Squadron	September 1917	Langley Field, Va.							
a. 11th Detachment Air Service Aircraft Production.	August 1918	do					May 1919	Langley Field, Va.	
120th Aero Squadron (service).									See 136th Aer. Sq. (cons.).

AERO SQUADRONS—Continued

Unit designation and redesignation	Organization		Stations in United States		Overseas		Demobilization		Remarks
	Month and year	Place	Month and year	Place	From—	To—	Month and year	Place	
121st (I) Aero Squadron	August 1917	Kelly Field, Tex.							
a. 121st Aero Squadron (supply).	September 1917	do	January 1918	Garden City, N. Y.					
			do	P. of E., Hoboken	January 1918.				
b. 640th Aero Squadron (supply).	February 1918	A. E. F				April 1919	April 1919	Mitchel Field. N. Y.	S.O.S. troops.
121st (II) Aero Squadron.	April 1918	Kelly Field, Tex	April 1918	Love Field, Tex.					
a. Squadron "B"	July 1918	Love Field, Tex					November 1918	Love Field, Tex.	
122d (I) Aero Squadron (supply).	September 1917	Kelly Field, Tex	January 1918	Garden City, N. Y.					
			do	P. of E., Hoboken	January 1918.				
a. 641st Aero Squadron (supply).	February 1918	A. E. F				May 1919	June 1919	Mitchel Field, N. Y.	Do.
122d (II) Aero Squadron service).	March 1918	Kelly Field, Tex	March 1918	Cp. Alfred Vail, N. J.					
			November 1918	Roosevelt Field, N. Y.					
			do	Henry J. Damm Field, N. Y.			January 1919	Garden City, N. Y.	
123d (I) Aero Squadron (supply).	September 1917	do	January 1918	Garden City, N. Y.					
			do	P. of E., Hoboken	January 1918.				
a. 642d Aero Squadron (supply).	February 1918	A. E. F				May 1919	June 1919	Mitchel Field, N. Y.	Do.
123d (II) Aero Squadron (service).	March 1918	Kelly Field, Tex	April 1918	Eberts Field, Ark.					
a. Squadron "B"	July 1918	Eberts Field, Ark					November 1918	Eberts Field, Ark.	

124th (I) Aero Squadron (supply).	September 1917	Kelly Field, Tex.	January 1918	Garden City, N. Y.					
			do	P. of E., Hoboken	January 1918.				
a. 643d Aero Squadron (supply).	February 1918	A. E. F.				June 1919	July 1919	Mitchel Field, N.Y.	Do.
124th (II) Aero Squadron (service).	March 1918	Kelly Field, Tex.	April 1918	Eberts Field, Ark.					
a. Squadron "C"	July 1918	Eberts Field, Ark.					November 1918	Eberts Field, Ark.	
125th (I) Aero Squadron (supply).	September 1917	Kelly Field, Tex.	January 1918	Garden City, N. Y.					
			do	P. of E., Hoboken	January 1918.				
a. 644th Aero Squadron (supply).	February 1918	A. E. F.				May 1919	June 1919	Mitchel Field, N.Y.	Do.
125th (II) Aero Squadron (service).	April 1918	Kelly Field, Tex.	April 1918	Eberts Field, Ark.					
a. Squadron "D"	July 1918	Eberts Field, Ark.					November 1918	Eberts Field, Ark.	
126th (I) Aero Squadron (supply).	September 1917	Kelly Field, Tex.	January 1918	Garden City, N. Y.					
			do	P. of E., Hoboken	January 1918.				
a. 645th Aero Squadron (supply).	February 1918	A. E. F.				June 1919	July 1919	Mitchel Field, N.Y.	Do.
126th (II) Aero Squadron (service).	April 1918	Kelly Field, Tex.	April 1918	Langley Field, Va.					
a. Squadron "B"	July 1918	Langley Field, Va.					November 1918	Langley Field, Va.	
127th (I) Aero Squadron (supply).	September 1917	Kelly Field, Tex.	January 1918	Garden City, N. Y.					
			do	P. of E., Hoboken	January 1918.				
a. 646th Aero Squadron (supply).	February 1918	A. E. F.				April 1919	April 1919	Mitchel Field, N.Y.	Do.
127th (II) Aero Squadron (service).	April 1918	Kelly Field, Tex.	April 1918	Langley Field, Va.					
a. Squadron "C"	July 1918	Langley Field, Va.					November 1918	Langley Field, Va.	
128th (I) Aero Squadron (supply).	September 1917	Kelly Field, Tex.	October 1917	Cp. Morrison, Va.					
a. 647th Aero Squadron (supply).	February 1918	Cp. Morrison, Va.					March 1919	Cp. Morrison, Va.	
128th (II) Aero Squadron.	April 1918	Kelly Field, Tex.	April 1918	Taylor Field, Ala.					
a. Squadron "A"	July 1918	Taylor Field, Ala.					November 1918	Taylor Field, Ala.	

AERO SQUADRONS—Continued

Unit designation and redesignation	Organization		Stations in United States		Overseas		Demobilization		Remarks
	Month and year	Place	Month and year	Place	From—	To—	Month and year	Place	
129th (I) Aero Squadron (supply).	September 1917	Kelly Field, Tex	December 1917	Waco, Tex.					
a. 648th Aero Squadron (supply).	February 1918	Cp. Morrison, Va.	March 1918	P. of E., Newport News.	March 1918	May 1919	June 1919	Mitchel Field, N.Y.	S.O.S. troops.
129th (II) Aero Squadron.	April 1918	Kelly Field, Tex	April 1918	Taylor Field, Ala.					
a. Squadron "D"	July 1918	Taylor Field, Ala.					November 1918	Taylor Field, Ala.	
130th (I) Aero Squadron (supply).	September 1917	Kelly Field, Tex	February 1918	Cp. Morrison, Va.					
a. 649th Aero Squadron (supply).	February 1918	Cp. Morrison, Va.	March 1918	P. of E., Newport News.	March 1918.				
			June 1919	Cp. Mills, N. Y.		June 1919	July 1919	Mitchel Field, N.Y.	Do.
130th (II) Aero Squadron (service).	March 1918	Cp. Sevier, S. C.	March 1918	Pratt Institute, Brooklyn, N. Y.					
			July 1918	Avn. Mec. Tng. Sch., St. Paul, Minn.			November 1918	Avn. Mec. Tng. Sch., St. Paul, Minn.	
131st (I) Aero Squadron (supply).	September 1917	Kelly Field, Tex	February 1918	Cp. Morrison, Va.					
a. 650th Aero Squadron (supply).	February 1918	Cp. Morrison, Va.	March 1918	P. of E., Newport News.	March 1918	May 1919	May 1919	Mitchel Field, N.Y.	Do.
131st (II) Aero Squadron.	March 1918	Cp. Sevier, S. C.	do	Taylor Field, Ala.					
a. Squadron "B"	July 1918	Taylor Field, Ala.					November 1918	Taylor Field, Ala.	
132d (I) Aero Squadron (supply).	September 1917	Kelly Field, Tex	February 1918	Cp. Morrison, Va.					
a. 651st Aero Squadron (supply).	February 1918	Cp. Morrison, Va.	October 1918	Garden City, N. Y.			December 1918	Garden City, N. Y.	Skeletonized July 1918.

132d (II) Aero Squadron	April 1918	Rockwell Field, Calif.							
a. Squadron "C"	July 1918	Rockwell Field, Calif.					November 1918	Rockwell Field, Calif.	
133d (I) Aero Squadron (supply).	September 1917	Kelly Field, Tex.	February 1918	Cp. Morrison, Va.					
a. 652d Aero Squadron (supply).	February 1918	Cp. Morrison, Va.	October 1918	Garden City, N. Y.			December 1918	Garden City, N. Y.	Do.
133d (II) Aero Squadron.	April 1918	Rockwell Field, Calif.							
a. Squadron "D"	July 1918	Rockwell Field, Calif.					November 1918	Rockwell Field, Calif.	
134th (I) Aero Squadron (supply).	September 1917	Kelly Field, Tex.	January 1918	Cp. Morrison, Va.					
a. 653d Aero Squadron (supply).	February 1918	Cp. Morrison, Va.					December 1918	Cp. Morrison, Va.	Do.
134th (II) Aero Squadron.	April 1918	Kelly Field, Tex.	April 1918	Brooks Field, Tex.					
a. Squadron "D"	July 1918	Brooks Field, Tex.					November 1918	Brooks Field, Tex.	
135th Aero Squadron (observation).	October 1917	Rockwell Field, Calif.	December 1917	Garden City, N. Y.					Cmpnt. of IV Corps Obsn. Gp.
			do	P. of E., Hoboken	December 1917				
			May 1919	Hazelhurst Field, N. Y.		May 1919.			
			do	Post Field, Okla.					Corps troops. Active through 1919.
136th (I) Aero Squadron (construction).	August 1917	Kelly Field, Tex.							
a. 120th Aero Squadron (supply).	September 1917	Do.							
b. 120th Aero Squadron (service).	October 1917	do	November 1917	Ellington Field, Tex.					
			February 1918	Garden City, N. Y.					
			do	P. of E., Hoboken	February 1918	May 1919	May 1919	Mitchel Field, N.Y.	S.O.S. troops.
136th (II) Aero Squadron.	September 1917	do	November 1917	Love Field, Tex.					
a. Squadron "C"	July 1918	Love Field, Tex.					November 1918	Love Field, Tex.	

AERO SQUADRONS—Continued

Unit designation and redesignation	Organization		Stations in United States		Overseas		Demobilization		Remarks
	Month and year	Place	Month and year	Place	From—	To—	Month and year	Place	
137th Aero Squadron (service).	September 1917	Kelly Field, Tex.	October 1917	Post Field, Okla.					
			February 1918	Garden City, N. Y.					
			March 1918	P. of E., Hoboken	March 1918	March 1919	March 1919	Garden City, N. Y.	S.O.S. troops.
138th Aero Squadron (pursuit).	do	do	October 1917	Post Field, Okla.					
			February 1918	Garden City, N. Y.					
			March 1918	P. of E., Hoboken	March 1918	July 1919	August 1919	Mitchel Field, N. Y.	Army troops.
139th Aero Squadron (pursuit).	do	do	October 1917	Taliaferro Field #1, Tex.					Cmpnt. of 2d Pur Gp.
			February 1918	Garden City, N. Y.					
			do	P. of E., Hoboken	February 1918	March 1919	April 1919	Garden City, N. Y.	Army troops.
140th Aero Squadron (service).	October 1917	do	November 1917	Park Field, Tex.					
			January 1918	Garden City, N. Y.					
			February 1918	P. of E., Hoboken	do	December 1918	December 1918	do	Cmpnt. of 4th Pur. Gp. S.O.S. troops.
141st Aero Squadron (pursuit).	do	Rockwell Field, Calif.	January 1918	Garden City, N. Y.					
			do	P. of E., Hoboken	January 1918	June 1919	July 1919	Hazelhurst Field, N. Y.	Army troops.
142d Aero Squadron (observation).	November 1917	do	February 1918	Garden City, N. Y.					
			do	P. of E., Hoboken	February 1918	March 1919	April 1919	Garden City, N. Y.	S.O.S. troops.
143d Aero Squadron (service).	October 1917	Chandler Field, Pa.	November 1917	Gerstner Field, La.					
a. Squadron "E"	July 1918	Gerstner Field, La.					November 1918	Gerstner Field, La.	
144th Aero Squadron (service).	October 1917	Kelly Field, Tex.					September 1919	Kelly Field, Tex.	
145th Aero Squadron (repair).	do	do					do	Do.	

146th Aero Squadron (supply).	October 1917	Garden City, N. Y.							
a. 654th Aero Squadron (supply).	January 1918	do	July 1918	Hazelhurst Field, N. Y.					
b. Air Park	November 1918	Hazelhurst Field, N. Y.					January 1919	Garden City, N. Y.	
147th Aero Squadron (pursuit).	November 1917	Kelly Field, Tex.	November 1917	Taliaferro Field #2, Tex.					Cmpnt. of 1st Pur. Gp.
			February 1918	Garden City, N. Y.					
			March 1918	P. of E., Hoboken	March 1918				
			March 1919	Garden City, N. Y.		March 1919.			
			April 1919	Selfridge Field, Mich.					
			August 1919	Kelly Field, Tex.					Active through 1919. Army troops.
148th Aero Squadron (pursuit).	do	do	November 1917	Taliaferro Field, #2, Tex.					Cmpnt. of 4th Pur. Gp.
			February 1918	Garden City, N. Y.					
			do	P. of E., Hoboken	February 1918	March 1919	April 1919	Garden City, N. Y.	Army troops.
149th Aero Squadron (pursuit).	December 1917	do	December 1917	Wilbur Wright Field, Ohio.					
			February 1918	Garden City, N. Y.					
			do	P. of E., Hoboken	do	do	March 1919	do	S.O.S. troops.
150th Aero Squadron	November 1917	do	November 1917	Rich Field, Tex.					
a. Squadron "B"	July 1918	Rich Field, Tex.					November 1918	Rich Field, Tex.	
151st Aero Squadron (service).	December 1917	Kelly Field, Tex.	December 1917	Wilbur Wright Field, Ohio.					
			February 1918	Garden City, N. Y.					
			do	P. of E., Hoboken	February 1918	March 1919	March 1919	Garden City, N. Y.	Do.
152d Aero Squadron (pursuit).	do	do	December 1917	Chanute Field, Ill.					
			February 1918	Garden City, N. Y.					
			do	P. of E., Hoboken	do	July 1919	July 1919	Mitchel Field, N. Y.	Do.
153d Aero Squadron (pursuit).	do	do	December 1917	Chanute Field, Ill.					
			January 1918	Garden City, N. Y.					
			do	P. of E, Hoboken	January 1918	March 1919	March 1919	Garden City, N. Y.	Do.
154th Aero Squadron (service).	do	do	December 1917	Scott Field, Ill.					
			January 1918	Garden City, N. Y.					
			February 1918	P. of E., Hoboken	February 1918	January 1919	February 1919	do	Do.

AERO SQUADRONS—Continued

Unit designation and redesignation	Organization		Stations in United States		Overseas		Demobilization		Remarks
	Month and year	Place	Month and year	Place	From—	To—	Month and year	Place	
155th Aero Squadron (night bombardment).	December 1917	Kelly Field, Tex.	December 1917	Scott Field, Ill.					
			January 1918	Garden City, N. Y.					
			February 1918	P. of E., Hoboken.	February 1918	March 1919	March 1919	Garden City, N. Y.	Army troops.
156th Aero Squadron (service).	do	do	December 1917	Selfridge Field, Mich.					
			February 1918	Garden City, N. Y.					
			March 1918	P. of E., Hoboken.	March 1918	December 1918	December 1918	do	S.O.S. troops.
157th Aero Squadron (construction).	do	do	December 1917	Selfridge Field, Mich.					
			February 1918	Garden City, N. Y.					
			do	P. of E., Hoboken.	February 1918	May 1919	June 1919	Mitchel Field, N. Y.	Do.
158th Aero Squadron (pursuit).	do	do	December 1917	Gerstner Field, La.					
			January 1918	Garden City, N. Y.					
			do	P. of E., Hoboken.	January 1918	March 1919	March 1919	Garden City, N. Y.	Do.
159th Aero Squadron (day bombardment).	do	do	December 1917	Wilbur Wright Field, Ohio.					
			February 1918	Garden City, N. Y.					
			do	P. of E., Hoboken.	February 1918	June 1919	June 1919	Mitchel Field, N. Y.	Do.
160th Aero Squadron	do	do	December 1917	Park Field, Tenn.			December 1918	Park Field, Tenn.	
a. Squadron "C"	July 1918	Park Field, Tenn.							
161st Aero Squadron (park).	December 1917	Kelly Field, Tex.	December 1917	Park Field, Tenn.					
			January 1918	Garden City, N. Y.					
			February 1918	P. of E., Hoboken.	February 1918	May 1919	May 1919	Mitchel Field, N.Y.	Do.
162d Aero Squadron (pursuit).	do	do	December 1917	Wilbur Wright Field, Ohio.					
			February 1918	Garden City, N. Y.					
			do	P. of E., Hoboken.	do	February 1919	February 1919	Garden City, N. Y.	Do.
163d Aero Squadron (day bombardment).	do	do	December 1917	Wilbur Wright Field, Ohio.					Cmpnt. of 2d Day Bombardment Gp.
			February 1918	Garden City, N. Y.					
			do	P. of E., Hoboken.	February 1918	June 1919	June 1919	Hazelhurst Field, N. Y	Army troops.

164th Aero Squadron	November 1917	do	November 1917	Call Field, Tex.					
a. Squadron "A"	July 1918	Call Field, Tex					November 1918	Call Field, Tex.	
165th Aero Squadron (service).	November 1917	Kelly Field, Tex	December 1917	Call Field, Tex.					
			February 1918	Garden City, N. Y.					
			do	P. of E., Hoboken	February 1918	June 1919	June 1919	Mitchel Field, N. Y.	S.O.S. troops.
166th Aero Squadron (day bombardment).	December 1917	do	December 1917	Wilbur Wright Field, Ohio.					Cmpnt. of 1st Day Bombardment Gp.
			February 1918	Garden City, N. Y.					
			March 1918	P. of E., Hoboken	March 1918.				
			June 1919	Mitchel Field, N. Y.		Do.			
			July 1919	Ellington Field, Tex.					
			September 1919	Kelly Field, Tex					Army troops. Active through 1919.
167th Aero Squadron (service).	do	do	December 1917	Hazelhurst Field, N. Y.					
			January 1918	Garden City, N. Y.					
			do	P. of E., Hoboken	January 1918	December 1918	December 1918	Garden City, N. Y.	S.O.S. troops.
168th Aero Squadron (observation).	do	do	December 1917	Hazelhurst Field, N. Y.					Cmpnt. of IV Corps Obsn. Gp.
			January 1918	Garden City, N. Y.					
			do	P. of E., Hoboken	January 1918	June 1919	July 1919	Hazelhurst Field, N. Y.	Army troops.
169th Aero Squadron (observation).	do	Love Field, Tex	do	Garden City, N. Y.					
			February 1918	P. of E., Hoboken	February 1918	May 1919	May 1919	do	S.O.S. troops.
170th Aero Squadron (service).	do	Kelly Field, Tex	December 1917	Selfridge Field, Mich.					
			February 1918	Hazelhurst Field, N. Y.					
			March 1918	P. of E., Hoboken	March 1918	June 1919	June 1919	Mitchel Field, N. Y.	Do.
171st Aero Squadron (service).	November 1917	do	December 1917	Rich Field, Tex.					
			January 1918	Garden City, N. Y.					
			February 1918	P. of E., Hoboken	February 1918	do	July 1919	do	Do.
172d Aero Squadron (observation).	December 1917	do	December 1917	Wilbur Wright Field, Ohio.					
			February 1918	Garden City, N. Y					
			do	P. of E., Hoboken	do	April 1919	April 1919	do	Do.

AERO SQUADRONS—Continued

Unit designation and redesignation	Organization		Stations in United States		Overseas		Demobilization		Remarks
	Month and year	Place	Month and year	Place	From—	To—	Month and year	Place	
173d Aero Squadron (service).	December 1917	Kelly Field, Tex.	December 1917	Chanute Field, Ill.					
			February 1918	Garden City, N. Y.					
			June 1918	P. of E., Hoboken.	June 1918	March 1919	March 1919	Garden City, N. Y.	S.O.S. troops.
174th Aero Squadron (observation).	do	do	December 1917	Chanute Field, Ill.					
			February 1918	Garden City, N. Y.					
			do	P. of E., Hoboken.	February 1918	April 1919	April 1919	Mitchel Field, N. Y	Do.
175th Aero Squadron	November 1917	do	December 1917	Ellington Field, Tex.					
			April 1918	Payne Field, Miss.					
a. Squadron "A"	July 1918	Payne Field, Miss.					November 1918	Payne Field, Miss.	
176th Aero Squadron (service).	December 1917	Kelly Field, Tex.	December 1917	Gerstner Field, La.					
			February 1918	Garden City, N. Y.					
			do	P. of E., Hoboken.	February 1918	March 1919	March 1919	Garden City, N. Y.	Do.
177th Aero Squadron (service).	do	do	December 1917	Gerstner Field, La.					
			February 1918	Garden City, N. Y.					
			do	P. of E., Hoboken.	do	December 1918	December 1918	Cp. Mills, N. Y.	Do.
178th Aero Squadron	January 1918	Do.							
a. Squadron "D"	July 1918	do					November 1918	Kelly Field, Tex.	
179th Aero Squadron	January 1918	do	March 1918	Brooks Field, Tex.					
a. Squadron "E"	July 1918	Brooks Field, Tex.					do	Brooks Field, Tex.	
180th Aero Squadron	December 1917	Kelly Field, Tex.							
a. Squadron "E"	July 1918	do					do	Kelly Field, Tex.	
181st Aero Squadron	December 1917	do	March 1918	Eberts Field, Ark.					
a. Squadron "E"	July 1918	Eberts Field, Ark.					do	Eberts Field, Ark.	
182d Aero Squadron (service).	November 1917	Kelly Field, Tex.	November 1917	Taliaferro Field #2, Tex.					
			January 1918	Taliaferro Field #1, Tex.					
			May 1918	Garden City, N. Y.					
			do	P. of E., Hoboken.	May 1918	March 1919	March 1919	Garden City, N. Y.	S.O.S. troops.

183d Aero Squadron	December 1917	do	December 1917	Taliaferro Field #2, Tex.					
			March 1918	Garden City, N. Y.					
			May 1918	P. of E., Hoboken	Do.				
a. 1st Park Co.	August 1918	A. E. F.							
b. 1st Air Park	October 1918	do				September 1919	September 1919	Camp Dix, N. J.	Cmpnt. of V Corps Obsn. Gp.
184th Aero Squadron (service).	December 1917	Kelly Field, Tex.	December 1917	Taliaferro Field #3, Tex.					
			March 1918	Garden City, N. Y.					
			June 1918	P. of E., Hoboken	June 1918	March 1919	March 1919	Garden City, N. Y.	S.O.S. troops.
185th Aero Squadron (night pursuit).	November 1917	do	January 1918	Garden City, N. Y.					Cmpnt. of 1st Pur. Gp.
			do	P. of E., Hoboken	January 1918	June 1919	June 1919	Mitchel Field, N.Y.	Army troops.
186th Aero Squadron (observation).	do	do	do	Garden City, N. Y.					Cmpnt. of First Army Obsn. Gp.
			do	P. of E., Hoboken	January 1918	August 1919	August 1919	do	Army troops.
187th Aero Squadron (service).	do	do	February 1918	Garden City, N. Y.					
			March 1918	P. of E., Hoboken	March 1918	December 1918	December 1918	Garden City, N. Y.	S.O.S. troops.
188th Aero Squadron (service).	do	do	February 1918	Garden City, N. Y.					
			March 1918	P. of E., Hoboken	do	do	do	do	Do.
189th Aero Squadron	do	do	December 1917	Ellington Field, Tex.			May 1919	Ellington Field, Tex.	
190th Aero Squadron	do	do	do	Do.					
			July 1918	Park Place, Houston, Tex.					
			January 1919	City Auditorium, Houston, Tex.			February 1919	City Auditorium, Houston, Tex.	
191st Aero Squadron	December 1917	Ellington Field, Tex.	July 1918	Park Place, Houston, Tex.			do	Park Place, Houston, Tex.	
192d Aero Squadron	do	Kelly Field, Tex.	December 1917	Call Field, Tex.					
a. Squadron "B"	July 1918	Call Field, Tex.					November 1918	Call Field, Tex.	
193d Aero Squadron	December 1917	Park Field, Tenn.	March 1918	Taylor Field, Ala.					
a. Squadron "C"	July 1918	Taylor Field, Ala.					do	Taylor Field, Ala.	
194th Aero Squadron	December 1917	Ellington Field, Tex.					May 1919	Ellington Field, Tex.	
195th Aero Squadron	November 1917	Kelly Field, Tex.	December 1917	Gerstner Field, La.					
a. Squadron "F"	July 1918	Gerstner Field, La.					November 1918	Gerstner Field, La.	

AERO SQUADRONS—Continued

Unit designation and redesignation	Organization		Stations in United States		Overseas		Demobilization		Remarks
	Month and year	Place	Month and year	Place	From—	To—	Month and year	Place	
196th Aero Squadron	December 1917	Kelly Field, Tex.	December 1917	Gerstner Field, La.					
a. Squadron "G"	July 1918	Gerstner Field, La.					November 1918	Gerstner Field, La.	
197th Aero Squadron	November 1917	Love Field, Tex.							
a. Squadron "D"	July 1918	do.					do.	Love Field, Tex.	
198th Aero Squadron	November 1917	Kelly Field, Tex.	December 1917	Call Field, Tex.					
a. Squadron "C"	July 1918	Call Field, Tex.					do.	Call Field, Tex.	
199th Aero Squadron (observation).	November 1917	Kelly Field, Tex.	December 1917	Love Field, Tex.					Cmpnt. of III Corps Obsn. Gp.
			January 1918	Garden City, N. Y.					
			February 1918	P. of E., Hoboken	February 1918	May 1919	June 1919	Mitchel Field, N. Y.	S.O.S. troops.
200th (I) Aero Squadron (construction).	October 1917	Garden City, N. Y.	October 1917	do.	October 1917.				
a. 496th Aero Squadron (construction).	February 1918	A. E. F.				April 1919	April 1919	Hazelhurst Field, N. Y.	Do.
200th (II) Aero Squadron.	June 1918	Avn. Mec. Tng. Sch., St. Paul, Minn.	June 1918	Mather Field, Calif.					
a. Squadron "A"	July 1918	Mather Field, Calif.					November 1918	Mather Field, Calif.	
201st (I) Aero Squadron (construction).	October 1917	Garden City, N. Y.	October 1917	P. of E., Hoboken	October 1917.				
a. 497th Aero Squadron (construction).	February 1918	A. E. F.				April 1919	April 1919	Hazelhurst Field, N. Y.	Do.
201st (II) Aero Squadron.	June 1918	Avn. Mec. Tng. Sch., St. Paul, Minn.	June 1918	Mather Field, Calif.					
a. Squadron "B"	July 1918	Mather Field, Calif.					November 1918	Mather Field, Calif.	

202d (I) Aero Squadron (construction).	December 1917	Cp. Morrison, Va.							
a. 498th Aero Squadron (construction).	February 1918	do	February 1918 August 1918 September 1918	Langley Field, Va. Garden City, N. Y. P. of E., Montreal	September 1918	January 1919	January 1919	Garden City, N. Y.	Do.
202d (II) Aero Squadron (service).	April 1918	Post Field, Okla.							
a. Squadron "E"	July 1918	do					do	Post Field, Okla.	
203d (I) Aero Squadron (construction).	December 1917	Cp. Morrison, Va.	December 1917	Langley Field, Va.					
a. 499th Aero Squadron (construction).	February 1918	Langley Field, Va.	October 1918 do	Cp. Hill, Va. P. of E., Newport News.	October 1918	March 1919	March 1919	Garden City, N. Y.	Do.
203d (II) Aero Squadron.	March 1918	Chanute Field, Ill.							
a. Squadron "C"	July 1918	do					December 1918	Chanute Field, Ill.	
204th (I) Aero Squadron (construction).	December 1917	Cp. Morrison, Va.							
a. 500th Aero Squadron (construction).	February 1918	do	February 1918 March 1918 August 1918 October 1918 do	Eberts Field, Ark. Payne Field, Miss. Langley Field, Va. Cp. Hill, Va. P. of E., Newport News.	October 1918	March 1919	March 1919	Garden City, N. Y.	Do.
204th (II) Aero Squadron.	March 1918	Rockwell Field, Calif.							
a. Squadron "E"	July 1918	do					November 1918	Rockwell Field, Calif.	
205th (I) Aero Squadron (construction).	December 1917	Cp. Morrison, Va.							
a. 501st Aero Squadron (construction).	February 1918	do	March 1918 do November 1918	Taylor Field, Ala. Souther Field, Ga. Langley Field, Va.			January 1919	Langley Field, Va.	
205th (II) Aero Squadron.	April 1918	Carlstrom Field, Fla.							
a. Squadron "D"	July 1918	do					November 1918	Carlstrom Field, Fla.	

AERO SQUADRONS—Continued

Unit designation and redesignation	Organization		Stations in United States		Overseas		Demobilization		Remarks
	Month and year	Place	Month and year	Place	From—	To—	Month and year	Place	
206th (I) Aero Squadron (construction).	December 1917	Cp. Morrison, Va.							
a. 502d Aero Squadron (construction).	February 1918	do	February 1918	Carlstrom Field, Fla.					
			March 1918	Dorr Field, Fla.					
			August 1918	Langley Field, Va.					
			October 1918	Brindley Field, N. Y.	--------	--------	January 1919	Garden City, N. Y.	
206th (II) Aero Squadron.	April 1918	Taliaferro Field #1, Tex.							
a. Squadron "D"	July 1918	Taliaferro Field, Tex.	--------	--------	--------	--------	November 1918	Taliaferro Field, Tex.	
207th (I) Aero Squadron (construction).	December 1917	Cp. Morrison, Va.							
a. 503d Aero Squadron (construction).	February 1918	do	February 1918	Dorr Field, Fla.					
			March 1918	Carlstrom Field, Fla.					
			do	Cp. Morrison, Va.					
			September 1918	Avn. Gen. Sup. Dep., Middletown, Pa.	--------	--------	March 1919	Avn. Gen. Sup. Dep., Middletown, Pa.	
207th (II) Aero Squadron.	April 1918	Taliaferro Field #2, Tex.	May 1918	Barron Field, Tex.	--------	--------	--------	--------	Taliaferro Field #2 redesignated Barron Field, May 1, 1918.
a. Squadron "C"	July 1918	Barron Field, Tex.	September 1918	Call Field, Tex.					
b. Squadron "D"	September 1918	Call Field, Tex.	--------	--------	--------	--------	November 1918	Call. Field, Tex.	
208th (I) Aero Squadron (construction).	December 1917	Cp. Morrison, Va.							
a. 504th Aero Squadron (construction).	February 1918	do	February 1918	Cp. Alfred Vail, N.J.					
			April 1918	Langley Field, Va.					
			July 1918	Cp. Morrison, Va.					
			November 1918	Langley Field, Va.	--------	--------	January 1919	Langley Field, Va.	

208th (II) Aero Squadron.	April 1918	Taliaferro Field #3, Tex.	May 1918	Carruthers Field, Tex.					Taliaferro Field #3 redesignated Carruthers Field, May 1, 1918.
a. Squadron "A"	July 1918	Carruthers Field, Tex.					November 1918	Carruthers Field, Tex.	
209th (I) Aero Squadron (construction).	December 1917	Kelly Field, Tex.	December 1917	Waco, Tex.					
a. 505th Aero Squadron (construction).	February 1918	Waco, Tex.	May 1918	Cp. Greene, N. C.					
			July 1918	Langley Field, Va.					
			October 1918	Roosevelt Field, N. Y.					
			November 1918	Henry J. Damm Field, N. Y.					
			January 1919	Hazelhurst Field, N. Y.			January 1919	Garden City, N. Y.	
209th (II) Aero Squadron.	April 1918	Taliaferro Field #3, Tex.	May 1918	Carruthers Field, Tex.					Taliaferro Field #3 redesignated Carruthers Field, May 1, 1918.
a. Squadron "B"	July 1918	Carruthers Field, Tex.					November 1918	Carruthers Field, Tex.	
210th Aero Squadron	December 1917	Chanute Field, Ill.	February 1918	Garden City, N. Y.					
			do	P. of E., Hoboken	February 1918	December 1918	December 1918	Garden City, N. Y.	S.O.S. troops.
211th Aero Squadron (service).	do.	Wilbur Wright Field, Ohio.	do	Garden City, N. Y.					
			June 1918	Commack Field, N. Y.					
			July 1918	Garden City, N. Y.					
			do	P. of E., Boston	July 1918	do	do	Cp. Devens, Mass.	Do.
212th Aero Squadron	June 1918	Kelly Field, Tex.					August 1919	Kelly Field, Tex.	
213th Aero Squadron (pursuit).	December 1917	Hazelhurst Field, N. Y.	January 1918	P. of E., Hoboken	January 1918				Cmpnt. of 3d Pur Gp.
			May 1919	Cp. Mills, N. Y.		May 1919	June 1919	Mitchel Field, N.Y.	Army troops.
214th Aero Squadron	do	Park Field, Tenn.							
a. Squadron "D"	July 1918	do					December 1918	Park Field, Tenn.	
215th Aero Squadron (service).	December 1917	Rockwell Field, Calif.	March 1918	March Field, Calif.					
a. Squadron "B"	July 1918	March Field, Calif.					November 1918	March Field, Calif.	

AERO SQUADRONS—Continued

Unit designation and redesignation	Organization		Stations in United States		Overseas		Demobilization		Remarks
	Month and year	Place	Month and year	Place	From—	To—	Month and year	Place	
216th Aero Squadron (service).	January 1918	Kelly Field, Tex.	March, 1918	Garden City, N. Y.					
			July 1918	P. of E., Hoboken	July 1918	December 1918	December 1918	Garden City, N. Y.	S.O.S. troops.
217th Aero Squadron (service).	do	do	March 1918	Garden City, N. Y.					
			August 1918	Mitchel Field, N.Y.			January 1919	Do.	
218th Aero Squadron (service).	do	do	March 1918	Garden City, N. Y.					
			June 1918	P. of E., Hoboken	June 1918.				
a. 4th Park Co.	August 1918	A. E. F.							
b. 4th Air Park	October 1918	do				June 1919	July 1919	Mitchel Field, N.Y.	Cmpnt. of 1st Pur. Gp.
219th Aero Squadron (service).	January 1918	Kelly Field, Tex.	March 1918	Garden City, N. Y.					
			June 1918	Commack Field, N. Y.					
			do	Garden City, N. Y.					
			July 1918	P. of E., Boston	July 1918	December 1918	December 1918	Garden City, N. Y.	S.O.S. troops.
220th Aero Squadron (service).	do	do	March 1918	Hazelhurst Field, N. Y.					
			do	P. of E., Hoboken	March 1918	do	do	do	Do.
221st Aero Squadron	December 1917	Scott Field, Ill.							
a. Squadron "B"	July 1918	do					November 1918	Scott Field, Ill.	
222d Aero Squadron (service).	December 1917	do	February 1918	Garden City, N. Y.					
			March 1918	P. of E., Halifax	March 1918.				
			June 1919	Cp. Mills, N. Y.		June 1919	July 1919	Mitchel Field, N.Y.	Do.
223d Aero Squadron (service).	January 1918	Kelly Field, Tex.	March 1918	Waco, Tex.					
			May 1918	Rich Field, Tex.					
			July 1918	Garden City, N. Y.					
			August 1918	P. of E., Hoboken	August 1918	do	June 1919	do	
224th Aero Squadron (service).	do	do	March 1918	Hazelhurst Field, N. Y.					
			do	P. of E., Hoboken	March 1918	December 1918	December 1918	Garden City, N. Y.	Do.

225th Aero Squadron (service).	do	do	do	Hazelhurst Field, N. Y.					
			July 1918	P. of E., Hoboken	July 1918	do	do	do	Do.
226th Aero Squadron (service).	do	do	March 1918	Garden City, N. Y.					
			June 1918	P. of E., Hoboken	June 1918	do	do	do	Do.
227th Aero Squadron (service).	January 1918	do	March 1918	Garden City, N. Y.					
			June 1918	P. of E., Hoboken	do	June 1919	July 1919	Hazelhurst Field, N. Y.	Do.
228th Aero Squadron (service).	do	do	March 1918	Garden City, N. Y.					
			July 1918	P. of E., Hoboken	July 1918	December 1918	December 1918	Garden City, N. Y.	Do.
229th (I) Aero Squadron (supply).	December 1917	do	January 1918	Garden City, N. Y.					
			do	P. of E., Hoboken	January 1918.				
a. 655th Aero Squadron (supply).	February 1918	A. E. F				May 1919	May 1919	Mitchel Field, N. Y.	Do.
229th (II) Aero Squadron.	April 1918	Taliaferro Field #3, Tex.	May 1918	Carruthers Field, Tex.					Taliaferro Field #3 redesignated Carruthers Field, May 1, 1918.
a. Squadron "C"	July 1918	Carruthers Field, Tex.	September 1918	Call Field, Tex.					
b. Squadron "E"	September 1918	Call Field, Tex					November 1918	Call Field, Tex.	
230th Aero Squadron (supply).	December 1917	Kelly Field, Tex	January 1918	Garden City, N. Y.					
			do	P. of E., Hoboken	January 1918.				
a. 656th Aero Squadron (supply).	February 1918	A. E. F				May 1919	May 1919	Mitchel Field, N. Y.	S.O.S. troops.
231st (I) Aero Squadron (supply).	December 1917	Kelly Field, Tex	February 1918	Garden City, N. Y.					
a. 657th Aero Squadron	February 1918	Garden City, N. Y.	do	P. of E., Hoboken	February 1918	March 1919	March 1919	Garden City, N. Y.	Do.
231st (II) Aero Squadron (service).	April 1918	Kelly Field, Tex	April 1918	Armorers' School, Wilbur Wright Field, Ohio.					
a. Squadron "A"	July 1918	Armorers' School, Wilbur Wright Field, Ohio.					December 1918	Armorers' School, Wilbur Wright Field, Ohio.	

AERO SQUADRONS—Continued

Unit designation and redesignation	Organization		Stations in United States		Overseas		Demobilization		Remarks
	Month and year	Place	Month and year	Place	From—	To—	Month and year	Place	
232d (I) Aero Squadron (supply).	December 1917	Kelly Field, Tex.	February 1918	Garden City, N. Y.					
a. 658th Aero Squadron (supply).	February 1918	Garden City, N. Y.	do	P. of E., Hoboken	February 1918	May 1919	May 1919	Mitchel Field, N. Y.	S.O.S. troops.
232d (II) Aero Squadron.	April 1918	Kelly Field, Tex.	April 1918	Ellington Field, Tex.					
a. Squadron "D"	July 1918	Ellington Field, Tex.					December 1918	Ellington Field, Tex.	
233d (I) Aero Squadron	December 1917	Kelly Field, Tex.							
a. 659th Aero Squadron (supply).	February 1918	do	February 1918	Garden City, N. Y.					
			March 1918	P. of E., Hoboken	March 1918	July 1919	July 1919	Mitchel Field, N. Y.	S.O.S. troops.
233d (II) Aero Squadron.	April 1918	do	April 1918	Ellington Field, Tex.					
a. Squadron "E"	July 1918	Ellington Field, Tex.					December 1918	Ellington Field, Tex.	
234th (I) Aero Squadron (supply).	December 1917	Kelly Field, Tex.							
a. 660th Aero Squadron (supply).	February 1918	do	April 1918	Garden City, N. Y.					
			May 1918	P. of E., Hoboken	May 1918	May 1919	June 1919	Mitchel Field, N. Y.	Do.
234th (II) Aero Squadron.	April 1918	do	June 1918	Brooks Field, Tex.					
a. Squadron "F"	July 1918	Brooks Field, Tex.					September 1918	Brooks Field, Tex.	
235th (I) Aero Squadron (supply).	December 1917	Kelly Field, Tex.							
a. 661st Aero Squadron (supply).	February 1918	do	May 1918	Garden City, N. Y.			December 1918	Garden City, N. Y.	

235th (II) Aero Squadron.	April 1918	Do.							
a. Squadron "F"	July 1918	do					November 1918	Kelly Field, Tex.	
236th (I) Aero Squadron (supply).	December 1917	Do.							
a. 662d Aero Squadron (supply).	February 1918	do	May 1918	Avn. Gen. Sup. Dep., San Antonio, Tex.			April 1919	Avn. Gen. Sup Dep., San Antonio, Tex.	
236th (II) Aero Squadron.	April 1918	do	do	Souther Field, Ga.					
a. Squadron "C"	July 1918	Souther Field, Ga					November 1918	Souther Field, Ga.	
237th (I) Aero Squadron	December 1917	Kelly Field, Tex.							
a. 663d Aero Squadron (supply).	February 1918	do	May 1918	Garden City, N. Y.			December 1918	Garden City, N. Y.	Skeletonized July 1918.
237th (II) Aero Squadron.	April 1918	do	do	Souther Field, Ga.					
a. Squadron "D"	July 1918	Souther Field, Ga.					November 1918	Souther Field, Ga.	
238th (I) Aero Squadron (supply).	December 1917	Kelly Field, Tex.							
a. 664th Aero Squadron (supply).	February 1918	do	May 1918	Garden City, N. Y.			December 1918	Garden City, N. Y.	Do.
238th (II) Aero Squadron.	April 1918	do	April 1918	Payne Field, Miss.					
a. Squadron "B"	July 1918	Payne Field, Miss.					November 1918	Payne Field, Miss.	
239th (I) Aero Squadron	December 1917	Kelly Field, Tex.							
a. 665th Aero Squadron (supply).	February 1918	do	May 1918	Garden City, N. Y.			December 1918	Garden City, N. Y.	Do.
239th (II) Aero Squadron.	April 1918	do	April 1918	Payne Field, Miss.					
a. Squadron "C"	July 1918	Payne Field, Miss.					November 1918	Payne Field, Miss.	
240th (I) Aero Squadron	December 1917	Kelly Field, Tex.							
a. 666th Aero Squadron (supply).	February 1918	do	March 1918	Garden City, N. Y.			December 1918	Garden City, N. Y.	Do.
240th (II) Aero Squadron.	April 1918	do	May 1918	Dorr Field, Fla.					
a. Squadron "D"	July 1918	Dorr Field, Fla.					November 1918	Dorr Field, Fla.	

AERO SQUADRONS—Continued

Unit designation and redesignation	Organization		Stations in United States		Overseas		Demobilization		Remarks
	Month and year	Place	Month and year	Place	From—	To—	Month and year	Place	
241st (I) Aero Squadron	December 1917	Kelly Field, Tex.							
a. 667th Aero Squadron (supply).	February 1918	do	March 1918	Garden City, N. Y.					
			do	P. of E., Hoboken	March 1918	June 1919	June 1919	Mitchel Field, N. Y.	S.O.S. troops.
241st (II) Aero Squadron.	April 1918	do	May 1918	Dorr Field, Fla.					
a. Squadron "E"	July 1918	Dorr Field, Fla					November 1918	Dorr Field, Fla.	
242d (I) Aero Squadron (supply).	December 1917	Kelly Field, Tex.							
a. 668th Aero Squadron (supply).	February 1918	do					August 1919	Kelly Field, Tex	Skeletonized March 1919.
242d (II) Aero Squadron.	April 1918	do	May 1918	Scott Field, Ill.					
a. Squadron "C"	July 1918	Scott Field, Ill					November 1918	Scott Field, Ill.	
243d (I) Aero Squadron (supply).	December 1917	Kelly Field, Tex.							
a. 669th Aero Squadron (supply).	February 1918	do	May 1918	Wilbur Wright Field, Ohio.			April 1919	Wilbur Wright Field, Ohio.	
243d (II) Aero Squadron.	April 1918	Do.							
a. Squadron "G"	July 1918	do					November 1918	Kelly Field, Tex.	
244th (I) Aero Squadron	November 1917	do	January 1918	Garden City, N. Y					
			do	P. of E., Hoboken	January 1918.				
a. 805th Aero Squadron (repair).	February 1918	A. E. F				June 1919	June 1919	Mitchel Field, N. Y.	S.O.S. troops.
244th (II) Aero Squadron.	April 1918	Kelly Field, Tex.							
a. Squadron "H"	July 1918	do					November 1918	Kelly Field, Tex.	

245th (I) Aero Squadron	November 1917	do	January 1918 do	Garden City, N. Y. P. of E., Hoboken	January 1918.				
a. 806th Aero Squadron (repair).	February 1918	A. E. F				December 1918	December 1918	Garden City, N. Y.	Do.
245th (II) Aero Squadron.	April 1917	Kelly Field, Tex.							
a. Squadron "I"	July 1918	do					November 1918	Kelly Field, Tex.	
246th (I) Aero Squadron	November 1917	do	November 1917	McCook Field, Ohio.					
a. 807th Aero Squadron (repair).	February 1918	McCook Field, Ohio.							
b. Squadron "A"	July 1918	do					August 1918	McCook Field, Ohio.	
246th (II) Aero Squadron.	April 1918	Kelly Field, Tex	May 1918	Wilbur Wright Field, Ohio.					
a. Squadron "L"	October 1918	Wilbur Wright Field, Ohio.					February 1919	Wilbur Wright Field, Ohio.	
247th Aero Squadron (service).	February 1918	Waco, Tex	February 1918	Garden City, N. Y.					
248th Aero Squadron (service).	do	do	March 1918 February 1918	P. of E., Hoboken Garden City, N. Y.	March 1918	March 1919	March 1919	Garden City, N. Y.	Do.
249th Aero Squadron (service).	November 1917	Kelly Field, Tex	March 1918 December 1917	P. of E., Hoboken Rich Field, Tex.	do	April 1919	May 1919	Mitchel Field, N. Y	Do.
a. Squadron "C"	July 1918	Rich Field, Tex					November 1918	Rich Field, Tex	
250th Aero Squadron	November 1917	Kelly Field, Tex	December 1917	Ellington Field, Tex.					
a. Squadron "F"	July 1918	Ellington Field, Tex.					December 1918	Ellington Field. Tex.	
251st Aero Squadron	December 1917	Post Field, Okla.							
a. Squadron "F"	July 1918	do					January 1919	Post Field, Okla.	
252d Aero Squadron	January 1918	Ellington Field, Tex.	April 1918	Payne Field, Miss.					
a. Squadron "D"	July 1918	Payne Field, Miss					November 1918	Payne Field, Miss.	
253d Aero Squadron	December 1917	Kelly Field, Tex	December 1917 August 1918	Gerstner Field, La. Henry J. Damm Field, N. Y.			January 1919	Garden City, N. Y	

AERO SQUADRONS—Continued

Unit designation and redesignation	Organization		Stations in United States		Overseas		Demobilization		Remarks
	Month and year	Place	Month and year	Place	From—	To—	Month and year	Place	
254th Aero Squadron (service).	February 1918	Waco, Tex	February 1918	Garden City, N. Y.					
			March 1918	P. of E., Hoboken	March 1918	December 1918	December 1918	Garden City, N. Y.	S.O.S. troops.
255th Aero Squadron (service).	do	do	do	Wilbur Wright Field, Ohio.					
			do	Garden City, N. Y.					
			June 1918	P. of E., Hoboken	June 1918.				
a. 3d Park Company.	July 1918	A. E. F.							
b. 3d Air Park	October 1918	do				June 1919	July 1919	Mitchel Field, N. Y.	
256th Aero Squadron	February 1918	Waco, Tex	March 1918	Wilbur Wright Field, Ohio.					
			do	Garden City, N. Y.					
			June 1918	Commack Field, N. Y.					
			July 1918	P. of E., Boston	July 1918	December 1918	December 1918	Garden City, N. Y.	Do.
257th Aero Squadron (training).	do	do	March 1918	Wilbur Wright Field, Ohio.					
			do	Garden City, N Y.					
			June 1918	P. of E., Hoboken	June 1918	April 1919	April 1919	Mitchel Field,. N Y.	Do.
258th Aero Squadron (observation).	do	do	March 1918	Wilbur Wright Field, Ohio					
			July 1918	Garden City, N. Y.					
			August 1918	P of E , Hoboken	August 1918				Cmpnt of VII Corps Obsn Gp.
			August 1919	Mitchel Field, N. Y.		August 1919.			
			do	Aberdeen Proving Ground, Md.					Army troops. Active through 1919.
259th Aero Squadron (service).	do	do	March 1918	Wilbur Wright Field, Ohio.					
			July 1918	Garden City, N. Y.					
			do	P. of E., Hoboken	July 1918	December 1918	December 1918	Garden City, N. Y.	S.O.S. troops.

260th Aero Squadron (service).	do	do	March 1918	Wilbur Wright Field, Ohio.					
			July 1918	Garden City, N. Y					
			do	P. of E., Hoboken	do	do	do	do	Do.
261st Aero Squadron (service).	do	Scott Field, Ill.	March 1918	Garden City, N. Y.					
			June 1918	Babylon, N. Y.					
			July 1918	Garden City, N. Y.					
			do	P. of E., Boston	do	do	do	do	Do.
262d Aero Squadron (service).	do	do	do	Garden City, N. Y.					
			do	P. of E., Boston	do	do	do	do	Do.
263d Aero Squadron (service).	do	do	do	Garden City, N. Y.					
			do	P. of E., Hoboken	do	do	do	do	Do.
264th Aero Squadron (service).	January 1918	Hazelhurst Field, N. Y.	February 1918	Garden City, N. Y.					
			do	P. of E., Hoboken	February 1918	March 1919	March 1919	do	Do.
265th Aero Squadron (service).	February 1918	Wilbur Wright Field, Ohio.	March 1918	Hazelhurst Field, N. Y.					
			July 1918	P. of E., Hoboken	July 1918	December 1918	December 1918	do	Do.
266th Aero Squadron (service).	January 1918	Selfridge Field, Mich.	do	Garden City, N. Y.					
			August 1918	P. of E., Hoboken	August 1918	May 1919	May 1919	Mitchel Field, N. Y.	Do.
267th Aero Squadron (service).	do	Chanute Field, Ill.	June 1918	Garden City, N. Y.					
			do	Babylon, N. Y.					
			July 1918	Garden City, N. Y.					
			do	P. of E., Boston	July 1918	December 1918	December 1918	Garden City, N. Y.	Do.
268th Aero Squadron (service).	do	do	June 1918	Garden City, N. Y.					
			do	Commack Field, N. Y.					
			July 1918	Garden City, N. Y.					
			do	P. of E., Boston	do	do	do	do	Do.
269th Aero Squadron (service).	February 1918	Gerstner Field, La.	do	Garden City, N. Y.					
			August 1918	P. of E., Hoboken	August 1918	July 1919	July 1919	Mitchel Field, N. Y.	Do.
270th Aero Squadron (service).	do	do	July 1918	Garden City, N. Y.					
			August 1918	P. of E., Hoboken	do	do	do	do	Do.
271st Aero Squadron	do	Ellington Field, Tex.	July 1918	Aberdeen Proving Ground, Md.			September 1919	Aberdeen Proving Ground, Md.	
272d Aero Squadron	April 1918	Do.							
a. Squadron "G"	July 1918	do					December 1918	Ellington Field, Tex.	

AERO SQUADRONS—Continued

Unit designation and redesignation	Organization		Stations in United States		Overseas		Demobilization		Remarks
	Month and year	Place	Month and year	Place	From—	To—	Month and year	Place	
273 Aero Squadron	February 1918	Taliaferro Field #2, Tex.	May 1918	Barron Field, Tex.					Taliaferro Field #2 redesignated Barron Field May 1, 1918.
a. Squadron "D"	July 1918	Barron Field, Tex.					November 1918	Barron Field, Tex.	
274th Aero Squadron	February 1918	Taliaferro Field #3, Tex.	do	Carruthers Field, Tex.					Taliaferro Field #3 redesignated Carruthers Field May 1, 1918.
a. Squadron "D"	July 1918	Carruthers Field, Tex.					November 1918	Carruthers Field, Tex.	
275th Aero Squadron	February 1918	Taliaferro Field #1, Tex.							
a. Squadron "E"	July 1918	Taliaferro Field, Tex.					do	Taliaferro Field, Tex.	
276th Aero Squadron (service).	February 1918	Cp. Sevier, S. C.	June 1918	Emerson Field, S. C.					
			April 1919	Pope Field, N. C			June 1919	Pope Field, N. C.	
277th Aero Squadron	do	Love Field, Tex.	August 1918	Garden City, N. Y.					
			do	Brindley Field, N. Y.			January 1919	Garden City, N. Y.	
278th Aero Squadron (service).	do	do	July 1918	Garden City, N. Y.					
			August 1918	P. of E., Hoboken	August 1918	July 1919	July 1919	Mitchel Field, N. Y.	Army troops.
279th Aero Squadron (service).	do	Gerstner Field, La.	July 1918	Garden City, N. Y.					
			do	P. of E., Hoboken	July 1918.				
a. 5th Park Company.	September 1918	A. E. F							Cmpnt. of 2d Pur Gp.
b. 5th Air Park	October 1918	do	March 1919	Cp. Stuart, Va		March 1919	March 1919	Langley Field, Va.	Demobilized at Langley Field, Va.; reconstituted at Kelly Field, Tex.
	July 1919	Kelly Field, Tex.							
280th Aero Squadron (service).	February 1918	Rich Field, Tex.	August 1918	Brindley Field, N. Y.			January 1919	Garden City, N. Y.	

281st Aero Squadron (service).	do	Park Field, Tenn.	July 1918 August 1918	Garden City, N. Y. P. of E., Hoboken.	August 1918	July 1919	July 1919	Mitchel Field, N. Y.	S.O.S. troops.
282d Aero Squadron	do	do	July 1918 August 1918	Garden City, N. Y. P. of E., Hoboken.	do	December 1918	December 1918	Cp. Devens, Mass.	Do.
283d Aero Squadron (service).	do	Rockwell Field, Calif.	April 1918	Mather Field, Calif.					
a. Squadron "C"	July 1918	Mather Field, Calif.					November 1918	Mather Field, Calif.	
284th Aero Squadron	February 1918	Scott Field, Ill.	February 1918	Carlstrom Field, Fla.					
a. Squadron "E"	July 1918	Carlstrom Field, Fla.					do	Carlstrom Field, Fla.	
285th Aero Squadron	March 1918	Ellington Field, Tex.							
a. Squadron "H"	July 1918	do					December 1918	Ellington Field, Tex.	
286th Aero Squadron	April 1918	Do.							
a. Squadron "I"	July 1918	do					do	Do.	
287th Aero Squadron (service).	April 1918	Kelly Field, Tex.	May 1918 June 1918	Wilbur Wright Field, Ohio. Chanute Field, Ill.					
a. Squadron "D"	July 1918	Chanute Field, Ill.							287th and 112th Aer. Sqs. consolidated into the Avn. Sup. Dep. Det., Americus, Ga., Jan. 1919.
b. 287th Aero Squadron.	December 1918	do					December 1918	Avn. Gen. Sup. Dep., Americus, Ga.	
288th Aero Squadron	April 1918	Kelly Field, Tex.	May 1918 June 1918	Wilbur Wright Field, Ohio. Chanute Field, Ill.					
a. Squadron "E"	July 1918	Chanute Field, Ill.					August 1918	Chanute Field, Ill.	
289th Aero Squadron	do	Rockwell Field, Calif.	August 1918	March Field, Calif.					
a. Squadron "C"	August 1918	March Field, Calif.					November 1918	March Field, Calif.	
290th Aero Squadron (provisional).	June 1918	Rockwell Field, Calif.							
a. Squadron "F"	July 1918	do					do	Rockwell Field, Calif.	

AERO SQUADRONS—Continued

Unit designation and redesignation	Organization		Stations in United States		Overseas		Demobilization		Remarks
	Month and year	Place	Month and year	Place	From—	To—	Month and year	Place	
291st Aero Squadron (provisional).	June 1918	Rockwell Field, Calif.							
a. Squadron "G"	July 1918	do					November 1918	Rockwell Field, Calif.	
292d Aero Squadron (provisional).	June 1918	Do.							
a. Squadron "H"	July 1918	do					do	Do.	
293d Aero Squadron	June 1918	March Field, Calif.							
a. Squadron "D"	July 1918	do					do	March Field, Calif.	
294th Aero Squadron	June 1918	Mather Field, Calif.							
a. Squadron "D"	July 1918	do					do	Mather Field, Calif	
295th Aero Squadron (provisional).	June 1918	Columbia Univ., N. Y.					February 1919	Columbia Univ., N. Y.	
296th Aero Squadron (provisional).	do	do					August 1918	Do.	
297th Aero Squadron (provisional).	August 1918	Carnegie Inst. of Tech., Pa.					January 1919	Carnegie Inst. of Tech., Pa.	
298th Aero Squadron (provisional).	do	do					do	Do.	
299th Aero Squadron (provisional).	do	do					do	Do.	
300th Aero Squadron									Never orgzd.
301st Aero Squadron									Do.
302d Aero Squadron (service).	June 1918	Carlstrom Field, Fla.							
a. Squadron "F"	July 1918	do					November 1918	Carlstrom Field, Fla.	
303d Aero Squadron (provisional).	May 1918	Ellington Field, Tex.							
a. 303d Aero Squadron (service).	June 1918	Do.							
b. Squadron "K"	July 1918	do					December 1918	Ellington, Field, Tex.	

304th Aero Squadron									Never orgzd.
305th Aero Squadron									Do.
306th Aero Squadron (service).	July 1918	Cp. Greene, N. C.	July 1918 do	Garden City, N. Y. P. of E., Hoboken	July 1918	December 1918	December 1918	Cp. Devens, Mass.	S.O.S. troops.
307th Aero Squadron (service).	do	do	do do	Garden City, N. Y. P. of E., Hoboken	do	do	do	Garden City, N. Y.	Do.
308th Aero Squadron (service).	do	do	do do	Garden City, N. Y. P. of E., Hoboken	do	do	do	do	Do.
309th Aero Squadron (service).	do	do	do do	Garden City, N. Y. P. of E., Hoboken	do	do	do	do	Do.
310th Aero Squadron (service).	do	do	do do	Garden City, N. Y. P. of E., Hoboken	do	do	do	do	Do.
311th Aero Squadron	June 1918	March Field, Calif.							
a. Squadron "E"	July 1918	do					November 1918	March Field, Calif.	
312th Aero Squadron (service).	do	Bolling Field, D. C.					September 1919	Bolling Field, D. C.	
313th Aero Squadron	June 1918	Kelly Field, Tex.					August 1919	Kelly Field, Tex.	
314th Aero Squadron (service).	July 1918	Garden City, N. Y.	July 1918	P. of E., Hoboken	July 1918	December 1918	December 1918	Garden City, N. Y.	Do.
315th Aero Squadron (service).	do	do	do	do	do	do	do	do	Do.
316th Aero Squadron (service).	do	do	do	do	do	do	do	do	Do.
317th Aero Squadron (service).	do	do	do	do	do	do	do	do	Do.
318th Aero Squadron (service).	do	do	do	do	do	do	do	do	Do.
319th Aero Squadron (service).	do	Cp. Morrison, Va.	do do	Garden City, N. Y. P. of E., Hoboken	do	do	do	do	Do.
320th Aero Squadron (service).	do	do	do do	Garden City, N. Y. P. of E., Hoboken	do	do	do	do	Do.
321st Aero Squadron (service).	July 1918	do	July 1918 do	Garden City, N. Y. P. of E., Hoboken	do	do	do	do	Do.
322d Aero Squadron	February 1918	Kelly Field, Tex.					February 1919	Kelly Field, Tex.	
323d Aero Squadron	December 1917	do					August 1919	Do.	
324th Aero Squadron	February 1918	do					do	Do.	
325th (I) Aero Squadron (service).	December 1917	Do.							
a. 869th Aero Squadron (repair).	April 1918	do					December 1918	Do.	

AERO SQUADRONS—Continued

Unit designation and redesignation	Organization		Stations in United States		Overseas		Demobilization		Remarks
	Month and year	Place	Month and year	Place	From—	To—	Month and year	Place	
325th (II) Aero Squadron (service).	July 1918	Cp. Morrison, Va.	July 1918 August 1918	Garden City, N. Y. P. of E., Hoboken.	August 1918	December 1918	December 1918	Garden City, N. Y.	S.O.S. troops.
326th (I) Aero Squadron	December 1917	Kelly Field, Tex.							
a. 870th Aero Squadron (repair).	April 1918	do					do	Kelly Field, Tex.	
326th (II) Aero Squadron (service).	July 1918	Cp. Morrison, Va.	July 1918 do	Garden City, N. Y. P. of E., Boston	July 1918	December 1918	do	Garden City, N. Y.	Do.
327th Aero Squadron	November 1917	Kelly Field, Tex.					August 1919	Kelly Field, Tex.	
328th Aero Squadron	do	do					do	Do.	
329th Aero Squadron (service).	July 1918	Cp. Morrison, Va.	July 1918 do	Garden City, N. Y. P. of E., Boston	July 1918	December 1918	December 1918	Garden City, N. Y.	Do.
330th Aero Squadron (service).	do	do	do do	Garden City, N. Y. P. of E., Philadelphia.	do	do	do	do	Do.
331st Aero Squadron (service).	do	do	do do	Garden City, N. Y. P. of E., Hoboken.	do	do	do	do	Do.
332d (I) Aero Squadron (supply).	December 1917	Kelly Field, Tex.	January 1918 do	Waco, Tex. Cp. Morrison, Va.					
a. 670th Aero Squadron (supply).	February 1918	Cp. Morrison, Va.					do	Cp. Morrison, Va.	Skeletonized July 1918.
332d (II) Aero Squadron (service).									See 339th (I) Aer. Sq.
333d (I) Aero Squadron	December 1917	Kelly Field, Tex.	January 1918 do	Waco, Tex. Cp. Morrison, Va.					
a. 671st Aero Squadron (supply).	February 1918	Cp. Morrison, Va.					December 1918	Cp. Morrison, Va.	Skeletonized July 1918.
333d (II) Aero Squadron (service).	July 1918	do	July 1918 do	Garden City, N. Y. P. of E., Hoboken.	July 1918	December 1918	do	Garden City, N. Y.	S.O.S. troops.

334th (I) Aero Squadron	December 1917	Kelly Field, Tex.	January 1918 do	Waco, Tex. Cp. Morrison, Va.					
a. 672d Aero Squadron (supply).	February 1918	Cp. Morrison, Va.					do	Cp. Morrison, Va.	**Skeletonized July 1918.**
334th (II) Aero Squadron (service).	July 1918	do	July 1918 do	Garden City, N. Y. P. of E., Hoboken	July 1918	December 1918	do	Garden City, N. Y.	**S.O.S. troops.**
335th (I) Aero Squadron	December 1917	Kelly Field, Tex.	January 1918 do	Waco, Tex. Cp Morrison, Va.					
a. 673d Aero Squadron (supply).	February 1918	Cp. Morrison, Va.					do	Cp. Morrison, Va.	
335th (II) Aero Squadron (service).	July 1918	do	July 1918 August 1918	Garden City, N. Y. P. of E., Hoboken	August 1918	December 1918	do	Garden City, N. Y.	Do.
336th (I) Aero Squadron (supply).	December 1917	Kelly Field, Tex.	January 1918 do	Waco, Tex. Cp .Morrison, Va.					
a. 674th Aero Squadron (supply).	February 1918	Cp. Morrison, Va.					do	Cp. Morrison, Va.	
336th (II) Aero Squadron (service).	July 1918	do	July 1918 August 1918	Garden City, N. Y. P. of E., Hoboken	August 1918	December 1918	do	Garden City, N. Y.	Do.
337th (I) Aero Squadron	December 1917	Kelly Field, Tex.	January 1918	Avn. Gen. Sup. Dep., San Antonio, Tex.					
a. 675th Aero Squadron (supply).	February 1918	Avn. Gen. Sup. Dep., San Antonio, Tex.					April 1919	Avn. Gen. Sup. Dep., San Antonio, Tex.	
337th (II) Aero Squadron (service).	July 1918	Cp. Morrison, Va.	July 1918 August 1918	Garden City, N Y. P. of E., Hoboken	August 1918	December 1918	December 1918	Garden City, N. Y.	Do.
338th Aero Squadron (supply).	do	do	July 1918 do	Garden City, N. Y. P. of E., Hoboken	July 1918	do	do	do	Do.
339th (I) Aero Squadron (supply).	do	Do.							
a. 332d Aero Squadron (service).	do	do	do do	Garden City, N. Y. P. of E., Hoboken	do	do	January 1919	do	Do.
339th (II) Aero Squadron (service).	August 1918	Garden City, N. Y.					April 1919	Do.	
340th Aero Squadron (service).	do	do					February 1919	Do.	

AERO SQUADRONS—Continued

Unit designation and redesignation	Organization		Stations in United States		Overseas		Demobilization		Remarks
	Month and year	Place	Month and year	Place	From—	To—	Month and year	Place	
341st Aero Squadron (service).	July 1918	Cp. Greene, N. C.	July 1918	Cp. Morrison, Va.	July 1918	March 1919	April 1919	Garden City, N. Y.	S.O.S. troops.
			do	P. of E., Newport News.					
342d Aero Squadron	August 1918	Wilbur Wright Field, Ohio.							
a. Squadron "M"	October 1918	Do.							
b. Squadron "Q"	November 1918	do					do	Wilbur Wright Field, Ohio.	
343d Aero Squadron	August 1918	Park Place, Houston, Tex.					February 1919	Park Place, Houston, Tex.	
344th Aero Squadron (service).	September 1918	Garden City, N. Y.					December 1918	Garden City, N. Y.	"Handley Page."
345th Aero Squadron (service).	do	do					January 1919	do	Do.
346th Aero Squadron (service).	do	do					do	do	Do.
347th Aero Squadron									Never orgzd.
348th Aero Squadron									Do.
349th Aero Squadron (service).	January 1918	Kelly Field, Tex.	March 1918	Garden City, N. Y.	May 1918	December 1918	January 1919	Garden City, N. Y.	S.O.S. troops.
			May 1918	P. of E., Hoboken.					
350th Aero Squadron (service).	do	do	March 1918	Garden City, N. Y.					
			June 1918	Babylon, N. Y.					
			July 1918	Garden City, N. Y.					
			do	P. of E., Boston	July 1918	do	December 1918	do	Do.
351st Aero Squadron (service).	do	do	March 1918	Waco, Tex.					
			April 1918	Taliaferro Field #2, Tex.					Taliaferro Field #2 redesignated Barron Field May 1, 1918.
			May 1918	Barron Field, Tex.					
			July 1918	Garden City, N. Y.					
			August 1918	P. of E., Hoboken.	August 1918	April 1919	April 1919	Mitchel Field, N.Y.	S.O.S. troops.

352d Aero Squadron	do	do	March 1918	Waco, Tex.					
			April 1918	Taliaferro Field #2, Tex.					Taliaferro Field #2 redesignated Barron Field May 1, 1918.
			May 1918	Barron Field, Tex.					
			July 1918	Mitchel Field, N. Y.					
			August 1918	Hazelhurst Field, N. Y.					
			September 1918	Roosevelt Field, N. Y.			January 1919	Garden City, N. Y.	
353d Aero Squadron (service).	do	do	March 1918	Waco, Tex.					
			April 1918	Taliaferro Field #3, Tex.					Taliaferro Field #3 redesignated Carruthers Field May 1, 1918.
			May 1918	Carruthers Field, Tex.					
			July 1918	Garden City, N. Y.					
			August 1918	P. of E., Hoboken	August 1918	May 1919	May 1919	Mitchel Field, N. Y.	S.O.S. troops.
354th Aero Squadron (observation).	do	do	March 1918	Waco, Tex.					Cmpnt. of VI Corps Obsn. Gp.
			April 1918	Taliaferro Field #1, Tex.					
			July 1918	Garden City, N. Y.					
			August 1918	P. of E., Hoboken	August 1918	June 1919	July 1919	Mitchel Field, N. Y.	Corps troops.
355th Aero Squadron	do	do	March 1918	Waco, Tex.					
			May 1918	Rich Field, Tex.					
			August 1918	Hazelhurst Field, N. Y.					
			September 1918	Roosevelt Field, N. Y.			December 1918	Roosevelt Field, N. Y.	
356th Aero Squadron (service).	do	do	March 1918	Garden City, N. Y.					
			May 1918	P. of E., Hoboken	May 1918	December 1918	do	Garden City, N. Y.	S.O.S. troops.
357th Aero Squadron	do	do	March 1918	Hazelhurst Field, N. Y.			September 1919	Hazelhurst Field, N. Y.	
358th Aero Squadron	do	do	do	Do.					
			April 1919	Roosevelt Field, N. Y.			do	Roosevelt Field, N. Y.	
359th Aero Squadron	February 1918	do	March 1918	Garden City, N. Y.					
			July 1918	Hazelhurst Field, N. Y.					
			August 1918	Brindley Field, N. Y.			January 1919	Garden City, N. Y.	

AERO SQUADRONS—Continued

Unit designation and redesignation	Organization		Stations in United States		Overseas		Demobilization		Remarks
	Month and year	Place	Month and year	Place	From—	To—	Month and year	Place	
360th Aero Squadron	January 1918	Kelly Field, Tex.	March 1918 June 1918	Garden City, N. Y. P. of E., Hoboken	June 1918.				
a. 2d Park Company.	August 1918	A. E. F.							Cmpnt. of 3d Pur. Gp.
b. 2d Air Park	October 1918	do	June 1919 July 1919 November 1919	Mitchel Field, N. Y. Ellington Field, Tex. Kelly Field, Tex.		June 1919.			
361st Aero Squadron (service).	January 1918	Kelly Field, Tex.	March 1918 July 1918	Garden City, N. Y. P. of E., Boston	July 1918	December 1918	December 1918	Garden City, N. Y.	S.O.S. troops.
362d Aero Squadron (depot).	do	NE Dept. Hq., Boston, Mass.							
a. 813th Aero Squadron (depot).	do	do					January 1919	NE Dept. Hq., Boston, Mass.	
363d Aero Squadron (depot).	do	E Dept. Hq., New York, N. Y.							
a. 814th Aero Squadron (depot).	February 1918	do					August 1919	E Dept. Hq., New York, N. Y.	
364th Aero Squadron (depot)	January 1918	S E Dept. Hq., Charleston, S. C.							
a. 815th Aero Squadron (depot).	February 1918	do					do	SE Dept. Hq., Charleston, S. C.	
365th Aero Squadron (depot).	January 1918	C Dept. Hq., Chicago, Ill.							
a. 816th Aero Squadron (depot).	February 1918	do					do	C Dept. Hq., Chicago, Ill.	

366th Aero Squadron (depot).	March 1918	Ft. Sill, Okla.							
a. 817th Aero Squadron (depot) Detachment.	April 1918	Do.							
b. 366th Aero Squadron (provisional).	May 1918	do					June 1918	Ft. Sill, Okla.	
367th Aero Squadron (depot).	January 1918	W Dept. Hq., San Francisco, Calif.							
a. 818th Aero Squadron (depot).	February 1918	do					August 1919	W Dept. Hq., San Francisco, Calif.	
368th Aero Squadron	January 1918	Langley Field, Va.							
a. Detachment #17, Air Service, Aircraft Production.	August 1918	do					January 1919	Langley Field, Va.	
369th Aero Squadron (service).	January 1918	Waco, Tex.	January 1918 February 1918	Hazelhurst Field, N. Y. P. of E., Hoboken	February 1918	May 1919	June 1919	Mitchel Field, N. Y.	S.O.S. troops.
370th Aero Squadron	do	do	January 1918 February 1918	Hazelhurst Field, N. Y. P. of E. Hoboken	do	do	do	do	Do.
371st Aero Squadron	do	do	January 1918 February 1918 March 1918	Hazelhurst Field, N. Y. Garden City, N. Y. P. of E., Halifax	March 1918	December 1918	December 1918	Garden City, N. Y.	Do.
372d Aero Squadron (service).	do	do	February 1918 March 1918	Hazelhurst Field, N. Y. P. of E., Halifax	March 1918	May 1919	May 1919	Mitchel Field, N. Y.	Do.
373d Aero Squadron (service).	do	do	February 1918 March 1918	Garden City, N. Y. P. of E., Halifax	do	March 1919	April 1919	Garden City, N. Y.	Do.
374th Aero Squadron (service).	do	do	February 1918 March 1918	Hazelhurst Field, N. Y. P. of E., Halifax	do	do	March 1919	do	Do.
375th Aero Squadron (service).	do	do	February 1918 March 1918	Garden City, N. Y. P. of E., Halifax	do	June 1919	June 1919	Mitchel Field, N. Y.	Do.

AERO SQUADRONS—Continued

Unit designation and redesignation	Organization		Stations in United States		Overseas		Demobilization		Remarks
	Month and year	Place	Month and year	Place	From—	To—	Month and year	Place	
376th Aero Squadron (training).	January 1918	Waco, Tex.	March 1918 June 1918	Garden City, N. Y. P. of E., Hoboken	June 1918	April 1919	April 1919	Mitchel Field, N. Y.	S.O.S. troops.
377th Aero Squadron (service).	do	do	March 1918 do	Garden City, N. Y. P. of E., Halifax	March 1918	December 1918	December 1918	Garden City, N. Y.	Do.
378th Aero Squadron (service).	do	do	do do	Garden City, N. Y. P. of E., Halifax	do	do	do	do	Do.
379th Aero Squadron	do	Taliaferro Field #3, Tex.	May 1918	Carruthers Field, Tex.					Taliaferro Field #3 redesignated Carruthers Field, May 1, 1918.
a. Squadron "E"	July 1918	Carruthers Field, Tex.					November 1918	Carruthers Field, Tex.	
380th Aero Squadron	January 1918	Selfridge Field, Mich.							
a. Squadron "B"	July 1918	do					do	Selfridge Field, Mich.	
381st to 399th Aero Squadrons.									Never orgzd.
400th Aero Squadron (construction).									See 29th Aer. Sq. (Prov.).
401st Aero Squadron (construction).	November 1917	Vancouver Bks. Wash.							
a. 15th Spruce Squadron.	July 1918	do					February 1919	Vancouver Bks., Wash.	
402d Aero Squadron (construction).	November 1917	Do.							
a. 16th Spruce Squadron.	July 1918	do					do	Do.	
403d Aero Squadron (construction).	November 1917	Do.							
a. 17th Spruce Squadron.	July 1918	do					January 1919	Do.	

404th Aero Squadron (construction).	November 1917	Do.						
a. 18th Spruce Squadron.	July 1918	do					do	Do.
405th Aero Squadron (construction).	November 1917	Do.						
a. 19th Spruce Squadron.	July 1918	do					February 1919	Do.
406th Aero Squadron (construction).	November 1917	Do.						
a. 20th Spruce Squadron.	July 1918	do					January 1919	Do.
407th Aero Squadron (construction).	November 1917	Do.						
a. 1st Spruce Squadron.	July 1918	do					do	Do.
408th Aero Squadron (construction).	November 1917	Do.						
a. 2d Spruce Squadron.	July 1918	do					do	Do.
409th Aero Squadron (construction).	November 1917	Do.						
a. 3d Spruce Squadron.	July 1918	do					February 1919	Do.
410th Aero Squadron (construction).	November 1917	Do.						
a. 4th Spruce Squadron.	July 1918	do					January 1919	Do.
411th Aero Squadron (construction).	November 1917	Do.						
a. 5th Spruce Squadron.	July 1918	do					February 1919	Do.
412th Aero Squadron (construction).	November 1917	Do.						
a. 6th Spruce Squadron.	July 1918	do					do	Do.
413th Aero Squadron (construction).	December 1917	do	December 1917	Aberdeen, Wash.				
a. 42d Spruce Squadron.	July 1918	Aberdeen, Wash.	December 1918	Vancouver Bks., Wash.			January 1919	Do.

AERO SQUADRONS—Continued

Unit designation and redesignation	Organization		Stations in United States		Overseas		Demobilization		Remarks
	Month and year	Place	Month and year	Place	From—	To—	Month and year	Place	
414th Aero Squadron (construction).	December 1917	Vancouver Bks., Wash.	December 1917	Powers, Oreg.					
a. 102d Spruce Squadron.	July 1918	Powers, Oreg	December 1918	Vancouver Bks., Wash.			January 1919	Vancouver Bks., Wash.	
415th Aero Squadron (construction).	December 1917	Vancouver Bks., Wash.	December 1917	Joyce, Wash.					
			April 1918	Twin, Wash.					
a. 32d Spruce Squadron.	July 1918	Twin, Wash	November 1918	Vancouver Bks., Wash.			do	Do.	
416th Aero Squadron (construction).	December 1917	Vancouver Bks., Wash.	December 1917	Ft. Lawton, Wash.					
			January 1918	Stillwater, Wash.					
a. 33d Spruce Squadron.	July 1918	Stillwater, Wash	September 1918	Everett, Wash.					
			November 1918	Vancouver Bks., Wash.			do	Vancouver Bks., Wash.	
417th Aero Squadron (construction).	December 1917	Vancouver Bks., Wash.	December 1917	Pysht, Wash.					
a. 34th Spruce Squadron.	July 1918	Pysht, Wash	December 1918	Vancouver Bks., Wash.			do	Do.	
418th Aero Squadron (construction).	January 1918	Vancouver Bks., Wash.	January 1918	Silvana, Wash.					
			March 1918	Arlington, Wash.					
a. 35th Spruce Squadron.	July 1918	Arlington, Wash	December 1918	Vancouver Bks., Wash.			do	Do.	
419th Aero Squadron (construction).	March 1918	Vancouver Bks., Wash.	March 1918	Lindberg, Wash.					
a. 43d Spruce Squadron.	July 1918	Lindberg, Wash	December 1918	Vancouver Bks., Wash.			do	Do.	
420th Aero Squadron (construction).	January 1918	Vancouver Bks., Wash.	January 1918	Hoquiam, Wash.					
a. 44th Spruce Squadron.	July 1918	Hoquiam, Wash	December 1918	Vancouver Bks., Wash.			do	Do.	

421st Aero Squadron (construction).	January 1918	Vancouver Bks., Wash.	January 1918	Carlisle, Wash.					
a. **45th Spruce** Squadron.	July 1918	Carlisle, Wash.	November 1918	Vancouver Bks., Wash.			do	Do.	
422d Aero Squadron (construction).	January 1918	Vancouver Bks., Wash.	January 1918	Blyn, Wash.					
a. 36th Spruce Squadron.	July 1918	Blyn, Wash	December 1918	Vancouver Bks., Wash.			do	Do.	
423d Aero Squadron (construction).	January 1918	Vancouver Bks., Wash.	January 1918	Bay City, Wash.					
a. 46th Spruce Squadron.	July 1918	Bay City, Wash	November 1918	Vancouver Bks., Wash.			do	Do.	
424th Aero Squadron (construction).	January 1918	Vancouver Bks., Wash.	January 1918	Blind Slough, Oreg.					
a. 66th Spruce Squadron.	July 1918	Blind Slough, Oreg.	December 1918	Vancouver Bks., Wash.			do	Do.	
425th Aero Squadron (construction).	December 1917	Vancouver Bks., Wash.							
a. 29th Spruce Squadron.	July 1918	do					March 1919	Do.	
426th Aero Squadron (construction).	December 1917	Do.							
a. 30th Spruce Squadron.	July 1918	do					January 1919	Do.	
427th Aero Squadron (construction).	January 1918	do	January 1918	Raymond, Wash.					
a. 47th Spruce Squadron.	July 1918	Raymond, Wash.	November 1918	Vancouver Bks., Wash.			do	Do.	
428th Aero Squadron (construction).	January 1918	Vancouver Bks., Wash.	January 1918	Seaside, Oreg.					
a. 67th Spruce Squadron.	July 1918	Seaside, Oreg	December 1918	Vancouver Bks., Wash.			do	Do.	
429th Aero Squadron (construction).	January 1918	Vancouver Bks., Wash.	January 1918	Aberdeen, Wash			February 1918	Aberdeen, Wash	Demobilized Aberdeen, Wash.; reconstituted Vancouver Bks., Wash.
	March 1918	Do.							
a. 31st Spruce Squadron.	July 1918	do					March 1919	Vancouver Bks., Wash.	

AERO SQUADRONS—Continued

Unit designation and redesignation	Organization		Stations in United States		Overseas		Demobilization		Remarks
	Month and year	Place	Month and year	Place	From—	To—	Month and year	Place	
430th Aero Squadron (construction).	January 1918	Vancouver Bks., Wash.	January 1918	Snoqualmie Falls, Wash.					
a. 37th Spruce Squadron.	July 1918	Snoqualmie Falls, Wash.	November 1918	Vancouver Bks., Wash.			January 1919	Vancouver Bks., Wash.	
431st Aero Squadron (construction).	January 1918	Vancouver Bks., Wash.	January 1918	Aberdeen, Wash.			February 1918	Aberdeen, Wash.	Demobilized Aberdeen, Wash.; reconstituted Vancouver Bks., Wash.
	February 1918	do	February 1918	Saginaw, Wash.					
a. 48th Spruce Squadron.	July 1918	Saginaw, Wash.	November 1918	Vancouver Bks., Wash.			January 1919	Vancouver Bks., Wash.	
432d Aero Squadron (construction).	January 1918	Vancouver Bks., Wash.	January 1918	Halmar, Wash.			February 1918	Halmar, Wash.	Demobilized Halmar, Wash.; reconstituted Vancouver Bks., Wash.
	March 1918	do	March 1918	Hoquiam, Wash.					
a. 49th Spruce Squadron.	July 1918	Hoquiam, Wash.	November 1918	Vancouver Bks., Wash.			January 1919	Vancouver Bks., Wash.	
433d Aero Squadron (construction).	January 1918	Vancouver Bks., Wash.	February 1918	Olney, Oreg.					
a. 68th Spruce Squadron.	July 1918	Olney, Oreg.	December 1918	Vancouver Bks., Wash.			do	Do.	
434th Aero Squadron (construction).	January 1918	Vancouver Bks., Wash.	February 1918	Clatsop, Oreg.					
a. 69th Spruce Squadron.	July 1918	Clatsop, Oreg.	November 1918	Vancouver Bks., Wash.			do	Do.	
435th (I) Aero Squadron (construction).	January 1918	Vancouver Bks., Wash.	March 1918	Hoquiam, Wash.					
a. 50th Spruce Squadron.	July 1918	Hoquiam, Wash.					do	Do.	
435th (II) Aero Squadron.									See 48th (I) Aer. Sq. (Cons.).
436th Aero Squadron (construction).	January 1918	Vancouver Bks., Wash.	February 1918	Hoquiam, Wash.					
			May 1918	Cosmopolis, Wash.					
a. 51st Spruce Squadron.	July 1918	Cosmopolis, Wash.	December 1918	Vancouver Bks., Wash.			January 1919	Vancouver Bks., Wash.	

437th Aero Squadron (construction).	January 1918	Vancouver Bks., Wash.	January 1918	Hoquiam, Wash.			February 1918	Hoquiam, Wash.	Demobilized Hoquiam, Wash.; reconstituted Vancouver Bks., Wash.
	March 1918	do	March 1918	Astoria, Oreg.					
			May 1918	Waldport, Oreg.					
a. 79th Spruce Squadron.	July 1918	Waldport, Oreg.	December 1918	South Beach, Oreg.			January 1919	Vancouver Bks., Wash.	
438th Aero Squadron (construction).	January 1918	Vancouver Bks., Wash.	January 1918	Raymond, Wash.					
a. 52d Spruce Squadron.	July 1918	Raymond, Wash.	November 1918	Vancouver Bks., Wash.			do	Do.	
439th Aero Squadron (construction).	January 1918	Vancouver Bks., Wash.							
a. 7th Spruce Squadron.	July 1918	do					do	Do.	
440th Aero Squadron (construction).	January 1918	Do.							
a. 8th Spruce Squadron.	July 1918	do					do	Do.	
441st Aero Squadron (construction).	January 1918	Do.							
a. 9th Spruce Squadron.	July 1918	do					February 1919	Do.	
442d Aero Squadron (construction).	January 1918	Do.							
a. 10th Spruce Squadron.	July 1918	do					January 1919	Do.	
443d Aero Squadron (construction).	January 1918	Do.							
a. 11th Spruce Squadron.	July 1918	do					February 1919	Do.	
444th Aero Squadron (construction).	January 1918	Do.							
a. 12th Spruce Squadron.	July 1918	do					January 1919	Do.	
445th Aero Squadron (construction).	February 1918	do	February 1918	Cp. Darrington, Wash.					
a. 38th Spruce Squadron.	July 1918	Cp. Darrington, Wash.	December 1918	Vancouver Bks., Wash.			do	Do.	

AERO SQUADRONS—Continued

Unit designation and redesignation	Organization		Stations in United States		Overseas		Demobilization		Remarks
	Month and year	Place	Month and year	Place	From—	To—	Month and year	Place	
446th Aero Squadron (construction).	February 1918	Vancouver Bks., Wash.	April 1918	Enumclaw, Wash.					
a. 53d Spruce Squadron.	July 1918	Enumclaw, Wash.	------	------	------	------	January 1919	Vancouver Bks., Wash.	
447th Aero Squadron (construction).	February 1918	Vancouver Bks., Wash.	March 1918	Miami, Oreg.					
a. 70th Spruce Squadron.	July 1918	Miami, Oreg.	December 1918	Vancouver Bks., Wash.	------	------	do	Do.	
448th Aero Squadron (construction).	February 1918	Vancouver Bks., Wash.	February 1918	Raymond, Wash.					
a. 54th Spruce Squadron.	July 1918	Raymond, Wash.	------	------	------	------	do	Do.	
449th Aero Squadron (construction).	February 1918	Vancouver Bks., Wash.	February 1918	South Bend, Wash.					
a. 55th Spruce Squadron.	July 1918	South Bend, Wash.	December 1918	Vancouver Bks., Wash.	------	------	do	Do.	
450th Aero Squadron (construction).	February 1918	Vancouver Bks., Wash.	March 1918	Clear Lake, Wash.					
a. 39th Spruce Squadron.	July 1918	Clear Lake, Wash.	November 1918	Sedro Woolley, Wash.					
			December 1918	Vancouver Bks., Wash.	------	------	do	Do.	
451st Aero Squadron (construction).	February 1918	Vancouver Bks., Wash.	February 1918	South Bend, Wash.					
			April 1918	Nemah, Wash.					
a. 56th Spruce Squadron.	July 1918	Nemah, Wash.	December 1918	Vancouver Bks., Wash.	------	------	do	Do.	
452d Aero Squadron (construction).	February 1918	Vancouver Bks., Wash.	February 1918	Seaside, Oreg.					
a. 71st Spruce Squadron.	July 1918	Seaside, Oreg.	November 1918	Vancouver Bks., Wash.	------	------	December 1918	Do.	

453d Aero Squadron (construction).	February 1918	Vancouver Bks., Wash.	April 1918	Toledo, Oreg.				
a. 80th Spruce Squadron.	July 1918	Toledo, Oreg	January 1919	Vancouver Bks., Wash.			February 1919	Do.
454th Aero Squadron (construction).	February 1918	Vancouver Bks., Wash.	March 1918	Raymond, Wash.				
a. 57th Spruce Squadron.	July 1918	Raymond, Wash	December 1918	Vancouver Bks., Wash.			January 1919	Do.
455th Aero Squadron (construction).	February 1918	Vancouver Bks., Wash.	February 1918 May 1918 June 1918	Pysht, Wash. South Beach, Oreg. Waldport, Oreg.				
a. 81st Spruce Squadron.	July 1918	Waldport, Oreg	December 1918	South Beach, Oreg			do	Do.
456th Aero Squadron (construction).	February 1918	Vancouver Bks., Wash.	February 1918	Clatsop, Oreg.				
a. 72d Spruce Squadron.	July 1918	Clatsop, Oreg	December 1918	Vancouver Bks., Wash.			do	Do.
457th Aero Squadron (construction).	February 1918	Vancouver Bks., Wash.	April 1918 July 1918	Youngs Falls, Oreg. Clatsop, Oreg.				
a. 73d Spruce Squadron.	July 1918	Clatsop, Oreg	November 1918	Vancouver Bks., Wash.			do	Do.
458th Aero Squadron (construction).	February 1918	Vancouver Bks., Wash.	March 1918	Clatsop, Oreg.				
a. 74th Spruce Squadron.	July 1918	Clatsop, Oreg	November 1918	Vancouver Bks., Wash.			do	Do
459th Aero Squadron (construction).	March 1918	Vancouver Bks., Wash.	March 1918 May 1918	Montesano, Wash. Aberdeen, Wash.				
a. 58th Spruce Squadron.	July 1918	Aberdeen, Wash	November 1918	Vancouver Bks., Wash.			do	Do.
460th Aero Squadron (construction).	December 1917	Portland, Oreg.						
a. 105th Spruce Squadron.	July 1918	do					February 1919	Portland, Oreg.
461st Aero Squadron (construction).	January 1918	Kelly Field, Tex	January 1918 April 1918 May 1918 August 1918	Brooks Field, Tex. Kelly Field, Tex. Ellington Field, Tex. Gerstner Field, La.			January 1919	GerstnerField, La.

AERO SQUADRONS—Continued

Unit designation and redesignation	Organization		Stations in United States		Overseas		Demobilization		Remarks
	Month and year	Place	Month and year	Place	From—	To—	Month and year	Place	
462d Aero Squadron (construction).									See 48th (I) Aer. Sq. (Cons.).
463d Aero Squadron (construction and repair).									See 51st (I) Aer. Sq. (Cons.).
464th (I) Aero Squadron (construction and repair).									See 52d (I) Aer. Sq. (Cons.).
464th (II) Aero Squadron (construction).	July 1919	Kelly Field, Tex.	July 1919 August 1919 do November 1919	McAllen, Tex. Laredo, Tex. Eagle Pass, Tex. Sanderson, Tex.					S.O.S. troops. Active through 1919.
465th Aero Squadron (construction and repair).									See 53d Aer. Sq. (Cons.).
466th Aero Squadron (construction).									See 54th Aer. Sq. (Cons.).
467th Aero Squadron (construction).									See 55th Aer. Sq. (Cons.).
468th Aero Squadron (construction).									See 56th Aer. Sq. (Cons.).
469th Aero Squadron (construction).									See 57th Aer. Sq. (Cons.).
470th Aero Squadron (construction).									See 58th Aer. Sq.
471st Aero Squadron (construction).									See 59th Aer. Sq.
472d Aero Squadron (construction).									See 60th Aer. Sq.

473d Aero Squadron (construction).									See 61st Aer. Sq.
474th Aero Squadron (construction).									See 62d Aer. Sq.
475th Aero Squadron (construction).									See 63d (I) Aer. Sq.
476th Aero Squadron (construction).									See 64th (I) Aer. Sq.
477th Aero Squadron (construction).									See 65th (I) Aer. Sq.
478th Aero Squadron (construction).									See 66th (I) Aer. Sq.
479th Aero Squadron (construction).									See 67th (I) Aer. Sq.
480th Aero Squadron (construction).									See 68th (I) Aer. Sq.
481st Aero Squadron (construction).									See 69th (I) Aer. Sq.
482d Aero Squadron (construction).									See 70th (I) Aer. Sq.
483d Aero Squadron (construction).									See 71st (I) Aer. Sq.
484th Aero Squadron (construction).									See 72d (I) Aer. Sq.
485th Aero Squadron (construction).									See 73d (I) Aer. Sq.
486th Aero Squadron (construction).									See 74th (I) Aer. Sq.
487th Aero Squadron (construction).									See 75th (I) Aer. Sq.
488th Aero Squadron (construction).									See 76th (I) Aer. Sq.
489th Aero Squadron (construction)									See 77th (I) Aer. Sq.
490th Aero Squadron (construction).									See 78th (I) Aer. Sq.
491st Aero Squadron (construction).									See 79th (I) Aer. Sq.
492d Aero Squadron (construction).									See 80th (I) Aer. Sq.

AERO SQUADRONS—Continued

Unit designation and redesignation	Organization		Stations in United States		Overseas		Demobilization		Remarks
	Month and year	Place	Month and year	Place	From—	To—	Month and year	Place	
493d Aero Squadron (construction).									See 45th (I) Aer. Sq.
494th Aero Squadron (construction).									See 82d (I) Aer. Sq.
495th Aero Squadron (construction).									See 83d (I) Aer. Sq.
496th Aero Squadron (construction).									See 200th (I) Aer. Sq (Cons.).
497th Aero Squadron (construction).									See 201st (I) Aer. Sq. (Cons.).
498th Aero Squadron (construction).									See 202d (I) Aer. Sq. (Cons.).
499th Aero Squadron (construction).									See 203d (I) Aer. Sq.
500th Aero Squadron (construction).									See 204th (I) Aer. Sq. (Cons.).
501st Aero Squadron (construction).									See 205th (I) Aer. Sq. (Cons.).
502d (I) Aero Squadron (construction).									See 206th (I) Aer. Sq. (Cons.).
502d (II) Aero Squadron (construction).	February 1918	Kelly Field, Tex.							
a. 29th Aero Squadron (service).	do	do	March 1918	Brooks Field, Tex.					
b. Squadron "A"	July 1918	Brooks Field, Tex.					November 1918	Brooks Field, Tex.	
503d Aero Squadron (construction).									See 207th (I) Aer. Sq. (Cons.).
504th Aero Squadron (construction).									See 208th (I) Aer. Sq. (Cons.).
505th Aero Squadron (construction).									See 209th (I) Aer. Sq. (Cons.).

506th Aero Squadron									Never orgzd.
507th Aero Squadron	February 1918	Kelly Field, Tex	July 1918	Wilbur Wright Field, Ohio.			April 1919	Wilbur Wright Field, Ohio.	
508th Aero Squadron	do	do	August 1918	Gerstner Field, La			January 1919	Gerstner Field, La.	
509th to 600th Aero Squadrons.									Do.
601st Aero Squadron (supply).	January 1918	Vancouver Bks., Wash.							
a. 13th Spruce Squadron.	July 1918	do					January 1919	Vancouver Bks., Wash.	
602d Aero Squadron (supply).	January 1918	do					May 1918	Do.	
603d Aero Squadron (supply).	February 1918	Do.							
a. 14th Spruce Squadron.	July 1918	do					January 1919	Do.	
604th Aero Squadron (supply).	March 1918	do					May 1918	Do.	
605th Aero Squadron									Do.
606th Aero Squadron (supply).	April 1918	Vancouver Bks., Wash.					May 1918	Vancouver Bks., Wash	
607th Aero Squadron (supply).	December 1917	Kelly Field, Tex	January 1918	Ft. Wayne, Mich			February 1919	Ft. Wayne, Mich.	
608th Aero Squadron (supply).	January 1918	do	March 1918	Waco, Tex.					
			May 1918 August 1918 April 1919	Cp. Greene, N. C. Garden City, N. Y. Mitchel Field, N. Y.			September 1919	Mitchel Field, N. Y.	
609th Aero Squadron (supply).	do	do	March 1918	Waco, Tex.					
			May 1918 August 1918 April 1919	Cp. Greene, N. C. Garden City, N. Y. Mitchel Field, N. Y.			do	Do.	
610th Aero Squadron (supply).	do	do	March 1918	Waco, Tex.					
			May 1918 July 1918	Cp. Greene, N. C. Avn. Gen. Sup. Dep., Middletown, Pa.			March 1919	Avn. Gen. Sup. Dep., Middletown, Pa.	

AERO SQUADRONS—Continued

Unit designation and redesignation	Organization		Stations in United States		Overseas		Demobilization		Remarks
	Month and year	Place	Month and year	Place	From—	To—	Month and year	Place	
611th Aero Squadron (supply).	January 1918	Kelly Field, Tex.	March 1918 May 1918 June 1918	Waco, Tex. Cp. Greene, N. C. Langley Field, Va.					
a. Detachment #18, Air Service, Aircraft Production.	August 1918	Langley Field, Va.					January 1919	Langley Field, Va.	
612th Aero Squadron (supply).	January 1918	Kelly Field, Tex.	March 1918 May 1918 July 1918	Waco, Tex. Cp. Greene, N. C. Wilbur Wright Field, Ohio.			March 1919	Wilbur Wright Field, Ohio.	
613th Aero Squadron (supply).	do	do	March 1918 May 1918 August 1918	Waco, Tex. Cp. Greene, N. C. Garden City, N. Y.			January 1919	Garden City, N. Y.	Skeletonized July 1918.
614th Aero Squadron (supply).	do	do	March 1918 May 1918 August 1918	Waco, Tex. Cp. Greene, N. C. Garden City, N. Y.			do	do	Do.
615th Aero Squadron (supply).	do	do	July 1918	Souther Field, Ga.			March 1919	Souther Field, Ga.	
616th Aero Squadron (supply).	do	do	March 1918 May 1918	Waco, Tex. Avn. Gen. Sup. Dep., Middletown, Pa.			do	Avn. Gen. Sup. Dep., Middletown, Pa.	
617th Aero Squadron (supply).	do	do	March 1918 October 1918	Cp. Morrison, Va. Garden City, N. Y.			December 1918	Garden City, N. Y.	Do.
618th Aero Squadron (supply).	do	do	March 1918 October 1918	Cp. Morrison, Va. Garden City, N. Y.			do	do	Do.
619th Aero Squadron (supply).	do	do	March 1918 May 1918	Waco, Tex. Detroit. Mich.					

a. Detachment #9, Air Service, Aircraft Production.	August 1918	Detroit, Mich.					January 1919	Detroit, Mich.	
620th Aero Squadron (supply).	January 1918	Kelly Field, Tex.	March 1918	Cp. Morrison, Va.					
621st Aero Squadron (supply).	do	do	October 1918 March 1918	Garden City, N. Y. Cp. Morrison, Va.			December 1918	Garden City, N. Y.	Do.
622d Aero Squadron (supply).	do	do	October 1918 March 1918	Garden City, N. Y. Cp. Morrison, Va.			do	do	Do.
623d Aero Squadron (supply).	February 1918	do	October 1918 March 1918	Garden City, N. Y. Waco, Tex.			do	do	Do.
624th Aero Squadron (supply).	do	do	May 1918 August 1918 March 1918	Cp. Greene, N. C. Garden City, N. Y. Cp. Morrison, Va.			do	do	Do.
625th Aero Squadron (supply).	do	do	October 1918 March 1918	Garden City, N. Y. Cp. Morrison, Va.			do	do	Do.
626th Aero Squadron (supply).	do	do	October 1918 March 1918	Garden City, N. Y. Cp. Morrison, Va.				do	Do.
627th Aero Squadron (supply).	do	do	June 1918 March 1918 May 1918	Langley Field, Va. Waco, Tex. Cp. Greene, N. C.			January 1919	Langley Field, Va.	
628th Aero Squadron	December 1917	Garden City, N. Y.	August 1918	Garden City, N. Y.			do	Garden City, N. Y.	Do.
629th Aero Squadron (supply).	January 1918	Taliaferro Field #1, Tex.	April 1919	Mitchel Field, N.Y.			October 1919	Mitchel Field, N.Y.	
a. Squadron 'F'	July 1918	Taliaferro Field, Tex.					November 1918	Taliaferro Field, Tex.	
630th Aero Squadron									Never orgzd.
631st Aero Squadron (supply).									See 46th (I) Aer. Sq.
632d Aero Squadron (supply).									See 111th (I) Aer. Sq.

AERO SQUADRONS—Continued

Unit designation and redesignation	Organization		Stations in United States		Overseas		Demobilization		Remarks
	Month and year	Place	Month and year	Place	From—	To—	Month and year	Place	
633d Aero Squadron (supply).									See 112th (I) Aer. Sq.
634th Aero Squadron (supply).									See 113th (I) Aer. Sq.
635th Aero Squadron (supply).									See 114th (I) Aer. Sq.
636th Aero Squadron (supply).									See 115th (I) Aer. Sq.
637th Aero Squadron (supply).									See 116th (I) Aer. Sq.
638th Aero Squadron (pursuit).									See 117th (I) Aer. Sq.
639th Aero Squadron (supply).									See 118th (I) Aer. Sq.
640th Aero Squadron (supply).									See 121st (I) Aer. Sq. (Sup.).
641st Aero Squadron (supply).									See 122d (I) Aer. Sq. (Sup.).
642d Aero Squadron (supply).									See 123d (I) Aer. Sq. (Sup.).
643d Aero Squadron (supply).									See 124th (I) Aer. Sq. (Sup.).
644th Aero Squad on (supply).									See 125th (I) Aer. Sq. (Sup.).
645th Aero Squadron (supply).									See 126th (I) Aer. Sq. (Sup.).
646th Aero Squadron (supply).									See 127th (I) Aer. Sq. (Sup.).
647th Aero Squadron (supply).									See 128th (I) Aer. Sq. (Sup.).

648th Aero Squadron (supply).									See 129th (I) Aer. Sq. (Sup.).
649th Aero Squadron (supply).									See 130th (I) Aer. Sq. (Sup.).
650th Aero Squadron (supply).									See 131st (I) Aer. Sq. (Sup.).
651st Aero Squadron (supply).									See 132d (I) Aer, Sq. (Sup.).
652d Aero Squadron (supply).									See 133d (I) Aer. Sq. (Sup.).
653d Aero Squadron (supply).									See 134th (I) Aer. Sq. (Sup.).
654th Aero Squadron (supply).									See 146th Aer. Sq. (Sup.).
655th Aero Squadron (supply).									See 229th (I) Aer. Sq. (Sup.).
656th Aero Squadron (supply).									See 230th Aer. Sq. (Sup.).
657th Aero Squadron (supply).									See 231st (I) Aer. Sq. (Sup.).
658th Aero Squadron (supply).									See 232d (I) Aer. Sq. (Sup.).
659th Aero Squadron (supply).									See 233d (I) Aer. Sq.
660th Aero Squadron (supply).									See 234th (I) Aer. Sq. (Sup.).
661st Aero Squadron (supply).									See 235th (I) Aer. Sq. (Sup.).
662d Aero Squadron (supply).									See 236th (I) Aer. Sq. (Sup.).
663d Aero Squadron (supply).									See 237th (I) Aer. Sq.
664th Aero Squadron (supply).									See 238th (I) Aer. Sq. (Sup.).
665th Aero Squadron (supply).									See 239th (I) Aer. Sq.
666th Aero Squadron (supply).									See 240th (I) Aer. Sq.
667th Aero Squadron (supply).									See 241st (I) Aer. Sq.

AERO SQUADRONS—Continued

Unit designation and redesignation	Organization		Stations in United States		Overseas		Demobilization		Remarks
	Month and year	Place	Month and year	Place	From—	To—	Month and year	Place	
668th Aero Squadron (supply).									See 242d (I) Aer. Sq. (Sup.).
669th Aero Squadron (supply).									See 243d (I) Aer. Sq. (Sup.).
670th Aero Squadron (supply).									See 332d (I) Aer. Sq. (Sup.).
671st Aero Squadron (supply).									See 333d (I) Aer. Sq.
672d Aero Squadron (supply).									See 334th (I) Aer. Sq.
673d Aero Squadron (supply).									See 335th (I) Aer. Sq.
674th Aero Squadron (supply).									See 336th (I) Aer. Sq. (Sup.).
675th Aero Squadron (supply).									See 337th (I) Aer. Sq.
676th Aero Squadron (supply).	February 1918	Cp. Dick, Tex	January 1919	Avn. Gen. Sup. Dep., Little Rock, Ark.			March 1919	Avn. Gen. Sup. Dep., Little Rock, Ark.	
677th Aero Squadron (supply).	January 1918	Cp. Morrison, Va.					June 1919	Cp. Morrison, Va.	
678th Aero Squadron (supply).	February 1918	Kelly Field, Tex	February 1918	Wilbur Wright Field, Ohio.			April 1919	Wilbur Wright Field, Ohio.	
679th Aero Squadron (supply).	do	Cp. Dick, Tex					January 1919	Cp. Dick, Tex.	
680th Aero Squadron (supply).	April 1918	Waco, Tex	May 1918	Cp. Greene, N. C.					
			August 1918	Garden City, N. Y.			September 1919	Garden City, N. Y.	
681st Aero Squadron (supply).	do	Kelly Field, Tex					August 1919	Kelly Field, Tex	

682d Aero Squadron (supply).	June 1918	do	June 1918	Avn. Gen. Sup. Dep., Houston, Tex.			March 1919	Avn. Gen. Sup. Dep., Houston, Tex.	
683d Aero Squadron (supply).	August 1918	220 Pavonia Ave., Jersey City, N. J.	November 1918	104 W. 14th St., New York, N. Y.			February 1919	104 W. 14th St., New York, N. Y.	
684th Aero Squadron (supply).	October 1918	Kelly Field, Tex					August 1919	Kelly Field, Tex	Skeletonized February 1919.
685th Aero Squadron (supply).	do	do					December 1918	do	Skeletonized during orgn.
686th to 799th Aero Squadrons.									Never orgzd.
800th Aero Squadron (repair).									See 106th (I) Aer. Sq.
801st Aero Squadron (repair).									See 107th (I) Aer. Sq.
802d Aero Squadron (repair).									See 108th (I) Aer. Sq.
803d Aero Squadron (repair).									See 109th (I) Aer. Sq.
804th Aero Squadron (repair).									See 110th (I) Aer. Sq.
805th Aero Squadron (repair).									See 244th (I) Aer. Sq.
806th Aero Squadron (repair).									See 245th (I) Aer. Sq.
807th Aero Squadron (repair).									See 246th (I) Aer. Sq.
808th Aero Squadron (repair).	August 1918	7th and B St., NW, Washington, D. C.					August 1919	7th and B St., NW, Washington, D. C.	
809th Aero Squadron (repair).	January 1918	Kelly Field, Tex	March 1918	Avn. Rep. Dep., Speedway, Indianapolis, Ind.			March 1919	Avn. Rep. Dep., Speedway, Indianapolis, Ind.	
810th Aero Squadron (repair).	do	do	February 1918	do			do	Do.	
811th Aero Squadron (repair).	do	do	March 1918	do			do	Do.	
812th Aero Squadron (repair).	do	do	October 1918 do	Garden City, N. Y. P. of E., Hoboken	October 1918	December 1918	December 1918	Garden City, N. Y.	S.O.S. troops.

AERO SQUADRONS—Continued

Unit designation and redesignation	Organization		Stations in United States		Overseas		Demobilization		Remarks
	Month and year	Place	Month and year	Place	From—	To—	Month and year	Place	
813th Aero Squadron (depot).									See 362d Aer. Sq. (Dep.).
814th Aero Squadron (depot).									See 363d Aer. Sq. (Dep.).
815th Aero Squadron (depot).									See 364th Aer. Sq. (Dep.).
816th Aero Squadron (depot).									See 365th Aer. Sq. (Dep.).
817th Aero Squadron (depot).	February 1918	S Dept. Hq., Ft. Sam Houston,					August 1919	S Dept. Hq., Ft. Sam Houston,	
818th Aero Squadron (depot).									See 367th Aer. Sq. (Dep.).
819th Aero Squadron (repair).	January 1918	Kelly Field, Tex					August 1919	Kelly Field, Tex	Skeletonized March 1919.
820th Aero Squadron (repair).	do	do					do	do	Do.
821st Aero Squadron (repair).	April 1918	Avn. Rep. Dep., Speedway, Indianapolis, Ind.					March 1919	Avn. Rep. Dep., Speedway, Indianapolis, Ind.	
822d Aero Squadron (repair).	January 1918	Waco, Tex	March 1918	Hazelhurst Field, N. Y.					
			April 1918	P. of E., Hoboken	April 1918.				
a. 6th Air Park Company.	August 1918	A. E. F							Cmpnt. of 4th Pur. Gp.
b. 6th Air Park	October 1918	do				July 1919	July 1919	Mitchel Field, N.Y.	
823d Aero Squadron (repair).	January 1918	Waco, Tex	March 1918	Garden City, N. Y.					
			May 1918	P. of E., Hoboken	May 1918	December 1918	December 1918	Garden City, N. Y.	S.O.S. troops.
824th Aero Squadron (repair).	do	do	March 1918	Garden City, N. Y.					
			May 1918	P. of E., Hoboken	do	do	do	do	Do.

825th Aero Squadron (repair).	do	do	March 1918	Garden City, N. Y.					
			August 1918	P. of E., Hoboken	August 1918	September 1919	September 1919	Cp. Dix, N. J	Do.
826th Aero Squadron (repair).	February 1918	do	March 1918	Mineola, N. Y.					
			April 1918	Garden City, N. Y.					
			May 1918	P. of E., Hoboken	May 1918	June 1919	June 1919	Mitchel Field, N. Y.	Do.
827th Aero Squadron (repair).	do	Kelly Field, Tex	February 1918	Wilbur Wright Field, Ohio.					
			March 1918	Garden City, N. Y.					
			May 1918	P. of E., Hoboken	do	do	do	do	Do.
828th Aero Squadron (repair).	do	do	February 1918	Selfridge Field, Mich.					
			May 1918	Garden City, N. Y.					
			August 1918	P. of E., Hoboken	August 1918	September 1919	September 1919	Cp. Dix, N. J	Do.
829th Aero Squadron (repair).	do	do	February 1918	Selfridge Field, Mich.					
			August 1918	Garden City, N. Y.					
			do	P. of E., Hoboken	do	do	do	do	Do.
830th Aero Squadron (repair).	do	do	February 1918	Selfridge Field, Mich.					
			August 1918	Hempstead Field, N. Y.					
			September 1918	P. of E., Quebec	September 1918	do	do	do	Do.
831st Aero Squadron (repair).	do	do	February 1918	Chanute Field, Ill.					
			March 1918	Garden City, N. Y.					
			May 1918	P. of E., Hoboken	May 1918	December 1918	December 1918	Garden City, N. Y.	Do.
832d Aero Squadron (repair).	do	do	February 1918	Chanute Field, Ill.					
			March 1918	Garden City, N. Y.					
			May 1918	P. of E., Hoboken	do	do	January 1919	do	Do.
833d Aero Squadron (repair).	do	Waco, Tex	March 1918	Garden City, N. Y.					
			May 1918	P. of E., Hoboken	do	do	December 1918	do	Do.
834th Aero Squadron (repair).	do	do	March 1918	Garden City, N. Y.					
			May 1918	P. of E., Hoboken	do	do	do	do	Do.
835th Aero Squadron (repair).	do	do	March 1918	Garden City, N. Y.					
			April 1918	P. of E., Hoboken	April 1918	March 1919	March 1919	do	Do.

AERO SQUADRONS—Continued

Unit designation and redesignation	Organization		Stations in United States		Overseas		Demobilization		Remarks
	Month and year	Place	Month and year	Place	From—	To—	Month and year	Place	
836th Aero Squadron (repair).	February 1918	Waco, Tex	March 1918 April 1918	Garden City, N. Y. P. of E., Hoboken	April 1918	December 1918	December 1918	Garden City, N. Y.	S.O.S. troops.
837th Aero Squadron (repair).	do	do	March 1918 May 1918	Garden City, N. Y. P. of E., Hoboken	May 1918	do	do	do	Do.
838th Aero Squadron (repair).	do	do	March 1918 April 1918	Garden City, N. Y. P. of E., Hoboken	April 1918	do	do	do	Do.
839th Aero Squadron (repair).	do	do	March 1918 April 1918	Garden City, N. Y. P. of E., Hoboken	do	do	do	do	Do.
840th Aero Squadron (repair).	do	do	March 1918 April 1918	Garden City, N. Y. P. of E., Hoboken	do	February 1919	March 1919	Langley Field, Va.	Do.
841st Aero Squadron (repair).	do	do	February 1918 March 1918 May 1918	Scott Field, Ill Garden City, N. Y. P. of E., Hoboken	May 1918	December 1918	December 1918	Garden City, N. Y.	Do.
842d to 849th Aero Squadrons.									Never orgzd.
850th Aero Squadron (repair).	February 1918	Ellington Field, Tex.							
a. Squadron "O"	July 1918	do					December 1918	Ellington Field, Tex.	
851st Aero Squadron (repair).	March 1918	Ellington Field, Tex.	March 1918	Wilbur Wright Field, Ohio.					
a. Squadron "B"	July 1918	Wilbur Wright Field, Ohio.					December 1918	Wilbur Wright Field, Ohio.	
852d Aero Squadron (repair).	February 1918	Waco, Tex	April 1918 August 1918	Garden City, N. Y. P. of E., Hoboken	August 1918	December 1918	do	Garden City, N. Y.	S.O.S. troops.

853d to 863d Aero Squadrons.									Never orgzd.
864th Aero Squadron (repair).	March 1918	A. S. Mec. Sch., St. Paul, Minn.					November 1918	A. S. Mec. Sch., St. Paul, Minn.	
865th Aero Squadron (repair).	do	Love Field, Tex.	April 1918	Avn. Rep. Dep., Dallas, Tex.			March 1919	Avn. Rep. Dep., Dallas, Tex.	
866th Aero Squadron (repair).	do	Garden City, N. Y.	April 1919	Mitchel Field, N. Y.			October 1919	Mitchel Field, N. Y.	
867th Aero Squadron (repair).	do	Avn. Rep. Dep., Dallas, Tex.					April 1919	Avn. Rep. Dep., Dallas, Tex.	
868th Aero Squadron (repair).	do	do					March 1919	Do.	
869th Aero Squadron (repair).									See 325th (I) Aer. Sq. (Serv.).
870th Aero Squadron (repair).									See 326th (I) Aer. Sq.
871st Aero Squadron (repair).	April 1918	A. S. Mec. Sch., St. Paul, Minn.					November 1918	A. S. Mec. Sch., St. Paul, Minn.	
872d Aero Squadron (repair).	do	do					do	Do.	
873d Aero Squadron (repair).	do	Avn. Rep. Dep., Dallas, Tex.					March 1919	Avn. Rep. Dep., Dallas, Tex.	
874th Aero Squadron (repair).	do	Wilbur Wright Field, Ohio.							
a. Squadron "C"	July 1918	do					December 1918	Wilbur Wright Field, Ohio.	
875th Aero Squadron (repair).	do	A. E. F.				June 1919	June 1919	Mitchel Field, N. Y.	S.O.S. troops.
876th Aero Squadron									Never orgzd.
877th Aero Squadron (repair).	June 1918	Avn. Rep. Dep., Dallas, Tex.					March 1919	Avn. Rep. Dep., Dallas, Tex.	
878th Aero Squadron (repair).	July 1918	do					do	Do.	
879th Aero Squadron (repair).	do	Cp. Greene, N. C.	July 1918	Avn. Rep. Dep. #3, Montgomery, Ala.			do	Avn. Rep. Dep. #3, Montgomery, Ala.	
880th Aero Squadron (repair).	do	do	do	do			do	Do.	

AERO SQUADRONS—Continued

Unit designation and redesignation	Organization		Stations in United States		Overseas		Demobilization		Remarks
	Month and year	Place	Month and year	Place	From—	To—	Month and year	Place	
881st Aero Squadron (repair).	July 1918	McCook Field, Ohio.							
a. Squadron "B"	do	do					August 1918	McCook Field, Ohio.	
882d Aero Squadron (repair).	do	Kelly Field, Tex.	July 1918	Avn. Rep. Dep. #3, Montgomery, Ala.			March 1919	Avn. Rep. Dep. #3, Montgomery, Ala.	
883d Aero Squadron	do	do	do	do			do	Do.	
884th to 1098th Aero Squadrons.									Never orgzd.
1099th Aero Squadron	May 1918	A. E. F.				March 1919	March 1919	Garden City, N. Y.	S.O.S. troops.
1100th Aero Squadron									Never orgzd.
1101st Aero Squadron (replacement).						April 1918	June 1919		Orgzd. and demobilized overseas. S.O.S. troops.
1102d Aero Squadron (replacement).	May 1918	A. E. F.				February 1919	March 1919	Cp. Lee, Va.	S.O.S. troops.
1103d Aero Squadron (replacement).	do	do				April 1919	May 1919	Mitchel Field, N. Y.	Do.
1104th Aero Squadron (replacement).	do	do				June 1919	July 1919	Roosevelt Field, N. Y.	Do.
1105th Aero Squadron (replacement).	do	do				May 1919	June 1919	Mitchel Field, N. Y.	Do.
1106th Aero Squadron (replacement).	June 1918	do				September 1919	September 1919	Cp. Dix, N. J.	Do.
1107th Aero Squadron (replacement).						July 1918	July 1919		Orgzd. and demobilized overseas. S.O.S. troops.
1108th Aero Squadron (replacement).	August 1918	A. E. F.				May 1919	June 1919	Mitchel Field, N. Y.	S.O.S. troops.
1109th Aero Squadron									Never orgzd.

1110th Aero Squadron (replacement).						October 1918	December 1918		Orgzd. and demobilized overseas. S.O.S. troops.
1111th Aero Squadron (replacement).						do	September 1919		Do.

LETTERED SQUADRONS AND FLYING SCHOOL DETACHMENTS (STATIONED AT AVIATION FIELDS)

Barron Field, Tex.:									
Squadron "A"									See 77th (II) Aer. Sq.
Squadron "B"									See 106th (II) Aer. Sq.
Squadron "C"									See 207th (II) Aer. Sq.
Squadron "D"									See 273d Aer. Sq.
Flying School Detachment.	November 1918	Barron Field, Tex.					March 1919	Barron Field, Tex.	Org. fr. pl. of former lettered sqs.
Brooks Field, Tex.:									
Squadron "A"									See 502d (II) Aer. Sq.
Squadron "B"									See 67th (II) Aer. Sq.
Squadron "C"									See 118th (II) Aer. Sq.
Squadron "D"									See 134th (II) Aer. Sq.
Squadron "E"									See 179th Aer. Sq.
Squadron "F"									See 234th (II) Aer. Sq.
Flying School Detachment.	November 1918	Brooks Field, Tex.					June 1919	Brooks Field, Tex.	Org. fr. pl. of former lettered sqs.
Call Field, Tex.:									
Squadron "A"									See 164th Aer. Sq.
Squadron "B"									See 192d Aer. Sq.
Squadron "C"									See 198th Aer. Sq.
Squadron "D"									See 207th (II) Aer. Sq.

LETTERED SQUADRONS AND FLYING SCHOOL DETACHMENTS—Continued

Unit designation and redesignation	Organization		Stations in United States		Overseas		Demobilization		Remarks
	Month and year	Place	Month and year	Place	From—	To—	Month and year	Place	
Call Field, Tex.—Con.									
Squadron "E"									See 229th (II) Aer. Sq.
Flying School Detachment.	November 1918	Call Field, Tex.					November 1919	Call Field, Tex.	Org. fr. pl. of former lettered sqs.
Carlstrom Field, Fla.:									
Squadron "A"									See 107th (II) Aer. Sq.
Squadron "B"									See 108th (II) Aer. Sq.
Squadron "C"									See 111th (II) Aer. Sq.
Squadron "D"									See 205th (II) Aer. Sq.
Squadron "E"									See 284th Aer. Sq.
Squadron "F"									See 302d Aer. Sq.
Flying School Detachment.	November 1918	Carlstrom Field, Fla.					August 1919	Carlstrom Field, Fla.	Org. fr. pl. of former lettered sqs.
Carruthers Field, Tex.:									
Squadron "A"									See 208th (II) Aer. Sq.
Squadron "B"									See 209th (II) Aer. Sq.
Squadron "C"									See 229th (II) Aer. Sq.
Squadron "D"									See 274th Aer. Sq.
Squadron "E"									See 379th Aer. Sq.
Flying School Detachment.	November 1918	Carruthers Field, Tex.					April 1919	Carruthers Field, Tex.	Org. fr. pl. of former lettered sqs.

Chanute Field, Ill.									
Squadron "A"									See 38th Aer. Sq.
Squadron "B"									See 112th (II) Aer. Sq.
Squadron "C"									See 203d (II) Aer. Sq.
Squadron "D"									See 287th Aer. Sq.
Squadron "E"									See 288th Aer. Sq.
Flying School Detachment.	December 1918	Chanute Field, Ill					November 1919	Chanute Field, Ill	Org. fr. pl. of former lettered sqs.
Dorr Field, Fla:									
Squadron "A"									See 76th (II) Aer. Sq.
Squadron "B"									See 109th (II) Aer. Sq.
Squadron "C"									See 110th (II) Aer. Sq.
Squadron "D"									See 240th (II) Aer. Sq.
Squadron "E"									See 241st (II) Aer Sq.
Flying School Detachment.	November 1918	Dorr Field, Fla.					November 1919	Dorr Field, Fla.	Org. fr. pl. of former lettered sqs.
Eberts Field, Ark:									
Squadron "A"									See 66th (II) Aer. Sq.
Squadron "B"									See 123d (II) Aer. Sq.
Squadron "C"									See 124th (II) Aer. Sq.
Squadron "D"									See 125th (II) Aer. Sq.
Squadron "E"									See 181st Aer. Sq.
Flying School Detachment.	November 1918	Eberts Field, Ark					November 1919	Eberts Field, Ark	Org. fr. pl. of former lettered sqs.
Ellington Field, Tex:									
Squadron "A"									See 69th (II) Aer. Sq.
Squadron "B"									See 70th (II) Aer. Sq.

LETTERED SQUADRONS AND FLYING SCHOOL DETACHMENTS—Continued

Unit designation and redesignation	Organization		Stations in United States		Overseas		Demobilization		Remarks
	Month and year	Place	Month and year	Place	From—	To—	Month and year	Place	
Ellington Field, Tex.—Continued.									
Squadron "C"									See 113th (II) Aer. Sq.
Squadron "D"									See 232d (II) Aer. Sq.
Squadron "E"									See 233d (II) Aer. Sq.
Squadron "F"									See 250th Aer. Sq.
Squadron "G"									See 272d Aer. Sq.
Squadron "H"									See 285th Aer. Sq.
Squadron "I"									See 286th Aer. Sq.
Squadron "K"									See 303d Aer. Sq.
Squadron "L"	August 1918	Ellington Field, Tex.					December 1918	Ellington Field, Tex.	
Squadron "M"	September 1918	do					do	Do.	
Squadron "N"	November 1918	do					do	Do.	
Squadron "O"									See 850th Aer. Sq.
Squadron "X"	September 1918	Ellington Field, Tex.					December 1918	Ellington Field, Tex.	
Squadron "Y"	do	do					do	Do.	
Squadron "Z"	September 1918	do					do	Do.	
Flying School Detachment.	December 1918	do					September 1919	do	Org. fr. pl. of former lettered sqs.
Gerstner Field, La:									
Squadron "A"									See 2d Res. Aer. Sq.
Squadron "B"									See 63d (II) Aer. Sq.
Squadron "C"									See 64th (II) Aer. Sq.

Squadron "D"									See 75th (II) Aer. Sq.
Squadron "E"									See 143d Aer. Sq.
Squadron "F"									See 195th Aer. Sq.
Squadron "G"									See 196th Aer. Sq.
Squadron "H"	July 1918	Gerstner Field, La.					September 1918	Gerstner Field, La.	
Flying School Detachment.	November 1918	do					November 1919	do	Org. fr. pl. of former lettered sqs.
Kelly Field, Tex:									
Squadron "A"									See 2d (I) Aer. Sq.
Squadron "B"									See 115th (II) Aer. Sq.
Squadron "C"									See 117th (II) Aer. Sq.
Squadron "D"									See 178th Aer. Sq.
Squadron "E"									See 180th Aer. Sq.
Squadron "F"									See 235th (II) Aer. Sq.
Squadron "G"									See 243d (II) Aer. Sq.
Squadron "H"									See 244th (II) Aer. Sq.
Squadron "I"									See 245th (II) Aer. Sq.
Squadron "K"									See 110th (I) Aer. Sq.
Flying School Detachment.	November 1918	Kelly Field, Tex.					November 1919	Kelly Field, Tex.	Org. fr. pl. of former lettered sqs.
Langley Field, Va:									
Squadron "A"									See 83d (II) Aer. Sq.
Squadron "B"									See 126th (II) Aer. Sq.
Squadron "C"									See 127th (II) Aer. Sq.
Flying School Detachment.	November 1918	Langley Field, Va.					November 1919	Langley Field, Va.	Org. fr. pl. of former lettered sqs.

LETTERED SQUADRONS AND FLYING SCHOOL DETACHMENTS—Continued

Unit designation and redesignation	Organization		Stations in United States		Overseas		Demobilization		Remarks
	Month and year	Place	Month and year	Place	From—	To—	Month and year	Place	
Love Field, Tex:									
Squadron "A"									See 71st (II) Aer. Sq.
Squadron "B"									See 121st (II) Aer. Sq.
Squadron "C"									See 136th (II) Aer. Sq.
Squadron "D"									See 197th Aer. Sq.
Flying School Detachment.	November 1918	Love Field, Tex					November 1919	Love Field, Tex	Org. fr. pl. of former lettered sqs.
March Field, Calif:									
Squadron "A"									See 68th (II) Aer. Sq.
Squadron "B"									See 215th Aer. Sq.
Squadron "C"									See 289th Aer. Sq.
Squadron "D"									See 293d Aer. Sq.
Squadron "E"									See 311th Aer. Sq.
Flying School Detachment.	November 1918	March Field, Calif.					November 1919	March Field, Calif.	Org. fr. pl. of former lettered sqs.
Mather Field, Calif:									
Squadron "A"									See 200th (II) Aer. Sq.
Squadron "B"									See 201st (II) Aer. Sq.
Squadron "C"									See 283d Aer. Sq.
Squadron "D"									See 294th Aer. Sq.
Squadron "E"	July 1918	Mather Field, Calif.					November 1918	Mather Field, Calif.	
Flying School Detachment.	November 1918	do					October 1919	do	Org. fr. pl. of former lettered sqs.

McCook Field, Ohio:									
Squadron "A"									See 246th (I) Aer. Sq.
Squadron "B"									See 881st Aer. Sq.
Park Field, Tenn:									
Squadron "A"									See 65th (II) Aer. Sq.
Squadron "B"									See 87th Aer. Sq.
Squadron "C"									See 160th Aer. Sq.
Squadron "D"									See 214th Aer. Sq.
Squadron "E"	August 1918	Park Field, Tenn.					December 1918	Park Field, Tenn.	
Flying School Detachment.	December 1918	do					July 1919	do	Org. fr. pl. of former lettered sqs.
Payne Field, Miss:									
Squadron "A"									See 175th Aer. Sq.
Squadron "B"									See 238th (II) Aer. Sq.
Squadron "C"									See 239th (II) Aer. Sq.
Squadron "D"									See 252d Aer. Sq.
Flying School Detachment.	November 1918	Payne Field, Miss.					November 1919	Payne Field, Miss.	Org. fr. pl. of former lettered sqs.
Post Field, Okla:									
Squadron "A"									See 3d (I) Aer. Sq.
Squadron "B"									See 4th (I) Aer. Sq.
Squadron "C"									See 80th (II) Aer. Sq.
Squadron "D"									See 81st (II) Aer. Sq.
Squadron "E"									See 202d (II) Aer. Sq.
Squadron "F"									See 251st Aer. Sq.
Flying School Detachment.	January 1919	Post Field, Okla.					September 1919	Post Field, Okla.	Org. fr. pl. of former lettered sqs.

LETTERED SQUADRONS AND FLYING SCHOOL DETACHMENTS—Continued

Unit designation and redesignation	Organization		Stations in United States		Overseas		Demobilization		Remarks
	Month and year	Place	Month and year	Place	From—	To—	Month and year	Place	
Rich Field, Tex:									
Squadron "A"									See 39th Aer. Sq.
Squadron "B"									See 150th Aer. Sq.
Squadron "C"									See 249th Aer. Sq.
Flying School Detachment.	November 1918	Rich Field, Tex.					December 1919	Rich Field, Tex.	Org. fr. pl. of former lettered sqs.
Rockwell Field, Calif:									
Squadron "A"									See 14th (I) Aer. Sq.
Squadron "B"									See 18th (I) Aer. Sq.
Squadron "C"									See 132d (II) Aer. Sq.
Squadron "D"									See 133d (II) Aer. Sq.
Squadron "E"									See 204th (II) Aer. Sq.
Squadron "F"									See 290th Prov. Aer. Sq.
Squadron "G"									See 291st Prov. Aer. Sq.
Squadron "H"									See 292d Prov. Aer. Sq.
Flying School Detachment.	November 1918	Rockwell Field, Calif.					September 1919	Rockwell Field, Calif.	Org. fr. pl. of former lettered sqs.
Scott Field, Ill:									
Squadron "A"									See 114th (II) Aer. Sq.
Squadron "B"									See 221st Aer. Sq.

Squadron "C"									See 242d (II) Aer. Sq.
Squadron "D"	July 1918	Scott Field, Ill					November 1918	Scott Field, Ill.	
Flying School Detachment.	November 1918	do					October 1919	do	Org. fr. pl. of former lettered sqs.
Selfridge Field, Mich:									
Squadron "A"									See 40th Aer. Sq.
Squadron "B"									See 380th Aer. Sq.
Squadron "C"	August 1918	Selfridge Field, Mich.					November 1918	Selfridge Field, Mich.	
Squadron "D"	do	do					do	Do.	
Squadron "E"	do	do					do	Do.	
Flying School Detachment.	November 1918	do					June 1919	do	Org. fr. pl. of former lettered sqs.
Souther Field, Ga:									
Squadron "A"									See 5th (I) Aer. Sq.
Squadron "B"									See 116th (II) Aer. Sq.
Squadron "C"									See 236th (II) Aer. Sq.
Squadron "D"									See 237th (II) Aer. Sq.
Flying School Detachment.	November 1918	Souther Field, Ga					November 1919	Souther Field, Ga	Org. fr. pl. of former lettered sqs.
Taliaferro Field, Tex:									
Squadron "A"									See 78th (II) Aer. Sq.
Squadron "B"									See 79th (II) Aer. Sq.
Squadron "C"									See 82d (II) Aer. Sq.
Squadron "D"									See 206th (II) Aer. Sq.
Squadron "E"									See 275th Aer. Sq.
Squadron "F"									See 629th Aer. Sq.
Flying School Detachment.	November 1918	Taliaferro Field, Tex.					November 1919	Taliaferro Field, Tex.	Org. fr. pl. of former lettered sqs.

LETTERED SQUADRONS AND FLYING SCHOOL DETACHMENTS—Continued

Unit designation and redesignation	Organisation		Stations in United States		Overseas		Demobilisation		Remarks
	Month and year	Place	Month and year	Place	From—	To—	Month and year	Place	
Taylor Field, Ala:									
Squadron "A"									See 128th (II) Aer. Sq.
Squadron "B"									See 131st (II) Aer. Sq.
Squadron "C"									See 193d Aer. Sq.
Squadron 'D"									See 129th (II) Aer. Sq.
Flying School Detachment.	November 1918	Taylor Field, Ala					November 1919	Taylor Field, Ala	Org. fr. pl. of former lettered sqs.
Wilbur Wright Field, Ohio:									
Squadron "A"									See 231st (II) Aer. Sq.
Squadron "B"									See 851st Aer. Sq.
Squadron "C"									See 874th Aer. Sq.
Squadron "I"									See 42d Aer. Sq.
Squadron "K"									See 44th Aer. Sq.
Squadron "L"									See 246th (II) Aer. Sq.
Squadron "M"									See 342d Aer. Sq.
Squadron "N"	October 1918	Wilbur Wright Field, Ohio.					February 1919	Wilbur Wright Field, Ohio.	
Squadron "O"	do	do					May 1919	do	Skeletonized February 1919.
Squadron "P"									See 44th Aer. Sq.
Squadron "Q"									See 342d Aer. Sq.
Flying School Detachment.	December 1918	Wilbur Wright Field, Ohio					March 1919	Wilbur Wright Field, Ohio.	Org. fr. pl. of former lettered sqs.

1st Provisional Squadron, Wilbur Wright Field.	April 1918	do					June 1918	Do.	
2d Provisional Squadron, Wilbur Wright Field.	do	do					do	Do.	
	October 1918	do					December 1918	do	Reorgzd. October 1918.
3d Provisional Squadron, Wilbur Wright Field.	April 1918	do					August 1918	Do.	
4th Provisonal Squadron, Wilbur Wright Field.	do	do					December 1918	Do.	
5th Provisional Squadron, Wilbur Wright Field.	May 1918	do					do	Do.	
6th Provisional Squadron, Wilbur Wright Field	do	do					September 1918	Do.	

PROVISIONAL SQUADRONS, SPRUCE PRODUCTION DIVISION

1st Provisional Squadron.	March 1918	Vancouver Bks., Wash.							
a. 21st Spruce Squadron.	July 1918	do					January 1919	Vancouver Bks., Wash.	
2d Provisional Squadron	March 1918	Do.							
a. 22d Spruce Squadron.	July 1918	do					do	Do.	
3d Provisional Squadron	March 1918	Do.							
a. 23d Spruce Squadron.	July 1918	do					do	Do.	
4th Provisional Squadron.	March 1918	Vancouver Bks., Wash.							
a. 24th Spruce Squadron.	July 1918	do					January 1919	Vancouver Bks., Wash.	
5th Provisional Squadron.	March 1918	Do.							
a. 25th Spruce Squadron.	July 1918	do					do	Do.	
6th Provisional Squadron.	March 1918	Do.							
a. 26th Spruce Squadron.	July 1918	do					do	Do.	

PROVISIONAL SQUADRONS, SPRUCE PRODUCTION DIVISION—Continued

Unit designation and redesignation	Organization		Stations in United States		Overseas		Demobilization		Remarks
	Month and year	Place	Month and year	Place	From—	To—	Month and year	Place	
7th Provisional Squadron.	March 1918	**Vancouver Bks., Wash.**	March 1918	Raymond, Wash.					
a. 59th Spruce Squadron.	July 1918	Raymond, Wash.	November 1918	Vancouver Bks., Wash.			January 1919	Vancouver Bks., Wash.	
8th Provisional Squadron.	March 1918	Vancouver Bks., Wash.	March 1918	Seaside, Oreg.					
			May 1918	Clatsop, Oreg.					
a. 75th Spruce Squadron.	July 1918	Clatsop Oreg	December 1918	Vancouver Bks., Wash.			do	Do.	
9th Provisional Squadron.	March 1918	Vancouver Bks., Wash.	March 1918	Hoquiam, Wash.					
a. 60th Spruce Squadron.	July 1918	Hoquiam, Wash.	November 1918	Vancouver Bks., Wash.			do	Do.	
10th Provisional Squadron.									Never orgzd.
11th Provisional Squadron.	March 1918	Vancouver Bks., Wash.	March 1918	Astoria, Oreg.					
a, 76th Spruce Squadron.	July 1918	Astoria, Oreg	November 1918	Vancouver Bks., Wash.			January 1919	Vancouver Bks., Wash.	
12th Provisional Squadron.	March 1918	Vancouver Bks., Wash.	March 1918	Carson, Wash.					
			May 1918	Cascade Locks, Oreg.					
			June 1918	Bridal Veil, Oreg.					
a. 104th Spruce Squadron.	July 1918	Bridal Veil, Oreg.	October 1918	Joyce, Wash.					
			December 1918	Vancouver Bks., Wash.			do	Do.	
13th Provisional Squadron.	April 1918	Vancouver Bks., Wash.	April 1918	Clatsop, Oreg.					
a. 77th Spruce Squadron.	July 1918	Clatsop, Oreg.	December 1918	Vancouver Bks., Wash.			do	Do.	

14th Provisional Squadron.	April 1918	Vancouver Bks., Wash.	April 1918	Astoria, Oreg.				
a. 78th Spruce Squadron.	July 1918	Astoria, Oreg	November 1918	Vancouver Bks., Wash.			do	Do.
15th Provisional Squadron.	April 1918	Vancouver Bks., Wash.	April 1918	Nemah, Wash.				
a. 61st Spruce Squadron.	July 1918	Nemah, Wash	September 1918 November 1918	South Bend, Oreg. Vancouver Bks., Wash.			do	Do.
16th Provisional Squadron.	April 1918	Vancouver Bks., Wash.	April 1918 May 1918	Toledo, Oreg. Yaquina, Oreg.				
a. 82nd Spruce Squadron.	July 1918	Yaquina, Oreg					do	Do.
17th Provisional Squadron.	April 1918	Vancouver Bks., Wash.	April 1918 June 1918	Aberdeen, Wash. Elma, Wash.				
a. 62d Spruce Squadron.	July 1918	Elma, Wash	September 1918 November 1918	Montesano, Wash. Vancouver Bks., Wash.			do	Do.
18th Provisional Squadron.	April 1918	Vancouver Bks., Wash.	April 1918	South Beach, Oreg.				
a. 83d Spruce Squadron.	July 1918	South Beach, Oreg.					do	Do.
19th Provisional Squadron.	April 1918	Vancouver Bks., Wash.	April 1918	Bay City, Wash.				
a. 63d Spruce Squadron.	July 1918	Bay City, Wash	December 1918	Vancouver Bks., Wash.			do	Do.
20th Provisional Squadron.	April 1918	Vancouver Bks., Wash.	April 1918	Waldport, Oreg.				
a. 84th Spruce Squadron.	July 1918	Waldport, Oreg					do	Do.
21st Provisional Squadron.	May 1918	Vancouver Bks., Wash.	May 1918	Waldport, Oreg.				
a. 85th Spruce Squadron.	July 1918	Waldport, Oreg	August 1918 September 1918 November 1918 December 1918	Newport, Oreg. Siemscarey, Wash. Port Angeles, Wash. Vancouver Bks., Wash.			do	Do.

PROVISIONAL SQUADRONS, SPRUCE PRODUCTION DIVISION—Continued

Unit designation and redesigantion	Organization		Stations in United States		Overseas		Demobilization		Remarks
	Month and year	Place	Month and year	Place	From—	To—	Month and year	Place	
22d Provisional Squadron.	May 1918	Vancouver Bks., Wash.	May 1918	South Beach, Oreg.					
a. 86th Spruce Squadron.	July 1918	South Beach, Oreg.					January 1919	Vancouver Bks., Wash.	
23d Provisional Squadron.	June 1918	Portland, Oreg.							
a. 106th Spruce Squadron.	July 1918	do					do	Portland, Oreg.	
24th Provisional Squadron.	June 1918	Vancouver Bks., Wash.	June 1918	South Beach, Oreg.					
a. 87th Spruce Squadron.	July 1918	South Beach, Oreg.	September 1918 December 1918	Siemscarey, Wash. Vancouver Bks., Wash.			do	Vancouver Bks., Wash.	
25th Provisional Squadron.	June 1918	Vancouver Bks., Wash.	June 1918	South Beach, Oreg.					
a. 88th Spruce Squadron.	July 1918	South Beach, Oreg.	October 1918 December 1918	Waldport, Oreg. Vancouver Bks., Wash.			do	Do.	
26th Provisional Squadron.	June 1918	Vancouver Bks., Wash.	June 1918	Waldport, Oreg.					
a. 89th Spruce Squadron.	July 1918	Waldport, Oreg.					do	Do.	
27th Provisional Squadron.	June 1918	Vancouver Bks., Wash.	June 1918	Newport, Oreg.					
a. 90th Spruce Squadron.	July 1918	Newport, Oreg.	December 1918	Vancouver Bks., Wash.			do	Do.	
28th Provisional Squadron.	June 1918	Vancouver Bks., Wash.	June 1918	Yaquina, Oreg.					
a. 91st Spruce Squadron.	July 1918	Yaquina, Oreg.	November 1918	Newport, Oreg.			do	Do.	

29th Provisional Squadron.	June 1918	Vancouver Bks., Wash.	June 1918	Agate Beach, Oreg.				
a. 92d Spruce Squadron.	July 1918	Agate Beach, Oreg.	November 1918	Newport, Oreg.				
			December 1918	Vancouver Bks., Wash.			do	Do.
30th Provisional Squadron.	do	Vancouver Bks., Wash.	July 1918	Newport, Oreg.				
a. 93d Spruce Squadron.	do	Newport, Oreg	November 1918	Yaquina, Oreg			do	Do.
31st Provisional Squadron.	June 1918	Vancouver Bks., Wash.						
a. 27th Spruce Squadron.	July 1918	do					February 1919	Do.
32d Provisional Squadron.	June 1918	Do.						
a. 28th Spruce Squadron.	July 1918	do					January 1919	Do.
33d Provisional Squadron.	do	do	July 1918	South Beach, Oreg.				
a. 94th Spruce Squadron.	do	South Beach, Oreg.	August 1918	Toledo, Oreg			do	Do.
34th Provisional Squadron.	do	Vancouver Bks., Wash.	July 1918	Waldport, Oreg.				
a. 95th Spruce Squadron.	do	Waldport, Oreg	August 1918	Newport, Oreg.				
			December 1918	Vancouver Bks., Wash.			do	Do.
35th Provisional Squadron.	do	Vancouver Bks., Wash.	July 1918	Coquille, Oreg.				
a. 103d Spruce Squadron.	do	Coquille, Oreg	December 1918	Vancouver Bks., Wash.			do	Do.
36th Provisional Squadron.	do	Vancouver Bks., Wash.	July 1918	South Beach, Oreg.				
a. 96th Spruce Squadron.	do	South Beach, Oreg.	August 1918	Lake Pleasant, Wash.				
			September 1918	Siemscarey, Wash.				
			December 1918	Vancouver Bks., Wash.			do	Do.

PROVISIONAL SQUADRONS, SPRUCE PRODUCTION DIVISION—Continued

Unit designation and redesignation	Organization		Stations in United States		Overseas		Demobilization		Remarks
	Month and year	Place	Month and year	Place	From—	To—	Month and year	Place	
37th Provisional Squadron.	July 1918	Vancouver Bks., Wash.	July 1918	Newport, Oreg.					
a. 97th Spruce Squadron.	do	Newport, Oreg.					January 1919	Vancouver Bks., Wash.	
38th Provisional Squadron.	do	Vancouver Bks., Wash.	July 1918	Newport, Oreg.					
a. 98th Spruce Squadron.	do	Newport, Oreg.	October 1918 December 1918	Waldport, Oreg. South Beach, Oreg.			do	Do.	
39th Provisional Squadron.	do	Vancouver Bks., Wash.	July 1918	Do.					
a. 99th Spruce Squadron.	do	South Beach, Oreg.	August 1918 October 1918	Wendling, Oreg. Beaver Hill, Oreg.			November 1918	Beaver Hill, Oreg.	
40th Provisional Squadron.	do	Vancouver Bks., Wash.	July 1918	South Beach, Oreg.					
a. 100th Spruce Squadron.	do	South Beach, Oreg.	August 1918 December 1918	Stillwater, Wash. Vancouver Bks., Wash.			January 1919	Vancouver Bks., Wash.	
41st Provisional Squadron.	do	Vancouver Bks., Wash.	July 1918	Joyce, Wash.					
a. 40th Spruce Squadron.	do	Joyce, Wash.					do	Do.	
42d Provisional Squadron.	do	Vancouver Bks., Wash.	July 1918	Toledo, Oreg.					
a. 101st Spruce Squadron.	do	Toledo, Oreg.					do	Do.	
43d Provisional Squadron.	do	Vancouver Bks., Wash.	July 1918	Joyce, Wash.					
a. 41st Spruce Squadron.	do	Joyce, Wash.					do	Do.	

44th Provisional Squadron.	do	Vancouver Bks., Wash.	July 1918	Aberdeen, Wash.					
a. 64th Spruce Squadron.	do	Aberdeen, Wash	November 1918	Vancouver Bks., Wash.			do	Do.	
45th Provisional Squadron.	do	Vancouver Bks., Wash.	July 1918	Raymond, Wash.					
a. 65th Spruce Squadron.	do	Raymond, Wash	November 1918	Vancouver Bks., Wash.			do	Do.	
46th Provisional Squadron.	do	Vancouver Bks., Wash.	July 1918	Cosmopolis, Wash.					
a. 107th Spruce Squadron.	do	Cosmopolis, Wash.	November 1918	Vancouver Bks., Wash.			do	Do.	
47th Provisional Squadron.	do	Vancouver Bks., Wash.	July 1918	Humptulips, Wash.					
a. 108th Spruce Squadron.	do	Humptulips, Wash.	November 1918	Vancouver Bks., Wash.			do	Do.	

SPRUCE SQUADRONS

1st Spruce Squadron									See 407th Aer. Sq.
2d Spruce Squadron									See 408th Aer. Sq.
3d Spruce Squadron									See 409th Aer. Sq.
4th Spruce Squadron									See 410th Aer. Sq.
5th Spruce Squadron									See 411th Aer. Sq.
6th Spruce Squadron									See 412th Aer. Sq.
7th Spruce Squadron									See 439th Aer. Sq.
8th Spruce Squadron									See 440th Aer. Sq.
9th Spruce Squadron									See 441st Aer. Sq.
10th Spruce Squadron									See 442d Aer. Sq.
11th Spruce Squadron									See 443d Aer. Sq.
12th Spruce Squadron									See 444th Aer. Sq.
13th Spruce Squadron									See 601st Aer. Sq.
14th Spruce Squadron									See 603d Aer. Sq.
15th Spruce Squadron									See 401st Aer. Sq.
16th Spruce Squadron									See 402d Aer. Sq.
17th Spruce Squadron									See 403d Aer. Sq.
18th Spruce Squadron									See 404th Aer. Sq.
19th Spruce Squadron									See 405th Aer. Sq.
20th Spruce Squadron									See 406th Aer. Sq.

SPRUCE SQUADRONS—Continued

Unit designation and redesignation	Organization		Stations in United States		Overseas		Demobilization		Remarks
	Month and year	Place	Month and year	Place	From—	To—	Month and year	Place	
21st Spruce Squadron									See 1st Prov. Sq.
22d Spruce Squadron									See 2d Prov. Sq.
23d Spruce Squadron									See 3d Prov. Sq.
24th Spruce Squadron									See 4th Prov. Sq.
25th Spruce Squadron									See 5th Prov. Sq.
26th Spruce Squadron									See 6th Prov. Sq.
27th Spruce Squadron									See 31st Prov. Sq.
28th Spruce Squadron									See 32d Prov. Sq.
29th Spruce Squadron									See 425th Aer. Sq.
30th Spruce Squadron									See 426th Aer. Sq.
31st Spruce Squadron									See 429th Aer. Sq.
32d Spruce Squadron									See 415th Aer. Sq.
33d Spruce Squadron									See 416th Aer. Sq.
34th Spruce Squadron									See 417th Aer. Sq.
35th Spruce Squadron									See 418th Aer. Sq.
36th Spruce Squadron									See 422d Aer. Sq.
37th Spruce Squadron									See 430th Aer. Sq.
38th Spruce Squadron									See 445th Aer. Sq.
39th Spruce Squadron									See 450th Aer. Sq.
40th Spruce Squadron									See 41st Prov. Sq.
41st Spruce Squadron									See 43d Prov. Sq.
42d Spruce Squadron									See 413th Aer. Sq.
43d Spruce Squadron									See 419th Aer. Sq.
44th Spruce Squadron									See 420th Aer. Sq.
45th Spruce Squadron									See 421st Aer. Sq.
46th Spruce Squadron									See 423d Aer. Sq.
47th Spruce Squadron									See 427th Aer. Sq.
48th Spruce Squadron									See 431st Aer. Sq.
49th Spruce Squadron									See 432d Aer. Sq.
50th Spruce Squadron									See 435th (I) Aer. Sq.

51st Spruce Squadron									See 436th Aer. Sq.
52d Spruce Squadron									See 438th Aer. Sq.
53d Spruce Squadron									See 446th Aer. Sq.
54th Spruce Squadron									See 448th Aer. Sq.
55th Spruce Squadron									See 449th Aer. Sq.
56th Spruce Squadron									See 451st Aer. Sq.
57th Spruce Squadron									See 454th Aer. Sq.
58th Spruce Squadron									See 459th Aer. Sq.
59th Spruce Squadron									See 7th Prov. Sq.
60th Spruce Squadron									See 9th Prov. Sq.
61st Spruce Squadron									See 15th Prov. Sq.
62d Spruce Squadron									See 17th Prov. Sq.
63d Spruce Squadron									See 19th Prov. Sq.
64th Spruce Squadron									See 44th Prov. Sq.
65th Spruce Squadron									See 45th Prov. Sq.
66th Spruce Squadron									See 424th Aer. Sq.
67th Spruce Squadron									See 428th Aer. Sq.
68th Spruce Squadron									See 433d Aer. Sq.
69th Spruce Squadron									See 434th Aer. Sq.
70th Spruce Squadron									See 447th Aer. Sq.
71st Spruce Squadron									See 452d Aer. Sq.
72d Spruce Squadron									See 456th Aer. Sq.
73d Spruce Squadron									See 457th Aer. Sq.
74th Spruce Squadron									See 458th Aer. Sq.
75th Spruce Squadron									See 8th Prov. Sq.
76th Spruce Squadron									See 11th Prov. Sq.
77th Spruce Squadron									See 13th Prov. Sq.
78th Spruce Squadron									See 14th Prov. Sq.
79th Spruce Squadron									See 437th Aer. Sq.
80th Spruce Squadron									See 453d Aer. Sq.
81st Spruce Squadron									See 455th Aer. Sq.
82d Spruce Squadron									See 16th Prov. Sq.
83d Spruce Squadron									See 18th Prov. Sq.
84th Spruce Squadron									See 20th Prov. Sq.
85th Spruce Squadron									See 21st Prov. Sq.
86th Spruce Squadron									See 22d Prov. Sq.
87th Spruce Squadron									See 24th Prov. Sq.
88th Spruce Squadron									See 25th Prov. Sq.
89th Spruce Squadron									See 26th Prov. Sq.

SPRUCE SQUADRONS—Continued

Unit designation and redesignation	Organization		Stations in United States		Overseas		Demobilization		Remarks
	Month and year	Place	Month and year	Place	From—	To—	Month and year	Place	
90th Spruce Squadron									See 27th Prov. Sq.
91st Spruce Squadron									See 28th Prov. Sq.
92d Spruce Squadron									See 29th Prov. Sq.
93d Spruce Squadron									See 30th Prov. Sq.
94th Spruce Squadron									See 33d Prov. Sq.
95th Spruce Squadron									See 34th Prov. Sq.
96th Spruce Squadron									See 36th Prov. Sq.
97th Spruce Squadron									See 37th Prov. Sq.
98th Spruce Squadron									See 38th Prov. Sq.
99th Spruce Squadron									See 39th Prov. Sq.
100th Spruce Squadron									See 40th Prov. Sq.
101st Spruce Squadron									See 42d Prov. Sq.
102d Spruce Squadron									See 414th Aer. Sq.
103d Spruce Squadron									See 35th Prov. Sq.
104th Spruce Squadron									See 12th Prov. Sq.
105th Spruce Squadron									See 460th Aer. Sq.
106th Spruce Squadron									See 23d Prov. Sq.
107th Spruce Squadron									See 46th Prov. Sq.
108th Spruce Squadron									See 47th Prov. Sq.
109th Spruce Squadron	July 1918	Vancouver Bks., Wash.	July 1918	Toledo, Oreg.			January 1919	Vancouver Bks., Wash.	
110th Spruce Squadron	do	do	do	Yaquina, Oreg.			do	Do.	
111th Spruce Squadron	do	do	do	Do.					
			September 1918	Newport, Oreg.			do	Do.	
112th Spruce Squadron	August 1918	do					do	Do.	
113th Spruce Squadron	do	do					February 1919	Do.	
114th Spruce Squadron	July 1918	do	August 1918	Astoria, Oreg.					
			November 1918	Vancouver Bks., Wash.			January 1919	Vancouver Bks., Wash.	
115th Spruce Squadron	do	do	July 1918	Joyce, Wash.					
			October 1918	Siemscarey, Wash.			do	Do.	

116th Spruce Squadron	do	do	July 1918	South Bend, Wash.				
			November 1918	Vancouver Bks., Wash.			do	Do.
117th Spruce Squadron	do	do	July 1918	Joyce, Wash.				
			December 1918	Vancouver Bks., Wash.			do	Do.
118th Spruce Squadron	do	do	July 1918	Joyce, Wash.				
			August 1918	Lake Crescent, Wash.				
			October 1918	Joyce, Wash.				
			December 1918	Vancouver Bks., Wash.			do	Do.
119th Spruce Squadron	August 1918	do	August 1918	Joyce, Wash.				
			do	Port Angeles, Wash.				
			December 1918	Vancouver Bks., Wash.			do	Do.
120th Spruce Squadron	do	do	August 1918	Port Angeles, Wash.				
			November 1918	Vancouver Bks., Wash.			do	Do.
121st Spruce Squadron	do	do	August 1918	Bellingham, Wash.				
			November 1918	Vancouver Bks., Wash.			do	Do.
122d Spruce Squadron	do	do	August 1918	Joyce, Wash.				
			September 1918	Siemscarey, Wash.				
			November 1918	Port Angeles, Wash.				
			December 1918	Vancouver Bks., Wash.			do	Do.
123d Spruce Squadron	do	do	August 1918	Lake Pleasant, Wash.				
			September 1918	Siemscarey, Wash.				
			November 1918	Port Angeles, Wash.				
			December 1918	Vancouver Bks., Wash.			do	Do.

SPRUCE SQUADRONS—Continued

Unit designation and redesignation	Organization		Stations in United States		Overseas		Demobilization		Remarks
	Month and year	Place	Month and year	Place	From—	To—	Month and year	Place	
124th Spruce Squadron	August 1918	Vancouver Bks., Wash.	August 1918	Joyce, Wash.					
			September 1918	Siemscarey, Wash.					
			December 1918	Vancouver Bks., Wash.			January 1919	Vancouver Bks., Wash.	
125th Spruce Squadron	do	do	August 1918	Eagle Gorge, Wash.					
			December 1918	Vancouver Bks., Wash.			do	Do.	
126th Spruce Squadron	do	do	August 1918	Joyce, Wash			do	Do.	
127th Spruce Squadron	do	do	do	do			do	Do.	
128th Spruce Squadron	do	do	do	Do.					
			December 1918	Siemscarey, Wash			do	Do.	
129th Spruce Squadron	do	do	August 1918	Timber, Oreg.					
			December 1918	Vancouver Bks., Wash.			do	Do.	
130th Spruce Squadron	do	do	August 1918	Seattle, Wash.					
			November 1918	Vancouver Bks., Wash.			do	Do.	
131st Spruce Squadron	do	do	August 1918	Falls City, Oreg.					
			October 1918	Dallas, Oreg			October 1918	Dallas, Oreg.	
132d Spruce Squadron	do	do	August 1918	Skykomish, Wash			do	Skykomish, Wash.	
133d Spruce Squadron	do	do	do	Knappton, Wash.					
			December 1918	Vancouver Bks., Wash.			January 1919	Vancouver Bks., Wash.	
134th Spruce Squadron	September 1918	Tillamook, Oreg	November 1918	do			do	Do.	
135th Spruce Squadron	do	Garibaldi, Oreg	December 1918	do			do	Do.	
136th Spruce Squadron	do	Vancouver Bks., Wash.	September 1918	Joyce, Wash			do	Do.	
137th Spruce Squadron	August 1918	Port Orchard, Wash.					September 1918	Port Orchard, Wash.	Demblzd. Port Orchard, Wash.; reconstituted Vancouver Bks., Wash.
	October 1918	Vancouver Bks., Wash.	October 1918	North Portland, Oreg.					
			December 1918	Vancouver Bks., Wash.			January 1919	Vancouver Bks., Wash.	

138th Spruce Squadron	September 1918	Vancouver Bks., Wash.	September 1918	Joyce, Wash.					
			December 1918	Vancouver Bks., Wash.			January 1918	Vancouver Bks., Wash.	
139th Spruce Squadron	do	do	September 1918	North Bend, Oreg.					
			December 1918	Vancouver Bks., Wash.			do	Do.	
140th Spruce Squadron	do	do	September 1918	Joyce, Wash			do	Do.	
141st Spruce Squadron	October 1918	do	October 1918	Port Gamble, Wash.					
			December 1918	Vancouver Bks., Wash.			do	Do.	
142d Spruce Squadron	September 1918	do	September 1918	Beaver Hill, Oreg.					
			November 1918	Vancouver Bks., Wash.			do	Do.	
143d Spruce Squadron	do	Joyce, Wash	December 1918	do			do	Do.	
144th Spruce Squadron	do	Vancouver Bks.,	September 1918	Joyce, Wash.					
			December 1918	Vancouver Bks., Wash.			do	Do.	
145th Spruce Squadron	do	Seaside, Oreg	November 1918	do			do	Do.	
146th Spruce Squadron	do	Astoria, Oreg	do	do			do	Do.	
147th Spruce Squadron	do	Warrenton, Oreg	do	do			do	Do.	
148th Spruce Squadron	do	Clatsop, Oreg	do	do			do	Do.	
149th Spruce Squadron	do	Garibaldi, Oreg	September 1918	Wheeler, Oreg.					
			November 1918	Vancouver Bks., Wash.			do	Do.	
150th Spruce Squadron	do	Astoria, Oreg	do	do			do	Do.	

AVIATION SCHOOL SQUADRONS

1st Aviation School Squadron.	May 1917	Rockwell Field, Calif.							Orgzd. fr. Avn. Co. "A", Rockwell Field, Calif. Redesignated 14th (I) Aer. Sq. August 1917.
2d Aviation School Squadron.	do	Mineola, N. Y.							Orgzd. fr. Avn. Co. "B", Mineola, N.Y. Redesignated 15th Aer. Sq. August 1917.

AVIATION SCHOOL SQUADRONS—Continued

Unit designation and redesignation	Organization		Stations in United States		Overseas		Demobilization		Remarks
	Month and year	Place	Month and year	Place	From—	To—	Month and year	Place	
3d Aviation School Squadron.	May 1917	Memphis, Tenn	May 1917	Chicago, Ill					Orgzd. fr. Avn. Co. "C", Memphis, Tenn. Redesignated 16th (I) Aer. Sq. August 1917.
			July 1917	Chanute Field, Ill.					
4th Aviation School Squadron.	do	Chicago, Ill	do	do					Orgzd. fr. Avn. Co. "C". Redesignated 16th (I) Aer. Sq. August 1917.
5th Aviation School Squadron.	do	Hampton, Va							Redesignated 119th Aer. Sq. September 1917.

BALLOON COMPANIES

Unit designation and redesignation	Organization		Stations in United States		Overseas		Demobilization		Remarks
	Month and year	Place	Month and year	Place	From—	To—	Month and year	Place	
Balloon Company "A"	August 1917	Ft. Omaha, Nebr	September 1917	Post Field, Okla					
a. 1st Balloon Squadron.	September 1917	Post Field, Okla					February 1918	Post Field, Okla	
1st Balloon Company	June 1918	A. E. F	June 1919	Cp. Lee, Va		June 1919			Orgzd. fr. Co. "A", 2d Bln. Sq. Active through 1919 Army troops.
			July 1919	Ross Field, Calif.					
2d Balloon Company	do	do	June 1919	Mitchel Field, N.Y.		do			Orgzd. fr. Co. "B", 2d Bln. Sq. Active through 1919 Corps troops.
			August 1919	Ross Field, Calif.					
3d Balloon Company	do	do	June 1919	Cp. Lee, Va		do			Orgzd. fr. Co. "C", 2d Bln. Sq. Active through 1919 Army troops.
			July 1919	Ross Field, Calif.					

4th Balloon Company	do	do	May 1919	Cp. Lee, Va		May 1919			Orgzd. fr. Co. "D", 2d Bln. Sq. Active through 1919.
			do	Brooks Field, Tex.					Army troops.
5th Balloon Company	do	do	do	Cp. Lee, Va		do			Orgzd. fr. Co. "A", 3d Bln. Sq. Active through 1919.
			do	Brooks Field, Tex.					Army troops.
6th Balloon Company	do	do	do	Cp. Lee, Va		do			Orgzd. fr. Co. "B", 3d Bln. Sq. Active through 1919.
			do	Brooks Field, Tex.					Army troops.
7th Balloon Company	do	do	do	Cp. Lee, Va		do			Orgzd. fr. Co. "C", 3d Bln. Sq. Active through 1919.
			do	Brooks Field, Tex.					Army troops.
8th Balloon Company	do	do	do	Cp. Lee, Va		do			Orgzd. fr. Co. "D", 3d Bln. Sq. Active through 1919.
			do	Brooks Field, Tex.					
			November 1919	Cp. Owen Beirne, Tex.					Army troops.
9th Balloon Company	July 1918	do	May 1919	Cp. Lee, Va		do			Orgzd. fr. Co. "A", 4th Bln. Sq. Active through 1919.
			do	Ft. Omaha, Nebr.					Army troops.
10th Balloon Company	do	A. E. F				do	May 1919	Cp. Lee, Va	Orgzd. fr. Co. "B", 4th Bln. Sq. Active through 1919. Corps troops.
11th Balloon Company	February 1918	Ft. Omaha, Nebr	February 1918	Cp. Morrison, Va					Orgzd. fr. Co. "A", 5th Bln. Sq.
			June 1918	P. of E., Newport News.	June 1918.				
			May 1919	Cp. Lee, Va		May 1919.			
			do	Brooks Field, Tex.					Army troops. Active through 1919.
12th Balloon Company	do	do	February 1918	Cp. Morrison, Va					Orgzd. fr. Co. "B", 5th Bln. Sq.
			June 1918	P. of E., Newport News.	June 1918.				
			March 1919	Langley Field, Va		March 1919.			
			April 1919	Ft. Omaha, Nebr					Army troops. Active through 1919.

BALLOON COMPANIES—Continued

Unit designation and redesignation	Organization		Stations in United States		Overseas		Demobilization		Remarks
	Month and year	Place	Month and year	Place	From—	To—	Month and year	Place	
13th Balloon Company	January 1918	Ft. Omaha, Nebr.	June 1918	Cp. Morrison, Va.					Orgzd. fr. Co. "C", 4th Bln. Sq. Army troops.
			July 1918	P. of E., Newport News.	July 1918.				
			June 1919	Mitchel Field, N. Y.		June 1919.			
			July 1919	Ross Field, Calif.					Active through 1919.
14th Balloon Company	do	do	July 1918	Cp. Morrison, Va.					Orgzd. fr. Co. "D", 4th Bln. Sq.
			do	P. of E., Newport News.	July 1918.				
			August 1919	Mitchel Field, N. Y.		August 1919.			
			September 1919	Ft. Omaha, Nebr.					Corps troops. Active through 1919.
15th Balloon Company	do	do	July 1918	Cp. Morrison, Va.					Orgzd. fr. Co. "C", 5th Bln. Sq. Corps troops.
			do	P. of E., Newport News.	July 1918.				
			June 1919	Cp. Lee, Va.		June 1919.			
			July 1919	Ross Field, Calif.					Active through 1919.
16th Balloon Company	do	do	July 1918	Cp. Morrison, Va.					Orgzd. fr. Co. "D", 5th Bln. Sq.
			do	P. of E., Newport News.	July 1918.				
			June 1919	Cp. Lee, Va.		June 1919.			
			July 1919	Ft. Omaha, Nebr.					
			August 1919	Brooks Field, Tex.					Corps troops. Active through 1919.
17th Balloon Company	do	do	September 1918	Cp. Morrison, Va.					
			October 1918	P. of E., Newport News.	October 1918.				
			May 1919	Cp. Lee, Va.		May 1919.			

			May 1919	Ft. Crook, Nebr.					
			June 1919	Ft. Omaha, Nebr.					Army troops. Active through 1919.
18th Balloon Company	do	do	September 1918	Cp. Morrison, Va.					
			October 1918	P. of E., Newport News.	October 1918.				
			May 1919	Cp. Lee, Va.		May 1919.			
			do	Lee Hall, Va.					
			August 1919	Aberdeen Proving Ground, Md.					Do.
19th Balloon Company	do	do	September 1918	Cp. Morrison, Va.					
			October 1918	P. of E., Newport News.	October 1918.				
			April 1919	Mitchel Field, N. Y.		April 1919.			
			July 1919	Lee Hall, Va.					
			do	Langley Field, Va.					Do.
20th Balloon Company	do	do	September 1918	Cp. Morrison, Va.					
			October 1918	P. of E., Newport News.	October 1918.				
			April 1919	Mitchel Field, N. Y.		April 1919.			
			July 1919	Lee Hall, Va.					Do.
21st Balloon Company	February 1918	Waco, Tex.	March 1918	Cp. Morrison, Va.					
			July 1918	Lee Hall, Va.					
			November 1918	Cp. Morrison, Va.			December 1918	Cp. Morrison, Va.	Demblzd. December 1918; reorgzd. June 1919. Active through 1919.
	June 1919	Ross Field, Calif.							
22d Balloon Company	February 1918	Waco, Tex.	March 1918	Cp. Morrison, Va.					
			July 1918	Lee Hall, Va.					
			April 1919	Cp. Victory, New York, N. Y.					
			May 1919	Boston, Mass.					
			do	Lee Hall, Va.					
			do	Ft. Hancock, N. J.					
			July 1919	Lee Hall, Va.					Active through 1919.

BALLOON COMPANIES—Continued

Unit designation and redesignation	Organization		Stations in United States		Overseas		Demobilization		Remarks
	Month and year	Place	Month and year	Place	From—	To—	Month and year	Place	
23d Balloon Company	February 1918	Waco, Tex	March 1918 July 1918 October 1918 do	Cp. Morrison, Va. Lee Hall, Va. Cp. Morrison, Va. P. of F., Newport News.	October 1918	January 1919	January 1919	Cp. Devens, Mass.	Army troops. Demobilized January 1919; reorganized June 1919; skeletonized fr. June to August 1919 when again demobilized.
	June 1919	Ross Field, Calif					August 1919	Ross Field, Calif.	
	September 1919	Post Field, Okla							Reorgzd. September 1919. Active through 1919.
24th Balloon Company	January 1918	Ft. Monroe, Va	March 1918 June 1918 August 1919 do	Cp. Morrison, Va. P. of E., Newport News. Mitchel Field, N. Y. Ft. Omaha, Nebr	June 1918.	August 1919.			Army troops. Active through 1919.
25th Balloon Company	February 1918	Post Field, Okla	March 1918 June 1918 June 1919 July 1919	Cp. Morrison, Va. P. of E., Newport News. Mitchel Field, N. Y. Ross Field, Calif	June 1918.	June 1919.			Do.
26th Balloon Company	do	do	June 1918 July 1918	Cp. Morrison, Va. P. of E., Newport News.	July 1918.				

			June 1919	Cp. Lee, Va.		June 1919.		
			July 1919	Lee Hall, Va.				Do.
27th Balloon Company	do	Waco, Tex.	March 1918	Cp. Morrison, Va.				
			July 1918	Lee Hall, Va.				
			November 1918	Cp. Morrison, Va.			December 1918	Cp. Morrison, Va.	Demblzd. December 1918; reorganized June 1919.
	June 1919	Ft. Omaha, Nebr.						Active through 1919.
28th Balloon Company	February 1918	Waco, Tex.	March 1918	Cp. Morrison, Va.				
			July 1918	Lee Hall, Va.				
			December 1918	Aberdeen Proving Ground, Md.				
			June 1919	Langley Field, Va.				
			October 1919	Lee Hall, Va.				Active through 1919.
29th Balloon Company	March 1918	Ft. Monroe, Va.	August 1919	Langley Field, Va.				
			do	Ft. Story, Va.				
			November 1919	Lee Hall, Va.				Do.
30th Balloon Company	do	Waco, Tex.	April 1918	Ft. Omaha, Nebr.				
			September 1918	Cp. Morrison, Va.				
			October 1918	P. of E., Newport News.	October 1918.			
			April 1919	Mitchel Field, N. Y.		April 1919.		
			July 1919	Lee Hall, Va.				Army troops. Active through 1919.
31st Balloon Company	do	do	April 1918	Post Field, Okla.				
			July 1918	West Point, Ky.				
			October 1918	Godman Field, Ky.				Active through 1919.
32d Balloon Company	do	do	April 1918	Post Field, Okla.				
			September 1918	Cp. McClellan, Ala.				
			February 1919	Pope Field, N. C.				
			August 1919	Lee Hall, Va.				Do.
33d Balloon Company	do	do	May 1918	Post Field, Okla.				
			November 1918	Cp. Jackson, S. C.				
			March 1919	Lee Hall, Va.			September 1919	Lee Hall, Va.	

BALLOON COMPANIES—Continued

Unit designation and redesignation	Organisation		Stations in United States		Overseas		Demobilization		Remarks
	Month and year	Place	Month and year	Place	From—	To—	Month and year	Place	
34th Balloon Company	March 1918	Cp. John Wise, Tex.	September 1918	Cp. Morrison, Va.					
			October 1918	P. of E., Newport News.	October 1918.				
			March 1919	Langley Field, Va.		March 1919	September 1919	Langley Field, Va.	Corps troops.
35th Balloon Company	do	do	September 1918	Cp. Morrison, Va.					
			October 1918	P. of E., Newport News.	October 1918.				
			April 1919	Mitchel Field, N. Y.		April 1919.			
			July 1919	Lee Hall, Va.			September 1919	Lee Hall, Va.	Corps troops. Skeletonized April 1919.
36th Balloon Company	do	do	September 1918	Cp. Morrison, Va.					
			October 1918	P. of E., Newport News.	October 1918.				
			April 1919	Mitchel Field, N. Y.		April 1919	August 1919	Mitchel Field, N. Y.	Corps troops.
37th Balloon Company									See 61st (I) Bln. Co.
38th Balloon Company	February 1918	Cp. John Wise, Tex.	July 1918	Ross Field, Calif.			September 1919	Ross Field, Calif.	
39th Balloon Company	do	do	April 1918	Post Field, Okla.			do	Post Field, Okla.	Skeletonized May 1919.
40th Balloon Company	do	do	May 1919	Brooks Field, Tex.			August 1919	Brooks Field, Tex.	Skeletonized June 1919.
41st Balloon Company	March 1918	do	May 1918	Cp. Morrison, Va.					
			do	Cp. Jackson, S. C.					
			November 1918	Cp. Morrison, Va.					
			do	Lee Hall, Va.			December 1918	Cp. Morrison, Va.	
42d Balloon Company	do	do	May 1918	Cp. Morrison, Va.					
			June 1918	P. of E., Newport News.	June 1918.				

			May 1919	Cp. Lee, Va.		May 1919.			
			do	Brooks Field, Tex.			August 1919	Brooks Field, Tex.	Army troops. Skeletonised May 1919.
43d Balloon Company	do	do	May 1918	Cp. Morrison, Va.					
			June 1918	P. of E., Newport News.	June 1918	May 1919	May 1919	Cp. Lee, Va.	Army troops.
44th Balloon Company	do	do	July 1918	Cp. Morrison, Va.					
			do	P. of E., Newport News.	July 1918	August 1919	August 1919	Mitchel Field, N. Y.	Corps troops.
45th Balloon Company	do	do	August 1918	Cp. Morrison, Va.					
			September 1918	P. of E., Newport News.	September 1918	April 1919	April 1919	do	Do.
46th Balloon Company	July 1918	Ft. Omaha, Nebr.	November 1918	Cp. Morrison, Va.			December 1918	Cp. Morrison, Va.	
47th Balloon Company	do	do					June 1919	Ft. Omaha, Nebr.	
48th Balloon Company	August 1918	do					January 1919	Do.	
49th Balloon Company	do	do	November 1918	Cp. Morrison, Va.			December 1918	Cp. Morrison, Va.	
50th Balloon Company	do	do					May 1919	Ft. Omaha, Nebr.	
51st Balloon Company	April 1918	Kelly Field, Tex.	June 1918	Ross Field, Calif.			January 1919	Ross Field, Calif.	
52d Balloon Company	do	do	do	do			do	Do.	
53d Balloon Company	July 1918	Ft. Omaha, Nebr.	November 1918	Cp. Morrison, Va.			December 1918	Cp. Morrison, Va.	
54th Balloon Company	August 1918	Cp. John Wise, Tex.	do	Do.					
			do	Lee Hall, Va.			do	Do.	
55th Balloon Company (provisional).	do	Do.							
a. 55th Balloon Company.	do	do	do	Cp. Morrison, Va.			do	Do.	
56th Balloon Company	do	do	do	do			do	Do.	
57th Balloon Company	do	do	do	do			do	Do.	
58th Balloon Company	March 1918	Do.	August 1918	Cp. Morrison, Va.					
			October 1918	P. of E., Newport News.	October 1918.				
			June 1919	Cp. Hill, Va.		June 1919	July 1919	Cp. Lee, Va.	Corps troops.
59th Balloon Company	August 1918	Ft. Omaha, Nebr.	March 1919	Wingfoot Lake, Akron, Ohio.			do	Langley Field, Va.	
60th Balloon Company	do	do	December 1918	Ft. Crook, Nebr.			June 1919	Ft. Crook, Nebr.	
61st (I) Balloon Company.	January 1918	Cp. John Wise, Tex.							
a. 37th Balloon Company.	February 1918	do	July 1918	Ross Field, Calif.			September 1919	Ross Field, Calif.	

BALLOON COMPANIES—Continued

Unit designation and redesignation	Organization		Stations in United States		Overseas		Demobilization		Remarks
	Month and year	Place	Month and year	Place	From—	To—	Month and year	Place	
61st (II) Balloon Company.	August 1918	Ft. Omaha Nebr.	September 1918	Ft. Crook, Nebr.					
			October 1918	Ft. Omaha, Nebr.					
			March 1919	Langley Field, Va.			April 1919	Langley Field, Va.	
62d Balloon Company	March 1918	do					January 1919	Ft. Omaha, Nebr.	
63d Balloon Company	do	do					June 1919	Do.	
64th Balloon Company	do	do	July 1918	Ross Field, Calif.			do	Ross Field, Calif.	
65th Balloon Company	do	do	do	do			January 1919	Do.	
66th Balloon Company	do	do	June 1918	do			June 1919	Do.	
67th Balloon Company	August 1918	Cp. John Wise, Tex.	May 1919	Brooks Field, Tex.			do	Brooks Field, Tex.	Skeletonized January 1919.
68th Balloon Company	do	do	May 1919	do			do	Do.	
69th Balloon Company	July 1918	A. E. F.				May 1919	May 1919	Cp. Lee, Va.	Army troops.
70th Balloon Company	August 1918	Post Field, Okla.	November 1918	Lee Hall, Va.			June 1919	Lee Hall, Va.	
71st Balloon Company	September 1918	Lee Hall, Va.					do	Do.	
72d Balloon Company	August 1918	Cp. John Wise, Tex.	May 1919	Brooks Field, Tex.			do	Brooks Field, Tex.	Skeletonized January 1919.
73d Balloon Company	do	Ft. Omaha, Nebr.					January 1919	Ft. Omaha, Nebr.	
74th Balloon Company	do	do	November 1918	Ft. Crook, Nebr.			June 1919	Ft. Crook, Nebr.	
75th Balloon Company	do	do					January 1919	Ft. Omaha, Nebr.	
76th Balloon Company	September 1918	Cp. John Wise, Tex.	May 1919	Brooks Field, Tex.			June 1919	Brooks Field, Tex.	Skeletonized January 1919.
77th Balloon Company	do	do	do	do			do	do	Do.
78th Balloon Company	do	do	do	do			do	Do.	
79th Balloon Company	October 1918	do	March 1919	do			do	do	Skeletonized March 1919.
80th Balloon Company	do	do	May 1919	do			do	do.	Skeletonized January 1919.
81st Balloon Company	do	Ft. Omaha, Nebr.					April 1919	Ft. Omaha, Nebr.	

82d Balloon Company									Ordered orgzd. at Ft. Omaha, Nebr. October 1918; orgn. order rescinded November 1918.
83d to 90th Balloon Companies.									Never orgzd.
91st Balloon Company	September 1918	Post Field, Okla	November 1918	Lee Hall, Va			June 1919	Lee Hall, Va	Skeletonized April 1919.
92d Balloon Company	do	do	do	do			do	Do.	
93d Balloon Company	October 1918	Cp. John Wise, Tex.	May 1919	Brooks Field, Tex.			do	Brooks Field, Tex.	Skeletonized January 1919.
94th Balloon Company	do	do	do	do			do	do	Do.
95th Balloon Company	do	do	do	do			do	do	Do.
96th Balloon Company	do	do	do	do			do	do	Do.
97th Balloon Company	do	do	do	do			do	do	Do.
98th Balloon Company	do	do	do	do			do	do	Do.
99th Balloon Company	do	do	do	do			do	do	Do.
100th Balloon Company									Never orgzd.
101st Balloon Company (replacement).	June 1918	A. E. F				July 1919	July 1919	Cp. Lee, Va	S.O.S. troops.
102d Balloon Company	October 1918	do				May 1919	May 1919	do	Do.

BALLOON GROUPS

1st Balloon Group, First Army.					November 1918	December 1918			Orgzd. and demobilized overseas.
2d Balloon Group, First Army.					do	do			Do.
Balloon Group, Third Army.					April 1919	May 1919			Do.
Balloon Group, I Army Corps.					October 1918	December 1918			Orgzd. and demobilized overseas. Corps troops.
Balloon Group, III Army Corps.	September 1918	A. E. F				August 1919	August 1919	Mitchel Field, N.Y.	Corps troops.

BALLOON GROUPS—Continued

Unit designation and redesignation	Organization		Stations in United States		Overseas		Demobilization		Remarks
	Month and year	Place	Month and year	Place	From—	To—	Month and year	Place	
Balloon Group, IV Army Corps.					October 1918	May 1919			Orgzd. and demobilized overseas. Corps troops.
Balloon Group, V Army Corps.					do	December 1918			Do.
Balloon Group, VI Army Corps.					November 1918	April 1919			Do.
Balloon Group, VII Army Corps.					May 1919	May 1919			Orgzd. and demobilized overseas.
Balloon Group, IX Army Corps.					December 1918	April 1919			Do.

BALLOON SQUADRONS

Unit designation and redesignation	Organization Month and year	Organization Place	Stations Month and year	Stations Place	Overseas From—	Overseas To—	Demobilization Month and year	Demobilization Place	Remarks
1st Balloon Squadron									See Bln. Co. "A".
2d Balloon Squadron	September 1917	Ft. Omaha, Nebr.	November 1917 December 1917	Garden City, N. Y. P. of E., Halifax	December 1917		June 1918	A. E. F.	
3d Balloon Squadron	November 1917	do	January 1918 do	Garden City, N. Y. P. of E., Hoboken	January 1918		do	Do.	
4th Balloon Squadron	do	do	February 1918 June 1918	Cp. Morrison, Va. P. of E., Newport News.	June 1918		July 1918	Do.	
5th Balloon Squadron	December 1917	do	February 1918	Cp. Morrison, Va.			February 1918	Cp. Morrison, Va.	

BALLOON SCHOOL SQUADRON

Unit designation and redesignation	Organization Month and year	Organization Place	Stations Month and year	Stations Place	Overseas From—	Overseas To—	Demobilization Month and year	Demobilization Place	Remarks
1st Balloon School Squadron.	May 1917	Ft. Omaha, Nebr.					March 1918	Ft. Omaha, Nebr.	

BALLOON WINGS

Balloon Wing, First Army.									Orgsd. and demobilised overseas.
Balloon Wing, Second Army.									Do.

BALLOON WING COMPANIES

Balloon Wing Company "A"					June 1918	October 1918			Do.
Balloon Wing Company "B"					July 1918	do			Do.
Balloon Wing Company "C".					do	do			Do.
Balloon Wing Company "D".	August 1918	A. E. F.				March 1919	March 1919	Langley Field, Va.	
Balloon Wing Company "E".	do	do				do	do	Do.	
Balloon Wing Company "F".	do	do				do	do	Do.	

DAY BOMBARDMENT GROUPS

1st Day Bombardment Group.					September 1918	November 1918			Orgsd. and demobilised overseas. Cmpnt. of 1st Pur. Wg. Army troops.
2d Day Bombardment Group.					November 1918	April 1919			Orgsd. and demobilised overseas. Army troops.

BUREAU OF AIRCRAFT PRODUCTION DETACHMENTS

Detachment #1, Air Service, Aircraft Production.	August 1918	Washington, D. C.					April 1919	Washington, D. C.	
Detachment #2, Air Service, Aircraft Production.	do	New York, N. Y.					do	New York, N. Y.	

BUREAU OF AIRCRAFT PRODUCTION DETACHMENTS—Continued

Unit designation and redesignation	Organization		Stations in United States		Overseas		Demobilization		Remarks
	Month and year	Place	Month and year	Place	From—	To—	Month and year	Place	
Detachment #3, Air Service, Aircraft Production.	August 1918	Springfield, Mass.	December 1918	Boston, Mass.			April 1919	Boston, Mass.	
Detachment #4, Air Service, Aircraft Production.	do	Buffalo, N. Y.					do	Buffalo, N. Y.	
Detachment #5, Air Service, Aircraft Production.	do	Pittsburgh, Pa.					March 1919	Pittsburgh, Pa.	
Detachment #6, Air Service, Aircraft Production.	do	Detroit, Mich.					April 1919	Detroit, Mich.	
Detachment #7, Air Service, Aircraft Production.	do	Dayton, Ohio					March 1919	Dayton, Ohio.	
Detachment #8, Air Service, Aircraft Production.	do	Chicago, Ill.					April 1919	Chicago, Ill.	
Detachment #9, Air Service, Aircraft Production.									See 619th Aer. Sq. (sup.).
Detachment #10, Air Service, Aircraft Production.	August 1918	McCook Field, Ohio.					May 1919	McCook Field, Ohio.	Orgzd. fr. Sqs. A and B McCook Field.
Detachment #11, Air Service, Aircraft Production.									See 119th Aer. Sq.
Detachment #12, Air Service, Aircraft Production.	August 1918	Kelly Field, Tex.					October 1918	Washington, D. C.	Merged with Det. #1, A. S. P. October 1918.

Detachment #13, Air Service, Aircraft Production.	November 1918	Detroit, Mich					January 1919	Detroit, Mich.	
Detachment #14, Air Service, Aircraft Production.	September 1918	Dayton, Ohio					do	Dayton, Ohio	
Detachment #15, Air Service, Aircraft Production.	do	Buffalo, N. Y					March 1919	Buffalo, N. Y.	
Detachment #16, Air Service, Aircraft Production.									Never orgzd.
Detachment #17, Air Service, Aircraft Production.									See 368th Aer. Sq.
Detachment #18, Air Service, Aircraft Production.									See 611th Aer. Sq. (sup.).

CONSTRUCTION COMPANIES

1st Construction Company.	January 1918	Kelly Field, Tex	January 1918 March 1918 do March 1919	Cp. Sevier, S. C. Garden City, N. Y. P. of E., Hoboken Garden City, N. Y	March 1918.	March 1919	April 1919	Garden City, N. Y	S.O.S. troops.
2d Construction Company.	do	do	January 1918 March 1918 do March 1919	Cp. Sevier, S. C. Avn. Field No. 1, Hempstead, N. Y. P. of E., Hoboken Garden City, N. Y	March 1918.	do	do	do	Do.
3d Construction Company.	do	do	January 1918 March 1918 do	Cp. Sevier, S. C. Garden City, N. Y. P. of E., Hoboken	March 1918	December 1918	December 1918	do	Do.
4th Construction Company.	do	do	January 1918 March 1918 do	Cp. Sevier, S. C. Garden City, N. Y. P. of E., Hoboken	do	do	do	do	Do.
5th Construction Company.	do	do	January 1918 March 1918 do	Cp. Sevier, S. C. Hazelhurst Field, N. Y. P. of E., Hoboken	do	do	do	do	Do.

CONSTRUCTION COMPANIES—Continued

Unit designation and redesignation	Organization		Stations in United States		Overseas		Demobilization		Remarks
	Month and year	Place	Month and year	Place	From—	To—	Month and year	Place	
6th Construction Company.	January 1918	Kelly Field, Tex.	January 1918	Cp. Sevier, S. C.					
			March 1918	Mineola, N. Y.					
			do	P. of E., Hoboken	March 1918	December 1918	December 1918	Garden City, N. Y.	S.O.S. troops.
7th Construction Company.	January 1918	Kelly Field, Tex.	February 1918	Cp. Sevier, S. C.					
			March 1918	Garden City, N. Y.					
			do	P. of E., Hoboken	do	do	do	do	Do.
8th Construction Company.	do	do	January 1918	Cp. Sevier, S. C.					
			March 1918	Mineola, N. Y.					
			do	P. of E., Hoboken	do	do	do	do	Do.
9th Construction Company.	do	do	February 1918	Cp. Sevier, S. C.					
			March 1918	Garden City, N. Y.					
			April 1918	P. of E., Hoboken	April 1918	do	do	do	Do.
10th Construction Company.	do	do	February 1918	Cp. Sevier, S. C.					
			May 1918	Garden City, N. Y.					
			August 1918	P. of E., Hoboken	August 1918	do	do	do	Do.
11th Construction Company.	January 1918	Kelly Field, Tex.	February 1918	Cp. Sevier, S. C.					
			May 1918	Garden City, N. Y.					
			August 1918	P. of E., Hoboken	August 1918.				
			March 1919	Garden City, N. Y.		March 1919	April 1919	Garden City, N. Y.	S.O.S. troops.
12th Construction Company.	do	do	February 1918	Cp. Sevier, S. C.					
			June 1918	Garden City, N. Y.					
			August 1918	P. of E., Hoboken	August 1918	April 1919	do	do	Do.
13th Construction Company.	May 1918	Garden City, N. Y.	June 1918	P. of E., Hoboken	June 1918	December 1918	December 1918	do	Do.
14th Construction Company.	do	Cp. Sevier, S. C.	June 1918	Garden City, N. Y.					
			August 1918	P. of E., Hoboken	August 1918	do	do	do	Do.
15th Construction Company.	do	do	June 1918	Garden City, N. Y.					
			July 1918	Hazelhurst Field, N. Y.					
			August 1918	P. of E., Hoboken	do	do	do	do	Do.

16th Construction Company.	do	do	June 1918	Garden City, N. Y.					
			July 1918	Chapman Field, N. Y.					
			August 1918	P. of E., Hoboken	do	April 1919	April 1919	Mitchel Field, N.Y.	Do.
17th Construction Company.	do	Waco, Tex	June 1918	Garden City, N. Y.					
			August 1918	P. of E., Hoboken	Do.				
			November 1918	Garden City, N. Y.		November 1918	January 1919	Garden City, N. Y.	Do.
18th Construction Company.	do	do	June 1918	Garden City, N. Y.					
			August 1918	P. of E., Hoboken	August 1918	December 1918	December 1918	do	Do.
19th Construction Company.	do	do	June 1918	Garden City, N. Y.					
			August 1918	P. of E., Hoboken	do	do	do	do	Do.
20th Construction Company.	do	do	July 1918	Lee Hall, Va.					
			November 1918	Langley Field, Va.			January 1919	Langley Field, Va.	
21st Construction Company.	June 1918	do	August 1918	Lee Hall, Va.					
			November 1918	Langley Field, Va.			do	Do.	
22d Construction Company.	do	do	August 1918	Lee Hall, Va.			April 1919	Lee Hall, Va.	
23d Construction Company.	do	do	July 1918	do			do	Do.	
24th Construction Company.	do	do	August 1918	Lufberry Field, N. Y.					
			November 1918	Brindley Field, N. Y.					
			December 1918	Chapman Field, Fla.			March 1919	Chapman Field, Fla.	
25th Construction Company.	do	do	August 1918	Henry J. Damm Field, N. Y.					
			December 1918	Avn. Gen. Sup. Dep., Middletown, Pa.			January 1919	Avn. Gen. Sup. Dep., Middletown, Pa.	
26th Construction Company.	do	do	August 1918	Garden City, N. Y.					
			October 1918	Hazelhurst Field, N. Y.					
			January 1919	Garden City, N. Y.			February 1919	Garden City, N. Y.	
27th Construction Company.	do	do	August 1918	Hazelhurst Field, N. Y.					
			September 1918	Roosevelt Field, N. Y.			December 1918	do	
28th Construction Company.	April 1918	Ft. Wayne, Mich.	August 1918	Langley Field, Va.			do	Langley Field, Va.	

CONSTRUCTION COMPANIES—Continued

Unit designation and redesignation	Organization		Stations in United States		Overseas		Demobilization		Remarks
	Month and year	Place	Month and year	Place	From—	To—	Month and year	Place	
29th Construction Company.	April 1918	Ft. Wayne, Mich.	August 1918	Langley Field, Va.			December 1918	Langley Field, Va.	
30th Construction Company.	do	do	do	do			do	Do.	
31st Construction Company.	June 1918	do	do	do			do	Do.	
32d Construction Company.	do	do	do	do			do	Do.	
33d Construction Company.	do	do	do	do			do	Do.	
34th Construction Company.	April 1918	do	July 1918	do			do	Do.	
35th Construction Company.	do	do	do	do			do	Do.	
36th Construction Company.	do	do	do	do			do	Do.	
37th Construction Company.	June 1918	do	August 1918	do			do	Do.	
38th Construction Company.	do	do	do	do			do	Do.	
39th Construction Company.	do	do	do	do			do	Do.	

AIR SERVICE MECHANICS REGIMENTS

Unit designation and redesignation	Organization		Stations in United States		Overseas		Demobilization		Remarks
	Month and year	Place	Month and year	Place	From—	To—	Month and year	Place	
First Regiment of Motor Mechanics, Signal Corps, Aviation Section.	December 1917	Cp. Hancock, Ga.	January 1918	Cp. Merritt, N. J.					
a. 1st Air Service Mechanics Regiment.	October 1918	A. E. F.	February 1918	P. of E., Hoboken.	February 1918.	June 1919	June 1919	Cp. Mills, N. Y.	S.O.S. troops.

Second Regiment of Motor Mechanics, Signal Corps, Aviation Section.	December 1917	Cp. Hancock, Ga.	February 1918	Cp. Merritt, N. J.					
a. 2d Air Service Mechanics Regiment.	October 1918	A. E. F.	March 1918	P. of E., Hoboken	March 1918.	do	July 1919	Mitchel Field, N.Y.	Do.
Third Regiment of Motor Mechanics, Signal Corps, Aviation Section.	December 1917	Cp. Hancock, Ga.	March 1918	Cp. Greene, N. C.					
a. 3d Air Service Mechanics Regiment.	September 1918	A. E. F.	June 1918 June 1919	P. of E., Hoboken Cp. Mills, N. Y.	June 1918.	do	do	do	Do.
Fourth Regiment of Motor Mechanics, Signal Corps, Aviation Section.	December 1917	Cp. Hancock, Ga.	March 1918	Cp. Greene, N. C.					
a. 4th Air Service Mechanics Regiment.	September 1918	A. E. F.	July 1918 do	Cp. Upton, N. Y. P. of E., Hoboken	July 1918.	do	do	do	Do.

OBSERVATION GROUPS

First Army Observation Group.					September 1918	April 1919			Orgzd. and demobilized overseas. Army troops.
Second Army Observation Group.					November 1918	do			Orgzd. and demobilized overseas.
I Corps Observation Group.					April 1918	December 1918			Orgzd. and demobilized overseas. Corps troops.
III Corps Observation Group.					September 1918	do			Do.
IV Corps Observation Group.					July 1918	May 1919			Do.
V Corps Observation Group.					August 1918	December 1918			Do.
VI Corps Observation Group.					October 1918	February 1919			Do.

PURSUIT GROUPS

Unit designation and redesignation	Organization		Stations in United States		Overseas		Demobilization		Remarks
	Month and year	Place	Month and year	Place	From—	To—	Month and year	Place	
First Pursuit Group					May 1918	December 1918			Orgzd. and demobilized overseas. Army troops.
Second Pursuit Group					June 1918	April 1919			Orgzd. and demobilized overseas. Cmpnt. of 1st Pur. Wg. Army troops.
Third Pursuit Group					July 1918	January 1919			Do.
Fourth Pursuit Group					November 1918	April 1919			Orgzd. and demobilized overseas. Army troops.
Fifth Pursuit Group					do	May 1919			Orgzd. and demobilized overseas

PURSUIT WING

Unit designation and redesignation	Organization: Month and year	Organization: Place	Stations in United States: Month and year	Stations in United States: Place	Overseas: From—	Overseas: To—	Demobilization: Month and year	Demobilization: Place	Remarks
First Pursuit Wing					July 1918	December 1918			Orgzd. and demobilized overseas. Cmpnt. of First Army. Army troops.
Spruce Production Division.	November 1917	Portland, Oreg					August 1919	Vancouver Bks., Wash.	

SPECIAL AND TECHNICAL UNITS

Units	Unit No.	Active service	Unit No.	Active service	Unit No.	Active service	Unit No.	Active service	Unit No.	Active service	Remarks
Photo Section	[aj] 1	April 1918–July 1919	[ai] 2	May 1918–June 1919	[bi] 3	March 1918–June 1919	[bj] 4	March 1918–June 1919	[bj] 5	April 1918–August 1919	a Orgzd. overseas; demobilized in U. S.
	[bj] 6	April 1918–June 1919	[bci] 7	July 1918–June 1919	[bdi] 8	July 1918 July 1919	[bi] 9	July 1918–July 1919	[ibe] 10	July 1918–May 1919	b Served overseas.
	[jb] 11	July 1918–July 1919	[bfi] 12(I)	July 1918–May 1919	12(II)	September 1919–thru December 1919	[ib] 13	July 1918–June 1919	[bi] 14	August 1918–June 1919	c Redes. 10th Photo Sec. September 1918.
	[bi] 15	August 1918–April 1919	[bi] 16	July 1918–August 1919	[ib] 17	July 1918–May 1919	[ib] 18	July 1918–June 1919	[bj] 19	July 1918–March 1919	d Redes. 12th Photo Sec. September 1918.
	[jb] 20	July 1918–April 1919	[bj] 21	July 1918–March 1919	[jb] 22	July 1918–April 1919	[ib] 23	July 1918–May 1919	[bi] 24	do	e Redes. 7th Photo Sec. September 1918.
	[jb] 25	August 1918–May 1919	[bi] 26	do	27	October 1918–November 1919	28	October 1918–January 1919	29	July 1918–December 1918	f Redes. 8th Photo Sec. September 1918.
	30	July 1918–January 1919	31	Never orgzd.	32	August 1918–March 1919	33	July 1918–March 1919	34	Never orgzd.	
	35	August 1918–January 1919	36	September 1918–March 1919	37	October 1918–January 1919	38	November 1918 March 1919	39	September 1918–September 1919	g Redes. 76th Photo Sec. December 1918.
	40	July 1918–October 1919	41	July 1918–February 1919	[g] 42	July 1918–December 1918	43	November 1918–April 1919	44	November 1918–April 1919	h G.H.Q. Troops.
	45	November 1918–March 1919	46	October 1918–October 1919	47	July 1918–July 1919	48	October 1918–November 1919	49	July 1918–January 1919	i Army Troops. j Corps Troops.
	50	August 1918–April 1919	51	October 1918–March 1919	52	October 1918–December 1918	53	October 1918–December 1918	54	October 1918–January 1919	
	55	August 1918–December 1918	56	August 1918–September 1919	57	October 1918 September 1919	58	July 1918–February 1919	59	September 1918–June 1919	
	60	July 1918–March 1919	61	do	62	November 1918–December 1918	63	November 1918–December 1918	64	February 1919–October 1919	
	65	November 1918–September 1919	66	September 1918–June 1919	67	November 1918–September 1919	68	October 1918–January 1919	[i] 69	September 1918–December 1918	
	[ib] 70	October 1918–December 1918	[bi] 71	October 1918–December 1918	[ib] 72	October 1918–January 1919	73	October 1918–December 1918	74	November 1918–January 1919	

SPECIAL AND TECHNICAL UNITS—Continued

Units	Unit No.	Active service	Unit No.	Active service	Unit No.	Active service	Unit No.	Active service	Unit No.	Active service	Remarks
Photo Section—Continued.	75	November 1918–March 1919	76	December 1918–January 1919	77 to 83	Never orgzd.	84	March 1919–October 1919	85 to 87	Never orgzd.	a Orgzd. overseas; demobilized in U. S.
	88	February 1919–October 1919	89 to 100	Never orgzd.	ia 101	November 1918–August 1919	ia 102	November 1918–May 1919	ia 103	November 1918–May 1919	h G. H. Q. Troops.
	ha 104	December 1918–August 1919	ha 105	November 1918–July 1919	ha 106	November 1918–May 1919	ha 107	do	ha 108	January 1919–July 1919	i Army Troops.
	ha 109	October 1918–May 1919									

ARMY SERVICE CORPS

SPECIAL AND TECHNICAL UNITS

Units	Unit No.	Active service	Unit No.	Active service	Unit No.	Active service	Unit No.	Active service	Unit No.	Active service	Remarks
Administrative Labor Company.	ac 1	May 1918–March 1919	ac 2	May 1918–May 1919	ac 3	June 1918–March 1919	a 4	June 1919–March 1919	ac 5	March 1918–March 1919	a Orgzd. and demblzd. overseas.
	ac 6	do	ac 7	March 1918–April 1919	ac 8	April 1918–August 1919	ac 9	April 1918–June 1919	ac 10	February 1918–June 1919	b Orgzd. overseas; demobilized in U. S.
	ac 11	do	ac 12	May 1918–June 1919	13	July 1919–October 1919	ac 14	March 1918–October 1919	c 15	July 1918–October 1919	c S. O. S. Troops.
	ac 16	do	ac 17	March 1918–March 1919	ac 18	March 1918–March 1919	ac 19	March 1918–March 1919	ac 20	March 1918–March 1919	
	ac 21	do	ac 22	do	ac 23	do	ac 24	May 1918–July 1919	ac 25	May 1918–September 1919	
	ac 26	May 1918–December 1919	bc 27	June 1918–September 1919	ac 28	May 1918–May 1919	ac 29	June 1918–June 1919	ac 30	June 1918–June 1919	
	a 31	July 1918–September 1919	32–45	Never orgzd.	a 46	March 1918–March 1919	ac 47	February 1918–September 1919	ac 48	Do.	
	ac 49	March 1918–March 1919	ac 50	August 1918–May 1919	ac 51	August 1918–December 1919	ac 52	August 1918–February 1919	53–85	Never orgzd.	

	No.	Dates	No.	Dates	No.	Dates	No.	Dates	No.	Dates	
	[a,c] 86	March 1918–March 1919	[a,c] 87	April 1918–March 1919	[a,c] 88	April 1918–March 1919	[a,c] 89	April 1918–February 1919	[a,c] 90	April 1918–May 1919	
	[a,c] 91	June 1918–May 1919	[a,c] 92	May 1918–June 1919	[a,c] 93	April 1918–June 1919	94–100	Never orgzd.	[a,c] 101	May 1918–February 1919	
	[a,c] 102	April 1918–February 1919	[a,c] 103	May 1918–March 1919	[a,c] 104	May 1918–March 1919	[a,c] 105	June 1918–June 1919	[a,c] 106	June 1918–June 1919	
	[a,c] 107	July 1918–October 1919	[a,c] 108	March 1918–June 1919	[a,c] 109	August 1918–June 1919	110–115	Never orgzd.	[a,c] 116	July 1918–March 1919	
	[a,c] 117	May 1918–March 1919	[a,c] 118	June 1918–March 1919	[c] 119	April 1918–March 1919	[a,c] 120	May 1918–March 1919	[a,c] 121	June 1918–March 1919	
	[a,c] 122	April 1918–March 1919	[a,c] 123	July 1918–October 1919	[a,c] 124	April 1918–April 1919	[a,c] 125	July 1918–February 1919	[a,c] 126	May 1918–May 1919	
	[a,c] 127	July 1918–September 1919	[a,c] 128	June 1918–October 1919	[a,c] 129	July 1918–October 1919	[a,c] 130	June 1918–September 1919	[a,c] 131	September 1918–October 1919	
	[a,c] 132	June 1918–June 1919	[a,c] 133	July 1918–March 1919	[a,c] 134	May 1918–May 1919	[a,c] 135	July 1918–June 1919	[a,c] 136	July 1918–August 1919	
	[a,c] 137	July 1918–February 1919	[a,c] 138	August 1918–March 1919	[a,c] 139	August 1918–March 1919	[a] 140	October 1918–March 1919	[a] 141	October 1918–March 1919	
	[a] 142	October 1918–March 1919	[a] 143	October 1918–March 1919	[a] 144	September 1918–August 1919	[a] 145	September 1918–December 1919	[a] 146	May 1918–March 1919	
	[a] 147	do	[a] 148	November 1918–October 1919	[a] 149	December 1918–March 1919	150 to 160	Never orgzd.	[a,c] 161	Do.	
	[a,c] 162	May 1918–August 1919	[a] 163	October 1918–March 1919	164 & 165	Never orgzd.	[a,c] 166	July 1918–March 1919	[a,c] 167	July 1918–March 1919	
	[a,c] 168	July 1918–March 1919	[a,c] 169	September 1918–March 1919	[a,c] 170	August 1918–March 1919	[a,c] 171	August 1918–March 1919	[a,c] 172	August 1918–March 1919	
	[a,c] 173	August 1918–March 1919	[a,c] 174	September 1918–March 1919	[a,c] 175	September 1918–March 1919	[a,c] 176	September 1918–March 1919	[a,c] 177	October 1918–March 1919	
	[a,c] 178	October 1918–March 1919	[a] 179	October 1918–August 1919	[a,c] 180	July 1918–December 1919	[a] 181	October 1918–March 1919	[a] 182	October 1918–May 1919	
	[a] 183	October 1918–February 1919	[a] 184	October 1918–June 1919	[a] 185	September 1918–April 1919	[a] 186	October 1918–August 1919	[a] 187	October 1918–April 1919	
	[a] 188	September 1918–April 1919	[a] 189	September 1918–April 1919	[a] 190	September 1918–September 1919					
Cement Mills Company.	[b] 1	October 1918–April 1919	[b] 2	September 1918–May 1919	[b] 3	September 1918–March 1919	[b] 4	September 1918–May 1919	[b] 5	September 1918–April 1919	a Orgzd. and demblzd. overseas.
	[b] 6	August 1918–May 1919	7	Never orgzd.	[a] 8	September 1918–February 1919					b Orgzd. overseas; demobilized in U. S. S.O.S. troops.

SPECIAL AND TECHNICAL UNITS—Continued

Units	Unit No.	Active service	Unit No.	Active service	Unit No.	Active service	Unit No.	Active service	Unit No.	Active service	Remarks
Censor and Press Company.	[a] 1	December 1918–June 1919	[a] 2	January 1919–July 1919	-------	-------	-------	-------	-------	-------	a Orgzd. and demblzd. overseas.
Cook Company.	[a] 1	December 1918–October 1919	[b] 2	December 1918–September 1919	[b] 3	December 1918–October 1919	[b] 4	February 1919–August 1919	[a] 5	March 1919–September 1919	a Orgzd. and demblzd. overseas.
	[a] 6	March 1919–June 1919	[a] 7	March 1919–June 1919	[a] 8	March 1919–June 1919	[b] 9	March 1919–August 1919	-------	-------	b Orgzd. overseas; demobilized. in U. S.
Depot Labor and Service Company.	[a,c] 1	September 1918–June 1919	[b,c] 2	September 1918–October 1919	[a,c] 3	September 1918–June 1919	[a,c] 4	September 1918–July 1919	[a,c] 5	September 1918–June 1919	a Orgzd. and demblzd. overseas.
	[a,c] 6	do	[a,c] 7	September 1918–June 1919	[a,c] 8	do	[a,c] 9	September 1918–June 1919	[a,c] 10	September 1918–July 1919	b Orgzd. overseas; demobilized in U. S.
	[a,c] 11	September 1918–July 1919	[a,c] 12	October 1918–July 1919	[a,c] 13	October 1918–June 1919	[a,c] 14	October 1918–June 1919	[a,c] 15	October 1918–June 1919	c S. O. S. Troops.
	[a,c] 16	October 1918–June 1919	[a,c] 17	October 1918–June 1919	[a,c] 18	October 1918–July 1919	[a,c] 19	do	[a,c] 20	Do.	
	[b,c] 21	October 1918–August 1919	[a,c] 22	do	[a,c] 23	October 1918–June 1919	[b,c] 24	October 1918–July 1919	[a,c] 25	November 1918–June 1919	
	[a] 26	November 1918–June 1919	[a] 27	November 1918–June 1919	[b] 28	November 1918–September 1919	[a] 29	November 1918–June 1919	[a] 30	November 1918–July 1919	
	[a] 31	do	[a] 32	December 1918–June 1919	[a] 33	November 1918–June 1919	[a] 34	December 1918–June 1919	[a] 35	December 1918–June 1919	
	[b] 36	December 1918–September 1919	[a] 37	December 1918–June 1919	[a] 38	November 1918–June 1919	[a] 39	December 1918–July 1919	[b] 40	November 1918–July 1919	
	[a] 41	December 1918–June 1919	[a] 42	March 1919–June 1919	[a] 43	March 1919–June 1919	[a] 44	March 1919–June 1919	[a] 45	March 1919–June 1919	
	[a] 46	March 1919–June 1919	[a] 47	do	[a] 48	do	[a] 49	do	[a] 50	Do.	
	[a] 51	do	[a] 52	do	[a] 53	do	[a] 54	do	[a] 55	Do.	
	[a] 56	do	[a] 57	do	[a] 58	do	[a] 59	do	[a] 60	Do.	
	[a] 61	do	[a] 62	do	[a] 63	do	[a] 64	do	[a] 65	Do.	
	[a] 66	do	[a] 67	do	[a] 68	do	[a] 69	do	[a] 70	May 1919–August 1919	

	[a] 71	May 1919–August 1919	[a] 72	May 1919–August 1919	[a] 73	May 1919–August 1919	[a] 74	May 1919–August 1919	[a] 75	May 1919–June 1919	
	[a] 76	do	[a] 77	March 1919–June 1919	[a] 78	March 1919–June 1919	[a] 79	March 1919–June 1919	[a] 80	May 1919–August 1919	
	[a] 81	do	[a] 82	May 1919–August 1919	[a] 83	do	[a] 84	do	[a] 85	March 1919–June 1919	
	[a] 86	March 1919–June 1919	[a] 87	March 1919–June 1919	[a] 88	do	[a] 89	do	[a] 90	Do.	
	[a] 91	do	[a] 92	do	[a] 93	do	[a] 94	do	[a] 95	Do.	
	[a] 96	do	[a] 97	do	[a] 98	do	[a] 99	do	[a] 100	April 1919–June 1919	
Garden Service Company.	[b] 1	July 1918–July 1919	2	Never orgzd.	[a] 3	November 1918–May 1919	[a] 4	November 1918–April 1919			a Orgzd. and demblzd. overseas. b Orgzd. overseas; demobilized in U. S. S. O. S. troops.
Guard Company.	[a, c] 1	September 1918–July 1919	[b, c] 2	March 1919–April 1919	[b, c] 3	March 1919–April 1919	[b, c] 4	March 1919–April 1919	[b, c] 5	March 1919–April 1919	a Orgzd. and demblzd. overseas. b Orgzd. overseas; demobilized in U. S. c S. O. S. Troops.
	[b, c] 6	March 1919–April 1919	[b, c] 7	do	8 to 12	Never orgzd.	[a, c] 13	October 1918–July 1919	14 to 50	Never orgzd.	
	[b] 51	December 1918–June 1919	[b] 52	December 1918–September 1919	[b] 53	December 1918–June 1919	[b] 54	November 1918–September 1919	[b] 55	November 1918–June 1919	
	[b] 56	November 1918–June 1919	[b] 57	November 1918–June 1919	[b] 58	November 1918–June 1919	[b] 59	December 1918–June 1919	[b] 60	December 1918–September 1919	
	[a] 61	December 1918–October 1919	[a] 62	March 1919–August 1919	[a] 63	March 1919–August 1919	[a] 64	March 1919–August 1919	[a] 65	March 1919–August 1919	
	[a] 66	March 1919–August 1919	[a] 67	July 1919–August 1919	[a] 68	July 1919–August 1919	[a] 69	July 1919–August 1919	70 to 100	Never orgzd.	
	[b] 101	March 1919–June 1919	[b] 102	March 1919–June 1919	[a] 103	April 1919–August 1919	[a] 104	March 1919–May 1919	[a] 105	March 1919–July 1919	
	[a] 106	March 1919–August 1919	[b] 107	do	[b] 108	March 1919–June 1919	[b] 109	March 1919–June 1919	[b] 110	March 1919–June 1919	
	[b] 111	March 1919–June 1919	[b] 112	March 1919–June 1919	[b] 113	March 1919–June 1919	[b] 114	March 1919–June 1919	[b] 115	March 1919–June 1919	
	[b] 116	do	[b] 117	April 1919–June 1919	118 to 125	Never orgzd.	[a] 126	March 1919–July 1919	[a] 127	March 1919–July 1919	
	[a] 128	May 1919–June 1919	[a] 129	May 1919–June 1919	[a] 130	April 1919–July 1919	[a] 131	April 1919–July 1919	[a] 132	April 1919–June 1919	

SPECIAL AND TECHNICAL UNITS—Continued

Units	Unit No.	Active service	Unit No.	Active service	Unit No.	Active service	Unit No.	Active service	Unit No.	Active service	Remarks
Guard Company —Continued.	[b] 103	May 1919–August 1919	[b] 134	July 1919–September 1919	[b] 135	June 1919–October 1919	[b] 136	July 1919–September 1919	[b] 137	July 1919–August 1919	a Orgzd. and demblzd. overseas. b Orgzd. overseas; demobilized in U. S.
	[a] 138	July 1919–October 1919	[a] 139	----do----	[a] 140	July 1919–September 1919	[a] 141	----do----	[a] 142	July 1919–September 1919	
	[a] 143	----do----	[a] 144	July 1919–October 1919	[a] 145	----do----	[a] 146	August 1919–October 1919	[a] 147	August 1919–October 1919	
	148	Never orgzd.	[a] 149	----do----	[a] 150	July 1919–October 1919					
Prisoner of War Escort Company.	[b c] 1	May 1918–October 1919	[b c] 2	June 1918–October 1919	[a c] 3	June 1918–February 1919	[a c] 4	July 1918–February 1919	[a c] 5	July 1918–February 1919	a Orgzd. and demblzd. overseas. b Orgzd. overseas; demobilized in U. S. c S. O. S. Troops.
	[a c] 6	July 1918–February 1919	[a c] 7	August 1918–February 1919	[a c] 8	August 1918–February 1919	[a c] 9	August 1918–October 1919	[a c] 10	August 1918–February 1919	
	[a c] 11	August 1918–February 1919	[a c] 12	July 1918–February 1919	[a c] 13	August 1918–March 1919	[a c] 14	February 1919–March 1919	[a c] 15	August 1918–March 1919	
	[a c] 16	August 1918–January 1919	[a c] 17	August 1918–January 1919	[a c] 18	----do----	[a c] 19	December 1918–March 1919	[a c] 20	Do.	
	[a c] 21	August 1918–March 1919	[a c] 22	August 1918–March 1919	[a c] 23	----do----	[a c] 24	August 1918–March 1919	[a c] 25	September 1918–March 1919	
	[a c] 26	October 1918–March 1919	[a c] 27	September 1918–March 1919	[a c] 28	September 1918–March 1919	[a c] 29	September 1918–March 1919	[a c] 30	Do.	
	[a c] 31	September 1918–February 1919	[a c] 32	----do----	[a c] 33	September 1918–October 1919	[a c] 34	----do----	[b c] 35	September 1918–October 1919	
	[a c] 36	September 1918–February 1919	[a c] 37	September 1918–March 1919	[a c] 38	September 1918–March 1919	[a c] 39	September 1918–February 1919	[a c] 40	September 1918–March 1919	
	[a c] 41	----do----	[a c] 42	----do----	[a c] 43	----do----	[a c] 44	September 1918–March 1919	[a c] 45	----do----	
	[a c] 46	September 1918–March 1919	[a c] 47	----do----	[a c] 48	September 1918–January 1919	[a c] 49	----do----	[a c] 50	September 1918–January 1919	
	[a c] 51	September 1918–April 1919	[a c] 52	September 1918–April 1919	[a c] 53	September 1918–April 1919	[a c] 54	November 1918–February 1919	[a c] 55	September 1918–September 1919	
	[a c] 56	September 1918–February 1919	[a c] 57	September 1918–February 1919	[a c] 58	September 1918–February 1919	[a c] 59	September 1918–February 1919	[b c] 60	September 1918–October 1919	

bc 61	September 1918–October 1919	bc 62	September 1918–October 1919	bc 63	September 1918–October 1919	bc 64	September 1918–October 1919	bc 65	Do.
bc 66	do	ac 67	September 1918–September 1919	bc 68	September 1918–November 1919	ac 69	September 1918–December 1918	ac 70	September 1918–February 1919
bc 71	October 1918–October 1919	bc 72	October 1918–October 1919	bc 73	October 1918–October 1919	ac 74	October 1918–July 1919	bc 75	October 1918–October 1919
bc 76	do	bc 77	do	bc 78	do	bc 79	October 1918–October 1919	ac 80	October 1918–June 1919
bc 81	do	bc 82	do	ac 83	October 1918–February 1919	ac 84	October 1918–February 1919	bc 85	October 1918–October 1919
ac 86	October 1918–February 1919	bc 87	do	ac 88	do	ac 89	do	ac 90	November 1918–February 1919
ac 91	October 1918–January 1919	ac 92	November 1918–March 1919	b 93	October 1918–October 1919	ac 94	do	ac 95	October 1918–February 1919
bc 96	October 1918–October 1919	ac 97	October 1918–February 1919	a 98	November 1918–February 1919	a 99	November 1918–February 1919	a 100	November 1918–February 1919
ca 101	November 1918–February 1919	ca 102	November 1918–April 1919	ca 103	do	ca 104	November 1918–March 1919	ac 105	Do.
ac 106	November 1918–February 1919	ac 107	November 1918–February 1919	ac 108	November 1918–February 1919	ac 109	November 1918–February 1919	ac 110	November 1918–April 1919
ac 111	November 1918–March 1919	ac 112	November 1918–April 1919	ac 113	November 1918–April 1919	ac 114	do	ac 115	do
ac 116	November 1918–April 1919	ac 117	November 1918–February 1919	cb 118	November 1918–October 1919	ac 119	November 1918–April 1919	ac 120	Do.
ac 121	do	bc 122	November 1918–October 1919	123 to 200	Never orgzd.	a 201	December 1918–September 1919	b 202	December 1918–October 1919
b 203	December 1918–October 1919	b 204	December 1918–October 1919	b 205	December 1918–October 1919	b 206	December 1918–November 1919	b 207	Do.
b 208	do	b 209	do	b 210	December 1918–November 1919	b 211	December 1918–October 1919	b 212	Do.
b 213	do	b 214	do	b 215	December 1918–October 1919	b 216	do	a 217	December 1918–July 1919
b 218	December 1918–October 1919	b 219	December 1918–October 1919	b 220	December 1918–October 1919	b 221	December 1918–October 1919	a 222	December 1918–July 1919
b 223	do	b 224	do	a 225	December 1918–September 1919	a 226	December 1918–July 1919	b 227	December 1918–October 1919
b 228	do	b 229	do	b 230	December 1918–October 1919	a 231	December 1918–September 1919	b 232	Do.

SPECIAL AND TECHNICAL UNITS—Continued

Units	Unit No.	Active service	Unit No.	Active service	Unit No.	Active service	Unit No.	Active service	Unit No.	Active service	Remarks
Prisoner of War Escort Company—Continued.	b 233	December 1918–October 1919	b 234	December 1918–October 1919	b 235	December 1918–October 1919	b 236	December 1918–October 1919	b 237	December 1918–October 1919	a Orgzd. and demblzd. overseas. b Orgzd. overseas; demobilized in U. S.
	b 238	do	b 239	do	b 240	do	b 241	do	b 242	Do.	
	b 243	do	a 244	December 1918–July 1919	b 245	do	b 246	do	b 247	Do.	
	b 248	do	b 249	December 1918–October 1919	b 250	do	b 251	do	b 252	Do.	
	b 253	December 1918–October 1919	b 254	December 1918–November 1919	b 255	December 1918–October 1919	b 256	December 1918–October 1919	b 257	December 1918–October 1919	
	b 258	do	b 259	December 1918–October 1919	b 260	do	b 261	do	b 262	do	
	b 263	do	b 264	January 1919–October 1919	b 265	do	a 266	December 1918–August 1919	b 267	Do.	
	b 268	do	b 269	December 1918–October 1919	a 270	December 1918–September 1919	a 271	December 1918–September 1919	b 272	Do.	
	b 273	do	b 274	do	a 275	December 1918–July 1919	a 276	January 1919–July 1919			
Rents, Requisitions and Claims Service Company.	a 1	January 1919–June 1919	a 2	January 1919–August 1919	a 3	December 1918–April 1919	a 4	November 1918–May 1919	a 5	November 1918–April 1919	a Orgzd. and demblzd. overseas. b Orgzd. overseas; demobilized in U. S. S. O. S. troops.
	a 6	December 1918–June 1919	a 7	December 1918–May 1919	a 8	October 1918–February 1919	a 9	December 1918–July 1919	a 10	December 1918–October 1919	
	a 11	December 1918–February 1919	a 12	December 1918–August 1919	a 13	December 1918–July 1919	a 14	February 1919–July 1919	a 15	October 1918–April 1919	
	a 16	December 1918–June 1919	a 17	December 1918–May 1919	a 18	December 1918–May 1919	a 19	December 1918–May 1919	a 20	December 1918–May 1919	
	a 21	December 1918–July 1919	b 22	December 1918–June 1919	a 23	December 1918–June 1919	a 24	December 1918–June 1919	a 25	December 1918–June 1919	
	a 26	October 1918–March 1919	a 27	October 1918–February 1919	a 28	November 1918–May 1919	a 29	October 1918–February 1919	a 30	November 1918–May 1919	
	a 31	October 1918–June 1919	a 32	October 1918–May 1919	a 33	October 1918–May 1919	a 34	October 1918–June 1919	a 35	October 1918–June 1919	

[a] 36	October 1918–May 1919	[a] 37	October 1918–May 1919	[a] 38	October 1918–April 1919	[a] 39	October 1918–July 1919	[a] 40	October 1918–February 1919
[a] 41	January 1919–June 1919	[a] 42	January 1919–June 1919	[a] 43	November 1918–July 1919	[a] 44	November 1918–July 1919	[a] 45	October 1918–June 1919
[a] 46	December 1918–June 1919	[a] 47	December 1918–February 1919	[a] 48	November 1918–February 1919	[a] 49	December 1918–June 1919	[a] 50	December 1918–June 1919
[a] 51	do	[a] 52	December 1918–June 1919	[a] 53	December 1918–June 1919	[a] 54	do	[a] 55	Do.
[a] 56	do	[a] 57	do	[a] 58	December 1918–March 1919	[a] 59	December 1918–March 1919		

ARTILLERY PARKS

ARMY ARTILLERY PARKS

Unit designation and redesignation	Organization		Stations in United States		Overseas		Demobilization		Remarks
	Month and year	Place	Month and year	Place	From—	To—	Month and year	Place	
Army Artillery Park, First Army.	March 1918	Ft. Winfield Scott, Calif.	May 1918 June 1918 May 1919	Cp. Mills, N. Y. P. of E., Hoboken Cp. Mills, N. Y.	June 1918.	May 1919	May 1919	Presidio of San Francisco, Calif.	Army troops.
Army Artillery Park, Second Army.	October 1918	Ft. MacArthur, Calif.					December 1918	Ft. MacArthur, Calif.	

CORPS ARTILLERY PARKS

Unit designation and redesignation	Organization month	Organization place	Stations month	Stations place	Overseas from	Overseas to	Demobilization month	Demobilization place	Remarks
I Corps Artillery Park.	January 1918	Cp. Jackson, S. C.	May 1918 do	Cp. Merritt, N. J. P. of E., Hoboken	May 1918	August 1919	August 1919	Cp. Stuart, Va	Corps troops.
II Corps Artillery Park.	May 1918	do	July 1918 do	Cp. Stuart, Va. P. of E., Newport News.	July 1918	March 1919	March 1919	Cp. Upton, N. Y.	Skeletonized February 1919. Corps troops.

CORPS ARTILLERY PARKS—Continued

Unit designation and redesignation	Organization		Stations in United States		Overseas		Demobilization		Remarks
	Month and year	Place	Month and year	Place	From—	To—	Month and year	Place	
III Corps Artillery Park	July 1918	Cp. Wadsworth, S. C.	August 1918	Cp. Hill, Va.					
			do	P. of E., Newport News.	August 1918	June 1919	June 1919	Cp. Stuart, Va	Corps troops.
IV Corps Artillery Park.	do	do	September 1918	P. of E., Hoboken	September 1918	do	July 1919	Cp. Mills, N. Y.	Do.
V Corps Artillery Park.	August 1918	do	do	Cp. Upton, N. Y.					
			do	P. of E., Hoboken	Do.				
			April 1919	Cp. Upton, N. Y.		April 1919	April 1919	Cp. Grant, Ill	Do.
VI Corps Artillery Park.	September 1918	Do.							
a. VIII Corps Artillery Park.	October 1918	do					January 1919	Cp. Wadsworth, S. C.	
VII Corps Artillery Park.									Never orgzd.
VIII Corps Artillery Park.									See VI Corps Arty. Park.

COAST ARTILLERY

AMMUNITION TRAINS

Unit designation and redesignation	Organization		Stations in United States		Overseas		Demobilization		Remarks
	Month and year	Place	Month and year	Place	From—	To—	Month and year	Place	
Coast Artillery Ammunition Train, Motor Section (6″ Gun and 8″ Howitzer).	January 1918	Ft. MacArthur, Calif.							Redes. 52d and 53d Am. Tns. February 1918.
a. 52d Ammunition Train.	February 1918	do	May 1918	Cp. Merritt, N. J.					Redes. fr. 6″ Gun M. Sec.
			do	P. of E., Hoboken	May 1918.				
			January 1919	Cp. Merritt, N. J.		January 1919.			
			do	Ft. MacArthur, Calif.			February 1919	Ft. MacArthur, Calif.	Army troops.
b. 53d Ammunition Train.	do	do	May 1918	Cp. Merritt, N. J.					Redes. fr. 8″ How. M. Sec.
			June 1918	P. of E., Hoboken	June 1918.				
			January 1919	Cp. Merritt, N. J.		January 1919	January 1919	Ft. Hamilton, N.Y.	Army troops.
52d Ammunition Train									See C.A. Am. Tn., M. Sec.
53d Ammunition Train									See C.A. Am. Tn., M. Sec.
54th Ammunition Train.	May 1918	Ft. Rosecrans, Calif.	August 1918	Cp. Mills, N.Y.					
			do	P. of E., Hoboken	August 1918.				
			February 1919	Cp. Stuart, Va		February 1919	February 1919	Ft. Monroe, Va	Army troops.
55th Ammunition Train (Motor Battalion).	do	Ft. MacArthur, Calif.	August 1918	Cp. Upton, N. Y.					
			September 1918	P. of E., Hoboken	September 1918.				
			March 1919	Cp. Stuart, Va		March 1919.			
			do	Cp. Kearny, Calif.			April 1919	Cp. Kearny, Calif.	Do.
56th Ammunition Train.	July 1918	Cp. Eustis, Va					December 1918	Cp. Eustis, Va.	
57th Ammunition Train.	do	do					do	Do.	
58th Ammunition Train.	August 1918	Ft. Adams, R. I.					do	Ft. Adams, R. I.	
59th Ammunition Train.	do	do					do	Do.	
60th Ammunition Train.	October 1918	Ft. Stark, N. H.					do	Ft. Stark, N. H.	
61st Ammunition Train.	do	Ft. Banks, Mass.					do	Ft. Banks, Mass.	
62d Ammunition Train.	do	Ft. Washington, Md.					do	Ft. Washington, Md.	

ANTIAIRCRAFT BATTALIONS

Unit designation and redesignation	Organization		Stations in United States		Overseas		Demobilization		Remarks
	Month and year	Place	Month and year	Place	From—	To—	Month and year	Place	
Antiaircraft Battalion (San Francisco).	November 1917	Ft. Winfield Scott, Calif.	December 1917	Cp. Merritt, N. J.					
a. 1st Antiaircraft Battalion.	December 1917	A. E. F	do	P. of E., Hoboken	December 1917.				
b. 1st Antiaircraft Sector.	November 1918	do	March 1919	Cp. Stuart, Va		March 1919	March 1919	Presidio of San Francisco, Calif.	Army troops.
1st Antiaircraft Battalion,									See A.A. Bn. (San Francisco).
2d Antiaircraft Battalion.	January 1918	Ft. MacArthur, Calif.	June 1918	Cp. Merritt, N. J.					Never reorgzd. as 2d A.A. Sector.
			do	P. of E., Hoboken	June 1918.				
			December 1918	Cp. Merritt, N. J.		December 1918.			
			do	Cp. Dix, N. J			January 1919	Cp. Dix, N.J	Army troops.
3d Antiaircraft Battalion.	April 1918	Ft. Morgan, Ala	July 1918	Cp. Merritt, N. J.					
			August 1918	P. of E., Hoboken	August 1918.				
a. 3d Antiaircraft Sector.	November 1918	A. E. F	January 1919	Cp. Stuart, Va		January 1919	do	Ft. Monroe, Va	Do.
4th Antiaircraft Battalion.	June 1918	Cp. Eustis, Va	September 1918	Cp. Hill, Va.					
			October 1918	P. of E., Newport News.	October 1918.				
a. 4th Antiaircraft Sector.	November 1918	A. E. F	January 1919	Cp. Mills, N.Y.		do	do	Ft. Totten, N.Y.	Do.
5th Antiaircraft Battalion.	September 1918	Ft. Williams, Maine	September 1918	Cp. Merritt, N. J.					
			October 1918	P. of E., Hoboken	October 1918.				
a. 5th Antiaircraft Sector.	November 1918	A. E. F	January 1919	Cp. Mills, N.Y.		do	do	Cp. Devens, Mass.	Do.
6th Antiaircraft Battalion.	September 1918	Ft. Hamilton, N. Y.	September 1918	Cp. Mills, N. Y.					
			do	P. of E., Hoboken	September 1918.				

a. 6th Antiaircraft Sector.	November 1918	A. E. F	January 1919	Cp. Merritt, N.J.		Do.			
			do	Ft. Wadsworth, N. Y.			February 1919	Ft. Wadsworth, N. Y.	Do.
7th Antiaircraft Battalion.	October 1918	Ft. Howard, Md.	October 1918	Cp. Merritt, N. J.					
			do	P. of E., Hoboken	October 1918.				
a. 7th Antiaircraft Sector.	November 1918	A. E. F	January 1919	Cp. Stuart, Va		do	January 1919	Ft. Monroe, Va	Do.
8th Antiaircraft Battalion.	October 1918	Cp. Eustis, Va.							
a. 15th Antiaircraft Sector.	November 1918	do					December 1918	Cp. Eustis, Va.	
9th Antiaircraft Battalion.	do	Ft. Dade, Fla.							
a. 18th Antiaircraft Sector.	do	do					do	Ft. Dade, Fla.	
10th Antiaircraft Battalion.	October 1918	Ft. Morgan, Ala.							
a. 19th Antiaircraft Sector.	November 1918	do					do	Ft. Morgan, Ala.	
11th to 23d Antiaircraft Battalions.									Authorized but never orgzd.

ANTIAIRCRAFT SECTORS

1st Antiaircraft Sector.									See A.A. Bn. (San Francisco).
2d Antiaircraft Sector									See 2d A.A. Bn.
3d Antiaircraft Sector									See 3d A.A. Bn.
4th Antiaircraft Sector									See 4th A.A. Bn.
5th Antiaircraft Sector									See 5th A.A. Bn.
6th Antiaircraft Sector									See 6th A.A. Bn.
7th Antiaircraft Sector									See 7th A.A. Bn.
8th Antiaircraft Sector	November 1918	A. E. F	January 1919	Cp. Mills, N. Y.		January 1919	January 1919	Ft. Totten, N. Y.	Army troops.
9th Antiaircraft Sector	do	do	do	Cp. Hill, Va		do	do	Cp. Eustis, Va	Do.
10th Antiaircraft Sector	do	do	March 1919	Cp. Merritt, N. J		March 1919	March 1919	Cp. Lee, Va	Do.
11th Antiaircraft Sector					November 1918	December 1918			Orgzd.anddemblzd. overseas. Army troops.

ANTIAIRCRAFT SECTORS—Continued

Unit designation and redesignation	Organization		Stations in United States		Overseas		Demobilization		Remarks
	Month and year	Place	Month and year	Place	From—	To—	Month and year	Place	
12th Antiaircraft Sector	November 1918	A. E. F	January 1919	Cp. Merritt, N. J		January 1919.			
			do	Ft. Wadsworth, N. Y.			February 1919	Ft. Wadsworth, N. Y.	Army troops.
13th Antiaircraft Sector	do	do	December 1918	Cp. Hill, Va		December 1918	January 1919	Cp. Eustis, Va	Do.
14th Antiaircraft Sector									Authorized but never orgzd.
15th Antiaircraft Sector									See 8th A.A. Bn.
16th Antiaircraft Sector	November 1918	Cp. Eustis, Va					December 1918	Cp. Eustis, Va	
17th Antiaircraft Sector	do	Ft. Hancock, N. J	November 1918	Cp. Eustis, Va			do	Do.	
18th Antiaircraft Sector									See 9th A.A. Bn.
19th Antiaircraft Sector									See 10th A.A. Bn.
20th Antiaircraft Sector									Authorized but never orgzd.

BRIGADE HEADQUARTERS

Unit designation and redesignation	Organization: Month and year	Organization: Place	Stations in United States: Month and year	Stations in United States: Place	Overseas: From—	Overseas: To—	Demobilization: Month and year	Demobilization: Place	Remarks
1st Expeditionary Brigade.	July 1917	Ft. Adams, R. I	August 1917	P. of E., Hoboken	August 1917.				
a. 1st Separate Brigade.	September 1917	A. E. F.							
b. 30th Separate Artillery Brigade (Railway).	March 1918	do	January 1919	Cp. Hill, Va		January 1919.			
			do	Cp. Eustis, Va					G.H.Q. troops.
1st Separate Brigade									See 1st Expeditionary Brig.
2d to 29th Artillery Brigades.									Never orgzd.
30th Separate Artillery Brigade (Railway).									See 1st Expeditionary Brig.

31st Heavy Artillery Brigade.	January 1918	Key West Bks., Fla.	March 1918	Cp. Merritt, N. J.					
			do	P. of E., Hoboken	March 1918.				
			February 1919	Ft. Winfield Scott, Calif.		February 1919.			
			October 1919	Cp. Lewis, Wash					Army troops.
32d Artillery Brigade	do	do	March 1918	Cp. Merritt, N. J.					
			do	P. of E., Hoboken	March 1918	December 1918	January 1919	Cp. Hill, Va.	Do.
33d Artillery Brigade	March 1918	Ft. Winfield Scott, Calif.	June 1918	Cp. Mills, N. Y.					
			July 1918	P. of E. Hoboken	July 1918.				
			February 1919	Cp. Stuart, Va		February 1919	February 1919	Ft. Monroe, Va	Do.
34th Artillery Brigade	February 1918	Ft. Adams, R. I.	July 1918	P. of E., Boston	July 1918.				
			February 1919	Cp. Merritt, N. J.		do	do	Ft. Hamilton, N.Y.	Do.
35th Artillery Brigade	June 1918	Ft. Hunt, Va	July 1918	Do.					
			August 1918	P. of E., Hoboken	August 1918.				
			March 1919	Cp. Mills, N. Y.		March 1919	March 1919	Ft. Totten, N. Y.	Do.
36th Artillery Brigade	do	Ft. DuPont, Del.	August 1918	Cp. Merritt, N. J.					
			do	P. of E., Hoboken	August 1918.				
			March 1919	Cp. Mills, N. Y.		do	do	do	Do.
37th Artillery Brigade	October 1918	Cp. Eustis, Va	October 1918	Cp. Stuart, Va.					
			do	P. of E., Newport News.	October 1918.				
			February 1919	Cp. Mills, N. Y.		February 1919	February 1919	do	Do.
38th Artillery Brigade	September 1918	do	September 1918	Cp. Stuart, Va.					
			October 1918	P. of E., Newport News.	October 1918.				
			February 1919	Cp. Stuart, Va		do	do	Ft. Monroe, Va	Do.
39th Artillery Brigade	August 1918	A. E. F	January 1919	Cp. Merritt, N. J.		January 1919.			
			do	Ft. Wadsworth, N. Y.					
			February 1919	Ft. Hamilton, N. Y.					
			October 1919	Cp. Jackson, S. C.					Do.
40th Artillery Brigade	do	Ft. Hamilton, N. Y.	September 1918	Cp. Mills, N. Y.					
			do	P. of E., Hoboken	September 1918.				
			December 1918	Cp. Mills, N. Y.		December 1918	December 1918	Ft. Hamilton, N. Y.	G.H.Q. troops.
41st Artillery Brigade	September 1918	Ft. Totten, N. Y.	September 1918	Cp. Eustis, Va.					
			November 1918	Cp. Stuart, Va.					
			do	Ft. Wadsworth, N. Y.			do	Ft. Wadsworth, N. Y.	

BRIGADE HEADQUARTERS—Continued

Unit designation and redesignation	Organization		Stations in United States		Overseas		Demobilization		Remarks
	Month and year	Place	Month and year	Place	From—	To—	Month and year	Place	
42d Artillery Brigade	October 1918	Ft. Strong, Mass.	October 1918	Cp. Eustis, Va.			December 1918	Cp. Eustis, Va.	
43d Artillery Brigade	do	Ft. Hamilton, N. Y.	November 1918	do			do	Do.	
44th Artillery Brigade	November 1918	Ft. Monroe, Va.					do	Ft. Monroe, Va.	
45th Artillery Brigade	do	Ft. Strong, Mass.	November 1918	Ft. Warren, Mass.					
			do	Ft. Revere, Mass.			do	Ft. Revere, Mass.	
46th Artillery Brigade									Authorized but never orgzd.
47th Artillery Brigade									Never orgzd.
48th Artillery Brigade									Authorized but never orgzd.

PROVISIONAL REGIMENTS

Unit designation and redesignation	Organization: Month and year	Organization: Place	Stations: Month and year	Stations: Place	Overseas: From—	Overseas: To—	Demobilization: Month and year	Demobilization: Place	Remarks
1st to 5th Provisional Regiments.									Never orgzd.
6th Provisional Regiment.	July 1917	Ft. Adams, R. I.	August 1917	P. of E., Hoboken	August 1917.				
a. 51st Regiment	February 1918	A. E. F.	February 1919	Cp. Mills, N. Y.		February 1919.			
			do	Ft. Hamilton, N. Y.					
			October 1919	Cp. Jackson, S. C.					Army troops.
7th Provisional Regiment.	July 1917	Ft. Adams, R. I.	August 1917	P. of E., Hoboken	August 1917.				
a. 52d Regiment	February 1918	A. E. F.	January 1919	Cp. Stuart, Va.		January 1919.			
			do	Cp. Eustis, Va.					G.H.Q. troops.
8th Provisional Regiment.	July 1917	Ft. Adams, R. I.	August 1917	P. of E., Hoboken	August 1917.				
a. 53d Regiment	February 1918	A. E. F.	March 1919	Cp. Stuart, Va.		March 1919.			
			do	Cp. Eustis, Va.					Do.

REGIMENTS

Howitzer Regiment, 30th Separate Artillery Brigade (Railway).	March 1918	A. E. F.							
a. 44th Regiment	August 1918	do	February 1919 do	Cp. Mills, N. Y. Ft. Totten, N. Y.		February 1919.			
1st to 14th Regiments									Army troops. Never orgzd.
15th Regiment	October 1918	Ft. Crockett, Tex.					November 1918	Ft. Crockett, Tex.	
16th Regiment									Do.
17th Regiment	October 1918	Ft. Monroe, Va.					January 1919	Ft. Monroe, Va.	
18th Regiment	do	Ft. Winfield Scott, Calif.					December 1918	Ft. Winfield Scott, Calif.	
19th Regiment	do	Ft. MacArthur, Calif.					do	Ft. MacArthur, Calif.	
20th Regiment	do	Ft. Crockett, Tex.					November 1918	Ft. Crockett, Tex.	
21st Regiment	November 1918	Ft. Pickens, Fla.					December 1918	Ft. Pickens, Fla.	
22d Regiment									Do.
23d Regiment									Do.
24th Regiment									Do.
25th Regiment	October 1918	Ft. Rosecrans, Calif.					December 1918	Ft. Rosecrans, Calif.	
26th Regiment	November 1918	Ft. Screven, Ga.					do	Ft. Screven, Ga.	
27th Regiment	October 1918	Ft. Stevens, Oreg.	November 1918	Cp. Eustis, Va.			do	Cp. Eustis, Va.	
28th Regiment	November 1918	Ft. Strong, Mass.	do	Ft. Revere, Mass.			do	Ft. Revere, Mass.	
29th Regiment	do	Ft. Williams, Maine.					do	Ft. Williams, Maine.	
30th Regiment	do	Ft. H. G. Wright, N. Y.	November 1918	Cp. Eustis, Va.			do	Cp. Eustis, Va.	
31st Regiment	October 1918	Ft. Hancock, N. J.	do	do			do	Do.	
32d Regiment	do	Ft. Hamilton, N. Y.	do	do			do	Do.	
33d Regiment	September 1918	Ft. Strong, Mass.	October 1918	do			do	Do.	
34th Regiment	October 1918	Ft. Totten, N. Y.	do	do			do	Do.	
35th Regiment	November 1918	Ft. DuPont, Del.					do	Ft. DuPont, Del., and Cp. Meade, Md.	
36th Regiment	September 1918	Ft. Moultrie, S. C.	October 1918 November 1918	Cp. Eustis, Va. Cp. Stuart, Va.			do	Ft. Monroe, Va.	

REGIMENTS—Continued

Unit designation and redesignation	Organization		Stations in United States		Overseas		Demobilization		Remarks
	Month and year	Place	Month and year	Place	From—	To—	Month and year	Place	
37th Regiment	September 1918	Ft. Hancock, N. J.	October 1918	Cp. Eustis, Va.					
			November 1918	Cp. Stuart, Va.					
			do	Ft. Hancock, N. J.			December 1918	Ft. Hancock, N. J.	
38th Regiment	do	Ft. Hamilton, N. Y.	October 1918	Cp. Eustis, Va.					
			November 1918	Cp. Stuart, Va.					
			do	Ft. Hamilton, N. Y.			do	Ft. Hamilton, N. Y.	
39th Regiment	do	Ft. Worden, Wash.	do	Cp. Upton, N. Y.					
			do	Cp. Grant, Ill.			do	Cp. Grant, Ill.	
40th Regiment	do	Ft. Winfield Scott, Calif.	do	Cp. Upton, N. Y.					
			do	Cp. Grant, Ill.					
			December 1918	Presidio of San Francisco, Calif.			January 1919	Presidio of San Francisco, Calif.	
41st Regiment	October 1918	Ft. Monroe, Va.					December 1918	Ft. Monroe, Va.	
42d Regiment	August 1918	A. E. F.	February 1919	Cp. Stuart, Va.		February 1919			G.H.Q. troops.
			do	Cp. Eustis, Va.					
43d Regiment	do	do	December 1918	Cp. Hill, Va.		December 1918			Do.
			do	Cp. Eustis, Va.					
44th Regiment									See How. Regt., 30th Sep. Arty. Brig. (Ry.).
45th Regiment	July 1918	Cp. Eustis, Va.	October 1918	Cp. Stuart, Va.					
			do	P. of E., Newport News.	October 1918.				
			January 1919	Cp. Mills, N. Y.		January 1919	February 1919	Cp. Dix, N. J.	Army troops.
46th Regiment	do	Cp. Eustis, Va.	October 1918	Cp. Stuart, Va.					
			do	P. of E., Newport News.	October 1918	February 1919	March 1919	Cp. Dix, N. J.	Do.
47th Regiment	do	do	do	Cp. Stuart, Va.					
			do	P. of E., Newport News.	Do.				
			February 1919	Cp. Stuart, Va.		Do.			
			do	Cp. Eustis, Va.			do	Cp. Eustis, Va.	Do.

48th Regiment	do	do	September 1918	Cp. Stuart, Va.					
			October 1918	P. of E., Newport, News.	October 1918.				
			March 1919	Cp. Stuart, Va.		March 1919	do	Cp. Grant, Ill	Do.
49th Regiment	do	do	September 1918	Cp. Stuart, Va.					
			October 1918	P. of E., Newport News.	October 1918.				
			March 1919	Cp. Merritt, N. J.		do	do	do	Do.
50th Regiment	do	do	September 1918	Cp. Stuart, Va.					
			October 1918	P. of E., Newport News.	October 1918	February 1919	March 1919	Cp. Dix, N. J	Do.
51st Regiment									
52d Regiment									See 6th Prov. Regt.
53d Regiment									See **7th Prov. Regt.**
54th Regiment	January 1918	C. D. of Portland (Hq., Fort Williams, Maine).	March 1918	P. of E., Hoboken	March 1918.				See 8th Prov. Regt.
	December 1918	A. E. F.				March 1919	March 1919	Cp. Devens, Mass.	During September, October and November 1918, Regt. converted into Repl. Bns. for Hv. Arty. Reorg. in December 1918.
55th Regiment	December 1917	C. D. of Boston (Hq., Fort Warren, Mass.).	March 1918	Cp. Merritt, N. J.					
			do	P. of E., Hoboken	March 1918.				
			January 1919	Cp. Mills, N. Y		January 1919.			
			do	Ft. H. G. Wright, N. Y.					
			February 1919	Ft. Winfield Scott, Calif.					
			October 1919	Cp. Lewis, Wash					
56th Regiment	do	Ft. H. G. Wright, N. Y.	March 1918	P. of E., Hoboken	March 1918.				Army troops.
			January 1919	Cp. Mills, N. Y		January 1919.			
			do	Ft. Schuyler, N. Y.					
			October 1919	Cp. Jackson, S. C.					Do.

REGIMENTS—Continued

Unit designation and redesignation	Organization		Stations in United States		Overseas		Demobilization		Remarks
	Month and year	Place	Month and year	Place	From—	To—	Month and year	Place	
57th Regiment	January 1918	Ft. Hancock, N. J.	May 1918	P. of E., Hoboken	May 1918.				
			January 1919	Cp. Merritt, N. J.		January 1919.			
			do	Ft. Hancock, N. J.					
			February 1919	Ft. Winfield Scott, Calif.					
			October 1919	Cp. Lewis, Wash.					Army troops.
58th Regiment	February 1918	Ft. Totten, N. Y.	May 1918	P. of E., Hoboken	May 1918	April 1919	May 1919	Cp. Upton, N. Y.	Do.
59th Regiment	January 1918	Ft. Hamilton, N. Y.	March 1918	do	March 1918.				
			January 1919	Cp. Upton, N. Y.		January 1919.			
			February 1919	Ft. Winfield Scott, Calif.					
			October 1919	Cp. Lewis, Wash.					Do.
60th Regiment	February 1918	Ft. Monroe, Va.	April 1918	Cp. Stuart, Va.					
			do	P. of E., Newport News.	April 1918.				
			February 1919	Cp. Merritt, N. J.		February 1919	February 1919	Ft. Washington, Md.	Do.
61st Regiment	May 1918	Ft. Moultrie, S. C.	June 1918	Cp. Eustis, Va.					
			July 1918	Cp. Stuart, Va.					
			do	P. of E., Newport News.	July 1918	do	do	Cp. Upton, N. Y.	Do.
62d Regiment	January 1918	C.D. of San Francisco. (Hq., Ft. Winfield Scott, Calif.)	June 1918	Cp. Mills, N. Y.					
			July 1918	P. of E., Hoboken	Do.				
			February 1919	Cp. Stuart, Va.		Do.			
			do	Cp. Eustis, Va.			March 1919	Cp. Eustis, Va.	Do.
63d Regiment	December 1917	C. D. of Puget Sound. (Hq., Ft. Worden, Wash.)	June 1918	Cp. Mills, N. Y.					
			July 1918	P. of E., Hoboken	July 1918.				
			February 1919	Cp. Mills, N. Y.		February 1919	do	Cp. Lewis, Wash.	Do.

64th Regiment	January 1918	C.D. of Tampa. (Hq., Ft. Dade, Fla.)	July 1918	Cp. Upton, N. Y.					
			do	P. of E., Hoboken	July 1918.				
			February 1919	Cp. Stuart, Va		Do.			
			do	Cp. Eustis, Va			April 1919	Cp. Eustis, Va	Do.
65th Regiment	December 1917	Ft. Stevens, Oreg.	March 1918	San Francisco, Calif.					Regt. assembled at San Francisco, Calif., from several posts, March 1918.
			do	Cp. Merritt, N. J.					
			do	P. of E., Hoboken	March 1918.				
			January 1919	Cp. Dix, N. J.		January 1919	February 1919	Cp. Lewis, Wash.	Army troops.
66th Regiment	March 1918	C.D. of Narragansett Bay. (Hq., Ft. Adams, R.I.)	July 1918	P. of E., Boston	July 1918	March 1919	March 1919	Cp. Upton, N. Y.	Do.
67th Regiment	May 1918	Ft. Winfield Scott, Calif.	August 1918	Cp. Mills, N. Y.					
			do	**P. of E., Hoboken**	**August 1918.**				
			March 1919	**Cp. Mills, N. Y.**		**Do.**			
			do	**Presidio of San Francisco, Calif.**			**April 1919**	**Presidio of San Francisco, Calif.**	**Do.**
68th Regiment	**June 1918**	**Ft. Terry, N. Y.**	**August 1918**	**P. of E., Boston**	**August 1918.**				
			February 1919	**Cp. Mills, N. Y.**		**February 1919.**			
			do	**Ft. Wadsworth, N. Y.**			**March 1919**	**Ft. Wadsworth, N. Y.**	**Do.**
69th Regiment	**May 1918**	**C.D. of Puget Sound. (Hq., Ft. Worden, Wash.)**	**August 1918**	**Cp. Mills, N. Y.**					
			do	P. of E., Philadelphia	August 1918	February 1919	do	Cp. Eustis, Va	Do.
70th Regiment	June 1918	Ft. Hamilton, N. Y.	June 1918	Ft. Wadsworth, N. Y.					
			July 1918	P. of E., Hoboken	July 1918.				
			February 1919	Cp. Merritt, N. J.		February 1919	March 1919	Cp. Sherman, Ohio.	Army troops.
71st Regiment	May 1918	C.D. of Boston. (Hq., Ft. Strong, Mass.)	July 1918	P. of E., Boston	July 1918.				
			February 1919	Cp. Merritt, N. J.		do	do	Cp. Devens, Mass.	Do.
72d Regiment	June 1918	C.D. of Portland, (Hq., Ft. Williams, Maine.)	August 1918	P. of E., Montreal	August 1918.				
			March 1919	Cp. Upton, N. Y.		March 1919	April 1919	Cp. Grant, Ill.	Do.
73d Regiment	July 1918	Ft. Banks, Mass.	September 1918	Cp. Mills, N. Y.					
			do	P. of E., Hoboken	September 1918.				
			December 1918	Cp. Mills, N. Y.		December 1918	January 1919	Cp. Devens, Mass.	G.H.Q. troops.

REGIMENTS—Continued

Unit designation and redesignation	Organization: Month and year	Organization: Place	Stations in United States: Month and year	Stations in United States: Place	Overseas: From—	Overseas: To—	Demobilization: Month and year	Demobilization: Place	Remarks
74th Regiment	June 1918	Ft. Schuyler, N. Y.	September 1918	Cp. Upton, N. Y.					
			do	P. of E., Hoboken	September 1918.				
			December 1918	Cp. Mills, N. Y.		December 1918.			
			do	Ft. Totten, N. Y.			January 1919	Ft. Totten, N. Y.	G.H.Q. troops
75th Regiment	September 1918	Ft. Moultrie, S. C.	September 1918	Cp. Merritt, N. J.					
			October 1918	P. of E., Hoboken	October 1918.				
			March 1919	Cp. Stuart, Va.		March 1919	March 1919	Cp. Grant, Ill.	Do.

COAST DEFENSE COMMANDS [1]
(As Constituted During and After July 1917)

Unit designation and redesignation	Organization: Month and year	Organization: Place	Stations in United States: Month and year	Stations in United States: Place	Overseas: From—	Overseas: To—	Demobilization: Month and year	Demobilization: Place	Remarks
C. D. of Balboa									
1st Company									See 1st Co. Ft. Grant.
2d Company									See 2d Co. Ft. Grant.
3d Company									See 3d Co. Ft. Grant.
4th Company									See 4th Co. Ft. Grant.
5th Company									See 5th Co. Ft. Grant.
6th Company									See 6th Co. Ft. Grant.
7th Company									See 7th Co. Ft. Grant.
8th Company									See 8th Co. Ft. Grant.
9th Company									See 9th Co. Ft. Grant.

10th Company									See 10th Co. Ft. Grant.
11th Company									See 11th Co. Ft. Grant.
C. D. of Baltimore									
1st (I) Company									See 1st Co. Ft. Howard.
1st (II) Company	September 1919	Ft. Howard, Md							Active through 1919.
2d (I) Company									See 2d Co. Ft. Howard.
2d (II) Company	September 1919	Ft. Howard, Md							Active through 1919.
3d Company									See 3d Co. Ft. Howard.
4th Company									See 4th Co. Ft. Howard.
5th (I) Company									See 1st Co. Ft. Smallwood.
5th (II) Company	January 1918	Locust Point, Baltimore, Md.	May 1918	Ft. Howard, Md			December 1918	Ft. Howard, Md	Orgzd. fr. 1st Co. Md. C.A. N.G.
6th Company	do	do	do	do			September 1919	do	Orgzd. fr. 2d Co. Md. C.A. N.G.
7th (Hq.) Company	June 1918	Ft. Howard, Md					do	Do.	
C. D. of Boston									
1st (I) Company									See 1st Co. Ft. Revere.
1st (II) Company	March 1918	Ft. Revere, Mass.							
2d Company									See 1st Co. Ft. Andrews.
3d Company	July 1918	East Boston, Mass	July 1918	Ft. Standish, Mass					Orgzd. fr. 2d Prov. Co. C.A.C.
			March 1919	Ft. Strong, Mass					Active through 1919.
4th Company	do	Ft. Warren, Mass							Do.
5th Company	August 1918	Ft. Revere, Mass	September 1919	Ft. Andrews, Mass					Do.

[1] Arranged in alphabetical order. Prior to 1916, numerical designation of coast defense companies was in a single series. Thereafter they were numbered serially within separate garrisons. Beginning in July 1917, serial and separate numbering of companies was applied to coast defense commands.

COAST DEFENSE COMMANDS—Continued

Unit designation and redesignation	Organization		Stations in United States		Overseas		Demobilization		Remarks
	Month and year	Place	Month and year	Place	From—	To—	Month and year	Place	
C. D. of Boston—Con.									
6th Company									See 5th Co. Ft. Andrews.
7th Company									See 1st Co. Ft. Warren.
8th (I) Company									See 4th Co. Ft. Strong.
8th (II) Company	March 1918	Ft. Banks, Mass.	November 1918	Ft. Andrews, Mass.					Active through 1919.
9th Company									See 1st Co. Ft. Strong.
10th Company									See 2d Co. Ft. Strong.
11th Company	August 1918	Ft. Andrews, Mass.	September 1918 January 1919	Ft. Standish, Mass. Ft. Strong, Mass.					Active through 1919.
12th Company	do	do	September 1918 November 1918 September 1919 December 1919	Deer Island, Mass. Ft. Strong, Mass. Ft. Andrews, Mass. Ft. Banks, Mass.					
13th (I) Company									See 2d Co. Ft. Banks.
13th (II) Company	March 1918	Ft. Andrews, Mass.					September 1919	Ft. Andrews, Mass.	
14th Company	August 1918	Ft. Standish, Mass.	August 1918 September 1918 November 1918 December 1918	Ft. Heath, Mass. Nahant, Mass. Ft. Heath, Mass. Ft. Banks, Mass.			do	Ft. Banks, Mass.	
15th Company									See 27th Co. Boston.
16th Company	August 1917	Ft. Revere, Mass.					December 1918	Ft. Revere, Mass.	Orgzd. fr. 1st Co. Mass. C.A. N.G.

17th Company	do	do					do	do	Orgzd. fr. 2d Co. Mass. C.A. N.G.
18th (I) Company	do	Ft. Strong, Mass.							Orgzd. fr. 3d Co. Mass. C.A. N.G. Redes. Btry. F, 55th Regiment, C.A.C. December 1917.
18th (II) Company	March 1918	do					December 1918	Ft. Strong, Mass.	
19th (I) Company	August 1917	Ft. Banks, Mass.							Orgzd. fr. 4th Co. Mass. C.A. N.G. Redes. Btry. D, 55th Regiment, C.A.C. December 1917.
19th (II) Company	December 1917	do					December 1918	Ft. Banks, Mass.	
20th (I) Company	August 1917	Ft. Andrews, Mass.							Orgzd. fr. 5th Co. Mass. C.A. N.G. Redes. Sup. Co. 55th Regiment, C.A.C. December 1917.
20th (II) Company	March 1918	do					November 1918	Ft. Andrews, Mass.	
21st Company	August 1917	Ft. Strong, Mass.					do	Ft. Strong, Mass.	Orgzd. fr. 6th Co. Mass. C.A. N.G.
22d Company	do	Ft. Banks, Mass.	October 1917	Watertown Arsenal, Mass.					Orgzd. fr. 7th Co. Mass. C.A. N.G.
			October 1918	Ft. Revere, Mass.			November 1918	Ft. Revere, Mass.	
23d Company	do	Ft. Andrews, Mass.					do	Ft. Andrews, Mass.	Orgzd. fr. 8th Co. Mass. C.A. N.G.
24th Company	do	Ft. Heath, Mass.	December 1917	Ft. Banks, Mass.					Orgzd. fr. 9th Co. Mass. C.A. N.G.
			March 1918	Ft. Heath, Mass.					
			July 1918	Ft. Banks, Mass.					
			August 1918	Ft. Heath, Mass.			November 1918	Ft. Heath, Mass.	
25th Company	do	Springfield Armory, Mass.	March 1918	Watertown Arsenal, Mass.					Orgzd. fr. 10th Co. Mass. C.A. N.G.
			October 1918	Ft. Standish, Mass.			November 1918	Ft. Standish, Mass.	
26th Company	do	Ft. Andrews, Mass.					do	Ft. Andrews, Mass.	Orgzd. fr. 11th Co. Mass. C.A. N.G.

COAST DEFENSE COMMANDS—Continued

Unit designation and redesignation	Organization		Stations in United States		Overseas		Demobilization		Remarks
	Month and year	Place	Month and year	Place	From—	To—	Month and year	Place	
C. D. of Boston—Con.									
27th Company	**August 1917**	Springfield Armory, Mass.	March 1918	Watertown Arsenal, Mass.					Orgzd. fr. 12th Co. Mass. C.A. N.G.
a. 15th Co. Boston	November 1918	Ft. Andrews, Mass.					September 1919	Ft. Andrews, Mass	
28th Company	August 1917	Ft. Standish, Mass.	September 1917 October 1917 August 1918	Cp. Devens, Mass. Ft. Standish, Mass. Ft. Heath, Mass.			November 1918	Ft. Heath, Mass.	Orgzd. fr. 2d Co. R. I. C.A. N.G.
29th (I) Company	do	do							Orgzd. fr. 9th Co. R. I. C.A. N.G. Redes. Btry. E, 55th Regiment, C.A.C. December 1917.
29th (II) Company	March 1918	do					November 1918	Ft. Standish, Mass.	
30th Company	August 1917	do					do	do	**Orgzd. fr. 10th Co. R. I. C.A. N.G.**
31st Company	do	Ft. Warren, Mass.					do	Ft. Warren, Mass.	Orgzd. fr. 13th Co. R. I. C.A. N.G.
32d Company	do	**Ft. Standish, Mass.**					do	Ft. Standish, Mass.	**Orgzd. fr. 20th Co.** R. I. C.A. N.G.
C. D. of The Cape Fear									
1st Company									See 1st Co. Ft. Caswell.
2d Company									See 3d Co. Ft. Caswell.
3d Company	September 1917	Ft. Caswell, N. C.					October 1919	Ft. Caswell, N. C.	Orgzd. fr. 3d Co. N. C. C.A. **N.G.**
4th Company	do	do					April 1919	do	**Orgzd. fr. 4th Co.** N. C. C.A. N.G.

5th Company	do	do					November 1918	do	Orgzd. fr. 5th Co. N. C. C.A. N.G.
6th Company	do	do					do	do	Orgzd. fr. 6th Co. N. C. C.A. N.G.
7th Company	do	do					do	do	Orgzd. fr. 1st Co. N. C. C.A. N.G.
8th Company	do	do					do	do	Orgzd. fr. 2d Co. N. C. C.A. N.G.
9th Company	January 1918	do					do	Do.	
10th Company	do	do					do	Do.	
11th Company	do	do					do	Do.	
12th Company	do	do					do	Do.	
C. D. of Charleston									
1st Company									See 1st Co. Ft. Moultrie.
2d Company									See 5th Co. Ft. Moultrie.
3d Company									See 3d Co. Ft. Moultrie.
4th Company									See 4th Co. Ft. Moultrie.
5th Company	April 1918	Ft. Moultrie, S.C.					September 1919	Ft. Moultrie, S. C.	
6th Company	August 1917	do					December 1918	do	Orgzd. fr. 1st Co. S. C. C.A. N.G.
7th Company	do	do					do	do	Orgzd. fr. 2d Co. S. C. C.A. N.G.
8th Company	do	do	June 1918	Ft. Sumter, S. C.			September 1918	Ft. Sumter, S.C.	Orgzd. fr. 3d Co. S. C. C.A. N.G.
9th Company	do	do					do	Ft. Moultrie, S. C.	Orgzd. fr. 4th Co. S. C. C.A. N.G.
10th (I) Company	do	do					June 1918	do	Orgzd. fr. 5th Co. S. C. C.A. N.G.
10th (II) Company									See Hq. Co. Charleston.
11th Company	April 1918	Ft. Moultrie, S. C.					June 1918	Ft. Moultrie, S. C.	
12th Company	do	do					do	Do.	
Hq. Company	do	Do.							
a. 10th (II) Company Charleston.	August 1918	do					September 1918	Do.	

COAST DEFENSE COMMANDS—Continued

Unit designation and redesignation	Organization		Stations in United States		Overseas		Demobilization		Remarks
	Month and year	Place	Month and year	Place	From—	To—	Month and year	Place	
C. D. of Chesapeake Bay									
1st Company									See 1st Co. Ft. Monroe.
2d Company									See 2d Co. Ft. Monroe.
3d Company									See 3d Co. Ft. Monroe.
4th Company									See 4th Co. Ft. Monroe.
5th Company									See 13th Co. Ft. Monroe.
6th (I) Company									See 6th Co. Ft. Monroe.
6th (II) Company	February 1918	Ft. Monroe, Va.							Orgsd. fr. 6th Co. Va. C.A. N.G. Active through 1919.
7th Company									See 7th Co. Ft. Monroe.
8th (I) Company									See 8th Co. Ft. Monroe.
8th (II) Company	February 1918	Fisherman's Island, Va.	February 1919	Ft. Monroe, Va.					Orgsd. fr. 4th Co. Va. C.A. N.G. Active through 1919.
9th Company									See 9th Co. Ft. Monroe.
10th Company	February 1918	Ft. Story, Va.					August 1919	Ft. Story, Va.	Orgsd. fr. 3d Co. Va. C.A. N.G.
11th Company	do	Ft. Monroe, Va.					do	Ft. Monroe, Va.	Orgsd. fr. 7th Co. Va. C.A. N.G.

Unit	Col 2	Col 3	Col 4	Col 5	Col 6	Col 7	Col 8	Col 9	Col 10
12th Company	do	do	March 1918	Ft. Wool, Va			do	Ft. Wool, Va	Orgsd. fr. 8th Co. Va. C.A. N.G.
13th Company	do	do	January 1919	Fisherman's Island, Va.					
			February 1919	Ft. Monroe, Va					
14th Company	March 1918	do					do	Ft. Monroe, Va.	
15th Company	April 1918	do					December 1918	Do.	
16th Company	do	do					do	Do.	
17th Company	July 1918	do					do	Do.	
C. D. of The Columbia									
1st Company									See 1st Co. Ft. Stevens.
2d Company									See 2d Co. Ft. Stevens.
3d Company									See 3d Co. Ft. Stevens.
4th Company									See 1st Co. Ft. Columbia.
5th Company	January 1918	Ft. Canby, Wash					December 1918	Ft. Canby, Wash	Orgsd. fr. 5th Co. Oreg. C.A. N.G.
6th (I) Company	do	Ft. Stevens, Oreg					November 1918	Ft. Stevens, Oreg	Orgsd. fr. 6th Co. Oreg. C.A. N.G.
6th (II) Company	November 1918	do					December 1918	do	Formed by consolidation of the 8th, 9th, 19th and 21st Cos. Columbia.
7th (I) Company	January 1918	Ft. Columbia, Wash.					November 1918	Ft. Columbia, Wash.	Orgsd. fr. 7th Co. Oreg. C.A. N.G.
7th (II) Company	November 1918	Ft. Stevens, Oreg					December 1918	Ft. Stevens, Oreg	Formed by consolidation of the 6th, 14th, 16th, 17th and 23d Cos. Columbia.
8th Company	January 1918	do					November 1918	do	Orgsd. fr. 8th Co. Oreg. C.A. N.G.
9th Company	do	do					do	do	Orgsd. fr. 9th Co. Oreg. C.A. N.G.

COAST DEFENSE COMMANDS—Continued

Unit designation and redesignation	Organization		Stations in United States		Overseas		Demobilization		Remarks
	Month and year	Place	Month and year	Place	From—	To—	Month and year	Place	
C. D. of The Columbia—Continued									
10th Company	January 1918	Ft. Columbia, Wash.					November 1918	Ft. Columbia, Wash.	Orgzd. fr. 10th Co. Oreg. C.A. N.G.
11th Company	do	Ft. Stevens, Oreg					do	Ft. Stevens, Oreg.	Orgzd. fr. 11th Co. Oreg. C.A. N.G.
12th Company	do	Ft. Canby, Wash					do	Ft. Canby, Wash	Orgzd fr. 12th Co. Oreg. C.A. N.G.
13th Company	do	Ft. Stevens, Oreg					do	Ft. Stevens, Oreg	Orgzd. fr. 1st Co. Oreg. C.A. N.G.
14th Company	do	do					do	do	Orgzd. fr. 2d Co. Oreg. C.A. N.G.
15th Company	do	do					do	do	Orgzd. fr. 3d Co. Oreg. C.A. N.G.
16th Company	do	Astoria, Oreg	February 1918	Ft. Stevens, Oreg			do	do	Orgzd. fr. 4th Co. Oreg. C.A. N.G.
17th Company	February 1918	Ft. Stevens, Oreg					do	Do.	
18th Company	do	do					do	Do.	
19th Company	April 1918	do					do	Do.	
20th Company	do	Ft. Canby, Wash					do	Ft. Canby, Wash.	
21st Company	do	do	November 1918	Ft. Stevens, Oreg			do	Ft. Stevens, Oreg.	
22d Company	do	Ft. Columbia, Wash.	do	do			do	Do.	
23d Company	May 1918	Ft. Stevens, Oreg					do	Do.	
C. D. of Cristobal									
1st Company									See 1st Co. Ft. Sherman.
2d Company									See 2d Co. Ft. Sherman.
3d Company									See 3d Co. Ft. Sherman.

4th Company									See 4th Co. Ft. Sherman.
5th Company									See 5th Co. Ft. Sherman.
6th Company									See 1st Co. Ft. De Lesseps.
7th Company									See 1st Co. Ft. Randolph.
8th Company									See 2d Co. Ft. Randolph.
9th Company									See 3d Co. Ft. Randolph.
10th Company									See 4th Co. Ft. Randolph.
11th Company									See 11th Co. Balboa.
C. D. of The Delaware									
1st Company									See 1st Co. Ft. Du Pont.
2d Company									See 2d Co. Ft. Du Pont.
3d (I) Company									See 3d Co. Ft. Du Pont.
3d (II) Company	January 1919	Ft. Delaware, Del.	September 1919	Ft. Du Pont, Del.					
4th (I) Company									See 4th Co. Ft. Du Pont.
4th (II) Company	February 1918	Ft. Mott, N. J.	May 1918 February 1919	Cape May, N. J. Ft. Mott, N. J.					
5th Company							December 1919	Ft. Mott, N. J.	
6th Company									See 11th Co. Delaware.
7th Company									See 6th Co. Ft. Du Pont.
8th Company									See 1st Co. Ft. Mott.
	April 1918	Ft. Du Pont, Del.					December 1918	Ft. Du Pont, Del.	Demblzd. December 1918; reorgzd. January 1919.
	January 1919	do					September 1919	Do.	

COAST DEFENSE COMMANDS—Continued

Unit designation and redesignation	Organization		Stations in United States		Overseas		Demobilization		Remarks
	Month and year	Place	Month and year	Place	From—	To—	Month and year	Place	
C. D. of The Delaware— Continued									
9th Company	August 1918	Ft. Du Pont, Del					December 1918	Ft. Du Pont, Del.	
10th Company	do	do					do	Do.	
11th (I) Company	February 1918	Ft. Mott, N. J							Orgsd. fr. 1st Co. N. J. C.A. N.G. Demblsd. December 1918; reorgsd. January 1919.
a. 5th Co. Delaware.	March 1918	do					December 1918	Ft. Mott, N. J	
	January 1919	do					September 1919	Do.	
11th (II) Company	August 1918	do					October 1919	Do.	
C. D. of Eastern New York									
1st (I) Company									See 4th Co. Ft. Totten.
1st (II) Company									See 3d Co. Ft. Totten.
2d (I) Company									See 7th Co. Ft. Totten.
2d (II) Company									See 5th Co. Ft. Totten.
3d Company									See 3d Co. Ft. Totten.
4th Company									See 1st Co. Ft. Schuyler.
5th Company									See 5th Co. Ft. Totten.
6th (I) Company									See 1st Co. Ft. Totten.

6th (II) Company	January 1919	Ft. Totten, N. Y.					September 1919	Ft. Totten, N. Y.	
7th (I) Company	May 1918	do					December 1918	Do.	
7th (II) Company	January 1919	do					September 1919	Do.	
8th (I) Company	July 1918	do					December 1918	Do.	
8th (II) Company	January 1919	do					September 1919	Do.	
9th (I) Company	July 1918	do					December 1918	Do.	
9th (II) Company	January 1919	do					September 1919	Do.	
10th Company	January 1918	do					December 1918	do	Orgsd. fr. 34th Co. N. Y. C.A. N.G.
11th Company	July 1918	do					do	Do.	
12th Company	do	do					do	Do.	
13th Company	October 1918	do					do	Do.	
C. D. of Galveston									
1st Company									See 1st Co. Ft. Crockett.
2d Company									See 2d Co. Ft. Crockett.
3d Company									See 3d Co. Ft. Crockett.
4th Company	August 1917	Ft. Crockett, Tex.					December 1918	Ft. Crockett, Tex.	Orgsd. fr. 1st Co. Tex. C.A. N.G.
5th Company	do	do					do	do	Orgsd. fr. 2d Co. Tex. C.A. N.G.
6th Company	do	do	July 1918	Sabine, Tex.			do	do	Orgsd. fr. 3d Co. Tex. C.A. N.G.
7th Company	do	do					do	do	Orgsd. fr. 4th Co. Tex. C.A. N.G.
8th Company	do	do	February 1918	Ft. San Jacinto, Tex.					Orgsd. fr. 5th Co. Tex. C.A. N.G.
			July 1918	Ft. Crockett, Tex.					
9th Company	January 1918	Ft. Travis, Tex.					December 1918	Ft. Crockett, Tex.	
10th Company	do	Ft. San Jacinto, Tex.					do	Do.	
							do	Ft. San Jacinto, Tex.	
11th Company	do	do					do	Do.	
12th Company	do	do	July 1918	Ft. Crockett, Tex.			do	Ft. Crockett, Tex.	
13th Company	do	Ft. Crockett, Tex.	do	Freeport, Tex.			do	Do.	
14th Company	do	do					do	Do.	

COAST DEFENSE COMMANDS—Continued

Unit designation and redesignation	Organization		Stations in United States		Overseas		Demobilization		Remarks
	Month and year	Place	Month and year	Place	From—	To—	Month and year	Place	
C. D. of Key West									
1st Company									See 1st Co. Key West Bks.
2d Company									See 2d Co. Key West Bks.
3d Company	October 1917	Key West Bks., Fla.					December 1918	Key West Bks., Fla.	Orgzd. fr. 1st Co. Fla. C.A. N.G.
4th Company	January 1918	do					do	Do.	
C. D. of Long Island Sound									
1st Company									See 3d Co. Ft. H. G. Wright.
2d Company									See 4th Co. Ft. H. G. Wright.
3d (I) Company									See 5th Co. Ft. H. G. Wright.
3d (II) Company									See 28th Co. Long Island Sound.
4th Company									See 7th Co. Ft. H. G. Wright.
5th (I) Company									See 30th Co. Long Island Sound.
5th (II) Company	January 1919	Ft. H. G. Wright, N. Y.							Active through 1919.
6th (I) Company									See 31st Co. Long Island Sound.
6th (II) Company	January 1919	Ft. H. G. Wright, N. Y.							Active through 1919.
7th (I) Company									See 32d Co. Long Island Sound.

7th (II) Company	January 1919	Ft. H. G. Wright, N. Y.						Active through 1919.
8th (I) Company	March 1918	do				December 1918	Ft. H. G. Wright, N. Y.	
8th (II) Company								See 1st Co. Ft. Terry.
9th (I) Company	March 1918	Ft. H. G. Wright, N. Y.				December 1918	Ft. H. G. Wright, N. Y.	
9th (II) Company								See **5th** Co. Ft. Terry.
10th (I) Company	March 1918	Ft. H. G. Wright, N. Y.				December 1918	Ft. H. G. Wright, N. Y.	
10th (II) Company								See 24th Co. Long Island Sound.
11th (I) Company	March 1918	Ft. H. G. Wright, N. Y.				December 1918	Ft. H. G. Wright, N. Y.	
11th (II) Company	January 1919	Ft. Terry, N. Y.				September 1919	Ft. Terry, N. Y.	
12th (I) Company								See 1st Co. Ft. Terry.
12th (II) Company	January 1919	Ft. Terry, N. Y.				September 1919	Ft. Terry, N. Y.	
13th (I) Company								See 3d Co. Ft. Terry.
13th (II) Company								See 34th Co. Long Island Sound.
13th (III) Company	January 1919	Ft. Terry, N. Y.				October 1919	Ft. Terry, N. Y.	
14th (I) Company								See 4th Co. Ft. Terry.
14th (II) Company								See 35th Co. Long Island Sound.
14th (III) Company	January 1919	Ft. H. G. Wright, N. Y.				September 1919	Ft. H. G. Wright, N. Y.	
15th (I) Company								See 5th Co. Ft. Terry.
15th (II) Company								See 1st Co. Ft. Michie.
16th (I) Company								See 7th Co. Ft. Terry.
16th (II) Company								See 36th Co. Long Island Sound.
17th Company	March 1918	Ft. Terry, N. Y.				December 1918	Ft. Terry, N. Y.	

COAST DEFENSE COMMANDS—Continued

Unit designation and redesignation	Organization		Stations in United States		Overseas		Demobilization		Remarks
	Month and year	Place	Month and year	Place	From—	To—	Month and year	Place	
C. D. of Long Island Sound—Continued									
18th Company									See 1st Co. Ft. Michie.
19th Company									See 33d Co. Long Island Sound.
20th Company									See 24th Co. Long Island Sound.
21st Company	March 1918	Ft. Terry, N. Y.					December 1918	Ft. Terry, N. Y.	
22d Company	do	do					do	Do.	
23d Company									See 1st Co. Ft. Michie.
24th Company	March 1918	Ft. Terry, N. Y.							
a. 20th Co. Long Island Sound.	April 1918	Do.							
b. 10th (II) Co. Long Island Sound.	December 1918	do					October 1919	Ft. Terry, N. Y.	
25th Company									Never orgzd.
26th Company	August 1917	Ft. H. G. Wright, N. Y.							Orgzd. fr. 3d Co. Conn. C.A. N.G. Redes. Sup. Co. 56th Regt., C.A.C. December 1917.
27th Company	do	do							Orgzd. fr. 4th Co. Conn. C.A. N.G. Redes. Btry. F, 56th Regt., C.A.C. December 1917.

28th Company	do	do							
a. 3d (II) Co. Long Island Sound.	April 1918	do							Orgzd. fr. 8th Co. Conn. C.A. N.G. **Active through 1919.**
29th Company	August 1917	do							Orgzd. fr. 9th Co. Conn. C.A. N.G. Redes. Btry. E, 56th Regt., C.A.C. December 1917.
30th Company	do	do							Orgzd. fr. 10th Co. Conn. C.A. N.G.
a. 5th (I) Co. Long Island Sound.	April 1918	do					December 1918	Ft. H. G. Wright, N. Y.	
31st Company	August 1917	do							Orgzd. fr. 12th Co. Conn. C.A. N.G.
a. 6th (I) Co. Long Island Sound.	April 1918	do					December 1918	Ft. H. G. Wright, N. Y.	
32d Company	August 1917	Ft. Terry, N. Y							Orgzd. fr. 1st Co. Conn. C.A. N.G.
a. 7th (I) Co. Long Island Sound.	April 1918	do					December 1918	Ft. Terry, N. Y.	
33d Company	August 1917	do							Orgzd. fr. 2d Co. Conn. C.A. N.G.
a. 19th Co. Long Island Sound.	April 1918	Ft. Michie, N. Y					December 1918	Ft. Michie, N. Y.	
34th Company	August 1917	Ft. Terry, N. Y							Orgzd. fr. 5th Co. Conn. C.A. N.G.
a. 13th (II) Co. Long Island Sound.	April 1918	do					December 1918	Ft. Terry, N. Y.	
35th Company	August 1917	do							Orgzd. fr. 6th Co. Conn. C.A. N.G.
a. 14th (II) Co. Long Island Sound.	April 1918	do					December 1918	Ft. Terry, N. Y.	

COAST DEFENSE COMMANDS—Continued

Unit designation and redesignation	Organization		Stations in United States		Overseas		Demobilization		Remarks
	Month and year	Place	Month and year	Place	From—	To—	Month and year	Place	
C. D. of Long Island Sound—Continued									
36th Company	August 1917	**Ft. Terry, N. Y.**							Orgzd. fr. 7th Co. Conn. C.A. N.G.
a. 16th (II) Co. Long Island Sound.	April 1918	do					December 1918	Ft. Terry, N. Y.	
37th Company	August 1917	do							Orgzd. fr. 11th Co. Conn. C.A. N.G. Redes. Btry. B, 56th Regt., C.A.C. December 1917.
38th Company	do	do							Orgzd. fr. 13th Co. Conn. C.A. N.G. Redes. Btry. D, 56th Regt., C.A.C. December 1917.
C. D. of Los Angeles									
1st (I) Company									See 4th (I) Co. Ft. Winfield Scott.
1st (II) Company	February 1918	Ft. MacArthur, Calif.					December 1918	Ft. MacArthur, Calif.	
2d (I) Company									**See 2d Co. Ft. MacArthur.**
2d (II) Company	**February 1918**	**Ft. MacArthur, Calif.**							**Active through 1919.**
3d (I) Company									**See 3d Co. Ft. MacArthur.**

3d (II) Company	February 1918	Ft. MacArthur, Calif.							Active through 1919.
4th (I) Company									See 4th Co. Ft. MacArthur.
4th (II) Company	February 1918	Ft. MacArthur, Calif.							Redes. Hq. Co. 19th Regt., C.A.C. October 1918.
5th (I) Company	September 1917	do							Orgzd. fr. 16th Co. Calif. C.A. N.G. Redes. Btry. D, 2d A.A. Bn. January 1918.
5th (II) Company	February 1918	do							Redes. Btry. A, 55th Am. Tn. May 1918.
5th (III) Company									See 9th (II) Co. Los Angeles.
6th (I) Company	September 1917	Ft. MacArthur, Calif.	October 1917	Long Beach, Calif			January 1918	Ft. MacArthur, Calif.	Orgzd. fr. 17th Co. Calif. C.A. N.G.
6th (II) Company	February 1918	do					December 1918	Do.	
7th (I) Company	September 1917	do					January 1918	do	Orgzd. fr. 19th Co. Calif. C.A. N.G.
7th (II) Company	February 1918	do							Redes. Co. B, 55th Am. Tn. May 1918.
7th (III) Company									See 10th (II) Co. Los Angeles.
8th (I) Company	September 1917	Ft. MacArthur, Calif.					January 1918	Ft. MacArthur, Calif.	Orgzd. fr. 20th Co. Calif. C.A. N.G.
8th (II) Company	February 1918	do							Redes. Co. C, 55th Am. Tn. May 1918.
8th (III) Company									See 11th (II) Co. Los Angeles.
9th (I) Company	September 1917	Ft. MacArthur, Calif.					January 1918	Ft. MacArthur, Calif.	Orgzd. fr. 21st Co. Calif. C.A. N.G.
9th (II) Company	February 1918	Do.							
a. 5th (III) Co. Los Angeles.	June 1918	do					December 1918	Do.	

COAST DEFENSE COMMANDS—Continued

Unit designation and redesignation	Organization		Stations in United States		Overseas		Demobilization		Remarks
	Month and year	Place	Month and year	Place	From—	To—	Month and year	Place	
C. D. of Los Angeles—Continued									
9th (III) Company									See 12th (II) Co. Los Angeles.
10th (I) Company	September 1917	Ft. MacArthur, Calif.	October 1917	San Pedro, Calif			January 1918	Ft. MacArthur, Calif.	Orgzd. fr. 22d Co. Calif. C.A. N.G.
10th (II) Company	February 1918	Do.							
a. 7th (III) Co. Los Angeles.	June 1918	do							Active through 1919.
10th (III) Company									See 13th (I) Co. Los Angeles.
11th (I) Company	September 1917	Ft. MacArthur, Calif.	October 1917	San Luis Obispo, Calif.			January 1918	Ft. MacArthur, Calif.	Orgzd. fr. 23d Co. Calif. C.A. N.G.
11th (II) Company	February 1918	Do.							
a. 8th (III) Co. Los Angeles.	June 1918	do					September 1919	Do.	
11th (III) Company									See 14th (I) Co. Los Angeles.
12th (I) Company	September 1917	Ft. MacArthur, Calif.					January 1918	Ft. MacArthur, Calif.	Orgzd. fr. 24th Co. Calif. C.A. N.G.
12th (II) Company	February 1918	Do.							
a. 9th (III) Co. Los Angeles.	June 1918	do					December 1918	Do.	
12th (III) Company	July 1918	do					do	Do.	
13th (I) Company	February 1918	Do.							
a. 10th (III) Co. Los Angeles.	June 1918	do							Redes. Sup. Co. 19th Regt., C.A.C. October 1918.

13th (II) Company	August 1918	do							Redes. Btry. B, 19th Regt., C.A.C. October 1918.
14th (I) Company	February 1918	Do.							
a. 11th (III) Co. Los Angeles.	June 1918	do							Redes. Btry. A, 19th Regt., C.A.C. October 1918.
14th (II) Company	August 1918	do							Redes. Btry. C, 19th Regt., C.A.C. October 1918.
15th Company	February 1918	Ft. MacArthur, Calif.							Redes. Co. D, 55th Am. Tn. October 1918.
16th and 17th Companies.									Never orgzd.
18th Company	October 1918	Ft. MacArthur, Calif.							Redes. Btry. D, 19th Regt., C.A.C. October 1918.
19th Company	do	do							Redes. Btry. E, 19th Regt., C.A.C. October 1918.
20th Company	do	do							Redes. Btry. F, 19th Regt., C.A.C. October 1918.
21st to 28th Companies									Never orgzd.
29th Company	September 1918	Ft. MacArthur, Calif.							Redes. Co. A, Second Army Arty. Park October 1918.
30th Company	do	do							Redes. Co. B, Second Army Arty. Park October 1918.

COAST DEFENSE COMMANDS—Continued

Unit designation and redesignation	Organization		Stations in United States		Overseas		Demobilization		Remarks
	Month and year	Place	Month and year	Place	From—	To—	Month and year	Place	
C. D. of Los Angeles—Continued									
31st Company	September 1918	Ft. MacArthur, Calif.							Redes. Co. C, Second Army Arty. Park October 1918.
32d Company	do	do							Redes. Btry. G, Second Army Arty. Park October 1918.
33d Company	do	do							Redes. Btry. H, Second Army Arty. Park October 1918.
34th Company	September 1918	Ft. MacArthur, Calif.							Redes. Co. D, Second Army Arty. Park October 1918.
35th Company	do	do							Redes. Btry. I, Second Army Arty. Park October 1918.
36th Company	do	do							Redes. Co. E, Second Army Arty. Park October 1918.
37th Company	do	do							Redes. Co. F, Second Army Arty. Park October 1918.

C. D. of Manila and Subic Bays									
1st Company									See 1st Co. Ft. Mills.
2d Company									See 2d Co. Ft. Mills.
3d Company									See 3d Co. Ft. Mills.
4th Company									See 4th Co. Ft. Mills.
5th Company									See 5th Co. Ft. Mills.
6th Company									See 6th Co. Ft. Mills.
7th Company									See 7th Co. Ft. Mills.
8th Company									See 8th Co. Ft. Mills.
9th Company									See 9th Co. Ft. Mills.
10th Company									See 10th Co. Ft. Mills.
11th Company									See 11th Co. Ft. Mills.
12th Company									See 12th Co. Ft. Mills.
13th Company									See 13th Co. Ft. Mills.
14th Company									See 14th Co. Ft. Mills.
15th Company									See 15th Co. Ft. Mills.
16th Company									See 16th Co. Ft. Mills.
17th Company									See 17th (II) Co. Ft. Mills.
18th Company									See 18th Co. Ft. Mills.
19th Company									See 19th Co. Ft. Mills.

COAST DEFENSE COMMANDS—Continued

Unit designation and redesignation	Organization		Stations in United States		Overseas		Demobilization		Remarks
	Month and year	Place	Month and year	Place	From—	To—	Month and year	Place	
***C. D. of Manila and Subic Bays*—Continued**									
20th Company									See 20th Co. Ft. Mills.
21st Company									See 21st Co. Ft. Mills.
C. D. of Mobile									
1st Company									See 1st Co. Ft. Morgan.
2d Company									See 2d Co. Ft. Morgan.
3d Company									See 3d Co. Ft. Morgan.
4th (I) Company									See 4th Co. Ft. Morgan.
4th (II) Company	January 1918	Ft. Morgan, Ala.	September 1918 November 1918	Ft. Gaines, Ala. Ft. Morgan, Ala.			September 1919	Ft. Morgan, Ala.	
5th (I) Company	October 1917	do							Redes. Btry. B, 1st T.M. Bn. December 1917.
5th (II) Company	January 1918	do					December 1918	Ft. Morgan, Ala.	
6th Company	February 1918	do					do	Do.	
C. D. of Narragansett Bay									
1st Company									See Hq. Co. Ft. Adams.
2d Company									See Arty Engr. Co. Ft. Adams.

3d Company									See 3d Co. Ft. Adams.
4th (I) Company									See 4th Co. Ft. Greble.
4th (II) Company									See 1st Co. Ft. Adams.
5th (I) Company									See 5th Co. Ft. Adams.
5th (II) Company	September 1919	Ft. Greble, R. I.							Active through 1919.
6th (I) Company									See 1st Co. Ft. Adams.
6th (II) Company	September 1919	Ft. Greble, R. I.							Active through 1919.
7th Company									See 1st Co. Ft. Greble.
8th Company									See 3d Co. Ft. Greble.
9th (I) Company	August 1917	Ft. Adams, R. I.					December 1918	Ft. Adams, R. I.	Orgzd. fr. 1st Co. R. I. C.A. N.G.
9th (II) Company									See 26th (I) Co. Narragansett Bay.
10th (I) Company	August 1917	Ft. Wetherill, R. I.					December 1918	Ft. Wetherill, R. I.	Orgzd. fr. 3d Co. R. I. C.A. N.G.
10th (II) Company									See 27th (I) Co. Narragansett Bay.
11th (I) Company	August 1917	Ft. Wetherill, R. I.					December 1918	Ft. Wetherill, R. I.	Orgzd. fr. 11th Co. R. I. C.A. N.G.
11th (II) Company									See 28th (I) Co. Narragansett Bay.
12th Company	August 1917	Ft. Kearny, R. I.					December 1918	Ft. Kearny, R. I.	Orgzd. fr. 12th Co. R. I. C.A. N.G.
13th Company	do	Ft. Getty, R. I.					do	Ft. Getty, R. I.	Orgzd. fr. 4th Co. R. I. C.A. N.G.
14th Company	do	Ft. Kearny, R. I.	August 1917	Springfield Armory, Mass.					Orgzd. fr. 14th Co. R. I. C.A. N.G.
			March 1918	Ft. Getty, R. I.			December 1918	Ft. Getty, R. I.	

COAST DEFENSE COMMANDS—Continued

Unit designation and redesignation	Organization		Stations in United States		Overseas		Demobilization		Remarks
	Month and year	Place	Month and year	Place	From—	To—	Month and year	Place	
C. D. of Narragansett Bay—Continued									
15th Company	August 1917	Ft. Greble, R. I.	August 1917 June 1918	Springfield Armory, Mass. Ft. Greble, R. I.			December 1918	Ft. Greble, R. I.	Orgzd. fr. 15th Co. R. I. C.A. N.G.
16th Company	do	Ft. Wetherill, R. I.					do	Ft. Wetherill, R. I.	Orgzd. fr. 16th Co. R. I. C.A. N.G.
17th Company	do	Ft. Greble, R. I.					do	Ft. Greble, R. I.	Orgzd. fr. 17th Co. R. I. C.A. N.G.
18th Company	do	Ft. Wetherill, R. I.					do	Ft. Wetherill, R. I.	Orgzd. fr. 18th Co. R. I. C.A. N.G.
19th Company	do	Ft. Getty, R. I.					do	Ft. Getty, R. I.	Orgzd. fr. 5th Co. R. I. C.A. N.G.
20th Company	do	Ft. Greble, R. I.	August 1917 March 1918	Springfield Armory, Mass. Ft. Getty, R. I.			December 1918	Ft. Getty, R. I.	Orgzd. fr. 6th Co. R. I. C.A. N.G.
21st Company	do	Ft. Wetherill, R. I.					do	Ft. Wertherill, R. I	Orgzd. fr. 7th Co. R. I. C.A. N.G.
22d Company	August 1918	Ft. Greble, R. I.					do	Ft. Greble, R. I.	Orgzd. fr. 8th Co. R. I. C.A. N.G.
23d Company									See 26th (I) Co. Narragansett Bay.
24th Company									See 27th (I) Co. Narragansett Bay.
25th Company									See 28th (I) Co. Narragansett Bay.
26th (I) Company	December 1917	Ft. Adams, R. I.							
a. 23d Co. Narragansett Bay.	May 1918	do	December 1918	Ft. Wetherill, R. I.					

b. 9th (II) Co. Narragansett Bay.	July 1919	Ft. Wetherill, R. I.					September 1919	Ft. Wetherill, R. I.	
26th (II) Company									See 29th (I) Co. Narragansett Bay.
27th (I) Company	December 1917	Ft. Adams, R. I.							
a. 24th Co. Narragansett Bay.	May 1918	do	December 1918	Ft. Getty, R. I.					
b. 10th (II) Co. Narragansett Bay.	July 1919	Ft. Getty, R. I.					September 1919	Ft. Getty, R. I.	
27th (II) Company									See 30th Co. Narragansett Bay.
27th (III) Company	October 1918	Ft. Adams, R. I.					December 1918	Ft. Adams, R. I.	Officer candidate Co.
28th (I) Company	December 1917	Ft. Adams, R. I.							
a. 25th Co. Narragansett Bay.	May 1918	do	December 1918	Ft. Kearny, R. I.					
b. 11th (II) Co. Narragansett Bay.	July 1919	Ft. Kearny, R. I.					September 1919	Ft. Kearny, R. I.	
28th (II) Company									See 31st Co. Narragansett Bay.
29th (I) Company	December 1917	Ft. Greble, R. I.							
a. 26th (II) Co. Narragansett Bay.	May 1918	Ft. Adams, R. I.					December 1918	Ft. Adams, R. I.	
29th (II) Company									See 32d Co. Narragansett Bay.
30th Company	December 1917	Ft. Greble, R. I.							
a. 27th (II) Co. Narragansett Bay.	May 1918	do					July 1918	Ft. Greble, R. I.	
31st Company	December 1917	Ft. Getty, R. I.							
a. 28th (II) Co. Narragansett Bay.	May 1918	Ft. Adams, R. I.					do	Ft. Adams, R. I.	
32d Company	December 1917	Ft. Getty, R. I.							
a. 29th (II) Co. Narragansett Bay.	May 1918	Ft. Adams, R. I.					do	Do.	

COAST DEFENSE COMMANDS—Continued

Unit designation and redesignation	Organization		Stations in United States		Overseas		Demobilization		Remarks
	Month and year	Place	Month and year	Place	From—	To—	Month and year	Place	
C. D. of New Bedford									
1st Company									See 1st Co. Ft. Rodman.
2d Company									See 2d Co. Ft. Rodman.
3d Company	September 1917	Ft. Rodman, Mass.					December 1918	Ft. Rodman, Mass.	Orgzd. fr. 19th Co. R. I. C.A. N.G.
4th (Hq.) Company	June 1918	do					do	Do.	
5th (Arty. Engr.) Company.	October 1918	do					do	Do.	
C. D. of New Orleans									
1st Company									See 1st Co. Jackson Bks.
2d Company									See 2d Co. Jackson Bks.
3d Company									See 3d Co. Jackson Bks.
4th Company									See 4th Co. Jackson Bks.
5th Company									See 5th Co. Jackson Bks.
6th Company	January 1918	Ft. St. Philip, La.	April 1918	Jackson Bks., La.			December 1918	Jackson Bks., La.	Orgzd. fr. 301st Co. C.A. N.A.
7th Company	do	Cp. Nicholls, La.	March 1918	do			do	do	Orgzd. fr. 302d Co. C.A. N.A.
8th Company	do	do	February 1918	Ft. St. Philip, La.					Orgzd. fr. 303d Co. C.A. N.A.
			April 1918	Jackson Bks., La.			December 1918	Jackson Bks., La.	
9th Company	do	do	March 1918	Ft. St. Philip, La.					Orgzd. fr. 304th Co. C.A. N.A.
			June 1918	Cp. Nicholls, La.			December 1918	Cp. Nicholls, La.	

10th Company	do	do	March 1918	Ft. St. Philip, La.					Orgzd. fr. 305th Co. C.A. N.A.
11th Company	do	do	June 1918	Cp. Nicholls, La.			December 1918	Cp. Nicholls, La.	Orgzd. fr. 306th Co. C.A. N.A.
			March 1918	Jackson Bks., La.					
12th Company	do	do	April 1918	Ft. St. Philip, La.					Orgzd. fr. 307th Co. C.A. N.A.
			June 1918	Cp. Nicholls, La.			December 1918	Cp. Nicholls, La.	
			do	Ft. St. Philip, La.					
13th Company	do	do	August 1918	Cp. Nicholls, La.			December 1918	Cp. Nicholls, La.	Orgzd. fr. 308th Co. C.A. N.A.
			do	Ft. St. Philip, La.			do	Ft. St. Philip, La.	
14th Company	do	do					do	Cp. Nicholls, La.	Orgzd. fr. 309th Co. C.A. N.A.
15th Company	do	do	June 1918	Ft. St. Philip, La.					Orgzd. fr. 310th Co. C.A. N.A.
			August 1918	Jackson Bks., La.			December 1918	Jackson Bks., La.	
C. D. of Oahu									
1st Company									See 1st Co. Ft. Kamehameha.
2d Company									See 2d Co. Ft. Kamehameha.
3d Company									See 3d Co. Ft. Kamehameha.
4th Company									See 4th Co. Ft. Kamehameha.
5th Company									See 5th Co. Ft. Kamehameha.
6th Company									See 6th Co. Ft. Kamehameha.
7th Company									See Hq. Co. Ft. Kamehameha.
8th Company									See 1st Co. Ft. Armstrong.
9th Company									See 1st Co. Ft. De Russy.
10th Company									See 2d Co. Ft. De Russy.

COAST DEFENSE COMMANDS—Continued

Unit designation and redesignation	Organization		Stations in United States		Overseas		Demobilization		Remarks
	Month and year	Place	Month and year	Place	From—	To—	Month and year	Place	
C. D. of Oahu—Con.									
11th Company									See 1st Co. Ft. Ruger.
12th Company									See 2d Co. Ft. Ruger.
13th Company									See 3d Co. Ft. Ruger.
14th Company									See 4th Co. Ft. Ruger.
C. D. of Pensacola									
1st Company									See 1st Co. Ft. Pickens.
2d Company									See 2d Co. Ft. Barrancas.
3d Company									See 3d Co. Ft. Barrancas.
4th Company									See 4th Co. Ft. Barrancas.
5th Company									See 1st Co. Ft. Barrancas.
6th Company	September 1917	Ft. Barrancas, Fla	August 1918	Ft. McRee, Fla					Orgzd. fr. 3d Co. Fla. C.A. N.G.
			September 1918	Ft. Barrancas, Fla.					
			November 1918	Ft. McRee, Fla			December 1918	Ft. McRee, Fla.	
7th Company	March 1918	do					do	Ft. Barrancas, Fla	
8th Company	do	do					do	Do.	
9th Company	May 1918	do					do	Do.	
10th Company	June 1918	do					January 1919	Do.	
11th Company	do	do					December 1918	Do.	
12th Company	do	do					do	Do.	

13th Company	do	do					do	Do.	
14th Company	do	do					do	Do.	
15th Company	do	do					do	Do.	
16th Company	do	do					do	Do.	
17th Company	do	do					January 1919	Do.	
18th Company	do	Ft. Pickens, Fla.	July 1918	Ft. Barrancas, Fla.			December 1918	Do.	
19th Company	do	Ft. Barrancas, Fla.					do	Do.	
20th Company	do	do					January 1919	Do.	
C. D. of Portland									
1st (I) Company									See 5th Co. Ft. Williams.
1st (II) Company	April 1918	Ft. Williams, Me.							Active through 1919.
2d Company									See 6th Co. Ft. Williams.
3d Company									See 1st Co. Ft. Williams.
4th Company	April 1918	Ft. Williams, Me.							Active through 1919.
5th Company	do	do							Do.
6th Company	do	Ft. Preble, Me.							Do.
7th Company	do	do							Do.
8th (I) Company									See 2d Co. Ft. Preble.
8th (II) Company	March 1918	Ft. Preble, Me.							Active through 1919.
9th Company									See 1st Co. Ft. Levett.
10th Company	April 1918	Ft. McKinley, Me.							Active through 1919.
11th Company	do	do					September 1919	Ft. McKinley, Me.	
12th (I) Company									See 2d Co. Ft. McKinley.
12th (II) Company	March 1918	Ft. McKinley, Me.					September 1919	Ft. McKinley, Me.	
13th Company									See 3d Co. Ft. McKinley.
14th Company									See 4th Co. Ft. McKinley.
15th Company	April 1918	Ft. McKinley, Me.					September 1919	Ft. McKinley, Me.	

COAST DEFENSE COMMANDS—Continued

Unit designation and redesignation	Organization		Stations in United States		Overseas		Demobilization		Remarks
	Month and year	Place	Month and year	Place	From—	To—	Month and year	Place	
C. D. of Portland—Con.									
16th (I) Company									See 6th Co. Ft. McKinley.
16th (II) Company	March 1918	Ft. McKinley, Me.					September 1919	Ft. McKinley, Me.	
17th Company									See 7th Co. Ft. Williams.
18th (I) Company									See 8th Co. Ft. Williams.
18th (II) Company	March 1918	Ft. Williams, Me.					December 1918	Ft. Williams, Me.	
19th (I) Company									See 9th Co. Ft. Williams.
19th (II) Company	April 1918	Ft. Williams, Me.					December 1918	Ft. Williams, Me.	
20th (I) Company									See 3d Co. Ft Preble.
20th (II) Company	April 1918	Ft. Preble, Me.					December 1918	Ft. Preble, Me.	
21st Company									See 4th Co. Ft. Preble.
22d (I) Company									See 2d Co. Ft. Levett.
22d (II) Company	March 1918	Ft. Levett, Me.					December 1918	Ft. Levett, Me.	
23d Company									See 3d Co. Ft. Levett.
24th (I) Company									See 7th Co. Ft. McKinley.
24th (II) Company	March 1918	Ft. McKinley, Me.					December 1918	Ft. McKinley, Me.	
25th (I) Company									See 8th Co. Ft. McKinley.
25th (II) Company	April 1918	Ft. McKinley, Me.					December 1918	Ft. McKinley, Me.	
26th (I) Company									See 9th Co. Ft. McKinley.

26th (II) Company	April 1918	Ft. McKinley, Me.					December 1918	Ft. McKinley, Me.	
27th (I) Company									See 1st Co. Ft. Lyon.
27th (II) Company	April 1918	Ft. McKinley, Me.					December 1918	Ft. McKinley, Me.	
28th Company									See 10th (I) Co. Ft. McKinley.
29th (I) Company									See 1st Co. Ft. Baldwin.
29th (II) Company	April 1918	Ft. Levett, Me.					December 1918	Ft. Levett, Me.	
C. D. of Portsmouth									
1st Company									See Hq. Co. Portsmouth.
2d Company									See Arty. Engr. Co. Portsmouth.
3d Company									See 1st Co. Ft. Constitution.
4th Company									See 2d Co. Ft. Constitution.
5th Company									See 3d Co. Ft. Constitution.
6th Company									See 5th Co. Ft. Constitution.
7th Company									See 6th Co. Ft. Constitution.
8th Company									See 7th Co. Ft. Constitution.
9th Company									See 4th Co. Ft. Constitution.
10th Company	January 1918	Ft. Constitution, N. H.					September 1918	Ft. Constitution, N. H.	
Hq. Company	July 1917	Do.							
a. 1st Co. Portsmouth	August 1917	do							Active through 1919.
Arty. Engr. Company	July 1917	Do.							
a. 2d Co. Portsmouth.	August 1917	do							Do.

COAST DEFENSE COMMANDS—Continued

Unit designation and redesignation	Organization		Stations in United States		Overseas		Demobilization		Remarks
	Month and year	Place	Month and year	Place	From—	To—	Month and year	Place	
C. D. of The Potomac									
1st Company									See 1st Co. Ft. Hunt.
2d Company									See 2d Co. Ft. Hunt.
3d Company									See 1st Co. Ft. Washington.
4th (I) Company									See 3d (I) Co. Ft. Washington.
4th (II) Company	April 1918	Ft. Washington, Md.					December 1918	Ft. Washington. Md.	
4th (III) Company	January 1919	do					September 1919	Do.	
5th (I) Company	January 1918	do					December 1918	do	Orgzd. fr. 2d Co. D. C. C.A. N.G.
5th (II) Company	January 1919	do					September 1919	Do.	
6th (I) Company	April 1918	do					December 1918	do	Demblzd. October 1, 1918; reorgzd. October 19, 1918.
6th (II) Company	January 1919	do					September 1919	Do.	
7th Company	April 1918	do					December 1918	Do.	
8th Company	do	do							Active through 1919.
C. D. of Puget Sound									
1st Company									See 1st Co. Ft. Worden.
2d Company									See 2d Co. Ft Worden.
3d Company									See 3d Co. Ft. Worden.
4th Company									See 4th Co. Ft. Worden.
5th Company									See 5th Co. Ft. Worden.

6th Company									
7th Company									See 6th Co. Ft. Worden.
8th Company									See 7th Co. Ft. Worden.
9th Company									See 8th Co. Ft. Worden.
10th Company									See 1st Co. Ft. Casey.
11th Company									See 2d Co. Ft. Casey.
12th Company									See 3d Co. Ft. Casey.
13th Company									See 4th Co. Ft. Casey.
14th Company									See 1st Co. Ft. Flagler.
15th Company									See 2d Co. Ft. Flagler.
16th Company									See 3d Co. Ft. Flagler.
17th (I) Company	January 1918	Anaconda, Mont	January 1918 July 1918 October 1918	Ft. Worden, Wash Ft. Flagler, Wash Ft. Worden, Wash					See 1st Co. Ft. Ward.
17th (II) Company	March 1919	Ft. Worden, Wash					December 1918	Ft. Worden, Wash.	Orgzd. fr. 1st Co. Wash. C.A. N.G.
18th Company	January 1918	Ft. Casey, Wash					August 1919 January 1919	Do. Ft. Casey, Wash	Orgzd. fr. 2d Co. Wash. C.A. N.G.
19th Company	do	Great Falls, Mont	January 1918	Ft. Worden, Wash			December 1918	Ft. Worden, Wash	Orgzd. fr. 3d Co. Wash. C.A. N.G.
20th Company	do	Ft. Flagler, Wash					do	Ft. Flagler, Wash	Orgzd. fr. 4th Co. Wash. C.A. N.G.
21st Company	do	Ft. Worden, Wash					do	Ft. Worden, Wash	Orgzd. fr. 5th Co. Wash. C.A. N.G.
22d Company	do	Butte, Mont	January 1918 July 1918 October 1918	Ft. Worden, Wash Ft. Flagler, Wash. Ft. Worden, Wash					Orgzd. fr. 6th Co. Wash. C.A. N.G.
23d Company	do	do	January 1918 July 1918 November 1918	do Ft. Flagler, Wash. Ft. Worden, Wash			December 1918	Ft. Worden, Wash.	Orgzd. fr. 7th Co. Wash. C.A. N.G.
24th Company	do	Ft. Flagler, Wash					December 1918 do	Ft. Worden, Wash. Ft. Flagler, Wash	Orgzd. fr. 8th Co. Wash. C.A. N.G.

COAST DEFENSE COMMANDS—Continued

Unit designation and redesignation	Organization		Stations in United States		Overseas		Demobilization		Remarks
	Month and year	Place	Month and year	Place	From—	To—	Month and year	Place	
C. D. of Puget Sound—Continued									
25th Company	January 1918	Ft. Casey, Wash					December 1918	Ft. Casey, Wash	Orgzd. fr. 9th Co. Wash. C.A. N.G.
26th Company	do	Ft. Flagler, Wash	November 1918	Ft. Worden, Wash			do	Ft. Worden, Wash	Orgzd. fr. 10th Co. Wash. C.A. N.G.
27th Company	do	do					do	Ft. Flagler, Wash	Orgzd. fr. 11th Co. Wash. C.A. N.G.
28th Company	do	Ft. Casey, Wash					do	Ft. Casey, Wash	Orgzd. fr. 12th Co. Wash. C.A. N.G.
29th Company	April 1918	Ft. Casey, Wash					do	Do.	
30th Company	March 1918	Ft. Worden, Wash					do	Ft. Worden, Wash.	
31st Company	October 1918	Ft. Flagler, Wash					do	Ft. Flagler, Wash.	
32d Company	do	do					do	Do.	
33d Company	do	do					do	Do.	
34th Company	do	Ft. Casey, Wash					do	Ft. Casey, Wash.	
35th Company	do	do					do	Do.	
36th Company	do	do					do	Do.	
37th Company	do	do					do	Do.	
38th Company	do	do					do	Do.	
39th Company	do	do					do	Do.	
40th Company	do	Ft. Worden, Wash					do	Ft. Worden, Wash.	
41st Company	do	do					do	Do.	
C. D. of San Diego									
1st Company									See 1st Co. Ft. Rosecrans.
2d (I) Company									See 2d Co. Ft. Rosecrans.
2d (II) Company									See 4th Co. Ft. Rosecrans.

3d Company									See 3d Co. Ft. Rosecrans.
4th (I) Company									See 4th Co. Ft. Rosecrans.
4th (II) Company	January 1918	Ft. Rosecrans, Calif.							Redes. Btry. A, 25th Regt., C.A.C. October 1918.
5th (I) Company	August 1917	Ft. Rosecrans, Calif.					January 1918	Ft. Rosecrans, Calif.	Orgzd. fr. 5th Co. Calif. C.A. N.G.
5th (II) Company	February 1918	do					October 1918	do	Orgzd. fr. 15th Co. Calif. C.A. N.G.
6th (I) Company	August 1917	do							Orgzd. fr. 8th Co. Calif. C.A. N.G. Redes. Btry. B, 65th Regt., C.A.C. January 1918.
6th (II) Company	January 1918	do							Orgzd. fr. 18th Co. Calif. C.A. N.G. Redes. Btry. E, 25th Regt., C.A.C. October 1918.
7th Company	September 1917	do							Orgzd. fr. 13th Co. Calif. C.A. N.G. Redes. Btry. B, 25th Regt., C.A.C. October 1918.
8th Company	do	do							Orgzd. fr. 14th Co. Calif. C.A. N.G. Redes. Btry. F, 25th Regt., C.A.C. October 1918.
9th Company	April 1918	do							Redes. Co. A, 54th Am. Tn. May 1918.
10th Company	do	do							Redes. Co. B, 54th Am. Tn. May 1918.

COAST DEFENSE COMMANDS—Continued

Unit designation and redesignation	Organization		Stations in United States		Overseas		Demobilization		Remarks
	Month and year	Place	Month and year	Place	From—	To—	Month and year	Place	
C. D. of San Diego—Continued									
11th Company	April 1918	**Ft. Rosecrans, Calif.**							Redes. Co. C, **54th** Am. Tn. **May** 1918.
12th Company	do	do							Redes. Co. D, **54th** Am. Tn. **May** 1918.
13th Company	August 1918	do					August 1918	Ft. Rosecrans, Calif.	
C. D. of San Francisco									
1st Company									See 1st Co. Ft. Winfield Scott.
2d Company									See 2d Co. Ft. Winfield Scott.
3d Company									See 3d Co. Ft. Winfield Scott.
4th Company									See 4th (II) Co. Ft. Winfield Scott.
5th (I) Company									See 5th Co. Ft. Winfield Scott.
5th (II) Company									See 46th (I) Co. San Francisco.
6th Company									See 6th Co. Ft. Winfield Scott.
7th (I) Company									See 7th Co. Ft. Winfield Scott.
7th (II) Company									See 45th (I) Co. San Francisco.

8th Company									See 8th Co. Ft. Winfield Scott.
9th Company									See 9th Co. Ft. Winfield Scott
10th (I) Company									See 10th Co. Ft. Winfield Scott
10th (II) Company									See 44th (I) Co. San Francisco.
11th (I) Company									See 2d Co. Ft. Baker.
11th (II) Company									See 43d Co. San Francisco.
12th Company									See 3d Co. Ft. Baker.
13th Company									See 4th Co. Ft. Baker.
14th (I) Company									See 1st Co. Ft. Baker.
14th (II) Company	January 1918	Ft. Barry, Calif							Redes. Btry. E, 67th Regt., C.A.C. May 1918.
14th (III) Company									See 47th Co. San Francisco.
15th Company									See 1st Co. Ft. Barry.
16th Company									See 2d Co. Ft. Barry.
17th Company									See 3d Co. Ft. Barry.
18th Company									See 1st Co. Ft. Miley.
19th Company									See 2d Co. Ft. Miley.
20th Company									See 3d Co. Ft. Miley.
21st Company	August 1917	Ft. Winfield Scott, Calif.	October 1917 January 1918	Benicia Arsenal Calif. Ft. Winfield Scott, Calif.			March 1918	Ft. Winfield Scott, Calif.	Orgzd. fr. 1st Co. Calif. C.A. N.G.

COAST DEFENSE COMMANDS—Continued

Unit designation and redesignation	Organization		Stations in United States		Overseas		Demobilization		Remarks
	Month and year	Place	Month and year	Place	From—	To—	Month and year	Place	
C. D. of San Francisco—Continued									
22d Company	August 1917	Ft. Winfield Scott, Calif.	October 1917	West Berkeley, Calif.					Orgzd. fr. 2d Co. Calif. C.A. N.G.
			February 1918	Ft. Winfield Scott, Calif.			March 1918	Ft. Winfield Scott, Calif.	
23d Company	do	do					April 1918	do	Orgzd. fr. 3d Co. Calif. C.A. N.G.
24th Company	do	do					do	do	Orgzd. fr. 4th Co. Calif. C.A. N.G.
25th Company	do	do	October 1917	Garfield, Utah					Orgzd. fr. 11th Co. Calif. C.A. N.G.
			February 1918	Ft. Winfield Scott, Calif.			March 1918	Ft. Winfield Scott, Calif.	
26th Company	do	do							Orgzd. fr. 6th Co. Calif. C.A. N.G. Redes. Btry. B, 67th Regt., C.A.C. May 1918.
27th Company	do	do					September 1919	Ft. Winfield Scott, Calif.	Orgzd. fr. 7th Co. Calif. C.A. N.G. Redes. Btry. D, 18th Regt., C.A.C. October 1918; reverted to former designation December 1918.

28th Company	do	do							Orgzd. fr. 12th Co. Calif. C.A. N.G. Redes. Btry. D, 67th Regt., C.A.C. May 1918.
29th Company	do	do							Orgzd. fr. 9th Co. Calif. C.A. N.G. Redes. Btry. F, 40th Regt., C.A.C. September 1918.
30th Company	do	do							Orgzd. fr. 10th Co. Calif. C.A. N.G. Redes. Sup. Co. 67th Regt., C.A.C. May 1918.
31st Company	December 1917	Presidio of San Francisco, Calif.	January 1918	Ft. Winfield Scott, Calif.			May 1918	Ft. Winfield Scott, Calif.	
32d Company	do	do	do	do					
33d Company	do	do	do	Do.			do	Do.	
34th Company	do	do	April 1918 January 1918	Ft. Funston, Calif. Ft. Winfield Scott, Calif.			do March 1918	Ft. Funston, Calif. Ft. Winfield Scott, Calif.	
35th Company	do	do	do	do			do	Do.	
36th Company	do	do	do	do			do	Presidio of San Francisco, Calif.	
37th Company	do	do	do	do			do	Ft. Winfield Scott, Calif.	
38th Company	do	do	do	do					
39th Company	do	do	do	do			do	Do.	
40th Company	do	do	do	do			do	Do.	
41st Company	do	do	do	do			do	Do.	
42d Company	do	do	do	do			do	Do.	
43d (I) Company	do	Do.					do	Do.	
a. 11th (II) Co. San Francisco.	January 1918	Ft. Winfield Scott, Calif.	February 1918	Ft. Baker, Calif.					Active through 1919.
43d (II) Company	March 1918	do					January 1919	Ft. Winfield Scott, Calif.	

COAST DEFENSE COMMANDS—Continued

Unit designation and redesignation	Organization		Stations in United States		Overseas		Demobilization		Remarks
	Month and year	Place	Month and year	Place	From—	To—	Month and year	Place	
C. D. of San Francisco—Continued									
44th (I) Company	December 1917	Presidio of San Francisco, Calif.							
a. 10th (II) Co. San Francisco.	January 1918	Ft. Winfield Scott, Calif.	February 1918	Ft. Barry, Calif					Active through 1919.
44th (II) Company	April 1918	do					April 1919	Ft. Winfield Scott, Calif.	
45th (I) Company	December 1917	Presidio of San Francisco, Calif.							
a. 7th (II) Co. San Francisco.	January 1918	Ft. Winfield Scott, Calif.							Redes. Btry. 'C 67th Regt., C.A.C. May 1918.
45th (II) Company	April 1918	do	July 1918	Ft. Baker, Calif			September 1919	Ft. Baker, Calif	Redes. Btry. F, 18th Regt., C.A.C. October 1918; reverted to former designation December 1918.
46th (I) Company	December 1917	Presidio of San Francisco, Calif.							
a. 5th (II) Co. San Francisco.	January 1918	Ft. Winfield Scott, Calif.					do	Ft. Winfield Scott, Calif.	
46th (II) Company	April 1918	do					do	Do.	
47th Company	June 1918	Do.							
a. 14th (III) Co. San Francisco.	April 1919	do	April 1919	Ft. Barry, Calif.					
			December 1919	Ft. Winfield Scott, Calif.					
48th Company	July 1918	do					January 1919	Do.	
49th Company	do	do	November 1918	Ft. Miley, Calif			do	Ft. Miley, Calif.	

50th Company	do	do	do	Ft. Barry, Calif			do	Ft. Barry, Calif.	
51st Company	do	do					do	Ft. Winfield Scott, Calif.	
52d Company	do	do					December 1918	Do.	
53d Company	August 1918	do					do	Do.	
54th to 56th Companies									Never orgzd.
57th Company	August 1918	Ft. Winfield Scott, Calif.					September 1918	Ft. Winfield Scott, Calif.	
58th Company	do	do					do	Do.	
59th Company	do	do					do	Do.	
60th Company	September 1918	do					December 1918	do	Formerly Enlisted Specialists' Preparatory School.
C. D. of Sandy Hook									
1st Company									See 1st Co. Ft. Hancock.
2d Company									See 2d Co. Ft. Hancock.
3d Company									See 3d Co. Ft. Hancock.
4th Company									See 4th Co. Ft. Hancock.
5th Company									See 5th Co. Ft. Hancock.
6th Company									See 6th Co. Ft. Hancock.
7th Company									See 7th Co. Ft. Hancock.
8th Company	April 1918	Ft. Hancock, N. J.					December 1918	Ft. Hancock, N. J.	
9th Company	do	do					do	Do.	
10th Company	do	do					do	Do.	
11th Company	do	do					do	Do.	
12th Company	do	do					do	Do.	
13th Company	January 1918	Jersey City, N. J	April 1918	Ft. Hancock, N. J			do	do	Orgzd. fr. 13th Co. N. Y. C.A. N.G.
14th Company	do	Picatinny Arsenal, N. J.	March 1918	do			do	do	Orgzd. fr. 14th Co. N. Y. C.A. N.G.
15th Company	do	Tuckahoe, N. J	do	do			do	do	Orgzd. fr. 15th Co. N. Y. C.A. N.G.

COAST DEFENSE COMMANDS—Continued

Unit designation and redesignation	Organization		Stations in United States		Overseas		Demobilization		Remarks
	Month and year	Place	Month and year	Place	From—	To—	Month and year	Place	
C. D. of Sandy Hook—Continued									
16th Company	January 1918	Picatinny Arsenal, N. J.	March 1918	Ft. Hancock, N. J.			December 1918	Ft. Hancock, N. J.	Orgzd. fr. 16th Co. N. Y. C.A. N.G.
17th Company	do	Ft. Hancock, N.J.					do	do	Orgzd. fr. 17th Co. N. Y. C.A. N.G.
18th Company	do	do					do	do	Orgzd. fr. 18th Co. N. Y. C.A. N.G.
19th Company	do	do					do	do	Orgzd. fr. 19th Co. N. Y. C.A. N.G.
20th Company	do	do					do	do	Orgzd. fr. 20th Co. N. Y. C.A. N.G.
21st Company	do	do					do	do	Orgzd. fr. 21st Co. N. Y. C.A. N.G.
22d Company	do	do					do	do	Orgzd. fr. 22d Co. N. Y. C.A. N.G.
23d Company	do	do					do	do	Orgzd. fr. 23d Co. N. Y. C.A. N.G.
24th Company	do	do					do	do	Orgzd. fr. 24th Co. N. Y. C.A. N.G.
C. D. of Savannah									
1st Company									See 1st Co. Ft. Screven.
2d (I) Company									See 1st Co. Ft. Fremont.
2d (II) Company	December 1918	Ft. Screven, Ga							Active through 1919.
3d (I) Company									See 3d Co. Ft. Screven.
3d (II) Company	February 1918	Ft. Screven, Ga					September 1918	Ft. Screven, Ga.	

3d (III) Company									See 13th Co. Savannah.
3d (IV) Company	January 1919	Ft. Screven, Ga					September 1919	Ft. Screven, Ga.	
4th (I) Company									See 4th (II) Co. Ft. Screven.
4th (II) Company									See 8th (I) Co. Savannah.
4th (III) Company	March 1918	Ft. Screven, Ga					November 1918	Ft. Screven, Ga.	
5th (I) Company	August 1917	do					December 1917	do	Orgzd. fr. 1st Co. Ga. C.A. N.G.
5th (II) Company	April 1918	do					November 1918	Do.	
6th (I) Company	August 1917	do					December 1917	do	Orgzd. fr. 2d Co. Ga. C.A. N.G.
6th (II) Company	April 1918	do					November 1918	Do.	
7th (I) Company	August 1917	do					December 1917	do	Orgzd. fr. 3d Co. Ga. C.A. N.G.
7th (II) Company	April 1918	do					September 1918	Do.	
7th (III) Company									See 14th Co. Savannah.
8th (I) Company	August 1917	Ft. Screven, Ga							Orgzd. fr. 4th Co. Ga. C.A. N.G.
a. 4th (II) Co. Savannah.	November 1917	do					December 1917	Ft. Screven, Ga.	
8th (II) Company	April 1918	do					September 1918	Do.	
9th Company	June 1918	do					do	Do.	
10th Company	July 1918	do					do	Do.	
11th Company	do	do					do	Do.	
12th Company	do	do					do	Do.	
13th Company	August 1918	Ft. Fremont, S.C.							
a. 3d (III) Co. Savannah.	September 1918	do					November 1918	Ft. Fremont, S. C.	
14th Company	August 1918	Mayport, Fla.							
a. 7th (III) Co. Savannah.	September 1918	do					do	Mayport, Fla.	

COAST DEFENSE COMMANDS—Continued

Unit designation and redesignation	Organization		Stations in United States		Overseas		Demobilization		Remarks
	Month and year	Place	Month and year	Place	From—	To—	Month and year	Place	
C. D. of Southern New York									
1st (I) Company									See 1st Co. Ft. Hamilton.
1st (II) Company									See 33d Co. South ern N. Y.
1st (III) Company									See 43d Co. Southern N. Y.
2d (I) Company									See 2d Co. Ft. Hamilton.
2d (II) Company									See 34th Co. Southern N. Y.
3d Company									See 5th Co. Ft. Hamilton.
4th (I) Company									See 7th Co. Ft. Hamilton.
4th (II) Company									See 35th Co. Southern N. Y.
4th (III) Company									See 30th Co. Southern N. Y.
5th Company									See 1st Co. Ft. Wadsworth.
6th Company									See 2d Co. Ft. Wadsworth.
7th Company									See 4th Co. Ft. Wadsworth.
8th Company									See 5th Co. Ft. Wadsworth.
9th Company									See 1st Co. Rockaway Beach.
10th Company									See 2d Co. Rockaway Beach.

11th Company									See 36th Co. Southern N. Y.
12th Company									See 37th Co. Southern N. Y.
13th Company									See 38th Co. Southern N. Y.
14th Company									See 39th Co. Southern N. Y.
15th (I) Company									See 40th Co. Southern N. Y.
15th (II) Company									See 44th Co. Southern N. Y.
16th Company									See 41st Co. Southern N. Y.
17th Company	January 1918	Ft. Wadsworth, N. Y.					December 1918	Ft. Wadsworth, N. Y.	Orgzd. fr. 2d Co. N. Y. C.A. N.G.
18th Company									See 42d Co. Southern N. Y.
19th Company									See 43d Co. Southern N. Y.
20th Company	January 1918	Ft. Hamilton, N. Y.					December 1918	Ft. Hamilton, N. Y.	Orgzd. fr. 5th Co. N. Y. C.A. N.G.
21st Company									See 44th Co. Southern N. Y.
22d Company	January 1918	Ft. Hamilton, N. Y.					December 1918	Ft. Hamilton, N. Y.	Orgzd. fr. 7th Co. N. Y. C.A. N.G.
23d Company	do	do					do	do	Orgzd. fr. 8th Co. N. Y. C.A. N.G.
24th Company	do	do	March 1918	Ft. Tilden, N. Y.			do	Ft. Tilden, N. Y.	Orgzd. fr. 9th Co. N. Y. C.A. N.G.
25th Company	do	Iona Island, N. Y.	February 1918	Ft. Hamilton, N. Y.					Orgzd. fr. 10th Co. N. Y. C.A. N.G.
			April 1918	Ft. Tilden, N. Y.			December 1918	Ft. Tilden, N. Y.	
26th Company	do	Ft. Hamilton, N. Y.					do	Ft. Hamilton, N. Y.	Orgzd. fr. 11th Co. N. Y. C.A. N.G.
27th Company									See 45th Co. Southern N. Y.
28th Company	January 1918	Ft. Wadsworth, N. Y.					December 1918	Ft. Wadsworth, N. Y.	Orgzd. fr. 26th Co. N. Y. C.A. N.G

COAST DEFENSE COMMANDS—Continued

Unit designation and redesignation	Organization		Stations in United States		Overseas		Demobilization		Remarks
	Month and year	Place	Month and year	Place	From—	To—	Month and year	Place	
C. D. of Southern New York—Continued									
29th Company	January 1918	Ft. Wadsworth, N. Y.					December 1918	Ft. Wadsworth, N. Y.	Orgzd. fr. 30th Co. N. Y. C.A. N.G.
30th Company	do	Constable Hook, Bayonne, N. J.	March 1918	Ft. Wadsworth, N. Y.					Orgzd. fr. 33d Co. N. Y. C.A. N.G.
			April 1918	Ft. Hamilton, N. Y.					Demblzd. December 1918; reorgzd. January 1919.
	January 1919	Ft. Hamilton, N. Y.							
a. 4th (III) Co. Southern New York.	February 1919	do							Active through 1919
31st Company	January 1918	Ft. Wadsworth, N. Y.					December 1918	Ft. Wadsworth, N. Y.	Orgzd. fr. 35th Co. N. Y. C.A. N.G.
32d Company	do	do					do	Do.	
33d Company	do	Do.							
a. 1st (II) Co. Southern New York.	March 1918	do					do	Do.	
34th Company	January 1918	Do.							
a. 2d (II) Co. Southern New York.	March 1918	do					do	do	Demblzd. December 1918; reorgzd. January 1919.
	January 1919	do	September 1919	Ft. Hamilton, N. Y.					
35th Company	January 1918	Do.							
a. 4th (II) Co. Southern New York.	March 1918	do					do	Do.	
36th Company	January 1918	Ft. Hamilton, N.Y.							
a. 11th Co. Southern New York.	March 1918	do					September 1919	Ft. Hamilton, N. Y.	
37th Company	January 1918	Do.							
a. 12th Co. Southern New York.	March 1918	do					December 1918	do	Demblzd. December 1918; reorgzd. January 1919.
	January 1919	do					September 1919	Do	

38th Company	January 1918	Constable Hook, Bayonne, N. J.	March 1918	Ft. Hamilton, N. Y.					
a. 13th Co. Southern New York.	March 1918	Ft. Hamilton, N.Y.					December 1918	do	Demblzd. December 1918; reorgzd. January 1919.
	January 1919	do					September 1919	Do.	
39th Company	January 1918	Iona Island, N. Y.	February 1918	Ft. Hamilton, N.Y.					
a. 14th Co. Southern New York.	March 1918	Ft. Hamilton, N.Y.					December 1918	do	Demblzd. December 1918; reorgzd. January 1919.
	January 1919	do					September 1919	Do.	
40th Company	January 1918	Do.							
a. 15th (I) Co. Southern New York.	March 1918	do					December 1918	Do.	
41st Company	January 1918	Tomkinsville, Staten Island, N. Y.	March 1918	Ft. Hamilton, N.Y.					
a. 16th Co. Southern New York.	March 1918	do					do	Do.	
42d Company	January 1918	Ft. Hamilton, N.Y.							
a. 18th Co. Southern New York.	March 1918	do					do	Do.	
43d Company	January 1918	Do.							
a. 19th Co. Southern New York.	March 1918	Do.							
b. 1st (III) Co. Southern New York.	February 1919	do							Active through 1919.
44th Company	January 1918	Ft. Tilden, N. Y.							
a. 21st Co. Southern New York.	March 1918	Do.							
b. 15th (II) Co. Southern New York.	February 1919	do					September 1919	Ft. Tilden, N. Y.	
45th Company	January 1918	Do.							
a. 27th Co. Southern New York.	March 1918	do					December 1918	Do.	

COAST DEFENSE COMMANDS—Continued

Unit designation and redesignation	Organization		Stations in United States		Overseas		Demobilization		Remarks
	Month and year	Place	Month and year	Place	From—	To—	Month and year	Place	
C. D. of Tampa									
1st Company									See 1st Co. Ft. Dade.
2d Company									See 2d Co. Ft. Dade.
3dCompany									See 3d Co. Ft. Dade.
4th Company	August 1917	St. Petersburg, Fla.	September 1917	Ft. Dade, Fla.			December 1918	Ft. Dade, Fla.	Orgzd. fr. 2d Co. Fla. C.A. N.G.
5th Company	February 1918	Ft. Dade, Fla.					do	Do.	
6th Company	do	do					do	Do.	

COAST DEFENSE COMPANIES [1]
(As Constituted During 1916 and first half of 1917)

Unit designation and redesignation	Organization		Stations in United States		Overseas		Demobilization		Remarks
	Month and year	Place	Month and year	Place	From—	To—	Month and year	Place	
1st Co. Ft. Adams	Orgzd. 1901		April 1917	Ft. Adams, R. I.					Orgzd. fr. 97th Co C.A.C.
a. 6th (I) Co. Narragansett Bay.	August 1917	Ft. Adams, R. I.							
b. 4th (II) Co. Narragansett Bay.	September 1919	do							Active through 1919.
2d Co. Ft. Adams	Orgzd. 1901		April 1917	Ft. Adams, R. I.					Orgzd. fr. 117th Co. C.A.C. Redes. Btry. K, 7th Prov. Regt., C.A.C., July 1917.
3d Co. Ft. Adams	Orgzd. 1907		do	do					Orgzd. fr. 129th Co. C.A.C.
a. 3d Co. Narragansett Bay.	August 1917	Ft. Adams, R. I.							Active through 1919.

4th Co. Ft. Adams	Orgzd. 1907		April 1917	Ft. Adams, R. I						Orgzd. fr. 130th Co.C.A.C.Redes. Btry. I, 7th Prov. Regt., C.A.C., July 1917.
5th Co. Ft. Adams	Orgzd. 1901		do	do						Orgzd. fr. 102d Co., C.A.C.
a. 5th (I) Co. Narragansett Bay.	August 1917	Ft. Adams, R. I						September 1919	Ft. Adams, R. I.	
Hq. Co. Ft. Adams	July 1917	Do.								
a. 1st Co. Narragansett Bay.	August 1917	do								**Active through 1919.**
Arty. Engr. Co. Ft. Adams.	July 1917	Do.								
a. 2d Co. Narragansett Bay.	August 1917	do								Do.
1st Co. Ft. Andrews	Orgzd. 1899		April 1917	Ft. Andrews, Mass.						Orgzd. fr. 59th Co., C.A.C.
a. Hq. Co. NE Dept.	July 1917	South Armory, Boston, Mass.								
b. 2d Co. Boston	August 1917	do	June 1918	Ft. Banks, Mass						Special Duty as Hq. Co. NE Dept. Active through 1919.
2d Co. Ft. Andrews	Orgzd. 1907		April 1917	Ft. Andrews, Mass.						Orgzd. fr. 151st Co. C.A.C. Redes. Btry. I, 6th Prov. Regt., C.A.C., July 1917.
3d Co. Ft. Andrews	do		do	do						Orgzd. fr. 153d Co. C.A.C. Redes. Btry. L, 6th Prov. Regt., C.A.C., July 1917.
4th Co. Ft. Andrews	Orgzd. 1916		do	do						Redes. Btry. M, 6th Prov. Regt., C. A.C., July 1917.

[1] **Arranged according to their stations in alphabetical order. Prior to 1916, numerical designation of coast defense companies was in a single series. Thereafter they were numbered serially within separate garrisons. Beginning in July 1917, serial and separate numbering of companies was applied to coast defense commands.**

COAST DEFENSE COMPANIES—Continued

Unit designation and redesignation	Organization		Stations in United States		Overseas		Demobilization		Remarks
	Month and year	Place	Month and year	Place	From—	To—	Month and year	Place	
5th Co. Ft. Andrews	July 1917	Ft. Andrews, Mass.							
a. 6th Co. Boston	August 1917	do	December 1917	Ft. Banks, Mass.					
			November 1918	Ft. Andrews, Mass.					Active through 1919.
1st Co. Ft. Armstrong	Organized 1901		April 1917	Ft. Armstrong, T.H.					Orgzd. fr. 104th Co., C.A.C.
a. 8th Co. Oahu	August 1917	Ft. Armstrong, T.H.							Active through 1919.
1st Co. Ft. Baker	Organized 1901		April 1917	Ft. Baker, Calif.					Orgzd. fr. 148th Co., C.A.C.
			do	Ft. Barry, Calif.					
a. 14th (I) Co. San Francisco.	August 1917	Ft. Barry, Calif.	November 1917	Ft. Winfield Scott, Calif.					Redes. Btry. D, 1st A.A. Bn. November 1917.
2d Co. Ft. Baker	Organized 1898		April 1917	Cp. John H. Beacon, Calexico, Calif.					Orgzd. fr. 61st Co., C.A.C.
			July 1917	Ft. Baker, Calif.					Redes. Btry. C, 1st A.A. Bn. November 1917.
a. 11th (I) Co. San Francisco.	August 1917	Ft. Baker, Calif.							
3d Co. Ft. Baker	Organized 1838		April 1917	do					Orgzd. fr. 32d Co., C.A.C.
a. 12th Co. San Francisco.	August 1917	Ft. Baker, Calif.	September 1919	Ft. Winfield Scott, Calif.					Redes. Btry. A, 18th Arty., C.A.C., October 1918; reverted to previous designation December 1918. Active through 1919.

4th (Hq.) Co. Ft. Baker	February 1917		April 1917	Ft. Baker, Calif.					
a. 13th Co. San Francisco.	August 1917	Ft. Baker, Calif.							Redes. Btry. A, 67th Arty., C.A.C. May 1918.
1st Co. Ft. Baldwin	August 1917	Ft. Baldwin, Maine							Orgzd. fr. 4th Co. Maine C.A. N.G.
a. 29th (I) Co. Portland.	do	do							Redes. Btry. D, 54th Arty., C.A.C. December 1917.
1st Co. Ft. Banks	Orgzd. 1813		April 1917	Ft. Banks, Mass					Orgzd. fr. 7th Co., C.A.C. Redes. Btry. K, 6th Prov. Regt., C.A.C., July 1917.
2d Co. Ft. Banks	Orgzd. 1916		do	do					Orgzd. fr. 152d Co., C.A.C. Redes. Hq. Co. 55th Regt. C.A.C., December 1917.
a. 13th (I) Co. Boston	August 1917	Ft. Banks, Mass.							
1st Co. Ft. Barrancas	Orgzd. 1847		April 1917	Ft. Barrancas, Fla.					Orgzd. fr. 22d Co., C.A.C.
a. 5th Co. Pensacola	August 1917	Ft. Barrancas, Fla.	October 1917 January 1919	Ft. Pickens, Fla. Ft. Barrancas, Fla.					Active through 1919
2d Co. Ft. Barrancas	Orgzd. 1838		April 1917	Ft. Barrancas, Fla.					Orgzd. fr. 20th Co. C.A.C.
a. 2d Co. Pensacola	August 1917	Ft. Pickens, Fla.	August 1917 October 1917 January 1918 July 1918 August 1918 September 1918	Ft. Pickens, Fla. Ft. Barrancas, Fla. Ft. McRee, Fla. Ft. Barrancas, Fla. Ft. McRee, Fla. Ft. Barrancas, Fla.					Active through 1919.
3d Co. Ft. Barrancas	Orgzd. 1898		April 1917	do					Orgzd. fr. 77th Co., C.A.C.
a. 3d Co. Pensacola	August 1917	Ft. Barrancas, Fla.					November 1919	Ft. Barrancas, Fla.	

COAST DEFENSE COMPANIES—Continued

Unit designation and redesignation	Organization		Stations in United States		Overseas		Demobilization		Remarks
	Month and year	Place	Month and year	Place	From—	To—	Month and year	Place	
4th Co. Ft. Barrancas	June 1917	**Ft. Barrancas, Fla.**							
a. 4th Co. Pensacola	August 1917	do	November 1917 September 1918 December 1918 July 1919	Ft. Pickens, Fla. Ft. Barrancas, Fla. Ft. Pickens, Fla. Ft. Barrancas, Fla.			November 1919	Ft. Barrancas, Fla.	
1st Co. Ft. Barry	Orgzd. 1898		April 1917	Ft. Barry, Calif					Orgzd. fr. 66th Co. C.A.C. Redes. Btry. D, 40th Regt., C.A.C. September 1918; reverted to previous designation December 1918. Active through 1919.
a. 15th Co. San Francisco.	August 1917	Ft. Barry, Calif	September 1919	Ft. Winfield Scott, Calif.					
2d Co. Ft. Barry	Organized 1907		April 1917	Ft. Barry, Calif					Orgzd. fr. 161st Co., C.A.C.
a. 16th Co. San Francisco.	August 1917	Ft. Barry, Calif	September 1919	Ft. Winfield Scott, Calif.					Redes. Btry, B, 18th Regt., C.A.C., October 1918; reverted to previous designation December 1918. Active through 1919.
3d (Hq.) Co. Ft. Barry	February 1917		April 1917	Ft. Barry, Calif.					
a. 17th Co. San Francisco.	August 1917	Ft. Barry, Calif	December 1917	Ft. Baker, Calif					Redes. Btry. F, 67th Regt., C.A.C., May 1918.

1st Co. Ft. Casey	Organized 1899		April 1917	Ft. Casey, Wash.					Orgzd. fr. 71st Co., C.A.C.
a. 9th Co. Puget Sound.	August 1917	Ft. Casey, Wash.	October 1917	Seattle, Wash.					
			January 1918	Ft. Casey, Wash.					Active through 1919.
2d Co. Ft. Casey	Organized 1901		April 1917	Ft. Casey, Wash.					Orgzd. fr. 85th Co., C.A.C.
a. 10th Co. Puget Sound.	August 1917	Cp. Lewis, Wash.	August 1917	Cp. Lewis, Wash.					
			October 1917	Ft. Casey, Wash.					Active through 1919.
3d Co. Ft. Casey	Organized 1907		April 1917	do					Orgzd. fr. 149th Co., C.A.C.
a. 11th Co. Puget Sound.	August 1917	Ft. Casey, Wash.							Active through 1919.
4th Co. Ft. Casey	July 1917	Do.							
a. 12th Co. Puget Sound.	August 1917	do					September 1919	Ft. Casey, Wash.	
1st Co. Ft. Caswell	Organized 1812		April 1917	Ft. Caswell, N. C.					Orgzd. fr. 19th Co., C.A.C.
a. 1st Co. Cape Fear.	August 1917	Ft. Caswell, N. C.							Active through 1919.
2d Co. Ft. Caswell	Organized 1812		April 1917	Ft. Caswell, N. C.					Orgzd. fr. 31st Co., C.A.C. Redes. Btry. L, 8th Prov. Regt., C.A.C. July 1917.
3d Co. Ft. Caswell	June 1917	Ft. Caswell, N. C.							
a. 2d Co. Cape Fear.	August 1917	do							Active through 1919.
1st Co. Ft. Columbia	May 1917	Ft. Stevens, Oreg.	May 1917	Ft. Columbia, Wash.					
a. 4th Co. Columbia.	August 1917	Ft. Columbia, Wash.							Active through 1919.

COAST DEFENSE COMPANIES—Continued

Unit designation and redesignation	Organization		Stations in United States		Overseas		Demobilization		Remarks
	Month and year	Place	Month and year	Place	From—	To—	Month and year	Place	
1st Co. Ft. Constitution	Organized 1907		April 1917	Ft. Constitution, N. H.					Orgzd. fr. 156th Co., C.A.C.
a. 3d Co. Portsmouth.	August 1917	Ft. Constitution, N. H.					September 1919	Ft. Constitution, N. H.	
2d Co. Ft. Constitution	June 1917	do	June 1917	Ft. Foster, Maine.					
a. 4th Co. Portsmouth.	August 1917	Ft. Foster, Maine	November 1917	Ft. Stark, N. H.					
			January 1918	Ft. Constitution, N. H.			do	Do.	
3d Co. Ft. Constitution	June 1917	Ft. Constitution, N. H.							
a. 5th Co. Portsmouth.	August 1917	do	September 1917	Ft. Stark, N. H			December 1918	Ft. Stark, N. H.	
4th Co. Ft. Constitution.	June 1917	do	August 1917	Cp. Devens, Mass					Orgzd. fr. 1st. Co. N.H. C.A. N.G.
a. 9th Co. Portsmouth.	August 1917	Cp. Devens, Mass.	October 1917	Springfield, Mass.					
			July 1918	Ft. Constitution, N. H.			December 1918	Ft. Constitution, N. H.	
5th Co. Ft. Constitution	do	Ft. Stark, N. H							Orgzd. fr. 2d Co., N.H. C.A. N.G.
a. 6th Co. Portsmouth.	do	do	September 1917	Cp. Devens, Mass.					
			October 1917	Springfield, Mass.					
			May 1918	Ft. Constitution, N. H.			December 1918	Ft. Constitution, N. H.	
6th Co. Ft. Constitution	do	Ft. Constitution, N. H.							Orgzd. fr. 3d Co., N.H. C.A. N.G.
a. 7th Co. Portsmouth.	do	do					December 1918	Ft. Constitution, N. H.	
7th Co. Ft. Constitution	do	do							Orgzd. fr. 4th Co. N.H. C.A. N.G.
a. 8th Co. Portsmouth.	do	do	November 1917	Ft. Foster, Maine.					
			October 1918	Ft. Constitution, N. H.			December 1918	Ft. Constitution, N. H.	

1st Co. Ft. Crockett	Organized 1907		April 1917	Ft. San Jacinto, Tex.					Orgzd. fr. 128th Co., C.A.C.
a. 1st Co. Galveston.	August 1917	Ft. San Jacinto, Tex.	February 1918	Ft. Crockett, Tex					Active through 1919.
2d Co. Ft. Crockett	Organized 1907		April 1917	Ft. Crockett, Tex					Orgzd. fr. 127th Co., C.A.C.
			do	Ft. San Jacinto, Tex.					
a. 2d Co. Galveston.	August 1917	Ft. San Jacinto, Tex.	February 1918	Ft. Crockett, Tex					Active through 1919.
3d Co. Ft. Crockett	June 1917	Ft. San Jacinto, Tex.							
a. 3d Co. Galveston.	August 1917	Ft. San Jacinto, Tex.	July 1918	Ft. Crockett, Tex					Do.
1st Co. Ft. Dade	Organized 1907		April 1917	Ft. Dade, Fla					Orgzd. fr. 162d Co., C.A.C.
a. 1st Co. Tampa	August 1917	Ft. Dade, Fla							Active through 1919.
2d Co. Ft. Dade	Organized 1916		April 1917	Ft. Dade, Fla.					
a. 2d Co. Tampa	August 1917	Ft. Dade, Fla							Do.
3d Co. Ft. Dade	June 1917	Ft. Dade, Fla.							
a. 3d Co. Tampa	August 1917	do					October 1919	Ft. Dade, Fla.	
1st Co. Ft. De Lesseps	June 1917	Ft. De Lesseps, C. Z.							
a. 6th Co. Cristobal	August 1917	do							Active through 1919.
1st Co. Ft. De Russy	Organized 1847		April 1917	Ft. De Russy, T. H.					Orgzd. fr. 10th Co., C.A.C.
a. 9th Co. Oahu	August 1917	Ft. De Russy, T. H.							Active through 1919.
2d Co. Ft. De Russy	Organized 1861		April 1917	Ft. De Russy, T. H.					Orgzd. fr. 55th Co., C.A.C.
a. 10th Co. Oahu	August 1917	Ft. De Russy, T. H.	June 1918 October 1918	Ft. Armstrong, T.H. Ft. De Russy, T. H.					Active through 1919.

COAST DEFENSE COMPANIES—Continued

Unit designation and redesignation	Organization		Stations in United States		Overseas		Demobilization		Remarks
	Month and year	Place	Month and year	Place	From—	To—	Month and year	Place	
1st Co. Ft. Du Pont	Organized 1916		April 1917 June 1917	Ft. Mott, N. J. Ft. Du Pont, Del.					
a. 1st Co. Delaware	August 1917	Ft. Du Pont, Del.	January 1918 March 1918 December 1919	Pigeon Point, Del. Ft. Du Pont, Del. Ft. Mott, N. J.					
2d Co. Ft. Du Pont	Organized 1907		April 1917	Ft. Du Pont, Del.					Orgzd. fr. 139th Co., C.A.C.
a. 2d Co. Delaware	August 1917	Ft. Du Pont, Del.							Active through 1919.
3d Co. Ft. Du Pont	Organized 1916		April 1917	Ft. Delaware, Del.					
a. 3d (I) Co. Delaware.	August 1917	Ft. Delaware, Del.					December 1918	Ft. Delaware, Del.	
4th Co. Ft. Du Pont	Organized 1901		April 1917	Ft. Du Pont, Del.					Orgzd. fr. 112th Co., C.A.C.
a. 4th (I) Co. Delaware.	August 1917	Ft. Du Pont, Del.							Redes. Btry. A, 60th Regt., C.A.C., January 1918.
5th Co. Ft. Du Pont	June 1917	Ft. Delaware, Del.							Redes. 1st T.M. Btry. June 1917.
6th Co. Ft. Du Pont	do	Ft. Du Pont, Del.							
a. 6th Co. Delaware.	August 1917	do					October 1919	Ft. Du Pont, Del.	
1st Co. Ft. Flagler	Organized 1794		April 1917	Ft. Flagler, Wash.					Orgzd. fr. 26th Co., C.A.C.
a. 13th Co. Puget Sound.	August 1917	Cp. Lewis, Wash.	September 1917	do					Active through 1919.
2d Co. Ft. Flagler	Organized 1901		April 1917	do					Orgzd. fr. 92d Co., C.A.C.
a. 14th Co. Puget Sound.	August 1917	Ft. Flagler, Wash.							Active through 1919.

3d Co. Ft. Flagler	Organized 1901		April 1917	Ft. Lawton, Wash.					Orgzd. fr. 94th Co., C.A.C.
a. 15th Co. Puget Sound.	August 1917	Ft. Lawton, Wash.	March 1918	Ft. Flagler, Wash.			September 1919	Ft. Flagler, Wash.	
1st Co. Ft. Fremont	April 1917	Ft. Fremont, S. C.	June 1917	Ft. Screven, Ga.					
a. Hq. Co. Ft. Screven.	June 1917	Ft. Screven, Ga.							
b. 2d (III) Co. Ft. Screven.	July 1917	do					November 1918	Ft. Screven, Ga.	
c. 2d (I) Co. Savannah.	August 1917	Ft. Screven, Ga.					November 1918	Fr. Screven, Ga.	
1st Co. Ft. Grant	Organized 1898		April 1917	Ft. Grant, C. Z.					Orgzd. fr. 81st Co., C.A.C.
a. 1st Co. Balboa	August 1917	Ft. Grant, C. Z.	October 1917	Ft. Amador, C. Z.					Active through 1919.
2d Co. Ft. Grant	Organized 1901		April 1917	Ft. Grant, C. Z.					Orgzd. fr. 87th Co., C.A.C.
a. 2d Co. Balboa	August 1917	Ft. Grant, C. Z.	October 1917	Ft. Amador, C. Z.					Active through 1919.
3d Co. Ft. Grant	Organized 1847		April 1917	Ft. Grant, C. Z.					Orgzd. fr. 45th Co., C.A.C.
a. 3d Co. Balboa	August 1917	Ft. Grant, C. Z.	October 1917	Ft. Amador, C. Z.					Active through 1919.
4th Co. Ft. Grant	Organized 1901		April 1917	Ft. Grant, C. Z.					Orgzd. fr. 116th Co., C.A.C.
a. 4th Co. Balboa	August 1917	Ft. Grant, C. Z.	do June 1917 October 1917	Ft. De Lesseps, C. Z. Ft. Grant, C. Z. Ft. Amador, C. Z.					Active through 1919.
5th Co. Ft. Grant	Organized 1812		April 1917	Ft. Grant, C. Z.					Orgzd. fr. 40th Co., C.A.C.
a. 5th Co. Balboa	August 1917	Ft. Grant, C. Z.	October 1917	Ft. Amador, C. Z.					Active through 1919.
6th Co. Ft. Grant	Organized 1898		April 1917	Ft. Grant, C. Z.					Orgzd. fr. 73d Co. C.A.C.
a. 6th Co. Balboa	August 1917	Ft. Grant, C. Z.	October 1917 October 1918 November 1918	Ft. Amador, C. Z. Ft. Grant, C. Z. Ft. Amador, C. Z.					Active through 1919.

COAST DEFENSE COMPANIES—Continued

Unit designation and redesignation	Organization		Stations in United States		Overseas		Demobilization		Remarks
	Month and year	Place	Month and year	Place	From—	To—	Month and year	Place	
7th Co. Ft. Grant	June 1917	Ft. Grant, C. Z.							
a. 7th Co. Balboa	August 1917	do							Active through 1919.
8th Co. Ft. Grant	Organized 1907		April 1917	Ft. Grant, C. Z.					Orgzd. fr. 144th Co., C.A.C.
a. 8th Co. Balboa	August 1917	Ft. Grant, C. Z.	October 1917	Ft. Amador, C. Z.					Active through 1919.
9th Co. Ft. Grant	Organized 1798		April 1917	Ft. Grant, C. Z.					Orgzd. fr. 8th Co., C.A.C.
a. 9th Co. Balboa	August 1917	Ft. Grant, C. Z.	October 1917	Ft. Amador, C. Z.					Active through 1919.
10th Co. Ft. Grant	June 1917	Do.							
a. 10th Co. Balboa	August 1917	do	do	do					Do.
11th Co. Ft. Grant	June 1917	Do.							
a. 11th Co. Balboa	August 1917	do	do	Do.					
b. 11th Co. Cristobal.	September 1919	Ft. Sherman, C. Z.							Do.
1st Co. Ft. Greble	Organized 1810		April 1917	Ft. Greble, R. I.					Orgzd. fr. 14th Co., C.A.C.
a. 7th Co. Narragansett Bay.	August 1917	Ft. Greble, R. I.					September 1919	Ft. Greble, R. I.	
2d Co. Ft. Greble	Organized 1901		April 1917	Ft. Greble, R. I.					Orgzd. fr. 109th Co., C.A.C. Redes. Btry. B, 6th Prov. Regt., C.A.C. July 1917.
3d Co. Ft. Greble	Organized 1901		April 1917	Ft. Greble, R. I.					Orgzd. fr. 110th Co., C.A.C.
a. 8th Co. Narragansett Bay.	August 1917	Ft. Greble, R. I.					September 1919	Ft. Greble, R. I.	

4th Co. Ft. Greble	July 1917	Do.							
a. 4th (I) Co. Narragansett Bay.	August 1917	do					do	Do.	
1st Co. Ft. Hamilton	Organized 1916		April 1917	Ft. Hamilton, N. Y.					
a. 1st (I) Co. Southern New York.	August 1917	Ft. Hamilton, N. Y.							Redes. Hq. Co., 59th Regt., C.A.C., January 1918.
2d Co. Ft. Hamilton	Organized 1808		April 1917	Ft. Hamilton, N. Y.					Orgzd. fr. 3d Co., C.A.C.
a. 2d (I) Co. Southern New York.	August 1917	Ft. Hamilton, N. Y.							Redes. Btry. C, 59th Regt., C.A.C., January 1918.
3d Co. Ft. Hamilton	Organized 1901		April 1917	Ft. Hamilton, N. Y.					Orgzd. fr. 84th Co., C.A.C. Redes. Btry. F, 8th Prov. Regt., C.A.C. July 1917.
4th (I) Co. Ft. Hamilton	Organized 1916		do	Rockaway Beach, N. Y.			June 1917	Rockaway Beach, N. Y.	
4th (II) Co. Ft. Hamilton.	June 1917	Ft. Hamilton, N. Y.							Redes. Btry. M, 7th Prov. Regt., C.A.C. July 1917.
5th Co. Ft. Hamilton	Organized 1901		April 1917	Ft. Hamilton, N. Y.					Orgzd. fr. 123d Co., C.A.C.
a. 3d Co. Southern New York.	August 1917	Ft. Hamilton, N. Y.							
6th Co. Ft. Hamilton	Organized 1901		do	do					Orgzd. fr. 122d Co., C.A.C. Redes Btry. L, 7th Prov. Regt., C. A. C. July 1917.
7th Co. Ft. Hamilton	June 1917	Ft. Hamilton, N. Y.							
a. 4th (I) Co. Southern New York.	August 1917	do							Redes. Btry. A, 59th Regt., C.A.C. January 1918.

COAST DEFENSE COMPANIES—Continued

Unit designation and redesignation	Organization		Stations in United States		Overseas		Demobilization		Remarks
	Month and year	Place	Month and year	Place	From—	To—	Month and year	Place	
1st Co. Ft. Hancock	Organized 1899		April 1917	Ft. Hancock, N. J.					Orgzd. fr. 48th Co., C.A.C.
a. 1st Co. Sandy Hook.	August 1917	Ft. Hancock, N. J.							
2d Co. Ft. Hancock	Organized 1898		do	do					Orgzd. fr. 76th Co., C.A.C.
a. 2d Co. Sandy Hook.	August 1917	Ft. Hancock, N. J.							
3d Co. Ft. Hancock	Organized 1901		do	do					Orgzd. fr. 113th Co., C.A.C.
a. 3d Co. Sandy Hook.	August 1917	Ft. Hancock, N. J.							
4th Co. Ft. Hancock	Organized 1907		do	do					Orgzd. fr. 136th Co., C.A.C.
a. 4th Co. Sandy Hook.	August 1917	Ft. Hancock, N. J.							
5th Co. Ft. Hancock	Organized 1907		do	do					Orgzd. fr. 137th Co., C.A.C.
a. 5th Co. Sandy Hook.	August 1917	Ft. Hancock, N. J.							**Active through 1919.**
6th Co. Ft. Hancock	Organized 1861		April 1917	Ft. Hancock, N. J.					Orgzd. fr. 56th Co., C.A.C.
a. 6th Co. Sandy Hook.	August 1917	Ft. Hancock, N. J.							**Active through 1919.**
7th Co. Ft. Hancock	June 1917	Do.							Do.
a. 7th Co. Sandy Hook.	August 1917	do							
1st Co. Ft. Howard	Organized 1907		April 1917	Ft. Howard, Md.					Orgzd. fr. 140th Co., C.A.C.
a. 1st (I) Co. Baltimore.	August 1917	Ft. Howard, Md.					December 1918	Ft. Howard, Md.	Demblzd. December 1918; reorgzd. January 1919.
	January 1919	do					September 1919	Do.	

2d Co. Ft. Howard	Organized 1901		April 1917	Ft. Howard, Md.					Orgzd. fr. 103d Co., C.A.C.
a. 2d (I) Co. Baltimore.	August 1917	Ft. Howard, Md.					December 1918	Ft. Howard, Md.	
3d Co. Ft. Howard	Organized 1916		April 1917	Ft. Howard, Md.					
a. **3d Co. Baltimore**	August 1917	Ft. Howard, Md.	July 1918	Ft. Smallwood, Md.					
			September 1918	Aberdeen Proving Ground, Md.			do	do	Demblzd. December 1918; reorgzd. January 1919.
	January 1919	do					September 1919	Do.	
4th Co. Ft. Howard	Organized 1916		April 1917	Fisherman's Island, Va.					
			July 1917	Ft. Howard, Md.					
a. **4th Co. Baltimore**	**August 1917**	**Ft. Howard, Md.**					do	**Do.**	
1st Co. Ft. Hunt	Organized 1899		April 1917	Ft. Hunt, Va.					Orgzd. fr. 47th Co., C.A.C.
a. 1st Co. Potomac	September 1917	Ft. Hunt, Va.	September 1919	Ft. Washington, Md.					Active through 1919.
2d Co. Ft. Hunt	June 1917	Do.							
a. 2d Co. Potomac	September 1917	do							Demblzd. October 1, 1918; reorgzd. October 19, 1918.
	October 1918	do	December 1918	Ft. Washington, Md.					**Active through 1919.**
1st Co. Jackson Barracks	Organized 1907		April 1917	Jackson Bks., La.					Orgzd. fr. 164th Co., C.A.C.
a. 1st Co. New Orleans.	August 1917	Jackson Bks., La.	December 1917	Ft. St. Philip, La.					
			March 1918	Cp. Nicholls, La.					
			December 1918	Jackson Bks., La.					
			April 1919	Ft. St. Philip, La.					
			October 1919	Jackson Bks., La.					**Active through 1919.**
2d Co. Jackson Barracks	Organized 1916		April 1917	Ft. St. Philip, La.					
			May 1917	Jackson Bks., La.					
a. 2d Co. New Orleans.	August 1917	Ft. St. Philip, La.	November 1917	Do.					
			August 1918	Ft. St. Philip, La.					
			January 1919	Jackson Bks., La.					Do.

COAST DEFENSE COMPANIES—Continued

Unit designation and redesignation	Organization		Stations in United States		Overseas		Demobilization		Remarks
	Month and year	Place	Month and year	Place	From—	To—	Month and year	Place	
3d Co. Jackson Barracks	June 1917	Jackson Bks., La.							
a. 3d Co. New Orleans.	August 1917	do	November 1917 February 1918 December 1918	Ft. St. Philip, La. Cp. Nicholls, La. Jackson Bks., La.			October 1919	Jackson Bks., La.	
4th Co. Jackson Barracks	June 1917	Do.							
a. 4th Co. New Orleans.	August 1917	Ft. St. Philip, La.	November 1917 January 1919 April 1919 August 1919	Jackson Bks., La. Ft. St. Philip, La. Jackson Bks., La. Ft. St. Philip, La.			do	Ft. St. Philip, La.	
5th Co. Jackson Barracks	May 1917	Jackson Bks., La.							Redes. fr. Hq. Det. Jackson Bks., July 1917.
a. 5th Co. New Orleans.	August 1917	do					December 1918	Jackson Bks., La.	
1st Co. Ft. Kamehameha	Organized 1898		April 1917	Ft. Kamehameha, T. H.					Orgzd. fr. 68th Co., C.A.C.
a. 1st Co. Oahu	August 1917	Ft. Kamehameha, T. H.	January 1918 February 1918	Pearl Harbor Naval Station, T. H. Ft. Kamehameha, T. H.					Active through 1919.
2d Co. Ft. Kamehameha	Organized 1898		April 1917	do					Orgzd. fr. 75th Co., C.A.C.
a. 2d Co. Oahu	August 1917	Ft. Kamehameha, T. H.							Active through 1919.
3d Co. Ft. Kamehameha	Organized 1901		April 1917	Ft. Kamehameha, T. H.					Orgzd. fr. 91st Co., C.A.C.
a. 3d Co. Oahu	August 1917	Ft. Kamehameha, T. H.	January 1918 February 1918	Pearl Harbor Naval Station, T. H. Ft. Kamehameha, T. H.					Active through 1919.

4th Co. Ft. Kamehameha	Organized 1901		April 1917	do					Orgzd. fr. 125th Co., C.A.C.
a. 4th Co. Oahu	August 1917	Ft. Kamehameha, T. H.	February 1918	Ft. Armstrong, T. H.					
			June 1918	Ft. Kamehameha, T. H.					
			January 1919	Ft. Armstrong, T. H.					
			April 1919	Ft. Kamehameha, T. H.					Active through 1919.
5th Co. Ft. Kamehameha	Organized 1907		April 1917	do					Orgzd. fr. 143d Co., C.A.C.
a. 5th Co. Oahu	August 1917	Ft. Kamehameha, T. H.	January 1918	Pearl Harbor Naval Station, T. H.					
			February 1918	Ft. Kamehameha, T. H.					Active through 1919.
6th Co. Ft. Kamehameha	July 1917	Do.							
a. 6th Co. Oahu	August 1917	do	December 1917	Ft. Armstrong T. H.					
			do	Ft. Kamehameha, T. H.					
			June 1918	Ft. Armstrong, T. H.					
			October 1918	Ft. Kamehameha, T. H.					
			January 1919	Ft. Armstrong, T. H.					
			March 1919	Ft. Kamehameha, T. H.					
			June 1919	Ft. Armstrong, T. H.					
			July 1919	Ft. Kamehameha, T. H.					Do.
Hq. Co. Ft. Kamehameha	July 1917	Ft. Kamehameha, T. H.							
a. 7th Co. Oahu	August 1917	do							Do.
1st Co. Key West Barracks.	Organized 1898		April 1917	Key West Bks., Fla.					Orgzd. fr. 80th Co., C.A.C.
a. 1st Co. Key West	August 1917	Key West Bks., Fla.							Active through 1919.
2d Co. Key West Barracks.	July 1917	Do.							
a. 2d Co. Key West	August 1917	do							Active through 1919.

COAST DEFENSE COMPANIES—Continued

Unit designation and redesignation	Organization		Stations in United States		Overseas		Demobilization		Remarks
	Month and year	Place	Month and year	Place	From—	To—	Month and year	Place	
1st Co. Ft. Levett	Organized 1861		April 1917	Ft. Levett, Maine					Orgzd. fr. 50th Co. C.A.C.
a. 9th Co. Portland	August 1917	Ft. Levett, Maine							Active through 1919.
2d Co. Ft. Levett	July 1917	do							Orgzd. fr. 2d Co. Maine C.A. N.G.
a. 22d (I) Co. Portland.	August 1917	do							Redes. Btry. D, 54th Regt., C.A.C. December 1917.
3d Co. Ft. Levett	July 1917	do	August 1917	Cp. Devens, Mass.					Orgzd. fr. 6th Co. Maine C.A. N.G.
a. 23d Co. Portland	August 1917	Cp. Devens, Mass.	October 1917	Watertown Arsenal, Mass.					
			March 1918	Ft. Williams, Maine			December 1918	Ft. Levett, Maine.	
1st Co. Ft. Lyon	July 1917	Ft. McKinley, Me.							Orgzd. fr. 13th Co. Maine C.A.N.G.
a. 10th (II) Co. Ft. McKinley.	August 1917	do	August 1917	Cp. Devens, Mass.					
b. 27th (I) Co. Portland.	do	Cp. Devens, Mass.	October 1917	Ft. McKinley, Me.					Redes. Btry. E, 54th Regt., C.A.C. December 1917.
1st Co. Ft. MacArthur									See 4th (I) Co. Ft. Winfield Scott.
2d Co. Ft. MacArthur	July 1917	Ft. MacArthur, Calif.							
a. 2d (I) Co. Los Angeles.	August 1917	do							Redes. Hq. and Sup. Co. 2d A.A. Bn. January 1918.
3d Co. Ft. MacArthur	July 1917	Do.							
a. 3d (I) Co. Los Angeles.	August 1917	do					February 1918	Ft. MacArthur, Calif.	

4th Co. Ft. MacArthur	July 1917	Do.							
a. 4th (I) Co. Los Angeles.	August 1917	do							Redes. Btry. C, 2d A.A. Bn. January 1918.
1st Co. Ft. McKinley	Organized 1808		April 1917	Ft. McKinley, Me.					Orgzd. fr. 1st Co., C.A.C. Redes. Btry. A, 6th Prov. Regt., C.A.C. July 1917.
2d Co. Ft. McKinley	Organized 1861		do	do					Orgzd. fr. 51st Co., C.A.C.
a. 12th (I) Co. Portland.	August 1917	Ft. McKinley, Me.							Redes. Btry. C, 54th Regt., C.A.C. December 1917.
3d Co. Ft. McKinley	Organized 1815		April 1917	Ft. Baldwin, Maine					Orgzd. fr. 37th Co., C.A.C.
a. 13th Co. Portland	August 1917	Ft. Baldwin, Me.	February 1919	Ft. McKinley, Me.			August 1919	Ft. McKinley, Me.	
4th Co. Ft. McKinley	Organized 1907		April 1917	do					Orgzd. fr. 154th Co., C.A.C.
a. 14th Co. Portland	August 1917	Ft. McKinley, Me.					August 1919	Ft. McKinley, Me.	
5th Co. Ft. McKinley	April 1917	do							Redes. Btry. D, 6th Prov. Regt., C.A. C. July 1917.
6th Co. Ft. McKinley	do	Do.							
a. 16th (I) Co. Portland.	August 1917	do							Redes. Btry. C, 54th Regt., C.A.C. December 1917.
7th Co. Ft. McKinley	July 1917	do							Orgzd. fr. 3d Co. Maine C.A. N.G.
a. 24th (I) Co. Portland.	August 1917	do							Redes. Btry. E, 54th Regt., C.A.C. December 1917.
8th Co. Ft. McKinley	July 1917	do							Orgzd. fr. 9th Co. Maine C.A. N.G.
a. 25th (I) Co. Portland.	August 1917	do							Redes. Btry. F, 54th Regt., C.A.C. December 1917.

COAST DEFENSE COMPANIES—Continued

Unit designation and redesignation	Organization		Stations in United States		Overseas		Demobilization		Remarks
	Month and year	Place	Month and year	Place	From—	To—	Month and year	Place	
9th Co. Ft. McKinley	July 1917	Ft. McKinley, Me.							Orgzd. fr. 11th Co. Maine C.A. N.G.
a. 26th (I) Co. Portland.	August 1917	do							Redes. Btry. F, 54th Regt., C.A.C. December 1917.
10th (I) Co. Ft. McKinley.	July 1917	do							Orgzd. fr. 12th Co. Maine C.A. N.G.
a. 28th Co. Portland	August 1917	do	November 1917 November 1918	Ft. Lyon, Me. Ft. McKinley, Me.			December 1918	Ft. McKinley, Me.	
10th (II) Co. Ft. McKinley.									See 1st Co. Ft. Lyon.
1st Co. Ft. Michie	Organized 1898		April 1917	Ft. Michie, N. Y.					Orgzd. fr. 79th Co., C.A.C.
a. 23d Co. Long Island Sound.	August 1917	Ft. Michie, N. Y.							
b. 18th Co. Long Island Sound.	April 1918	Do.							
c. 15th (II) Co. Long Island Sound.	December 1918	do	September 1919	Ft. Terry, N. Y.			October 1919	Ft. Terry, N. Y.	
1st Co. Ft. Miley	Organized 1812		April 1917	Ft. Miley, Calif.					Orgzd. fr. 13th Co., C.A.C.
a. 18th Co. San Francisco.	August 1917	Ft. Miley, Calif.							Redes. Btry. E, 40th Regt., C.A.C. September 1918; reverted to original designation December 1918. Active through 1919.

[c]Co. Ft. Miley	Organized 1812		April 1917	Ft. Miley, Calif					Orgzd. fr. 25th Co., C.A.C.
a. 19th Co. San Francisco.	August 1917	Ft. Miley, Calif	September 1919	Ft. Winfield Scott, Calif.					Redes. Btry. C, 18th Regt., C.A.C. October 1918; reverted to original designation December 1918.
			December 1919	Ft. Barry, Calif.					
3d (Hq.) Co. Ft. Miley	February 1917		April 1917	Ft. Miley, Calif.					
a. 20th Co. San Francisco.	August 1917	Ft. Miley, Calif	December 1917	Ft. Winfield Scott, Calif.					
			February 1918	Ft. Miley, Calif			September 1919	Ft. Miley, Calif.	
1st Co. Ft. Mills	Organized 1907		April 1917	Ft. Mills, P. I					Orgzd. fr. 138th Co., C.A.C.
a. 1st Co. Manila Bay.	September 1917	Ft. Mills, P. I	December 1919	Ft. Drum, P. I.					
2d Co. Ft. Mills	Organized 1901		April 1917	Ft. Hughes, P. I					Orgzd. fr. 95th Co., C.A.C.
			August 1917	Ft. Mills, P. I.					
a. 2d Co. Manila Bay.	September 1917	Ft. Mills, P. I					November 1917	Ft. Mills, P. I	Demblzd. November 1917; reorgzd. June 1918.
	June 1918	Ft. Mills, P. I	June 1918	Ft. Drum, P. I.					
			November 1918	Ft. Mills, P. I.					
			August 1919	Ft. Drum, P. I.					
			December 1919	Ft. Mills, P. I.					
3d Co. Ft. Mills	Organized 1907		April 1917	Ft. Mills, P. I					Orgzd. fr. 142d Co., C.A.C.
a. 3d Co. Manila Bay.	September 1917	Ft. Mills, P. I							Active through 1919.
4th Co. Ft. Mills	Organized 1798		April 1917	Ft. Wint, P. I					Orgzd. fr. 17th Co., C.A.C.
			May 1917	Ft. Mills, P. I.					
a. 4th Co. Manila Bay.	September 1917	Ft. Mills, P. I							Active through 1919.
5th Co. Ft. Mills	Organized 1899		April 1917	Ft. Mills, P. I					Orgzd. fr. 36th Co. C.A.C.
			August 1917	Ft. Wint, P. I.					
a. 5th Co. Manila Bay.	September 1917	Ft. Wint, P. I	November 1917	Ft. Mills, P. I.					
			May 1918	Ft. Wint, P. I.					
			August 1918	Ft. Mills, P. I					Active through 1919.

COAST DEFENSE COMPANIES—Continued

Unit designation and redesignation	Organization		Stations in United States		Overseas		Demobilization		Remarks
	Month and year	Place	Month and year	Place	From—	To—	Month and year	Place	
6th Co. Ft. Mills	Organized 1901		April 1917	Ft. Mills, P. I.					Orgzd. fr. 86th Co., C.A.C.
a. 6th Co. Manila Bay.	September 1917	Ft. Mills, P. I.	November 1918 February 1918 August 1918 November 1918 August 1919	Ft. Wint, P. I. Ft. Mills, P. I. Ft. Wint, P. I. Ft. Mills, P. I. Ft. Wint, P. I.					Active through 1919.
7th Co. Ft. Mills	Organized 1899		April 1917	Ft. Mills, P. I.					Orgzd. fr. 70th Co., C.A.C.
a. 7th Co. Manila Bay.	September 1917	Ft. Mills, P. I.	February 1918 May 1918 November 1918 April 1919	Ft. Wint, P. I. Ft. Mills, P. I. Ft. Wint, P. I. Ft. Mills, P. I.					Active through 1919.
8th Co. Ft. Mills	Organized 1901		April 1917	do					Orgzd. fr. 90th Co., C.A.C.
a. 8th Co. Manila Bay.	September 1917	Ft. Mills, P. I.	May 1919 August 1919	Ft. Wint, P. I. Ft. Mills, P. I.					Active through 1919.
9th Co. Ft. Mills	Organized 1899		April 1917	do					Orgzd. fr. 11th Co., C.A.C.
a. 9th Co. Manila Bay.	September 1917	Ft. Mills, P. I.	April 1918 July 1918 November 1918 April 1919 August 1919	Ft. Hughes, P. I. Ft. Mills, P. I. Ft. Hughes, P. I. Ft. Mills, P. I. Ft. Hughes, P. I.					Active through 1919.

10th Co. Ft. Mills	Organized 1899		April 1917	Ft. Mills, P. I.					Orgzd. fr. 23d Co., C.A.C.
a. 10 th Co. Manila Bay.	September 1917	Ft. Mills, P. I.	July 1918	Ft. Hughes, P. I.					
			November 1918	Ft. Mills, P. I.					
			August 1919	Ft. Frank, P. I.					**Active through 1919.**
11th Co. Ft. Mills	Organized 1821		April 1917	Ft. Mills, P. I.					Orgzd. fr. 42d Co., C.A.C.
a. 11th Co. Manila Bay.	September 1917	Ft. Mills, P. I.	April 1919	Ft. Hughes, P. I.					
			August 1919	Ft. Mills, P. I.					**Active through 1919.**
12th Co. Ft. Mills	Organized 1798		April 1917	Ft. Mills, P. I.					Orgzd. fr. 18th Co., C.A.C.
a. 12th Co. Manila Bay.	September 1917	Ft. Mills, P. I.					November 1917	Ft. Mills, P. I.	
13th Co. Ft. Mills	Organized 1815		April 1917	Ft. Mills, P. I.					Orgzd. fr. 4th Co., C.A.C.
			May 1917	Ft. Wint, P. I.					
a. 13th Co. Manila Bay.	September 1917	Ft. Mills, P. I.					November 1917	Ft. Mills, P. I.	
14th Co. Ft. Mills	Organized 1847		April 1917	Ft. Frank, P. I.					Orgzd. fr. 33d Co., C.A.C.
a. 14th Co. Manila Bay.	September 1917	Ft. Mills, P. I.	May 1917	Ft. Mills, P. I.					
			November 1917	Ft. Frank, P. I.					
			February 1918	Ft. Mills, P. I.					
			June 1919	Ft. Frank, P. I.					
			August 1919	Ft. Mills, P. I.					**Active through 1919.**
15th Co. Ft. Mills	Organized 1901		April 1917	do.					Orgzd. fr. 11th Co., C.A.C.
a. 15th Co. Manila Bay.	September 1917	Ft. Mills, P. I.							**Active through 1919.**
16th Co. Ft. Mills	Organized 1901		April 1917	Ft. Mills, P. I.					Orgzd. fr. 99th Co., C.A.C.
a. 16th Co. Manila Bay.	September 1917	Ft. Mills, P. I.							**Active through 1919.**

COAST DEFENSE COMPANIES—Continued

Unit designation and redesignation	Organization		Stations in United States		Overseas		Demobilization		Remarks
	Month and year	Place	Month and year	Place	From—	To—	Month and year	Place	
17th (I) Co. Ft. Mills	Organized 1916		April 1917	Ft. Mills, P. I.			June 1917	Ft. Mills, P. I.	Orgzd. fr. Fort Command Co. Ft. Mills.
17th (II) Co. Ft. Mills	July 1917	Ft. Mills, P. I.	August 1917	Ft. Hughes, P. I.					
a. 17th Co. Manila Bay.	September 1917	Ft. Hughes, P. I.	January 1918	Ft. Mills, P. I.					Demblzd. April 1918; reorgzd. July 1918.
	July 1918	Ft. Mills, P. I.							**Active through 1919.**
18th Co. Ft. Mills	July 1917	do	August 1917	Ft. Hughes, P. I.					
a. 18th Co. Manila Bay.	September 1917	Ft. Hughes, P. I.	January 1918	Ft. Mills, P. I.					
			September 1918	Ft. Drum, P. I.					
			February 1919	Ft. Mills, P. I.					
			July 1919	Ft. Drum, P. I.					
			September 1919	Ft. Mills, P. I.					Do.
19th Co. Ft. Mills	July 1917	Ft. Mills, P. I.	July 1917	Ft. Frank, P. I.					
a. 19th Co. Manila Bay.	September 1917	Ft. Frank, P. I.	November 1917	Ft. Mills, P. I.					
			February 1918	Ft. Frank, P. I.					
			May 1918	Ft. Mills, P. I.					
			September 1919	Ft. Drum, P. I.					Do.
20th Co. Ft. Mills	July 1917	Ft. Mills, P. I.	August 1917	Ft. Frank, P. I.					
a. 20th Co. Manila Bay.	September 1917	Ft. Frank, P. I.	November 1917	Ft. Mills, P. I.					Do.
21st Co. Ft. Mills	July 1917	Ft. Mills, P. I.					November 1917	Ft. Mills, P. I.	
a. 21st Co. Manila Bay.	September 1917	do							
1st Co. Ft. Monroe	Organized 1899		April 1917	Ft. Monroe, Va					Orgzd. fr. 35th Co., C.A.C.
a. 1st Co. Chesapeake Bay.	August 1917	Ft. Monroe, Va							**Active through 1919.**

2d Co. Ft. Monroe	Organized 1815		April 1917	Ft. Story, Va					Orgzd. fr. 41st Co., C.A.C.
a. 2d Co. Chesapeake Bay.	August 1917	Ft. Story, Va							Active through 1919.
3d Co. Ft. Monroe	Organized 1899		April 1917	Ft. Monroe, Va					Orgzd. fr. 58th Co., C.A.C.
a. 3d Co. Chesapeake Bay.	August 1917	Ft. Monroe, Va							Active through 1919.
4th Co. Ft. Monroe	Organized 1898		April 1917	Ft. Monroe, Va					Orgzd. fr. 69th Co., C.A.C.
a. 4th Co. Chesapeake.			May 1917 November 1918	Washington, D. C. Ft. Monroe, Va					Active through 1919.
5th Co. Ft. Monroe	Organized 1901		April 1917	Ft. Story, Va					Orgzd. fr. 118th Co., C.A.C. Redes. Hq. and Sup. Co. 8th Prov. Regt., C.A.C. July 1917.
6th Co. Ft. Monroe	Organized 1812		do	Ft. Monroe, Va					Orgzd. fr. 6th Co., C.A.C.
a. 6th (I) Co. Chesapeake Bay.	August 1917	Ft. Wool, Va	July 1917 September 1917	Ft. Wool, Va. Ft. Monroe, Va					Redes. Btry. E, 60th Regt., C.A.C. December 1917.
7th Co. Ft. Monroe	Organized 1907		April 1917	do					Orgzd. fr. 166th Co. C.A.C.
a. 7th Co. Chesapeake Bay.	August 1917	Washington, D. C.	June 1917 November 1918	Washington, D. C. Ft. Monroe, Va					Active through 1919.
8th Co. Ft. Monroe	Organized 1907		April 1917 do do July 1917	Ft. Monroe, Va Ft. Wool, Va. Ft. Monroe, Va. Fisherman's Island, Va.					Orgzd. fr. 168th Co., C.A.C.
a. 8th (I) Co. Chesapeake Bay.	August 1917	Fisherman's Island, Va.							Redes. Hq. Btry. 60th Regt., C.A.C. December 1917.

COAST DEFENSE COMPANIES—Continued

Unit designation and redesignation	Organization		Stations in United States		Overseas		Demobilization		Remarks
	Month and year	Place	Month and year	Place	From—	To—	Month and year	Place	
9th Co. Ft. Monroe	Organized 1907		April 1917	Ft. Monroe, Va					Orgzd. fr. 169th Co., C.A.C.
a. 9th Co. Chesapeake Bay.	August 1917	Ft. Monroe, Va					August 1919	Ft. Monroe, Va.	
10th Co. Ft. Monroe	May 1917	Ft. Monroe, Va							Redes. Btry. D, 8th Prov. Regt., C.A.C. July 1917.
11th Co. Ft. Monroe	do	do							Redes. Btry. B, 8th Prov. Regt., C.A.C. July 1917.
12th Co. Ft. Monroe	June 1917	do							Redes, Btry. C, 8th Prov. Regt., C.A.C. July 1917.
13th Co. Ft. Monroe	do	Do.							
a. 5th Co. Chesapeake Bay.	August 1917	do							Active through 1919.
1st Co. Ft. Morgan	Organized 1786		April 1910	Ft. Morgan, Ala					Orgzd. fr. 39th Co., C.A.C.
a. 1st Co. Mobile	August 1917	Ft. Morgan, Ala	January 1918	Mobile, Ala.					
			March 1918	Ft. Morgan, Ala.					
			November 1919	Bogalusa, La.					
			December 1919	Ft. Morgan, Ala.					
2d Co. Ft. Morgan	Organized 1916		April 1917	Ft. Morgan, Ala.					
a. 2d Co. Mobile	August 1917	Ft. Morgan, Ala	November 1919	Bogalusa, La.					
			December 1919	Ft. Morgan, Ala.					
3d Co. Ft. Morgan	June 1917	Do.							
a. 3d Co. Mobile	August 1917	do	October 1917	Ft. Gaines, Ala.					
			March 1919	Ft. Morgan, Ala			September 1919	Ft. Morgan, Ala.	
4th Co. Ft. Morgan	June 1917	Do.							
a. 4th (I) Co. Mobile.	August 1917	do							Redes. Btry. B, 1st T.M. Bn. December 1917.

1st Co. Ft. Mott	June 1917	Ft. Mott, N. J.							
a. 7th Co. Delaware	August 1917	do	December 1917	Cramp Shipyard. Philadelphia, Pa.					
			March 1918	Ft. Mott, N. J			December 1918	Ft. Mott, N. J.	
2d Co. Ft. Mott	June 1917	do							Redes. Hq. and Sup. Co. 6th Prov. Regt., C.A.C. July 1917.
1st Co. Ft. Moultrie	Organized 1908		April 1917	Ft. Moultrie, S. C					Orgzd. fr. 170th Co., C.A.C.
a. 1st Co. Charleston	August 1917	Ft. Moultrie, S.C							Active through 1919.
2d Co. Ft. Moultrie	Organized 1898		April 1917	Ft. Moultrie, S. C					Orgzd. fr. 78th Co., C.A.C. Redes. Btry. H, 8th Prov. Regt., C.A.C. July 1917.
3d Co. Ft. Moultrie	Organized 1907		do	do					Orgzd. fr. 145th Co., C.A.C.
a. 3d Co. Charleston	August 1917	Ft. Moultrie, S. C.							Active through 1919.
4th Co. Ft. Moultrie	Organized 1916		April 1917	Ft. Moultrie, S. C.					
a. 4th Co. Charleston.	August 1917	Ft. Moultrie, S. C							Do.
5th Co. Ft. Moultrie	June 1917	Do.							
a. 2d Co. Charleston.	August 1917	do							Do.
1st Co. Ft. Pickens	Organized 1907		April 1917	Ft. Pickens, Fla					Orgzd. fr. 163d Co., C.A.C.
a. 1st Co. Pensacola	August 1917	Ft. Pickens, Fla							Active through 1919.
1st Co. Ft. Preble	Organized 1901		April 1917	Ft. Preble, Maine					Orgzd. fr. 107th Co., C.A.C. Redes. Btry. E, 6th Prov. Regt., C.A.C. July 1917.

COAST DEFENSE COMPANIES—Continued

Unit designation and redesignation	Organization		Stations in United States		Overseas		Demobilization		Remarks
	Month and year	Place	Month and year	Place	From—	To—	Month and year	Place	
2d Co. Ft. Preble	Organized 1899		April 1917	Ft. Preble, Maine					Orgzd. fr. 24th Co., C.A.C.
a. 8th (I) Co. Portland.	August 1917	Ft. Preble, Me							Redes. Btry. D, 54th Regt., C.A.C. December 1917.
3d Co. Ft. Preble	July 1917	do							Orgzd. fr. 8th Co. Me. C.A. N.G.
a. 20th (I) Co. Portland.	August 1917	do							Redes. Sup. Co., 54th Regt., C.A.C. December 1917.
4th Co. Ft. Preble	July 1917	do	August 1917	Cp. Devens, Mass.					Orgzd. fr. 10th Co. Me. C.A. N.G.
a. 21st Co. Portland.	August 1917	Cp. Devens, Mass.	October 1917	Watertown Arsenal, Mass.					
			March 1918	Ft. Preble, Me			December 1918	Ft. Preble, Me.	
1st Co. Ft. Randolph	Organized 1847		April 1917	Ft. Randolph, C.Z.					Orgzd. fr. 21st Co., C.A.C.
a. 7th Co. Cristobal	August 1917	Ft. Randolph, C. Z.							Active through 1919.
2d Co. Ft. Randolph	June 1917	Do.							
a. 8th Co. Cristobal	August 1917	do							Do.
3d Co. Ft. Randolph	Organized 1798		April 1917	Ft. Randolph, C. Z.					Orgzd. fr. 15th Co., C.A.C.
a. 9th Co. Cristobal	August 1917	Ft. Randolph, C. Z.							Active through 1919.
4th Co. Ft. Randolph	June 1917	Do.							
a. 10th Co. Cristobal.	August 1917	do							Do.

1st Co. Ft. Revere	Organized 1901		April 1917	Ft. Revere, Mass.					Orgzd. fr. 96th Co., C.A.C.
a. 1st (I) Co. Boston.	August 1917	Ft. Revere, Mass.							Redes. Btry. A, 55th Regt., C.A.C. December 1917. Active through 1919.
1st Co. Rockaway Beach	June 1917	Rockaway Beach, N. Y.	August 1917	Ft. Tilden, N. Y.					
a. 9th Co. Southern New York.	August 1917	Ft. Tilden, N. Y.	April 1918	Ft. Hamilton, N. Y.					Demblzd. December 1918; reorganized January 1919.
	January 1919	Ft. Hamilton, N. Y.	February 1919	Ft. Tilden, N. Y.					Active through 1919.
2d Co. Rockaway Beach	June 1917	Rockaway Beach, N. Y.	August 1917	do					Orgzd. fr. 34th Co., N.Y. C.A. N.G.
a. 10th Co. Southern New York.	August 1917	Ft. Tilden, N. Y.	April 1918	Ft. Hamilton, N. Y.			December 1918	Ft. Hamilton, N. Y.	Demblzd. December 1918; reorganized January 1919.
	January 1919	Ft. Hamilton, N. Y.					September 1919	Do.	
3d Co. Rockaway Beach	June 1917	do	June 1917	Rockaway Beach, N. Y.					
			July 1917	Ft. Adams, R. I.					Redes. Btry. G, 8th Prov. Regt., C.A.C. July 1917.
1st Co. Ft. Rodman	Organized 1861		April 1917	Ft. Rodman, Mass.					
a. 1st Co. New Bedford.	August 1917	Ft. Rodman, Mass.							Orgzd. fr. 52d Co., C.A.C. Active through 1919.
2d Co. Ft. Rodman	June 1917	Do.							
a. 2d Co. New Bedford.	August 1917	do					September 1919	Ft. Rodman, Mass.	
1st Co. Ft. Rosecrans	Organized 1798		April 1917	Ft. Rosecrans, Calif.					
a. 1st Co. San Diego.	August 1917	Ft. Rosecrans, Calif.							Orgzd. fr. 28th Co., C.A.C. Active through 1919.

COAST DEFENSE COMPANIES—Continued

Unit designation and redesignation	Organization		Stations in United States		Overseas		Demobilization		Remarks
	Month and year	Place	Month and year	Place	From—	To—	Month and year	Place	
2d Co. Ft. Rosecrans	Organized 1901		April 1917	Ft. Rosecrans, Calif.					Orgzd. fr. 115th Co., C.A.C.
a. 2d (I) Co. San Diego.	August 1917	Ft. Rosecrans, Calif.							Redes. Btry. A, 65th Regt., C.A.C. January 1918.
3d Co. Ft. Rosecrans	May 1917	Do.							Active through 1919.
a. 3d Co. San Diego	August 1917	do							
4th (Hq.) Co. Ft. Rosecrans.	May 1917	Do.							
a. 4th (I) Co. San Diego.	August 1917	Do.							
b. 2d (II) Co. San Diego.	January 1918	do					October 1919	Ft. Rosecrans, Calif.	
1st Co. Ft. Ruger	Organized 1812		April 1917	Ft. Ruger, T. H.					Orgzd. fr. 2d Co., C.A.C.
a. 11th Co. Oahu	August 1917	Ft. Ruger, T. H.	June 1918	Ft. Armstrong, T. H.					
			October 1918	Ft. Ruger, T. H.					Active through 1919.
2d Co. Ft. Ruger	Organized 1901		April 1917	do					Orgzd. fr. 105th Co., C.A.C.
a. 12th Co. Oahu	August 1917	Ft. Ruger, T. H.							Active through 1919.
3d Co. Ft. Ruger	Organized 1907		April 1917	Ft. Ruger, T. H.					Orgzd. fr. 159th Co., C.A.C.
a. 13th Co. Oahu	August 1917	Ft. Ruger, T. H.							Active through 1919.
4th Co. Ft. Ruger	July 1917	Do.							Do.
a. 14th Co. Oahu	August 1917	do							

1st Co. Ft. Schuyler	June 1917	Ft. Schuyler, N. Y.	August 1917	Ft. Totten, N. Y.					
a. 4th Co. Eastern New York.	August 1917	Ft. Totten, N. Y.	December 1917	Weehawken, N. J.					
			April 1918	Ft. Totten, N. Y.	——	——	September 1919	Ft. Totten, N. Y.	
2d Co. Ft. Schuyler	June 1917	Ft. Schuyler, N. Y.	——	——	——	——	——	——	Redes. Btry. F, 7th Prov. Regt., C.A.C. July 1917.
1st Co. Ft. Winfield Scott.	Organized 1907	——	April 1917	Ft. Winfield Scott, Calif.	——	——	——	——	Orgzd. fr. 147th Co., C.A.C.
a. 1st Co. San Francisco.	August 1917	Ft. Winfield Scott, Calif.	September 1919	Ft. Barry, Calif.	——	——	——	——	Redes. Hq. Co. 18th Regt. C.A.C. October 1918; reverted to previous designation December 1918.
			December 1919	Ft. Winfield Scott, Calif.					
2d Co. Ft. Winfield Scott.	Organized 1898	——	April 1917	Ft. Winfield Scott, Calif.	——	——	——	——	Orgzd. fr. 60th Co., C.A.C.
a. 2d Co. San Francisco.	August 1917	Ft. Winfield Scott, Calif.	December 1919	Ft. Barry, Calif.	——	——	——	——	Redes. Btry. A, 40th Regt., C.A.C. September 1918; reverted to previous designation December 1918. Active through 1919.
3d Co. Ft. Winfield Scott.	Organized 1861	——	April 1917	Ft. Winfield Scott, Calif.	——	——	——	——	Orgzd. fr. 57th Co., C.A.C.
a. 3d Co. San Francisco.	August 1917	Ft. Winfield Scott, Calif.	——	——	——	——	——	——	Active through 1919.
4th (I) Co. Ft. Winfield Scott.	Organized 1812	——	March 1917	Ft. Winfield Scott, Calif.	——	——	——	——	Orgzd. fr. 38th Co., C.A.C.
			do	Ft. MacArthur, Calif.					
a. 1st Co. Ft. MacArthur.	March 1917	Ft. MacArthur, Calif.							
b. 1st (I) Co. Los Angeles.	August 1917	do	December 1917	Cp. Merritt, N. J.					
			do	P. of E., Hoboken	December 1917	——	——	——	Redes. 3d Sep. A.A. Btry. December 1917.

COAST DEFENSE COMPANIES—Continued

Unit designation and redesignation	Organization		Stations in United States		Overseas		Demobilization		Remarks
	Month and year	Place	Month and year	Place	From—	To—	Month and year	Place	
4th (II) Co. Ft. Winfield Scott.	March 1917		April 1917	Ft. Winfield Scott, Calif.					
a. 4th Co. San Francisco.	April 1917	Ft. Winfield Scott, Calif.	July 1917	Cp. Fremont, Calif.					Redes. Btry. B, 40th Regt., C.A.C. September 1918 reverted to former designation December 1918.
			October 1917	Ft. Winfield Scott, Calif.			September 1919	Ft. Winfield Scott, Calif.	
5th Co. Ft. Winfield Scott.	Organized 1907		April 1917	Presidio of San Francisco, Calif.					Orgzd. fr. 158th Co., C.A.C.
			May 1917	Ft. Winfield Scott, Calif.					
a. 5th (I) Co. San Francisco.	August 1917	Ft. Winfield Scott, Calif.	September 1917	Cp. Fremont, Calif.					
			October 1917	Ft. Winfield Scott, Calif.					Redes. Hq. & Sup. Co. A.A. Bn. San Francisco November 1917.
6th Co. Ft. Winfield Scott.	Organized 1898		April 1917	Lake Merced, Calif.					Orgzd. fr. 65th Co., C.A.C. Lake Merced renamed Ft. Funston June 26, 1917.
			June 1917	Ft. Funston, Calif.					
a. 6th Co. San Francisco.	August 1917	Ft. Funston, Calif.	December 1918	Ft. Winfield Scott, Calif.					Redes. Btry. C, 40th Regt., C.A.C. September 1918; reverted to former designation December 1918.
			September 1919	Ft. Barry, Calif.					
			December 1919	Ft. Winfield Scott, Calif.					

7th Co. Ft. Winfield Scott.	Organized 1794		April 1917 May 1917	Presidio of San Francisco, Calif. Ft. Winfield Scott, Calif.					Orgzd. fr. 27th Co., C.A.C.
a. 7th (I) Co. San Francisco.	August 1917	Ft. Winfield Scott, Calif.	September 1917 October 1917	Cp. Fremont, Calif. Ft. Winfield Scott, Calif.					Redes. 4th Sep. A.A. Btry. October 1917.
8th (Hq.) Co. Ft. Winfield Scott.	Organized 1898		April 1917	Ft. Winfield Scott, Calif.					Orgzd. fr. 64th Co., C.A.C.
a. 8th Co. San Francisco.	August 1917	Ft. Winfield Scott, Calif.							Active through 1919.
9th Co. Ft. Winfield Scott.	Organized 1808		April 1917	Ft. Winfield Scott, Calif.					Orgzd. fr. 29th Co., C.A.C.
a. 9th Co. San Francisco.	August 1917	Ft. Winfield Scott, Calif.	September 1917 October 1917 September 1918 September 1919	Cp. Fremont, Calif. Ft. Winfield Scott, Calif. Ft. Funston, Calif. Ft. Winfield Scott, Calif.					Active through 1919.
10th Co. Ft. Winfield Scott.	Organized 1898		April 1917	do					Orgzd. fr. 67th Co., C.A.C.
			do	Ft. Miley, Calif.					
a. 10th (I) Co. San Francisco.	August 1917	Ft. Miley, Calif	November 1917	Ft. Winfield Scott, Calif.					Redes. Btry. B, 1st A.A. Bn. November 1917.
1st Co. Ft. Screven	Organized 1898		April 1917	Ft. Screven, Ga					Orgzd. fr. 72d Co., C.A.C.
a. 1st Co. Savannah	August 1917	Ft. Screven, Ga							Active through 1919.
2d (I) Co. Ft. Screven	Organized 1901		do	do			April 1917	Ft. Screven, Ga	Orgzd. fr. 121st Co., C.A.C.
2d (II) Co. Ft. Screven									See 4th (I) Co. Ft. Screven.
2d (III) Co. Ft. Screven									See 1st Co. Ft. Fremont.
3d Co. Ft. Screven	Organized 1916		April 1917	Ft. Screven, Ga.					
a. 3d (I) Co. Savannah.	August 1917	Ft. Screven, Ga							Redes. Btry. C, 61st Regt., C.A.C. December 1917.

COAST DEFENSE COMPANIES—Continued

Unit designation and redesignation	Organization		Stations in United States		Overseas		Demobilization		Remarks
	Month and year	Place	Month and year	Place	From—	To—	Month and year	Place	
4th (I) Co. Ft. Screven	Organized 1898		April 1917	Ft. Screven, Ga					Orgzd. fr. 74th Co., C.A.C.
a. 2d (II) Co. Ft. Screven.	April 1917	Ft. Screven, Ga							Redes. Btry. M, 8th Prov. Regt., C.A.C., July 1917.
4th (II) Co. Ft. Screven	June 1917	Do.							
a. 4th (I) Co. Savannah.	August 1917	do					November 1917	Ft. Screven, Ga.	
Hq. Co. Ft. Screven									See 1st Co. Ft. Fremont.
1st Co. Ft. Sherman	Organized 1838		April 1917	Ft. Sherman, C. Z.					Orgzd. fr. 44th Co., C.A.C.
a. 1st Co. Cristobal.	August 1917	Ft. Sherman, C. Z.							Active through 1919.
2d Co. Ft. Sherman	Organized 1901		April 1917	Ft. Sherman, C. Z.					Orgzd. fr. 124th Co., C.A.C.
a. 2d Co. Cristobal	August 1917	Ft. Sherman, C. Z.							Active through 1919.
3d Co. Ft. Sherman	Organized 1901		April 1917	Ft. Sherman, C. Z.					Orgzd. fr. 119th Co., C.A.C.
a. 3d Co. Cristobal	August 1917	Ft. Sherman, C. Z.							Active through 1919.
4th Co. Ft. Sherman	June 1917	Do.							Do.
a. 4th Co. Cristobal	August 1917	do							
5th Co. Ft. Sherman	Organized 1815		April 1917	Ft. Sherman, C. Z.					Orgzd. fr. 16th Co., C.A.C.
a. 5th Co. Cristobal	August 1917	Ft. Sherman, C. Z.							Active through 1919.

1st Co. Ft. Smallwood	June 1917	Ft. Smallwood, Md.							
a. 5th (I) Co. Baltimore.	August 1917	do							Redes. Btry. E, 58th Regt., C.A.C. December 1917.
1st Co. Ft. Stevens	Organized 1847		April 1917	Ft. Stevens, Oreg					Orgzd. fr. 34th Co., C.A.C.
a. 1st Co. Columbia	August 1917	Ft. Stevens, Oreg							Active through 1919.
2d Co. Ft. Stevens	Organized 1907		April 1917	Ft. Stevens, Oreg					Orgzd. fr. 160th Co., C.A.C.
a. 2d Co. Columbia	August 1917	Ft. Stevens, Oreg							Active through 1919.
3d Co. Ft. Stevens	Organized 1916		April 1917 May 1917	Vancouver Bks., Wash. Ft. Stevens, Oreg.					
a. 3d Co. Columbia	August 1917	Ft. Stevens, Oreg							Active through 1919.
1st Co. Ft. Strong	Organized 1916		April 1917	Ft. Strong, Mass.					
a. 9th Co. Boston	August 1917	Ft. Strong, Mass							Active through 1919.
2d Co. Ft. Strong	Organized 1916		April 1917	Ft. Strong, Mass.					
a. 10th Co. Boston	August 1917	Ft. Strong, Mass							Active through 1919.
3d Co. Ft. Strong	Organized 1847		April 1917	Ft. Strong, Mass					Orgzd. fr. 46th Co., C.A.C. Redes. Btry. C, 6th Prov. Regt., C.A.C. July 1917.
4th Co. Ft. Strong	Organized 1916		do	Do.					
a. 8th (I) Co. Boston.	August 1917	Ft. Strong, Mass							Redes. Btry. C, 55th Regt., C.A.C. December 1917.

COAST DEFENSE COMPANIES—Continued

Unit designation and redesignation	Organization		Stations in United States		Overseas		Demobilization		Remarks
	Month and year	Place	Month and year	Place	From—	To—	Month and year	Place	
1st Co. Ft. Terry	Organized 1817		April 1917	Ft. Terry, N. Y.					Orgzd. fr. 43d Co., C.A.C.
a. 12th (I) Co. Long Island Sound.	August 1917	Ft. Terry, N. Y.							
b. 8th (II) Co. Long Island Sound.	December 1918	do							Active through 1919.
2d Co. Ft. Terry	Organized 1901		April 1917	Ft. Terry, N. Y.					Orgzd. fr. 88th Co., C.A.C. Redes Btry. C, 7th Prov. Regt., C.A.C. July 1917.
3d Co. Ft. Terry	Organized 1907		do	do					Orgzd. fr. 133d Co., C.A.C.
a. 13th (I) Co. Long Island Sound.	August 1917	Ft. Terry, N. Y.							Redes. Btry. A, 56th Regt., C.A.C. December 1917.
4th Co. Ft. Terry	Organized 1901		April 1917	Ft. Terry, N. Y.					Orgzd. fr. 100th Co., C.A.C.
a. 14th (I) Co. Long Island Sound.	August 1917	Ft. Terry, N. Y.							Redes. Hq. Btry. 56th Regt., C.A.C. December 1917.
5th Co. Ft. Terry	Organized 1907		April 1917	Ft. Terry, N. Y.					Orgzd. fr. 157th Co., C.A.C.
a. 15th (I) Co. Long Island Sound.	August 1917	Ft. Terry, N. Y.							
b. 9th (II) Co. Long Island Sound.	December 1918	do							Active through 1919.

6th Co. Ft. Terry	April 1917	do							Redes. Btry. B, 7th Prov. Regt., C.A.C. July 1917.
7th Co. Ft. Terry	June 1917	Do.							
a. 16th (I) Co. Long Island Sound.	August 1917	do							Redes. Btry. B, 56th Regt., C.A.C. December 1917.
1st Co. Ft. Totten	Organized 1899		April 1917 May 1917	Rockaway Beach, N. Y. Ft. Totten, N. Y.					Orgzd. fr. 82d Co., C.A.C.
a. 6th (I) Co. Eastern New York.	August 1917	Ft. Totten, N. Y.	April 1918	Ft. Schuyler, N. Y.			December 1918	Ft. Schuyler, N. Y.	
2d Co. Ft. Totten	Organized 1901		April 1917	Ft. Totten, N. Y.					Orgzd. fr. 101st Co., C.A.C. Redes. Btry. G, 7th Prov. Regt., C.A.C. July 1917.
3d Co. Ft. Totten	Organized 1907		do	do					Orgzd. fr. 135th Co., C.A.C.
a. 3d Co. Eastern New York.	August 1917	Ft. Totten, N. Y.							
b. 1st (II) Co. Eastern New York.	October 1919	do							Active through 1919.
4th Co. Ft. Totten	Organized 1907		April 1917	Ft. Totten, N. Y.					Orgzd. fr. 165th Co., C.A.C.
a. 1st (I) Co. Eastern New York.	August 1917	Ft. Totten, N. Y.					September 1919	Ft. Totten, N. Y.	
5th Co. Ft. Totten	Organized 1907		April 1917	Ft. Totten, N. Y.					Orgzd. fr. 167th Co., C.A.C.
a. 5th Co. Eastern New York.	August 1917	Ft. Totten, N. Y.	December 1917 April 1918 January 1919	Jersey City, N. J. Ft. Schuyler, N. Y. Ft. Totten, N. Y.					
b. 2d (II) Co. Eastern New York.	October 1919	do							Active through 1919.

COAST DEFENSE COMPANIES—Continued

Unit designation and redesignation	Organization		Stations in United States		Overseas		Demobilization		Remarks
	Month and year	Place	Month and year	Place	From—	To—	Month and year	Place	
6th Co. Ft. Totten	April 1917	Ft. Schuyler, N. Y	June 1917	Ft. Totten, N. Y					Redes. Btry. H, 7th Prov. Regt., C.A.C. July 1917.
7th Co. Ft. Totten	June 1917	Ft. Totten, N. Y.							
a. 2d (I) Co. Eastern New York.	August 1917	do					September 1919	Ft. Totten, N. Y.	
1st Co. Ft. Wadsworth	Organized 1861		April 1917	Ft. Wadsworth, N. Y.					Orgzd. fr. 53d Co., C.A.C.
a. 5th Co. Southern New York.	August 1917	Ft. Wadsworth, N. Y.							Active through 1919.
2d Co. Ft. Wadsworth	Organized 1861		April 1917	Ft. Wadsworth, N. Y.					Orgzd. fr. 54th Co., C.A.C.
a. 6th Co. Southern New York.	August 1917	Ft. Wadsworth, N. Y.							Active through 1919.
3d Co. Ft. Wadsworth	Organized 1901		April 1917	Ft. Wadsworth, N. Y.					Orgzd. fr. 114th Co., C.A.C. Redes. Btry. E, 8th Prov. Regt., C.A.C. July 1917.
4th Co. Ft. Wadsworth	June 1917	Ft. Wadsworth, N. Y.							
a. 7th Co. Southern New York.	August 1917	do	September 1919	Ft. Hamilton, N. Y					Active through 1919.
5th Co. Ft. Wadsworth	June 1917	Do.							
a. 8th Co. Southern New York.	August 1917	do	do	do					Do.

1st Co. Ft. Ward	Organized 1907		April 1917	Ft. Ward, Wash.					Orgzd. fr. 150th Co., C.A.C.
a. 16th Co. Puget Sound.	August 1917	Ft. Ward, Wash.							Active through 1919.
1st Co. Ft. Warren	Organized 1847		April 1917	Ft. Warren, Mass.					Orgzd. fr. 9th Co., C.A.C.
a. 7th Co. Boston	August 1917	Ft. Warren, Mass.							Active through 1919.
1st Co. Ft. Washington	Organized 1916		April 1917	Ft. Washington, Md.					
a. 3d (II) Co. Ft. Washington.	July 1917	Ft. Washington, Md.							
b. 3d Co. Potomac	September 1917	do					September 1919	Ft. Washington, Md.	
2d Co. Ft. Washington ton.	Organized 1916		April 1917	Ft. Wool, Va.			July 1917	Ft. Wool, Va.	
3d (I) Co. Ft. Washington.	June 1917	Ft. Washington, Md.							
a. 4th Co. Ft. Washington.	July 1917	Do.							
b. 4th (I) Co. Potomac.	September 1917	do					January 1918	Ft. Washington, Md.	
3d (II) Co. Ft. Washington.									See 1st Co. Ft. Washington.
4th Co. Ft. Washington									See 3d (I) Co. Ft. Washington.
1st Co. Ft. Williams	Organized 1907		April 1917	Ft. Williams, Maine.					Orgzd. fr. 155th Co., C.A.C.
a. 3d Co. Portland	August 1917	Ft. Williams, Maine.							Active through 1919.
2d Co. Ft. Williams	Organized 1812		April 1917	Ft. Williams, Maine.					Orgzd. fr. 5th Co., C.A.C. Redes. Btry. H, 6th Prov. Regt., C.A.C. July 1917.

COAST DEFENSE COMPANIES—Continued

Unit designation and redesignation	Organization		Stations in United States		Overseas		Demobilization		Remarks
	Month and year	Place	Month and year	Place	From—	To—	Month and year	Place	
3d Co. Ft. Williams	Organized 1861		April 1917	Ft. Williams Maine.					Orgzd. fr. 49th Co., C.A.C. Redes. Btry. G, 6th Prov. Regt., C.A.C. July 1917.
4th Co. Ft. Williams	Organized 1901		do	do					Orgzd. fr. 89th Co., C.A.C. Redes. Btry. F, 6th Prov. Regt., C.A.C. July 1917.
5th (Hq.) Co. Ft. Williams.	July 1917	Ft. Williams, Maine.							
a. 1st (I) Co. Portland.	August 1917	do							Redes. Hq. Co. 54th Regt., C.A.C. December 1917.
6th Co. Ft. Williams	July 1917	Do.							
a. 2d Co. Portland	August 1917	Do.							
7th Co. Ft. Williams	July 1917	do							Orgzd. fr. 1st Co. Maine C.A. N.G.
a. 17th Co. Portland	August 1917	do					January 1919	Ft. Williams, Maine.	
8th Co. Ft. Williams	July 1917	do							Orgzd. fr. 5th Co. Maine C.A. N.G.
a. 18th (I) Co. Portland.	August 1917	do							Redes. Btry. B, 54th Regt., C.A.C. December 1917.
9th Co. Ft. Williams	July 1917	do							Orgzd. fr. 7th Co. Maine C.A. N.G.
a. 19th (I) Co. Portland.	August 1917	do							Redes. Btry. B, 54th Regt., C.A.C. December 1917.

1st Co. Ft. Worden	Organized 1813		April 1917	Ft. Worden, Wash.					Orgzd. fr. 30th Co., C.A.C.
			August 1917	Cp. Lewis, Wash.					
a. 1st Co. Puget Sound.	August 1917	Cp. Lewis, Wash.	October 1917	Ft. Flagler, Wash.					
			January 1919	Ft. Worden, Wash.					Active through 1919.
2d Co. Ft. Worden	Organized 1898		April 1917	Ft. Worden, Wash.					Orgzd. fr. 62d Co., C.A.C.
			July 1917	Cp. Lewis, Wash.					
a. 2d Co. Puget Sound.	August 1917	Cp. Lewis, Wash.	September 1917	Ft. Worden, Wash.					Active through 1919.
3d Co. Ft. Worden	Organized 1898		April 1917	Ft. George Wright, Wash.					Orgzd. fr. 63d Co., C.A.C.
a. 3d Co. Puget Sound.	August 1917	Ft. George Wright, Wash.	January 1918	Ft. Worden, Wash.					Active through 1919.
4th Co. Ft. Worden	Organized 1901		April 1917	do					Orgzd. fr. 106th Co., C.A.C.
a. 4th Co. Puget Sound.	August 1917	Ft. Worden, Wash.							Active through 1919.
5th Co. Ft. Worden	Organised 1901		April 1917	Ft. Worden, Wash.					Orgzd. fr. 108th Co., C.A.C.
a. 5th Co. Puget Sound.	August 1917	Ft. Worden, Wash.	November 1917	Seattle, Wash.					
			January 1918	Ft. Worden, Wash.					Active through 1919.
6th Co. Ft. Worden	Organized 1901		April 1917	do					Orgzd. fr. 126th Co. C.A.C.
a. 6th Co. Puget Sound.	August 1917	Ft. Worden, Wash.					September 1919	Ft. Worden, Wash.	
7th Co. Ft. Worden	July 1917	Do.							
a. 7th Co. Puget Sound.	August 1917	do					do	Do.	
8th Co. Ft. Worden	July 1917	Do.							
a. 8th Co. Puget Sound.	August 1917	do					do	Do.	
1st Co. Ft. H. G. Wright.	Organized 1907		April 1917	Ft. H. G. Wright, N. Y.					Orgzd. fr. 134th Co., C.A.C. Redes. Btry. A, 7th Prov. Regt., C.A.C. July 1917.

COAST DEFENSE COMPANIES—Continued

Unit designation and redesignation	Organization		Stations in United States		Overseas		Demobilization		Remarks
	Month and year	Place	Month and year	Place	From—	To—	Month and year	Place	
2d Co. Ft. H. G. Wright	Organized 1899		April 1917	Ft. H. G. Wright, N. Y.					Orgzd. fr. 12th Co. C.A.C. Redes. Btry. E, 7th Prov. Regt., C.A.C. July 1917.
3d Co. Ft. H. G. Wright	Organized 1907		do	do					Orgzd. fr. 132d Co.
a. 1st Co. Long Island Sound.	August 1917	Ft. H. G. Wright, N. Y.							Active through 1919.
4th Co. Ft. H. G. Wright.	Organized 1907		April 1917	Ft. H. G. Wright, N. Y.					Orgzd. fr. 131st Co., C.A.C.
a. 2d Co. Long Island Sound.	August 1917	Ft. H. G. Wright, N. .Y.							Active through 1919
5th Co. Ft. H. G. Wright.	Organized 1907		April 1917	Ft. H. G. Wright, N. .Y.					Orgzd. fr. 146th Co., C.A.C.
a. 3d (I) Co. Long Island Sound.	August 1917	Ft. H. G. Wright, N. Y.							Redes. Btry. C, 56th Regt., C.A.C. December 1917.
6th Co. Ft. H. G. Wright	April 1917	do							Redes. Btry. D, 7th Prov. Regt., C. A.C., July 1917.
7th Co. Ft. H. G. Wright.	June 1917	Do.							
a. 4th Co. Long Island Sound.	August 1917	do							Active through 1919.

SPECIAL AND TECHNICAL UNITS

Units	Unit No.	Active service	Unit No.	Active service	Unit No.	Active service	Unit No.	Active service	Unit No.	Active service	Remarks
Bands, Coast Artillery Corps.	1	April 1917–December 1919	2	April 1917–December 1919	3	April 1917–December 1919	4	April 1917–December 1919	5	April 1917–December 1919	
	6	do	7	do	8	do	9	do	10	Do.	
	11	do	12	do	13	do	14	do	15	Do.	
	16	July 1917–December 1919	17	September 1917–December 1919	18	June 1917–December 1919	19	January 1918–December 1918	20	January 1918–December 1918	
	21	January 1918–December 1918	22	January 1918–December 1918	23	January 1918–December 1918	24	January 1918–February 1919	25	Do.	
	26	do	27	February 1918–December 1918	28	February 1918–December 1918	29	February 1918–December 1918	30	February 1918–January 1919	

FIELD ARTILLERY

BRIGADE HEADQUARTERS

Unit designation and redesignation	Organization		Stations in United States		Overseas		Demobilization		Remarks
	Month and year	Place	Month and year	Place	From—	To—	Month and year	Place	
1st Field Artillery Brigade.	August 1917	A. E. F.	September 1919	Cp. Mills, N. Y.		September 1919			Cmpnt. of 1st Div.
			do	Cp. Meade, Md.					
			October 1919	Cp. Zachary Taylor, Ky.					
2d Field Artillery Brigade.	January 1918	A. E. F.	August 1919	Cp. Mills, N. Y.		August 1919			Cmpnt. of 2d Div.
			do	Cp. Travis, Tex.					
3d Field Artillery Brigade.	November 1917	Cp. Stanley, Tex.	December 1917	Cp. Travis, Tex.					Cmpnt. of 3d Div.
			March 1918	Cp. Merritt, N. J.					
			April 1918	P. of E., Hoboken	April 1918.				
			August 1919	Cp. Merritt, N. J.		August 1919.			
			do	Cp. Pike, Ark.					

BRIGADE HEADQUARTERS—Continued

Unit designation and redesignation	Organization		Stations in United States		Overseas		Demobilization		Remarks
	Month and year	Place	Month and year	Place	From—	To—	Month and year	Place	
4th Field Artillery Brigade.	January 1918	Cp. Greene, N. C.	May 1918	Cp. Merritt, N. J.					Cmpnt. of 4th Div.
			do	P. of E., Hoboken	May 1918.				
			July 1919	Cp. Merritt, N. J.		July 1919.			
			August 1919	Cp. Dodge, Iowa.					
5th Field Artillery Brigade.	December 1917	Cp. Stanley, Tex.	February 1918	Cp. MacArthur, Tex.					Cmpnt. of 5th Div.
			May 1918	Cp. Upton, N. Y.					
			do	P. of E., Hoboken	May 1918.				
			July 1919	Cp. Merritt, N. J.		July 1919.			
			do	Cp. Bragg, N. C.					
6th Field Artillery Brigade.	April 1918	Ft. Sam Houston, Tex.	April 1918	Cp. Doniphan, Okla.					Cmpnt. of 6th Div.
			July 1918	Cp. Mills, N. Y.					
			do	P. of E., Hoboken	July 1918.				
			June 1919	Cp. Mills, N. Y.		June 1919.			
			do	Cp. Grant, Ill.					
7th Field Artillery Brigade.	January 1918	Cp. Wheeler, Ga.	June 1918	Cp. McClellan, Ala.					Cmpnt. of 7th Div.
			August 1918	Cp. Merritt, N. J.					
			do	P. of E., Hoboken	August 1918.				
			June 1919	Cp. Mills, N. Y.		June 1919.			
			do	Cp. Funston, Kans.					
8th Field Artillery Brigade.	February 1918	Cp. Fremont, Calif.	July 1918	Ft. Sill, Okla.					Cmpnt. of 8th Div.
			October 1918	Cp. Mills, N. Y.					
			do	P. of E., Hoboken	October 1918.				
			January 1919	Cp. Mills, N. Y.		January 1919.			
			do	Cp. Knox, Ky.					
9th Field Artillery Brigade.	August 1918	Cp. McClellan, Ala.					February 1919	Cp. McClellan, Ala.	Cmpnt. of 9th Div.
10th Field Artillery Brigade.	do	Cp. Funston, Kans.					do	Cp. Funston, Kans.	Cmpnt. of 10th Div.

11th Field Artillery Brigade.	do	Cp. Meade, Md.					December 1918	Cp. Meade, Md.	Cmpnt. of 11th Div. until September 1918; thereafter Corps Arty.
12th Field Artillery Brigade.	do	Cp. McClellan, Ala.					February 1919	Cp. McClellan, Ala.	Cmpnt. of 12th Div.
13th Field Artillery Brigade.	do	Cp. Lewis, Wash.					March 1919	Cp. Lewis, Wash.	Cmpnt. of 13th Div.
14th Field Artillery Brigade.	do	Cp. Custer, Mich.					February 1919	Cp. Custer, Mich.	Cmpnt. of 14th Div.
15th Field Artillery Brigade.	September 1918	Cp. Stanley, Tex.					do	Cp. Stanley, Tex.	Cmpnt. of 15th Div.
16th Field Artillery Brigade.	do	Cp. Kearny, Calif.					do	Cp. Kearny, Calif.	Cmpnt. of 16th Div.
17th Field Artillery Brigade.	August 1918	Cp. Bowie, Tex.	November 1918	Ft. Sill, Okla.			do	Ft. Sill, Okla.	Cmpnt. of 17th Div.
18th Field Artillery Brigade.	do	Cp. Travis, Tex.					do	Cp. Travis, Tex.	Cmpnt. of 18th Div.
19th Field Artillery Brigade.	August 1918	Cp. Bowie, Tex.	October 1918	Ft. Sill, Okla.			February 1919	Ft. Sill, Okla.	Cmpnt. of 19th Div.
20th Field Artillery Brigade.	November 1918	Cp. Jackson, S. C.					do	Cp. Jackson, S. C.	Cmpnt. of 20th Div.
21st Field Artillery Brigade.	October 1918	Cp. Sheridan, Ala.					December 1918	Cp. Sheridan, Ala.	
22d Field Artillery Brigade.	September 1918	Cp. Meade, Md.					October 1918	Cp. Meade, Md.	
23d Field Artillery Brigade.	October 1918	Cp. Sheridan, Ala.					December 1918	Cp. Sheridan, Ala.	Corps Arty.
24th Field Artillery Brigade.	September 1918	Cp. Knox, Ky.					February 1919	Cp. Knox, Ky.	Cmpnt. of 11th Div.
25th to 50th Field Artillery Brigades.									Never orgzd.
51st Field Artillery Brigade.	August 1917	Boxford, Mass.	September 1917	P. of E., Hoboken	September 1917	April 1919	April 1919	Cp. Devens, Mass.	Cmpnt. of 26th Div.
52d Field Artillery Brigade.	October 1917	Cp. Wadsworth, S. C.	May 1918	Cp. Stuart, Va.					Cmpnt. of 27th Div.
			June 1918	P. of E., Newport News.	June 1918.				
			March 1919	Cp. Mills, N. Y.		March 1919.			
			do	Cp. Upton, N. Y.			April 1919	Cp. Upton, N. Y.	

BRIGADE HEADQUARTERS—Continued

Unit designation and redesignation	Organization		Stations in United States		Overseas		Demobilization		Remarks
	Month and year	Place	Month and year	Place	From—	To—	Month and year	Place	
53d Field Artillery Brigade.	August 1917	Cp. Hancock, Ga.	May 1918	Cp. Mills, N. Y.					Cmpnt. of 28th Div.
			do	P. of E., Hoboken.	May 1918	May 1919	May 1919	Cp. Dix, N. J.	
54th Field Artillery Brigade.	September 1917	Cp. McClellan, Ala	June 1918	Cp. Mills, N. Y.					Cmpnt. of 29th Div.
			do	P. of E., Philadelphia.	June 1918.				
			May 1919	Cp. Stuart, Va.		May 1919	May 1919	Cp. Lee, Va.	
55th Field Artillery Brigade.	do	Cp. Sevier, S. C.	May 1918	Cp. Mills, N. Y.					Cmpnt. of 30th Div.
			do	P. of E., Hoboken.	May 1918.				
			March 1919	Cp. Stuart, Va.		March 1919	April 1919	Ft. Oglethorpe, Ga.	
56th Field Artillery Brigade.	do	Cp. Wheeler, Ga.	July 1918	Cp. Jackson, S. C.					Cmpnt. of 31st Div.
			October 1918	Cp. Mills, N. Y.					
			do	P. of E., Hoboken.	October 1918.				
			December 1918	Cp. Merritt, N. J.		December 1918	January 1919	Cp. Gordon, Ga.	
57th Field Artillery Brigade.	do	Cp. MacArthur, Tex.	February 1918	do					Cmpnt. of 32d Div.
			do	P. of E., Hoboken.	February 1918	May 1919	May 1919	Cp. Devens, Mass.	
58th Field Artillery Brigade.	do	Cp. Logan, Tex.	May 1918	Cp. Merritt, N. J.					Cmpnt. of 33d Div.
			do	P. of E., Hoboken.	May 1918.				
			May 1919	Cp. Mills, N. Y.		May 1919	June 1919	Cp. Grant, Ill.	
59th Field Artillery Brigade.	October 1917	Cp. Cody, N. Mex.	July 1918	Ft. Sill, Okla.					Cmpnt. of 34th Div.
			September 1918	Cp. Upton, N. Y.					
			do	P. of E., Hoboken.	September 1918.				
			January 1919	Cp. Merritt, N. J.		January 1919	January 1919	Cp. Dodge, Iowa.	
60th Field Artillery Brigade.	September 1917	Cp. Doniphan, Okla.	May 1918	Cp. Mills, N. Y.					Cmpnt. of 35th Div.
			do	P. of E., Hoboken.	May 1918.				
			April 1919	Cp. Mills, N. Y.		April 1919	April 1919	Cp. Pike, Ark.	

61st Field Artillery Brigade.	October 1917	Cp. Bowie, Tex.	July 1918	do					Cmpnt. of 36th Div.
62d Field Artillery Brigade.	September 1917	Cp. Sheridan, Ala.	do March 1919 June 1918	P. of E., Hoboken Cp. Stuart, Va. Cp. Upton, N. Y.	July 1918.	March 1919	March 1919	Cp. Bowie, Tex.	Cmpnt. of 37th Div.
63d Field Artillery Brigade.	October 1917	Cp. Shelby, Miss.	do March 1919 September 1918	P. of E., Hoboken Cp. Stuart, Va. Cp. Mills, N. Y.	June 1918.	March 1919	April 1919	Cp. Sherman, Ohio	Corps troops. Cmpnt. of 38th Div.
64th Field Artillery Brigade.	December 1917	Cp. Beauregard, La	October 1918 December 1918 August 1918	P. of E., Hoboken Cp. Merritt, N. J. Cp. Mills, N. Y.	October 1918.	December 1918	January 1919	Ft. Benjamin Harrison, Ind.	Cmpnt. of 39th Div.
65th Field Artillery Brigade.	October 1917	Cp. Kearny, Calif.	do April 1919 do August 1918	P. of E., Hoboken Cp. Merritt, N. J. Cp. Shelby, Miss. Cp. Mills, N. Y.	August 1918.	April 1919	May 1919	Cp. Shelby, Miss.	Cmpnt. of 40th Div.
66th Field Artillery Brigade.	do	Cp. Greene, N. C.	do December 1918 October 1917	P. of E., Hoboken Cp. Merritt, N. J. Cp. Mills, N. Y.	August 1918.	December 1918	January 1919	Presidio of San Francisco, Calif.	Cmpnt. of 41st Div.
67th Field Artillery Brigade.	September 1917	Cp. Mills, N. Y.	December 1917 January 1918 June 1919 October 1917	Cp. Merritt, N. J. P. of E., Hoboken Cp. Merritt, N. J. P. of E., Hoboken	January 1918. October 1917	June 1919	June 1919	Cp. Lewis, Wash.	Cmpnt. of 42d Div.
			April 1919	Cp. Merritt, N. J.		April 1919	May 1919	Cp. Grant, Ill.	
68th to 150th Field Artillery Brigades.									Never Orgzd.
151st Field Artillery Brigade.	August 1917	Cp. Devens, Mass.	July 1918	P. of E., Boston	July 1918				Cmpnt. of 76th Div.
152d Field Artillery Brigade.	September 1917	Cp. Upton, N Y	April 1919 April 1918	Cp. Devens, Mass. P. of E., Hoboken	 April 1918	April 1919	May 1919	Cp. Devens, Mass.	Corps troops. Cmpnt. of 77th Div.
			April 1919	Cp. Mills, N. Y.		April 1919	May 1919	Cp. Upton, N. Y.	

BRIGADE HEADQUARTERS—Continued

Unit designation and redesignation	Organization		Stations in United States		Overseas		Demobilization		Remarks
	Month and year	Place	Month and year	Place	From—	To—	Month and year	Place	
153d Field Artillery Brigade.	October 1917	Cp. Dix, N. J.	May 1918	P. of E., Hoboken.	May 1918	May 1919	May 1919	Cp. Dix, N. J.	Cmpnt. of 78th Div.
154th Field Artillery Brigade.	September 1917.	Cp. Meade, Md.	July 1918	P. of E., Philadelphia.	July 1918	do	do	do	Cmpnt. of 79th Div.
155th Field Artillery Brigade.	do	Cp. Lee, Va.	May 1918	P. of E., Newport News.	May 1918				Cmpnt. of 80th Div.
			May 1919	Cp. Stuart, Va.		May 1919	June 1919	Cp. Stuart, Va.	
156th Field Artillery Brigade.	do	Cp. Jackson, S. C.	July 1918	Cp. Mills, N. Y.					Cmpnt. of 81st Div.
			August 1918	P. of E., Hoboken.	August 1918.				
			June 1919	Cp. Mills, N. Y.		June 1919	June 1919	Cp. Lee, Va.	
157th Field Artillery Brigade.	do	Cp. Gordon, Ga.	May 1918	do					Cmpnt. of 82d Div.
			do	P. of E., Hoboken.	May 1918	May 1919	May 1919	Cp. Upton, N. Y.	
158th Field Artillery Brigade.	August 1917	Cp. Sherman, Ohio.	June 1918	Cp. Mills, N. Y.					Cmpnt. of 83d Div.
			do	P. of E., Hoboken.	June 1918	May 1919	May 1919	Cp. Sherman, Ohio.	
159th Field Artillery Brigade.	November 1917.	Cp. Zachary Taylor, Ky.	do	Cp. Knox, Ky.					Cmpnt. of 84th Div.
			August 1918	Cp. Mills, N. Y.					
			September 1918.	P. of E., Hoboken.	September 1918.				
			January 1919	Cp. Merritt, N. J.		January 1919	January 1919	Cp. Zachary Taylor, Ky.	
160th Field Artillery Brigade.	September 1917.	Cp. Custer, Mich.	July 1918	Cp. Mills, N. Y.					Cmpnt. of 85th Div.
			do	P. of E., Hoboken.	July 1918.				
			April 1919	Cp. Mills, N. Y.		April 1919	April 1919	Cp. Custer, Mich.	Corps troops.
161st Field Artillery Brigade.	do	Cp. Grant, Ill.	May 1918	Cp. Robinson, Wis.					Cmpnt. of 86th Div.
			September 1918.	Cp. Mills, N. Y.					
			do	P. of E., Hoboken.	September 1918.				
			January 1919	Cp. Mills, N. Y.		January 1919	January 1919	Cp. Grant, Ill.	

162d Field Artillery Brigade.	do	Cp. Pike, Ark.	June 1918	Cp. Dix, N. J.					Cmpnt. of 87th Div.
			August 1918	P. of E., Hoboken	August 1918.				
			February 1919	Cp. Dix, N. J.		February 1919	March 1919	Cp. Dix, N. J.	
163d Field Artillery Brigade.	do	Cp. Dodge, Iowa	August 1918	Cp. Mills, N. Y.					Cmpnt. of 88th Div.
			do	P. of E., Hoboken	August 1918.				
			January 1919	Cp. Stuart, Va.		January 1919	January 1919	Cp. Dodge, Iowa.	
164th Field Artillery Brigade.	September 1917	Cp. Funston, Kans.	June 1918	Cp. Mills, N. Y.					Cmpnt. of 89th Div.
			do	P. of E., Hoboken	June 1918.				
			May 1919	Cp. Upton, N. Y.		May 1919	June 1919	Cp. Upton, N. Y.	
165th Field Artillery Brigade.	August 1917	Cp. Travis, Tex.	June 1918	Cp. Mills, N. Y.					Cmpnt. of 90th Div.
			do	P. of E. Philadelphia, Pa.	June 1918.				
			June 1919	Cp. Mills, N. Y.		June 1919	June 1919	Cp. Bowie, Tex.	
166th Field Artillery Brigade.	September 1917	Cp. Lewis, Wash.	July 1918	do					Cmpnt. of 91st Div.
			do	P. of E., Hoboken	July 1918.				
			March 1919	Cp. Merritt, N. J.		March 1919	April 1919	Cp. Kearny, Calif.	Corps troops.
167th Field Artillery Brigade.	November 1917	Cp. Dix, N. J.	June 1918	P. of E., Hoboken	June 1918				Cmpnt. of 92d Div.
			February 1919	Cp. Mills, N. Y.		February 1919	February 1919	Cp. Meade, Md.	
168th Field Artillery Brigade.									Never orgzd.
169th Field Artillery Brigade.									Do.
170th Field Artillery Brigade.	September 1918	Cp. Knox, Ky.					December 1918	Cp. Knox, Ky.	Cmpnt. of 95th Div.
171st Field Artillery Brigade.	do	Cp. Kearny, Calif.					do	Cp. Kearny, Calif.	Cmpnt. of 96th Div.
172d Field Artillery Brigade.	October 1918	Cp. Jackson, S. C.					January 1919	Cp. Jackson, S. C.	Cmpnt. of 97th Div.

REGIMENTS

Unit designation and redesignation	Organization		Stations in United States		Overseas		Demobilization		Remarks
	Month and year	Place	Month and year	Place	From—	To—	Month and year	Place	
1st Field Artillery	Organized 1907		April 1917	Schofield Bks., T. H.					
			December 1917	Ft. Sill, Okla.					
2d Field Artillery	do		April 1917	Cp. Stotsenburg, P. I.					Cmpnt. of 8th F. A. Brig.
			October 1917	Presidio of San Francisco, Calif.					
			February 1918	Cp. Fremont, Calif.					
			July 1918	Ft. Sill, Okla.					
			October 1918	Cp. Mills, N. Y.					
			do	P. of E., Hoboken	October 1918.				
			January 1919	Cp. Mills, N. Y.		January 1919.			
			do	Cp. Knox, Ky.					
			February 1919	Cp. Zachary Taylor, Ky.					
3d Field Artillery	do		April 1917	Ft. Sam Houston, Tex.					Cmpnt. of 6th F. A. Brig.
			June 1917	Cp. Funston, Tex.					
			August 1917	Ft. Sam Houston, Tex.					
			April 1918	Cp. Doniphan, Okla.					
			July 1918	Cp. Mills, N. Y.					
			do	P. of E., Hoboken	July 1918.				
			June 1919	Cp. Mills, N. Y.		June 1919.			
			do	Cp. Grant, Ill.					
4th Field Artillery	do		April 1917	Cp. Stewart, Tex.					Units of the regt. were stationed at various camps throughout the U. S. and Canal Zone until July 1918.
			May 1917	Syracuse, N. Y.					
			August 1917	Pine Camp, N. Y.					
			October 1917	Cp. Shelby, Miss.					
	July 1918	Regt. assembled at Cp. Logan, Tex.	July 1918	Cp. Logan, Tex.					
			September 1918	Corpus Christi, Tex.					
			January 1919	Cp. Stanley, Tex.					

5th Field Artillery	Organized 1907		April 1917	Ft. Bliss, Tex					Cmpnt. of 1st F. A. Brig.
			July 1917	P. of E., Hoboken	July 1917.				
			September 1919	Cp. Mills, N. Y		September 1919			
			do	Cp. Leach, D. C.					
			do	Cp. Meade, Md.					
			October 1919	Cp. Zachary Taylor, Ky.					
6th Field Artillery	Organized 1907		April 1917	Douglas, Ariz					Cmpnt. of 1st F. A. Brig.
			July 1917	P. of E., Hoboken	July 1917.				
			September 1919	Cp. Mills, N. Y		September 1919.			
			do	Cp. Leach, D. C.					
			do	Cp. Meade, Md.					
			October 1919	Cp. Zachary Taylor, Ky.					
7th Field Artillery	Organized 1916		April 1917	Ft. Sam Houston, Tex.					Cmpnt. of 1st F. A. Brig.
			July 1917	P. of E., Hoboken	July 1917.				
			September 1919	Cp. Mills, N. Y		September 1919.			
			do	Cp. Leach, D. C.					
			do	Cp. Meade, Md.					
			October 1919	Cp. Zachary Taylor, Ky.					
8th Field Artillery	do		April 1917	Ft. Bliss, Tex					Cmpnt. of 7th F. A. Brig.
			May 1917	Cp. Robinson, Wis.					
			November 1917	Cp. Wheeler, Ga.					
			June 1918	Cp. McClellan, Ala.					
			August 1918	Cp. Merritt, N. J.					
			do	P. of E., Hoboken	August 1918.				
			June 1919	Cp. Mills, N. Y		June 1919.			
			do	Cp. Funston, Kans.					
9th Field Artillery	do		April 1917	Schofield Bks., T. H.					
			January 1918	Ft. Sill, Okla.					
10th Field Artillery	June 1917	Douglas, Ariz	March 1918	Cp. Merritt, N. J					Cmpnt. of 3d F. A. Brig.
			April 1918	P. of E., Hoboken	April 1918.				
			August 1919	Cp. Merritt, N. J		August 1919.			
			do	Cp. Pike, Ark.					

REGIMENTS—Continued

Unit designation and redesignation	Organization: Month and year	Organization: Place	Stations in United States: Month and year	Stations in United States: Place	Overseas: From—	Overseas: To—	Demobilization: Month and year	Demobilization: Place	Remarks
11th Field Artillery	June 1917	Douglas, Ariz.	April 1918	Cp. Doniphan, Okla.					Cmpnt. of 6th F. A. Brig.
			July 1918	Cp. Mills, N. Y.					
			do	P. of E., Hoboken	July 1918.				
			June 1919	Cp. Mills, N. Y.		June 1919.			
			do	Cp. Grant, Ill.					Army troops.
12th Field Artillery	do	Ft. Myer, Va.	December 1917	Cp. Merritt, N. J.					Cmpnt. of 2d F. A. Brig.
			January 1918	P. of E., Hoboken	January 1918.				
			August 1919	Cp. Mills, N. Y.		August 1919.			
			do	Cp. Travis, Tex.					
13th Field Artillery	do	Cp. Stewart, Tex.	July 1917	Ft. Bliss, Tex.					Cmpnt. of 4th F. A. Brig.
			December 1917	Cp. Greene, N. C.					
			May 1918	Cp. Merritt, N. J.					
			do	P. of E., Hoboken	May 1918.				
			July 1919	Cp. Merritt, N. J.		July 1919.			
			August 1919	Cp. Dodge, Iowa					
14th Field Artillery	do	Ft. Sill, Okla.							
15th Field Artillery	do	Syracuse, N. Y.	August 1917	Pine Camp, N. Y.					Cmpnt. of 2d F. A. Brig.
			November 1917	Cp. Merritt, N. J.					
			December 1917	P. of E., Hoboken	December 1917.				
			August 1919	Cp. Mills, N. Y.		August 1919.			
			do	Cp. Travis, Tex.					
16th Field Artillery	do	Cp. Robinson, Wis.	October 1917	Plattsburg Bks., N. Y.					Cmpnt. of 4th F. A. Brig.
			November 1917	Cp. Greene, N. C.					
			May 1918	P. of E., Hoboken	May 1918.				
			July 1919	Cp. Merritt, N. J.		July 1919.			
			August 1919	Cp. Dodge, Iowa.					

17th Field Artillery	do	do	December 1917	P. of E., Newport News.	December 1917				Cmpnt. of 2d F. A. Brig.
			August 1919	Cp. Mills, N. Y.		August 1919.			
			do	Cp. Travis, Tex.					
18th Field Artillery	do	Ft. Bliss, Tex.	March 1918	Cp. Merritt, N. J.					Cmpnt. of 3d F. A. Brig.
			April 1918	P. of E., Hoboken	April 1918.				
			August 1919	Cp. Merritt, N. J.		August 1919.			
			do	Cp. Pike, Ark.					
19th Field Artillery	do	Cp. Wilson, Tex.	July 1917	Ft. Sam Houston, Tex.					Cmpnt. of 5th F. A. Brig.
			November 1917	Cp. Stanley, Tex.					
			February 1918	Cp. MacArthur, Tex.					
			May 1918	Cp. Upton, N. Y.					
			do	P. of E., Hoboken	May 1918.				
			July 1919	Cp. Mills, N. Y.		July 1919.			
			do	Cp. Bragg, N. C.					
20th Field Artillery	do	do	June 1917	Cp. Funston, Tex.					Do.
			February 1918	Cp. MacArthur, Tex.					
			May 1918	Cp. Upton, N. Y.					
			do	P. of E., Montreal	May 1918.				
			July 1919	Cp. Merritt, N. J.		July 1919.			
			do	Cp. Bragg, N. C.					
21st Field Artillery	do	do	July 1917	Cp. Funston, Tex.					Do.
			February 1918	Cp. MacArthur, Tex.					
			May 1918	Cp. Upton, N. Y.					
			do	P. of E., Montreal	May 1918.				
			July 1919	Cp. Merritt, N. J.		July 1919.			
			do	Cp. Bragg, N. C.					
22d Field Artillery									Never orgzd.
23d Field Artillery									Do.
24th Field Artillery									Do.
25th Field Artillery	August 1918	Cp. McClellan, Ala.					February 1919	Cp. McClellan, Ala.	Cmpnt. of 9th F. A. Brig.
26th Field Artillery	do	do					do	do	Do.
27th Field Artillery	do	do					do	do	Do.

REGIMENTS—Continued

Unit designation and redesignation	Organization		Stations in United States		Overseas		Demobilization		Remarks
	Month and year	Place	Month and year	Place	From—	To—	Month and year	Place	
28th Field Artillery	August 1918	Cp. Funston, Kans.					February 1919	Cp. Funston, Kans.	Cmpnt. of 10th F. A. Brig.
29th Field Artillery	do	do					do	do	Do.
30th Field Artillery	do	do					do	do	Do.
31st Field Artillery	do	Cp. Meade, Md					December 1918	Cp. Meade, Md	Cmpnt. of 11th F. A. Brig.
32d Field Artillery	do	do					do	do	Do.
33d Field Artillery	do	do					do	do	Do.
34th Field Artillery	do	Cp. McClellan, Ala.					February 1919	Cp. McClellan, Ala.	Cmpnt. of 12th F. A. Brig.
35th Field Artillery	do	do					do	do	Do.
36th Field Artillery	do	do					do	do	Do.
37th Field Artillery	do	Cp. Lewis, Wash					do	Cp. Lewis, Wash	Cmpnt. of 13th F. A. Brig.
38th Field Artillery	do	do					do	do	Do.
39th Field Artillery	do	do					do	do	Do.
40th Field Artillery	do	Cp. Custer, Mich					do	Cp. Custer, Mich	Cmpnt. of 14th F. A. Brig.
41st Field Artillery	do	do					do	do	Do.
42d Field Artillery	do	do					do	do	Do.
43d Field Artillery	do	Cp. Stanley, Tex					do	Cp. Stanley, Tex	Orgzd. fr. 304th Cav. Cmpnt. of 15th F. A. Brig.
44th Field Artillery	do	do					do	do	Orgzd. fr. 305th Cav. Cmpnt. of 15th F. A. Brig.
45th Field Artillery	do	do					do	do	Do.
46th Field Artillery	do	Cp. Kearny, Calif.					do	Cp. Kearny, Calif.	Orgzd. fr. 301st Cav. Cmpnt. of 16th F. A. Brig.
47th Field Artillery	do	do					do	do	Do.

48th Field Artillery	do	do					do	do	Orgzd. fr. 302d Cav. Cmpnt. of 16th F. A. Brig.
49th Field Artillery	do	Cp. Bowie, Tex	November 1918	Ft. Sill, Okla			do	Ft. Sill, Okla	Orgzd. fr. 306th Cav. Cmpnt. of 17th F. A. Brig.
50th Field Artillery	do	do	do	do			do	do	Do.
51st Field Artillery	do	do	do	do			do	do	Orgzd. fr. 307th Cav. Cmpnt. of 17th F. A. Brig.
52d Field Artillery	do	Cp. Stanley, Tex	August 1918	Cp. Travis, Tex			do	Cp. Travis, Tex	Orgzd. fr. 303d Cav. Cmpnt. of 18th F. A. Brig.
53d Field Artillery	do	do	do	do			do	do	Do.
54th Field Artillery	do	do	do	do			do	do	Orgzd. fr. 304th Cav. Cmpnt. of 18th F. A. Brig.
55th Field Artillery	do	Cp. Bowie, Tex	October 1918	Ft. Sill, Okla			do	Ft. Sill, Okla	Orgzd. fr. 307th Cav. Cmpnt. of 19th F. A. Brig.
56th Field Artillery	do	do	do	do			do	do	Orgzd. fr. 309th Cav. Cmpnt. of 19th F. A. Brig.
57th Field Artillery	do	do	do	do			do	do	Do.
58th Field Artillery	October 1918	Ft. Ethan Allen, Vt.	November 1918	Cp. Jackson, S. C			do	Cp. Jackson, S. C	Orgzd. fr. 310th Cav. Cmpnt. of 20th F. A. Brig.
59th Field Artillery	do	do	do	do			do	do	Do.
60th Field Artillery	August 1918	Fts. Myer, Va. and D. A. Russell, Wyo.	September 1918	do			do	do	Orgzd. fr. 312th Cav. Cmpnt. of 20th F. A. Brig.
61st Field Artillery	do	Fts. Sheridan, Ill. and D. A. Russell, Wyo.	September and October 1918.	do			January 1919	do	Orgzd. fr. 312th Cav. Cmpnt. of 172d F. A. Brig.
62d Field Artillery	October 1918	Cp. Owen Beirne, Tex.	November 1918	do			do	do	Orgzd. fr. 314th Cav. Cmpnt. of 172d F. A. Brig.
63d Field Artillery	do	do	do	do			do	do	Do.

REGIMENTS—Continued

Unit designation and redesignation	Organization		Stations in United States		Overseas		Demobilization		Remarks
	Month and year	Place	Month and year	Place	From—	To—	Month and year	Place	
64th Field Artillery	August 1918	Cp. Kearny, Calif.					December 1918	Cp. Kearny, Calif.	Orgzd. fr. 302d Cav. Cmpnt. of 171st F. A. Brig.
65th Field Artillery	September 1918	do					do	do	Orgzd. fr. 308th Cav. Cmpnt. of 171st F. A. Brig.
66th Field Artillery	do	do					do	do	Do.
67th Field Artillery	do	Cp. Knox, Ky.					do	Cp. Knox, Ky.	Orgzd. fr. 311th Cav. Cmpnt. of 170th F. A. Brig.
68th Field Artillery	do	do					do	do	Do.
69th Field Artillery	August 1918	Cp. Del Rio, Tex.	September 1918	Cp. Knox, Ky.			do	do	Orgzd. fr. 313th Cav. Cmpnt. of 170th F. A. Brig.
70th Field Artillery	do	do	do	do			February 1919	do	Orgzd. fr. 313th Cav. Cmpnt. of 24th F. A. Brig.
71st Field Artillery	do	Ft. D. A. Russell, Wyo.	do	do			do	do	Orgzd. fr. 315th Cav. Cmpnt. of 24th F. A. Brig.
72d Field Artillery	do	do	do	do			do	do	Do.
73d Field Artillery	October 1918	Cp. Jackson, S. C.					December 1918	Cp. Jackson, S. C.	Cmpnt. of 22d F. A. Brig.
74th Field Artillery	do	Cp. Sheridan, Ala.					do	Cp. Sheridan, Ala.	Cmpnt. of 23d F. A. Brig. (Corps Troops).
75th Field Artillery	do	do					do	do	Do.
76th Field Artillery	November 1917	Ft. Ethan Allen, Vt.	November 1917 March 1918 April 1918 August 1919 do	Cp. Shelby, Miss. Cp. Merritt, N. J. P. of E., Hoboken Cp. Merritt, N. J. Cp. Pike, Ark.	April 1918.	August 1919.			Orgzd. fr. 18th Cav. Cmpnt. of 3d F. A. Brig.

77th Field Artillery	October 1917	do	November 1917	Cp. Shelby, Miss.					Orgzd. fr. 19th Cav. Cmpnt. of 4th F. A. Brig.
			December 1917	Cp. Greene, N. C.					
			May 1918	Cp. Merritt, N. J.					
			do	P. of E., Hoboken	May 1918.				
			July 1919	Cp. Merritt, N. J.		July 1919.			
			August 1919	Cp. Dodge, Iowa.					
78th Field Artillery	November 1917	Cp. Logan, Tex.	April 1918	Cp. Doniphan, Okla.					Orgzd. fr. 20th Cav. Cmpnt. of 6th F. A. Brig.
			July 1918	Cp. Mills, N. Y.					
			do	P. of E., Hoboken	July 1918.				
			June 1919	Cp. Mills, N. Y.		June 1919.			
			do	Cp. Grant, Ill.					
79th Field Artillery	do	do	June 1918	Cp. McClellan, Ala.					Orgzd. fr. 21st Cav. Cmpnt. of 7th F. A. Brig.
			August 1918	Cp. Merritt, N. J.					
			do	P. of E., Hoboken	August 1918.				
			June 1919	Cp. Mills, N. Y.		June 1919.			
			do	Cp. Funston, Kans.					
80th Field Artillery	do	Ft. Oglethorpe, Ga.	February 1918	Cp. MacArthur, Tex.					Orgzd. fr. 22d Cav. Cmpnt. of 7th F. A. Brig.
			June 1918	Cp. McClellan, Ala.					
			August 1918	Cp. Merritt, N. J.					
			do	P. of E., Hoboken	August 1918.				
			June 1919	Cp. Mills, N. Y.		June 1919.			
			do	Cp. Funston, Kans.					
81st Field Artillery	do	do	February 1918	Cp. Fremont, Calif.					Orgzd. fr. 23d Cav. Cmpnt. of 8th F. A. Brig.
			July 1918	Ft. Sill, Okla.					
			October 1918	Cp. Mills, N. Y.					
			November 1918	P. of E., Hoboken	November 1918.				
			January 1919	Cp. Merritt, N. J.		January 1919.			
			do	Cp. Knox, Ky.					
82d Field Artillery	do	Cp. Logan, Tex.	December 1917	Ft. Bliss, Tex.					Orgzd. fr. 24th Cav. Cmpnt. of 15th Cav. Div.

REGIMENTS—Continued

Unit designation and redesignation	Organization		Stations in United States		Overseas		Demobilization		Remarks
	Month and year	Place	Month and year	Place	From—	To—	Month and year	Place	
83d Field Artillery	November 1917	Ft. D. A. Russell, Wyo.	February 1918	Cp. Fremont, Calif.					Orgzd. fr. 25th Cav. Cmpnt. of 8th F. A. Brig.
			July 1918	Ft. Sill, Okla.					
			October 1918	Cp. Mills, N. Y.					
			do	P. of E., Hoboken	October 1918.				
			January 1919	Cp. Mills, N. Y.		January 1919.			
			do	Cp. Knox, Ky.					
84th Field Artillery	October 1918	Cp. Sheridan, Ala.					December 1918	Cp. Sheridan, Ala.	Cmpnt. of 21st F. A. Brig.
85th Field Artillery	do	do					do	do	Do.
86th to 100th Field Artillery.									Never orgzd.
101st Field Artillery	August 1917	Boxford, Mass.	September 1917	P. of E., Hoboken	September 1917	April 1919	April 1919	Cp. Devens, Mass.	Cmpnt. of 51st F. A. Brig.
102d Field Artillery	do	do	do	do	do	do	do	do	Do.
103d Field Artillery	do	do	October 1917	do	October 1917	do	do	do	Do.
104th Field Artillery	October 1917	Cp. Wadsworth, S. C.	May 1918	Cp. Stuart, Va.					Cmpnt. of 52d F. A. Brig.
			June 1918	P. of E., Newport News.	June 1918.				
			March 1919	Cp. Upton, N. Y.		March 1919	April 1919	Cp. Upton, N. Y.	
105th Field Artillery	do	do	May 1918	Cp. Stuart, Va.					Cmpnt. of 52d F. A. Brig.
			June 1918	P. of E., Newport News.	June 1918.				
			March 1919	Cp. Mills, N. Y.		March 1919.			
			do	Cp. Upton, N. Y.			April 1919	Cp. Upton, N. Y.	
106th Field Artillery	September 1917	do	May 1918	Cp. Stuart, Va.					Cmpnt. of 52d F. A. Brig.
			June 1918	P. of E., Newport News.	June 1918.				
			March 1919	Cp. Mills, N. Y.		March 1919	March 1919	Cp. Upton, N. Y.	

107th Field Artillery	do	Cp. Hancock, Ga.	May 1918	do					Cmpnt. of 53d F. A. Brig.
			do	P. of E., Hoboken	May 1918	May 1919	May 1919	Cp. Dix, N. J.	
108th Field Artillery	do	do	do	Cp. Mills, N. Y.					Do.
			do	P. of E., Hoboken	May 1918	May 1919	May 1919	Cp. Dix, N. J.	
109th Field Artillery	do	do	do	Cp. Mills, N. Y.					Do.
			do	P. of E., Hoboken	May 1918	May 1919	May 1919	Cp. Dix, N. J.	
110th Field Artillery	do	Cp. McClellan, Ala.							
a. 112th Field Artillery.	November 1917	do	June 1918	Cp. Mills, N. Y.					Cmpnt. of 54th F. A. Brig.
			do	P. of E., Hoboken	June 1918.				
			May 1919	Cp. Stuart, Va.		May 1919	May 1919	Cp. Dix, N. J.	
111th Field Artillery	September 1917	do	June 1918	Cp. Mills, N. Y.					Do.
			do	P. of E., Philadelphia.	June 1918	June 1919	June 1919	Cp. Lee, Va.	
112th Field Artillery	do	Do.							
a. 110th Field Artillery.	November 1917	do	June 1918	Cp. Mills, N. Y.					Do.
			do	P. of E., Baltimore	June 1918.				
			May 1919	Cp. Stuart, Va.		May 1919.			
			do	Cp. Meade, Md.			June 1919	Cp. Meade, Md.	
113th Field Artillery	September 1917	Cp. Sevier, S. C.	May 1918	Cp. Mills, N. Y.					Cmpnt. of 55th F. A. Brig.
			do	P. of E., Hoboken	May 1918.				
			March 1919	Cp. Stuart, Va.		March 1919	March 1919	Cp. Jackson, S. C.	
114th Field Artillery	do	do	May 1918	Cp. Mills, N. Y.					Do.
			do	P. of E., Hoboken	May 1918.				
			March 1919	Cp. Stuart, Va.		March 1919	April 1919	Ft. Ogelthorpe, Ga.	
115th Field Artillery	do	do	May 1918	Cp. Mills, N. Y.					Do.
			June 1918	P. of E., Hoboken	June 1918.				
			March 1919	Cp. Jackson, S. C.		March 1919	April 1919	Ft. Ogelthorpe, Ga.	
116th Field Artillery	October 1917	Cp. Wheeler, Ga.	July 1918	do					Cmpnt. of 56th F. A. Brig.
			October 1918	Cp. Mills, N. Y.					
			do	P. of E., Hoboken	October 1918.				
			December 1918	Cp. Merritt, N. J.		December 1918.			
			do	Cp. Gordon, Ga.			January 1919	Cp. Gordon, Ga.	
117th Field Artillery	do	do	July 1918	Cp. Jackson, S. C.					Do.
			October 1918	Cp. Mills, N. Y.					
			do	P. of E., Hoboken	October 1918.				
			December 1918	Cp. Merritt, N. J.		December 1918.			
			do	Cp. Gordon, Ga.			January 1919	Cp. Gordon, Ga.	

REGIMENTS—Continued

Unit designation and redesignation	Organization		Stations in United States		Overseas		Demobilization		Remarks
	Month and year	Place	Month and year	Place	From—	To—	Month and year	Place	
118th Field Artillery	September 1917	Cp. Wheeler, Ga.	July 1918	Cp. Jackson, S. C.					Cmpnt. of 56th F. A. Brig.
			October 1918	Cp. Mills, N. Y.					
			do	P. of E., Hoboken	October 1918.				
			December 1918	Cp. Stuart, Va.		December 1918.			
			do	Cp. Gordon, Ga.			January 1919	Cp. Gordon, Ga.	
119th Field Artillery	do	Cp. MacArthur, Tex.	February 1918	Cp. Merritt, N. J.					Cmpnt. of 57th F. A. Brig.
			do	P. of E., Hoboken	February 1918.				
			May 1919	Cp. Mills, N. Y.		May 1919	May 1919	Cp. Custer, Mich.	
120th Field Artillery	do	do	February 1918	Cp. Merritt, N. J.					Do.
			March 1918	P. of E., Hoboken	March 1918.				
			May 1919	Cp. Devens, Mass.		May 1919	May 1919	Cp. Grant, Ill.	
121st Field Artillery	do	do	February 1918	Cp. Merritt, N. J.					Do.
			March 1918	P. of E., Hoboken	March 1918.				
			May 1919	Cp. Devens, Mass.		May 1919	May 1919	Cp. Grant, Ill.	
122d Field Artillery	do	Cp. Logan, Tex.	May 1918	Cp. Merritt, N. J.					Cmpnt. of 58th F. A. Brig.
			do	P. of E., Hoboken	May 1918.				
			May 1919	Cp. Mills, N. Y.		May 1919	June 1919	Cp. Grant, Ill.	
123d Field Artillery	do	do	May 1918	Cp. Merritt, N. J.					Do.
			do	P. of E., Hoboken	May 1918.				
			May 1919	Cp. Mills, N. Y.		May 1919	June 1919	Cp. Grant, Ill.	
124th Field Artillery	September 1917	Cp. Logan, Tex.	May 1918	Cp. Merritt, N. J.					Cmpnt. of 58th F. A. Brig.
			do	P. of E., Hoboken	May 1918.				
			May 1919	Cp. Mills, N. Y.		May 1919	June 1919	Cp. Grant, Ill.	
125th Field Artillery	do	Cp. Cody, N. Mex.	July 1918	Ft. Sill, Okla.					Cmpnt. of 59th F. A. Brig.
			September 1918	Cp. Upton, N. Y.					
			do	P. of E., Hoboken	September 1918.				
			January 1919	Cp. Stuart, Va.		January 1919	January 1919	Cp. Dodge, Iowa.	

126th Field Artillery	do	do	July 1918	Ft. Sill, Okla					Do.
			September 1918	Cp. Upton, N. Y.					
			do	P. of E., Hoboken	September 1918.				
			January 1919	Cp. Stuart, Va		January 1919	January 1919	Cp. Dodge, Iowa.	
127th Field Artillery	October 1917	do	July 1918	Ft. Sill, Okla					Do.
			September 1918	Cp. Upton, N. Y.					
			do	P. of E., Hoboken	September 1918.				
			January 1919	Cp. Stuart, Va		January 1919	January 1919	Cp. Dodge, Iowa.	
128th Field Artillery	September 1917	Cp. Doniphan, Okla.	May 1918	Cp. Mills, N. Y.					Cmpnt. of 60th F. A. Brig.
			do	P. of E., Hoboken	May 1918.				
			April 1919	Cp. Devens, Mass.		April 1919.			
			do	Cp. Funston, Kans.			May 1919	Cp. Funston, Kans.	
129th Field Artillery	October 1917	do	May 1918	Cp. Mills, N. Y.					Do.
			do	P. of E., Hoboken	May 1918.				
			April 1919	Cp. Mills, N. Y.		April 1919	May 1919	Cp. Funston, Kans.	
130th Field Artillery	do	do	May 1918	do					Do.
			do	P. of E., Hoboken	May 1918.				
			April 1919	Cp. Upton, N. Y.		April 1919	May 1919	Cp. Funston, Kans.	
131st Field Artillery	do	Cp. Bowie, Tex.	July 1918	Cp. Mills, N. Y.					Cmpnt. of 61st F. A. Brig.
			do	P. of E., Hoboken	July 1918.				
			March 1919	Cp. Stuart, Va.		March 1919.			
			do	Cp. Travis, Tex.			April 1919	Cp. Travis, Tex.	
132d Field Artillery	do	do	July 1918	Cp. Mills, N. Y.					Do.
			do	P. of E., Hoboken	July 1918.				
			March 1919	Cp. Stuart, Va.		March 1919	April 1919	Cp. Bowie, Tex.	
133d Field Artillery	do	do	July 1918	Cp. Mills, N. Y.					Do.
			do	P. of E., Hoboken	July 1918.				
			March 1919	Cp. Morrison, Va.		March 1919.			
			do	Cp. Bowie, Tex.			April 1919	Cp. Bowie, Tex.	
134th Field Artillery	September 1917	Cp. Sheridan, Ala.	June 1918	Cp. Upton, N. Y.					Cmpnt. of 62d F. A. Brig.
			do	P. of E., Hoboken	June 1918.				
			March 1919	Cp. Stuart, Va.		March 1919	April 1919	Cp. Sherman, Ohio	Army troops.
135th Field Artillery	do	do	June 1918	Cp. Upton, N. Y.					Cmpnt. of 62d F A. Brig.
			do	P. of E., Hoboken	June 1918.				
			March 1919	Cp. Stuart, Va.		March 1919	April 1919	Cp. Sherman, Ohio	Corps troops.

REGIMENTS—Continued

Unit designation and redesignation	Organization		Stations in United States		Overseas		Demobilization		Remarks
	Month and year	Place	Month and year	Place	From—	To—	Month and year	Place	
136th Field Artillery	September 1917	Cp. Sheridan, Ala.	June 1918	Cp. Upton, N. Y.					Cmpnt. of 62d F. A. Brig.
			do	P. of E., Montreal	June 1918.				
			March 1919	Cp. Stuart, Va.		March 1919	April 1919	Cp. Sherman, Ohio	Corps troops.
137th Field Artillery	October 1917	Cp. Shelby, Miss.	September 1918	Cp. Mills, N. Y.					Cmpnt. of 63d F. A. Brig.
			October 1918	P. of E., Hoboken	October 1918.				
			December 1918	Cp. Merritt, N. J.		December 1918	January 1919	Ft. Benjamin Harrison, Ind.	
138th Field Artillery	do	do	September 1918	Cp. Upton, N. Y					Do.
			October 1918	P. of E., Hoboken	October 1918.				
			December 1918	Cp. Mills, N. Y.		December 1918	January 1919	Cp. Zachary Taylor, Ky.	
139th Field Artillery	do	do	September 1918	Cp. Upton, N. Y					Do.
			October 1918	P. of E., Hoboken	October 1918.				
			December 1918	Cp. Merritt, N. J.		December 1918	January 1919	Ft. Benjamin Harrison, Ind.	
140th Field Artillery	September 1917	Cp. Jackson, Miss.	November 1917	Cp. Beauregard, La.					Cmpnt. of 64th F. A. Brig.
			August 1918	Cp. Mills, N. Y.					
			do	P. of E., Hoboken	August 1918.				
			June 1919	Cp. Mills, N. Y.		June 1919	June 1919	Cp. Shelby, Miss.	
141st Field Artillery	do	Cp. Nicholls, La.	October 1917	Cp. Beauregard, La					Do.
			August 1918	Cp. Mills, N. Y.					
			do	P. of E., Hoboken	August 1918.				
			April 1919	Cp. Merritt, N. J.		April 1919.			
			do	Cp. Shelby, Miss.			May 1919	Cp. Shelby, Miss.	
142d Field Artillery	November 1917	Ft. Logan H. Roots, Ark.	November 1917	Cp. Beauregard, La.					Do.
			August 1918	Cp. Mills, N. Y.					
			do	P. of E., Hoboken	August 1918.				
			June 1919	Cp. Morrison, Va.		June 1919	June 1919	Cp. Pike, Ark.	

143d Field Artillery	September 1917	Presidio of San Francisco, Calif.	October 1917	Cp. Kearny, Calif.					Cmpnt. of 65th F. A. Brig.
			August 1918	Cp. Mills, N. Y.					
			do	P. of E., Hoboken	August 1918.				
			December 1918	Cp. Merritt, N. J.		December 1918	January 1919	Presidio of San Francisco, Calif.	
144th Field Artillery	October 1917	Cp. Kearny, Calif.	August 1918	Cp. Mills, N. Y.					Do.
			do	P. of E., Hoboken	August 1918.				
			January 1919	Cp. Merritt, N. J.		January 1919	January 1919	Presidio of San Francisco, Calif.	
145th Field Artillery	do	Ft. Douglas, Utah	October 1917	Cp. Kearny, Calif.					Do.
			August 1918	Cp. Mills, N. Y.					
			do	P. of E., Hoboken	August 1918.				
			January 1919	Cp. Merritt, N. J.		January 1919	January 1919	Logan, Utah.	
146th Field Artillery	September 1917	Cp. Greene, N. C.	October 1917	Cp. Mills, N. Y.					Cmpnt. of 66th F. A. Brig.
			December 1917	Cp. Merritt, N. J.					
			do	P. of E., Hoboken	December 1917.				
			June 1919	Cp. Merritt, N. J.		June 1919	June 1919	Ft. D. A. Russell, Wyo.	Army troops.
147th Field Artillery	October 1917	do	October 1917	Cp. Mills, N. Y.					Cmpnt. of 66th F. A. Brig.
			December 1917	Cp. Merritt, N. J.					
			January 1918	P. of E., Hoboken	January 1918.				
			May 1919	Cp. Dix, N. J.		May 1919	May 1919	Cp. Dodge, Iowa.	
148th Field Artillery	September 1917	do	October 1917	Cp. Mills, N. Y.					Do.
			December 1917	Cp. Merritt, N. J.					
			January 1918	P. of E., Hoboken	January 1918.				
			June 1919	Cp. Mills, N. Y.		June 1919	June 1919	Ft. D. A. Russell, Wyo.	Army troops.
149th Field Artillery	August 1917	Ft. Sheridan, Ill.	September 1917	do					Cmpnt. of 67th F. A. Brig.
			October 1917	P. of E., Hoboken	October 1917.				
			April 1919	Cp. Merritt, N. J.		April 1919	May 1919	Cp. Grant, Ill.	
150th Field Artillery	do	Ft. Benjamin Harrison, Ind.	September 1917	Cp. Mills, N. Y.					Do.
			October 1917	P. of E., Hoboken	October 1917.				
			April 1919	Cp. Merritt, N. J.		April 1919	May 1919	Cp. Zachary Taylor, Ky.	

REGIMENTS—Continued

Unit designation and redesignation	Organization		Stations in United States		Overseas		Demobilization		Remarks
	Month and year	Place	Month and year	Place	From—	To—	Month and year	Place	
151st Field Artillery	August 1917	Ft. Snelling, Minn.	September 1917	Cp. Mills, N. Y.					Cmpnt. of 67th F. A. Brig.
			October 1917	P. of E., Hoboken	October 1917.				
			April 1919	Cp. Merritt, N. J.		April 1919	May 1919	Cp. Dodge, Iowa.	
152d to 300th Field Artillery.									Never orgzd.
301st Field Artillery	August 1917	Cp. Devens, Mass.	July 1918	P. of E., Boston	July 1918				Cmpnt. of 151st F. A. Brig.
			January 1919	Cp. Mills, N. Y.		January 1919	January 1919	Cp. Devens, Mass.	
302d Field Artillery	do	do	July 1918	P. of E., Boston	July 1918				Do.
			April 1919	Cp. Devens, Mass.		April 1919	May 1919	Cp. Devens, Mass.	Corps troops.
303d Field Artillery	do	do	July 1918	P. of E., Boston	July 1918				Cmpnt. of 151st F. A. Brig.
			April 1919	Cp. Devens, Mass.		April 1919	May 1919	Cp. Devens, Mass.	Corps troops.
304th Field Artillery	do	Cp. Upton, N. Y.	April 1[illegible]	P. of E., Hoboken	April 1918				Cmpnt. of 152d F. A. Brig.
			April 1919	Cp. Mills, N. Y.		April 1919	May 1919	Cp. Upton, N. Y.	
305th Field Artillery	September 1917	do	April 1918	P. of E., Hoboken	April 1918				Do.
			April 1919	Cp. Mills, N. Y.		April 1919	May 1919	Cp. Upton, N. Y.	
306th Field Artillery	August 1917	Cp. Upton, N. Y.	April 1918	P. of E., Hoboken	April 1918				Do.
			April 1919	Cp. Mills, N. Y.		April 1919	May 1919	Cp. Upton, N. Y.	
307th Field Artillery	September 1917	Cp. Dix, N. J.	May 1918	P. of E., Hoboken	May 1918	May 1919	do	Cp. Dix, N. J.	Cmpnt. of 153d F. A. Brig.
308th Field Artillery	do	do	do	do	do	do	do	do	Do.
309th Field Artillery	do	do	do	P. of E., Boston	do	do	do	do	Do.
310th Field Artillery	August 1917	Cp. Meade, Md.	July 1918	P. of E., Philadelphia.	July 1918	do	do	do	Cmpnt. of 154th F. A. Brig.
311th Field Artillery	do	do	do	do	do				Do.
			May 1919	Cp. Dix, N. J.		May 1919	June 1919	Cp. Dix, N. J.	
312th Field Artillery	do	do	July 1918	P. of E., Philadelphia.	July 1918				Do.
			May 1919	Cp. Morrison, Va.		May 1919	May 1919	Cp. Dix, N. J.	

313th Field Artillery	do	Cp. Lee, Va	May 1918	P. of E., Newport News.	May 1918				Cmpnt. of 155th F. A. Brig.
314th Field Artillery	do	do	May 1919 May 1918	Cp. Stuart, Va. P. of E., Newport News.	 May 1918	May 1919	June 1919	Cp. Lee, Va.	Do.
315th Field Artillery	September 1917	do	May 1919 May 1918	Cp. Stuart, Va. P. of E., Newport News.	 May 1918	May 1919	June 1919	Cp. Lee, Va.	Do.
316th Field Artillery	do	Cp. Jackson, S. C.	May 1919 July 1918	Cp. Stuart, Va. Cp. Mills, N. Y.		May 1919	June 1919	Cp. Lee, Va.	Cmpnt. of 156th F. A. Brig.
317th Field Artillery	do	do	August 1918 June 1919 July 1918	P. of E., Hoboken. Cp. Stuart, Va. Cp. Mills, N. Y.	August 1918.	June 1919	June 1919	Cp. Lee, Va.	Do.
318th Field Artillery	do	do	August 1918 July 1918	P. of E., Hoboken. Cp. Mills, N. Y.	August 1918	June 1919	June 1919	Cp. Morrison, Va.	Do.
319th Field Artillery	do	Cp. Gordon, Ga.	August 1918 June 1919 May 1918	P. of E., Hoboken. Cp. Stuart, Va. Cp. Mills, N. Y.	August 1918.	June 1919	June 1919	Ft. Oglethorpe, Ga.	Cmpnt. of 157th F. A. Brig.
320th Field Artillery	do	do	do May 1919 May 1918	P. of E., Hoboken. Cp. Upton, N. Y. Cp. Mills, N. Y.	May 1918.	May 1919	May 1919	Cp. Dix, N. J.	Do.
321st Field Artillery	do	do	do do	P. of E., Hoboken. Cp. Mills, N. Y.	May 1918	May 1919	May 1919	Cp. Dix, N. J.	Do.
322d Field Artillery	do	Cp. Sherman, Ohio.	do May 1919 June 1918	P. of E., Hoboken. Cp. Merritt, N. J. Cp. Mills, N. Y.	May 1918.	May 1919	May 1919	Cp. Dix, N. J.	Cmpnt. of 158th F. A. Brig.
323d Field Artillery	do	do	do May 1919 June 1918	P. of E., Hoboken. Cp. Merritt, N. J. Cp. Mills, N. Y.	June 1918.	May 1919	June 1919	Cp. Sherman, Ohio.	Do.
324th Field Artillery	do	do	do May 1919 June 1918 do May 1919 do	P. of E., Philadelphia. Cp. Merritt, N. J. Cp. Mills, N. Y. P. of E., Hoboken. Cp. Mills, N. Y. Cp. Sherman, Ohio.	June 1918. June 1918.	May 1919 May 1919.	May 1919 June 1919	Cp. Dix, N. J. Cp. Sherman, Ohio.	Do.

REGIMENTS—Continued

Unit designation and redesignation	Organization		Stations in United States		Overseas		Demobilization		Remarks
	Month and year	Place	Month and year	Place	From—	To—	Month and year	Place	
325th Field Artillery	September 1917	Cp. Zachary Taylor, Ky.	June 1918	Cp. Knox, Ky.					Cmpnt. of 159th F. A. Brig.
			September 1918	Cp. Mills, N. Y.					
			do	P. of E., Hoboken	September 1918.				
			February 1919	Cp. Stuart, Va.		February 1919.			
			do	Cp. Sherman, Ohio			March 1919	Cp. Sherman, Ohio	
326th Field Artillery	August 1917	do	June 1918	Cp. Knox, Ky.					Do.
			September 1918	Cp. Mills, N. Y.					
			do	P. of E., Hoboken	September 1918.				
			February 1919	Cp. Stuart, Va.		February 1919.			
			do	Cp. Zachary Taylor, Ky.			March 1919	Cp. Zachary Taylor, Ky.	
327th Field Artillery	do	do	April 1918	Cp. Knox, Ky.					Do.
			September 1918	Cp. Mills, N. Y.					
			do	P. of E., Hoboken	September 1918.				
			February 1919	Cp. Merritt, N. J.		February 1919	February 1919	Cp. Grant, Ill.	
328th Field Artillery	September 1917	Cp. Custer, Mich.	July 1918	Cp. Mills, N. Y.					Cmpnt. of 160th F. A. Brig.
			do	P. of E., Hoboken	July 1918.				
			April 1919	Cp. Mills, N. Y.		April 1919	April 1919	Cp. Custer, Mich.	Corps troops.
329th Field Artillery	do	do	July 1918	do					Cmpnt. of 160th F. A. Brig.
			do	P. of E., Hoboken	July 1918.				
			April 1919	Cp. Mills, N. Y.		April 1919	April 1919	Cp. Custer, Mich.	
330th Field Artillery	do	do	July 1918	do					Do.
			do	P. of E., Hoboken	July 1918.				
			April 1919	Cp. Mills, N. Y.		April 1919	April 1919	Cp. Custer, Mich.	Corps troops.
331st Field Artillery	August 1917	Cp. Grant, Ill.	May 1918	Cp. Robinson, Wis.					Cmpnt. of 161st F. A. Brig.
			September 1918	Cp. Mills, N. Y.					
			do	P. of E., Hoboken	September 1918.				
			February 1919	Cp. Merritt, N. J.		February 1919	February 1919	Cp. Grant, Ill.	

332d Field Artillery	do	do	May 1918	Cp. Robinson, Wis.					Do.
			September 1918	Cp. Mills, N. Y.					
			do	P. of E., Hoboken	September 1918.				
			February 1919	Cp. Stuart, Va.		February 1919	February 1919	Cp. Grant, Ill.	
333d Field Artillery	do	do	May 1918	Cp. Robinson, Wis.					Do.
			September 1918	Cp. Mills, N. Y.					
			do	P. of E., Hoboken	September 1918.				
			January 1919	Cp. Mills, N. Y.		January 1919	January 1919	Cp. Grant, Ill.	
334th Field Artillery	September 1917	Cp. Pike, Ark.	June 1918	Cp. Dix, N. J.					Cmpnt. of 162d F. A. Brig.
			August 1918	P. of E., Hoboken	August 1918.				
			February 1919	Cp. Merritt, N. J.		February 1919	March 1919	Cp. Dix, N. J.	
335th Field Artillery	do	do	June 1918	Cp. Dix, N. J.					Do.
			August 1918	P. of E., Hoboken	August 1918.				
			March 1919	Cp. Merritt, N. J.		March 1919	March 1910	Cp. Dix, N. J.	
336th Field Artillery	do	Ft. Logan H. Roots, Ark.	September 1917	Cp. Pike, Ark.					Do.
			June 1918	Cp. Dix, N. J.					
			August 1918	P. of E., Hoboken	August 1918.				
			March 1919	Cp. Stuart, Va.		March 1919	March 1919	Cp. Dix, N. J.	
337th Field Artillery	do	Cp. Dodge, Iowa	August 1918	Cp. Mills, N. Y.					Cmpnt. of 163d F. A. Brig.
			do	P. of E., Hoboken	August 1918.				
			January 1919	Cp. Merritt, N. J.		January 1919	February 1919	Cp. Dodge, Iowa.	
338th Field Artillery	do	do	August 1918	Cp. Mills, N. Y.					Do.
			do	P. of E., Hoboken	August 1918.				
			January 1919	Cp. Stuart, Va.		January 1919	January 1919	Cp. Dodge, Iowa.	
339th Field Artillery	do	do	August 1918	Cp. Mills, N. Y.					Do.
			do	P. of E., Hoboken	August 1918.				
			January 1919	Cp. Merritt, N. J.		January 1919	February 1919	Cp. Dodge, Iowa.	
340th Field Artillery	do	Cp. Funston, Kans.	June 1918	Cp. Mills, N. Y.					Cmpnt. of 164th F. A. Brig.
			do	P. of E., Hoboken	June 1918.				
			May 1919	Cp. Upton, N. Y.		May 1919	June 1919	Ft. Bliss, Tex.	
341st Field Artillery	do	do	June 1918	Cp. Mills, N. Y.					Do.
			do	P. of E., Boston	June 1918.				
			May 1919	Cp. Upton, N. Y.		May 1919	June 1919	Ft. D. A. Russell, Wyo.	
342d Field Artillery	do	do	June 1918	Cp. Mills, N. Y.					Cmpnt. of 164th F. A. Brig.
			do	P. of E., Hoboken	June 1918.				
			May 1919	Cp. Upton, N. Y.		May 1919	June 1919	Cp. Funston, Kans.	

REGIMENTS—Continued

Unit designation and redesignation	Organization		Stations in United States		Overseas		Demobilization		Remarks
	Month and year	Place	Month and year	Place	From—	To—	Month and year	Place	
343d Field Artillery	August 1917	Cp. Travis, Tex	June 1918	Cp. Mills, N. Y					Cmpnt. of 165th F. A. Brig.
			do	P. of E., Philadelphia.	June 1918.				
			June 1919	Cp. Merritt, N. J		June 1919	June 1919	Cp. Pike, Ark.	
344th Field Artillery	do	do	June 1918	Cp. Mills, N. Y					Do.
			do	P. of E., Boston	June 1918.				
			June 1919	Cp. Jackson, S. C		June 1919	June 1919	Cp. Bowie, Tex.	
345th Field Artillery	do	do	June 1918	Cp. Mills, N. Y					Do.
			do	P. of E., Boston	June 1918.				
			June 1919	Cp. Merritt, N. J		June 1919	June 1919	Cp. Bowie, Tex.	
346th Field Artillery	September 1917	Cp. Lewis, Wash	July 1918	Cp. Mills, N. Y					Cmpnt. of 166th F. A. Brig.
			do	P. of E., Hoboken	July 1918.				
			January 1919	Cp. Merritt, N. J		January 1919.			
			do	Cp. Lewis, Wash			February 1919	Cp. Lewis, Wash.	
347th Field Artillery	do	do	July 1918	Cp. Mills, N. Y					Do.
			do	P. of E., Hoboken	July 1918.				
			March 1919	Cp. Merritt, N. J		March 1919	April 1919	Presidio of San Francisco, Calif.	Corps troops.
348th Field Artillery	do	do	July 1918	Cp. Mills, N. Y					Cmpnt. of 166th F. A. Brig.
			do	P. of E., Hoboken	July 1918.				
			March 1919	Cp. Merritt, N. J		March 1919	April 1919	Ft. D. A. Russell, Wyo.	Corps troops.
349th Field Artillery	November 1917	Cp. Dix, N. J	June 1918	P. of E., Hoboken	June 1918				Cmpnt. of 167th F. A. Brig.
			March 1919	Cp. Upton, N. Y		March 1919	March 1919	Cp. Dix, N. J.	
350th Field Artillery	do	do	June 1918	Cp. Mills, N. Y					Do.
			do	P. of E., Hoboken	June 1918.				
			March 1919	Cp. Upton, N. Y		March 1919	March 1919	Cp. Dix, N. J.	
351st Field Artillery	October 1917	Cp. Meade, Md	June 1918	P. of E., Hoboken	June 1918				Do.
			February 1919	Cp. Mills, N. Y		February 1919.			
			do	Cp. Meade, Md			March 1919	Cp. Meade, Md.	

AMMUNITION TRAINS

1st Ammunition Train	November 1917	A. E. F	September 1919	Cp. Mills, N. Y.		September 1919			Cmpnt. of 1st Div.
			do	Cp. Meade, Md.					
			October 1919	Cp. Zachary Taylor, Ky.					
2d Ammunition Train	October 1917	Chickamauga Park, Ga.	December 1917	Cp. Merritt, N. J.					Cmpnt. of 2d Div.
			January 1918	P. of E., Hoboken	January 1918.				
			August 1919	Cp. Mills, N. Y.		August 1919.			
			do	Cp. Travis, Tex.					
3d Ammunition Train	December 1917	Cp. Forrest, Ga.	March 1918	Cp. Merritt, N. J.					Cmpnt. of 3d Div.
			do	P. of E., Hoboken	March 1918.				
			August 1919	Cp. Merritt, N. J.		August 1919.			
			September 1919	Cp. Pike, Ark.					
4th Ammunition Train	January 1918	Cp. Greene, N. C.	May 1918	Cp. Merritt, N. J.					Cmpnt. of 4th Div.
			do	P. of E., Hoboken	May 1918.				
			August 1919	Cp. Stuart, Va.		August 1919.			
			do	Cp. Dodge, Iowa.					
5th Ammunition Train	do	Cp. Logan, Tex.	May 1918	Cp. Upton, N. Y.					Cmpnt. of 5th Div.
			do	P. of E., Hoboken	May 1918.				
			July 1919	Cp. Merritt, N. J.		July 1919.			
			do	Cp. Gordon, Ga.					
6th Ammunition Train	February 1918	Cp. McClellan, Ala.	March 1918	Cp. Forrest, Ga.					Cmpnt. of 6th Div.
			May 1918	Cp. Wadsworth, S. C.					
			July 1918	Cp. Mills, N. Y.					
			do	P. of E., Hoboken	July 1918.				
			June 1919	Cp. Stuart, Va.		June 1919.			
			do	Cp. Grant, Ill.					
7th Ammunition Train	March 1918	Cp. Wheeler, Ga.	May 1918	Cp. MacArthur, Tex.					Cmpnt. of 7th Div.
			August 1918	Cp. Merritt, N. J.					
			do	P. of E., Hoboken	August 1918.				
			June 1919	Cp. Mills, N. Y.		June 1919.			
			do	Cp. Funston, Kans.					
8th Ammunition Train	April 1918	Cp. Fremont, Calif.	October 1918	Cp. Mills, N. Y.					Cmpnt. of 8th Div.
			November 1918	Cp. Lee, Va.			February 1919	Cp. Lee, Va.	
9th Ammunition Train	August 1918	Cp. McClellan, Ala.					do	Cp. McClellan, Ala.	Cmpnt. of 9th Div

AMMUNITION TRAINS—Continued

Unit designation and redesignation	Organization		Stations in United States		Overseas		Demobilization		Remarks
	Month and year	Place	Month and year	Place	From—	To—	Month and year	Place	
10th Ammunition Train	August 1918	Cp. Funston, Kans.					February 1919	Cp. Funston, Kans.	Cmpnt. of 10th Div.
11th Ammunition Train	do	Cp. Meade, Md.					December 1918	Cp. Meade, Md.	Cmpnt. of 11th Div.
12th Ammunition Train	do	Cp. McClellan, Ala.					January 1919	Cp. McClellan, Ala.	Cmpnt. of 12th Div.
13th Ammunition Train	September 1918	Cp. Lewis, Wash.					February 1919	Cp. Lewis, Wash.	Cmpnt. of 13th Div.
14th Ammunition Train	August 1918	Cp. Custer, Mich.					do	Cp. Custer, Mich.	Cmpnt. of 14th Div.
15th (I) Ammunition Train.	September 1918	Cp. Stanley, Tex.					do	Cp. Stanley, Tex.	Cmpnt. of 15th Div.
15th (II) Ammunition Train.	January 1918	Cp. Owen Beirne, Tex.	April 1918	Ft. Bliss, Tex.			do	Ft. Bliss, Tex.	Cmpnt. of 15th Cav. Div.
16th Ammunition Train	September 1918	Cp. Kearny, Calif.					do	Cp. Kearny, Calif.	Cmpnt. of 16th Div.
17th Ammunition Train	do	Cp. Bowie, Tex.	November 1918	Ft. Sill, Okla.			do	Ft. Sill, Okla.	Cmpnt. of 17th Div.
18th Ammunition Train	do	Cp. Travis, Tex.					do	Cp. Travis, Tex.	Cmpnt. of 18th Div.
19th Ammunition Train	do	Cp. Bowie, Tex.	October 1918	Ft. Sill, Okla.			do	Ft. Sill, Okla.	Cmpnt. of 19th Div.
20th Ammunition Train	November 1918	Cp. Jackson, S. C.					January 1919	Cp. Jackson, S. C.	Cmpnt. of 20th Div.
21st to 100th Ammunition Trains.									Never orgzd.
101st Ammunition Train	August 1917	Cp. Bartlett, Mass.	October 1917	P. of E., Hoboken.	October 1917	April 1919	April 1919	Cp. Devens, Mass.	Cmpnt. of 26th Div.
102d Ammunition Train	October 1917	Cp. Wadsworth, S. C.	May 1918 June 1918	Cp. Stuart, Va. P. of E., Newport News.	June 1918.				Cmpnt. of 27th Div.

			March 1919	Cp. Merritt, N. J.		March 1919.			
			do	Cp. Upton, N. Y.			April 1919	Cp. Upton, N. Y.	
103d Ammunition Train	September 1917	Cp. Hancock, Ga.	May 1918	Cp. Mills, N. Y.					Cmpnt. of 28th Div.
			do	P. of E., Hoboken	May 1918	May 1919	May 1919	Cp. Dix, N. J.	
104th Ammunition Train	October 1917	Cp. McClellan, Ala.	June 1918	Cp. Mills, N. Y.					Cmpnt. of 29th Div.
			do	P. of E., Hoboken	June 1918.				
			May 1919	Cp. Hill, Va.		May 1919	May 1919	Cp. Dix, N. J.	
105th Ammunition Train	September 1917	Cp. Sevier, S. C.	May 1918	Cp. Mills, N. Y.					Cmpnt. of 30th Div.
			do	P. of E., Montreal	May 1918.				
			March 1919	Cp. Jackson, S. C.		March 1919	April 1919	Cp. Jackson, S. C.	
106th Ammunition Train	October 1917	Cp. Wheeler, Ga.	September 1918	Cp. Mills, N. Y.					Cmpnt. of 31st Div.
			October 1918	P. of E., Hoboken	October 1918.				
			July 1919	Cp. Merritt, N. J.		July 1919	July 1919	Cp. Gordon, Ga.	
107th Ammunition Train	do	Cp. MacArthur, Tex.	January 1918	Cp. Merritt, N. J.					Cmpnt. of 32d Div.
			February 1918	P. of E., Hoboken	February 1918.				
			May 1919	Cp. Merritt, N. J.		May 1919	May 1919	Cp. Grant, Ill.	
108th Ammunition Train	do	Cp. Logan, Tex.	May 1918	do					Cmpnt. of 33d Div.
			do	P. of E., Montreal	May 1918.				
			May 1919	Cp. Mills, N. Y.		May 1919	June 1919	Cp. Grant, Ill.	
109th Ammunition Train	do	Cp. Cody, N. Mex.	September 1918	Cp. Dix, N. J.					Cmpnt. of 34th Div.
			October 1918	P. of E., Hoboken	October 1918.				
			May 1919	Cp. Jackson, S. C.		May 1919	May 1919	Cp. Dodge, Iowa.	
110th Ammunition Train.	do	Cp. Doniphan, Okla.	May 1918	Cp. Mills, N. Y.					Cmpnt. of 35th Div.
			do	P. of E., Hoboken	May 1918.				
			April 1919	Cp. Mills, N. Y.		April 1919	May 1919	Cp. Funston, Kans.	
111th Ammunition Train.	do	Cp. Bowie, Tex.	July 1918	Cp. Mills, N. Y.					Cmpnt. of 36th Div.
			do	P. of E., Hoboken	July 1918.				
			March 1919	Cp. Stuart, Va.		March 1919	March 1919	Cp. Bowie, Tex.	
112th Ammunition Train.	September 1917	Columbus, Ohio	September 1917	Cp. Sheridan, Ala.					Cmpnt. of 37th Div
			June 1918	Cp. Upton, N. Y.					
			do	P. of E., Philadelphia.	June 1918.				
			April 1919	Cp. Stuart, Va.		April 1919	April 1919	Cp. Sherman, Ohio.	
113th Ammunition Train.	October 1917	Cp. Shelby, Miss.	September 1918	Cp. Mills, N. Y.					Cmpnt. of 38th Div.
			October 1918	P. of E., Hoboken	October 1918.				
			January 1919	Cp. Mills, N. Y.		January 1919.			
			do	Cp. Dix, N. J.			February 1919	Cp. Dix, N. J.	
114th Ammunition Train.	November 1917	Cp. Beauregard, La.	August 1918	Cp. Mills, N. Y.					Cmpnt. of 39th Div.
			do	P. of E., Hoboken	August 1918.				
			December 1918	Cp. Stuart, Va.		December 1918	January 1919	Cp. Beauregard, La.	

AMMUNITION TRAINS—Continued

Unit designation and redesignation	Organization		Stations in United States		Overseas		Demobilization		Remarks
	Month and year	Place	Month and year	Place	From—	To—	Month and year	Place	
115th Ammunition Train.	October 1917	Cp. Kearny, Calif.	August 1918	Cp. Mills, N. Y.					Cmpnt of 40th Div.
			do.	P. of E., Hoboken.	August 1918.				
			April 1919	Cp. Mills, N. Y.		April 1919	May 1919	Presidio of San Francisco, Calif.	
116th Ammunition Train.	do.	Cp. Greene, N. C.	November 1917.	do.					Cmpnt. of 41st Div.
			December 1917.	P. of E., Hoboken.	December 1917.				
			February 1919.	Cp. Dix, N. J.		February 1919.	March 1919	Cp. Dix, N. J.	
117th Ammunition Train.	August 1917	Cp. Martin, Kans.	September 1917.	Cp. Mills, N. Y.					Cmpnt. of 42d Div.
			October 1917	P. of E., Hoboken.	October 1917.				
			May 1919	Cp. Morrison, Va.		May 1919	May 1919	Cp. Funston, Kans.	
118th to 300th Ammunition Trains.									Never orgzd.
301st Ammunition Train.	September 1917.	Cp. Devens, Mass.	July 1918	P. of E., Montreal.	July 1918	January 1919	January 1919	Cp. Devens, Mass.	Cmpnt. of 76th Div.
302d Ammunition Train.	do.	Cp. Upton, N. Y.	April 1918	P. of E., Hoboken.	April 1918				Cmpnt. of 77th Div.
			May 1919	Cp. Mills, N. Y.		May 1919	May 1919	Cp. Upton, N. Y.	
303d Ammunition Train.	December 1917.	Cp. Dix, N. J.	May 1918	P. of E., Philadelphia.	May 1918	do.	do.	Cp. Dix, N. J.	Cmpnt. of 78th Div.
304th Ammunition Train.	September 1917.	Cp. Meade, Md.	July 1918	do.	July 1918				Cmpnt. of 79th Div.
			May 1919	Cp. Jackson, S. C.		May 1919	June 1919	Cp. Jackson, S. C.	
305th Ammunition Train.	do.	Cp. Lee, Va.	May 1918	P. of E., Newport News.	May 1918	June 1919	do.	Cp. Dix, N. J.	Cmpnt. of 80th Div.
306th Ammunition Train.	October 1917	Cp. Jackson, S. C.	July 1918	Cp. Mills, N. Y.					Cmpnt. of 81st Div.
			August 1918	P. of E., Hoboken.	August 1918	June 1919	June 1919	Cp. Jackson, S. C.	
307th Ammunition Train.	do.	Cp. Gordon, Ga.	May 1918	Cp. Mills, N. Y.					Cmpnt. of 82d Div.
			do.	P. of E., Hoboken.	May 1918	May 1919	May 1919	Cp. Upton, N. Y.	
308th Ammunition Train.	do.	Cp. Sherman, Ohio.	June 1918	Cp. Mills, N. Y.					Cmpnt. of 83d Div.
			do.	P. of E., Boston.	June 1918.				
			April 1919	Cp. Upton, N. Y.		April 1919	May 1919	Cp. Sherman, Ohio.	
309th Ammunition Train.	September 1917.	Cp. Zachary Taylor, Ky.	June 1918	Cp. Sherman, Ohio.					Cmpnt. of 84th Div.
			August 1918	Cp. Mills, N. Y.					
			September 1918.	P. of E., Hoboken.	September 1918.				
			February 1919.	Cp. Mills, N. Y.		February 1919.	February 1919.	Cp. Sherman, Ohio.	

310th Ammunition Train	do	Cp. Custer, Mich.	July 1918	do					Cmpnt. of 85th Div.
			do	P. of E., Hoboken	July 1918.				
			April 1919	Cp. Mills, N. Y.		April 1919	April 1919	Cp. Custer, Mich.	
311th Ammunition Train	do	Cp. Grant, Ill.	August 1918	do					Cmpnt. of 86th Div.
			September 1918	P. of E., Hoboken	September 1918.				
			January 1919	Cp. Stuart, Va.		January 1919	February 1919	Cp. Grant, Ill.	
312th Ammunition Train	do	Ft. Logan H. Roots, Ark.	September 1917	Cp. Pike, Ark.					Cmpnt. of 87th Div.
			June 1918	Cp. Dix, N. J.					
			August 1918	P. of E., Montreal	August 1918.				
			March 1919	Cp. Merritt, N. J.		March 1919	March 1919	Cp. Dix, N. J.	
313th Ammunition Train	October 1917	Cp. Dodge, Iowa	August 1918	Cp. Mills, N. Y.					Cmpnt. of 88th Div.
			do	P. of E., Hoboken	August 1918.				
			May 1919	Cp. Mills, N. Y.		May 1919	June 1919	Cp. Dodge, Iowa.	
314th Ammunition Train	do	Cp. Funston, Kans.	June 1918	do					Cmpnt. of 89th Div.
			do	P. of E., Hoboken	June 1918.				
			May 1919	Cp. Upton, N. Y		May 1919	June 1919	Cp. Dodge, Iowa.	
315th Ammunition Train	September 1917	Cp. Travis, Tex.	June 1918	Cp. Mills, N. Y.					Cmpnt. of 90th Div.
			July 1918	P. of E., Hoboken	July 1918	June 1919	June 1919	Cp. Devens, Mass.	
316th Ammunition Train	do	Cp. Lewis, Wash.	do	Cp. Mills, N. Y.					Cmpnt. of 91st Div.
			do	P. of E., Hoboken	July 1918.				
			April 1919	Cp. Upton, N. Y.		April 1919	May 1919	Presidio of San Francisco, Calif.	
317th Ammunition Train	November 1917	Cp. Funston, Kans.	June 1918	do					Cmpnt. of 92d Div.
			do	P. of E., Hoboken	June 1918.				
			March 1919	Cp. Upton, N. Y.		March 1919	March 1919	Cp. Zachary Taylor, Ky.	
318th Ammunition Train									Never orgzd.
319th Ammunition Train									Do.
320th Ammunition Train	October 1918	Cp. Knox, Ky.					December 1918	Cp. Knox, Ky.	Cmpnt. of 95th Div.
321st Ammunition Train	September 1918	Cp. Kearny, Calif.					do	Cp. Kearny, Calif.	Cmpnt. of 96th Div.

TRENCH ARTILLERY

TRENCH MORTAR BATTALIONS

Unit designation and redesignation	Organization		Stations in United States		Overseas		Demobilization		Remarks
	Month and year	Place	Month and year	Place	From—	To—	Month and year	Place	
1st Trench Mortar Battalion.	December 1917	Jackson Bks., La.	March 1918 do February 1919	Cp. Merritt, N. J. P. of E., Hoboken Cp. Stuart, Va.	March 1918.	February 1919	March 1919	Cp. Upton, N. Y.	Corps troops.
2d Trench Mortar Battalion.	January 1918	Ft. Monroe, Va.	May 1918 do do	Lee Hall, Va. Cp. Mills, N. Y. P. of E., Boston	May 1918	April 1919	April 1919	do	Do.
3d Trench Mortar Battalion.	April 1918	Ft. Crockett, Tex.	July 1918 do January 1919	Cp. Upton, N. Y. P. of E., Hoboken Cp. Mills, N. Y.	July 1918.	January 1919	January 1919	Ft. DuPont, Del.	Do.
4th Trench Mortar Battalion.	June 1918	Cp. Eustis, Va.	September 1918 October 1918 January 1919	Cp. Hill, Va. P. of E., Newport News. Cp. Mills, N. Y.	October 1918.	do	February 1919	Ft. Howard, Md.	Do.
5th Trench Mortar Battalion.	August 1918	Ft. Hancock, N. J.	September 1918 do	Do. P. of E., Hoboken	September 1918	do	January 1919	Ft. Hamilton, N. Y.	Do.
6th Trench Mortar Battalion.	October 1918	Ft. Caswell, N. C.	October 1918 November 1918 January 1919	Cp. Merritt, N. J. P. of E., Hoboken Cp. Stuart, Va.	November 1918.	do	do	Ft. Monroe, Va.	Do.
7th Trench Mortar Battalion.	do	Ft. DuPont, Del.	October 1918 do January 1919	Cp. Merritt, N. J. P. of E., Hoboken Cp. Stuart, Va.	October 1918.	do	do	do	Do.
8th Trench Mortar Battalion.	November 1918	Ft. Moultrie, S. C.					December 1918	Ft. Moultrie, S. C.	
9th Trench Mortar Battalion.	do	Cp. Nicholls, La.					do	Cp. Nicholls, La.	

TRENCH MORTAR BATTERIES

1st Trench Mortar Battery.	June 1917	Ft. DuPont, Del.	June 1917	Ft. Wadsworth, N. Y.					Cmpnt. of 1st F. A. Brig. Orgzd. fr. 5th Co. Ft. DuPont, C.A.C.
			August 1917	P. of E., Hoboken	August 1917.				
			April 1919	Cp. Mills, N. Y.		April 1919	May 1919	Cp. Upton, N. Y.	
2d Trench Mortar Battery.	October 1917	Gettysburg, Pa.	December 1917	Cp. Merritt, N. J.					Cmpnt. of 2d F. A. Brig.
			do	P. of E., Portland	December 1917	April 1919	April 1919	Cp. Dix, N. J.	
3d Trench Mortar Battery.	November 1917	Cp. Stanley, Tex.	do	Cp. Travis, Tex.					Cmpnt. of 3d F. A. Brig.
			March 1918	Cp. Merritt, N. J.					
			April 1918	P. of E., Hoboken	April 1918	March 1919	March 1919	Cp. Stuart, Va.	
4th Trench Mortar Battery.	December 1917	Cp. Greene, N. C.	May 1918	Cp. Merritt, N. J.					Cmpnt. of 4th F.A. Brig.
			do	P. of E., Hoboken	May 1918.				
			April 1919	Cp. Merritt, N. J.		April 1919	April 1919	Cp. Dix, N. J.	
5th Trench Mortar Battery.	do	Cp. Stanley, Tex.	February 1918	Cp. MacArthur, Tex.					Cmpnt. of 5th F.A. Brig.
			May 1918	Cp. Upton, N. Y.					
			June 1918	P. of E., Hoboken	June 1918.				
			March 1919	Cp. Merritt, N. J.		March 1919	March 1919	Cp. Upton, N. Y.	
6th Trench Mortar Battery.	February 1918	Cp. McClellan, Ala.	April 1918	Cp. Doniphan, Okla.					Cmpnt. of 6th F.A. Brig.
			July 1918	Cp. Mills, N. Y.					
			do	P. of E., Hoboken	July 1918.				
			April 1919	Cp. Merritt, N. J.		April 1919	April 1919	Cp. Dix, N. J.	
7th Trench Mortar Battery.	April 1918	Cp. Wheeler, Ga	June 1918	Cp. McClellan, Ala.					Cmpnt. of 7th F.A. Brig.
			August 1918	Cp. Merritt, N. J.					
			do	P. of E., Hoboken	August 1918	January 1919	January 1919	Cp. Merritt, N. J.	
8th Trench Mortar Battery.	May 1918	Cp. Fremont, Calif.	July 1918	Cp. Doniphan, Okla.					Cmpnt. of 8th F.A. Brig.
			October 1918	Cp. Mills, N. Y.					
			do	P. of E., Hoboken	October 1918.				
			January 1919	Cp. Mills, N. Y.		January 1919	February 1919	Cp. Knox, Ky.	
9th Trench Mortar Battery.	August 1918	Cp. McClellan, Ala.					February 1919	Cp. McClellan, Ala.	Cmpnt. of 9th F.A. Brig.
10th Trench Mortar Battery.	do	Cp. Funston, Kans.					January 1919	Cp. Funston, Kans.	Cmpnt. of 10th F.A. Brig.

TRENCH MORTAR BATTERIES—Continued

Unit designation and redesignation	Organization		Stations in United States		Overseas		Demobilization		Remarks
	Month and year	Place	Month and year	Place	From—	To—	Month and year	Place	
11th Trench Mortar Battery.	August 1918	Cp. Meade, Md					December 1918	Cp. Meade, Md	Cmpnt. of 11th F.A. Brig.
12th Trench Mortar Battery.	do	Cp. McClellan, Ala.					January 1919	Cp. McClellan, Ala.	Cmpnt. of 12th F.A. Brig.
13th Trench Mortar Battery.	do	Cp. Lewis, Wash					February 1919	Cp. Lewis, Wash	Cmpnt. of 13th F.A. Brig.
14th Trench Mortar Battery.	do	Cp. Custer, Mich					do	Cp. Custer, Mich	Cmpnt. of 14th F.A. Brig.
15th Trench Mortar Battery.	do	Cp. Stanley, Tex					do	Cp. Stanley, Tex	Cmpnt. of 15th F.A. Brig. Orgzd. fr. elements 305th Cav.
16th Trench Mortar Battery.	do	Cp. Kearny, Calif					do	Cp. Kearny, Calif	Cmpnt. of 16th F.A. Brig. Orgzd. fr. M. G. Tr., 301st Cav.
17th Trench Mortar Battery.	do	Cp. Bowie, Tex	November 1918	Ft. Sill, Okla			January 1919	Ft. Sill, Okla	Cmpnt. of 17th F.A. Brig. Orgzd. fr. M. G. Tr. 306th Cav.
18th Trench Mortar Battery.	do	Cp. Travis, Tex					February 1919	Cp. Travis, Tex	Cmpnt. of 18th F.A. Brig. Orgzd. fr. elements 303d Cav.
19th Trench Mortar Battery.	do	Cp. Bowie, Tex	October 1918	Ft. Sill, Okla			do	Ft. Sill, Okla	Cmpnt. of 19th F.A. Brig. Orgzd. fr. M.G. Tr. 309th Cav.
20th Trench Mortar Battery.	October 1918	Ft. Ethan Allen, Vt.	November 1918	Cp. Jackson, S. C			do	Cp. Jackson, S. C	Cmpnt. of 20th F.A. Brig. Orgzd. fr. M.G. Tr. 310th Cav.

21st Trench Mortar Battery.	do	Ft. Bliss, Tex.	do	do			January 1919	do	Cmpnt. of 172d F.A. Brig. Orgzd. fr. M.G. Tr. 314th Cav.
22d Trench Mortar Battery.	September 1918	Cp. Kearny, Calif.					December 1918	Cp. Kearny, Calif.	Cmpnt. of 171st F.A. Brig. Orgzd. fr. elements 308th Cav.
23d Trench Mortar Battery.	do	Cp. Knox, Ky.					do	Cp. Knox, Ky.	Cmpnt. of 170th F.A. Brig. Orgzd. fr. M.G. Tr., 311th Cav.
24th Trench Mortar Battery.	August 1918	Ft. D. A. Russell, Wyo.	September 1918	Cp. Knox, Ky.			January 1919	Do.	
25th Trench Mortar Battery.	do	Cp. Stanley, Tex.					December 1918	Cp. Stanley, Tex.	Cmpnt. of 175th F.A. Brig., but never joined.
26th Trench Mortar Battery.	do	Del Rio, Tex.	September 1918	Cp. Knox, Ky.			February 1919	Cp. Knox, Ky.	Cmpnt. of 173d F.A. Brig., but never joined.
27th Trench Mortar Battery.	do	Cp. Bowie, Tex.					December 1918	Cp. Bowie, Tex.	Cmpnt. of 176th F.A. Brig., but never joined.
28th Trench Mortar Battery.	do	Ft. Sheridan, Ill.	October 1918	Cp. Jackson, S. C.			November 1918	Cp. Jackson, S. C.	Cmpnt. of 174th F.A. Brig., but never joined.
29th Trench Mortar Battery.	do	Cp. Kearny, Calif.					December 1918	Cp. Kearny, Calif.	Cmpnt. of 177th F.A. Brig., but never joined.
30th to 100th Trench Mortar Batteries.									Never orgzd.
101st Trench Mortar Battery.	August 1917	Brunswick, Maine.	August 1917	Boxford, Mass.					Cmpnt. of 51st F.A. Brig.
			October 1917	P. of E., Boston	October 1917.				
			March 1919	Cp Merritt, N. J.		March 1919	March 1919	Cp. Devens, Mass.	
102d Trench Mortar Battery.	October 1917	Cp. Wadsworth, S. C.	May 1918	Cp. Stuart, Va.					Cmpnt. of 52d F.A. Brig.
			June 1918	P. of E., Newport News.	June 1918.				
			January 1919	Cp. Mills, N. Y.		January 1919	February 1919	Cp. Upton, N. Y.	

TRENCH MORTAR BATTERIES—Continued

Unit designation and redesignation	Organization		Stations in United States		Overseas		Demobilization		Remarks
	Month and year	Place	Month and year	Place	From—	To—	Month and year	Place	
103d Trench Mortar Battery.	December 1917	Cp. Hancock, Ga.	May 1918	Cp. Mills, N. Y.					Cmpnt. of 53d F.A. Brig.
			do	P. of E., Hoboken	May 1918	March 1919	April 1919	Cp. Dix, N. J.	
104th Trench Mortar Battery.	September 1917	Cp. McClellan, Ala.	June 1918	Cp. Mills, N. Y.					Cmpnt. of 54th F.A. Brig.
			July 1918	P. of E., Hoboken	July 1918.				
			March 1919	Cp. Merritt, N. J.		March 1919	March 1919	Cp. Dix, N. J.	
105th Trench Mortar Battery.	do	Cp. Sevier, S. C.	May 1918	Cp. Mills, N. Y.					Cmpnt. of 55th F.A. Brig.
			do	P. of E., Hoboken	May 1918.				
			March 1919	Cp. Stuart, Va.		March 1919	March 1919	Cp. Oglethorpe, Ga.	
106th Trench Mortar Battery.	do	Cp. Wheeler, Ga.	July 1918	Cp. Jackson, S. C.					Cmpnt. of 56th F.A. Brig.
			October 1918	Cp. Mills, N. Y.					
			do	P. of E., Hoboken	October 1918.				
			January 1919	Cp. Mills, N. Y.		January 1919	January 1919	Cp. Gordon, Ga.	
107th Trench Mortar Battery.	October 1917	Cp. MacArthur, Tex.	February 1918	Cp. Merritt, N. J.					Cmpnt. of 57th F.A. Brig.
			do	P. of E., Hoboken	February 1918.				
			May 1919	Cp. Dix, N. J.		May 1919	May 1919	Cp. Grant, Ill.	
108th Trench Mortar Battery.	do	Cp. Logan, Tex.	May 1918	Cp. Merritt, N. J.					Cmpnt. of 58th F.A. Brig.
			do	P. of E., Hoboken	May 1918.				
			March 1919	Cp. Merritt, N. J.		March 1919	March 1919	Cp. Grant, Ill.	
109th Trench Mortar Battery.	do	Cp. Cody, N. Mex.	July 1918	Ft. Sill, Okla.					Cmpnt. of 59th F.A. Brig.
			September 1918	Cp. Upton, N. Y.					
			do	P. of E., Hoboken	September 1918.				
			January 1919	Cp. Merritt, N. J.		January 1919	January 1919	Cp. Dodge, Iowa.	
110th Trench Mortar Battery.	do	Cp. Doniphan, Okla.	May 1918	Cp. Mills, N. Y.					Cmpnt. of 60th F.A. Brig.
			do	P. of E., Hoboken	May 1918.				

111th Trench Mortar Battery.	do	Cp. Bowie, Tex.	April 1919 July 1918	Cp. Dix, N. J Cp. Mills, N. Y.		April 1919	May 1919	Cp. Funston, Kans.	Cmpnt. of 61st F.A. Brig.
112th Trench Mortar Battery.	September 1917	Cp. Sheridan, Ala.	August 1918 March 1919 June 1918	P. of E., Hoboken Cp. Stuart, Va. Cp. Upton, N. Y.	August 1918.	March 1919	April 1919	Cp. Travis, Tex.	Cmpnt. of 62d F.A. Brigade.
113th Trench Mortar Battery.	October 1917	Cp. Shelby, Miss.	do April 1919 September 1918	P. of E., Hoboken Cp. Dix, N. J. Cp. Mills, N. Y.	June 1918.	April 1919	May 1919	Cp. Sherman, Ohio.	Cmpnt. of 63d F.A. Brig.
114th Trench Mortar Battery.	November 1917	Cp. Beauregard, La.	October 1918 January 1919 August 1918	P. of E., Hoboken Cp. Mills, N. Y. do	October 1918.	January 1919	January 1919	Cp. Zachary Taylor, Ky.	Cmpnt. of 64th F.A. Brig.
115th Trench Mortar Battery.	October 1917	Cp. Kearny, Calif.	do January 1919 August 1918	P. of E., Hoboken Cp. Merritt, N. J. Cp. Mills, N. Y.	August 1918.	January 1919	February 1919	Cp. Beauregard, La.	Cmpnt. of 65th F.A. Brig.
116th Trench Mortar Battery.	October 1917	Cp. Greene, N. C.	do January 1919 October 1917	P. of E., Hoboken Cp. Stuart, Va. Cp. Mills, N. Y.	August 1918.	January 1919	January 1919	Presidio of San Francisco, Calif.	Cmpnt. of 66th F.A. Brig.
117th Trench Mortar Battery.	September 1917	Cp. Mills, N. Y.	December 1917 January 1918 March 1919 October 1917	Cp. Merritt, N. J. P. of E., Hoboken Cp. Merritt, N. J. P. of E., Hoboken	January 1918. October 1917	March 1919	March 1919	Cp. Dodge, Iowa.	Cmpnt. of 67th F.A. Brig.
			April 1919	Cp. Merritt, N. J.		April 1919	May 1919	Cp. Meade, Md.	
118th to 300th Trench Mortar Batteries.									Never orgzd.
301st Trench Mortar Battery.	August 1917	Cp. Devens, Mass.	July 1918	P. of E., Boston	July 1918				Cmpnt. of 151st F. A. Brig.
302d Trench Mortar Battery	September 1917	Cp. Upton, N. Y.	January 1919 April 1918	Cp. Merritt, N. J. P. of E., Hoboken	 April 1918	January 1919	February 1919	Cp. Devens, Mass.	Cmpnt. of 152d F. A. Brig.
			February 1919	Cp. Upton, N. Y.		February 1919	March 1919	Cp. Upton, N. Y.	

TRENCH MORTAR BATTERIES—Continued

Unit designation and redesignation	Organization		Stations in United States		Overseas		Demobilization		Remarks
	Month and year	Place	Month and year	Place	From—	To—	Month and year	Place	
303d Trench Mortar Battery.	September 1917	Cp. Dix, N. J.	May 1918	P. of E., Philadelphia.	May 1918				Cmpnt. of 153d F. A. Brig.
			April 1919	Cp. Dix, N. J.		April 1919	May 1919	Cp. Dix, N. J.	
304th Trench Mortar Battery.	do	Cp. Meade, Md.	July 1918	P. of E., Philadelphia.	July 1918				Cmpnt. of 154th F. A. Brig.
			March 1919	Cp. Merritt, N. J.		March 1919	March 1919	Cp. Dix, N. J.	
305th Trench Mortar Battery.	do	Cp. Lee, Va.	May 1918	P. of E., Newport News.	May 1918				Cmpnt. of 155th F. A. Brig.
			February 1919	Cp. Stuart, Va.		February 1919	March 1919	Cp. Lee, Va.	
306th Trench Mortar Battery.	do	Cp. Jackson, S. C.	July 1918	Cp. Mills, N. Y.					Cmpnt. of 156th F. A. Brig.
			do	P. of E., Hoboken.	July 1918.				
			March 1919	Cp. Stuart, Va.		March 1919	April 1919	Cp. Lee, Va.	
307th Trench Mortar Battery.	do	Cp. Gordon, Ga.	May 1918	Cp. Mills, N. Y.					Cmpnt. of 157th F. A. Brig.
			do	P. of E., Hoboken.	May 1918.				
			March 1919	Cp. Stuart, Va.		March 1919	March 1919	Cp. Dix, N. J.	
308th Trench Mortar Battery.	do	Cp. Sherman, Ohio.	June 1918	Cp. Mills, N. Y.					Cmpnt. of 158th F. A. Brig.
			do	P. of E., Hoboken.	June 1918.				
			April 1919	Cp. Mills, N. Y.		April 1919	May 1919	Cp. Sherman, Ohio.	
309th Trench Mortar Battery.	August 1917	Cp. Zachary Taylor, Ky.	June 1918	West Point, Ky.					Cmpnt. of 159th F. A. Brig.
			September 1918	Cp. Mills, N. Y.					
			do	P. of E., Hoboken.	September 1918.				
			January 1919	Cp. Mills, N. Y.		January 1919	January 1919	Cp. Zachary Taylor, Ky.	
310th Trench Mortar Battery.	November 1917	Cp. Custer, Mich.	July 1918	do					Cmpnt. of 160th F. A. Brig.
			do	P. of E., Hoboken.	July 1918.				
			March 1919	Cp. Merritt, N. J.		March 1919	March 1919	Cp. Custer, Mich.	

311th Trench Mortar Battery.	September 1917	Cp. Grant, Ill	May 1918	Cp. Robinson, Wis.					Cmpnt. of 161st F. A. Brig.
312th Trench Mortar Battery.	do	Cp. Pike, Ark	September 1918 do June 1918	Cp. Mills, N. Y. P. of E., Hoboken Cp. Dix, N. J	September 1918	January 1919	January 1919	Cp. Stuart, Va.	Cmpnt. of 162d F. A. Brig.
313th Trench Mortar Battery.	do	Cp. Dodge, Iowa	August 1918 March 1919 August 1918	P. of E., Hoboken Cp. Merritt, N. J Cp. Mills, N. Y	August 1918.	March 1919	March 1919	Cp. Dodge, Iowa.	Cmpnt. of 163d F. A. Brig.
314th Trench Mortar Battery.	do	Cp. Funston, Kans.	do January 1919 June 1918	P. of E., Hoboken Cp. Merritt, N. J Cp. Mills, N. Y	August 1918.	January 1919	January 1919	Cp. Dodge, Iowa.	Cmpnt. of 164th F. A. Brig.
315th Trench Mortar Battery.	do	Cp. Travis, Tex	do March 1919 June 1918	P. of E., Hoboken Cp. Merritt, N. J Cp. Mills, N. Y	June 1918.	March 1919	March 1919	Cp. Dodge, Iowa.	Cmpnt. of 165th F. A. Brig.
316th Trench Mortar Battery.	October 1917	Cp. Lewis, Wash	do March 1919 July 1918	P. of E., Hoboken Cp. Merritt, N. J Cp. Mills, N. Y	June 1918.	March 1919	April 1919	Cp. Bowie, Tex.	Cmpnt. of 166th F. A. Brig.
317th Trench Mortar Battery.	May 1918	Cp. Dix, N. J	do March 1919 June 1918	P. of E., Hoboken Cp. Merritt, N. J P. of E., Hoboken	July 1918. June 1918	March 1919	March 1919	Cp. Lewis, Wash.	Cmpnt. of 167th F. A. Brig.
			February 1919	Cp. Upton, N. Y		February 1919	March 1919	Cp. Shelby, Miss.	

CAVALRY

BRIGADES

Unit designation and redesignation	Organization		Stations in United States		Overseas		Demobilization		Remarks
	Month and year	Place	Month and year	Place	From—	To—	Month and year	Place	
1st Cavalry Brigade	February 1918	Ft. Sam Houston, Tex.	November 1918	Brownsville, Tex.			July 1919	Brownsville, Tex.	Cmpnt. of 15th Cav. Div.
2d Cavalry Brigade	December 1917	Ft. Bliss, Tex.					do	Ft. Bliss, Tex.	Do.
3d Cavalry Brigade	do	Cp. Harry J. Jones, Douglas, Ariz.					do	Cp. Harry J. Jones, Douglas, Ariz.	Do.

REGIMENTS

Unit designation and redesignation	Organization		Stations in United States		Overseas		Demobilization		Remarks
	Month and year	Place	Month and year	Place	From—	To—	Month and year	Place	
1st Cavalry	Organized 1833		April 1917	Cp. Harry J. Jones, Douglas, Ariz.					1833, Regt. of Dragoons; 1861, 1st Cav. Cmpnt. of 3d Cav. Brig.
			May 1917	Ft. D. A. Russell, Wyo.					
			December 1917	Cp. Harry J. Jones, Douglas, Ariz.					
2d Cavalry	Organized 1836		April 1917	Ft. Ethan Allen, Vt.					1836, 2d Dragoons; 1861, 2d Cav.
			March 1918	Cp. Merritt, N. J.					
			do	P. of E., Hoboken	March 1918.				
			June 1919	Cp. Mills, N. Y.		June 1919.			
			July 1919	Ft. Riley, Kans.					Corps troops.
3d Cavalry	Organized 1846		April 1917	Ft. Sam Houston, Tex.					1846, Regt. of Mtd. Riflemen; 1861, 3d Cav.
			October 1917	P. of E., Philadelphia.	October 1917.				
			June 1919	Cp. Devens, Mass.		June 1919.			
			July 1919	Ft. Myer, Va.					Corps troops.
4th Cavalry	Organized 1855		April 1917	Schofield Bks., T. H.					1855, 1st Cav.; 1861, 4th Cav.
			November 1918	Ft. Ringgold, Tex.					

5th Cavalry	do		April 1917	Cp. Stewart, Tex					1855, 2d Cav.; 1861, 5th Cav. Cmpnt. of 2d Cav. Brig.
			October 1917	Ft. Bliss, Tex					
			September 1919	Marfa, Tex.					
6th Cavalry	Organized 1861		April 1917	do					1861, 3d Cav.; 1861, 6th Cav.
			November 1917	Ft. Sam Houston, Tex.					
			March 1918	Cp. Merritt, N. J.					
			do	P. of E., Hoboken	March 1918.				
			June 1919	Cp. Stuart, Va		June 1919			Corps troops.
			July 1919	Ft. Oglethorpe, Ga.					
7th Cavalry	Organized 1866		April 1917	Cp. Stewart, Tex.					Cmpnt. of 2d Cav. Brig.
			May 1917	Ft. Bliss, Tex.					
8th Cavalry	do		April 1917	do					Do.
			October 1917	Marfa, Tex.					
			October 1919	Ft. Bliss, Tex.					
9th Cavalry	do		April 1917	Cp. Stotsenburg, P. I.					
10th Cavalry	do		do	Ft. Huachuca, Ariz.					
11th Cavalry	Organized 1901		do	Cp. Stewart, Tex.					
			May 1917	Ft. Oglethorpe, Ga.					
			January 1918	Cp. Forrest, Ga.					
			May 1918	Ft. Oglethorpe, Ga.					
			September 1918	Ft. Myer, Va.					
			July 1919	Presidio of Monterey, Calif.					
12th Cavalry	do		April 1917	Columbus, N. Mex.					
13th Cavalry	do		do	Cp. Stewart, Tex.					
			May 1917	Ft. Riley, Kans.					
			December 1917	Ft. Ringgold, Tex.					
			January 1918	Brownsville, Tex.					
			October 1918	Ft. Ringgold, Tex.					
			December 1918	Ft. Clark, Tex.					
14th Cavalry	do		April 1917	Cp. Del Rio, Tex.					Cmpnt. of 1st Cav. Brig.
			April 1918	Ft. Sam Houston, Tex.					
			June 1918	Cp. Travis, Tex.					
			August 1918	Ft. Sam Houston, Tex.					

REGIMENTS—Continued

Unit designation and redesignation	Organization		Stations in United States		Overseas		Demobilization		Remarks
	Month and year	Place	Month and year	Place	From—	To—	Month and year	Place	
15th Cavalry	Organized 1901		April 1917	Ft. McKinley, P. I.					Cmpnt. of 3d Cav. Brig.
			October 1917	Cp. Fremont, Calif.					
			December 1917	Cp. Harry J. Jones, Douglas, Ariz.					
			March 1918	Cp. Merritt, N. J.					
			do	P. of E., Hoboken	March 1918.				
			June 1919	Cp. Mills, N. Y.		June 1919.			
			do	Ft. D. A. Russell, Wyo.					
16th Cavalry	Organized 1916		April 1917	Llano Grande, Tex.					
			May 1917	Mercedes, Tex.					
			January 1919	Brownsville, Tex.					
			June 1919	Ft. Brown, Tex.					
17th Cavalry	do		April 1917	Ft. Bliss, Tex.					Do.
			May 1917	Cp. Harry J. Jones, Douglas, Ariz.					
			April 1919	Schofield Bks., T.H.					
18th Cavalry	June 1917	Ft. Ethan Allen, Vt.							Converted into 76th F. A. November 1917.
19th Cavalry	do	do							Converted into 77th F. A. October 1917.
20th Cavalry	do	Ft. Riley, Kans.	November 1917	Cp. Logan, Tex.					Converted into 78th F. A. November 1917.
21st Cavalry	do	do	do	do					Converted into 79th F. A. November 1917.

22d Cavalry	do	Ft. Oglethorpe, Ga.							Converted into 80th F. A. November 1917.
23d Cavalry	do	do							Converted into 81st F. A. November 1917.
24th Cavalry	do	Ft. D. A. Russell, Wyo.							Converted into 82d F. A. November 1917.
25th Cavalry	do	do							Converted into 83d F. A. November 1917.
26th to 100th Cavalry									Never orgzd.
101st Cavalry	November 1917	Cp. Hancock, Ga.					November 1917	Cp. Hancock, Ga.	
102d to 300th Cavalry									Do.
301st Cavalry	February 1918	Cp. Fremont, Calif.	April 1918	Presidio of Monterey, Calif.					Converted into 46th and 47th F. A. August 1918.
302d Cavalry	do	do	August 1918 May 1918 August 1918	Cp. Kearny, Calif. Cp. Harry J. Jones, Douglas, Ariz. Cp. Kearny, Calif.					Converted into 48th and 64th F. A. August 1918.
303d Cavalry	do	Cp. Stanley, Tex.							Converted into 52d and 53d F. A. August 1918.
304th Cavalry	do	do							Converted into 43d and 54th F. A. August 1918.
305th Cavalry	do	do							Converted into 44th and 45th F. A. August 1918.
306th Cavalry	do	Ft. Clark, Tex.	August 1918	Cp. Bowie, Tex.					Converted into 49th and 50th F. A. August 1918.
307th Cavalry	do	Cp. Del Rio, Tex.	do	do					Converted into 51st and 55th F. A. August 1918.
308th Cavalry	do	Cp. Harry J. Jones, Douglas, Ariz.	September 1918	Cp. Kearny, Calif.					Converted into 65th and 66th F. A. September 1918.

REGIMENTS—Continued

Unit designation and redesignation	Organization		Stations in United States		Overseas		Demobilization		Remarks
	Month and year	Place	Month and year	Place	From—	To—	Month and year	Place	
309th Cavalry	February 1918	Ft. Sam Houston, Tex.	August 1918	Cp. Bowie, Tex					Converted into 56th and 57th F. A. August 1918.
310th Cavalry	do	Ft. Ethan Allen, Vt							Converted into 58th and 59th F. A. October 1918.
311th Cavalry	do	Ft. Riley, Kans	September 1918	Cp. Knox, Ky					Converted into 67th and 68th F. A. September 1918.
312th Cavalry	March 1918	Ft. Myer, Va., Ft. Sheridan, Ill., and Ft. D. A. Russell, Wyo.							Converted into 60th and 61st F. A. August 1918.
313th Cavalry	April 1918	Cp. Del Rio, Tex							Converted into 69th and 70th F. A. August 1918.
314th Cavalry	do	Cp. Owen Beirne, Tex.							Converted into 62d and 63d F. A. October 1918.
315th Cavalry	do	Ft. D. A. Russell, Wyo.							Converted into 71st and 72d F. A. August 1918.

DIVISIONAL HEADQUARTERS TROOP

Unit designation and redesignation	Organization: Month and year	Organization: Place	Stations: Month and year	Stations: Place	Overseas: From—	Overseas: To—	Demobilization: Month and year	Demobilization: Place	Remarks
Headquarters Troop 15th Cavalry Division.	December 1917	Cp. Owen Beirne, Tex.	April 1918	Cp. Fort Bliss, Tex			March 1919	Cp. Fort Bliss, Tex	

CHEMICAL WARFARE SERVICE

1ST GAS REGIMENT [1]

Company A	October 1917	Cp. American Univ., D. C.	December 1917	P. of E., Hoboken	December 1917.				
			February 1919	Cp. Mills, N. Y.		February 1919	February 1919	Cp. Kendrick, N. J.	G. H. Q. troops.
Company B	November 1917	do	December 1917	P. of E., Hoboken	December 1917.				
			February 1919	Cp. Mills, N. Y.		do	do	do	Do.
Company C	December 1917	do	December 1917	Cp. Belvoir, Va.					
			do	Ft. Myer, Va.					
			February 1918	P. of E., Hoboken	February 1918.				
			February 1919	Cp. Mills, N. Y.		do	do	do	Do.
Company D	do	do	December 1917	Ft. Myer, Va.					
			February 1918	P. of E., Hoboken	February 1918.				
			February 1919	Cp. Mills, N. Y.		do	do	do	Do.
Company E	January 1918	Ft. Myer, Va.	June 1918	Cp. Merritt, N. J.					
			do	P. of E., Hoboken	June 1918.				
			February 1919	Cp. Mills, N. Y.		do	do	do	Do.
Company F	March 1918	do	June 1918	Cp. Merritt, N. J.					
			do	P. of E., Hoboken	June 1918.				
			February 1919	Cp. Mills, N. Y.		do	do	do	Do.
Company G	October 1918	Cp. Sherman, Ohio					December 1918	Cp. Sherman, Ohio	
Company H	do	do					do	Do.	
Company I	do	do					do	Do.	
Company K	do	do					do	Do.	
Company L	do	do					do	Do.	
Company M	do	do					do	Do.	
Company Q					August 1918	January 1919			Orgzd. and dembl'zd. overseas.

EDGEWOOD PLANT ORGANIZATION

1st Battalion									
Headquarters	June 1918	Edgewood Arsenal, Md.					May 1919	Edgewood Arsenal, Md.	
Company A	do	do					April 1919	Do.	
Company B	do	do					May 1919	Do.	

[1] **30th Engineers (Gas & Flame) Regiment authorized and organized October 1917; redesignated 1st Gas Regiment July 13, 1918. Companies A to F, inclusive organized as components of 30th Engineers.**

EDGEWOOD PLANT ORGANIZATION—Continued

Unit designation and redesignation	Organization		Stations in United States		Overseas		Demobilization		Remarks
	Month and year	Place	Month and year	Place	From—	To—	Month and year	Place	
1st Battalion—Continued									
Company C	June 1918	Edgewood Arsenal, Md.					August 1918	Edgewood Arsenal, Md.	Demblzd. August 1918; reorgzd. February 1919.
	February 1919	do					April 1919	Do.	
Company D	June 1918	do					January 1919	Do.	
Company E	September 1918	do					May 1919	Do.	
Company F	do	do					do	Do.	
Company G	do	do					November 1918	Do.	
2d Battalion									
Headquarters	June 1918	do					March 1919	Do.	
Company A	do	do					do	Do.	
Company B	do	do					do	Do.	
Company C	do	do					do	Do.	
Company D	do	do					do	Do.	
Company E	August 1918	do					do	Do.	
Company F	do	do					do	Do.	
Company G	do	do					January 1919	Do.	
Company H	do	do					do	Do.	
Company K	October 1918	do					do	Do.	
Company L	do	do					do	Do.	
Company M	do	do					do	Do.	
Company N	November 1918	do					do	Do.	
Company O	January 1919	do					March 1919	Do.	
Casual Company	July 1918	do					do	Do.	
3d Battalion									
Headquarters	June 1918	do					January 1919	Do.	
Companies A to G									Never orgzd.
Company H	November 1918	Edgewood Arsenal, Md.					December 1918	Edgewood Arsenal, Md.	

Company I	August 1918	do					January 1919	Do.	
Company K	do	do					December 1918	Do.	
Company L	do	do					January 1919	Do.	
Company M	do	do					December 1918	Do.	
Company N	September 1918	do					do	Do.	
Company O	do	do					January 1919	Do.	
Casual Company X	June 1918	do					September 1918	Do.	
4th Battalion									
Headquarters	do	do					January 1919	Do.	
Company A	do	do					do	Do.	
Company B	September 1918	do					December 1918	Do.	

DEPOT BRIGADES[1]

1st to 50th Depot Brigades.									Never orgzd.
51st Depot Brigade	August 1917	Framingham, Mass.	November 1917	Cp. Greene, N. C.			January 1918	Cp. Greene, N. C.	Cmpnt. of 26th Div. No record of tng. units.
52d Depot Brigade									Never orgzd.
53d Depot Brigade	September 1917	Cp. Hancock, Ga.					November 1917	Cp. Hancock, Ga.	Cmpnt. of 28th Div. No record of tng. units.
54th Depot Brigade	do	Cp. McClellan, Ala.					do	Cp. McClellan, Ala	Cmpnt. of 29th Div. No record of tng. units.
55th Depot Brigade	do	Cp. Sevier, S. C.					October 1917	Cp. Sevier, S. C.	Cmpnt. of 30th Div. No record of tng. units.
56th Depot Brigade	October 1917	Cp. Wheeler, Ga.					do	Cp. Wheeler, Ga.	Cmpnt. of 31st Div. No record of tng. units.
57th Depot Brigade	September 1917	Cp. MacArthur, Tex.					November 1917	Cp. MacArthur, Tex.	Cmpnt. of 32d Div. No record of tng. units.

[1] Depot brigades were at first organized as part of tactical divisions, but were later detached and placed directly under the several camp and cantonment commanders as independent units. The National Guard depot brigades, numbering from 51 to 63, inclusive, existed for a very brief period only, at the termination of which they were absorbed by their respective divisions during process of organization.

DEPOT BRIGADES—Continued

Unit designation and redesignation	Organization		Stations in United States		Overseas		Demobilization		Remarks
	Month and year	Place	Month and year	Place	From—	To—	Month and year	Place	
58th Depot Brigade									Never orgzd.
59th Depot Brigade	September 1917	Cp. Cody, N. Mex.					December 1917	Cp. Cody, N. Mex.	Cmpnt. of 34th Div. No record of tng. units.
60th Depot Brigade	do	Cp. Doniphan, Okla.					November 1917	Cp. Doniphan, Okla.	Cmpnt. of 35th Div. No record of tng. units.
61st Depot Brigade	October 1917	Cp. Bowie, Tex.					March 1918	Cp. Bowie, Tex.	Cmpnt. of 36th Div. No record of tng. units.
62d Depot Brigade	September 1917	Cp. Sheridan, Ala.					October 1917	Cp. Sheridan, Ala.	Cmpnt. of 37th Div. No record of tng. units.
63d Depot Brigade	do	Cp. Shelby, Miss.					do	Cp. Shelby, Miss.	Cmpnt. of 38th Div. No record of tng. units.
64th to 150th Depot Brigades.									Never orgzd.
151st Depot Brigade	August 1917	Cp. Devens, Mass.					May 1919	Cp. Devens, Mass.	Cmpnt. of 76th Div.
1st Training Battalion.	do	do					do	do	Cmpnt. of 151st Dep. Brig.
2d Training Battalion.	do	do					do	do	Do.
3d Training Battalion.	do	do					do	do	Do.
4th Training Battalion.	do	do					December 1918	do	Do.
5th Training Battalion.	do	do					do	do	Do.

6th Training Battalion.	do	do					do	do	Do.
7th Training Battalion.	do	do					do	do	Do.
8th Training Battalion.	do	do					do	do	Do.
9th Training Battalion.	do	do					do	do	Do.
10th Training Battalion.	May 1918	do					do	do	Do.
11th Training Battalion.	do	do					do	do	Do.
12th Training Battalion.	do	do					do	do	Do.
13th Training Battalion.	August 1918	do					April 1919	do	Do.
1st Development Battalion.	June 1918	do					do	do	Do.
2d Development Battalion.	July 1918	do					January 1919	do	Do.
3d Development Battalion.	do	do					December 1918	do	Do.
4th Development Battalion.	October 1918	do					do	do	Do.
152d Depot Brigade	August 1917	Cp. Upton, N. Y.					May 1919	Cp. Upton, N. Y.	Cmpnt. of 77th Div.
1st Training Group	September 1917	do					December 1917	do	Cmpnt. of 152d Dep. Brig.
2d Training Group	do	do					do	do	Do.
3d Training Group	do	do					November 1917	do	Do.
4th Training Group	do	do					do	do	Do.
1st Provisional Training Regiment.	November 1917	do					December 1917	do	Do.
2d Provisional Training Regiment.	do	do					do	do	Do.
1st Training Battalion.	September 1917	do					May 1919	do	Do.

DEPOT BRIGADES—Continued

Unit designation and redesignation	Organization		Stations in United States		Overseas		Demobilization		Remarks
	Month and year	Place	Month and year	Place	From—	To—	Month and year	Place	
152d Depot Brigade—Continued									
2d Training Battalion.	September 1917	Cp. Upton, N. Y.					May 1919	Cp. Upton, N. Y.	Cmpnt. of 152d Dep. Brig.
3d Training Battalion.	do	do					do	do	Do.
4th Training Battalion.	do	do					do	do	Do.
5th Training Battalion.	do	do					December 1918	do	Do.
6th Training Battalion.	do	do					do	do	Cmpnt. of 152d Dep. Brig. Demobilized November 1917; reorganized April 1918.
7th Training Battalion.	do	do					do	do	Cmpnt. of 152d Dep. Brig.
8th Training Battalion.	do	do					do	do	Do.
9th Training Battalion.	do	do					do	do	Do.
10th Training Battalion.	do	do					do	do	Cmpnt. of 152d Dep. Brig. Demobilized November 1917; reorganized April 1918.

11th Training Battalion.	do	do					do	do	**Cmpnt. of 152d Dep. Brig. Demobilized November 1917; reorganized June 1918.**
12th Training Battalion.	do	do					do	do	Do.
13th Training Battalion.	do	do					do	do	Cmpnt. of 152d Dep. Brig. Demobilized November 1917; reorganized July 1918.
14th Training Battalion.	do	do					November 1917	do	Cmpnt. of 152d Dep. Brig.
15th Training Battalion.	do	do					do	do	Do.
16th Training Battalion.	do	do					do	do	Do.
17th Training Battalion.	do	do					do	do	Do.
18th Training Battalion.	do	do					do	do	Do.
19th Training Battalion.	do	do					do	do	Do.
20th Training Battalion.	do	do					do	do	Do.
1st Development Battalion.	June 1918	do					December 1918	do	Do.
2d Development Battalion.	do	do					do	do	Do.
3d Development Battalion.	do	do					do	do	Do.
4th Development Battalion.	August 1918	do					do	do	Do.
5th Development Battalion.									Never orgzd.
6th Development Battalion.	August 1918	Cp. Upton, N. Y.					December 1918	Cp. Upton, N. Y.	Cmpnt. of 152d Dep. Brig.

DEPOT BRIGADES—Continued

Unit designation and redesignation	Organization		Stations in United States		Overseas		Demobilization		Remarks
	Month and year	Place	Month and year	Place	From—	To—	Month and year	Place	
153d Depot Brigade	August 1917	Cp. Dix, N. J					May 1919	Cp. Dix, N. J	Cmpnt. of 78th Div.
1st Provisional Training Regiment.	October 1917	do					December 1917	do	Cmpnt. of 153d Dep. Brig.
2d Provisional Training Regiment.	do	do					do	do	Do.
3d Provisional Training Regiment.	do	do					do	do	Do.
1st Training Battalion.	September 1917	do					May 1919	do	Do.
2d Training Battalion.	do	do					do	do	Do.
3d Training Battalion.	do	do					December 1918	do	Do.
4th Training Battalion.	do	do					May 1919	do	Do.
5th Training Battalion.	do	do					December 1918	do	Do.
6th Training Battalion.	do	do					May 1919	do	Do.
7th Training Battalion.	May 1918	do					December 1918	do	Do.
8th Training Battalion.	do	do					do	do	Do.
9th Training Battalion.	do	do					May 1919	do	Cmpnt. of 153d Dep. Brig. Converted into Development Bn. June 1918.

10th Training Battalion.	do	do					December 1918	do	Cmpnt. of 153d Dep. Brig.
11th Training Battalion.	do	do	October 1918	Cp. Wheeler, Ga			do	Cp. Wheeler, Ga	Do.
12th Training Battalion.	do	do					February 1919	Cp. Dix, N. J	Cmpnt. of 153d Dep. Brig. Converted into Development Bn. August 1918.
13th Training Battalion.	June 1918	do					May 1919	do	Cmpnt. of 153d Dep. Brig.
14th Training Battalion.	August 1918	do					December 1918	do	Do.
15th Training Battalion	September 1918	do					do	do	Do.
16th Training Battalion.	October 1918	do					March 1919	do	Do.
17th Training Battalion.	do	do					April 1919	do	Do.
18th Training Battalion	do	do					December 1918	do	Do
154th Depot Brigade	September 1917	Cp. Meade, Md					May 1919	Cp. Meade, Md	Cmpnt. of 79th Div.
1st (I) Training Battalion.	do	do							Cmpnt. of 154th Dep. Brig. Converted into 1st Development Bn. September 1918.
1st (II) Training Battalion.	September 1918	do					March 1919	Cp. Meade, Md	Cmpnt. of 154th Dep. Brig.
2d Training Battalion.	September 1917	do					May 1919	do	Do.
3d Training Battalion.	do	do					do	do	Do.
4th (I) Training Battalion.	do	do							Cmpnt. of 154th Dep. Brig. Converted into 2d Development Bn. September 1918.
4th (II) Training Battalion.	September 1918	do					May 1919	Cp. Meade, Md	Cmpnt. of 154th Dep. Brig.

DEPOT BRIGADES—Continued

Unit designation and redesignation	Organization		Stations in United States		Overseas		Demobilization		Remarks
	Month and year	Place	Month and year	Place	From—	To—	Month and year	Place	
154th Depot Brigade—Continued									
5th (I) Training Battalion.	September 1917	Cp. Meade, Md.					November 1918	Cp. Meade, Md.	Cmpnt. of 154th Dep. Brig.
5th (II) Training Battalion.	January 1919	do					May 1919	do	Do.
6th Training Battalion.	September 1917	do							Cmpnt. of 154th Dep. Brig. Converted into 3d Development Bn. September 1918.
7th Training Battalion.	do	do					November 1918	Cp. Meade, Md.	Cmpnt. of 154th Dep. Brig.
8th Training Battalion.	do	do							Cmpnt. of 154th Dep. Brig. Converted into 4th Development Bn. September 1918.
9th Training Battalion.	June 1918	do					November 1918	do	Cmpnt. of 154th Dep. Brig.
10th Training Battalion.	do	do					do	do	Do.
11th Training Battalion.	do	do					do	do	Do.
12th Training Battalion.	do	do					do	do	Do.
1st Development Battalion.	September 1918	do					December 1918	do	Do.
2d Development Battalion.	do	do					do	do	Do.

3d Development Battalion.	do	do					February 1919	do	Do.
4th Development Battalion.	do	do					April 1919	do	Do.
5th Development Battalion.	do	do					December 1918	do	Do.
6th Development Battalion.	do	do					do	do	Do.
155th Depot Brigade	September 1917	Cp. Lee, Va					May 1919	Cp. Lee, Va	Cmpnt. of 80th Div.
1st Training Battalion.	do	do					do	do	Cmpnt. of 155th Dep. Brig.
2d Training Battalion.	do	do					do	do	Do.
3d Training Battalion.	do	do					do	do	Do.
4th Training Battalion.	do	do					do	do	Do.
5th Training Battalion.	do	do					November 1918	do	Do.
6th Training Battalion.	do	do					do	do	Do.
7th Training Battalion.	do	do					do	do	Do.
8th Training Battalion.	do	do					do	do	Do.
9th Training Battalion.	do	do					do	do	Do.
10th Training Battalion.	October 1917	do					do	do	Do.
11th Training Battalion.	do	do					January 1918	do	Do.
12th Training Battalion.	do	do					do	do	Do.
13th Training Battalion.	do	do					do	do	Do.
14th Training Battalion.	do	do					do	do	Do.
15th Training Battalion.	do	do					do	do	Do.

DEPOT BRIGADES—Continued

Unit designation and redesignation	Organization		Stations in United States		Overseas		Demobilization		Remarks
	Month and year	Place	Month and year	Place	From—	To—	Month and year	Place	
155th Depot Brigade—Continued									
16th Training Battalion.	October 1917	Cp. Lee, Va					January 1918	Cp. Lee, Va	Cmpnt. of 155th Dep. Brig.
17th Training Battalion.	do	do					do	do	Do.
18th Training Battalion.	do	do					do	do	Do.
19th Training Battalion.	do	do					do	do	Do.
20th Training Battalion.	do	do					do	do	Do.
21st Training Battalion.	do	do					do	do	Do.
22d Training Battalion.	do	do					do	do	Do.
23d Training Battalion.	November 1917	do					do	do	Do.
24th Training Battalion.	October 1917	do					do	do	Do.
25th Training Battalion.	November 1917	do					do	do	Do.
1st to 10th Provisional Training Battalions.									Never orgzd.
11th Provisional Training Battalion.	April 1918	Cp. Lee, Va					November 1918	Cp. Lee ,Va	Cmpnt. of 155th Dep. Brig.
12th Provisional Training Battalion.	do	do					do	do	Do.

13th Provisional Training Battalion.	July 1918	do					September 1918	do	Do.
14th Provisional Training Battalion.	do	do					do	do	Do.
15th Provisional Training Battalion.	do	do					August 1918	do	Do.
1st Development Battalion.	June 1918	do					December 1918	do	Do.
2d Development Battalion.	do	do					do	do	Do.
3d Development Battalion.	July 1918	do					do	do	Do.
4th Development Battalion.	November 1918	do					November 1918	do	Do.
156th Depot Brigade	September 1917	Cp. Jackson, S. C.	September 1918	Cp. Sevier, S. C.					
1st Provisional Regiment.	July 1918	do	January 1919 September 1918	Cp. Jackson, S. C. Cp. Sevier, S. C.			May 1919 November 1918	Cp. Jackson, S. C. Cp. Sevier, S. C.	Cmpnt. of 81st Div. Cmpnt. of 156th Dep. Brig.
2d Provisional Regiment.	do	do	do	do			do	do	Do.
3d Provisional Regiment.	do	do	do	do			do	do	Do.
4th Provisional Regiment.	do	do	do	do			do	do	Do.
1st Training Battalion.	October 1917	do	do	Do.					
2d Training Battalion.	do	do	January 1919 September 1918	Cp. Jackson, S. C. Cp. Sevier, S. C.			April 1919	Cp. Jackson, S. C.	Do.
3d Training Battalion.	April 1918	do	January 1919 September 1918	Cp. Jackson, S. C. Cp. Sevier, S. C.			do	do	Do.
4th Training Battalion.	November 1917	do	January 1919 September 1918	Cp. Jackson, S. C. Cp. Sevier, S. C.			do	do	Do.
5th Training Battalion.	do	do	January 1919 September 1918	Cp. Jackson, S. C. Cp. Sevier, S. C.			March 1919 November 1918	do Cp. Sevier, S. C.	Do. Do.

DEPOT BRIGADES—Continued

Unit designation and redesignation	Organization		Stations in United States		Overseas		Demobilization		Remarks
	Month and year	Place	Month and year	Place	From—	To—	Month and year	Place	
156th Depot Brigade—Continued									
6th Training Battalion.	November 1917	Cp. Jackson, S. C.	September 1918	Cp. Sevier, S. C.			November 1918	Cp. Sevier, S. C.	Cmpnt. of 156th Dep. Brig.
7th Training Battalion.	April 1918	do	do	do			do	do	Do.
8th Training Battalion.	do	do	do	do			do	do	Do.
9th Training Battalion.	do	do	do	do			do	do	Do.
10th Training Battalion.	May 1918	do	do	do			do	do	Do.
11th Training Battalion.	do	do	do	do			do	do	Do.
12th Training Battalion.	do	do	do	do			do	do	Do.
1st Development Battalion.	July 1918	do	do	do			December 1918	do	Do.
2d Development Battalion.	do	do	do	do			do	do	Do.
3d Development Battalion.	do	do					do	Cp. Jackson, S. C.	Cmpnt. of 156th Dep. Brig. Relvd. fr. duty with Dep. Brig. September 1918.
4th Development Battalion.	do	do	September 1918	Cp. Sevier, S. C.			do	Cp. Sevier, S. C.	Cmpnt. of 156th Dep. Brig.
5th Development Battalion.	September 1918	Cp. Sevier, S. C.					do	do	Do.
6th Development Battalion.	do	do	January 1919	Cp. Jackson, S. C.			April 1919	Cp. Jackson, S. C.	Do.

7th Development Battalion.	do	do					December 1918	Cp. Sevier, S. C.	Do.
8th Development Battalion.	December 1918	do	January 1919	Cp. Jackson, S. C.			March 1919	Cp. Jackson, S. C.	Do.
157th Depot Brigade	September 1917	Cp. Gordon, Ga.	September 1918 December 1918	Cp. McClellan, Ala. Cp. Gordon, Ga.			May 1919	Cp. Gordon, Ga.	Cmpnt. of 82d Div.
1st Training Battalion.	do	do	September 1918	Cp. McClellan, Ala.			October 1918	Cp. McClellan, Ala.	Cmpnt. of 157th Dep. Brig.
2d Training Battalion.	October 1917	do	do	do			do	do	Do.
3d Training Battalion.	do	do	do	do			do	do	Do.
4th Training Battalion.	do	do	do	do			do	do	Do.
5th Training Battalion.	November 1917	do	do	do			do	do	Do.
6th Training Battalion.	April 1918	do	do	do			do	do	Do.
7th Training Battalion.	do	do	do	do			do	do	Do.
8th Training Battalion.	do	do	do	do			do	do	Do.
9th Training Battalion.	June 1918	do	do	do			do	do	Do.
10th Training Battalion.	November 1917	do	do	do			do	do	Do.
11th Training Battalion.	do	do					January 1919	Cp. Gordon, Ga.	Do.
12th Training Battalion.	do	do					do	do	Do.
13th Training Battalion.	do	do					September 1918	do	Do.
1st Development Battalion.	July 1918	do					May 1919	do	Do.
2d Development Battalion.	do	do					March 1919	do	Do.
1st Receiving Battalion.	October 1918	Cp. McClellan, Ala.					November 1919	Cp. McClellan, Ala.	Cmpnt. of 157th Dep. Brig. Orgzd. fr. 1st Tng. Bn.

DEPOT BRIGADES—Continued

Unit designation and redesignation	Organization		Stations in United States		Overseas		Demobilization		Remarks
	Month and year	Place	Month and year	Place	From—	To—	Month and year	Place	
157th Depot Brigade—Continued									
2d Receiving Battalion.	October 1918	Cp. McClellan, Ala.	December 1918	Cp. Gordon, Ga.			March 1919	Cp. Gordon, Ga.	Cmpnt. of 157th Dep. Brig. Orgzd. fr. 2d Tng. Bn.
3d Receiving Battalion.	do	do					November 1919	Cp. McClellan, Ala.	Cmpnt. of 157th Dep. Brig. Orgzd. fr. 3d Tng. Bn.
4th Receiving Battalion.	do	do					do	do	Cmpnt. of 157th Dep. Brig. Orgzd. fr. 4th Tng. Bn.
5th Receiving Battalion.	do	do	December 1918	Cp. Gordon, Ga.			April 1919	Cp. Gordon, Ga.	Cmpnt. of 157th Dep. Brig. Orgzd. fr. 5th Tng. Bn.
6th Receiving Battalion.	do	do					November 1918	Cp. McClellan, Ala.	Cmpnt. of 157th Dep. Brig. Orgzd. fr. 6th Tng. Bn.
7th Receiving Battalion.	do	do					do	do	Cmpnt. of 157th Dep. Brig. Orgzd. fr. 7th Tng. Bn.
8th Receiving Battalion.	do	do					do	do	Cmpnt. of 157th Dep. Brig. Orgzd. fr. 8th Tng. Bn.
9th Receiving Battalion.	do	do					do	do	Cmpnt. of 157th Dep. Brig. Orgzd. fr. 9th Tng. Bn.
10th Receiving Battalion.	do	do	December 1918	Cp. Gordon, Ga.			April 1919	Cp. Gordon, Ga.	Cmpnt. of 157th Dep. Brig. Orgzd. fr. 10th Tng. Bn.
11th Receiving Battalion.	do	do					December 1918	Cp. McClellan, Ala.	Cmpnt. of 157th Dep. Brig. Orgzd. fr. 11th Tng. Bn.

12th Receiving Battalion.	do	Cp. Gordon, Ga					November 1918	Cp. Gordon, Ga	Cmpnt. of 157th Dep. Brig. Orgzd. fr. 12th Tng. Bn.
13th Receiving Battalion.	November 1918	Cp. McClellan, Ala.	December 1918	Cp. Gordon, Ga			April 1919	do	Cmpnt. of 157th Dep. Brig.
14th Receiving Battalion.	do	do					November 1918	Cp. McClellan, Ala.	Do.
158th Depot Brigade	August 1917	Cp. Sherman, Ohio					May 1919	Cp. Sherman, Ohio	Cmpnt. of 83d Div.
1st Training Battalion.	September 1917	do					do	do	Cmpnt. of 158th Dep. Brig.
2d Training Battalion.	do	do					do	do	Do.
3d Training Battalion.	do	do					March 1919	do	Do.
4th Training Battalion.	do	do					December 1918	do	Do.
5th Training Battalion.	do	do					do	do	Do.
6th Training Battalion.	do	do					do	do	Do.
7th Training Battalion.	do	do					do	do	Do.
8th Training Battalion.	do	do					do	do	Do.
9th Training Battalion.	do	do					do	do	Do.
10th Training Battalion.	do	do					May 1919	do	Do.
11th Training Battalion.	do	do					December 1918	do	Do.
12th Training Battalion.	do	do					do	do	Do.
1st Development Battalion.	July 1918	do					January 1919	do	Do.
2d Development Battalion.	do	do					December 1918	do	Do.
3d Development Battalion.	do	do					January 1919	do	Do.
4th Development Battalion.	August 1918	do					December 1918	do	Do.

DEPOT BRIGADES—Continued

Unit designation and redesignation	Organization		Stations in United States		Overseas		Demobilization		Remarks
	Month and year	Place	Month and year	Place	From—	To—	Month and year	Place	
158th Depot Brigade—Continued									
5th Development Battalion.	August 1918	Cp. Sherman, Ohio.					December 1918	Cp. Sherman, Ohio.	Cmpnt. of 158th Dep. Brig.
6th Development Battalion.	do	do					do	do	Do.
159th Depot Brigade	August 1917	Cp. Zachary Taylor, Ky.					May 1919	Cp. Zachary Taylor, Ky.	Cmpnt. of 84th Div.
1st (I) Training Battalion.	do	do					October 1917	do	Cmpnt. of 159th Dep. Brig.
1st (II) Training Battalion.	October 1917	do					May 1919	do	Cmpnt. of 159th Dep. Brig. Orgzd. fr. 33d Tng. Bn.
2d (I) Training Battalion.	August 1917	do					October 1917	do	Cmpnt. of 159th Dep. Brig.
2d (II) Training Battalion.	October 1917	do					March 1919	do	Cmpnt. of 159th Dep. Brig. Orgzd. fr. 32d Tng. Bn.
3d Training Battalion.	August 1917	do					do	do	Cmpnt. of 159th Dep. Brig.
4th (I) Training Battalion.	do	do					January 1918	do	Do.
4th (II) Training Battalion.	January 1918	do					May 1919	do	Cmpnt. of 159th Dep. Brig. Orgzd. fr. 7th Tng. Bn.
5th (I) Training Battalion.	August 1917	do					October 1917	do	Cmpnt. of 159th Dep. Brig.
5th (II) Training Battalion.	October 1917	do					January 1918	do	Do.

5th (III) Training Battalion.	January 1918	do					December 1918	do	Cmpnt. of 159th Dep. Brig. Orgzd. fr. 10th and 11th Tng. Bns.
6th (I) Training Battalion.	August 1917	do					November 1917	do	Cmpnt. of 159th Dep. Brig.
6th (II) Training Battalion.	November 1917	do					January 1918	do	Cmpnt. of 159th Dep. Brig. Orgzd. fr. 19th and 20th Tng. Bns.
6th (III) Training Battalion.	January 1918	do					December 1918	do	Cmpnt. of 159th Dep. Brig. Orgzd. fr. 12th and 13th Tng. Bns.
7th (I) Training Battalion.	August 1917	do					January 1918	do	Cmpnt. of 159th Dep. Brig.
7th (II) Training Battalion.	January 1918	do					December 1918	do	Cmpnt. of 159th Dep. Brig. Orgzd. fr. 14th Tng. Bn.
8th Training Battalion.	August 1917	do					do	do	Cmpnt. of 159th Dep. Brig.
9th (I) Training Battalion.	do	do					October 1917	do	Do.
9th (II) Training Battalion.	October 1917	do					January 1918	do	Cmpnt. of 159th Dep. Brig. Orgzd. fr. 30th Tng. Bn.
9th (III) Training Battalion.	April 1918	do					December 1918	do	Cmpnt. of 159th Dep. Brig.
10th (I) Training Battalion.	August 1917	do					November 1917	do	Do.
10th (II) Training Battalion.	November 1917	do					January 1918	do	Cmpnt. of 159th Dep. Brig. Orgzd. fr. 15th and 18th Tng. Bns.
10th (III) Training Battalion.	April 1918	do					December 1918	do	Cmpnt. of 159th Dep. Brig.
11th (I) Training Battalion.	August 1917	do					October 1917	do	Do.

DEPOT BRIGADES—Continued

Unit designation and redesignation	Organization		Stations in United States		Overseas		Demobilization		Remarks
	Month and year	Place	Month and year	Place	From—	To—	Month and year	Place	
159th Depot Brigade—Continued									
11th (II) Training Battalion.	October 1917	Cp. Zachary Taylor, Ky.					January 1918	Cp. Zachary Taylor, Ky.	Cmpnt. of 159th Dep. Brig. Orgzd. fr. 29th Tng. Bn.
11th (III) Training Battalion.	May 1918	do					December 1918	do	Cmpnt. of 159th Dep. Brig.
12th (I) Training Battalion.	August 1917	do					October 1917	do	Do.
12th (II) Training Battalion.	October 1917	do					January 1918	do	Cmpnt. of 159th Dep. Brig. Orgzd. fr. 28th Tng. Bn.
12th (III) Training Battalion.	May 1918	do					December 1918	do	Cmpnt. of 159th Dep. Brig.
13th (I) Training Battalion.	August 1917	do					October 1917	do	Do.
13th (II) Training Battalion.	October 1917	do					January 1918	do	Cmpnt. of 159th Dep. Brig. Orgzd. fr. 27th Tng. Bn.
13th (III) Training Battalion.	May 1918	do					October 1918	do	Cmpnt. of 159th Dep. Brig.
14th (I) Training Battalion.	August 1917	do					Jauary 1918	do	Do.
14th (II) Training Battalion.	June 1918	do					October 1918	do	Do.
15th (I) Training Battalion.	August 1917	do					October 1917	do	Do.
15th (II) Training Battalion.	October 1917	do					November 1917	do	Cmpnt. of 159th Dep. Brig. Orgzd. fr. 26th Tng. Bn.

15th (III) Training Battalion.	June 1918	do					October 1918	do	Cmpnt. of 159th Dep. Brig.
16th (I) Training Battalion.	August 1917	do					October 1917	do	Do.
16th (II) Training Battalion.	October 1917	do					November 1917	do	Do.
16th (III) Training Battalion.	June 1918	do					October 1918	do	Do.
17th (I) Training Battalion.	August 1917	do					November 1917	do	Do.
17th (II) Training Battalion.	June 1918	do					October 1918	do	Do.
18th (I) Training Battalion.	August 1917	do					October 1917	do	Do.
18th (II) Training Battalion.	October 1917	do					November 1917	do	Cmpnt. of 159th Dep.Brig.Orgzd. fr. 22d Tng. Bn.
18th (III) Training Battalion.	June 1918	do					October 1918	do	Cmpnt. of 159th Dep. Brig.
19th (I) Training Battalion.	August 1917	do					October 1917	do	Do.
19th (II) Training Battalion.	October 1917	do					November 1917	do	Cmpnt. of 159th Dep.Brig.Orgzd. fr. 21st Tng. Bn.
20th Training Battalion.	August 1917	do					do	do	Cmpnt. of 159th Dep. Brig.
21st Training Battalion.	do	do					October 1917	do	Do.
22d Training Battalion.	do	do					do	do	Do.
23d Training Battalion.	do	do					do	do	Do.
24th Training Battalion.	do	do					do	do	Do.
25th Training Battalion.	do	do					do	do	Do.
26th Training Battalion	do	do					do	do	Do.
27th Training Battalion.	do	do					do	do	Do.

DEPOT BRIGADES—Continued

Unit designation and redesignation	Organization		Stations in United States		Overseas		Demobilization		Remarks
	Month and year	Place	Month and year	Place	From—	To—	Month and year	Place	
159th Depot Brigade—Continued									
28th Training Battalion.	August 1917	Cp. Zachary Taylor, Ky.					October 1917	Cp. Zachary Taylor, Ky.	Cmpnt. of 159th Dep. Brig.
29th Training Battalion.	do	do					do	do	Do.
30th Training Battalion.	do	do					do	do	Do.
31st Training Battalion.	do	do					do	do	Do.
32d Training Battalion.	do	do					do	do	Do.
33d Training Battalion.	do	do					do	do	Do.
1st Development Battalion.	June 1918	do					November 1918	do	Do.
2d Development Battalion.	August 1918	do					do	do	Do.
3d Development Battalion.	do	do	October 1918	Cp. Beauregard, La.			do	Cp. Beauregard, La.	Do.
160th Depot Brigade	September 1917	Cp. Custer, Mich.					May 1919	Cp. Custer, Mich.	Cmpnt. of 85th Div.
1st Training Battalion.	do	do					February 1919	do	Cmpnt. of 160th Dep. Brig.
2d Training Battalion.	do	do					do	do	Do.
3d Training Battalion.	do	do					March 1919	do	Do.
4th Training Battalion.	do	do					December 1918	do	Do.
5th Training Battalion.	do	do					do	do	Do.

6th Training Battalion.	do	do					do	do	Do.
7th (I) Training Battalion.	do	do					January 1918	do	Do.
7th (II) Training Battalion.	June 1918	do					December 1918	do	Do.
8th (I) Training Battalion.	September 1917	do					January 1918	do	Do.
8th (II) Training Battalion.	June 1918	do					December 1918	do	Do.
9th (I) Training Battalion.	September 1917	do					January 1918	do	Do.
9th (II) Training Battalion.	June 1918	do					December 1918	do	Do.
10th (I) Training Battalion.	September 1917	do					January 1918	do	Do.
10th (II) Training Battalion.	June 1918	do					December 1918	do	Do.
11th Training Battalion.	do	do					do	do	Do.
12th Training Battalion.	do	do					do	do	Do.
1st Development Battalion.	do	do					do	do	Do.
2d Development Battalion.	July 1918	do					do	do	Do.
3d Development Battalion.	do	do					do	do	Do.
4th Development Battalion.	September 1918	do	October 1918	Cp. Beauregard, La.			October 1918	Cp. Beauregard, La.	Do.
161st Depot Brigade	August 1917	Cp. Grant, Ill					May 1919	Cp. Grant, Ill	Cmpnt. of 86th Div.
1st Provisional Training Regiment.	June 1918	do					January 1919	do	Cmpnt. of 161st Dep. Brig.
2d Provisional Training Regiment.	do	do					December 1918	do	Do.
3d Provisional Training Regiment.	do	do					November 1918	do	Do.

DEPOT BRIGADES—Continued

Unit designation and redesignation	Organization		Stations in United States		Overseas		Demobilization		Remarks
	Month and year	Place	Month and year	Place	From—	To—	Month and year	Place	
161st Depot Brigade—Continued									
4th Provisional Training Regiment.	**June 1918**	Cp. Grant, Ill					November 1918	Cp. Grant, Ill	Cmpnt. of 161st Dep. Brig.
1st Training Battalion.	November 1917	do					May 1919	do	Do.
2d Training Battalion.	March 1918	do					do	do	Do.
3d Training Battalion.	do	do					April 1919	do	Do.
4th Training Battalion.	do	do					do	do	Do.
5th Training Battalion.	do	do					December 1918	do	Do.
6th Training Battalion.	do	do					do	do	Do.
7th Training Battalion.	**May 1918**	do					November 1918	do	Do.
8th Training Battalion.	do	do					do	do	Do.
9th Training Battalion.	do	do					do	do	Do.
10th Training Battalion.	do	do					do	do	Do.
11th Training Battalion.	do	do					do	do	Do.
12th Training Battalion.	do	do					do	do	Do.
13th Training Battalion.	September 1918	do					January 1919	do	Do.

1st Development Battalion.	do	do					February 1919	do	Do.
2d Development Battalion.	do	do					May 1919	do	Do.
3d Development Battalion.	do	do					January 1919	do	Do.
4th Development Battalion.	do	do					February 1919	do	Do.
5th Development Battalion.	do	do					do	do	Do.
6th Development Battalion.	do	do	October 1918	Cp. Logan, Tex			November 1918	Cp. Logan, Tex	Do.
7th Development Battalion.	do	do					February 1919	Cp. Grant, Ill	Do.
162d Depot Brigade	August 1917	Cp. Pike, Ark					May 1919	Cp. Pike, Ark	Cmpnt. of 87th Div.
1st (I) Training Battalion.	September 1917	do					January 1918	do	Cmpnt. of 162d Dep. Brig.
1st (II) Training Battalion.	January 1918	do							Do.
a. 1st Receiving Battalion.	September 1918	do					November 1918	Cp. Pike, Ark.	
2d (I) Training Battalion.	September 1917	do					January 1918	do	Do.
2d (II) Training Battalion.	January 1918	do							Do.
a. 2d Receiving Battalion.	September 1918	do					March 1919	Cp. Pike, Ark.	
3d (I) Training Battalion.	September 1917	do					January 1918	do	Do.
3d (II) Training Battalion.	January 1918	do							Do.
a. 3d Receiving Battalion.	September 1918	do					December 1918	Cp. Pike, Ark.	
4th (I) Training Battalion.	September 1917	do					January 1918	do	Do.
4th (II) Training Battalion.	January 1918	do							Do.
a. 4th Receiving Battalion.	September 1918	do					May 1919	Cp. Pike, Ark.	

DEPOT BRIGADES—Continued

Unit designation and redesignation	Organization		Stations in United States		Overseas		Demobilization		Remarks
	Month and year	Place	Month and year	Place	From—	To—	Month and year	Place	
162d Depot Brigade—Continued									
5th (I) Training Battalion.	September 1917	**Cp. Pike, Ark**					January 1918	**Cp. Pike, Ark**	**Cmpnt. of 162d Dep. Brig.**
5th (II) Training Battalion.	January 1918	do							Do.
a. 5th Receiving Battalion.	September 1918	do					November 1918	Cp. Pike, Ark.	
6th (I) Training Battalion.	September 1917	do					January 1918	do	Do.
6th (II) Training Battalion.	January 1918	do							Do.
a. 6th Receiving Battalion.	September 1918	do					November 1918	Cp. Pike, Ark.	
7th (I) Training Battalion.	October 1917	do					January 1918	do	Do.
7th (II) Training Battalion.	March 1918	do							Do.
a. 7th Receiving Battalion.	September 1918	do					December 1918	Cp. Pike, Ark.	
8th (I) Training Battalion.	October 1917	do					January 1918	do	Do.
8th (II) Training Battalion.	April 1918	do							Do.
a. 8th Receiving Battalion.	September 1918	do					December 1918	Cp. Pike, Ark.	

9th Training Battalion.	June 1918	do							Do.
a. 9th Receiving Battalion.	September 1918	do					December 1918	Cp. Pike, Ark.	
10th Training Battalion.	June 1918	do							Do.
a. 10th Receiving Battalion.	September 1918	do					December 1918	Cp. Pike, Ark.	
11th Training Battalion.	June 1918	do							Do.
a. 11th Receiving Battalion.	September 1918	do					May 1919	Cp. Pike, Ark.	
12th Training Battalion.	June 1918	do							Do.
a. 12th Receiving Battalion.	September 1918	do					December 1918	Cp. Pike, Ark.	
13th Training Battalion.	August 1918	do							Do.
a. 13th Receiving Battalion.	September 1918	do					November 1918	Cp. Pike, Ark.	
14th Training Battalion.	August 1918	do							Do.
a. 14th Receiving Battalion.	September 1918	do					November 1918	Cp. Pike, Ark.	
15th Training Battalion.	August 1918	do							Do.
a. 15th Receiving Battalion.	September 1918	do					November 1918	Cp. Pike, Ark.	
1st to 15th Receiving Battalions.									See 1st to 15th Tng. Bns.
16th Receiving Battalion.	September 1918	Cp. Pike, Ark					May 1919	Cp. Pike, Ark	Cmpnt. of 162d Dep. Brig.

DEPOT BRIGADES—Continued

Unit designation and redesignation	Organization		Stations in United States		Overseas		Demobilization		Remarks
	Month and year	Place	Month and year	Place	From—	To—	Month and year	Place	
162d Depot Brigade—Continued									
17th Receiving Battalion.	October 1918	Cp. Pike, Ark					December 1918	Cp. Pike, Ark	Cmpnt. of 162 Dep. Brig.
18th Receiving Battalion.	do	do					do	do	Do.
19th Receiving Battalion.	do	do					do	do	Do.
20th Receiving Battalion.	do	do					do	do	Do.
21st Receiving Battalion.	do	do					do	do	Do.
22d Receiving Battalion.	do	do					November 1918	do	Do.
23d Receiving Battalion.	do	do					December 1918	do	Do.
24th Receiving Battalion.	do	do					October 1918	do	Do.
1st Development Battalion.	do	do					December 1918	do	Do.
2d Development Battalion.	do	do					do	do	Do.
3d Development Battalion.	November 1918	do					do	do	Do.
4th Development Battalion.									Never orgzd.
5th Development Battalion.	November 1918	Cp. Pike, Ark					December 1918	Cp. Pike, Ark	Cmpnt. of 162d Dep. Brig.
6th Development Battalion.	do	do					do	do	Do.

7th Development Battalion.	do	do					do	do	Do.
8th Development Battalion.	do	do					March 1919	do	Do.
9th Development Battalion.	do	do					do	do	Do.
163d Depot Brigade	August 1917	Cp. Dodge, Iowa					May 1919	Cp. Dodge, Iowa	Cmpnt. of 88th Div.
1st Provisional Regiment.	September 1917	do					October 1917	do	Cmpnt. of 163d Dep. Brig.
2d Provisional Regiment.	do	do					do	do	Do.
1st Battalion	November 1917	do					March 1919	do	Do.
2d Battalion	do	do					do	do	Do.
3d Battalion	do	do					do	do	Do.
4th Battalion	do	do					December 1918	do	Do.
5th Battalion	do	do					November 1918	do	Do.
6th (I) Battalion	March 1918	do					April 1918	do	Do.
6th (II) Battalion	June 1918	do					March 1919	do	Do.
7th (I) Battalion	March 1918	do					April 1918	do	Do.
7th (II) Battalion	June 1918	do					December 1918	do	Do.
8th Battalion	do	do					do	do	Do.
9th Battalion	July 1918	do					do	do	Do.
10th Battalion	do	do					November 1918	do	Do.
11th Battalion	do	do					do	do	Do.
12th Battalion	do	do					do	do	Do.
1st to 12th Provisional Battalions.									Never orgzd.
13th Provisional Battalion.	July 1918	Cp. Dodge, Iowa					November 1918	Cp. Dodge, Iowa	Cmpnt. of 163d Dep. Brig.
14th Provisional Battalion.	do	do					do	do	Do.
15th Provisional Battalion.	do	do					do	do	Do.
16th Provisional Battalion.	do	do					October 1918	do	Do.
17th Provisional Battalion.	August 1918	do					do	do	Do.
18th Provisional Battalion.	do	do					do	do	Do.

DEPOT BRIGADES—Continued

Unit designation and redesignation	Organization		Stations in United States		Overseas		Demobilization		Remarks
	Month and year	Place	Month and year	Place	From—	To—	Month and year	Place	
163d Depot Brigade—Continued									
19th Provisional Battalion.	August 1918	Cp. Dodge, Iowa					October 1918	Cp. Dodge, Iowa	Cmpnt. of 163d Dep. Brig.
1st Development Battalion.	do	do					January 1919	do	Do.
2d Development Battalion.	do	do					February 1919	do	Do.
3d Development Battalion.	September 1918	do	November 1918	Cp. Cody, N. Mex.			December 1918	Cp. Cody, N. Mex.	Do.
164th Depot Brigade	September 1917	Cp. Funston, Kans.					May 1919	Cp. Funston, Kans.	Cmpnt. of 89th Div.
1st (I) Battalion	do	do					November 1918	do	Cmpnt. of 164th Dep. Brig.
1st (II) Battalion	December 1918	do					March 1919	do	Do.
2d (I) Battalion	September 1917	do					November 1918	do	Do.
2d (II) Battalion	December 1918	do					March 1919	do	Do.
3d (I) Battalion	September 1917	do					November 1918	do	Do.
3d (II) Battalion	December 1918	do							Do.
a. Depot Brigade Battalion.	March 1919	do					May 1919	Cp. Funston, Kans.	
4th (I) Battalion	September 1917	do					November 1918	do	Do.
4th (II) Battalion	December 1918	do					March 1919	do	Do.
5th Battalion	September 1917	do					November 1918	do	Do.
6th Battalion	do	do					do	do	Do.
7th Battalion	do	do					do	do	Do.
8th Battalion	do	do					do	do	Do.
9th Battalion	do	do					do	do	Do.
10th Battalion	do	do					do	do	Do.
11th Battalion	do	do					do	do	Do.

12th Battalion	do	do					do	do	Do.
13th Battalion	do	do					June 1918	do	Do.
14th Battalion	do	do					do	do	Do.
15th Battalion	do	do					December 1918	do	Do.
16th Battalion	do	do					June 1918	do	Do.
17th Battalion	do	do					do	do	Do.
18th Battalion	do	do					do	do	Do.
19th Battalion	do	do					do	do	Do.
20th Battalion	do	do					December 1917	do	Do.
21st Battalion	do	do					do	do	Do.
22d Battalion	do	do					do	do	Do.
23d Battalion	do	do					do	do	Do.
24th Battalion	do	do					do	do	Do.
1st (I) Development Battalion.	June 1918	do					August 1918	do	Do.
1st (II) Development Battalion.	August 1918	do					March 1919	do	Do.
2d (I) Development Battalion.	June 1918	do					August 1918	do	Do.
2d (II) Development Battalion.	August 1918	do					December 1918	do	Do.
3d Development Battalion.	do	do					do	do	Do.
1st Development Battalion (colored).	do	do					do	do	Do.
2d (I) Development Battalion (colored).	June 1918	do					August 1918	do	Do.
2d (II) Development Battalion (colored).	August 1918	do					March 1919	do	Do.
3d Development Battalion (colored).	do	do					December 1918	do	Do.
165th Depot Brigade	August 1917	Cp. Travis, Tex.					May 1919	Cp. Travis, Tex.	Cmpnt. of 90th Div.
1st Battalion	September 1917	do					December 1918	do	Cmpnt. of 165th Dep. Brig.

DEPOT BRIGADES—Continued

Unit designation and redesignation	Organization		Stations in United States		Overseas		Demobilization		Remarks
	Month and year	Place	Month and year	Place	From—	To—	Month and year	Place	
165th Depot Brigade—Continued									
2d Battalion	September 1917	Cp. Travis, Tex.					December 1918	Cp. Travis, Tex.	Cmpnt. of 165th Dep. Brig.
3d Battalion	do	do					do	do	Do.
4th Battalion	do	do					do	do	Do.
5th Battalion	do	do					do	do	Do.
6th Battalion	do	do					March 1919	do	Do.
7th Battalion	do	do					do	do	Do.
8th Battalion	do	do					May 1919	do	Do.
9th Battalion	do	do					do	do	Do.
10th Battalion	do	do					December 1918	do	Do.
11th Battalion	do	do					do	do	Do.
12th Battalion	do	do					do	do	Do.
13th (I) Battalion	do	do					August 1918	do	Do.
13th (II) Battalion	September 1918	do					October 1918	do	Do.
14th (I) Battalion	September 1917	do					August 1918	do	Do.
14th (II) Battalion	September 1918	do					October 1918	do	Do.
15th (I) Battalion	September 1917	do					August 1918	do	Do.
15th (II) Battalion	September 1918	do					October 1918	do	Do.
16th Battalion	October 1917	do					do	do	Do.
17th Battalion	do	do					do	do	Do.
18th (I) Battalion	do	do					August 1918	do	Do.
18th (II) Battalion	September 1918	do					October 1918	do	Do.
19th Battalion	June 1918	do					August 1918	do	Do.
20th Battalion	do	do					do	do	Do.
21st Battalion	do	do					do	do	Do.
22d Battalion	do	do					do	do	Do.
23d Battalion	do	do					do	do	Do.
1st Development Battalion.	October 1918	do					January 1919	do	Do.

2d Development Battalion.	do	do							**Do.**
a. White Development Battalion.	**January 1919**	do					**February 1919**	**Cp. Travis, Tex.**	
3d Development Battalion.	October 1918	do					**January 1919**	do	**Do.**
1st Development Battalion (colored).	**December 1918**	do							Do.
a. Colored Development Battalion.	**January 1919**	do					**February 1919**	Cp. Travis, Tex.	
2d Development Battalion (colored).	**December 1918**	do					**January 1919**	do	**Do.**
3d Development Battalion (colored).	do	do					do	do	Do.
166th Depot Brigade	September 1917	Cp. Lewis, Wash.					**May 1919**	Cp. Lewis, Wash.	**Cmpnt. of 91st Div.**
1st Battalion	do	do					April 1919	do	**Cmpnt. of 166th Dep. Brig.**
2d Battalion	do	do					December 1918	do	Do.
3d Battalion	do	do					do	do	Do.
4th Battalion	do	do					do	do	**Do.**
5th Battalion	do	do					do	do	**Do.**
6th Battalion	do	do					do	do	**Do.**
7th Battalion	do	do					**April 1919**	do	**Do.**
8th Battalion	do	do					December 1918	do	Do.
9th Battalion	do	do					do	do	Do.
10th Battalion	do	do					do	do	Do.
11th (I) Battalion	October 1917	do					January 1918	do	Do.
11th (II) Battalion	May 1918	do					March 1919	do	Do.
12th (I) Battalion	October 1917	do					January 1918	do	Do.
12th (II) Battalion	May 1918	do					May 1919	do	Do.
13th (I) Battalion	October 1917	do					February 1918	do	Do.

DEPOT BRIGADES—Continued

Unit designation and redesignation	Organization		Stations in United States		Overseas		Demobilization		Remarks
	Month and year	Place	Month and year	Place	From—	To—	Month and year	Place	
166th Depot Brigade—Continued									
13th (II) Battalion	June 1918	Cp. Lewis, Wash.					October 1918	Cp. Lewis, Wash.	Cmpnt. of 166th Dep. Brig.
14th (I) Battalion	October 1917	do					January 1918	do	Do.
14th (II) Battalion	June 1918	do					October 1918	do	Do.
15th (I) Battalion	October 1917	do					January 1918	do	Do.
15th (II) Battalion	June 1918	do					September 1918	do	Do.
16th Battalion	October 1917	do					January 1918	do	Do.
17th Battalion	do	do					do	do	Do.
18th Battalion	do	do					do	do	Do.
19th Battalion	do	do					do	do	Do.
1st Development Battalion.	July 1918	do					November 1918	do	Do.

DEPOT SPECIAL AND TECHNICAL UNITS

Units	Unit No.	Active service	Unit No.	Active service	Unit No.	Active service	Unit No.	Active service	Unit No.	Active service	Remarks
SEPARATE DEVELOPMENT BATTALIONS											
Camp Beauregard, La., Battalions.	1	August 1918–May 1919	2	September 1918–May 1919	3	August 1918–December 1918					
Camp Bowie, Tex., Battalions.	1	June 1918–April 1919	2	December 1918–February 1919							
Camp Cody, N. Mex., Battalions.	1	June 1918–December 1918	2	September 1918–December 1918							

Camp Doniphan, Okla., Battalion.	--------	July 1918–March 1919								
Camp Fremont, Calif., Battalion.	--------	June 1918–December 1918								
Camp Greene, N.C., Battalions.	1	August 1918–February 1919	2	September 1918–February 1919						
Camp Hancock, Ga., Battalion.	--------	June 1918–February 1919								
Camp Kearny, Calif., Battalion.	--------	June 1918–February 1919								
Camp Logan, Tex., Battalions.	1	September 1918–January 1919	2	August 1918–February 1919	3	August 1918–January 1919				
Camp MacArthur, Tex., Battalions.	1	August 1918–February 1919	2	September 1918–January 1919	3	September 1918–November 1918	4	September 1918–November 1918	5	September 1918–December 1918
Camp McClellan, Ala., Battalions.	1	July 1918–February 1919	2	November 1918–February 1919						
Camp Sevier, S. C., Battalion.	1	June 1918–September 1918								
Camp Shelby, Miss., Battalion.	--------	June 1918–March 1919								
Camp Sheridan, Ala., Battalion.	--------	July 1918–January 1919								
Camp Wadsworth, S. C., Battalions.	1	June 1918–February 1919	2	September 1918–February 1919						
Camp Wheeler, Ga., Battalions.	1	July 1918–December 1918	2	July 1918–December 1918	3	August 1918–December 1918	4	October 1918–December 1918		

DIVISIONS [1]

CAVALRY DIVISIONS

Unit designation and redesignation	Organization		Stations in United States		Overseas		Demobilization		Remarks
	Month and year	Place	Month and year	Place	From—	To—	Month and year	Place	
1st Provisional Cavalry Division.	March 1917	El Paso, Tex.							Orgzn. discontinued June 1917.
15th Cavalry Division	December 1917	Ft. Bliss, Tex.					May 1918	Ft. Bliss, Tex.	

INFANTRY DIVISIONS

Unit designation and redesignation	Organization		Stations in United States		Overseas		Demobilization		Remarks
	Month and year	Place	Month and year	Place	From—	To—	Month and year	Place	
1st Division	June 1917	New York, N. Y.	June 1917	P. of E., Hoboken	June 1917				Orgzn. directed by W.D. May 1917.
			September 1919	Cp. Meade, Md.		August 1919			Emergency pl. demobilized.
			do	Cp. Zachary Taylor, Ky.					Active through 1919.
1st Division, Philippine National Guard.	December 1918	Cp. Claudio, Ft. Wm. McKinley, P. I.					December 1918	Ft. Wm. McKinley, P. I.	
1st Provisional Infantry Division.	March 1917	Cp. Wilson, Tex.							Orgzn. discontinued June 1917.
2d Division	October 1917	A. E. F.							Orgzn. directed by W.D. September 1917.
			August 1919	Cp. Mills, N. Y.		August 1919			Emergency pl. demobilized.
			do	Cp. Travis, Tex.					Active through 1919.
2d Provisional Infantry Division.	March 1917	El Paso, Tex.							Orgzn. discontinued June 1917.
3d Division	November 1917	Cp. Greene, N. C.	March 1918	Cp. Merritt, N. J.	March 1918.				
			August 1919	do		August 1919			Emergency pl. demobilized.

			do	Cp. Pike, Ark					Active through 1919.
3d Provisional Infantry Division.	March 1917	Douglas, Ariz							Organ. discontinued June 1917.
4th Division	December 1917	Cp. Greene, N. C.	April 1918	Cp. Mills, N. Y.					
			do	P. of E., Hoboken	April 1918.				
			August 1919	Cp. Merritt, N. J.		August 1919			Emergency pl. demobilised.
			do	Cp. Dodge, Iowa					Active through 1919.
5th Division	do	Cp. Logan, Tex	April 1918	Cp. Merritt, N. J.					
			do	P. of E., Hoboken	April 1918.				
			July 1919	Hoboken, N. J.		July 1919			Emergency pl. demobilised.
			do	Cp. Gordon, Ga					Active through 1919.
6th Division	November 1917	Cp. McClellan, Ala.	March 1918	Cp. Forrest, Ga.					
			May 1918	Cp. Wadsworth, S. C.					
			July 1918	Cp. Mills, N. Y.					
			do	P. of E., Hoboken	July 1918.				
			June 1919	Cp. Mills, N. Y.		June 1919			Emergency pl. demobilized.
			do	Cp. Grant, Ill					Active through 1919.
7th Division	January 1918	Cp. Wheeler, Ga	May 1918	Cp. MacArthur, Tex.					
			July 1918	Cp. Merritt, N. J.					
			August 1918	P. of E., Hoboken	August 1918.				
			June 1919	Cp. Mills, N. Y.		June 1919			Emergency pl. and certain units demobilized.
			do	Cp. Funston, Kans.					Active through 1919.
8th Division	January 1918	Cp. Fremont, Calif.	October 1918	Cp. Mills, N. Y.					
			November 1918	P. of E., Hoboken	November 1918	September 1919	September 1919	Cp. Dix, N. J.	Only part of Div. sent overseas.

[1] **Data appearing under the various headings refer primarily to Division Headquarters. For other components consult proper unit tables.**

INFANTRY DIVISIONS—Continued

Unit designation and redesignation	Organization		Stations in United States		Overseas		Demobilization		Remarks
	Month and year	Place	Month and year	Place	From—	To—	Month and year	Place	
9th Division	July 1918	Cp. Sheridan, Ala.					February 1919	Cp. Sheridan, Ala.	
10th Division	August 1918	Cp. Funston, Kans.					do	Cp. Funston, Kans.	
11th Division	do	Cp. Meade, Md.					do	Cp. Meade, Md.	
12th Division	July 1918	Cp. Devens, Mass.					do	Cp. Devens, Mass.	
13th Division	do	Cp. Lewis, Wash.					March 1919	Cp. Lewis, Wash.	
14th Division	do	Cp. Custer, Mich.					February 1919	Cp. Custer, Mich.	
15th Division	August 1918	Cp. Logan, Tex.					do	Cp. Logan, Tex.	
16th Division	do	Cp. Kearny, Calif.					March 1919	Cp. Kearny, Calif.	
17th Division	do	Cp. Beauregard, La.					February 1919	Cp. Beauregard, La.	
18th Division	do	Cp. Travis, Tex.					do	Cp. Travis, Tex.	
19th Division	September 1918	Cp. Dodge, Iowa					do	Cp. Dodge, Iowa.	
20th Division	August 1918	Cp. Sevier, S. C.					do	Cp. Sevier, S. C.	
21st to 25th Divisions									Never orgzd.
26th Division	August 1917	Boston, Mass.	September 1917	P. of E., Hoboken	October 1917.				
			April 1919	Boston, Mass.		April 1919	May 1919	Cp. Devens, Mass.	
27th Division	September 1917	Cp. Wadsworth, S. C.	May 1918	Cp. Stuart, Va.					
			do	P. of E., Newport News.	May 1918.				
			March 1919	Cp. Mills, N. Y.		March 1919	April 1919	Cp. Upton, N. Y.	
28th Division	do	Cp. Hancock, Ga.	April 1918	Cp. Upton, N. Y.					
			May 1918	P. of E., Hoboken	May 1918.				
			April 1919	Philadelphia, Pa.		April 1919	May 1919	Cp. Dix, N. J.	
29th Division	July 1917	Cp. Edge, N. J.	August 1917	Cp. McClellan, Ala.					
			June 1918	Cp. Stuart, Va.					
			do	P. of E., Newport News.	June 1918.				
			May 1919	Newport News, Va.		May 1919	May 1919	Cp. Dix, N. J.	

30th Division	August 1917	Cp. Sevier, S. C.	May 1918	Cp. Mills, N. Y.					
			do	P. of E., Hoboken	May 1918.				
			April 1919	Charleston, S. C.		April 1919	May 1919	Cp. Jackson, S. C.	
31st Division	do	Cp. Wheeler, Ga.	September 1918	Cp. Mills, N. Y.					
			October 1918	P. of E., Hoboken	October 1918				Div. skeletonized November 1918. Record cadre only.
			December 1918	Cp. Merritt, N. J.		December 1918	January 1919	Cp. Gordon, Ga.	
32d Division	do	Cp. MacArthur, Tex.	January 1918	Do.					
			do	P. of E., Hoboken	January 1918.				
			May 1919	Cp. Upton, N. Y.		May 1919	May 1919	Cp. Custer, Mich.	
33d Division	do	Cp. Logan, Tex.	May 1918	do					
			do	P. of E., Hoboken	May 1918.				
			May 1919	Hoboken, N. J.		May 1919	June 1919	Cp. Grant, Ill.	
34th Division	do	Cp. Cody, N. Mex.	August 1918	Cp. Dix, N. J.					
			September 1918	P. of E., Hoboken	September 1918				Div. skeletonized November 1918. Record cadre only.
			January 1919	Cp. Merritt, N. J.		January 1919	February 1919	Cp. Grant, Ill.	
35th Division	do	Cp. Doniphan, Okla.	April 1918	Cp. Mills, N. Y.					
			do	P. of E., Hoboken	April 1918.				
			April 1919	Newport News, Va.		April 1919	May 1919	Cp. Funston, Kans.	
36th Division	do	Cp. Bowie, Tex.	July 1918	Cp. Mills, N. Y.					
			do	P. of E., Hoboken	July 1918.				
			June 1919	Cp. Mills, N. Y.		June 1919	June 1919	Cp. Bowie, Tex.	
37th Division	do	Cp. Sheridan, Ala.	May 1918	Cp. Lee, Va.					
			June 1918	P. of E., Hoboken	June 1918.				
			March 1919	Cp. Mills, N. Y.		March 1919.			
			April 1919	Cp. Sherman, Ohio			do	Cp. Sherman, Ohio.	
38th Division	do	Cp. Shelby, Miss.	September 1918	Cp. Mills, N. Y.					
			October 1918	P. of E., Hoboken	October 1918				Div. skeletonized November 1918. Record cadre only.
			December 1918	Newport News, Va.		December 1918.			
			do	Cp. Zachary Taylor, Ky.			January 1919	Cp. Zachary Taylor, Ky.	
39th Division	do	Cp. Beauregard, La.	August 1918	Cp. Merritt, N. J.					
			do	P. of E., Hoboken	August 1918				Functioned as 5th Depot Div. September–October 1918; skeletonized November 1918. Record cadre only.
			December 1918	Newport News, Va.		December 1918	January 1919	Cp. Beauregard, La.	

INFANTRY DIVISIONS—Continued

Unit designation and redesignation	Organization		Stations in United States		Overseas		Demobilization		Remarks
	Month and year	Place	Month and year	Place	From—	To—	Month and year	Place	
40th Division	August 1917	Cp. Kearny, Calif.	August 1918	Cp. Mills, N. Y.					Functioned as 6th Depot Div. August–October 1918.
			do	P. of E., Hoboken	August 1918				
			March 1919	Cp. Mills, N. Y.		March 1919	April 1919	Cp. Kearny, Calif.	
41st Division	September 1917	Cp. Greene, N. C.	October 1917	Cp. Mills, N. Y.					Functioned as 1st Depot Div. July–December 1918.
			December 1917	P. of E., Hoboken	December 1917				
			February 1919	Hoboken, N. J.		February 1919	February 1919	Cp. Dix, N. J.	
42d Division	do	Cp. Mills, N. Y.	October 1917	P. of E., Hoboken	October 1917	May 1919	May 1919	Do.	
43d to 75th Divisions									Never orgzd.
76th Division	August 1917	Cp. Devens, Mass.	July 1918	P. of E., Hoboken	July 1918				Functioned as 3d Depot Div. August–November 1918. Skeletonized November 1918. Record cadre only.
			December 1918	Cp. Merritt, N. J.		December 1918.			
			do	Cp. Devens, Mass.			January 1919	Cp. Devens, Mass.	
77th Division	do	Cp. Upton, N. Y.	March 1918	P. of E., Portland, Maine.	March 1918.				
			April 1919	Hoboken, N. J.		April 1919	May 1919	Cp. Upton, N. Y.	
78th Division	do	Cp. Dix, N. J.	May 1918	P. of E., Philadelphia.	May 1918.				
			June 1919	Brooklyn, N. Y.		June 1919	June 1919	Cp. Dix, N. J.	
79th Division	do	Cp. Meade, Md.	July 1918	P. of E., Hoboken	July 1918.				
			May 1919	Cp. Dix, N. J.		May 1919	do	Do.	
80th Division	do	Cp. Lee, Va.	May 1918	P. of E., Hoboken	May 1918.				
			May 1919	Newport News, Va.		do	do	Cp. Lee, Va.	
81st Division	do	Cp. Jackson, S. C.	May 1918	Cp. Sevier, S. C.					
			July 1918	Cp. Upton, N. Y.					
			do	P. of E., Hoboken	July 1918.				
			June 1919	Hoboken, N. J.		June 1919	do	Hoboken, N. J.	

82 Division	do	Cp. Gordon, Ga	April 1918	Cp. Upton, N. Y.					
			do	P. of E., Hoboken	April 1918.				
			May 1919	Cp. Upton, N. Y.		May 1919	May 1919	Cp. Upton, N. Y.	
83d Division	do	Cp. Sherman, Ohio.	May 1918	Cp. Merritt, N. J.					
			June 1918	P. of E., Hoboken	June 1918				Functioned as 2d Depot Div. August–December 1918.
			January 1919	Hoboken, N. J.		January 1919.			
			do	Cp. Sherman, Ohio.			October 1919	Cp. Sherman, Ohio.	
84th Division	do	Cp. Zachary Taylor, Ky.	June 1918	Cp. Sherman, Ohio.					
			August 1918	Cp. Mills, N. Y.					
			September 1918	P. of E., Hoboken	September 1918				Div. skeletonized October 1918. Record cadre only.
			January 1919	Hoboken, N. J.		January 1919.			
			do	Cp. Zachary Taylor, Ky.			July 1919	Cp. Zachary Taylor, Ky.	
85th Division	August 1917	Cp. Custer, Mich.	July 1918	Cp. Mills, N. Y.					
			do	P. of E., Hoboken	July 1918				Functioned as 4th Depot Division August - October 1918.
			March 1919	Cp. Mills, N. Y.		March 1919	April 1919	Cp. Custer, Mich.	
86th Division	do	Cp. Grant, Ill	Augu	Cp. Mills, N. Y.					
			September 1918	P. of E., Hoboken	September 1918				Div. skeletonized October 1918. Record cadre only.
			January 1919	Cp. Mills, N. Y.		January 1919	January 1919	Cp. Grant, Ill.	
87th Division	do	Cp. Pike, Ark	June 1918	Cp. Dix, N. J.					
			August 1918	P. of E., Hoboken	August 1918.				
			January 1919	Cp. Merritt, N. J.		Do.			
			do	Cp. Dix, N. J.			February 1919	Cp. Dix, N. J.	
88th Division	do	Cp. Dodge, Iowa	August 1918	Cp. Upton, N. Y.					
			do	P. of E., Quebec	August 1918.				
			June 1919	Newport News, Va.		June 1919	June 1919	Cp. Dodge, Iowa.	
89th Division	do	Cp. Funston, Kans.	May 1918	Cp. Mills, N. Y.					
			June 1918	P. of E., Hoboken	June 1918.				
			May 1919	Cp. Upton, N. Y.		May 1919.			
			June 1919	Cp. Funston, Kans.			July 1919	Cp. Funston, Kans.	
90th Division	do	Cp. Travis, Tex	June 1918	Cp. Mills, N. Y.					
			do	P. of E., Hoboken	June 1918.				
			June 1919	Cp. Devens, Mass.		June 1919	June 1919	Cp. Bowie, Tex.	

INFANTRY DIVISIONS—Continued

Unit designation and redesignation	Organization		Stations in United States		Overseas		Demobilization		Remarks
	Month and year	Place	Month and year	Place	From—	To—	Month and year	Place	
91st Division	August 1917	Cp. Lewis, Wash.	June 1918	Cp. Merritt, N. J.					
			July 1918	P. of E., Hoboken.	July 1918.				
			April 1919	Cp. Merritt, N. J.		April 1919.			
			do.	Presidio of San Francisco, Calif.			May 1919	Presidio of San Francisco, Calif.	
92d Division	October 1917	Cp. Funston, Kans.	June 1918	Cp. Upton, N. Y.					
			do.	P. of E., Hoboken.	June 1918.				
			February 1919	Cp. Upton, N. Y.		February 1919	February 1919	Cp. Meade, Md.	
93d Division (provisional).	December 1917	Cp. Stuart, Va.	February 1918	P. of E., Hoboken.	February 1918		May 1918	A. E. F.	
94th Division									Orgzn. contemplated but never effected.
95th Division	September 1918	Cp. Sherman, Ohio.					December 1918	Cp. Sherman, Ohio.	
96th Division	October 1918	Cp. Wadsworth, S. C.					January 1919	Cp. Wadsworth, S. C.	
97th Division	September 1918	Cp. Cody, N. Mex.					December 1918	Cp. Cody, N. Mex.	
98th Division	October 1918	Cp. McClellan, Ala.					November 1918	Cp. McClellan, Ala.	
99th Division	do.	Cp. Wheeler, Ga.					do.	Cp. Wheeler, Ga.	
100th Division	do.	Cp. Bowie, Tex.					do.	Cp. Bowie, Tex.	
101st Division	November 1918	Cp. Shelby, Miss.					do.	Cp. Shelby, Miss.	
102d Division									Orgzn. never progressed beyond assembly of cadre pl. at Cp. Dix, N. J.

TRAIN HEADQUARTERS AND MILITARY POLICE

1st Train Headquarters and Military Police.	August 1917	New York City, N. Y.	August 1917	P. of E., Hoboken	August 1917				Cmpnt. of 1st Div
			September 1919	Cp. Mills, N. Y		September 1919.			
			do	Cp. Meade, Md.					
			October 1919	Cp. Zachary Taylor, Ky.					Active through 1919.
2d Train Headquarters and Military Police.	October 1917	Ft. Oglethorpe, Ga.	December 1917	Cp. Merritt, N. J					Cmpnt. of 2d Div.
			January 1918	P. of E., Hoboken	January 1918.				
			August 1919	Cp. Merritt, N. J		August 1919.			
			do	Cp. Travis, Tex					Active through 1919.
3d Train Headquarters and Military Police.	December 1917	Chickamauga Park, Ga.	March 1918	Cp. Merritt, N. J					Cmpnt. of 3d Div.
			do	P. of E., Hoboken	March 1918.				
			August 1919	Cp. Merritt, N. J		August 1919.			
			do	Cp. Pike, Ark					Active through 1919.
4th Train Headquarters and Military Police.	January 1918	Cp. Greene, N. C	April 1918	Cp. Mills, N. Y					Cmpnt. of 4th Div.
			May 1918	P. of E., Hoboken	May 1918.				
			August 1919	Newport News, Va.		August 1919.			
			do	Cp. Dodge, Iowa					Active through 1919.
5th Train Headquarters and Military Police.	December 1917	Cp. Logan, Tex	April 1918	Cp. Merritt, N. J					Cmpnt. of 5th Div.
			do	P. of E., Hoboken	April 1918.				
			July 1919	Cp. Mills, N. Y		July 1919.			
			do	Cp. Gordon, Ga					Active through 1919.
6th Train Headquarters and Military Police.	February 1918	Cp. McClellan, Ala.	March 1918	Cp. Forrest, Ga					Cmpnt. of 6th Div.
			May 1918	Cp. Wadsworth, S. C.					
			June 1918	Cp. Mills, N. Y.					
			July 1918	P. of E., Hoboken	July 1918.				
			June 1919	Cp. Merritt, N. J		June 1919.			
			do	Cp. Grant, Ill					Active through 1919.

TRAIN HEADQUARTERS AND MILITARY POLICE—Continued

Unit designation and redesignation	Organization		Stations in United States		Overseas		Demobilization		Remark
	Month and year	Place	Month and year	Place	From—	To—	Month and year	Place	
7th Train Headquarters and Military Police.	April 1918	Cp. Wheeler, Ga.	May 1918	Cp. MacArthur, Tex.					Cmpnt. of 7th Div.
			July 1918	Cp. Merritt, N. J.					
			August 1918	P. of E., Hoboken	August 1918.				
			June 1919	Cp. Mills, N. Y.		June 1919.			
			July 1919	Cp. Funston, Kans.					Active through 1919.
8th Train Headquarters and Military Police.	do	Cp. Fremont, Calif.	October 1918	Cp. Mills, N. Y.					Cmpnt. of 8th Div.
			November 1918	Cp. Lee, Va.			February 1919	Cp. Lee, Va.	
9th Train Headquarters and Military Police.	July 1918	Cp. Sheridan, Ala.					do	Cp. Sheridan, Ala.	Cmpnt. of 9th Div.
10th Train Headquarters and Military Police.	August 1918	Cp. Funston, Kans.					do	Cp. Funston, Kans.	Cmpnt. of 10th Div.
11th Train Headquarters and Military Police.	do	Cp. Meade, Md.					do	Cp. Meade, Md.	Cmpnt. of 11th Div.
12th Train Headquarters and Military Police.	July 1918	Cp. Devens, Mass.					January 1919	Cp. Devens, Mass.	Cmpnt. of 12th Div.
13th Train Headquarters and Military Police.	September 1918	Cp. Lewis, Wash.					March 1919	Cp. Lewis, Wash.	Cmpnt. of 13th Div.
14th Train Headquarters and Military Police.	do	Cp. Custer, Mich.					February 1919	Cp. Custer, Mich.	Cmpnt. of 14th Div.
15th (I) Train Headquarters and Military Police.	do	Cp. Logan, Tex.					do	Cp. Logan, Tex.	Cmpnt. of 15th Div.
15th (II) Train Headquarters and Military Police.	January 1918	Cp. Owen Beirne, Tex.	April 1918	Cp. Fort Bliss, Tex.			March 1919	Cp. Fort Bliss, Tex.	Cmpnt. of 15th Cav. Div.
16th Train Headquarters and Military Police.	September 1918	Cp. Kearny, Calif.					February 1919	Cp. Kearny, Calif.	Cmpnt. of 16th Div.
17th Train Headquarters and Military Police.	August 1918	Cp. Beauregard, La.					January 1919	Cp. Beauregard, La.	Cmpnt. of 17th Div.

18th Train Headquarters and Military Police.	September 1918	Cp. Travis, Tex.					do.	Cp. Travis, Tex.	Cmpnt. of 18th Div.
19th Train Headquarters and Military Police.	do.	Cp. Dodge, Iowa.					do.	Cp. Dodge, Iowa.	Cmpnt. of 19th Div.
20th Train Headquarters and Military Police.	do.	Cp. Sevier, S. C.					February 1919	Cp. Sevier, S. C.	Cmpnt. of 20th Div.
21st to 100th Train Headquarters and Military Police.									Never orgzd.
101st Train Headquarters and Military Police.	August 1917	Cp. Devens, Mass.	September 1917	Cp. Bartlett, Mass.					Cmpnt. of 26th Div.
102d Train Headquarters and Military Police.	July 1917	New York City, N. Y.	October 1917	P. of E., Hoboken.	October 1917	April 1919	April 1919	Cp. Devens, Mass.	Cmpnt. of 27th Div.
			September 1917	Cp. Wadsworth, S. C.					
			May 1918	Cp. Hill, Va.					
			do.	P. of E., Newport News.	May 1918.				
103d Train Headquarters and Military Police.	August 1917	Mt. Gretna, Pa.	March 1919	Cp. Mills, N. Y.		March 1919	April 1919	Cp. Upton, N. Y.	Cmpnt. of 28th Div.
			September 1917	Cp. Hancock, Ga.					
104th Train Headquarters and Military Police.	September 1917	Cp. McClellan, Ala.	April 1918	Cp. Upton, N. Y.					Cmpnt. of 29th Div.
			May 1918	P. of E., Hoboken.	May 1918	April 1919	May 1919	Cp. Dix, N. J.	
			June 1918	Cp. Mills, N. Y.					
105th Train Headquarters and Military Police.	September 1917	Cp. Sevier, S. C.	July 1918	P. of E., Hoboken.	July 1918.				Cmpnt. of 30th Div.
			May 1919	Cp. Merritt, N. J.		May 1919	May 1919	Cp. Dix, N. J.	
			May 1918	P. of E., Philadelphia.	May 1918	April 1919	April 1919	Cp. Jackson, S.C.	
106th Train Headquarters and Military Police.	October 1917	Cp. Wheeler, Ga.	September 1918	Cp. Mills, N. Y.					Cmpnt. of 31st Div. Skeletonized November 1918. Record cadre only.
107th Train Headquarters and Military Police.	do.	Cp. MacArthur, Tex.	October 1918	P. of E., Hoboken.	October 1918	December 1918	January 1919	Cp. Gordon, Ga.	Cmpnt. of 32d Div
			January 1918	Cp. Merritt, N. J.					
			February 1918	P. of E., Hoboken.	February 1918.				
			May 1919	Cp. Morrison, Va.		May 1919	May 1919	Cp. Grant, Ill.	

TRAIN HEADQUARTERS AND MILITARY POLICE—Continued

Unit designation and redesignation	Organization		Stations in United States		Overseas		Demobilization		Remarks
	Month and year	Place	Month and year	Place	From—	To—	Month and year	Place	
108th Train Headquarters and Military Police.	October 1917	Cp. Logan, Tex.	May 1918	Cp. Upton, N. Y.					Cmpnt. of 33d Div.
			do	P. of E., Hoboken	May 1918.				
			May 1919	Cp. Mills, N. Y.		May 1919	June 1919	Cp. Grant, Ill.	
109th Train Headquarters and Military Police.	do	Cp. Cody, N. Mex.	September 1918	Cp. Dix, N. J.					Cmpnt. of 34th Div.
			October 1918	P. of E., Hoboken	October 1918				Skeletonized November 1918.
			January 1919	Cp. Merritt, N. J.		January 1919	February 1919	Cp. Grant, Ill.	Record cadre only.
110th Train Headquarters and Military Police.	do	Cp. Doniphan, Okla.	April 1918	Cp. Mills, N. Y.					Cmpnt. of 35th Div.
			May 1918	P. of E., Hoboken	May 1918.				
			April 1919	Cp. Stuart, Va.		April 1919	April 1919	Cp. Funston, Kans.	
111th Train Headquarters and Military Police.	August 1917	Houston, Tex.	August 1917	Cp. Bowie, Tex.					Cmpnt. of 36th Div
			July 1918	Cp. Mills, N. Y.					
			do	P. of E., Hoboken	July 1918.				
			June 1919	Cp. Mills, N. Y.		June 1919	June 1919	Cp. Bowie, Tex.	
112th Train Headquarters and Military Police.	do	Columbus, Ohio	September 1917	Cp. Sheridan, Ala.					Cmpnt. of 37th Div.
			June 1918	Cp. Upton, N. Y.					
			do	P. of E., Hoboken	June 1918.				
			March 1919	Cp. Mills, N. Y.		March 1919	April 1919	Cp. Sherman, Ohio.	
113th Train Headquarters and Military Police.	October 1917	Cp. Shelby, Miss.	September 1918	Cp. Mills, N. Y.					Cmpnt. of 38th Div.
			October 1918	P. of E., Hoboken	October 1918				Skeletonized November 1918.
			December 1918	Cp. Hill, Va.		December 1918	January 1919	Cp. Zachary Taylor, Ky.	Record cadre only.

114th Train Headquarters and Military Police.	do	Cp. Beauregard, La.	August 1918	Cp. Mills, N. Y.					Cmpnt. of 39th Div.
			do	P. of E., Hoboken	August 1918				Skeletonized November 1918.
			January 1919	Cp. Stuart, Va.		January 1919	January 1919	Cp. Beauregard, La.	Record cadre only.
115th Train Headquarters and Military Police.	do	Cp. Kearny, Calif.	August 1918	Cp. Mills, N. Y.					Cmpnt. of 40th Div.
			do	P. of E., Hoboken	August 1918.				
			April 1919	Cp. Mills, N. Y.		April 1919	April 1919	Cp. Kearny, Calif.	
116th Train Headquarters and Military Police.	September 1917	Cp. Greene, N. C.	November 1917	do					Cmpnt. of 41st Div.
			December 1917	P. of E., Hoboken	December 1917.				
			June 1919	Cp. Merritt, N. J.		June 1919	June 1919	Cp. Dix, N. J.	
117th Train Headquarters and Military Police.	August 1917	Cp. Mills, N. Y.	October 1917	P. of E., Hoboken	October 1917				Cmpnt. of 42d Div.
			April 1919	Cp. Merritt, N. J.		April 1919	May 1919	Cp. Meade. Md.	
118th to 300th Train Headquarters and Military Police.									Never orgzd.
301st Train Headquarters and Military Police.	August 1917	Cp. Devens, Mass.	July 1918	P. of E., Boston	July 1918				Cmpnt. of 76th Div. Skeletonized November 1918. Record Cadre only.
			December 1918	Cp. Merritt, N. J.		December 1918	December 1918	Cp. Devens, Mass.	
302d Train Headquarters and Military Police.	do	Cp. Upton, N. Y.	March 1918	P. of E., Portland	March 1918				Cmpnt. of 77th Div.
			May 1919	Cp. Mills, N. Y.		May 1919	May 1919	Cp. Upton, N. Y.	
303d Train Headquarters and Military Police.	October 1917	Cp. Dix, N. J.	May 1918	P. of E., Philadelphia.	May 1918	do	do	Cp. Dix, N. J.	Cmpnt. of 78th Div.
304th Train Headquarters and Military Police.	September 1917	Cp. Meade, Md.	July 1918	P. of E., Hoboken	July 1918	do	do	do	Cmpnt. of 79th Div.
305th Train Headquarters and Military Police.	do	Cp. Lee, Va.	May 1918	P. of E., Newport News.	May 1918.				Cmpnt. of 80th Div.
			June 1919	Cp. Stuart, Va.		June 1919	June 1919	Cp. Lee, Va.	

TRAIN HEADQUARTERS AND MILITARY POLICE—Continued

Unit designation and redesignation	Organization		Stations in United States		Overseas		Demobilization		Remarks
	Month and year	Place	Month and year	Place	From—	To—	Month and year	Place	
306th Train Headquarters and Military Police.	September 1917	Cp. Jackson, S. C.	May 1918	Cp. Sevier, S. C.					Cmpnt. of 81st Div.
			July 1918	Cp. Mills, N. Y.					
			do	P. of E., Hoboken	July 1918	June 1919	June 1919	Cp. Jackson, S. C.	
307th Train Headquarters and Military Police.	do	Cp. Gordon, Ga.	April 1918	Cp. Upton, N. Y.					Cmpnt. of 82d Div.
			May 1918	P. of E., Hoboken	May 1918	May 1919	May 1919	Cp. Upton, N. Y.	
308th Train Headquarters and Military Police.	do	Cp. Sherman, Ohio.	June 1918	Cp. Mills, N. Y.					Cmpnt. of 83d Div.
			do	P. of E., Hoboken	June 1918.				
			June 1919	Cp. Merritt, N. J.		June 1919	June 1919	Cp. Sherman, Ohio.	
309th Train Headquarters and Military Police.	do	Cp. Zachary Taylor, Ky.	June 1918	Cp. Sherman, Ohio.					Cmpnt. of 84th Div. Skeletonized November 1918. Record Cadre only.
			September 1918	Cp. Mills, N. Y.					
			do	P. of E., Hoboken	September 1918				
			January 1919	Cp. Merritt, N. J.		January 1919	January 1919	Cp. Zachary Taylor, Ky.	
310th Train Headquarters and Military Police.	do	Cp. Custer, Mich.	July 1918	Cp. Mills, N. Y.					Cmpnt. of 85th Div.
			do	P. of E., Hoboken	July 1918	April 1919	April 1919	Cp. Mills, N. Y.	
311th Train Headquarters and Military Police.	do	Cp. Grant, Ill.	August 1918	Cp. Mills, N. Y.					Cmpnt. of 86th Div.
			September 1918	P. of E., Hoboken	September 1918				Skeletonized November 1918.
			January 1919	Cp. Mills, N. Y.		January 1919	February 1919	Cp. Grant, Ill.	Record cadre only.

312th Train Headquarters and Military Police.	do	Cp. Pike, Ark.	June 1918	Cp. Dix, N. J.					Cmpnt. of 87th Div.
313th Train Headquarters and Military Police.	do	Cp. Dodge, Iowa	August 1918 January 1919 August 1918	P. of E., Hoboken Cp. Merritt, N. J. P. of E., Montreal	August 1918. August 1918	January 1919	February 1919	Cp. Dix, N. J.	Cmpnt. of 88th Div.
314th Train Headquarters and Military Police.	do	Cp. Funston, Kans.	June 1919 June 1918	Cp. Hill, Va. Cp. Mills, N. Y.		June 1919	June 1919	Cp. Dodge, Iowa.	Cmpnt. of 89th Div.
315th Train Headquarters and Military Police.	August 1917	Cp. Travis, Tex.	do May 1919 June 1918	P. of E., Hoboken Cp. Upton, N. Y. Cp. Mills, N. Y.	June 1918.	May 1919	June 1919	Cp. Funston, Kans.	Cmpnt. of 90th Div
316th Train Headquarters and Military Police.	September 1917	Cp. Lewis, Wash.	do June 1919 July 1918	P. of E., Hoboken Cp. Devens, Mass. Cp. Merritt, N. J.	June 1918.	June 1919	June 1919	Cp. Bowie, Tex.	Cmpnt. of 91st Div.
317th Train Headquarters and Military Police.	November 1917	Cp. Funston, Kans.	do April 1919 June 1918	P. of E., Hoboken Cp. Merritt, N. J. Cp. Upton, N. Y.	July 1918.	April 1919	May 1919	Presidio of San Francisco, Calif.	Cmpnt. of 92d Div.
318th and 319th Train Headquarters and Military Police.			do	P. of E., Hoboken	June 1918	February 1919	March 1919	Cp. Upton, N. Y.	Never orgzd.
320th Train Headquarters and Military Police.	September 1918	Cp. Sherman, Ohio.					December 1918	Cp. Sherman, Ohio.	Cmpnt. of 95th Div.
321st Train Headquarters and Military Police.									Never orgzd.
322d Train Headquarters and Military Police.	October 1918	Cp. Cody, N. Mex.					December 1918	Cp. Cody, N. Mex.	Cmpnt. of 97th Div.

DIVISIONAL HEADQUARTERS TROOPS

Unit designation and redesignation	Organization		Stations in United States		Overseas		Demobilization		Remarks
	Month and year	Place	Month and year	Place	From—	To—	Month and year	Place	
Headquarters Troop 1st Division.	June 1917	A. E. F.	September 1919	Cp. Mills, N. Y.	June 1917	September 1919.			
			do	Cp. Meade, Md.					
			October 1919	Cp. Z. Taylor, Ky.					Active through 1919.
Headquarters Troop 2d Division.	October 1917	Ft. Ethan Allen, Vt.	December 1917	P. of E., Hoboken.	December 1917.				
			August 1919	Cp. Mills, N. Y.		August 1919.			
			do	Cp. Travis, Tex.					Do.
Headquarters Troop 3d Division.	November 1917	Ft. Bliss, Tex.	December 1917	Cp. Greene, N. C.					
			March 1918	Cp. Merritt, N. J.					
			do	P. of E., Hoboken.	March 1918.				
			August 1919	Cp. Merritt, N. J.		August 1919.			
			do	Cp. Pike, Ark.					Do.
Headquarters Troop 4th Division.	December 1917	Cp. Greene, N. C.	April 1918	Cp. Mills, N. Y.					
			May 1918	P. of E., Hoboken.	May 1918.				
			August 1919	Cp. Merritt, N. J.		August 1919.			
			do	Cp. Dodge, Iowa.					Do.
Headquarters Troop 5th Division.	November 1917	Ft. Riley, Kans.	April 1918	Cp. Merritt, N. J.					
			do	P. of E., Hoboken.	April 1918.				
			July 1919	Cp. Merritt, N. J.		July 1919.			
			do	Cp. Gordon, Ga.					Do.
Headquarters Troop 6th Division.	December 1917	Ft. Sam Houston, Tex.	March 1918	Cp. Forrest, Ga.					
			May 1918	Cp. Wadsworth, S. C.					
			June 1918	Cp. Mills, N. Y.					
			July 1918	P. of E., Hoboken.	July 1918.				
			June 1919	Cp. Mills, N. Y.		June 1919.			
			do	Cp. Grant, Ill.					Do.

Headquarters Troop 7th Division.	March 1918	Cp. Forrest, Ga.	April 1918	Cp. MacArthur, Tex.					
			July 1918	Cp. Merritt, N. J.					
			August 1918	P. of E., Hoboken	August 1918.				
			June 1919	Cp. Mills, N. Y.		June 1919.			
			do	Cp. Funston, Kans.					Do.
Headquarters Troop 8th Division.	January 1918	Cp. Fremont, Calif.	October 1918	Cp. Mills, N. Y.					
			November 1918	P. of E., Hoboken	November 1918.				
			September 1919	Cp. Mills, N. Y.		September 1919	September 1919	Cp. Dix, N. J.	
Headquarters Troop 9th Division.	July 1918	Cp. Sheridan, Ala.					February 1919	Cp. Sheridan, Ala.	
Headquarters Troop 10th Division.	August 1918	Cp. Funston, Kans.					do	Cp. Funston, Kans.	
Headquarters Troop 11th Division.	do	Cp. Meade, Md.					do	Cp. Meade, Md.	
Headquarters Troop 12th Division.	do	Cp. Devens, Mass.					January 1919	Cp. Devens, Mass.	
Headquarters Troop 13th Division.	September 1918	Cp. Lewis, Wash.					March 1919	Cp. Lewis, Wash.	
Headquarters Troop 14th Division.	August 1918	Cp. Custer, Mich.					February 1919	Cp. Custer, Mich.	
Headquarters Troop 15th Division.	September 1918	Cp. Logan, Tex.					do	Cp. Logan, Tex.	
Headquarters Troop 16th Division.	August 1918	Cp. Kearny, Calif.					do	Cp. Kearny, Calif.	
Headquarters Troop 17th Division.	September 1918	Cp. Beauregard, La.					do	Cp. Beauregard, La.	
Headquarters Troop 18th Division.	do	Cp. Travis, Tex.					do	Cp. Travis, Tex.	
Headquarters Troop 19th Division.	do	Cp. Dodge, Iowa.					January 1919	Cp. Dodge, Iowa.	
Headquarters Troop 20th Division.	do	Cp. Sevier, S. C.					February 1919	Cp. Sevier, S. C.	
Headquarters Troop 26th Division.	August 1917	Allston, Mass.	October 1918	P. of E., Hoboken	October 1918	April 1919	April 1919	Cp. Devens, Mass.	
Headquarters Troop 27th Division.	do	New York City, N. Y.	September 1917	Cp. Wadsworth, S. C.					
			May 1918	Cp. Stuart, Va.					
			do	P. of E., Newport News.	May 1918.				
			March 1919	Cp. Mills, N. Y.		March 1919	do	Cp. Upton, N. Y.	

DIVISIONAL HEADQUARTERS TROOPS—Continued

Unit designation and redesignation	Organization		Stations in United States		Overseas		Demobilization		Remarks
	Month and year	Place	Month and year	Place	From—	To—	Month and year	Place	
Headquarters Troop 28th Division.	August 1917	Cp. Hancock, Ga.	April 1918	Cp. Upton, N. Y.					
			May 1918	P. of E., Hoboken.	May 1918	April 1919	May 1919	Cp. Dix, N. J.	
Headquarters Troop 29th Division.	do	Cp. Edge, N. J.	September 1917	Cp. McClellan, Ala.					
			June 1918	Cp. Stuart, Va.					
			do	P. of E., Newport News.	June 1918.				
			May 1919	Cp. Stuart, Va.		May 1919	do	Do.	
Headquarters Troop 30th Division.	do	Cp. Sevier, S. C.	May 1918	Cp. Mills, N. Y.					
			do	P. of E., Hoboken.	May 1918	April 1919	April 1919	Cp. Jackson, S. C.	
Headquarters Troop 31st Division.	September 1917	Cp. Wheeler, Ga.	September 1918	Cp. Mills, N. Y.			October 1918	Cp. Mills, N. Y.	
Headquarters Troop 32d Division.	do	Cp. MacArthur, Tex.	January 1918	Cp. Merritt, N. J.					
			do	P. of E., Hoboken.	January 1918.				
			May 1919	Cp. Upton, N. Y.		May 1919	May 1919	Cp. Custer, Mich.	
Headquarters Troop 33d Division.	do	Cp. Logan, Tex.	May 1918	Do.					
			do	P. of E., Hoboken.	May 1918.				
			May 1919	Cp. Mills, N. Y.		do	do	Cp. Grant, Ill.	
Headquarters Troop 34th Division.	do	Cp. Cody, N. Mex.	August 1918	Cp. Dix, N. J.					
			September 1918	P. of E., Hoboken.	September 1918	November 1918			Demblzd. overseas.
Headquarters Troop 35th Division.	October 1917	Cp. Doniphan, Okla.	April 1918	Cp. Mills, N. Y.					
			do	P. of E., Hoboken.	April 1918.				
			April 1919	Cp. Stuart, Va.		April 1919	May 1919	Cp. Funston, Kans.	
Headquarters Troop 36th Division.	September 1917	Cp. Bowie, Tex.	July 1918	Cp. Mills, N. Y.					
			do	P. of E., Hoboken.	July 1918.				
			June 1919	Cp. Mills, N. Y.		June 1919	June 1919	Cp. Bowie, Tex.	

Headquarters Troop 37th Division.	August 1917	Columbus, Ohio	September 1917	Cp. Sheridan, Ala.				
			May 1918	Cp. Lee, Va.				
			June 1918	P. of E., Hoboken	June 1918.			
			March 1919	Cp. Mills, N. Y.		March 1919	April 1919	Cp. Sherman, Ohio.
Headquarters Troop 38th Division.	September 1917	Cp. Shelby, Miss.	September 1918	Do.				
Headquarters Troop 39th Division.	October 1917	Cp. Beauregard, La.	October 1918	P. of E., Hoboken	October 1918	November 1918		Do.
			August 1918	Cp. Merritt, N. J.				
Headquarters Troop 40th Division.	September 1917	Cp. Kearny, Calif.	do	P. of E., Hoboken	August 1918	November 1918		Do.
			July 1918	Cp. Mills, N. Y.				
Headquarters Troop 41st Division.	August 1917	Murray, Wash.	August 1918	P. of E., Hoboken	August 1918.			
			April 1919	Cp. Mills, N. Y.		April 1919	April 1919	Cp. Kearny, Calif.
			September 1917	Cp. Greene, N. C.				
Headquarters Troop 42d Division.	do	Cp. Mills, N. Y.	October 1917	Cp. Mills, N. Y.				
			December 1917	P. of E., Hoboken	December 1917.			
			February 1919	Cp. Merritt, N. J.		February 1919	February 1919	Cp. Dix, N. J.
			October 1917	P. of E., Hoboken	October 1917.			
Headquarters Troop 76th Division.	do	Cp. Devens, Mass.	April 1919	Cp. Merritt, N. J.		April 1919	May 1919	Do.
			July 1918	P. of E., Hoboken	July 1918.			
Headquarters Troop 77th Division.	September 1917	Cp. Upton, N. Y.	December 1918	Cp. Merritt, N. J.		December 1918	December 1918	Cp. Devens, Mass.
			March 1918	P. of E., Hoboken	March 1918.			
Headquarters Troop 78th Division.	do	Cp. Dix, N. J.	April 1919	Cp. Mills, N. Y.		April 1919	May 1919	Cp. Upton, N. Y.
			May 1918	P. of E., Hoboken	May 1918	June 1919	June 1919	Cp. Dix, N. J.
Headquarters Troop 79th Division.	do	Cp. Meade, Md.	July 1918	do	July 1918	May 1919	May 1919	Do.
Headquarters Troop 80th Division.	do	Cp. Lee, Va.	May 1918	do	May 1918.			
Headquarters Troop 81st Division.	do	Cp. Jackson, S. C.	May 1919	Cp. Stuart, Va.		do	June 1919	Cp. Lee, Va.
			May 1918	Cp. Sevier, S. C.				
			July 1918	P. of E., Hoboken	July 1918.			
			June 1919	Cp. Mills, N. Y.		June 1919	do	Do.

DIVISIONAL HEADQUARTERS TROOPS—Continued

Unit designation and redesignation	Organization		Stations in United States		Overseas		Demobilization		Remarks
	Month and year	Place	Month and year	Place	From—	To—	Month and year	Place	
Headquarters Troop 82d Division.	September 1917	Cp. Gordon, Ga.	April 1918	Cp. Upton, N. Y.					
			do	P. of E., Hoboken	April 1918	May 1919	May 1919	Cp. Upton, N. Y.	
Headquarters Troop 83d Division.	do	Cp. Sherman, Ohio.	May 1918	Cp. Merritt, N. J.					
			June 1918	P. of E., Hoboken	June 1918.				
			January 1919	Cp. Merritt, N. J.		January 1919	February 1919	Cp. Sherman, Ohio.	
Headquarters Troop 84th Division.	do	Cp. Zachary, Taylor, Ky.	June 1918	Cp. Sherman, Ohio.					
			August 1918	Cp. Mills, N. Y.					
			September 1918	P. of E., Hoboken	September 1918	November 1918			Demblzd. overseas.
Headquarters Troop 85th Division.	do	Cp. Custer, Mich.	July 1918	Cp. Mills, N. Y.					
			do	P. of E., Hoboken	July 1918.				
			March 1919	Cp. Mills, N. Y.		March 1919	April 1919	Cp. Custer, Mich.	
Headquarters Troop 86th Division.	August 1917	Cp. Grant, Ill.	August 1918	Do.					
			September 1918	P. of E., Hoboken	September 1918.				
			January 1919	Cp. Mills, N. Y.		January 1919	January 1919	Cp. Grant, Ill.	
Headquarters Troop 87th Division.	September 1917	Cp. Pike, Ark.	June 1918	Cp. Dix, N. J.					
			August 1918	P. of E., Hoboken	August 1918.				
			January 1919	Cp. Merritt, N. J.		do	February 1919	Cp. Dix, N. J.	
Headquarters Troop 88th Division.	do	Cp. Dodge, Iowa.	August 1918	Cp. Upton, N. Y.					
			do	P. of E., Montreal,	August 1918				
			June 1919	Cp. Hill, Va.		June 1919	June 1919	Cp. Dodge, Iowa.	
Headquarters Troop 89th Division.	do	Cp. Funston, Kans.	May 1918	Cp. Mills. N. Y.					
			June 1918	P. of E., Hoboken	June 1918.				
			May 1919	Cp. Upton, N. Y.		May 1919	do	Cp. Zachary Taylor, Ky.	

Headquarters Troop 90th Division.	do	Cp. Travis, Tex.	June 1918	Cp. Mills, N. Y.					
			do	P. of E., Hoboken	June 1918.				
			June 1919	Cp. Devens, Mass.		June 1919	do	Cp. Bowie, Tex.	
Headquarters Troop 91st Division.	October 1917	Cp. Lewis, Wash.	June 1918	Cp. Merritt, N. J.					
			July 1918	P. of E., Hoboken	July 1918.				
			April 1919	Cp. Merritt, N. J.		April 1919	May 1919	Presidio of San Francisco, Calif.	
Headquarters Troop 92d Division.	December 1917	Cp. Funston, Kans.	May 1918	Cp. Upton, N. Y.					
			June 1918	P. of E., Hoboken	June 1918.				
			February 1919	Cp. Upton, N. Y.		February 1919	March 1919	Cp. Meade, Md.	
Headquarters Troop 93d, 94th, & 95th Divisions.									Never orgzd.
Headquarters Troop 96th Division.	November 1918	Cp. Wadsworth, S. C.					January 1919	Cp. Wadsworth, S. C.	

CORPS OF ENGINEERS

REGIMENTS, BATTALIONS, COMPANIES

1st Engineers (sapper regiment).	Organized 1916		April 1917	Washington Bks., D. C.					Cmpnt. of 1st Div
			August 1917	P. of E., Hoboken	August 1917.				
			August 1919	Cp. Mills, N. Y.		August 1919.			
			September 1919	Cp. Meade, Md.					
			October 1919	Cp. Zachary Taylor, Ky.					Active through 1919.
2d Engineers (sapper regiment).	do		April 1917	El Paso, Tex.					Cmpnt. of 2d Div.
			August 1917	Washington, D. C.					
			September 1917	P. of E., Hoboken	September 1917.				
			August 1919	Cp. Mills, N. Y.		August 1919.			
			do	Cp. Travis, Tex.					Active through 1919.
3d Engineers (sapper regiment).	do		April 1917	Manila, P. I.					1st Bn. in Philippines; 2d Bn. in Panama.
			October 1917	Ft. Shafter, T. H.					Active through 1919.

REGIMENTS, BATTALIONS, COMPANIES—Continued

Unit designation and redesignation	Organization		Stations in United States		Overseas		Demobilization		Remarks
	Month and year	Place	Month and year	Place	From—	To—	Month and year	Place	
4th Engineers (sapper regiment).	June 1917	Vancouver Bks., Wash.	December 1917	Cp. Greene, N. C.					Cmpnt. of 4th Div
			April 1918	P. of E., Hoboken	April 1918.				
			July 1919	Cp. Merritt, N. J.		July 1919.			
			August 1919	Cp. Dodge, Iowa					Active through 1919.
5th Engineers (sapper regiment).	May 1917	Cp. Newton D. Baker, Tex.	June 1917	Cp. Scurry, Tex.					Cmpnt. of 7th Div
			July 1918	P. of E., Hoboken	July 1918.				
			February 1919	Cp. Mills, N. Y.		February 1919.			
			March 1919	Cp. A. A. Humphreys, Va.					Active through 1919.
6th Engineers (sapper regiment).	do	Washington Bks., D. C.	December 1917	P. of E., Hoboken	December 1917				Cmpnt. of 3d Div.
			August 1919	Cp. Merritt, N. J.		August 1919.			
			do	Cp. Pike, Ark					Active through 1919.
7th Engineers (sapper regiment).	do	do	May 1917	Ft. Leavenworth, Kans.					Cmpnt. of 5th Div.
			February 1918	Cp. Merritt, N. J.					
			March 1918	P. of E., Hoboken	March 1918.				
			July 1919	Cp. Merritt, N. J.		July 1919.			
			do	Cp. Gordon, Ga.					Active through 1919.
8th Engineers (mounted battalion).	July 1917	Cp. Stewart, Tex.	October 1917	Cp. Courchesne, Tex.					Orgzd. fr. 1st Engr. Mtd. Bn.
			November 1917	Cp. Newton D. Baker, Tex.					Active through 1919.
9th Engineers (mounted battalion).	May 1917	Cp. Newton D. Baker, Tex.	May 1917	Cp. Stewart, Tex.					Cmpnt. of 15th Cav. Div. Orgzd. fr. 2d Engr. Mtd. Bn.
			October 1917	Cp. Courchesne, Tex.					
			January 1919	Cp. Cody, N. Mex.					

			April 1919	Cp. Courchesne, Tex.					Active through 1919.
10th Engineers (forestry regiment).	August 1917	American University, Washington, D. C.	September 1917	P. of E., Hoboken	September 1917		October 1918	A. E. F	Absorbed by 20th Engrs.
11th Engineers (standard gauge railway construction regiment).	June 1917	Ft. Totten, N. Y	July 1917	P. of E., Hoboken	July 1917				Orgzd. fr. 1st Engrs. N. A.
			April 1919	Cp. Mills, N. Y		April 1919	May 1919	Cp. Upton, N. Y	S.O.S. troops.
12th Engineers (standard gauge railway operation regiment).	May 1917	St. Louis, Mo	June 1917	Cp. Gaillard, Mo					Orgzd. fr. 2d Res. Engrs.
			July 1917	P. of E., Hoboken	July 1917.				
			April 1919	Cp. Upton, N. Y		April 1919	May 1919	Cp. Funston, Kans.	Army troops.
13th Engineers (standard gauge railway operation regiment).	do	Chicago, Ill	July 1917	P. of E., Hoboken	July 1917				Orgzd. fr. 3d Res. Engrs.
			April 1919	Cp. Mills, N. Y		April 1919	May 1919	Cp. Grant, Ill.	
14th Engineers (standard gauge railway operation regiment).	June 1917	Cp. Rockingham, N. H.	July 1917	P. of E., Hoboken	July 1917				Orgzd. fr. 4th Res. Engrs.
			April 1919	Cp. Devens, Mass		April 1919	May 1919	Cp. Devens, Mass	Army troops.
15th Engineers (standard gauge railway construction regiment).	May 1917	Oakmont, Pa	July 1917	P. of E., Hoboken	July 1917				Orgzd. fr. 5th Res. Engrs.
			April 1919	Cp. Upton, N. Y		April 1919	May 1919	Cp. Sherman, Ohio	Army troops.
16th Engineers (standard gauge railway construction regiment).	do	Detroit, Mich	August 1917	P. of E., Hoboken	August 1917				Orgzd. fr. 6th Res. Engrs.
			April 1919	Cp. Upton, N. Y		April 1919	May 1919	Cp. Custer, Mich.	S.O.S. troops.
17th Engineers (standard gauge railway construction regiment).	do	Atlanta, Ga	July 1917	P. of E., Hoboken	July 1917				Orgzd. fr. 7th Res. Engrs.
			March 1919	Cp. Merritt, N. J		March 1919	April 1919	Cp. Gordon, Ga	S.O.S. troops.

REGIMENTS, BATTALIONS, COMPANIES—Continued

Unit designation and redesignation	Organization		Stations in United States		Overseas		Demobilization		Remarks
	Month and year	Place	Month and year	Place	From—	To—	Month and year	Place	
18th Engineers (standard gauge railway construction regiment).	May 1917	American Lake, Wash.	August 1917	P. of E., Hoboken	August 1917				Orgzd. fr. 8th Res. Engrs.
			April 1919	Cp. Mills, N. Y.		April 1919	May 1919	Cp. Lewis, Wash.	S.O.S. troops.
19th Engineers (standard gauge railway shop regiment).	do	Philadelphia, Pa.	August 1917	P. of E., Hoboken	August 1917				Orgzd. fr. 9th Res. Engrs. Converted into 19th Regt. T. C. September 1918.
20th Engineers[1] (forestry regiment).	September 1917	American University, Washington, D. C.	November 1917	P. of E., Hoboken	November 1917.				
			July 1919	Cp. Mills, N. Y.		July 1919	July 1919	Cp. Grant, Ill.	S.O.S. troops.
21st Engineers (light railway operation regiment).	August 1917	Cp. Grant, Ill.	December 1917	P. of E., Hoboken	December 1917	June 1919	June 1919	Cp. Devens, Mass.	Army troops.
22d Engineers (light railway construction regiment).	March 1918	Cp. Sheridan, Ala.	June 1918	do	June 1918.				
			June 1919	Cp. Jackson, S. C.		do	July 1919	Cp. Zachary Taylor, Ky.	Do.
23d Engineers (highway regiment).	September 1917	Cp. Meade, Md.	January 1918	Cp. Laurel, Md.					
			March 1918	P. of E., Hoboken	March 1918	do	June 1919	Cp. Devens, Mass.	Do.
24th Engineers (supply and shop regiment).	November 1917	Cp. Dix, N. J.	do	do	do	May 1919	do	Cp. Jackson, S. C.	Do.
25th Engineers (general construction regiment).	September 1917	Cp. Devens, Mass.	February 1918	P. of E., Hoboken	February 1918.				
			May 1919	Cp. Merritt, N. J.		May 1919	May 1919	Cp. Upton, N. Y.	Do.

26th Engineers (water supply regiment).	do.	Cp. Dix, N. J.	June 1918	P. of E., Hoboken.	June 1918	March 1919	March 1919	Cp. Dix, N. J.	Do.
27th Engineers (mining regiment).	October 1917	Cp. Meade, Md.	do.	do.	Do.				
			March 1919	Cp. Merritt, N. J.		do.	April 1919	Cp. Grant, Ill.	Do.
28th Engineers (quarry regiment).	November 1917	do.	April 1918	Occoquan, Va.					
			August 1918	P. of E., Hoboken.	August 1918	July 1919	July 1919	Cp. Devens, Mass.	Do.
29th Engineers [2]									G.H.Q. troops. Army troops.
30th Engineers (gas and flame regiment).	October 1917	American University, Washington, D. C.	December 1917	P. of E., Hoboken.	December 1917				Converted into 1st Gas Regt. July 1918.
31st Engineers (standard gauge railway operation and maintenance regiment).	February 1918	Ft. Leavenworth, Kans.	June 1918	do.	June 1918				Converted into 31st Regt. T.C. September 1918.
32d Engineers (standard gauge railway construction regiment).	January 1918	Cp. Grant, Ill.	do.	do.	Do.				
			June 1919	Cp. Stuart, Va.		June 1919	June 1919	Cp. Grant, Ill.	S.O.S. troops.
33d Engineers (general construction regiment).	do.	Cp. Devens, Mass.	July 1918	P. of E., Hoboken.	July 1918.				
			July 1919	Cp. Mills, N. Y.		July 1919	July 1919	Cp. Upton, N. Y.	
34th Engineers (supply and shop regiment).	February 1918	Cp. Dix, N. J.	June 1918	Ft. Benjamin Harrison, Ind.					
			August 1918	P. of E., Hoboken.	August 1918	August 1919	August 1919	Newport News, Va.	Do.
35th Engineers (railway shop regiment).	October 1917	Cp. Grant, Ill.	January 1918	do.	January 1918				Converted into 35th Regt. T.C. September 1918.
36th Engineers (railway transportation battalion).	March 1918	do.	May 1918	Cp. Mills, N. Y.					
			June 1918	P. of E., Hoboken.	June 1918				Converted into 36th Regt. T.C. September 1918.

[1] Originally consisted of 10 Bns. of 3 cos. each. In October 1918, the 10th, 41st, 42d, and 43d Engrs. were merged with the 20th Engrs. Latest authorization provided for 29 battalion headquarters, 145 companies, and 46,025 enlisted men. See p. 190.

[2] In existence from October 1917 to August 1919, but during this period never functioned as a regiment. There was no regimental headquarters; battalions and companies were attached to the various armies and corps primarily for surveying and printing duties, one battalion (later known as 74th Engineers) being used for flash and sound ranging.

REGIMENTS, BATTALIONS, COMPANIES—Continued

Unit designation and redesignation	Organization		Stations in United States		Overseas		Demobilization		Remarks
	Month and year	Place	Month and year	Place	From—	To—	Month and year	Place	
37th Engineers (electrical and mechanical regiment).	January 1918	Ft. Myer, Va	June 1918	P. of E., Hoboken	June 1918	March 1919	April 1919	Cp. Stuart, Va	Army troops.
38th Engineers (crane operating battalion).	October 1917	do	February 1918	do	February 1918				Converted into 38th Regt. T.C. September 1918. S.O.S. troops.
39th Engineers (standard gauge railway operation battalion).	February 1918	Cp. Upton, N. Y	June 1918	do	June 1918				Converted into 39th Regt., T.C. September 1918.
40th Engineers (camouflage battalion).	December 1917	Cp. Leach, D. C	January 1918	do	January 1918.				
			January 1919	Cp. Merritt, N. J		January 1919	February 1919	Washington Bks., D. C.	Army troops.
41st Engineers (auxiliary forestry battalion).	January 1918	American University, Washington, D. C.	February 1918	Cp. Belvoir, Va.					
			do	American University, Washington, D. C.					
			do	P. of E., Hoboken	February 1918		October 1918	A. E. F	Absorbed by 20th Engrs.
42d Engineers (auxiliary forestry battalion).	February 1918	American University, Washington, D. C.	May 1918	do	May 1918		do	do	Do.
43d Engineers (auxiliary forestry battalion).	January 1918	do	do	do	do		do	do	Do.
44th Engineers (standard gauge railway maintenance of way battalion).	May 1918	Ft. Benjamin Harrison, Ind.	July 1918	Cp. Merritt, N. J.					
			do	P. of E., Hoboken	July 1918				Converted into 44th Regt. T.C. September 1918

45th Engineers (railway maintenance of way battalion)	March 1918	Cp. Meade, Md	April 1918 July 1918	Cp. A. A. Humphreys, Va. P. of E., Newport News.	do				Converted into 45th Regt. T.C. September 1918.
46th Engineers (railway maintenance of way battalion).	do	Cp. Sheridan, Ala	June 1918 July 1918	Cp. Merritt, N. J. P. of E., Hoboken	do				Converted into 46th Regt. T.C. September 1918.
47th Engineers (railway maintenance of way battalion).	do	do	do	do	do				Converted into 47th Regt. T.C. September 1918.
48th Engineers (railway maintenance of way battalion).	May 1918	Ft. Benjamin Harrison, Ind.	do do	Cp. Merritt, N. J. P. of E., Hoboken	do				Converted into 48th Regt. T.C. September 1918.
49th Engineers (railway shop, maintenance of equipment battalion).	March 1918	Ft. Myer, Va	do	do	do				Converted into 49th Regt. T.C. September 1918.
50th Engineers (railway maintenance of equipment battalion).	April 1918	Cp. Laurel, Md	do	do	do				Converted into 50th Regt. T.C. September 1918.
51st Engineers (trades and storekeepers battalion).	March 1918	Cp. Lee, Va	May 1918 June 1918	Cp. A. A. Humphreys, Va. P. of E., Hoboken	June 1918				Converted into 51st Regt. T.C September 1918.
52d Engineers (standard gauge railway operation battalion).	February 1918	Cp. Upton, N. Y	do	do	do				Converted into 52d Regt. T.C. September 1918.
53d Engineers (standard gauge railway operation battalion).	March 1918	Cp. Dix, N. J	do	do	do				Converted into 53d Regt. T.C. September 1918.
54th Engineers (standard gauge railway operation battalion).	do	do	do	do	do				Converted into 54th Regt. T.C. September 1918.

REGIMENTS, BATTALIONS, COMPANIES—Continued

Unit designation and redesignation	Organization		Stations in United States		Overseas		Demobilization		Remarks
	Month and year	Place	Month and year	Place	From—	To—	Month and year	Place	
55th Engineers (standard gauge railway construction regiment).	March 1918	Cp. Custer, Mich.	June 1918	Cp. Merritt, N. J.					
			do	P. of E., Hoboken.	June 1918.				
			July 1919	Cp. Mills, N. Y.		July 1919	July 1919	Cp. Dodge, Iowa	S.O.S. troops.
56th Engineers (searchlight regiment).	January 1918	Washington Bks., D. C.	May 1918	P. of E., Hoboken.	May 1918.				
			April 1919	Cp. Stuart, Va.		April 1919.			
			do	Cp. Lee, Va.					
			May 1919	Washington Bks., D. C.					
			June 1919	Cp. A. A. Humphreys, Va.			September 1919	Cp. A. A. Humphreys, Va.	Army troops.
57th Engineers (inland waterway regiment).	April 1918	Cp. Laurel, Md.	June 1918	P. of E., Hoboken.	June 1918				Converted into 57th Regt. T.C. September 1918. S.O.S. troops.
58th Engineers (standard gauge railway operation battalion).	June 1918	A. E. F.							Converted into 58th Regt. T.C September 1918.
59th Engineers (standard gauge railway operation battalion).	do	do							Converted into 59th Regt. T.C. September 1918.
60th Engineers (standard gauge railway operation battalion).	May 1918	Ft. Benjamin Harrison, Ind.	June 1918	P. of E., Hoboken.	June 1918				Converted into 60th Regt. T.C. September 1918.
61st Engineers (standard gauge railway operation battalion).	do	do	do	Cp. Upton, N. Y.					
			July 1918	P. of E., Hoboken.	July 1918				Converted into 61st Regt. T.C. September 1918.

62d Engineers (standard gauge railway operation battalion).	do.	do.	do. do.	Cp. Upton, N. Y. P. of E., Hoboken.	 do.				 Converted into 62d Regt. T.C. September 1918.
63d Engineers (standard gauge railway operation battalion).	do.	do.	do.	do.	do.				Converted into 63d Regt. T.C. September 1918.
64th Engineers (standard gauge railway operation battalion).	June 1918.	A. E. F.							Converted into 64th Regt. T.C. September 1918.
65th (I) Engineers (tank service regiment).	February 1918.	Cp. Upton, N. Y.	March 1918.	Cp. Meade, Md.					Absorbed by Tank Corps March 1918.
65th (II) Engineers (standard gauge railway operation battalion).	June 1918.	A. E. F.							Converted into 65th Regt. T.C. September 1918.
66th Engineers (standard gauge railway operation regiment).	April 1918.	Cp. Laurel, Md.	June 1918.	P. of E., Hoboken.	June 1918.				Converted into 66th Regt. T.C. September 1918.
67th Engineers (standard gauge railway transportation battalion).	June 1918.	A. E. F.							Converted into 67th Regt. T.C. September 1918.
68th Engineers (standard gauge railway operation battalion).	July 1918.	Cp. Leach, D. C.	August 1918. September 1918.	Cp. Merritt, N. J. P. of E., Hoboken.	 December 1918.				 Converted into T.C. Cos. December 1918.
69th Engineers (standard gauge railway operation battalion).	do.	Ft. Myer, Va.	do.	do.	do.				Do.
70th Engineers (railway construction battalion).	August 1918.	Ft. Douglas, Utah.	November 1918. do.	Cp. Upton, N. Y. Cp. A. A. Humphreys, Va.			January 1919.	Cp. A. A. Humphreys, Va.	
71st Engineers (domestic antiaircraft searchlight operation regiment).	September 1918.	Washington Bks., D. C.					do.	Washington Bks., D. C.	

REGIMENTS, BATTALIONS, COMPANIES—Continued

Unit designation and redesignation	Organization		Stations in United States		Overseas		Demobilization		Remarks
	Month and year	Place	Month and year	Place	From—	To—	Month and year	Place	
72d Engineers (standard gauge railway construction battalion).	November 1918	A. E. F.	July 1919	Cp. Mills, N. Y.		July 1919	July 1919	Cp. Dix, N. J.	
73d Engineers (searchlight regiment).	October 1918	Washington Bks., D. C.					December 1918	Washington Bks., D. C.	
74th Engineers (sound and flash ranging battalion).	December 1918	A. E. F.	March 1919	Cp. Stuart, Va.		March 1919	March 1919	Cp. Dix, N. J.	Orgzd. fr. 2d Bn. 29th Engrs.
75th Engineers (battalion).	October 1918	Ft. Benjamin Harrison, Ind.					November 1918	Ft. Benjamin Harrison, Ind.	Absorbed by 70th and 138th Engrs.
76th Engineers (general construction battalion).	do	Ft. Myer, Va.	November 1918	Cp. Leach, D. C.			December 1918	Cp. Leach, D. C.	
77th Engineers (general construction battalion).	do	do	do	do			do	Do.	
78th Engineers (general construction battalion).	do	Cp. Leach, D. C.					do	Do.	
79th Engineers (general construction battalion).	do	do					do	Do.	
80th Engineers									Never orgzd.
81st Engineers (locomotive repair battalion).	September 1918	Ft. Benjamin Harrison, Ind.					December 1918	Ft. Benjamin Harrison, Ind.	
82d to 86th Engineers									Never orgzd.
87th Engineers (car repair battalion).	October 1918	Ft. Benjamin Harrison, Ind.	October 1918 November 1918 do	Cp. Upton, N. Y. Cp. Merritt, N. J. Cp. A. A. Humphreys, Va.			January 1919	Cp. A. A. Humphreys, Va.	

88th to 92d Engineers									Never orgzd.
93d Engineers (standard gauge railway maintenance of way battalion).	October 1918	Ft. Benjamin Harrison, Ind.					December 1918	Ft. Benjamin Harrison, Ind.	
94th to 96th Engineers									Never orgzd.
97th Engineers (supply regiment).	September 1918	Cp. Leach, D. C.					December 1918	Cp. Leach, D. C.	
98th Engineers (road battalion).	do	do					do	Do.	
99th Engineers (battalion).	do	Ft. Myer, Va.	November 1918	Cp. Leach, D. C.			do	Do.	
100th Engineers									Never orgzd.
101st Engineers (sapper regiment).	August 1917	Boston, Mass.	September 1917	P. of E., Hoboken	September 1917	April 1919	April 1919	Cp. Devens, Mass.	Cmpnt. of 26th Div.
102d Engineers (sapper regiment).	do	Cp. Wadsworth, S. C.	March 1918	Cp. Belvoir, Va.					Orgzd. fr. 22d Engrs. N. Y. N. G.
			May 1918	P. of E., Newport News.	May 1918	March 1919	April 1919	Cp. Upton, N. Y.	Cmpnt. of 27th Div.
103d Engineers (sapper regiment).	do	Cp. Hancock, Ga.	do	P. of E., Hoboken	do	May 1919	May 1919	Cp. Dix, N. J.	Cmpnt. of 28th Div.
104th Engineers (sapper regiment).	do	Cp. McClellan, Ala.	June 1918	do	June 1918				Cmpnt. of 29th Div.
			May 1919	Cp. Merritt, N. J.		May 1919	May 1919	Cp. Dix, N. J.	
105th Engineers (sapper regiment).	September 1917	Cp. Sevier, S. C.	May 1918	P. of E., Montreal	May 1918	April 1919	April 1919	Cp. Jackson, S. C.	Cmpnt. of 30th Div.
106th Engineers (sapper regiment).	do	Cp. Wheeler, Ga.	September 1918	P. of E., Hoboken	September 1918	July 1919	July 1919	do	Cmpnt. of 31st Div.
107th Engineers (sapper regiment).	do	Cp. MacArthur, Tex.	January 1918	Cp. Merritt, N. J.					Cmpnt. of 32d Div.
			do	P. of E., Hoboken	January 1918.				
			May 1919	Cp. Dix, N. J.		May 1919	May 1919	Cp. Custer, Mich.	
108th Engineers (sapper regiment).	August 1917	Chicago, Ill.	September 1917	Cp. Logan, Tex.					Cmpnt. of 33d Div.
			April 1918	Cp. Merritt, N. J.					
			May 1918	P. of E., Hoboken	May 1918.				
			May 1919	Cp. Mills, N. Y.		May 1919	June 1919	Cp. Grant, Ill.	
109th Engineers (sapper regiment).	September 1917	Cp. Cody, N. Mex.	August 1918	Cp. Dix, N. J.					Cmpnt. of 34th Div.
			September 1918	P. of E., Hoboken	September 1918.				
			June 1919	Cp. Mills, N. Y.		June 1919.			
			do	Cp. Dodge, Iowa			July 1919	Cp. Dodge, Iowa.	

REGIMENTS, BATTALIONS, COMPANIES—Continued

Unit designation and redesignation	Organization		Stations in United States		Overseas		Demobilization		Remarks
	Month and year	Place	Month and year	Place	From—	To—	Month and year	Place	
110th Engineers (sapper regiment).	September 1917	Cp. Doniphan, Okla.	April 1918	Cp. Merritt, N. J.					Cmpnt. of 35th Div.
			May 1918	P. of E., Hoboken	May 1918.	April 1919	April 1919	Cp. Funston, Kans.	
			April 1919	Cp. Mills, N. Y.					
111th Engineers (sapper regiment).	August 1917	Cp. Bowie, Tex.	July 1918	do					Cmpnt. of 36th Div.
			do	P. of E., Hoboken	July 1918.	May 1919	June 1919	Cp. Bowie, Tex.	
			May 1919	Cp. Mills, N. Y.					
112th Engineers (sapper regiment).	do	Cp. Sheridan, Ala.	May 1918	Cp. Lee, Va.					Cmpnt. of 37th Div.
			June 1918	P. of E., Newport News.	June 1918.	April 1919	April 1919	Cp. Sherman, Ohio.	
			April 1919	Cp. Stuart, Va.					
113th Engineers (sapper regiment).	September 1917	Cp. Shelby, Miss.	September 1918	Cp. Mills, N. Y.					Cmpnt. of 38th Div.
			do	P. of E., Hoboken	September 1918.	June 1919	June 1919	Cp. Sherman, Ohio.	
			June 1919	Cp. Merritt, N. J.					
114th Engineers (sapper regiment).	August 1917	Cp. Beauregard, La.	August 1918	P. of E., Hoboken	August 1918				Cmpnt. of 39th Div.
			May 1919	Cp. Stuart, Va.		May 1919	May 1919	Cp. Shelby, Miss.	
115th Engineers (sapper regiment).	September 1917	Cp. Kearny, Calif.	July 1918	Cp. Mills, N. Y.					Cmpnt. of 40th Div.
			August 1918	P. of E., Hoboken	August 1918.	June 1919	July 1919	Ft. D. A. Russell, Wyo.	Corps troops.
			June 1919	Cp. Merritt, N. J.					
116th Engineers (sapper regiment).	do	Cp. Greene, N. C.	November 1917	P. of E., Hoboken	November 1917	February 1919	March 1919	Cp. Dix, N. J.	Cmpnt. of 41st Div.
117th Engineers (sapper regiment).	do	Cp. Mills, N. Y.	October 1917	do	October 1917				Cmpnt. of 42d Div.
			April 1919	Cp. Merritt, N. J.		April 1919	May 1919	Cp. Jackson, S. C.	
118th Engineers (standard gauge railway operation regiment).	September 1918	Ft. Benjamin Harrison, Ind.	September 1918	P. of E., Hoboken	September 1918		December 1918	A. E. F.	Absorbed by T.C

119th Engineers									Never orgzd.
120th Engineers (standard gauge railway shop regiment).	September 1918	Ft. Benjamin Harrison, Ind.					December 1918	Ft. Benjamin Harrison, Ind.	
121st Engineers (standard gauge railway construction battalion).	November 1918	A. E. F	July 1919	Cp. Mills, N. Y		July 1919	July 1919	Cp. Dix, N. J.	
122d Engineers (standard gauge railway construction battalion).	do	do	do	Cp. Upton, N. Y		do	do	Do.	
123d Engineers									Never orgzd.
124th Engineers (dock construction battalion).	November 1918	Cp. Forrest, Ga					January 1919	Cp. Forrest, Ga.	
125th Engineers (dock construction battalion).	do	do					do	Do.	
126th Engineers (general construction battalion).	do	A. E. F	August 1919	Newport News, Va.		August 1919	August 1919	Cp. Dix, N. J.	
127th Engineers (general construction barralion).	do	do	July 1919	Cp. Merritt, N. J		July 1919	July 1919	Do.	
128th Engineers (general construction battalion).	do	do	do	do		do	do	Do.	
129th Engineers (general construction battalion).	do	do	do	do		do	do	do	S.O.S. troops.
130th Engineers (general construction battalion).	do	do	do	Newport News, Va.		do	do	Do.	
131st Engineers (general construction battalion).	do	do	do	Cp. Merritt, N. J		do	do	Cp. Sherman, Ohio.	
132d Engineers (road battalion).	April 1919	do	do	Cp. Mills, N. Y		do	do	Cp. Grant, Ill.	

REGIMENTS, BATTALIONS, COMPANIES—Continued

Unit designation and redesignation	Organization		Stations in United States		Overseas		Demobilization		Remarks
	Month and year	Place	Month and year	Place	From—	To—	Month and year	Place	
133d Engineers									Never orgzd.
134th Engineers (road battalion).					November 1918	December 1918			Orgzd. and demobilized overseas.
135th Engineers (road battalion).					December 1918	do			Do.
136th Engineers (water supply battalion).					November 1918	do			Do.
137th Engineers (electrical and mechanical battalion).	December 1918	A. E. F	July 1919	Cp. Mills, N. Y		July 1919	July 1919	Cp. Dix, N. J.	
138th Engineers (railway construction regiment).	November 1918	Ft. Benjamin Harrison, Ind.					December 1918	Ft. Benjamin Harrison, Ind.	
139th Engineers (dock construction regiment).	do	Cp. Shelby, Miss					do	Cp. Shelby, Miss.	
140th Engineers (general construction regiment).	do	do					do	Do.	
141st Engineers (road battalion).	do	do					do	Do.	
142d Engineers (road battalion).	do	do					do	Do.	
143d Engineers (water supply battalion).	do	do					do	Do.	
144th Engineers (electrical and mechanical battalion).	do	do					do	Do.	
145th Engineers (light railway and shop regiment).	do	Ft. Leavenworth, Kans.					January 1919	Ft. Leavenworth, Kans.	

146th Engineers (quarry company).	do	Cp. Shelby, Miss.					December 1918	Cp. Shelby, Miss.	
147th Engineers (railway operation regiment).	do	Ft. Benjamin Harrison, Ind.					do	Ft. Benjamin Harrison, Ind.	
148th Engineers									Never orgzd.
149th Engineers (electrical and mechanical regiment).	November 1918	Cp. Shelby, Miss.					December 1918	Cp. Shelby, Miss.	
150th Engineers (general construction regiment).	do	do					do	Do.	
151st and 152d Engineers.									Do.
153d Engineers (dock construction battalion).	November 1918	Cp. Shelby, Miss.					December 1918	Cp. Shelby, Miss.	
154th Engineers (general construction battalion).	do	do					do	Do.	
155th to 208th Engineers.									Do.
209th Engineers (sapper regiment).	August 1918	Cp. Forrest, Ga.	September 1918	Cp. Sheridan, Ala.			January 1919	Cp. Sheridan, Ala.	Cmpnt. of 9th Div
210th Engineers (sapper regiment).	do	do	October 1918	Cp. Funston, Kans.					Cmpnt. of 10th Div.
			November 1918	Cp. Mills, N. Y.					
			January 1919	Cp. A. A. Humphreys, Va.			March 1919	Cp. A. A. Humphreys, Va.	
211th Engineers (sapper regiment).	do	do	October 1918	Cp. Meade, Md.			February 1919	Cp. Meade, Md.	Cmpnt. of 11th Div.
212th Engineers (sapper regiment).	do	do	August 1918	Cp. Devens, Mass.			January 1919	Cp. Devens, Mass.	Cmpnt. of 12th Div.
213th Engineers (sapper regiment).	do	do	October 1918	Cp. Lewis, Wash.			February 1919	Cp. Lewis, Wash.	Cmpnt. of 13th Div.
214th Engineers (sapper regiment).	do	do	do	Cp. Custer, Mich.			do	Cp. Custer, Mich.	Cmpnt. of 14th Div.
215th Engineers (sapper regiment).	September 1918	Cp. A. A. Humphreys, Va.	November 1918	Cp. Logan, Tex.			do	Cp. Logan, Tex.	Cmpnt. of 15th Div.

REGIMENTS, BATTALIONS, COMPANIES—Continued

Unit designation and redesignation	Organization		Stations in United States		Overseas		Demobilization		Remarks
	Month and year	Place	Month and year	Place	From—	To—	Month and year	Place	
216th Engineers (sapper regiment).	September 1918	Cp. A. A. Humphreys, Va.	October 1918	Cp. Kearny, Calif.			February 1919	Cp. Kearny, Calif.	Cmpnt. of 16th Div.
217th Engineers (sapper regiment).	do	do	November 1918	Cp. Beauregard, La.			January 1919	Cp. Beauregard, La.	Cmpnt. of 17th Div.
218th Engineers (sapper regiment).	do	do	do	Cp. Travis, Tex.			February 1919	Cp. Travis, Tex.	Cmpnt. of 18th Div.
219th Engineers (sapper regiment).	do	do	do	Cp. Dodge, Iowa			January 1919	Cp. Dodge, Iowa	Cmpnt. of 19th Div.
220th Engineers (sapper regiment).	do	do	October 1918	Cp. Sevier, S. C.					Cmpnt. of 20th Div.
			December 1918	Washington Bks., D. C.			June 1919	Washington Bks., D. C.	
221st to 300th Engineers									Never orgzd.
301st Engineers (sapper regiment).	August 1917	Cp. Devens, Mass.	July 1918	P. of E., Hoboken	July 1918	June 1919	June 1919	Cp. Devens, Mass.	Cmpnt. of 76th Div. Corps troops.
302d Engineers (sapper regiment).	do	Cp. Upton, N. Y.	March 1918	do	March 1918				Cmpnt. of 77th Div.
			May 1919	Cp. Mills, N. Y.		May 1919	May 1919	Cp. Upton, N. Y.	
303d Engineers (sapper regiment).	September 1917	Cp. Dix, N. J.	May 1918	P. of E., Boston	May 1918	June 1919	June 1919	Cp. Dix, N. J.	Cmpnt. of 78th Div.
304th Engineers (sapper regiment).	August 1917	Cp. Meade, Md.	July 1918	P. of E., Hoboken	July 1918	May 1919	do	do	Cmpnt. of 79th Div.
305th Engineers (sapper regiment).	September 1917	Cp. Lee, Va.	May 1918	P. of E., Newport News.	May 1918	June 1919	do	do	Cmpnt. of 80th Div.
306th Engineers (sapper regiment).	August 1917	Cp. Jackson, S. C.	do	Cp. Sevier, S. C.					Cmpnt. of 81st Div.
			July 1918	Cp. Upton, N. Y.					
			do	P. of E., Hoboken	July 1918	June 1919	June 1919	Cp. Jackson, S. C.	
307th Engineers (sapper regiment).	do	Cp. Gordon, Ga.	May 1918	Cp. Mills, N. Y.					Cmpnt. of 82d Div.
			do	P. of E., Hoboken	May 1918.				
			May 1919	Cp. Upton, N. Y.		May 1919	May 1919	Cp. Dix, N. J.	

308th Engineers (sapper regiment).	September 1917	Cp. Sherman, Ohio	May 1918	Cp. Merritt, N. J.					Cmpnt. of 83d Div.
			June 1918	P. of E., Hoboken	June 1918.				
309th Engineers (sapper regiment).	August 1917	Cp. Zachary Taylor, Ky.	June 1919	Cp. Jackson, S. C.		June 1919	July 1919	Cp. Sherman, Ohio	Corps troops.
			June 1918	Cp. Sherman, Ohio					Cmpnt. of 84th Div.
			August 1918	Cp. Mills, N. Y.					
			September 1918	P. of E., Hoboken	September 1918.				
310th Engineers (sapper regiment).	do	Cp. Custer, Mich.	July 1919	Cp. Mills, N. Y.		July 1919	July 1919	Cp. Sherman, Ohio.	
			July 1918	Do.					
			do	P. of E., Hoboken	July 1918				Cmpnt. of 85th Div.
			July 1919	Cp. Mills, N. Y.		July 1919	July 1919	Cp. Sherman, Ohio.	
311th Engineers (sapper regiment).	do	Cp. Grant, Ill.	August 1918	do					Cmpnt. of 86th Div.
			September 1918	P. of E., Hoboken	September 1918.				
312th Engineers (sapper regiment).	do	Cp. Pike, Ark.	June 1919	Cp. Dix, N. J.		June 1919	July 1919	Cp. Grant, Ill.	
			June 1918	do					Cmpnt. of 87th Div.
313th Engineers (sapper regiment).	September 1917	Cp. Dodge, Iowa	August 1918	P. of E., Hoboken	August 1918	June 1919	June 1919	Cp. Dix, N. J.	
			do	Cp. Mills, N. Y.					Cmpnt. of 88th Div.
			do	P. of E., Hoboken	August 1918.				
314th Engineers (sapper regiment).	do	Cp. Funston, Kans.	June 1919	Cp. Mills, N. Y.		June 1919	June 1919	Cp. Dodge, Iowa.	
			May 1918	do					Cmpnt. of 89th Div.
			June 1918	P. of E., Hoboken	June 1918.				
315th Engineers (sapper regiment).	August 1917	Cp. Travis, Tex.	May 1919	Cp. Devens, Mass.		May 1919	June 1919	Cp. Funston, Kans.	
			June 1918	Cp. Mills, N. Y.					Cmpnt. of 90th Div.
			do	P. of E., Hoboken	June 1918.				
316th Engineers (sapper regiment).	do	Cp. Lewis, Wash.	June 1919	Cp. Mills, N. Y.		June 1919	June 1919	Cp. Dodge, Iowa.	
			June 1918	Cp. Merritt, N. J.					
			July 1918	P. of E., Hoboken	July 1918.				Cmpnt. of 91st Div.
			April 1919	Cp. Merritt, N. J.		April 1919	May 1919	Presidio of San Francisco, Calif.	
317th Engineers (sapper regiment).	November 1917	Cp. Sherman, Ohio	June 1918	P. of E., Hoboken	June 1918				Cmpnt. of 92d Div.
			March 1919	Cp. Upton, N. Y.		March 1919	March 1919	Cp. Sherman, Ohio.	

REGIMENTS, BATTALIONS, COMPANIES—Continued

Unit designation and redesignation	Organization		Stations in United States		Overseas		Demobilization		Remarks
	Month and year	Place	Month and year	Place	From—	To—	Month and year	Place	
318th Engineers (sapper regiment).	December 1917	Vancouver Bks., Wash.	April 1918	Cp. Merritt, N. J.					Cmpnt. of 6th Div.
			May 1918	P. of E., Hoboken	May 1918.				
			June 1919	Cp. Stuart, Va.		June 1919			Active through 1919.
319th Engineers (sapper regiment).	January 1918	Cp. Fremont, Calif.	do	Cp. Grant, Ill.					
			September 1918	P. of E., Hoboken	September 1918				Cmpnt. of 8th Div
			August 1919	Cp. Merritt, N. J.		August 1919	September 1919	Presidio of San Francisco, Calif.	
320th to 400th Engineers.									Never orgzd.
401st Engineers (ponton park).	July 1918	Cp. Forrest, Ga.	September 1918	Cp. Upton, N. Y.					
			do	P. of E., Hoboken	September 1918.				
			March 1919	Cp. Merritt, N. J.		March 1919	March 1919	Cp. Meade, Md.	Army troops
402d to 441st Engineers.									Orgzd. as Depot Dets. See special form.
442d Engineers (truck company).	December 1917	Ft. Myer, Va.	March 1918	P. of E., Hoboken	March 1918				Converted into M. T.C. unit October 1918. S.O.S. troops.
443d Engineers (truck company).	do	do	January 1918	Cp. Lee, Va.					
			March 1918	Cp. A. A. Humphreys, Va.					
			July 1918	P. of E., Hoboken	July 1918				Do.
444th Engineers (truck company).	January 1918	do	January 1918	Cp. Lee, Va.					
			March 1918	Ft. Myer, Va.					
			do	P. of E., Philadelphia.	March 1918				Do.

445th Engineers (truck company).	April 1918	do	July 1918	P. of E., Hoboken	July 1918				Do.
446th and 447th Engineers.									Orgzd. as Depot Dets. See special form.
448th Engineers (truck company).	December 1917	Ft. Myer, Va	March 1918	P. of E., Hoboken	March 1918				Converted into M T.C. unit October 1918. S.O.S troops.
449th Engineers (truck company).	do	do	January 1918	Cp. Lee, Va.					
			February 1918	Cp. A. A. Humphreys, Va.					
			July 1918	P. of E., Hoboken	July 1918				Do.
450th Engineers (truck company).	April 1918	do	August 1918	do	August 1918.				Do.
451st Engineers (truck company).	January 1918	do	March 1918	do	March 1918				Do.
452d Engineers (truck company).	December 1917	do	do	P. of E., Philadelphia.	do				Do.
453d Engineers (truck company).	February 1918	do	July 1918	P. of E., Hoboken	July 1918				Do.
454th and 455th Engineers.									Orgzd. as Depot Dets. See special form.
456th Engineers (truck company).	January 1918	Cp. A. A. Humphreys, Va.	July 1918	P. of E., Hoboken	July 1918				Converted into M. T.C. unit October 1918. S.O.S troops.
457th Engineers (truck company).	do	Ft. Myer, Va.	May 1918	do	May 1918				Do.
458th Engineers (truck company).	April 1918	do	July 1918	do	July 1918				Do.
459th Engineers (limousine company).	December 1917	do	March 1918	do	March 1918				Do.
460th Engineers (all weather car company).	February 1918	do	do	do	do				Do.
461st Engineers (touring car company).	January 1918	do	do	do	do				Do.

REGIMENTS, BATTALIONS, COMPANIES—Continued

Unit designation and redesignation	Organization		Stations in United States		Overseas		Demobilization		Remarks
	Month and year	Place	Month and year	Place	From—	To—	Month and year	Place	
462d Engineers (motorcycle company).	February 1918	Ft. Myer, Va.	August 1918	P. of E., Hoboken	August 1918				Converted into M. T.C. unit October 1918.
463d Engineers (motorcycle company).	do.	do.	March 1918	P. of E., Philadelphia.	March 1918				Do.
464th Engineers (ponton train).	January 1918	Washington Bks., D. C.	July 1918	P. of E., Hoboken	July 1918.				
			April 1919	Cp. Merritt, N. J.		April 1919	May 1919	Cp. Sherman, Ohio.	Corps troops.
465th Engineers (ponton train).	March 1918	do.	August 1918	P. of E., Hoboken	August 1918.				
			May 1919	Cp. Mills, N. Y.		May 1919	do.	Cp. Dix, N. J.	Do.
466th Engineers (ponton train).	May 1918	do.	September 1918	P. of E., Hoboken	September 1918.				
			January 1919	Cp. Merritt, N. J.		January 1919	February 1919	Cp. A. A. Humphreys, Va.	Do.
467th Engineers (ponton train).	July 1918	Cp. Forrest, Ga.	September 1918	P. of E., Hoboken	September 1918				
			March 1919	Cp. Merritt, N. J.		March 1919	March 1919	Cp. Meade, Md.	Do.
468th Engineers (ponton train).	do.	do.	September 1918	P. of E., Hoboken	September 1918.				
			March 1919	Cp. Merritt, N. J.		March 1919	March 1919	Cp. Dodge, Iowa	Do.
469th Engineers (transportation corps battalion).	February 1918	Ft. Slocum, N. Y.	April 1918	Do.					
			do.	P. of E., Hoboken	April 1918				Converted into T. C. unit November 1918.
470th and 471st Engineers.									Orgzd. as Depot Dets. See special form.
472d Engineers (military mapping regiment).	May 1918	Washington, D. C.					April 1919	Washington, D. C.	
473d to 479th Engineers									Do.

480th Engineers (ponton train).	October 1918	Washington Bks., D. C.					January 1919	Washington Bks., D. C.	
481st Engineers									Orgzd. as Depot Det. See special form.
482d to 485th Engineers.									Authorized, but never orgzd.
486th Engineers (dredge operating detachment).	October 1918	New York, N. Y.					November 1918	New York, N. Y.	
487th Engineers									Do.
488th and 489th Engineers.									Orgzd. as Depot Dets. See special form.
490th to 500th Engineers.									Never orgzd.
501st Engineers (white service battalion)	September 1917	Washington, D. C.	October 1917	Cp. Merritt, N. J.					
			November 1917	P. of E., Hoboken	November 1917	May 1919	June 1919	Cp. Upton, N. Y.	S.O.S. troops.
502d Engineers (white service battalion).	September 1917	Washington, D. C.	October 1917	Cp. Merritt, N. J.					
			November 1917	P. of E., Hoboken	Do.				
			June 1919	Cp. Stuart, Va.		June 1919	do	do	Do.
503d Engineers (white service battalion).	do	Cp. Grant, Ill.	October 1917	Cp. Merritt, N. J.					
			November 1917	P. of E., Hoboken	November 1917		October 1918	A. E. F.	Absorbed by 20th Engineers. S.O.S. troops.
504th Engineers (white service battalion).	October 1917	Cp. Merritt, N. J.	November 1917	do	do	June 1919	June 1919	Cp. Devens, Mass.	S.O.S. troops.
505th Engineers (colored service battalion).	do	Cp. Lee, Va.	December 1917	P. of E., Newport News.	December 1917.				
			May 1919	Cp. Merritt, N. J.		May 1919	do	Cp. Meade, Md.	Army troops.
506th Engineers (colored service battalion).	do	do	January 1918	P. of E., Hoboken	January 1918.				
			May 1919	Cp. Merritt, N. J.		do	do	do	S.O.S. troops.
507th Engineers (colored service battalion).	November 1917	Cp. Travis, Tex.	February 1918	P. of E., Hoboken	February 1918		October 1918	A. E. F.	Absorbed by 20th Engineers. S.O.S. troops.
508th Engineers (colored service battalion).	October 1917	Cp. Pike, Ark.	January 1918	do	January 1918.				
			June 1919	Cp. Alexander, Va.		June 1919	June 1919	Cp. Shelby, Miss.	Army troops.

REGIMENTS, BATTALIONS, COMPANIES—Continued

Unit designation and redesignation	Organization		Stations in United States		Overseas		Demobilization		Remarks
	Month and year	Place	Month and year	Place	From—	To—	Month and year	Place	
509th Engineers (colored service battalion).	October 1917	Cp. Travis, Tex	February 1918	P. of E., Hoboken	February 1918.				
			June 1919	Cp. Upton, N. Y.		June 1919	June 1919	Cp. Travis, Tex	S.O.S. troops.
510th Engineers (colored service battalion).	January 1918	Cp. Lee, Va	March 1918	P. of E., Hoboken	March 1918	do	do	Cp. Lee ,Va	Do.
511th Engineers (colored service battalion).	do	do	do	do	Do.				
			June 1919	Cp. Alexander, Va.		do	do	do	Do.
512th Engineers (colored service battalion).	do	Cp. Pike, Ark	April 1918	P. of E., Hoboken	April 1918.				
			June 1919	Cp. Upton, N. Y.		do	do	Cp. Pike, Ark	Do.
513th Engineers (colored service battalion).	do	Cp. Travis, Tex	March 1918	Cp. Stuart, Va.					
			April 1918	P. of E., Newport News.	April 1918.				
			June 1919	Cp. Upton, N. Y.		do	do	Cp. Bowie, Tex	Army troops
514th Engineers (colored service battalion).	February 1918	Cp. Gordon, Ga	April 1918	Cp. Stuart, Va.					
			do	P. of E., Newport News.	April 1918.				
			June 1919	Cp. Upton, N. Y.		do	do	Cp. Gordon, Ga	S.O.S. troops.
515th Engineers (colored service battalion).	January 1918	Cp. Zachary Taylor, Ky.	May 1918	P. of E., Hoboken	May 1918.				
			July 1919	Cp. Mills, N. Y.		July 1919	July 1919	Cp. Zachary Taylor, Ky.	Do.
516th Engineers (colored service battalion).	April 1918	Cp. Gordon, Ga	June 1918	Cp. A. A. Humphreys, Va.					
			July 1918	P. of E., Hoboken	July 1918.				
			July 1919	Cp. Alexander, Va.		do	do	Cp. Gordon, Ga	Army troops.
517th Engineers (colored service battalion).	do	do	July 1918	P. of E., Newport News.	July 1918		October 1918	A. E. F	Absorbed by 20th Engineers. S.O.S troops.

518th Engineers (colored service battalion).	May 1918	do	September 1918	P. of E., Hoboken	September 1918				Converted into T. C. unit December 1918. S.O.S. troops.
519th Engineers (colored service battalion).	April 1918	Cp. Devens, Mass.	July 1918	do	July 1918		October 1918	A. E. F	Absorbed by 20th Engineers .S.O.S troops.
520th Engineers (colored service battalion).	do	do	June 1918	Cp. A. A. Humphreys, Va.					
			August 1918	P. of E., Hoboken	August 1918.				
			June 1919	Cp. Alexander, Va.		June 1919	July 1919	Cp. Sherman, Ohio.	S.O.S. troops.
521st Engineers (colored service battalion).	do	Cp. Meade, Md	April 1918	Cp. A. A. Humphreys, Va.					
			August 1918	P. of E., Hoboken	August 1918	do	June 1919	Cp. Jackson, S. C	Do.
522d Engineers (colored service battalion).	March 1918	do	April 1918	Cp. A. A. Humphreys, Va.					
			August 1918	P. of E., Hoboken	Do.				
			June 1919	Cp. Alexander, Va		do	do	Cp. Bowie, Tex	Army troops.
523d Engineers (colored service battalion).	do	Cp. Pike, Ark	May 1918	Cp. A. A. Humphreys, Va.					
			June 1918	Cp. Stuart, Va.					
			July 1918	P. of E., Newport News.	July 1918		October 1918	A. E. F	Absorbed by 20th Engineers. S.O.S. troops.
524th Engineers (colored service battalion).	April 1918	do	May 1918	Cp. A. A. Humphreys, Va.					
			June 1918	Cp. Stuart, Va.					
			July 1918	P. of E., Newport, News.	do	June 1919	July 1919	Cp. Jackson, S. C	Army troops.
525th Engineers (colored service battalion).	do	do	do	do	Do.				
			July 1919	Norfolk, Va		July 1919	do	Cp. Shelby, Miss.	S.O.S. troops.
526th Engineers (colored service battalion).	May 1918	do	July 1918	P. of E., Newport News.	July 1918.				
			July 1919	Norfolk, Va		do	do	do	Do.
527th Engineers (colored service battalion).	March 1918	Cp. Dodge, Iowa	April 1918	Cp. Upton, N. Y.					
			June 1918	P. of E., Hoboken	June 1918.				
			June 1919	Cp. Upton, N. Y.		June 1919	do	Cp. Gordon, Ga	Army troops.

REGIMENTS, BATTALIONS, COMPANIES—Continued

Unit designation and redesignation	Organization		Stations in United States		Overseas		Demobilization		Remarks
	Month and year	Place	Month and year	Place	From—	To—	Month and year	Place	
528th Engineers (colored service battalion).	April 1918	Cp. Dodge, Iowa	July 1918	P. of E., Hoboken	July 1918.				
			June 1919	Cp. Upton, N. Y.		June 1919	June 1919	Cp. Gordon, Ga.	Army troops.
529th Engineers (colored service battalion).	do	Cp. Funston, Kans.	June 1918	Do.					
			do	P. of E., Hoboken	June 1918	do	do	Cp. Upton, N. Y.	Do.
530th Engineers (colored service battalion).	do	do	July 1918	do	July 1918	do	do	do	Do.
531st Engineers (colored service battalion).	do	Cp. Travis, Tex.	June 1918	Cp. Upton, N. Y.					
			do	P. of E., Hoboken	June 1918		October 1918	A. E. F.	Absorbed by 20th Engineers. S.O.S. troops.
532d Engineers (colored service battalion).	May 1918	Cp. Zachary Taylor, Ky.	July 1918	Cp. Stuart, Va.					
			do	P. of E., Newport News.	July 1918.				
			July 1919	Cp. Mills, N. Y.		July 1919	July 1919	Cp. Zachary Taylor, Ky.	Army troops.
533d Engineers (colored service battalion).	June 1918	Cp. Pike, Ark.	August 1918	P. of E., Hoboken	August 1918		October 1918	A. E. F.	Absorbed by 20th Engineers. S.O.S. troops.
534th Engineers (colored service battalion).	May 1918	Cp. Jackson, S. C.	do	Cp. Upton, N. Y.					
			do	P. of E., Hoboken	do	July 1919	July 1919	Cp. Devens, Mass.	Army troops.
535th Engineers (colored service battalion).	do	Cp. Lee, Va.	do	P. of E., Newport News.	do	June 1919	do	Cp. Upton, N. Y.	Army troops.
536th Engineers (colored service battalion).	do	Cp. Custer, Mich.	do	Cp. Upton, N. Y.					
			do	P. of E., Hoboken	do	July 1919	do	Cp. Jackson, S. C.	S.O.S. troops.
537th Engineers (colored service battalion).	do	Cp. Travis, Tex.	July 1918	Cp. Mills, N. Y.					
			do	P. of E., Hoboken	July 1918.				
			July 1919	Cp. Devens, Mass.		do	do	Cp. Bowie, Tex.	Army troops.

538th Engineers (colored service battalion).	do	Cp. Meade, Md.	August 1918	P. of E., Hoboken	August 1918				Converted into T. C. unit December 1918. S.O.S. troops.
539th Engineers (colored service battalion).	do	Cp. Gordon, Ga.	September 1918	P. of E., Hoboken	September 1918.				
540th Engineers (colored service battalion).	August 1918	Cp. A. A. Humphreys, Va.	June 1919 October 1918	Cp. Upton, N. Y. Cp. Merritt, N. J.		June 1919	July 1919	Cp. Gordon, Ga.	Army troops.
541st Engineers (colored service battalion).	do	do	do June 1919 September 1918	P. of E., Hoboken Cp. Upton, N. Y. P. of E., Hoboken	October 1918. September 1918	do July 1919	June 1919 July 1919	Cp. Lee, Va. Cp. Dix, N. J.	S.O.S. troops. Army troops.
542d Engineers (colored service battalion).	do	do	do	do	Do.				
543d Engineers (colored service battalion).	do	do	June 1919 September 1918	Cp. Upton, N. Y. P. of E., Hoboken	 September 1918.	June 1919	June 1919	Cp. Dix, N. J.	Do.
544th Engineers (colored service battalion).	do	do	June 1919 September 1918	Cp. Alexander, Va. P. of E., Hoboken	 September 1918	June 1919 July 1919	July 1919 do	Cp. Lee, Va. Norfolk, Va.	Do.
545th Engineers (colored service battalion).	do	do	do	do	Do.				
546th Engineers (colored service battalion).	September 1918	do	June 1919 September 1918	Cp. Merritt, N. J. P. of E., Hoboken	 September 1918.	June 1919	do	Cp. Meade, Md.	S.O.S. troops.
547th Engineers (colored service battalion).	do	do	June 1919 October 1918	Newport News, Va. Cp. Merritt, N. J.		do	June 1919	Cp. Jackson, S. C.	Army troops.
548th Engineers (colored service battalion).	do	do	do July 1919 October 1918	P. of E., Hoboken Newport News, Va. Cp. Merritt, N. J.	October 1918.	July 1919	July 1919	Cp. Lee, Va.	S.O.S. troops.
549th Engineers (colored service battalion).	do	do	do July 1919 November 1918 do July 1919	P. of E., Hoboken Cp. Mills, N. Y. Cp. Merritt, N. J. P. of E., Hoboken Cp. Alexander, Va.	October 1918. November 1918.	do do	do do	Cp. Gordon, Ga. Cp. Lee, Va.	Do. Do.

REGIMENTS, BATTALIONS, COMPANIES—Continued

Unit designation and redesignation	Organization		Stations in United States		Overseas		Demobilization		Remarks
	Month and year	Place	Month and year	Place	From—	To—	Month and year	Place	
550th Engineers (colored service battalion).	September 1918	Cp. A. A. Humphreys, Va.	November 1918	Cp. Merritt, N. J.					
			do.	P. of E., Hoboken	November 1918.				
			July 1919	Cp. Mills, N. Y.		July 1919	July 1919	Cp. Gordon, Ga.	S.O.S. troops.
551st Engineers (colored service battalion).	October 1918	do.					January 1919	Cp. A. A. Humphreys, Va.	
552d Engineers (colored service battalion).	do.	do.					do.	Do.	
553d Engineers (colored service battalion).	do.	do.					do.	Do.	
554th Engineers (colored service battalion).	do.	do.					November 1918	Do.	
555th Engineers									Authorized, but never orgzd.
556th Engineers (colored service battalion).	October 1918	Cp. A. A. Humphreys, Va.					November 1918	Cp. A. A. Humphreys, Va.	
557th to 563d Engineers									Never orgzd.
564th Engineers (colored service battalion).	November 1918	Cp. Shelby, Miss.					December 1918	Cp. Shelby, Miss.	
565th Engineers (colored service battalion).	October 1918	do.					do.	Do.	
566th Engineers (colored service battalion).	do.	do.					do.	Do.	
567th Engineers (colored service battalion).	do.	Cp. Wheeler, Ga.					do.	Cp. Wheeler, Ga.	
568th to 600th Engineers									Authorized, but never orgzd.
601st Engineers (sapper regiment).	March 1918	Cp. Laurel, Md.	June 1918	P. of E., Hoboken	June 1918.				
			July 1919	Cp. Devens, Mass.		July 1919	July 1919	Cp. Dix, N. J.	Corps troops.
602d Engineers (sapper regiment).	do.	Cp. Devens, Mass.	July 1918	P. of E., Hoboken	July 1918.				
			June 1919	Cp. Merritt, N. J.		June 1919	do.	Cp. Grant, Ill.	Do.

603d Engineers (sapper regiment).	April 1918	Ft. Benjamin Harrison, Ind.	August 1918	P. of E., Hoboken	August 1918.				
604th Engineers (sapper regiment).	do	Vancouver Bks., Wash.	June 1919	Cp. Hill, Va		do	June 1919	do	Do.
			May 1918	Cp. Leach, D. C.					
605th Engineers (sapper regiment).	June 1918	Cp. Forrest, Ga	June 1918	Glenburnie, Md.					
			August 1918	P. of E., Hoboken	August 1918.				
			June 1919	Cp. Stuart, Va		June 1919	July 1919	Cp. Grant, Ill	Do.
			September 1918	Cp. Upton, N. Y.					
606th Engineers (sapper regiment).	October 1918	Cp. A. A. Humphreys, Va.	do	P. of E., Hoboken	September 1918.				
			June 1919	Cp. Merritt, N. J		do	June 1919	Cp. Dix, N. J	Do.
							January 1919	Cp. A. A. Humphreys, Va.	
607th to 700th Engineers									Never orgzd.
701st Engineers (stevedore battalion).	September 1918	Cp. Alexander, Va.	October 1918	P. of E., Newport News.	October 1918				Converted into T.C. unit December 1918.
702d Engineers (stevedore battalion).	October 1918	do	November 1918	do	November 1918				Do.

ENGINEER TRAINS

1st Engineer Train	June 1917	Washington Bks., D. C.	August 1917	P. of E., Hoboken	August 1917				Cmpnt. of 1st Div
			September 1919	Cp. Mills, N. Y		September 1919.			
			do	Cp. Meade, Md.					
			October 1919	Cp. Zachary Taylor, Ky.					
2d Engineer Train	April 1917	El Paso, Tex	August 1917	Washington, D. C					Cmpnt. of 2d Div.
			September 1917	P. of E., Newport News.	September 1917.				
			August 1919	Cp. Merritt, N. J		August 1919.			
			do	Cp. Travis, Tex.					
3d Engineer Train									Never orgzd.
4th Engineer Train	June 1917	Cp. Greene, N. C	April 1918	Cp. Merritt, N. J					Cmpnt. of 4th Div.
			do	P. of E., Hoboken	April 1918.				
			July 1919	Cp. Merritt, N. J		July 1919.			
			August 1919	Cp. Dodge, Iowa.					

ENGINEER TRAINS—Continued

Unit designation and redesignation	Organization		Stations in United States		Overseas		Demobilization		Remarks
	Month and year	Place	Month and year	Place	From—	To—	Month and year	Place	
5th Engineer Train	July 1917	Cp. Funston, Tex.	July 1918	P. of E., Hoboken	July 1918				Orgzd. fr. 1st Engr. Tn. (Inf. Div.).
			February 1919	Cp. Mills, N. Y.		February 1919			Cmpnt. of 7th Div.
			March 1919	Cp. A. A. Humphreys, Va.					
6th Engineer Train	do	Washington Bks., D. C.	December 1917	P. of E., Hoboken	January 1918				Cmpnt. of 3d Div.
			August 1919	Cp. Merritt, N. J.		August 1919.			
			do	Cp. Pike, Ark.					
7th Engineer Train	September 1917	Ft. Leavenworth, Kans.	February 1918	Cp. Merritt, N. J.					Cmpnt. of 5th Div.
			March 1918	P. of E., Hoboken	March 1918.				
			July 1919	Cp. Merritt, N. J.		July 1919.			
			do	Cp. Gordon, Ga.					
8th Engineer Train	August 1917	Cp. Stewart, Tex.							
9th Engineer Train	March 1917	do	October 1917	Cp. Courchesne, Tex.					Cmpnt. of 15th Cav. Div.
10th to 100th Engineer Trains.									Never orgzd.
101st Engineer Train	August 1917	Cp. Devens, Mass.	September 1917	Cp. Wentworth, Mass.					Cmpnt. of 26th Div.
			do	P. of E., Hoboken	September 1917	April 1919	April 1919	Cp. Devens, Mass.	
102d Engineer Train	October 1917	Cp. Wadsworth, S. C.	May 1918	Cp. Stuart, Va.					Cmpnt. of 27th Div.
			do	P. of E., Newport News.	May 1918.				
			March 1919	Cp. Mills, N. Y.		March 1919	April 1919	Cp. Upton, N. Y.	
103d Engineer Train	November 1917	Cp. Hancock, Ga.	May 1918	do					Cmpnt. of 28th Div.
			do	P. of E., Hoboken	May 1918	May 1919	May 1919	Cp. Dix, N. J.	
104th Engineer Train	October 1917	Cp. McClellan, Ala.	June 1918	do	June 1918				Cmpnt. of 29th Div.
			May 1919	Cp. Merritt, N. J.		May 1919	May 1919	Cp. Dix, N. J.	

105th Engineer Train	September 1917	Cp. Sevier, S. C.	May 1918	P. of E., Hoboken	May 1918	April 1919	April 1919	Cp. Jackson, S. C.	Cmpnt. of 30th Div.
106th Engineer Train	October 1917	Cp. Wheeler, Ga.	September 1918	Cp. Mills, N. Y.					Cmpnt. of 31st Div.
			do.	P. of E., Hoboken	September 1918.				
			July 1919	Cp. Mills, N. Y.		July 1919	July 1919	Cp. Gordon, Ga.	
107th Engineer Train	do.	Cp. MacArthur, Tex.	January 1918	Cp. Merritt, N. J.					Cmpnt. of 32d Div.
			do.	P. of E., Hoboken	January 1918.				
			May 1919	Cp. Dix, N. J.		May 1919	May 1919	Cp. Custer, Mich.	
108th Engineer Train	do.	Cp. Logan, Tex.	April 1918	Cp. Merritt, N. J.					Cmpnt. of 33d Div.
			May 1918	P. of E., Hoboken	May 1918.				
			May 1919	Cp. Mills, N. Y.		May 1919	June 1919	Cp. Grant, Ill.	
109th Engineer Train	do.	Cp. Cody, N. Mex.	September 1918	P. of E., Hoboken	September 1918				Cmpnt. of 34th Div.
			June 1919	Cp. Hill, Va.		June 1919	July 1919	Cp. Dodge, Iowa.	
110th Engineer Train	do.	Cp. Doniphan, Okla.	April 1918	Cp. Merritt, N. J.					Cmpnt. of 35th Div.
			May 1918	P. of E., Hoboken	May 1918.				
			April 1919	Cp. Mills, N. Y.		April 1919	May 1919	Cp. Funston, Kans.	
111th Engineer Train	do.	Cp. Bowie, Tex.	July 1918	do.					Cmpnt. of 36th Div.
			do.	P. of E., Hoboken	July 1918.				
			June 1919	Cp. Mills, N. Y.		June 1919	June 1919	Cp. Bowie, Tex.	
112th Engineer Train	August 1917	Cp. Sheridan, Ala.	May 1918	Cp. Lee, Va.					Cmpnt. of 37th Div.
			June 1918	P. of E., Newport News.	June 1918.				
			March 1919	Cp. Mills, N. Y.		March 1919	April 1919	Cp. Sherman, Ohio.	
113th Engineer Train	October 1917	Cp. Shelby, Miss.	September 1918	do.					Cmpnt. of 38th Div.
			do.	P. of E., Hoboken	September 1918	June 1919	July 1919	Cp. Devens, Mass.	
114th Engineer Train	November 1917	Cp. Beauregard, La.	August 1918	do.	August 1918				Cmpnt. of 39th Div.
			May 1919	Cp. Morrison, Va.		May 1919	May 1919	Cp. Shelby, Miss.	
115th Engineer Train	September 1917	Cp. Kearny, Calif.	August 1918	Cp. Mills, N. Y.					Cmpnt. of 40th Div.
			do.	P. of E., Hoboken	August 1918.				
			June 1919	Cp. Merritt, N. J.		June 1919	July 1919	Ft. D. A. Russell, Wyo.	Corps troops.
116th Engineer Train	October 1917	Cp. Greene, N. C.	October 1917	Cp. Mills, N. Y.					Cmpnt. of 41st Div.
			November 1917	P. of E., Hoboken	November 1917.				
			February 1919	Cp. Dix, N. J.		February 1919	May 1919	Cp. Dix, N. J.	
117th Engineer Train	August 1917	Cp. Mills, N. Y.	October 1917	P. of E., Hoboken	October 1917				Cmpnt. of 42d Div.
			April 1919	Cp. Merritt N. J.		April 1919	May 1919	Cp. Jackson, S. C.	
118th to 208th Engineer Trains.									Never orgsd.
209th Engineer Train	August 1918	Cp. Sheridan, Ala.					January 1919	Cp. Sheridan, Ala.	Cmpnt. of 9th Div.

ENGINEER TRAINS—Continued

Unit designation and redesignation	Organization		Stations in United States		Overseas		Demobilization		Remarks
	Month and year	Place	Month and year	Place	From—	To—	Month and year	Place	
210th Engineer Train	August 1918	Cp. Funston, Kans	November 1918	Cp. Mills, N. Y.					Cmpnt. of 10th Div.
			January 1919	Cp. A. A. Humphreys, Va.			March 1919	Cp. A. A. Humphreys, Va.	
211th Engineer Train	September 1918	Cp. Forrest, Ga	October 1918	Cp. Meade, Md			February 1919	Cp. Meade, Md	Cmpnt. of 11th Div.
212th Engineer Train	August 1918	do	August 1918	Cp. Devens, Mass			January 1919	Cp. Devens, Mass	Cmpnt. of 12th Div.
213th Engineer Train	do	do	October 1918	Cp. Lewis, Wash			February 1919	Cp. Lewis, Wash	Cmpnt. of 13th Div.
214th Engineer Train	November 1918	Cp. Custer, Mich					January 1919	Cp. Custer, Mich	Cmpnt. of 14th Div.
215th to 218th Engineer Trains.									Never orgzd.
219th Engineer Train	November 1918	Cp. Dodge, Iowa					January 1919	Cp. Dodge, Iowa	Cmpnt. of 19th Div.
220th to 300th Engineer Trains.									Never orgzd.
301st Engineer Train	August 1917	Cp. Devens, Mass	July 1918	P. of E., Hoboken	July 1918	June 1919	June 1919	Cp. Devens, Mass	Cmpnt. of 76th Div. Corps troops.
302d Engineer Train	do	Cp. Upton, N. Y	March 1918	do	March 1918	May 1919	May 1919	Cp. Upton, N. Y	Cmpnt. of 77th Div.
303d Engineer Train	do	Cp. Dix, N. J	May 1918	P. of E., Boston	May 1918	June 1919	June 1919	Cp. Dix, N. J	Cmpnt. of 78th Div.
304th Engineer Train	September 1917	Cp. Meade, Md	July 1918	P. of E., Hoboken	July 1918				Cmpnt. of 79th Div.
			May 1919	Cp. Dix, N. J		May 1919	June 1919	Cp. Dix, N. J.	
305th Engineer Train	August 1917	Cp. Lee, Va	May 1918	P. of E., Newport News.	May 1918				Cmpnt. of 80th Div.
			June 1919	Cp. Merritt, N. J		June 1919	June 1919	Cp. Dix, N. J	
306th Engineer Train	do	Cp. Jackson, S. C	May 1918	Cp. Sevier, S. C					Cmpnt. of 81st Div
			July 1918	P. of E., Hoboken	July 1918	June 1919	June 1919	Cp. Jackson, S. C.	

307th Engineer Train	do	Cp. Gordon, Ga.	May 1918	Cp. Mills, N. Y.					Cmpnt. of 82d Div.
			do	P. of E., Hoboken	May 1918	May 1919	May 1919	Cp. Dix, N. J.	
308th Engineer Train	September 1917	Cp. Sherman, Ohio	June 1918	do	June 1918				Cmpnt. of 83d Div.
			June 1919	Cp. Jackson, S. C.		June 1919	July 1919	Cp. Sherman, Ohio	Corps troops.
309th Engineer Train	August 1917	Cp. Zachary Taylor, Ky.	June 1918	Cp. Sherman, Ohio					Cmpnt. of 84th Div.
			August 1918	Cp. Mills, N. Y.					
			September 1918	P. of E., Hoboken	September 1918.				
			June 1919	Cp. Hill, Va.		June 1919	July 1919	Cp. Sherman, Ohio.	
310th Engineer Train	do	Cp. Custer, Mich.	July 1918	Cp. Mills, N. Y.					Cmpnt. of 85th Div.
			do	P. of E., Hoboken	July 1918.				
			June 1919	Cp. Devens, Mass.		June 1919	July 1919	Cp. Custer, Mich.	
311th Engineer Train	do	Cp. Grant, Ill.	August 1918	Cp. Mills, N. Y.					Cmpnt. of 86th Div.
			September 1918	P. of E., Hoboken	September 1918.				
			June 1919	Cp. Dix, N. J.		June 1919	July 1919	Cp. Grant, Ill.	
312th Engineer Train	do	Cp. Pike, Ark.	June 1918	do					Cmpnt. of 87th Div.
			August 1918	P. of E., Hoboken	August 1918	June 1919	June 1919	Cp. Dix, N. J	
313th Engineer Train	do	Cp. Dodge, Iowa	do	do	do				Cmpnt. of 88th Div.
			June 1919	Cp. Mills, N. Y.		June 1919	June 1919	Cp. Dodge, Iowa.	
314th Engineer Train	September 1917	Cp. Funston, Kans.	May 1918	do					Cmpnt. of 89th Div.
			June 1918	P. of E., Hoboken	June 1918.				
			May 1919	Cp. Upton, N. Y.		May 1919	June 1919	Cp. Funston, Kans.	
315th Engineer Train	August 1917	Cp. Travis, Tex.	June 1918	Cp. Mills, N. Y.					Cmpnt. of 90th Div.
			do	P. of E., Hoboken	June 1918.				
			June 1919	Cp. Mills, N. Y.		June 1919	June 1919	Cp. Dodge, Iowa.	
316th Engineer Train	do	Cp. Lewis, Wash.	June 1918	Cp. Merritt, N. J.					Cmpnt. of 91st D
			July 1918	P. of E., Hoboken	July 1918.				
			April 1919	Cp. Merritt, N. J.		April 1919	May 1919	Presidio of San Francisco, Calif.	
317th Engineer Train	November 1917	Cp. Sherman, Ohio	June 1918	P. of E., Hoboken	June 1918	March 1919	March 1919	Cp. Upton, N. Y.	Cmpnt. of 92d Div.
318th Engineer Train	December 1917	Vancouver Bks., Wash.	April 1918	Cp. Merritt, N. J.					Cmpnt. of 6th Div.
			May 1918	P. of E., Hoboken	May 1918.				
			June 1919	Cp. Mills, N. Y.		June 1919			Active through 1919.
319th Engineer Train	March 1918	Cp. Fremont, Calif.	September 1918	Cp. Upton, N. Y.					Cmpnt. of 8th Div.
			do	P. of E., Hoboken	September 1918.				
			August 1919	Cp. Merritt, N. J.		August 1919	September 1919	Presidio of San Francisco, Calif.	

SPECIAL AND TECHNICAL UNITS

Units	Unit No.	Active service	Unit No.	Active service	Unit No.	Active service	Unit No.	Active service	Unit No.	Active service	Remarks
Depot Detachments	402	October 1917–November 1918	[a] 403	October 1917–November 1918	[a] 404	October 1917–November 1918	[a] 405	October 1917–November 1918	[a] 406	September 1917–November 1918	a Converted into Q.M.C. unit November 1918.
	[a] 407	September 1917–November 1918	[a] 408	do	409	October 1917–August 1918	[a] 410	do	[a] 411	do	b Orgzd. in U. S.; demobilized overseas.
	[a] 412	November 1917–November 1918	[a] 413	September 1917–November 1918	[a] 414	September 1917–November 1918	[a] 415	September 1917–November 1918	[a] 416	October 1917–November 1918	c Orgzd. in C. Z; converted into Q.M.C. unit February 1919.
	[a] 417	September 1917–November 1918	[a] 418	October 1917–November 1918	[b] 419	November 1917–July 1919	[a] 420	November 1917–November 1918	[a] 421	November 1917–November 1918	d Orgzd. in U. S.; converted into T.C. unit November 1918 overseas.
	[a] 422	do	[a] 423	September 1917–November 1918	[a] 424	September 1917–November 1918	[a] 425	do	[a] 426	September 1917–November 1918	e Orgzd. and demblzd. in Philippines.
	[a] 427	do	[a] 428	do	[a] 429	October 1917–November 1918	[a] 430	October 1917–November 1918	[a] 431	Do.	f Orgzd. and demblzd. in Hawaii.
	[a] 432	October 1917–November 1918	[a] 433	do	[a] 434	do	435	September 1917–August 1918	[c] 436	November 1917–February 1919	g Converted into C.W.S. unit September 1918.
	[a] 437	do	[a] 438	October 1917–November 1918	[a] 439	do	[a] 440	December 1917–November 1918	[a] 441	December 1917–November 1918	h S.O.S. troops.
	442–445	Never orgzd.	[d h] 446	November 1917–November 1918	[b] 447	December 1917–August 1919	448–453	Never orgzd.	[e] 454	February 1918–December 1918	
	[f] 455	February 1918–December 1918	456–469	Never orgzd.	[a] 470	February 1918–November 1918	[a] 471	March 1918–November 1918	472	Never orgzd.	
	[g] 473	July 1918–September 1918	[a] 474	July 1918–November 1918	[a] 475	July 1918–December 1918	[a] 476	August 1918–November 1918	477	August 1918–January 1919	
	478	September 1918–through December 1919	479	Never orgzd.	480	Never orgzd.	481	September 1918–December 1918	482–485	Authorized, but never orgzd.	
	486	Never orgzd.	487	Authorized, but never orgzd.	488	November 1918 through December 1919	489	November 1918–February 1919			

INFANTRY

BRIGADE HEADQUARTERS

Unit designation and redesignation	Organization		Stations in United States		Overseas		Demobilization		Remarks
	Month and year	Place	Month and year	Place	From—	To—	Month and year	Place	
1st Infantry Brigade	June 1917	New York, N. Y.	June 1917	P. of E., Hoboken	June 1917				Cmpnt. of 1st Div.
			September 1919	Cp. Merritt, N. J.		September 1919.			
			do	Cp. Meade, Md.					
			October 1919	Cp. Zachary Taylor, Ky.					Active through 1919.
1st Infantry Brigade, Philippine National Guard.	November 1918	Cp. Tomas Claudio, P. I.					February 1919	Cp. Tomas Claudio, P. I.	In Federal service November–December 1918.
1st Brigade, 1st Provisional Infantry Division.	March 1917	Brownsville, Tex.						Brownsville, Tex.	Orgn. discontinued June 1917
1st Brigade, 2d Provisional Infantry Division.	do	El Paso, Tex.						El Paso, Tex.	Orgn. discontinued June 1917.
1st Brigade, 3d Provisional Infantry Division.	do	Nogales, Ariz.						Nogales, Ariz.	Do.
1st Hawaiian Brigade	April 1917	Schofield Bks., T. H.						Schofield Bks., T. H.	Orgn. discontinued October 1918.
2d Infantry Brigade	June 1917	New York, N. Y.	June 1917	P. of E., Hoboken	June 1917				Cmpnt. of 1st Div.
			September 1919	Cp. Meade, Md.		September 1919.			
			October 1919	Cp. Zachary Taylor, Ky.					Active through 1919.
2d Infantry Brigade, Philippine National Guard.	November 1918	Cp. Tomas Claudio, P. I.					February 1919	Cp. Tomas Claudio, P. I.	In Federal service November–December 1918.
2d Brigade, 1st Provisional Infantry Division.	March 1917	Laredo, Tex.						Laredo, Tex.	Orgn. discontinued June 1917.

BRIGADE HEADQUARTERS—Continued

Unit designation and redesignation	Organization		Stations in United States		Overseas		Demobilization		Remarks
	Month and year	Place	Month and year	Place	From—	To—	Month and year	Place	
2d Brigade, 2d Provisional Infantry Division.	March 1917	El Paso, Tex						El Paso, Tex	Orgn. discontinued June 1917.
2d Brigade, 3d Provisional Infantry Division.	do	Douglas, Ariz						Douglas, Ariz	Do.
3d Infantry Brigade	October 1917	A. E. F	August 1919	Cp. Merritt, N. J		August 1919			Cmpnt. of 2d Div.
			do	Cp. Travis, Tex					Active through 1919.
3d Infantry Brigade, Philippine National Guard.	November 1918	Cp. Tomas Claudio, P. I.					February 1919	Cp. Tomas Claudio, P. I.	In Federal service November–December 1918.
3d Brigade, 1st Provisional Infantry Division.	March 1917	Eagle Pass, Tex						Eagle Pass, Tex	Orgn. discontinued June 1917.
3d Brigade, 2d Provisional Infantry Division.	do	Columbus, N. Mex.						Columbus, N. Mex.	Do.
4th Infantry Brigade									U.S.M.C. orgn. Cmpnt. of 2d Div.
5th Infantry Brigade	January 1918	Cp. Greene, N. C	March 1918	Cp. Merritt, N. J					Cmpnt. of 3d Div.
			April 1918	P. of E., Hoboken	April 1918.				
			August 1919	Cp. Merritt, N. J		August 1919.			
			do	Cp. Pike, Ark					Active through 1919.
6th Infantry Brigade	do	do	March 1918	Cp. Merritt, N. J					Cmpnt. of 3d Div.
			April 1918	P. of E., Hoboken	April 1918.				
			August 1919	Cp. Merritt, N. J		August 1919.			
			do	Cp. Pike, Ark					Active through 1919.

7th Infantry Brigade	December 1917	do	April 1918	Cp. Mills, N. Y.					Cmpnt. of 4th Div.
			May 1918	P. of E., Hoboken	May 1918.				
			July 1919	Cp. Mills, N. Y.		July 1919.			
			August 1919	Cp. Dodge, Iowa					Active through 1919.
8th Infantry Brigade	do	do	April 1918	Cp. Mills, N. Y.					Cmpnt. of 4th Div.
			May 1918	P. of E., Hoboken	May 1918.				
			August 1919	Cp. Merritt, N. J.		August 1919.			
			do	Cp. Dodge, Iowa					Active through 1919.
9th Infantry Brigade	do	do	April 1918	Cp. Merritt, N. J.					Cmpnt. of 5th Div.
			do	P. of E., Hoboken	April 1918.				
			July 1919	Cp. Mills, N. Y.		July 1919.			
			do	Cp. Gordon, Ga.					Active through 1919.
10th Infantry Brigade	January 1918	Cp. Forrest, Ga.	April 1918	Cp. Upton, N. Y.					Cmpnt. of 5th Div.
			do	P. of E., Hoboken	April 1918.				
			July 1919	Cp. Mills, N. Y.		July 1919.			
			do	Cp. Gordon, Ga.					Active through 1919.
11th Infantry Brigade	December 1917	do	June 1918	Cp. Upton, N. Y.					Cmpnt. of 6th Div.
			July 1918	P. of E., Hoboken	July 1918.				
			June 1919	Cp. Merritt, N. J.		June 1919.			
			do	Cp. Grant, Ill.					Active through 1919.
12th Infantry Brigade	November 1917	do	May 1918	Cp. Wadsworth, S. C.					Cmpnt. of 6th Div.
			June 1918	Cp. Mills, N. Y.					
			July 1918	P. of E., Hoboken	July 1918.				
			June 1919	Cp. Merritt, N. J.		June 1919.			
			do	Cp. Grant, Ill.					Active through 1919.
13th Infantry Brigade	December 1917	Chickamauga Park, Ga.	February 1918	Cp. MacArthur, Tex.					Cmpnt. of 7th Div.
			July 1918	Cp. Merritt, N. J.					
			August 1918	P. of E., Hoboken	August 1918.				
			June 1919	Cp. Mills, N. Y.		June 1919.			
			do	Cp. Funston, Kans					Active through 1919.

BRIGADE HEADQUARTERS—Continued

Unit designation and redesignation	Organization		Stations in United States		Overseas		Demobilization		Remarks
	Month and year	Place	Month and year	Place	From—	To—	Month and year	Place	
14th Infantry Brigade	December 1917	Cp. Bliss, Tex.	June 1918	Cp. MacArthur, Tex.					Cmpnt. of 7th Div.
			July 1918	Cp. Merritt, N. J.					
			August 1918	P. of E., Hoboken	August 1918.				
			June 1919	Cp. Mills, N. Y.		June 1919.			
			do	Cp. Funston, Kans.					Active through 1919.
15th Infantry Brigade	January 1918	Cp. Fremont, Calif.	October 1918	Cp. Mills, N. Y.					Cmpnt. of 8th Div.
			November 1918	Cp. Lee, Va.			February 1919	Cp. Lee, Va.	
16th Infantry Brigade	December 1917	Cp. Fremont, Calif.	October 1918	Cp. Mills, N. Y.					Do.
			do	P. of E., Hoboken	October 1918		November 1918	A. E. F.	
17th Infantry Brigade	do	Cp. Zachary Taylor, Ky.	April 1918	Cp. Gordon, Ga.					Cmpnt. of 9th Div.
			June 1918	Cp. Sheridan, Ala.			February 1919	Cp. Sheridan, Ala.	
18th Infantry Brigade	July 1918	Cp. Sheridan, Ala.					do	do	Do.
19th Infantry Brigade	August 1918	Cp. Funston, Kans.					do	Cp. Funston, Kans.	Cmpnt. of 10th Div.
20th Infantry Brigade	do	do					do	do	Do.
21st Infantry Brigade	do	Cp. Meade, Md.					do	Cp. Meade, Md.	Cmpnt. of 11th Div.
22d Infantry Brigade	September 1918	Cp. Meade, Md.					do	Cp. Meade, Md.	Do.
23d Infantry Brigade	August 1918	Cp. Devens, Mass.					January 1919	Cp. Devens, Mass.	Cmpnt. of 12th Div.
24th Infantry Brigade	do	do					do	do	Do.
25th Infantry Brigade	do	Cp. Lewis, Wash.					March 1919	Cp. Lewis, Wash.	Cmpnt. of 13th Div.
26th Infantry Brigade	do	do					do	do	Do.
27th Infantry Brigade	July 1918	Cp. Custer, Mich.					February 1919	Cp. Custer, Mich.	Cmpnt. of 14th Div.
28th Infantry Brigade	do	do					do	do	Do.
29th Infantry Brigade	September 1918	Cp. Logan, Tex.					do	Cp. Logan, Tex.	Cmpnt. of 15th Div.

30th Infantry Brigade	do	do					do	do	Do.
31st Infantry Brigade	do	Cp. Kearny, Calif.					do	Cp. Kearny, Calif	Cmpnt. of 16th Div.
32d Infantry Brigade	do	do					do	do	Do.
33d Infantry Brigade									Never orgzd.
34th Infantry Brigade	January 1919	Cp. Beauregard, La.					February 1919	Cp. Beauregard, La.	Cmpnt. of 17th Div.
35th Infantry Brigade	August 1918	Cp. Travis, Tex.					do	Cp. Travis, Tex.	Cmpnt. of 18th Div.
36th Infantry Brigade	do	do					do	do	Cmpnt. of 18th Div.
37th Infantry Brigade	October 1918	Cp. Dodge, Iowa					January 1919	Cp. Dodge, Iowa	Cmpnt. of 19th Div.
38th Infantry Brigade	do	do					do	do	Do.
39th Infantry Brigade	do	Cp. Sevier, S. C.					February 1919	Cp. Sevier, S. C.	Cmpnt. of 20th Div.
40th Infantry Brigade	August 1918	do					do	do	Do.
41st to 50th Infantry Brigades.									Never orgzd.
51st Infantry Brigade	August 1917	Boston, Mass.	September 1917	P. of E., Hoboken	September 1917	April 1919	April 1919	Cp. Devens, Mass.	Cmpnt. of 26th Div.
52d Infantry Brigade	do	Westfield, Mass.	do	P. of E., Montreal	do	do	do	do	Do.
53d Infantry Brigade	October 1917	Cp. Wadsworth, S. C.	May 1918	Cp. Stuart, Va.					Cmpnt. of 27th Div.
			do	P. of E., Newport News.	May 1918.				
			March 1919	Cp. Mills, N. Y.		March 1919	April 1919	Cp. Upton, N. Y.	
54th Infantry Brigade	do	do	May 1918	Cp. Stuart, Va.					Do.
			do	P. of E., Newport News.	May 1918.				
			March 1919	Cp. Merritt, N. J.		March 1919	April 1919	Cp. Upton, N. Y.	
55th Infantry Brigade	September 1917	Cp. Hancock, Ga.	April 1918	do					Cmpnt. of 28th Div.
			May 1918	P. of E., Hoboken	May 1918	May 1919	May 1919	Cp. Dix, N. J.	
56th Infantry Brigade	do	do	April 1918	Cp. Upton, N. Y.					Do.
			May 1918	P. of E., Hoboken	May 1918.				
			April 1919	Cp. Stuart, Va.		April 1919	May 1919	Cp. Dix, N. J.	
57th Infantry Brigade	do	Cp. McClellan, Ala.	June 1918	do					Cmpnt. of 29th Div.
			do	P. of E., Newport News.	June 1918	May 1919	May 1919	Cp. Dix, N. J.	

BRIGADE HEADQUARTERS—Continued

Unit designation and redesignation	Organization		Stations in United States		Overseas		Demobilization		Remarks
	Month and year	Place	Month and year	Place	From—	To—	Month and year	Place	
58th Infantry Brigade	August 1917	**Cp. McClellan, Ala.**	June 1918	P. of E., Hoboken	June 1918				**Cmpnt. of 29th Div.**
			May 1919	Cp. Merritt, N. J.		May 1919	May 1919	Cp. Meade, Md.	
59th Infantry Brigade	September 1917	Cp. Sevier, S. C.	May 1918	Cp. Mills, N. Y.					Cmpnt. of 30th Div.
			do	P. of E., Hoboken	May 1918.				
			March 1919	Cp. Jackson, S. C.		March 1919	April 1919	Ft. Oglethorpe, Ga.	
60th Infantry Brigade	do	do	May 1918	Cp. Merritt, N. J.					Do.
			do	P. of E., Hoboken	May 1918	April 1919	April 1919	Cp. Jackson, S. C.	
61st Infantry Brigade	August 1917	Cp. Wheeler, Ga.	September 1918	Cp. Mills, N. Y.					Cmpnt. of 31st Div. Skeletonized November 1918.
			October 1918	P. of E., Hoboken	October 1918.				
			December 1918	Cp. Merritt, N. J.		December 1918	January 1919	Cp. Gordon, Ga.	Record cadre only.
62d Infantry Brigade	do	do	September 1918	Cp. Mills, N. Y.					Cmpnt. of 31st Div. Skeletonized November 1918.
			October 1918	P. of E., Hoboken	October 1918				Record cadre only.
			December 1918	Cp. Merritt, N. J.		December 1918	January 1919	Cp. Gordon, Ga.	
63d Infantry Brigade	September 1917	Cp. MacArthur, Tex.	January 1918	do					Cmpnt. of 32d Div.
			February 1918	P. of E., Hoboken	February 1918.				
			May 1919	Cp. Mills, N. Y.		May 1919	May 1919	Cp. Custer, Mich.	
64th Infantry Brigade	do	do	January 1918	Cp. Merritt, N. J.					Do.
			February 1918	P. of E., Hoboken	February 1918.				
			May 1919	Cp. Merritt, N. J.		May 1919	May 1919	Cp. Grant, Ill.	
65th Infantry Brigade	August 1917	Cp. Logan, Tex.	May 1918	Cp. Upton, N. Y.					Cmpnt. of 33d Div.
			do	P. of E., Hoboken	May 1918.				
			May 1919	Cp. Mills, N. Y.		May 1919	May 1919	Cp. Grant, Ill.	
66th Infantry Brigade	September 1917	do	May 1918	Cp. Upton, N. Y.					Do.
			do	P. of E., Hoboken	May 1918.				
			May 1919	Cp. Mills, N. Y.		May 1919	June 1919	Cp. Grant, Ill.	

67th Infantry Brigade	August 1917	Cp. Cody, N. Mex	August 1918	Cp. Dix, N. J.					Cmpnt. of 34th Div. Skeletonized November 1918.
68th Infantry Brigade	do	do	September 1918 January 1919 August 1918	P. of E., Hoboken Cp. Merritt, N. J. Cp. Dix, N. J.	September 1918	January 1919	February 1919	Cp. Grant, Ill.	Record cadre only.
69th Infantry Brigade	do	Cp. Doniphan, Okla.	October 1918 January 1919 April 1918	P. of E., Hoboken Cp. Merritt, N. J. Cp. Mills, N. Y.	October 1918.	January 1919	February 1919	Cp. Grant, Ill.	Cmpnt. of 34th Div. Skeletonized November 1918. Record cadre only.
70th Infantry Brigade	September 1917	do	May 1918 April 1919 April 1918	P. of E., Hoboken Cp. Stuart, Va. Cp. Mills, N. Y.	May 1918.	April 1919	May 1919	Cp. Funston, Kans	Cmpnt. of 35th Div.
71st Infantry Brigade	August 1917	Cp. Bowie, Tex.	do April 1919 July 1918	P. of E., Hoboken Cp. Stuart, Va. Cp. Mills, N. Y.	April 1918.	April 1919	May 1919	Cp. Funston, Kans	Do.
72d Infantry Brigade	September 1917	do	do June 1919 July 1918	P. of E., Hoboken Cp. Mills, N. Y. Cp. Mills, N. Y.	July 1918.	June 1919	June 1919	Cp. Bowie, Tex.	Cmpnt. of 36th Div.
73d Infantry Brigade	do	Cp. Sheridan, Ala.	do June 1919 May 1918	P. of E., Hoboken Cp. Mills, N. Y. Cp. Lee, Va.	July 1918.	June 1919	June 1919	Cp. Bowie, Tex.	Do.
74th Infantry Brigade	do	do	June 1918 March 1919 May 1918	P. of E., Newport News. Cp. Dix, N. J. Cp. Lee, Va.	June 1918.	March 1919	April 1919	Cp. Sherman, Ohio	Cmpnt. of 37th Div.
75th Infantry Brigade	do	Cp. Shelby, Miss.	June 1918 March 1919 September 1918	P. of E., Newport News. Cp. Mills, N. Y. do	June 1918.	March 1919	April 1919	Cp. Sherman, Ohio	Do.
76th Infantry Brigade	do	do	October 1918 December 1918 September 1918	P. of E., Hoboken Cp. Hill, Va. Cp. Mills, N. Y.	October 1918.	December 1918	January 1919	Cp. Zachary Taylor, Ky.	Cmpnt. of 38th Div. Skeletonized November 1918. Record cadre only. Cmpnt. of 38th Div. Skeletonized November 1918.

BRIGADE HEADQUARTERS—Continued

Unit designation and redesignation	Organization		Stations in United States		Overseas		Demobilization		Remarks
	Month and year	Place	Month and year	Place	From—	To—	Month and year	Place	
76th Infantry Brigade—Continued.			October 1918	P. of E., Montreal	October 1918.	December 1918	January 1919	Cp. Zachary Taylor, Ky.	Record cadre only.
			December 1918	Cp. Hill, Va					
77th Infantry Brigade	August 1917	Cp. Beauregard, La.	August 1918	Cp. Stuart, Va					Cmpnt. of 39th Div. Skeletonized November 1918.
			do	P. of E., Newport News.	August 1918.	January 1919	January 1919	Cp. Beauregard, La.	Record cadre only.
			January 1919	Cp. Stuart, Va					
78th Infantry Brigade	do	do	August 1918	Cp. Merritt, N. J					Cmpnt. of 39th Div. Skeletonized November 1918.
			do	P. of E., Hoboken	August 1918.	January 1919	January 1919	Cp. Beauregard, La.	Record cadre only.
			January 1919	Cp. Stuart, Va					
79th Infantry Brigade	do	Cp. Kearny, Calif	August 1918	Cp. Mills, N. Y					Cmpnt. of 40th Div.
			do	P. of E., Hoboken	August 1918.	April 1919	April 1919	Cp. Kearny, Calif.	
			April 1919	Cp. Mills, N. Y					
80th Infantry Brigade	do	do	August 1918	Cp. Mills, N. Y					Do.
			do	P. of E., Hoboken	August 1918.	April 1919	April 1919	Cp. Kearny, Calif.	
			April 1919	Cp. Mills, N. Y					
81st Infantry Brigade	September 1917	Cp. Greene, N. C	November 1917	Cp. Mills, N. Y					Cmpnt. of 41st Div.
			December 1917	P. of E., Hoboken	December 1917	March 1919	March 1919	Cp. Dix, N. J.	
82d Infantry Brigade	do	do	November 1917	Cp. Mills, N. Y					Do.
			December 1917	Cp. Merritt, N. J.					
			do	P. of E., Hoboken	December 1917.	February 1919	February 1919	Cp. Dix, N. J.	
			February 1919	Cp. Merritt, N. J					
83d Infantry Brigade	August 1917	Cp. Mills, N. Y	October 1917	P. of E., Hoboken	October 1917				Cmpnt. of 42d Div.
			April 1919	Cp. Merritt, N. J		April 1919	May 1919	Cp. Upton, N. Y.	

84th Infantry Brigade	September 1917	do	November 1917	P. of E., Hoboken	November 1917				Do.
			April 1919	Cp. Merritt, N. J.		April 1919	May 1919	Cp. Dodge, Iowa	
85th to 150th Infantry Brigades.									Never orgzd.
151st Infantry Brigade	August 1917	Cp. Devens, Mass.	July 1918	P. of E., Hoboken	July 1918				Cmpnt. of 76th Div. Skeletonized November 1918.
152d Infantry Brigade	do	do	January 1919	Cp. Hill, Va.		January 1919	February 1919	Cp. Devens, Mass.	Record cadre only.
			July 1918	P. of E., Hoboken	July 1918				
153d Infantry Brigade	do	Cp. Upton, N. Y.	January 1919	Cp. Hill, Va.		January 1919	February 1919	Cp. Devens, Mass.	Do.
			April 1918	P. of E., Boston	April 1918				Cmpnt. of 77th Div.
154th Infantry Brigade	do	do	April 1919	Cp. Mills, N. Y.		April 1919	May 1919	Cp. Upton, N. Y.	
			April 1918	P. of E., Hoboken	April 1918				Do.
155th Infantry Brigade	do	Cp. Dix, N. J.	April 1919	Cp. Mills, N. Y.		April 1919	May 1919	Cp. Upton, N. Y.	
			May 1918	P. of E., Hoboken	May 1918				Cmpnt. of 78th Div.
156th Infantry Brigade	do	do	May 1919	Cp. Merritt, N. J.		May 1919	June 1919	Cp. Dix, N. J.	
			May 1918	P. of E., Hoboken	May 1918				Do.
157th Infantry Brigade	do	Cp. Meade, Md.	May 1919	Cp. Hill, Va.		May 1919	May 1919	Cp. Dix, N. J.	
			July 1918	P. of E., Hoboken	July 1918				Cmpnt. of 79th Div.
158th Infantry Brigade	do	do	May 1919	Cp. Stuart, Va.		May 1919	June 1919	Cp. Dix, N. J.	
			July 1918	P. of E., Hoboken	July 1918				Do.
159th Infantry Brigade	do	Cp. Lee, Va.	May 1919	Cp. Stuart, Va.		May 1919	June 1919	Cp. Dix, N. J.	
			May 1918	P. of E., Newport News.	May 1918				Cmpnt. of 80th Div.
160th Infantry Brigade	do	do	May 1919	Cp. Stuart, Va.		May 1919	May 1919	Cp. Lee, Va.	
			May 1918	P. of E., Newport News.	May 1918				Do.
161st Infantry Brigade	do	Cp. Jackson, S. C.	May 1919	Cp. Mills, N. Y.		May 1919	June 1919	Cp. Dix, N. J.	
			May 1918	Cp. Sevier, S. C.					Cmpnt. of 81st Div.
162d Infantry Brigade	do	do	July 1918	Cp. Upton, N. Y.					
			do	P. of E., Hoboken	July 1918	June 1919	June 1919	Cp. Jackson, S. C.	
			May 1918	Cp. Sevier, S. C.					Do.
			July 1918	Cp. Mills, N. Y.					
			do	P. of E., Hoboken	July 1918	June 1919	June 1919	Cp. Devens, Mass.	

BRIGADE HEADQUARTERS—Continued

Unit designation and redesignation	Organization		Stations in United States		Overseas		Demobilization		Remarks
	Month and year	Place	Month and year	Place	From—	To—	Month and year	Place	
163d Infantry Brigade	September 1917	Cp. Gordon, Ga.	April 1918	Cp. Upton, N. Y.					Cmpnt. of 82d Div.
			do	P. of E., Hoboken	April 1918	May 1919	May 1919	Cp. Mills, N. Y.	
164th Infantry Brigade	August 1917	do	do	Cp. Upton, N. Y.					Do.
			May 1918	P. of E., Hoboken	May 1918	May 1919	May 1919	Cp. Mills, N. Y.	
165th Infantry Brigade	do	Cp. Sherman, Ohio	do	Cp. Merritt, N. J.					Cmpnt. of 83d Div.
			June 1918	P. of E., Hoboken	June 1918.				
			February 1919	Cp. Mills, N. Y.		February 1919	February 1919	Cp. Sherman, Ohio	
166th Infantry Brigade	do	do	May 1918	Cp. Merritt, N. J.					Do.
			June 1918	P. of E., Hoboken	June 1918.				
			January 1919	Cp. Merritt, N. J.		January 1919	February 1919	Cp. Sherman, Ohio	
167th Infantry Brigade	do	Cp. Zachary Taylor, Ky.	June 1918	Cp. Sherman, Ohio					Cmpnt. of 84th Div.
			August 1918	Cp. Mills, N. Y					Skeletonized November 1918.
			September 1918	P. of E., Hoboken	September 1918				
			January 1919	Cp. Merritt, N. J.		January 1919	February 1919	Cp. Zachary Taylor, Ky.	Record cadre only.
168th Infantry Brigade	do	do	June 1918	Cp. Sherman, Ohio					Cmpnt. of 84th Div.
			August 1918	Cp. Mills, N. Y.					
			September 1918	P. of E., Hoboken	September 1918				Skeletonized November 1918.
			January 1919	Cp. Merritt, N. J.		January 1919	February 1919	Cp. Zachary Taylor, Ky.	Record cadre only.
169th Infanty Brigade	do	Cp. Custer, Mich.	July 1918	Cp. Mills, N. Y.					Cmpnt. of 85th Div.
			do	P. of E., Hoboken	July 1918.				
			March 1919	Cp. Mills, N. Y.		March 1919	April 1919	Cp. Custer, Mich.	
170th Infantry Brigade	do	do	July 1918	do					Do.
			do	P. of E., Hoboken	July 1918.				
			April 1919	Cp. Upton, N. Y.		April 1919	April 1919	Cp. Custer, Mich.	

171st Infantry Brigade	September 1917	Cp. Grant, Ill	August 1918	do					Cmpnt. of 86th Div.
			September 1918	P. of E., Hoboken	September 1918				Skeletonised November 1918.
			January 1919	Cp. Mills, N. Y.		January 1919	January 1919	Cp. Grant, Ill.	Record cadre only.
172d Infantry Brigade	August 1917	do	August 1918	do					Cmpnt. of 86th Div.
			September 1918	P. of E., Hoboken	September 1918				Skeletonised November 1918.
			January 1919	Cp. Mills, N. Y.		January 1919	January 1919	Cp. Grant, Ill.	Record cadre only.
173d Infantry Brigade	do	Cp. Pike, Ark	June 1918	Cp. Dix, N. J.					Cmpnt. of 87th Div.
			August 1918	P. of E., Hoboken	August 1918.				
			January 1919	Cp. Stuart, Va.		January 1919	February 1919	Cp. Dix, N. J.	
174th Infantry Brigade	do	do	June 1918	Cp. Dix, N. J.					Do.
			August 1918	P. of E., Hoboken	August 1918.				
			January 1919	Cp. Stuart, Va.		January 1919	February 1919	Cp. Dix, N. J.	
175th Infantry Brigade	September 1917	Cp. Dodge, Iowa	August 1918	Cp. Upton, N. Y.					Cmpnt. of 88th Div.
			do	P. of E., Hoboken	August 1918.				
			May 1919	Cp. Merritt, N. J.		May 1919	June 1919	Cp. Dodge, Iowa.	
176th Infantry Brigade	August 1917	do	August 1918	Cp. Mills, N. Y.					Do.
			do	P. of E., Hoboken	August 1918.				
			May 1919	Cp. Morrison, Va.		May 1919	June 1919	Cp. Dodge, Iowa.	
177th Infantry Brigade	do	Cp. Funston, Kans.	May 1918	Cp. Mills, N. Y.					Cmpnt. of 89th Div.
			June 1918	P. of E., Hoboken	June 1918.				
			May 1919	Cp. Upton, N. Y.		May 1919	June 1919	Cp. Funston, Kans.	
178th Infantry Brigade	do	do	May 1918	Cp. Mills, N. Y.					Do.
			June 1918	P. of E., Hoboken	June 1918.				
			May 1919	Cp. Upton, N. Y.		May 1919	June 1919	Cp. Zachary Taylor, Ky.	
179th Infantry Brigade	do	Cp. Travis, Tex.	June 1918	Cp. Mills, N. Y.					Cmpnt. of 90th Div.
			do	P. of E., Hoboken	June 1918.				
			June 1919	Cp. Stuart, Va.		June 1919	June 1919	Cp. Pike, Ark.	
180th Infantry Brigade	do	do	June 1918	Cp. Mills, N. Y.					Do.
			do	P. of E., Hoboken	June 1918.				
			June 1919	Cp. Devens, Mass.		June 1919	June 1919	Cp. Bowie, Tex.	
181st Infantry Brigade	September 1917	Cp. Lewis, Wash.	June 1918	Cp. Merritt, N. J.					Cmpnt. of 91st Div.
			July 1918	P. of E., Hoboken	July 1918.				
			April 1919	Cp. Merritt, N. J.		April 1919	April 1919	Cp. Kearny, Calif.	

BRIGADE HEADQUARTERS—Continued

Unit designation and redesignation	Organization		Stations in United States		Overseas		Demobilization		Remarks
	Month and year	Place	Month and year	Place	From—	To—	Month and year	Place	
182d Infantry Brigade	September 1917	Cp. Lewis, Wash.	June 1918	Cp. Merritt, N. J.					Cmpnt. of 91st Div.
			July 1918	P. of E., Hoboken	July 1918.				
			April 1919	Cp. Merritt, N. J.		April 1919	April 1919	Cp. Lewis, Wash.	
183d Infantry Brigade	November 1917	Cp. Grant, Ill.	May 1918	Cp. Upton, N. Y.					Cmpnt. of 92d Div
			June 1918	P. of E., Hoboken	June 1918	February 1919	March 1919	Cp. Upton, N. Y.	
184th Infantry Brigade	do	Cp. Upton, N. Y.	do	do	do				Do.
			February 1919	Cp. Merritt, N. J.		February 1919	March 1919	Cp. Meade, Md.	
185th Infantry Brigade	December 1917	Cp. Logan, Tex.	March 1918	Cp. Stuart, Va.					Cmpnt. of 93d Div.
			April 1918	P. of E., Newport News.	April 1918		May 1918	A. E. F.	
186th Infantry Brigade	do	Cp. Jackson, S. C.	do	do	do		do	do	Do.
187th to 191st Infantry Brigades.									Never orgzd.
192d Infantry Brigade	September 1918	Cp. Wadsworth, S. C.					December 1918	Cp. Wadsworth, S. C.	Cmpnt. of 96th Div.
Provisional Tactical Brigade (Puerto Rican).	October 1918	Cp. Las Casas, P.R.					do	Cp. Las Casas, P.R.	

REGIMENTS

Unit designation and redesignation	Organization month and year	Organization place	Stations month and year	Stations place	Overseas from	Overseas to	Demobilization month and year	Demobilization place	Remarks
1st Infantry	Organized 1791		April 1917	Schofield Bks., T.H.					Cmpnt. of 25th In Brig.
			June 1918	Cp. Murray, Wash.					
			do	Cp. Lewis, Wash.					Active through 1919.
2d Infantry	Organised 1808		April 1917	Ft. Shafter, T.H.					Cmpnt. of 38th Inf. Brig.
			July 1918	Cp. Fr-mont, Calif.					
			September 1918	Cp. Dodge, Iowa.					
			November 1919	Cp. Sherman, Ohio.					Active through 1919.

3d Infantry	Organized 1784		April 1917	Cp. Eagle Pass, Tex.					Patrolling Mexican border through December 1919.
4th Infantry	Organized 1812		do	Brownsville, Tex					Cmpnt. of 5th Inf. Brig.
			June 1917	Gettysburg, Pa.					
			October 1917	Cp. Greene, N. C.					
			December 1917	Cp. Stuart, Va.					
			April 1918	P. of E., Newport News.	April 1918.				
			August 1919	Cp. Merritt, N. J.		August 1919.			
			do	Cp. Pike, Ark					Active through 1919.
5th Infantry	Organized 1808		April 1917	Empire, C. Z					Cmpnt. of 33d Inf. Brig.
			August 1918	Cp. Beauregard, La.					
			December 1918	Cp. Zachary Taylor, Ky.					
			September 1919	Cp. Meade, Md.					
			October 1919	P. of E., Hoboken	October 1919				Duty A. F. in G. through December 1919.
6th Infantry	Organized 1812		April 1917	Cp. Newton D. Baker, Tex.					Cmpnt. of 10th Inf. Brig.
			May 1917	Chickamauga Park, Ga.					
			April 1918	P. of E., Hoboken	April 1918.				
			July 1919	Cp. Mills, N. Y.		July 1919.			
			do	Cp. Gordon, Ga.					Active through 1919.
7th Infantry	do		April 1917	Cp. Fort Bliss Tex.					Cmpnt. of 5th Inf. Brig.
			June 1917	Gettysburg, Pa.					
			November 1917	Cp. Greene, N. C.					
			March 1918	Cp. Merritt, N. J.					
			April 1918	P. of E., Hoboken	April 1918.				
			August 1919	Cp. Merritt, N. J.		August 1919.			
			do	Cp. Pike, Ark					Active through 1919.

REGIMENTS—Continued

Unit designation and redesignation	Organization		Stations in United States		Overseas		Demobilization		Remarks
	Month and year	Place	Month and year	Place	From—	To—	Month and year	Place	
8th Infantry	Organized 1838		April 1917	Ft. McKinley, P. I.					Cmpnt. of 16th Inf. Brig.
			September 1917	Cp. Fremont, Calif.					
			October 1918	Cp. Mills, N. Y.					
			do	P. of E., Hoboken	October 1918				Duty A. E. F. and A.F.inG.through December 1919.
9th Infantry	Organized 1855		April 1917	Cp. Wilson, Tex					Cmpnt. of 3d Inf. Brig.
			May 1917	Syracuse, N. Y.					
			September 1917	P. of E., Hoboken	September 1917.				
			July 1919	Cp. Merritt, N. J.		July 1919.			
			August 1919	Cp. Travis, Tex					Active through 1919.
10th Infantry	do		April 1917	Cp. E. S. Otis, C. Z.					Cmpnt. of 27th Inf. Brig.
			May 1917	Ft. Benjamin Harrison, Ind.					
			July 1918	Cp. Custer, Mich					Active through 1919.
11th Infantry	Organized 1861		April 1917	Douglas, Ariz					Cmpnt. of 10th Inf. Brig.
			May 1917	Chickamauga Park, Ga.					
			April 1918	Cp. Merritt, N. J.					
			do	P. of E., Hoboken	April 1918.				
			July 1919	Cp. Mills, N. Y.		July 1919.			
			do	Cp. Gordon, Ga					Active through 1919.
12th Infantry	do		April 1917	Nogales, Ariz					Cmpnt. of 15th Inf. Brig.
			May 1917	Presidio of San Francisco, Calif.					
			January 1918	Cp. Fremont, Calif.					
			October 1918	Cp. Mills, N. Y.					
			November 1918	Cp. Stuart, Va.					

			October 1919	Ft. Jay, N. Y.					
			November 1919	Cp. Meade, Md					Active through 1919.
13th Infantry	do		April 1917	Ft. Mills, P. I					Cmpnt. of 16th Inf. Brig.
			August 1917	Presidio of San Francisco, Calif.					
			October 1917	Cp. Fremont, Calif.					
			October 1918	Cp. Mills, N. Y.					
			December 1918	Cp. Merritt, N. J					Active through 1919.
14th Infantry	do		April 1917	Yuma, Ariz					Cmpnt. of 37th Inf. Brig.
			November 1917	Vancouver Bks., Wash.					
			January 1918	Ft. George Wright, Wash.					
			March 1918	Ft. Lawton, Wash.					
			September 1918	Cp. Dodge, Iowa.					
			December 1918	Cp. Grant, Ill.					
			November 1919	Cp. Custer, Mich					Active through 1919.
15th Infantry	do		April 1917	Tientsin, China					At Tientsin through December 1919.
16th Infantry	do		do	Cp. Newton D. Baker, Tex.					Cmpnt. of 1st Inf. Brig.
			May 1917	Ft. Bliss, Tex.					
			June 1917	P. of E., Hoboken	June 1917.				
			September 1919	Cp. Merritt, N. J		September 1919.			
			do	Cp. Meade, Md.					
			October 1919	Cp. Zachary Taylor, Ky.					Active through 1919.
17th Infantry	do		April 1917	Ft. McPherson, Ga.					Cmpnt. of 21st Inf. Brig.
			August 1917	Chickamauga Park, Ga.					
			March 1918	Charleston, S. C.					
			June 1918	Cp. Sevier, S. C.					
			July 1918	Cp. Meade, Md					Active through 1919.

REGIMENTS—Continued

Unit designation and redesignation	Organization		Stations in United States		Overseas		Demobilization		Remarks
	Month and year	Place	Month and year	Place	From—	To—	Month and year	Place	
18th Infantry	Organized 1861		April 1917	Cp. Harry J. Jones, Douglas, Ariz.					Cmpnt. of 1st Inf. Brig.
			June 1917	P. of E., Hoboken	June 1917.				
			September 1919	Cp. Merritt, N. J.		September 1919.			
			do	Cp. Meade, Md.					
			October 1919	Cp. Zachary Taylor, Ky.					Active through 1919.
19th Infantry	do		April 1917	Ft. Sam Houston, Tex.					Cmpnt. of 35th Inf. Brig.
			June 1918	Cp. Travis, Tex.					
			March 1919	Cp. Harry J. Jones, Douglas, Ariz.					Active through 1919.
20th Infantry	do		April 1917	Cp. Fort Bliss, Tex.					Cmpnt. of 20th Inf. Brig.
			May 1917	Ft. Douglas, Utah.					
			June 1918	Cp. Funston, Kans.					
			December 1918	Ft. Leavenworth, Kans.					
			February 1919	Ft. Riley, Kans.					
			July 1919	Ft. Crook, Nebr.					Active through 1919.
21st Infantry	Organized 1862		April 1917	San Diego, Calif.					Cmpnt. of 31st Inf. Brig.
			August 1918	Cp. Kearny, Calif.					
			February 1919	Vancouver Bks., Wash.					
			March 1919	Ft. George Wright, Wash.					Active through 1919.
22d Infantry	Organized 1866		April 1917	Ft. Jay, N. Y.					Guarding installations in E. Dept. through 1919.

23d Infantry	Organized 1861		do	Cp. Cotton, Tex.					Cmpnt. of 3d Inf. Brig.
			May 1917	Syracuse, N. Y.					
			September 1917	P. of E., Hoboken	September 1917.				
			August 1919	Cp. Merritt, N. J.		August 1919.			
			do	Cp. Travis, Tex.					Active through 1919.
24th Infantry	Organized 1866		April 1917	Cp. Furlong, N. Mex.					At Cp. Furlong through December 1919.
25th Infantry	do		do	Schofield Bks., T.H.					
			October 1918	Cp. Stephen Little, Ariz.					Patrolling Mexican border.
26th Infantry	Organized 1901		April 1917	Harlingen, Tex.					Cmpnt. of 2d Inf. Brig.
			June 1917	P. of E., Hoboken	June 1917.				
			September 1919	Cp. Merritt, N. J.		September 1919.			
			do	Cp. Meade, Md.					
			October 1919	Cp. Zachary Taylor, Ky.					Active through 1919.
27th Infantry	do		April 1917	Manila, P. I.					
			August 1918	Vladivostok, Russia.					Duty A. E. F. Siberia, through December 1919.
28th Infantry	do		April 1917	Ft. Ringgold, Tex.					Cmpnt. of 2d Inf. Brig.
			June 1917	P. of E., Hoboken	June 1917.				
			August 1919	Cp. Merritt, N. J.		August 1919.			
			September 1919	Cp. Meade, Md.					
			October 1919	Cp. Zachary Taylor, Ky.					Active through 1919.
29th Infantry	do		April 1917	Cp. Gaillard, C. Z.					Cmpnt. of 34th Inf. Brig.
			September 1918	Cp. Beauregard, La.					
			March 1919	Cp. Shelby, Miss.					
			October 1919	Cp. Benning, Ga.					Active through 1919.

REGIMENTS—Continued

Unit designation and redesignation	Organization: Month and year	Organization: Place	Stations in United States: Month and year	Stations in United States: Place	Overseas: From—	Overseas: To—	Demobilization: Month and year	Demobilization: Place	Remarks
30th Infantry	Organized 1901		April 1917	Cp. Eagle Pass, Tex.					Cmpnt. of 6th Inf Brig.
			May 1917	Syracuse, N. Y.					
			October 1917	Cp. Greene, N. C.					
			March 1918	Cp. Merritt, N. J.					
			April 1918	P. of E., Hoboken	April 1918.				
			August 1919	Cp. Merritt, N. J.		August 1919.			
			do	Cp. Pike, Ark					Active through 1919.
31st Infantry	Organized 1916		April 1917	Manila, P. I.					
			August 1918	Vladivostok, Russia.					Duty A. E. F., Siberia, through December 1919.
32d Infantry	do		April 1917	SchofieldBks., T. H.					Cmpnt. of 32d Inf. Brig.
			July 1918	Cp. Kearny, Calif.					Active through 1919.
33d Infantry	do		April 1917	Gatun, C. Z					Duty Panama Canal Dept. through December 1919.
34th Infantry	do		do	Marfa, Tex					Cmpnt. of 14th Inf. Brig.
			May 1917	Cp. Fort Bliss, Tex.					
			June 1918	Cp. MacArthur, Tex.					
			July 1918	Cp. Merritt, N. J.					
			August 1918	P. of E., Hoboken	August 1918.				
			June 1919	Cp. Merritt, N. J.		June 1919.			
			do	Cp. Funston, Kans.					Active through 1919.
35th Infantry	do		April 1917	Nogales, Ariz.					Cmpnt. of 36th Inf. Brig.

			August 1918	Cp. Travis, Tex.					Patrolling Mexican Border.
			November 1918	Cp. Lewis, Wash.					Active through 1919.
36th Infantry	do		April 1917	Ft. Clark, Tex.					Cmpnt. of 23d Inf. Brig.
			June 1917	Ft. Snelling, Minn.					
			August 1918	Cp. Devens, Mass.					Active through 1919.
37th Infantry	do		April 1917	Ft. McIntosh, Tex.					Patrolling Mexican Border.
38th Infantry	June 1917	Syracuse, N. Y.	October 1917	Cp. Greene, N. C.					Orgzd. fr. 30th Inf.
			March 1918	Cp. Merritt, N. J.					Cmpnt. of 6th Inf. Brig.
			do	P. of E., Hoboken	March 1918.				
			August 1919	Cp. Merritt, N. J.		August 1919.			
			do	Cp. Pike, Ark.					Active through 1919.
39th Infantry	do	do	October 1917	Cp. Greene, N. C.					Orgzd. fr. 30th Inf.
			April 1918	Cp. Mills, N. Y.					Cmpnt. of 7th Inf. Brig.
			May 1918	P. of E., Hoboken	May 1918.				
			August 1919	Cp. Merritt, N. J.		August 1919.			
			do	Cp. Dodge, Iowa					Active through 1919.
40th Infantry	do	Ft. Snelling, Minn.	December 1917	Ft. Sheridan, Ill.					Orgzd. fr. 36th Inf.
			July 1918	Cp. Custer, Mich.					Cmpnt. of 28th Inf. Brig.
			December 1918	Cp. Sherman, Ohio.					Active through 1919.
41st Infantry	do	do	October 1917	Ft. Crook, Nebr.					Orgzd. fr. 36th Inf.
			June 1918	Cp. Funston, Kans.					Cmpnt. of 19th Inf. Brig.
			November 1919	Cp. Upton, N. Y.					Active through 1919.
42d Infantry	do	Ft. Douglas, Utah	November 1917	Cp. Dodge, Iowa					Orgzd. fr. 20th Inf.
			March 1918	Picatinny Arsenal, N. J.					Cmpnt. of 24th Inf. Brig.
			July 1918	Cp. Devens, Mass.					
			December 1918	Cp. Upton, N. Y.					Active through 1919.

REGIMENTS—Continued

Unit designation and redesignation	Organization		Stations in United States		Overseas		Demobilization		Remarks
	Month and year	Place	Month and year	Place	From—	To—	Month and year	Place	
43d Infantry	June 1917	Ft. Douglas, Utah	November 1917	Cp. Pike, Ark					Orgzd. fr. 20th Inf.
			February 1918	New Orleans, La					Cmpnt. of 29th Inf. Brig.
			July 1918	Cp. Logan, Tex.					
			March 1919	Cp. Travis, Tex.					
			August 1919	Cp. Lee, Va					Active through 1919.
44th Infantry	do	Vancouver Bks., Wash.	November 1917	Cp. Lewis, Wash					Orgzd. fr. 14th Inf.
			December 1918	Presidio of San Francisco, Calif.					Cmpnt. of 26th Inf. Brig. Active through 1919.
45th Infantry	May 1917	Ft. Benjamin Harrison, Ind.	November 1917	Cp. Zachary Taylor, Ky.					Orgzd. fr. 10th Inf.
			April 1918	Cp. Gordon, Ga					Cmpnt. of 17th Inf. Brig.
			June 1918	Cp. Sheridan, Ala.					
			December 1918	Cp. Gordon, Ga.					
			September 1919	Cp. Dix, N. J.					Active through 1919.
46th Infantry	June 1917	do	November 1917	Cp. Zachary Taylor, Ky.					Orgzd. fr. 10th Inf.
			April 1918	Cp. Gordon, Ga					Cmpnt. of 18th Inf. Brig.
			May 1918	Cp. Sheridan, Ala.					
			March 1919	Ft. Oglethorpe, Ga.					
			August 1919	Cp. Jackson, S. C					Active through 1919.
47th Infantry	do	Syracuse, N. Y	October 1917	Cp. Greene, N. C					Orgzd. fr. 9th Inf.
			April 1918	Cp. Mills, N. Y					Cmpnt. of 7th Inf. Brig.
			May 1918	P. of E., Hoboken	May 1918.				
			July 1919	Cp. Mills, N. Y		July 1919.			
			August 1919	Cp. Dodge, Iowa					Active through 1919.

48th Infantry	do	do	September 1917	Cp. Hill, Va.					Orgzd. fr. 9th Inf.
			December 1917	Cp. Stuart, Va.					Cmpnt. of 39th Inf. Brig.
			August 1918	Cp. Sevier, S. C.					
			December 1918	Cp. Jackson, S. C.					Active through 1919.
49th Infantry	do	do	September 1917	Cp. Merritt, N. J.					Orgzd. fr. 23d Inf.
			June 1918	Cp. Upton, N. Y.					
			July 1918	P. of E., Hoboken	July 1918				Attached to 83d Div. while overseas.
			January 1919	Cp. Merritt, N. J.		January 1919.			
			do	Ft. Leavenworth, Kans.					
			August 1919	Ft. Snelling, Minn.					Active through 1919.
50th Infantry	do	do	November 1917	Cp. Greene, N. C.					Orgzd. fr. 23d Inf.
			March 1918	Curtis Bay, Md.					Cmpnt. of 40th Inf. Brig.
			August 1918	Cp. Sevier, S. C.					
			December 1918	Cp. Dix, N. J.					
			October 1919	P. of E., Hoboken	October 1919				Duty A. F. in G. through December 1919.
51st Infantry	do	Chickamauga Park, Ga.	June 1918	Cp. Mills, N. Y.					Orgzd. fr. 11th Inf.
			July 1918	P. of E., Hoboken	July 1918				Cmpnt. of 11th Inf. Brig.
			June 1919	Cp. Merritt, N. J.		June 1919.			
			do	Cp. Grant, Ill.					Active through 1919.
52d Infantry	do	do	June 1918	Cp. Upton, N. Y.					Orgzd. fr. 11th Inf.
			July 1918	P. of E., Hoboken	July 1918				Cmpnt. of 11th Inf. Brig.
			June 1919	Cp. Merritt, N. J.		June 1919.			
			do	Cp. Grant, Ill.					Active through 1919.
53d Infantry	do	do	May 1918	Cp. Wadsworth, S. C.					Orgzd. fr. 6th Inf.
			June 1918	Cp. Mills, N. Y.					Cmpnt. of 12th Inf. Brig.
			July 1918	P. of E., Hoboken	July 1918.				
			June 1919	Cp. Mills, N. Y.		June 1919.			
			do	Cp. Grant, Ill.					Active through 1919.

REGIMENTS—Continued

Unit designation and redesignation	Organization		Stations in United States		Overseas		Demobilization		Remarks
	Month and year	Place	Month and year	Place	From—	To—	Month and year	Place	
54th Infantry	June 1917	Chicamauga Park, Ga.	May 1918	Cp. Wadsworth, S. C.					Orgzd. fr. 6th Inf.
			June 1918	Cp. Mills, N. Y.					Cmpnt. of 12th Inf. Brig.
			July 1918	P. of E., Hoboken	July 1918.				
			June 1919	Cp. Mills, N. Y.		June 1919.			
			do	Cp. Grant, Ill.					
			July 1919	Ft. Leavenworth, Kans.					
			August 1919	Cp. Grant, Ill					Active through 1919.
55th Infantry	do	Ft. McPherson, Ga.	July 1917	Chicamauga Park, Ga.					Orgzd. fr. 17th Inf.
			February 1918	Cp. MacArthur, Tex.					Cmpnt. of 13th Inf. Brig.
			July 1918	Cp. Merritt, N. J.					
			August 1918	P. of E., Hoboken	August 1918.				
			June 1919	Cp. Merritt, N. J.		June 1919.			
			do	Cp. Funston, Kans.					Active through 1919.
56th Infantry	do	Ft. Oglethorpe, Ga.	July 1917	Chickamauga Park, Ga.					Orgzd. fr. 17th Inf.
			February 1918	Cp. MacArthur, Tex.					Cmpnt. of 13th Inf. Brig.
			July 1918	Cp. Merritt, N. J.					
			August 1918	P. of E., Hoboken	August 1918.				
			June 1919	Cp. Mills, N. Y.		June 1919.			
			July 1919	Cp. Funston, Kans.					Active through 1919.
57th Infantry	do	Cp. Wilson, Tex	July 1917	Cp. Funston, Tex.					Orgzd. fr. 19th Inf.
			October 1917	San Benito, Tex					Cmpnt. of 30th Inf. Brig.
			November 1917	Brownsville, Tex.					

			December 1917	Houston, Tex.					
			May 1918	Cp. Logan, Tex.					
			December 1918	Cp. Pike, Ark.					
			November 1919	Cp. Dix, N. J.					Active through 1919.
58th Infantry	do	Gettysburg, Pa.	November 1917	Cp. Greene, N. C.					
			April 1918	Cp. Mills, N. Y.					Orgsd. fr. 4th Inf.
			May 1918	P. of E., Hoboken	May 1918.				Cmpnt. of 8th Inf. Brig.
			August 1919	Cp. Merritt, N. J.		August 1919.			
			do	Cp. Dodge, Iowa					Active through 1919.
59th Infantry	do	do	November 1917	Cp. Greene, N. C.					
			April 1918	Cp. Mills, N. Y.					Orgsd. fr. 4th Inf.
			May 1918	P. of E., Hoboken	May 1918.				Cmpnt. of 8th Inf. Brig.
			August 1919	Cp. Merritt, N. J.		August 1919.			
			do	Cp. Dodge, Iowa					Active through 1919.
60th Infantry	do	do	November 1917	Cp. Greene, N. C.					
			April 1918	Cp. Merritt, N. J.					Orgsd. fr. 7th Inf.
			do	P. of E., Hoboken	April 1918.				Cmpnt. of 9th Inf. Brig.
			July 1919	Cp. Mills, N. Y.		July 1919.			
			do	Cp. Gordon, Ga.					Active through 1919.
61st Infantry	do	do	November 1917	Cp. Greene, N. C.					
			April 1918	Cp. Merritt, N. J.					Orgsd. fr. 7th Inf.
			do	P. of E., Hoboken	April 1918.				Cmpnt. of 9th Inf. Brig.
			July 1919	Cp. Mills, N. Y.		July 1919.			
			do	Cp. Gordon, Ga.					Active through 1919.
62d Infantry	do	Presidio of San Francisco, Calif.	January 1918	Cp. Fremont, Calif.					Orgsd. fr. 12th Inf.
			October 1918	Cp. Mills, N. Y.					Cmpnt. of 15th Inf. Brig.
			November 1918	Cp. Lee, Va.					Active through 1919.
63d Infantry	do	do	August 1918	Cp. Meade, Md.					Orgsd. fr. 12th Inf.
			January 1919	East Potomac Park, D. C.					Cmpnt. of 22d Inf. Brig.
			June 1919	Madison Bks., N. Y.					Active through 1919.

REGIMENTS—Continued

Unit designation and redesignation	Organization		Stations in United States		Overseas		Demobilization		Remarks
	Month and year	Place	Month and year	Place	From—	To—	Month and year	Place	
64th Infantry	June 1917	Cp. Baker, Tex	June 1917	Cp. Fort Bliss, Tex.					Orgzd. fr. 34th Inf.
			June 1918	Cp. MacArthur, Tex.					Cmpnt. of 14th Inf. Brig.
			August 1918	Cp. Merritt, N. J.					
			do	P. of E., Hoboken	August 1918.				
			June 1919	Cp. Mills, N. Y		June 1919.			
			do	Cp. Funston, Kans.					Active through 1919.
65th Infantry									See Puerto Rico Regt. of Inf.
66th Infantry									Never orgzd.
67th Infantry	July 1918	Cp. Sheridan, Ala					February 1919	Cp. Sheridan, Ala	Orgzd. fr. 45th Inf. Cmpnt. of 17th Inf. Brig.
68th Infantry	do	do					do	do	Orgzd. fr. 46th Inf. Cmpnt. of 18th Inf. Brig.
69th Infantry	August 1918	Cp. Funston, Kans.					do	Cp. Funston, Kans.	Orgzd. fr. 41st Inf. Cmpnt. of 19th Inf. Brig.
70th Infantry	do	do					do	do	Orgzd. fr. 20th Inf. Cmpnt. of 20th Inf. Brig.
71st Infantry	do	Cp. Meade, Md					do	Cp. Meade, Md	Orgzd. fr. 17th Inf. Cmpnt. of 21st Inf. Brig.
72d Infantry	September 1918	do					do	do	Orgzd. fr. 63d Inf. Cmpnt. of 22d Inf. Brig.
73d Infantry	July 1918	Cp. Devens, Mass.					January 1919	Cp. Devens, Mass.	Cmpnt. of 23d Inf. Brig.

74th Infantry	do	do					do	do	Cmpnt. of 24th Inf. Brig.
75th Infantry	August 1918	Cp. Lewis, Wash					February 1919	Cp. Lewis, Wash	Orgzd. fr. 1st Inf. Cmpnt. of 25th Inf. Brig.
76th Infantry	do	do					March 1919	do	Orgzd. fr. 44th Inf. Cmpnt. of 26th Inf. Brig.
77th Infantry	do	Cp. Custer, Mich					February 1919	Cp. Custer, Mich	Orgzd. fr. 10th Inf. Cmpnt. of 27th Inf. Brig.
78th Infantry	do	do					do	do	Orgzd. fr. 40th Inf. Cmpnt. of 28th Inf. Brig.
79th Infantry	September 1918	Cp. Logan, Tex					do	Cp. Logan, Tex	Orgzd. fr. 43d Inf. Cmpnt. of 29th Inf. Brig.
80th Infantry	do	do					do	do	Orgzd. fr. 57th Inf. Cmpnt. of 30th Inf. Brig.
81st Infantry	do	Cp. Kearny, Calif					do	Cp. Kearny, Calif	Orgzd. fr. 21st Inf. Cmpnt. of 31st Inf. Brig.
82d Infantry	do	do					do	do	Orgzd. fr. 32d Inf. Cmpnt. of 32d Inf. Brig.
83d Infantry	August 1918	Cp. Beauregard, La.					January 1919	Cp. Beauregard, La.	Cmpnt. of 33d Inf. Brig.
84th Infantry	September 1918	do					do	do	Cmpnt. of 34th Inf. Brig.
85th Infantry	do	Cp. Travis, Tex					February 1919	Cp. Travis, Tex	Orgzd. fr. 19th Inf. Cmpnt. of 35th Inf. Brig.
86th Infantry	do	do					do	do	Orgzd. fr. 35th Inf. Cmpnt. of 36th Inf. Brig.
87th Infantry	do	Cp. Dodge, Iowa					January 1919	Cp. Dodge, Iowa	Orgzd. fr. 14th Inf. Cmpnt. of 37th Inf. Brig.

REGIMENTS—Continued

Unit designation and redesignation	Organization		Stations in United States		Overseas		Demobilization		Remarks
	Month and year	Place	Month and year	Place	From—	To—	Month and year	Place	
88th Infantry	September 1918	Cp. Dodge, Iowa					January 1918	Cp. Dodge, Iowa	Orgzd. fr. 2d Inf. Cmpnt. of 38th Inf. Brig.
89th Infantry	August 1918	Cp. Sevier, S. C					March 1919	Cp. Sevier, S. C	Orgzd. fr. 48th Inf. Cmpnt. of 39th Inf. Brig.
90th Infantry	do	do					do	do	Orgzd. fr. 50th Inf. Cmpnt. of 40th Inf. Brig.
91st to 100th Infantry									Never orgzd.
101st Infantry	August 1917	Framingham, Mass.	September 1917	P. of E., Hoboken	September 1917	April 1919	April 1919	Cp. Devens, Mass	Cmpnt. of 51st Inf. Brig.
102d Infantry	do	New Haven, Conn	do	P. of E., Montreal	do	do	do	do	Do.
103d Infantry	do	Westfield, Mass	do	P. of E., Hoboken	do	do	do	do	Cmpnt. of 52d Inf. Brig.
104th Infantry	do	Cp. Bartlett, Mass.	do	P. of E., Hoboken and Montreal.	do	do	do	do	Do.
105th Infantry	October 1917	Cp. Wadsworth, S. C.	May 1918	Cp. Stuart, Va					Cmpnt. of 53d Inf. Brig.
			do	P. of E., Newport News.	May 1918.				
			March 1919	Cp. Mills, N. Y		March 1919	April 1919	Cp. Upton, N. Y.	
106th Infantry	do	do	May 1918	P. of E., Hoboken	May 1918				Do.
			March 1919	Cp. Mills, N. Y		March 1919	April 1919	Cp. Upton, N. Y.	
107th Infantry	do	do	April 1918	Cp. Stuart, Va					Cmpnt. of 54th Inf. Brig.
			May 1918	P. of E., Newport News.	May 1918.				
			March 1919	Cp. Merritt, N. J		March 1919	April 1919	Cp. Upton, N. Y.	
108th Infantry	do	do	May 1918	Cp. Stuart, Va					Do.
			do	P. of E., Newport News.	May 1918.				
			March 1919	Cp. Merritt, N. J		March 1919	March 1919	Cp. Upton, N. Y.	

109th Infantry	September 1917	Cp. Hancock, Ga.	April 1918	Cp. Upton, N. Y.					Cmpnt. of 55th Inf. Brig.
			May 1918	P. of E., Hoboken	May 1918	May 1919	May 1919	Cp. Dix, N. J.	Do.
110th Infantry	do	do	April 1918	Cp. Merritt, N. J.					
			May 1918	P. of E., Hoboken	May 1918	May 1919	May 1919	Cp. Dix, N. J.	
111th Infantry	do	do	April 1918	Cp. Upton, N. Y.					Cmpnt. of 56th Inf. Brig.
			May 1918	P. of E., Hoboken	May 1918	April 1919	May 1919	Cp. Dix, N. J.	Do.
112th Infantry	do	do	do	Cp. Upton, N. Y.					
			do	P. of E., Hoboken	May 1918	April 1919	May 1919	Cp. Dix, N. J.	
113th Infantry	October 1917	Cp. McClellan, Ala.	June 1918	Cp. Stuart, Va.					Cmpnt. of 57th Inf. Brig.
			do	P. of E., Newport News.	June 1918	May 1919	May 1919	Cp. Merritt, N. J.	
114th Infantry	do	do	do	Cp. Stuart, Va.					Do.
			do	P. of E., Newport News.	June 1918.				
			May 1919	Cp. Stuart, Va.		May 1919	May 1919	Cp. Dix, N. J.	
115th Infantry	do	do	June 1918	P. of E., Hoboken	June 1918				Cmpnt. of 58th Inf. Brig.
			May 1919	Cp. Stuart, Va.		May 1919	June 1919	Cp. Meade, Md.	
116th Infantry	do	do	June 1918	P. of E., Hoboken	June 1918				Do.
			May 1919	Cp. Stuart, Va.		May 1919	May 1919	Cp. Lee, Va.	
117th Infantry	September 1917	Cp. Sevier, S. C.	May 1918	Cp. Mills, N. Y.					Cmpnt. of 59th Inf. Brig.
			do	P. of E., Hoboken	May 1918.				
			March 1919	Cp. Jackson, S. C.		March 1919	April 1919	Ft. Oglethorpe, Ga.	
118th Infantry	do	do	May 1918	Cp. Mills, N. Y.					Do.
			do	P. of E., Hoboken	May 1918	March 1919	April 1919	Cp. Jackson, S. C.	
119th Infantry	do	do	do	Cp. Merritt, N. J.					Cmpnt. of 60th Inf. Brig.
			do	P. of E., Hoboken	May 1918	April 1919	April 1919	Cp. Jackson, S. C.	
120th Infantry	do	do	do	Cp. Merritt, N. J.					Do.
			do	P. of E., Boston	May 1918	April 1919	April 1919	Cp. Jackson, S. C.	
121st Infantry	do	Cp. Wheeler, Ga.	September 1918	Cp. Mills, N. Y.					Cmpnt. of 61st Inf. Brig.
			October 1918	P. of E., Hoboken	October 1918				Skeletonized November 1918.
			December 1918	Cp. Merritt, N. J.		December 1918	January 1919	Cp. Gordon, Ga.	Record cadre only.

REGIMENTS—Continued

Unit designation and redesignation	Organization		Stations in United States		Overseas		Demobilization		Remarks
	Month and year	Place	Month and year	Place	From—	To—	Month and year	Place	
122d Infantry	September 1917	Cp. Wheeler, Ga.	September 1918	Cp. Mills, N. Y.					Cmpnt. of 61st Inf. Brig.
			October 1918	P. of E., Hoboken	October 1918				Skeletonized November 1918.
			December 1918	Cp. Merritt, N. J.		December 1918	January 1919	Cp. Gordon, Ga.	Record cadre only.
123d Infantry	do	do	September 1918	Cp. Mills, N. Y.					Cmpnt. of 62d Inf. Brig.
			October 1918	P. of E., Hoboken	October 1918				Skeletonized November 1918.
			December 1918	Cp. Merritt, N. J.		December 1918	January 1919	Cp. Gordon, Ga.	Record cadre only
124th Infantry	do	do	September 1918	Cp. Mills, N. Y.					Cmpnt. of 62d Inf. Brig.
			October 1918	P. of E., Hoboken	October 1918				Skeletonized November 1918.
			December 1918	Cp. Merritt, N. J.		December 1918	January 1919	Cp. Gordon, Ga.	Record cadre only.
125th Infantry	do	Cp. MacArthur, Tex.	January 1918	do					Cmpnt. of 63d Inf. Brig.
			February 1918	P. of E., Hoboken	February 1918.				
			May 1919	Cp. Mills, N. Y.		May 1919	May 1919	Cp. Custer, Mich.	
126th Infantry	do	do	January 1918	Cp. Merritt, N. J.					Do.
			February 1918	P. of E., Hoboken	February 1918.				
			May 1919	Cp. Devens, Mass.		May 1919	May 1919	Cp. Custer, Mich.	
127th Infantry	do	do	January 1918	Cp. Merritt, N. J.					Cmpnt. of 64th Inf. Brig.
			February 1918	P. of E., Hoboken	February 1918.				
			May 1919	Cp. Merritt, N. J.		May 1919	May 1919	Cp. Grant, Ill.	
128th Infantry	do	do	February 1918	do					Do.
			do	P. of E., Hoboken	February 1918.				
			May 1919	Cp. Mills, N. Y.		May 1919	May 1919	Cp. Grant, Ill.	
129th Infantry	do	Cp. Logan, Tex.	May 1918	Cp. Upton, N. Y.					Cmpnt. of 65th Inf. Brig.
			do	P. of E., Hoboken	May 1918.				
			May 1919	Cp. Merritt, N. J.		May 1919	June 1919	Cp. Grant, Ill.	

130th Infantry	October 1917	do	May 1918	Cp. Upton, N. Y.					Do.
			do	P. of E., Hoboken	May 1918.				
			May 1919	Cp. Mills, N. Y.		May 1919	May 1919	Cp. Grant, Ill.	
131st Infantry	do	do	May 1918	Cp. Upton, N. Y.					Cmpnt. of 66th Inf. Brig.
			do	P. of E., Hoboken	May 1918.				
			May 1919	Cp. Mills, N. Y.		May 1919	June 1919	Cp. Grant, Ill.	
132d Infantry	do	do	May 1918	Cp. Upton, N. Y.					Do.
			do	P. of E., Hoboken	May 1918.				
			May 1919	Cp. Mills, N. Y.		May 1919	May 1919	Cp. Grant, Ill.	
133d Infantry	do	Cp. Cody, N. Mex.	August 1918	Cp. Dix, N. J.					Cmpnt. of 67th Inf. Brig.
			October 1918	P. of E., Hoboken	October 1918				Skeletonized November 1918.
			January 1919	Cp. Merritt, N. J.		January 1919	February 1919	Cp. Grant, Ill.	Record cadre only.
134th Infantry	September 1917	do	August 1918	Cp. Dix, N. J.					Cmpnt. of 67th Inf. Brig.
			October 1918	P. of E., Hoboken	October 1918				Skeletonized November 1918.
			January 1919	Cp. Merritt, N. J.		January 1919	February 1919	Cp. Grant, Ill.	Record cadre only.
135th Infantry	do	Ft. Snelling, Minn.	October 1917	Cp. Cody, N. Mex.					Cmpnt. of 68th Inf. Brig.
			August 1918	Cp. Dix, N. J.					Skeletonized November 1918.
			October 1918	P. of E., Hoboken	October 1918.				
			January 1919	Cp. Merritt, N. J.		January 1919	February 1919	Cp. Grant, Ill.	Record cadre only.
136th Infantry	do	Cp. Cody, N. Mex.	August 1918	Cp. Dix, N. J.					Cmpnt. of 68th Inf. Brig.
			October 1918	P. of E., Hoboken	October 1918				Skeletonized November 1918.
			January 1919	Cp. Merritt, N. J.		January 1919	February 1919	Cp. Grant, Ill.	Record cadre only.
137th Infantry	October 1917	Cp. Doniphan, Okla.	April 1918	Cp. Mills, N. Y.					Cmpnt. of 69th Inf. Brig.
			do	P. of E., Hoboken	April 1918.				
			April 1919	Cp. Upton, N. Y.		April 1919	May 1919	Cp. Funston, Kans.	
138th Infantry	do	do	April 1918	Cp. Mills, N. Y.					Do.
			May 1918	P. of E., Hoboken	May 1918.				
			April 1919	Cp. Hill, Va.		April 1919	May 1919	Cp. Funston, Kans.	
139th Infantry	do	do	April 1918	Cp. Mills, N. Y.					Cmpnt. of 70th Inf. Brig.
			do	P. of E., Hoboken	April 1918.				
			April 1919	Cp. Stuart, Va.		April 1919	May 1919	Cp. Funston, Kans.	

REGIMENTS—Continued

Unit designation and redesignation	Organization		Stations in United States		Overseas		Demobilization		Remarks
	Month and year	Place	Month and year	Place	From—	To—	Month and year	Place	
140th Infantry	**October 1917**	**Cp. Doniphan, Okla.**	April 1918	Cp. Mills, N. Y.					**Cmpnt. of 70th Inf. Brig.**
			do	P. of E., Hoboken	April 1918.				
			April 1919	Cp. Stuart, Va.		April 1919	May 1919	Cp. Funston, Kans.	
141st Infantry	do	Cp. Bowie, Tex.	July 1918	Cp. Mills, N. Y.					Cmpnt. of 71st Inf. Brig.
			do	P. of E., Hoboken	July 1918.				
			June 1919	Cp. Mills, N. Y.		June 1919	July 1919	Cp. Travis, Tex.	
142d Infantry	do	do	July 1918	do					Do.
			do	P. of E., Hoboken	July 1918.				
			June 1919	Cp. Mills, N. Y.		June 1919	June 1919	Cp. Bowie, Tex.	
143d Infantry	do	do	July 1918	Cp. Stuart, Va.					Cmpnt. of 72d Inf. Brig.
			do	P. of E., Newport News.	July 1918.				
			June 1919	Cp. Stuart, Va.		June 1919	June 1919	Cp. Bowie, Tex.	
144th Infantry	do	do	July 1918	Cp. Mills, N. Y.					Do.
			do	P. of E., Hoboken	July 1918.				
			June 1919	Cp. Mills, N. Y.		June 1919	June 1919	Cp. Bowie, Tex.	
145th Infantry	September 1917	Cp. Sheridan, Ala.	May 1918	Cp. Lee, Va.					Cmpnt. of 73d Inf. Brig.
			June 1918	P. of E., Hoboken	June 1918.				
			March 1919	Cp. Mills, N. Y.		March 1919	May 1919	Cp. Sherman, Ohio.	
146th Infantry	do	do	May 1918	Cp. Lee, Va.					Do.
			June 1918	P. of E., Hoboken	June 1918.				
			March 1919	Cp. Dix, N. J.		March 1919	April 1919	Cp. Sherman, Ohio.	
147th Infantry	do	do	May 1918	Cp. Lee, Va.					Cmpnt. of 74th Inf. Brig.
			June 1918	P. of E., Newport News.	June 1918.				
			March 1919	Cp. Mills, N. Y.		March 1919	April 1919	Cp. Sherman, Ohio.	
148th Infantry	do	do	May 1918	Cp. Lee, Va.					Do.
			June 1918	P. of E., Newport News.	June 1918.				
			March 1919	Cp. Mills, N. Y.		March 1919	April 1919	Cp. Sherman, Ohio.	

149th Infantry	do	Cp. Shelby, Miss.	September 1918	do					Cmpnt. of 75th Inf. Brig.
			October 1918	P. of E., Hoboken	October 1918				Skeletonized November 1918.
			December 1918	Cp. Hill, Va.		December 1918	January 1919	Cp. Zachary Taylor, Ky.	Record cadre only.
150th Infantry	do	do	September 1918	Cp. Mills, N. Y.					Cmpnt. of 75th Inf. Brig.
			October 1918	P. of E., Montreal	October 1918				Skeletonized November 1918.
			December 1918	Cp. Hill, Va.				Cp. Zachary Taylor, Ky.	Record cadre only.
151st Infantry	do	do	September 1918	Cp. Mills, N. Y.					Cmpnt. of 76th Inf. Brig.
			October 1918	P. of E., Montreal	October 1918				Skeletonized November 1918.
			December 1918	Cp. Hill, Va.		December 1918	January 1919	Cp. Zachary Taylor, Ky.	Record cadre only.
152d Infantry	do	do	September 1918	Cp. Mills, N. Y.					Cmpnt. of 76th Inf. Brig.
			October 1918	P. of E., Hoboken	October 1918				Skeletonized November 1918.
			December 1918	Cp. Hill, Va.		December 1918	January 1919	Cp. Zachary Taylor, Ky.	Record cadre only.
153d Infantry	October 1917	Cp. Pike, Ark.	November 1917	Cp. Beauregard, La.					Cmpnt. of 77th Inf. Brig.
			August 1918	Cp. Stuart, Va.					Skeletonized November 1918.
			do	P. of E., Newport News.	August 1918.				
			December 1918	Cp. Stuart, Va.		December 1918	January 1919	Cp. Beauregard, La.	Record cadre only.
154th Infantry	do	Cp. Beauregard, La.	August 1918	do					Cmpnt. of 77th Inf. Brig.
			do	P. of E., Newport News.	August 1918				Skeletonized November 1918.
			December 1918	Cp. Stuart, Va.		December 1918	January 1919	Cp. Beauregard, La.	Record cadre only.

REGIMENTS—Continued

Unit designation and redesignation	Organization		Stations in United States		Overseas		Demobilization		Remarks
	Month and year	Place	Month and year	Place	From—	To—	Month and year	Place	
155th Infantry	October 1917	Cp. Beauregard, La.	August 1918	Cp. Merritt, N. J.					Cmpnt. of 78th Inf. Brig.
			do	P. of E., Hoboken	August 1918				Skeletonized November 1918.
			December 1918	Cp. Stuart, Va.		December 1918	January 1919	Cp. Beauregard, La.	Record cadre only.
156th Infantry	do	do	August 1918	Cp. Mills, N. Y.					Cmpnt. of 78th Inf. Brig.
			do	P. of E., Hoboken	August 1918				Skeletonized November 1918.
			December 1918	Cp. Stuart, Va.		December 1918	January 1919	Cp. Beauregard, La.	Record cadre only.
157th Infantry	do	Cp. Kearny, Calif.	August 1918	Cp. Mills, N. Y.					Cmpnt. of 79th Inf. Brig.
			do	P. of E., Hoboken	August 1918.				
			April 1919	Cp. Merritt, N. J.		April 1919	April 1919	Ft. D. A. Russell, Wyo.	
158th Infantry	do	do	August 1918	Cp. Mills, N. Y.					Do.
			do	P. of E., Hoboken	August 1918.				
			April 1919	Cp. Merritt, N. J.		April 1919	May 1919	Ft. Bliss, Tex.	
159th Infantry	do	do	August 1918	Cp. Mills, N. Y.					Cmpnt. of 80th Inf. Brig.
			do	P. of E., Hoboken	August 1918.				
			April 1919	Cp. Mills, N. Y.		April 1919	May 1919	Presidio of San Francisco, Calif.	
160th Infantry	September 1917	do	August 1918	do					Do.
			do	P. of E., Hoboken	August 1918.				
			March 1919	Cp. Mills, N. Y.		March 1919	April 1919	Cp. Kearny, Calif.	
161st Infantry	October 1917	Cp. Murray, Wash.	November 1917	do					Cmpnt. of 81st Inf. Brig.
			December 1917	P. of E., Hoboken	December 1917.				
			February 1919	Cp. Morrison, Va.		February 1919	March 1919	Cp. Dodge, Iowa.	
162d Infantry	do	Cp. Greene, N. C.	November 1917	Cp. Mills, N. Y.					Do.
			December 1917	P. of E., Hoboken	December 1917	February 1919	February 1919	Cp. Dix, N. J.	

163d Infantry	September 1917	do	November 1917	Cp. Mills, N. Y.					Cmpnt. of 82d Inf. Brig.
			December 1917	Cp. Merritt, N. J.					
			do	P. of E., Hoboken	December 1917.				
			February 1919	Cp. Merritt, N. J.		February 1919	February 1919	Cp. Dix, N. J.	
164th Infantry	October 1917	do	November 1917	Cp. Mills, N. Y.					Do.
			December 1917	Cp. Merritt, N. J.					
			do	P. of E., Hoboken	December 1917	February 1919	February 1919	Cp. Dix, N. J.	
165th Infantry	August 1917	Cp. Mills, N. Y.	October 1917	do	October 1917				Cmpnt. of 83d Inf. Brig.
			April 1919	Cp. Mills, N. Y.		April 1919	May 1919	Cp. Upton, N. Y.	
166th Infantry	do	Cp. Perry, Ohio	September 1917	do					Do.
			October 1917	P. of E., Hoboken	October 1917	April 1919	May 1919	Cp. Merritt, N. J.	
167th Infantry	do	Cp. Sheridan, Ala.	September 1917	Cp. Mills, N. Y.					Cmpnt. of 84th Inf. Brig.
			November 1917	P. of E., Hoboken	November 1917.				
			April 1919	Cp. Merritt, N. J.		April 1919	May 1919	Cp. Shelby, Miss.	
168th Infantry	do	Des Moines, Iowa	September 1917	Cp. Mills, N. Y.					Do.
			November 1917	P. of E., Hoboken	November 1917.				
			April 1919	Cp. Upton, N. Y.		April 1919	May 1919	Cp. Dodge, Iowa.	
169th to 300th Infantry									Never orgzd.
301st Infantry	August 1917	Cp. Devens, Mass.	July 1918	P. of E., Hoboken	July 1918				Cmpnt. of 151st Inf. Brig.
			January 1919	Cp. Hill, Va.		January 1919	January 1919	Cp. Devens, Mass.	Skeletonized November 1918. Record cadre only.
302d Infantry	do	do	July 1918	P. of E., Hoboken	July 1918				Cmpnt. of 151st Inf. Brig.
			January 1919	Cp. Hill, Va.		January 1919	January 1919	Cp. Devens, Mass.	Skeletonized November 1918. Record cadre only.
303d Infantry	do	do	July 1918	P. of E., Montreal	July 1918				Cmpnt. of 152d Inf. Brig.
			January 1919	Cp. Hill, Va.		January 1919	January 1919	Cp. Devens, Mass.	Skeletonized November 1918. Record cadre only.
304th Infantry	do	do	July 1918	P. of E., Boston	July 1918				Cmpnt. of 152d Inf. Brig.
			January 1919	Cp. Hill, Va.		January 1919	January 1919	Cp. Devens, Mass.	Skeletonized November 1918. Record cadre only.

REGIMENTS—Continued

Unit designation and redesignation	Organisation		Stations in United States		Overseas		Demobilisation		Remarks
	Month and year	Place	Month and year	Place	From—	To—	Month and year	Place	
305th Infantry	**August 1917**	Cp. Upton, N. Y.	April 1918	P. of E., Hoboken	April 1918				Cmpnt. of 153d Inf. Brig.
			April 1919	Cp. Mills, N. Y.		April 1919	May 1919	Cp. Upton, N. Y.	
306th Infantry	do	do	April 1918	P. of E., Boston	April 1918				Do.
			April 1919	Cp. Mills, N. Y.		April 1919	May 1919	Cp. Upton, N. Y.	
307th Infantry	September 1917	do	April 1918	P. of E., Hoboken	April 1918				Cmpnt. of 154th Inf. Brig.
			April 1919	Cp. Mills, N. Y.		April 1919	May 1919	Cp. Upton, N. Y.	
308th Infantry	do	do	April 1918	P. of E., Hoboken	April 1918				Do.
			April 1919	Cp. Mills, N. Y.		April 1919	May 1919	Cp. Upton, N. Y.	
309th Infantry	do	Cp. Dix, N. J.	May 1918	P. of E., Hoboken	May 1918				Cmpnt. of 155th Inf. Brig.
			May 1919	Cp. Merritt, N. J.		May 1919	June 1919	Cp. Upton, N. Y.	
310th Infantry	do	do	May 1918	P. of E., Hoboken	May 1918	do	do	Cp. Dix, N. J.	Do.
311th Infantry	do	do	do	do	do				Cmpnt. of 156th Inf. Brig.
			May 1919	Cp. Merritt, N. J.		May 1919	May 1919	Cp. Dix, N. J.	
312th Infantry	do	do	May 1918	P. of E., Hoboken	May 1918	do	do	do	Do.
313th Infantry	August 1917	Cp. Meade, Md.	July 1918	do	July 1918				Cmpnt. of 157th Inf. Brig.
			May 1919	Cp. Stuart, Va.		May 1919	June 1919	Cp. Meade, Md.	
314th Infantry	do	do	July 1918	P. of E., Hoboken	July 1918	do	May 1919	Cp. Dix, N. J.	Do.
315th Infantry	do	do	do	do	do	do	do	do	Cmpnt. of 158th Inf. Brig.
316th Infantry	do	do	do	do	do	do	do	do	Do.
317th Infantry	September 1917	Cp. Lee, Va.	May 1918	do	May 1918				Cmpnt. of 159th Inf. Brig.
			June 1919	Cp. Stuart, Va.		June 1919	June 1919	Cp. Lee, Va.	
318th Infantry	**August 1917**	**Cp. Lee, Va.**	May 1918	**P. of E., Hoboken**	**May 1918**				Cmpnt. of 159th Inf. Brig.
			May 1919	**Cp. Stuart, Va.**		**May 1919**	**June 1919**	Cp. Lee, Va.	

319th Infantry	do	do	May 1918	P. of E., Hoboken	May 1918				Cmpnt. of 160th Inf. Brig.
			June 1919	Cp. Dix, N. J.		June 1919	June 1919	Cp. Sherman, Ohio.	
320th Infantry	do	do	May 1918	P. of E., Newport News.	May 1918				Do.
			May 1919	Cp. Dix, N. J.		May 1919	June 1919	Cp. Sherman, Ohio.	
321st Infantry	September 1917	Cp. Jackson, S. C.	May 1918	Cp. Sevier, S. C.					Cmpnt. of 161st Inf. Brig.
			July 1918	Cp. Upton, N. Y.					
			do	P. of E., Hoboken	July 1918.				
			June 1919	Cp. Stuart, Va.		June 1919	June 1919	Cp. Lee, Va.	
322d Infantry	do	do	May 1918	Cp. Sevier, S. C.					Do.
			July 1918	Cp. Upton, N. Y.					
			do	P. of E., Hoboken	July 1918	June 1919	June 1919	Cp. Morrison, Va.	
323d Infantry	do	do	May 1918	Cp. Sevier, S. C.					Cmpnt. of 162d Inf. Brig.
			July 1918	Cp. Mills, N. Y.					
			do	P. of E., Hoboken	July 1918	June 1919	June 1919	Cp. Stuart, Va.	
324th Infantry	do	do	May 1918	Cp. Sevier, S. C.					Do.
			July 1918	Cp. Mills, N. Y.					
			August 1918	P. of E., Hoboken	August 1918	June 1919	June 1919	Cp. Jackson, S. C.	
325th Infantry	do	Cp. Gordon, Ga.	April 1918	Cp. Upton, N. Y.					Cmpnt. of 163d Inf. Brig.
			do	P. of E., Hoboken	April 1918	May 1919	May 1919	Cp. Upton, N. Y.	
326th Infantry	do	do	do	Cp. Upton, N. Y.					Do.
			do	P. of E., Hoboken	April 1918.				
			June 1919	Cp. Merritt, N. J.		June 1919	June 1919	Cp. Upton, N. Y.	
327th Infantry	do	do	April 1918	Cp. Upton, N. Y.					Cmpnt. of 164th Inf. Brig.
			May 1918	P. of E., Hoboken	May 1918	May 1919	May 1919	Cp. Upton, N. Y.	
328th Infantry	do	do	April 1918	Cp. Upton, N. Y.					Do.
			May 1918	P. of E., Hoboken	May 1918.				
			May 1919	Cp. Mills, N. Y.		May 1919	May 1919	Cp. Upton, N. Y.	
329th Infantry	do	Cp. Sherman, Ohio.	May 1918	Cp. Merritt, N. J.					Cmpnt. of 165th Inf. Brig.
			June 1918	P. of E., Hoboken	June 1918.				
			January 1919	Cp. Mills, N. Y.		January 1919	February 1919	Cp. Sherman, Ohio.	
330th Infantry	do	do	May 1918	Cp. Mills, N. Y.					Do.
			June 1918	P. of E., Hoboken	June 1918.				
			January 1919	Cp. Merritt, N. J.		January 1919	March 1919	Cp. Sherman, Ohio.	

REGIMENTS—Continued

Unit designation and redesignation	Organization: Month and year	Organization: Place	Stations in United States: Month and year	Stations in United States: Place	Overseas: From—	Overseas: To—	Demobilization: Month and year	Demobilization: Place	Remarks
331st Infantry	September 1917	Cp. Sherman, Ohio.	May 1918	Cp. Merritt, N. J.					Cmpnt. of 166th Inf. Brig.
			June 1918	P. of E., Hoboken.	June 1918.				
			January 1919	Cp. Mills, N. Y.		January 1919	March 1919	Cp. Sherman, Ohio.	
332d Infantry	do	do	May 1918	Cp. Merritt, N. J.					Do.
			June 1918	P. of E., Hoboken.	June 1918.				
			April 1919	Cp. Merritt, N. J.		April 1919	June 1919	Cp. Sherman, Ohio.	
333d Infantry	August 1917	Cp. Zachary Taylor, Ky.	June 1918	Cp. Sherman, Ohio.					Cmpnt. of 167th Inf. Brig. Skeletonized November 1918. Record cadre only.
			August 1918	Cp. Mills, N. Y.					
			September 1918	P. of E., Hoboken.	September 1918.				
			January 1919	Cp. Merritt, N. J.		January 1919	February 1919	Cp. Zachary Taylor, Ky.	
334th Infantry	do	do	June 1918	Cp. Sherman, Ohio.					Cmpnt. of 167th Inf. Brig. Skeletonized November 1918. Record cadre only.
			August 1918	Cp. Mills, N. Y.					
			September 1918	P. of E., Hoboken.	September 1918.				
			January 1919	Cp. Merritt, N. J.		January 1919	February 1919	Cp. Zachary Taylor, Ky.	
335th Infantry	do	do	June 1918	Cp. Sherman, Ohio.					Cmpnt. of 168th Inf. Brig. Skeletonized November 1918. Record cadre only.
			August 1918	Cp. Mills, N. Y.					
			September 1918	P. of E., Hoboken.	September 1918				
			January 1919	Cp. Merritt, N. J.		January 1919	February 1919	Cp. Zachary Taylor, Ky.	
336th Infantry	do	do	June 1918	Cp. Sherman, Ohio.					Cmpnt. of 168th Inf. Brig. Skeletonized November 1918. Record cadre only.
			August 1918	Cp. Mills, N. Y.					
			September 1918	P. of E., Hoboken.	September 1918.				
			January 1919	Cp. Merritt, N. J.		January 1919	February 1919	Cp. Zachary Taylor, Ky.	

337th Infantry	September 1917	Cp. Custer, Mich.	July 1918	Cp. Mills, N. Y.					Cmpnt. of 169th Inf. Brig.
			do	P. of E., Hoboken	July 1918.				
338th Infantry	do	do	April 1919	Cp. Upton, N. Y.		April 1919	April 1919	Cp. Custer, Mich.	
			July 1918	Cp. Mills, N. Y.					Do.
			do	P. of E., Hoboken	July 1918.				
339th Infantry	August 1917	do	April 1919	Cp. Dix, N. J.		April 1919	April 1919	Cp. Custer, Mich.	
			July 1918	Cp. Mills, N. Y.					Cmpnt. of 170th Inf. Brig.
			do	P. of E., Hoboken	July 1918.				
340th Infantry	September 1917	do	July 1919	Cp. Devens, Mass.		July 1919	July 1919	Cp. Custer, Mich.	Do.
			July 1918	Cp. Mills, N. Y.					
			do	P. of E., Boston	July 1918.				
341st Infantry	do	Cp. Grant, Ill.	April 1919	Cp. Upton, N. Y.		April 1919	April 1919	Cp. Grant, Ill.	
			August 1918	do					Cmpnt. of 171st Inf. Brig.
			September 1918	P. of E., Hoboken	September 1918				Skeletonized November 1918.
342d Infantry	do	do	January 1919	Cp. Mills, N. Y.		January 1919	January 1919	Cp. Grant, Ill.	Record cadre only.
			August 1918	Cp. Upton, N. Y.					Cmpnt. of 171st Inf. Brig.
			September 1918	P. of E., Hoboken	September 1918				Skeletonized November 1918.
343 Infantry	August 1917	do	January 1919	Cp. Mills, N. Y.		January 1919	January 1919	Cp. Grant, Ill.	Record cadre only.
			August 1918	do					Cmpnt. of 172d Inf. Brig.
			September 1918	P. of E., Hoboken	September 1918				Skeletonized November 1918.
344th Infantry	September 1917	do	January 1919	Cp. Mills, N. Y.		January 1919	January 1919	Cp. Grant, Ill.	Record cadre only.
			August 1918	do					Cmpnt. of 172d Inf. Brig.
			September 1918	P. of E., Hoboken	September 1918				Skeletonized November 1918.
345th Infantry	do	Cp. Pike, Ark.	January 1919	Cp. Mills, N. Y.		January 1919	January 1919	Cp. Grant, Ill.	Record cadre only.
			June 1918	Cp. Dix, N. J.					Cmpnt. of 173d Inf. Brig.
346th Infantry	do	do	August 1918	P. of E., Hoboken	August 1918	January 1919	January 1919	Cp. Merritt, N. J.	
			June 1918	Cp. Dix, N. J.					Do.
			August 1918	P. of E., Hoboken	August 1918	March 1919	April 1919	Cp. Merritt, N. J.	

REGIMENTS—Continued

Unit designation and redesignation	Organization		Stations in United States		Overseas		Demobilization		Remarks
	Month and year	Place	Month and year	Place	From—	To—	Month and year	Place	
347th Infantry	September 1917	Cp. Pike, Ark.	June 1918	Cp. Dix, N. J.					Cmpnt. of 174th Inf. Brig.
			August 1918	P. of E., Philadelphia.	August 1918.				
			December 1918	Cp. Merritt, N. J.		December 1918	January 1919	Cp. Dix, N. J.	
348th Infantry	do	do	June 1918	Cp. Dix, N. J.					Do.
			August 1918	P. of E., Montreal	August 1918	March 1919	March 1919	Cp. Dix, N. J.	
349th Infantry	do	Cp. Dodge, Iowa	do	Cp. Upton, N. Y.					Cmpnt. of 175th Inf. Brig.
			do	P. of E., Hoboken	August 1918.				
			May 1919	Cp. Mills, N. Y.		May 1919	June 1919	Cp. Dodge, Iowa.	
350th Infantry	do	do	August 1918	Cp. Upton, N. Y.					Do.
			do	P. of E., Hoboken	August 1918.				
			May 1919	Cp. Alexander, Va.		May 1919	June 1919	Cp. Dodge, Iowa.	
351st Infantry	do	do	August 1918	Cp. Mills, N. Y.					Cmpnt. of 176th Inf. Brig.
			do	P. of E., Hoboken	August 1918.				
			May 1919	Cp. Morrison, Va.		May 1919	June 1919	Cp. Dodge, Iowa.	
352d Infantry	do	do	August 1918	Cp. Mills, N. Y.					Do.
			do	P. of E., Hoboken	August 1918.				
			June 1919	Cp. Hill, Va.		June 1919	June 1919	Cp. Dodge, Iowa.	
353d Infantry	do	Cp. Funston, Kans.	May 1918	Cp. Mills, N. Y.					Cmpnt. of 177th Inf. Brig.
			June 1918	P. of E., Hoboken	June 1918.				
			May 1919	Cp. Upton, N. Y.		May 1919	June 1919	Cp. Funston, Kans.	
354th Infantry	do	do	May 1918	Cp. Mills, N. Y.					Do.
			June 1918	P. of E., Hoboken	June 1918.				
			May 1919	Cp. Upton, N. Y.		May 1919	June 1919	Cp. Funston, Kans.	
355th Infantry	do	do	May 1918	Cp. Mills, N. Y.					Cmpnt. of 178th Inf. Brig.
			June 1918	P. of E., Hoboken	June 1918.				
			May 1919	Cp. Upton, N. Y.		May 1919	June 1919	Cp. Funston, Kans.	

356th Infantry	do	do	May 1918	Cp. Mills, N. Y.					Do.
			June 1918	P. of E., Hoboken	June 1918.				
			May 1919	Cp. Upton, N. Y.					
357th Infantry	August 1917	Cp. Travis, Tex.				May 1919	June 1919	Cp. Funston, Kans.	
			June 1918	Cp. Mills, N. Y.					Cmpnt. of 179th Inf. Brig.
			do	P. of E., Hoboken	June 1918.				
			June 1919	Cp. Stuart, Va.					
358th Infantry	do	do				June 1919	June 1919	Cp. Pike, Ark.	
			June 1918	Cp. Mills, N. Y.					Do.
			do	P. of E., Hoboken	June 1918.				
			June 1919	Cp. Devens, Mass.					
359th Infantry	September 1917	do				June 1919	June 1919	Cp. Pike, Ark.	
			June 1918	Cp. Mills, N. Y.					Cmpnt. of 180th Inf. Brig.
			do	P. of E., Hoboken	June 1918.				
			June 1919	Cp. Stuart, Va.					
360th Infantry	August 1917	do				June 1919	June 1919	Cp. Bowie, Tex.	
			June 1918	Cp. Mills, N. Y.					Do.
			do	P. of E., Hoboken	June 1918.				
			June 1919	Cp. Devens, Mass.					
361st Infantry	September 1917	Cp. Lewis, Wash.				June 1919	June 1919	Cp. Travis, Tex.	
			June 1918	Cp. Merritt, N. J.					Cmpnt. of 181st Inf. Brig.
			July 1918	P. of E., Hoboken	July 1918				
362d Infantry	do	do				April 1919	April 1919	Cp. Merritt, N. J.	
			June 1918	Cp. Merritt, N. J.					Do.
			July 1918	P. of E., Hoboken	July 1918.				
			April 1918	Cp. Merritt, N. J.		April 1919	May 1919	Ft. D. A. Russell, Wyo.	
363d Infantry	do	do							
			June 1918	do					Cmpnt. of 182d Inf. Brig.
			July 1918	P. of E., Hoboken	July 1918.				
			April 1919	Cp. Merritt, N. J.		April 1919	May 1919	Presidio of San Francisco, Calif.	
364th Infantry	do	do							
			July 1918	do					Do.
			do	P. of E., Hoboken	July 1918.				
			March 1919	Cp. Upton, N. Y.					
365th Infantry	October 1917	Cp. Grant, Ill.				March 1919	April 1919	Cp. Kearny, Calif.	
			May 1918	do					Cmpnt. of 183d Inf. Brig.
			June 1918	P. of E., Hoboken	June 1918				
366th Infantry	November 1917	Cp. Dodge, Iowa				February 1919	March 1919	Cp. Upton, N. Y.	
			do	Cp. Upton, N. Y.					Do.
			do	P. of E., Hoboken	June 1918.				
			February 1919	Cp. Upton, N. Y.		February 1919	March 1919	Ft. Oglethorpe, Ga.	
367th Infantry	do	Cp. Upton, N. Y.	June 1918	P. of E., Hoboken	June 1918				
									Cmpnt. of 184th Inf. Brig.
			February 1919	Cp. Upton, N. Y.		February 1919	March 1919	Cp. Meade, Md.	

REGIMENTS—Continued

Unit designation and redesignation	Organization		Stations in United States		Overseas		Demobilization		Remarks
	Month and year	Place	Month and year	Place	From—	To—	Month and year	Place	
368th Infantry	October 1917	Cp. Meade, Md.	June 1918	P. of E., Hoboken	June 1918				Cmpnt. of 184th Inf. Brig.
			February 1919	Cp. Upton, N. Y.		February 1919	March 1919	Cp. Meade, Md.	
369th Infantry	November 1917	Cp. Merritt, N. J.	December 1917	P. of E., Hoboken	December 1917	do	February 1919	Cp. Upton, N. Y.	Cmpnt. of 185th Inf. Brig.
370th Infantry	December 1917	Cp. Logan, Tex.	March 1918	Cp. Stuart, Va.					Do.
			April 1918	P. of E., Newport News.	April 1918.				
			February 1919	Cp. Upton, N. Y.		February 1919	March 1919	Cp. Grant, Ill.	
371st Infantry	do	Cp. Jackson, S. C.	April 1918	P. of E., Newport News.	April 1918				Cmpnt. of 186th Inf. Brig.
			February 1919	Cp. Upton, N. Y.		February 1919	February 1919	Cp. Jackson, S. C.	
372d Infantry	January 1918	Cp. Stuart, Va.	March 1918	P. of E., Newport News.	March 1918				Do.
			February 1919	Cp. Upton, N. Y.		February 1919	March 1919	Cp. Sherman, Ohio.	
373d Infantry	July 1918	Cp. Las Casas, P. R.					January 1919	Cp. Las Casas, P. R.	
374th Infantry	do	do					do	do	
375th Infantry	do	do					do	do	
376th to 378th Infantry.									Never orgzd.
379th Infantry	September 1918	Cp. Sherman, Ohio.					December 1918	Cp. Sherman, Ohio.	
380th Infantry	do	do					do	Do.	
381st and 382d Infantry.									Do.
383d Infantry	September 1918	Cp. Wadsworth, S. C.					January 1919	Cp. Wadsworth, S. C.	Cmpnt. of 192d Inf. Brig.
384th Infantry	do	do					do	do	Do.
385th to 386th Infantry.									Never orgzd.
387th Infantry	October 1918	Cp. Cody, N. Mex.					December 1918	Cp. Cody, N. Mex.	Cmpnt. of 194th Inf. Brig.
388th Infantry	do	do					do	do	Do.

PIONEER REGIMENTS

1st Pioneer Infantry	January 1918	Cp. Wadsworth, S. C.	July 1918	Cp. Mills, N. Y.					Corps troops.
			do	P. of E., Hoboken	July 1918.				
			July 1919	Cp. Stuart, Va.		July 1919	July 1919	Cp. Zachary Taylor, Ky.	
2d Pioneer Infantry	do	do	June 1918	Do.					
			do	P. of E., Newport News.	June 1918	October 1919	November 1919	Cp. Dix. N. J.	Army troops.
3d Pioneer Infantry	February 1918	Cp. Greene, N. C.	February 1918	Cp. Wadsworth, S. C.					
			August 1918	Cp. Stuart, Va.					
			do	P. of E., Newport News.	August 1918.				
			July 1919	Cp. Merritt, N. J.		July 1919	July 1919	Cp. Dodge, Iowa	Do.
4th Pioneer Infantry	do	do	February 1918	Cp. Wadsworth, S. C.					Corps troops.
			September 1918	Cp. Stuart, Va.					
			do	P. of E., Newport News.	September 1918	February 1919	February 1919	Cp. Hill, Va.	
5th Pioneer Infantry	do	do	February 1918	Cp. Wadsworth, S. C.			January 1919	Cp. Wadsworth, S. C.	Do.
6th Pioneer Infantry	October 1918	Cp. Sherman, Ohio					February 1919	Cp. Sherman, Ohio	Do.
7th to 50th Pioneer Infantry.									Never orgzd.
51st Pioneer Infantry	January 1918	Cp. Wadsworth, S. C.	July 1918	Cp. Merritt, N. J.					
			do	P. of E., Hoboken	July 1918.				
			July 1919	Cp. Mills, N. Y.		July 1919	July 1919	Cp. Upton, N. Y.	Corps troops.
52d Pioneer Infantry	do	do	July 1918	Cp. Upton, N. Y.					
			August 1918	P. of E., Hoboken	August 1918	April 1919	April 1919	Cp. Dix, N. J.	Do.
53d Pioneer Infantry	do	do	July 1918	Cp. Upton, N. Y.					Do.
			August 1918	P. of E., Hoboken	August 1918.				
			May 1919	Cp. Stuart, Va.		May 1919	May 1919	Cp. Upton, N. Y.	
54th Pioneer Infantry	do	do	August 1918	do					Army troops.
			do	P. of E., Newport News.	August 1918.				
			June 1919	Cp. Stuart, Va.		June 1919	July 1919	Cp. Grant, Ill.	
55th Pioneer Infantry	do	do	September 1918	do					Do.
			do	P. of E., Newport News.	September 1918	February 1919	February 1919	Cp. Hill, Va.	

PIONEER REGIMENTS—Continued

Unit designation and redesignation	Organization		Stations in United States		Overseas		Demobilization		Remarks
	Month and year	Place	Month and year	Place	From—	To—	Month and year	Place	
56th Pioneer Infantry	February 1918	Cp. Greene, N. C.	February 1918	Cp. Wadsworth, S. C.					Army troops.
			September 1918	Cp. Merritt, N. J.					
			do	P. of E., Hoboken	September 1918.				
			June 1919	Cp. Stuart, Va.		June 1919	July 1919	Cp. Dix, N. J.	
57th Pioneer Infantry	do	do	February 1918	Cp. Wadsworth, S. C.					Do.
			September 1918	Cp. Merritt, N. J.					
			do	P. of E., Hoboken	September 1918.				
			February 1919	Cp. Hill, Va.		February 1919	February 1919	Cp. Devens, Mass.	
58th Pioneer Infantry	do	do	February 1918	Cp.Wadsworth, S. C.			January 1919	Cp. Wadsworth, S. C.	Do.
59th Pioneer Infantry	January 1918	Cp. Dix, N. J	August 1918	P. of E., Hoboken	August 1918				Do.
			July 1919	Cp. Mills, N. Y		July 1919	July 1919	Cp. Dix, N. J.	
60th Pioneer Infantry	July 1918	Cp. Wadsworth, S. C.					January 1919	Cp. Wadsworth, S. C.	
61st Pioneer Infantry	do	do					do	Do.	
62d Pioneer Infantry	do	do					do	Do.	
63d Pioneer Infantry	October 1918	Cp. Dix, N. J					do	Cp. Dix, N. J.	
64th Pioneer Infantry	do	Cp. Zachary Taylor, Ky.					February 1919	Cp. Zachary Taylor, Ky.	
65th Pioneer Infantry	do	Cp. Funston, Kans.					December 1918	Cp. Funston, Kans.	
66th to 74th Pioneer Infantry.									Authorized, but never orgzd.
75th to 800th Pioneer Infantry.									Never orgzd.
801st Pioneer Infantry	June 1918	Cp. Zachary Taylor, Ky.	September 1918	Cp. Merritt, N. J.					
			do	P. of E., Hoboken	September 1918.				
			June 1919	Cp. Alexander, Va.		June 1919	June 1919	Cp. Zachary Taylor, Ky.	Corps troops.

802d Pioneer Infantry	July 1918	Cp. Sherman, Ohio.	August 1918	Cp. Mills, N. Y.					Army troops.
			do	P. of E., Hoboken	August 1918.				
803d Pioneer Infantry	do	Cp. Grant, Ill.	July 1919	Cp. Mills, N. Y.		July 1919	July 1919	Cp. Gordon, Ga.	
			September 1918	Cp. Upton, N. Y.					
			do	P. of E., Hoboken	September 1918.				
804th Pioneer Infantry	do	Cp. Dodge, Iowa	July 1919	Newport News, Va.		do	do	Cp. Grant, Ill.	Do.
			August 1918	Cp. Upton, N. Y.					
			September 1918	P. of E., Hoboken	September 1918.				
805th Pioneer Infantry	June 1918	Cp. Funston, Kans.	July 1919	Cp. Mills, N. Y.		do	do	Cp. Gordon, Ga.	Corps troops.
			August 1918	Cp. Upton, N. Y.					Army troops.
			September 1918	P. of E., Quebec	September 1918.				
806th Pioneer Infantry	July 1918	do	June 1919	Cp. Upton, N. Y.		June 1919	July 1919	Cp. Shelby, Miss.	Do.
			September 1918	Cp. Mills, N. Y.					
			do	P. of E., Hoboken	September 1918.				
807th Pioneer Infantry	do	Cp. Dix, N. J.	June 1919	Cp. Upton, N. Y.		June 1919	July 1919	Cp. Shelby, Miss.	Do.
			September 1918	P. of E., Hoboken	September 1918				
808th Pioneer Infantry	do	Cp. Meade, Md.	July 1919	Newport News, Va.		July 1919	July 1919	Cp. Jackson, S. C.	Do.
			August 1918	P. of E., Hoboken	August 1918				
809th Pioneer Infantry	August 1918	Cp. Dodge, Iowa	June 1919	Cp. Alexander, Va.		June 1919	June 1919	Cp. Lee, Va.	Corps troops.
			September 1918	Cp. Upton, N. Y.					
			do	P. of E., Hoboken	September 1918.				
810th Pioneer Infantry	September 1918	Cp. Greene, N. C.	July 1919	Cp. Mills, N. Y.		July 1919	July 1919	Cp. Sherman, Ohio.	
811th Pioneer Infantry	August 1918	Cp. Dix, N. J.					December 1918	Cp. Greene, N. C.	
			October 1918	P. of E., Hoboken	October 1918.				
812th Pioneer Infantry	do	Cp. Grant, Ill.	July 1919	Cp. Mills, N. Y.		July 1919	July 1919	Cp. Dix, N. J.	Do.
			November 1918	Cp. Merritt, N. J.					
813th Pioneer Infantry	do	Cp. Sherman, Ohio.					January 1919	Cp. Grant, Ill.	Army troops.
			September 1918	Cp. Mills, N. Y.					
			do	P. of E., Hoboken	September 1918.				
814th Pioneer Infantry	do	Cp. Zachary Taylor, Ky.	July 1919	Cp. Alexander, Va.		July 1919	July 1919	Cp. Dix, N. J.	
			October 1918	Cp. Upton, N. Y.					
			do	P. of E., Hoboken	October 1918.				
815th Pioneer Infantry	September 1918	Cp. Funston, Kans.	December 1918	Cp. Mills, N. Y.		December 1918	do	Cp. Zachary Taylor, Ky.	Corps troops.
			September 1918	Cp. Merritt, N. J.					
			October 1918	P. of E., Hoboken	October 1918.				
816th Pioneer Infantry	do	do	July 1919	Cp. Stuart, Va.		July 1919	do	Cp. Travis, Tex.	Army troops.
			October 1918	Cp. Upton, N. Y.					
			do	P. of E., Hoboken	October 1918.				
817th Pioneer Infantry			August 1919	Cp. Alexander, Va.		August 1919	August 1919	Cp. Shelby, Miss.	Do.
									Authorized, but never orgzd.

PHILIPPINE SCOUTS

Unit designation and redesignation	Organization		Stations in United States		Overseas		Demobilization		Remarks
	Month and year	Place	Month and year	Place	From—	To—	Month and year	Place	
1st Battalion, P.S.	Organized 1904		April 1917	Augur Bks., P.I.			April 1918	Ft. McKinley, P.I.	Absorbed by 1st Phil. Inf. (Prov.)
2d Battalion, P. S	Organized 1905		do	Cp. John Hay, P. I.					
3d Battalion, P. S	do		do	Cp. McGrath, P. I.			do	Cp. McGrath, P. I.	Absorbed by 3d Phil. Inf. (Prov.)
4th Battalion, P. S	do		do	Pettit Bks., P. I.			do	Ft. McKinley, P. I.	Absorbed by 2d Phil. Inf. (Prov.)
5th Battalion, P. S.	do		do	Ft. Mills, P. I.					
6th Battalion, P. S	do		do	Ludlow Bks., P. I.			do	do	Absorbed by 1st Phil. Inf. (Prov.)
7th Battalion, P. S	do		do	Regan Bks., P. I.			do	Cp. Eldridge, P. I.	Absorbed by 3d Phil. Inf. (Prov.)
8th Battalion, P. S	do		do	Ludlow Bks., P. I.			do	Ft. Mills, P. I.	Absorbed by 4th Phil. Inf. (Prov.)
9th Battalion, P. S	Organized 1908		do	Warwick Bks., P. I.			do	do	Do.
10th Battalion, P. S	do		do	Ft. San Pedro, P. I.			do	Ft. McKinley, P. I.	Absorbed by 2d Phil. Inf. (Prov.)
11th Battalion, P. S	do		do	Ft. Mills, P. I.			do	Cp. Stotsenburg, P. I.	Absorbed by 1st Phil F.A. (Prov.) (Mtn.)
12th Battalion, P. S	Organized 1909		do	Cp. Keithley, P. I.			do	do	Do.
13th Battalion, P. S	Organized 1914		do	Augur Bks., P. I.					
14th Battalion, P. S									Authorized, but never orgzd.

PHILIPPINE NATIONAL GUARD

Unit designation and redesignation	Organization Month and year	Organization Place	Stations Month and year	Stations Place	Overseas From—	Overseas To—	Demobilization Month and year	Demobilization Place	Remarks
1st Infantry, P.N.G.	December 1918	Cp. Claudio, P. I.					December 1918	Cp. Claudio, P. I.	Cmpnt. of 1st Inf. Brig.
2d Infantry, P.N.G.	do	do					do	do	Do.
3d Infantry, P.N.G.	do	do					do	do	Do.
4th Infantry, P.N.G.	do	do					do	do	Cmpnt. of 2d Inf. Brig.

5th Infantry, P.N.G.	do.	do.					do.	do.	Do.
6th Infantry, P.N.G.	do.	do.					do.	do.	Do.
7th Infantry, P.N.G.	do.	do.					do.	do.	Cmpnt. of 3d Inf. Brig.
8th Infantry, P.N.G.	do.	do.					do.	do.	Do.
9th Infantry, P.N.G.	do.	do.					do.	do.	Do.

PHILIPPINE INFANTRY (PROVISIONAL)

1st Philippine Infantry (provisional).	April 1918	Ft. McKinley, P. I.							
2d Philippine Infantry (provisional).	do.	Do.							
3d Philippine Infantry (provisional).	do.	Cp. McGrath, P. I.							
4th Philippine Infantry (provisional).	do.	Ft. Mills, P. I.							

HAWAIIAN INFANTRY

1st Hawaiian Infantry	June 1918	Ft. Armstrong, T. H.					July 1919	Ft. Shafter, T. H.	
2d Hawaiian Infantry	do.	Schofield Bks., T. H.					February 1919	Schofield Bks., T. H.	

PUERTO RICAN INFANTRY

Puerto Rico Regiment of Infantry.	Organized 1899		April 1917 May 1917 March 1919	San Juan, P. R. Cp. Otis, C. Z. San Juan, P. R.					

MISCELLANEOUS REGIMENTS

First Army Headquarters Regiment.	November 1917	Cp. Greene, N. C.	March 1918 do.	Cp. Merritt, N. J. P. of E., Hoboken	March 1918.				Orgzd. fr. 1st N.H Inf.
Third Army Composite Regiment.	May 1919	A. E. F.	June 1919 September 1919	Cp. Merritt, N. J. Cp. Mills, N. Y.		June 1919 September 1919	June 1919 September 1919	Cp. Devens, Mass. Cp. Meade, Md.	

INFANTRY SPECIAL AND TECHNICAL UNITS

Units	Unit No.	Active service	Unit No.	Active service	Unit No.	Active service	Unit No.	Active service	Unit No.	Active service	Remarks
CAMP GRANT, ILL., REPLACEMENT AND TRAINING UNITS											
Regiment	1	October 1918–January 1919									
Battalions	1	September 1918–January 1919	2	September 1918–January 1919	3	September 1918–January 1919	4–17	Never orgzd.	18	October 1918–January 1919	
CAMP GORDON, GA., REPLACEMENT AND TRAINING UNITS											
Brigades	1	May 1918–December 1918	2	May 1918–December 1918	3	May 1918–December 1918					
Regiments	1	April 1918–December 1918	2	April 1918–December 1918	3	do	4	May 1918–December 1918	5	May 1918–December 1918	
	6	May 1918–December 1918									
Battalion	1	December 1918–February 1919									
CAMP LEE, VA., REPLACEMENT AND TRAINING UNITS											
Battalions	1	June 1918–February 1919	2	June 1918–January 1919	3	June 1918–January 1919	4	June 1918–January 1919	5	June 1918–January 1919	
	6	June 1918–January 1919	7	do	8	June 1918–December 1918	9	do	10	Do.	
	11	do	12	do	13	July 1918–January 1919	14	July 1918–November 1918	15	July 1918–November 1918	
	16	July 1918–November 1918	17	July 1918–January 1919	18	do	19	September 1918–November 1918	20	September 1918–November 1918	

CAMP MAC ARTHUR, TEX., REPLACEMENT AND TRAINING UNITS											
Battalions	1	June 1918–March 1919	2	June 1918–January 1919	3	June 1918–January 1919	4	June 1918–January 1919	5	June 1918–December 1918	
	6	June 1918–January 1919	7	June 1918–December 1918	8	do	9	June 1918–December 1918	10	Do.	
	11	June 1918–December 1918	12	do	13	August 1918–December 1918					
CAMP PIKE, ARK., REPLACEMENT AND TRAINING UNITS											
Brigades	1	June 1918–November 1918	2	June 1918–November 1918							
Regiments	a 1	July 1918–January 1919	b 2	July 1918–January 1919	c 3	July 1918–January 1919	d 4	July 1918–December 1918			a Redes. 1st Tng. Gp. b Redes. 2d Tng. Gp. c Redes. 3d Tng. Gp. d Redes. 4th Tng. Gp.
Battalions	1	June 1918–January 1919	2	June 1918–January 1919	3	June 1918–January 1919	4	June 1918–February 1919	5	June 1918–February 1919	
	6	June 1918–December 1918	7	do	8	do	9	June 1918–January 1919	10	June 1918–December 1918	
	11	do	12	June 1918–December 1918	13	August 1918–January 1919	14	August 1918–January 1919	15	September 1918–December 1918	

MACHINE GUN UNITS

MACHINE GUN BATTALIONS

Unit designation and redesignation	Organization		Stations in United States		Overseas		Demobilization		Remarks
	Month and year	Place	Month and year	Place	From—	To—	Month and year	Place	
1st Machine Gun Battalion.	November 1917	A. E. F	September 1919	Cp. Mills, N. Y		September 1919			Cmpnt. of 1st Div.
			do	Cp. Meade, Md.					
			October 1919	Cp. Zachary Taylor, Ky.					Active through 1919.

MACHINE GUN BATTALIONS—Continued

Unit designation and redesignation	Organization		Stations in United States		Overseas		Demobilization		Remarks
	Month and year	Place	Month and year	Place	From—	To—	Month and year	Place	
2d Machine Gun Battalion.	January 1918	A. E. F	September 1919	Cp. Mills, N. Y.		September 1919			Cmpnt. of 1st Inf. Brig.
			do	Cp. Meade, Md.					
			October 1919	Cp. Zachary Taylor, Ky.					Active through 1919.
3d Machine Gun Battalion.	do	do	September 1919	Cp. Mills, N. Y.		September 1919			Cmpnt. of 2d Inf. Brig.
			do	Cp. Meade, Md.					
			October 1919	Cp. Zachary Taylor, Ky.					Active through 1919.
4th Machine Gun Battalion.	October 1917	Gettysburg, Pa.	December 1917	P. of E., Portland	December 1917				Cmpnt. of 2d Div.
			August 1919	Cp. Mills, N. Y.		August 1919.			
			do	Cp. Travis, Tex.					Active through 1919.
5th Machine Gun Battalion.	January 1918	A. E. F	do	Cp. Mills, N. Y.		August 1919			Orgzd. as Prov. M. G. Bn. August 1917. Cmpnt. of 3d Inf. Brig. Active through 1919.
			do	Cp. Travis, Tex.					
6th Machine Gun Battalion.									U.S.M.C. orgn.
7th Machine Gun Battalion.	November 1917	Cp. Greene, N. C.	March 1918	Cp. Merritt, N. J.					Cmpnt. of 3d Div.
			April 1918	P. of E., Hoboken	April 1918				A. F. in G. through December 1919.
8th Machine Gun Battalion.	do	do	March 1918	Cp. Merritt, N. J.					Cmpnt. of 5th Inf. Brig.
			April 1918	P. of E., Hoboken	April 1918.				
			August 1919	Cp. Merritt, N. J.		August 1919.			
			do	Cp. Pike, Ark.					Active through 1919.

9th Machine Gun Battalion.	do	do	**March 1918**	**Cp. Merritt, N. J.**					Cmpnt. of 6th Inf. Brig.
			April 1918	P. of E., Hoboken	April 1918.				
			August 1919	Cp. Merritt, N. J.		August 1919.			
			do	Cp. Pike, Ark					Active through 1919.
10th Machine Gun Battalion.	do	do	April 1918	Cp. Mills, N. Y.					Cmpnt. of 4th Div
			May 1918	P. of E., Hoboken	May 1918.				
			July 1919	Cp. Mills, N. Y.		July 1919.			
			August 1919	Cp. Dodge, Iowa					Active through 1919.
11th Machine Gun Battalion.	December 1917	do	April 1918	Cp. Mills, N. Y.					Cmpnt. of 7th Inf. Brig.
			May 1918	P. of E., Hoboken	May 1918.				
			July 1919	Cp. Merritt, N. J.		July 1919.			
			August 1919	Cp. Dodge, Iowa					Active through 1919.
12th Machine Gun Battalion.	do	do	April 1918	Cp. Mills, N. Y.					Cmpnt. of 8th Inf. Brig.
			May 1918	P. of E., Hoboken	May 1918.				
			July 1919	Cp. Merritt, N. J.		July 1919.			
			August 1919	Cp. Dodge, Iowa					Active through 1919.
13th Machine Gun Battalion.	November 1917	Ft. Sam Houston, Tex.	April 1918	Cp. Merritt, N. J.					Cmpnt. of 5th Div.
			do	P. of E., Hoboken	April 1918.				
			July 1919	Cp. Merritt, N. J.		July 1919.			
			do	Cp. Gordon, Ga.					Active through 1919.
14th Machine Gun Battalion.	December 1917	Cp. Greene, N. C.	April 1918	Cp. Merritt, N. J.					Cmpnt. of 9th Inf. Brig.
			do	P. of E., Hoboken	April 1918.				
			July 1919	Cp. Mills, N. Y.		July 1919.			
			do	Cp. Gordon, Ga.					Active through 1919.
15th Machine Gun Battalion.	January 1918	Cp. Forrest, Ga.	April 1918	Cp. Merritt, N. J.					Cmpnt. of 10th Inf. Brig.
			do	P. of E., Hoboken	April 1918.				
			July 1919	Cp. Merritt, N. J.		July 1919.			
			do	Cp. Gordon, Ga.					Active through 1919.

MACHINE GUN BATTALIONS—Continued

Unit designation and redesignation	Organization		Stations in United States		Overseas		Demobilization		Remarks
	Month and year	Place	Month and year	Place	From—	To—	Month and year	Place	
16th Machine Gun Battalion.	January 1918	Cp. Forrest, Ga.	April 1918	Cp. Wadsworth, S. C.					Cmpnt. of 6th Div.
			June 1918	Cp. Mills, N. Y.					
			July 1918	P. of E., Hoboken	July 1918.				
			June 1919	Cp. Merritt, N. J.		June 1919.			
			do	Cp. Grant, Ill.					Active through 1919.
17th Machine Gun Battalion.	December 1917	do	June 1918	Cp. Wadsworth, S. C.					Cmpnt. of 11th Inf. Brig.
			July 1918	Cp. Mills, N. Y.					
			do	P. of E., Hoboken	July 1918.				
			June 1919	Cp. Stuart, Va.		June 1919.			
			do	Cp. Grant, Ill.					Active through 1919.
18th Machine Gun Battalion.	do	do	May 1918	Cp. Wadsworth, S. C.					Cmpnt. of 12th Inf. Brig.
			July 1918	Cp. Mills, N. Y.					
			do	P. of E., Hoboken	July 1918.				
			June 1919	Cp. Merritt, N. J.		June 1919.			
			do	Cp. Grant, Ill.					Active trhough 1919.
19th Machine Gun Battalion.	January 1918	do	May 1918	Cp. MacArthur, Tex.					Cmpnt. of 7th Div.
			July 1918	Cp. Merritt, N. J.					
			August 1918	P. of E., Hoboken	August 1918.				
			June 1919	Cp. Morrison, Va.		June 1919.			
			do	Cp. Funston, Kans.					Active through 1919.
20th Machine Gun Battalion.	do	do	February 1918	Cp. MacArthur, Tex.					Cmpnt. of 13th Inf. Brig.
			July 1918	Cp. Merritt, N. J.					

			August 1918	P. of E., Hoboken	August 1918.				
			June 1919	Cp. Merritt, N. J.		June 1919.			
			do	Cp. Funston, Kans.					Active through 1919.
21st Machine Gun Battalion.	do	Cp. Fort Bliss, Tex.	February 1918	Cp. Newton D. Baker, Tex.					Cmpnt. of 14th Inf. Brig.
			June 1918	Cp. MacArthur, Tex.					
			August 1918	Cp. Merritt, N. J.					
			do	P. of E., Hoboken	August 1918.				
			June 1919	Cp. Mills, N. Y.		June 1919.			
			do	Cp. Funston, Kans.					Active through 1919.
22d Machine Gun Battalion.	March 1918	Cp. Fremont, Calif.	October 1918	Cp. Mills, N. Y.					Cmpnt. of 8th Div.
23d Machine Gun Battalion.	February 1918	do	November 1918	Cp. Lee, Va.			February 1919	Cp. Lee, Va.	
			October 1918	Cp. Mills, N. Y.					Cmpnt. of 15th Inf. Brig.
24th Machine Gun Battalion.	January 1918	do	November 1918	Cp. Lee, Va.			February 1919	Cp. Lee, Va.	
			October 1918	Cp. Mills, N. Y.					Cmpnt. of 16th Inf. Brig.
25th Machine Gun Battalion.	August 1918	Cp. Sheridan, Ala.	November 1918	Cp. Lee, Va.			February 1919	Cp. Lee, Va.	
							do	Cp. Sheridan, Ala.	Cmpnt. of 9th Div.
26th Machine Gun Battalion.	December 1917	Cp. Zachary Taylor, Ky.	April 1918	Cp. Gordon, Ga.					Cmpnt. of 17th Inf. Brig.
27th (I) Machine Gun Battalion.	do	Ft. Sam Houston, Tex.	June 1918	Cp. Sheridan, Ala.			February 1919	Cp. Sheridan, Ala.	
			February 1918	Cp. Travis, Tex.					Cmpnt. of 19th Inf. Brig.
			April 1918	Ft. Sam Houston, Tex.					
a. 29th Machine Gun Battalion.	July 1918	do	July 1918	Cp. Funston, Kans.			February 1919	Cp. Funston, Kans.	
27th (II) Machine Gun Battalion.	do	Cp. Sheridan, Ala.					do	Cp. Sheridan, Ala.	Cmpnt. of 18th Inf. Brig.
28th Machine Gun Battalion.	August 1918	Cp. Funston, Kans.					do	Cp. Funston, Kans.	Cmpnt. of 10th Div.
29th Machine Gun Battalion.									See 27th (I) M.G. Bn.

MACHINE GUN BATTALIONS—Continued

Unit designation and redesignation	Organization		Stations in United States		Overseas		Demobilization		Remarks
	Month and year	Place	Month and year	Place	From—	To—	Month and year	Place	
30th Machine Gun Batralion.	August 1918	Cp. Funston, Kans.					February 1919	Cp. Funston, Kans.	Cmpnt. of 20th Inf. Brig.
31st Machine Gun Battalion.	September 1918	Cp. Meade, Md.					Januaey 1919	Cp. Meade, Md.	Cmpnt. of 11th Div.
32d Machine Gun Battalion.	do	do					do	do	Cmpnt. of 21st Inf. Brig.
33d Machine Gun Battalion.	do	do					do	do	Cmpnt. of 22d Inf. Brig.
34th Machine Gun Battalion.	August 1918	Cp. Devens, Mass.					do	Cp. Devens, Mass.	Cmpnt. of 12th Div.
35th Machine Gun Battalion.	do	do					do	do	Cmpnt. of 23d Inf. Brig.
36th Machine Gun Battalion.	do	do					do	do	Cmpnt. of 24th Inf. Brig.
37th Machine Gun Battalion.	September 1918	Cp. Lewis, Wash.					February 1919	Cp. Lewis, Wash.	Cmpnt. of 13th Div.
38th Machine Gun Battalion.	do	do					do	do	Cmpnt. of 25th Inf. Brig.
39th Machine Gun Battalion.	September 1918	Cp. Lewis, Wash.					February 1919	Cp. Lewis, Wash.	Cmpnt. of 26th Inf. Brig.
40th Machine Gun Battalion.	do	Cp. Custer, Mich.					do	Cp. Custer, Mich.	Cmpnt. of 14th Div.
41st Machine Gun Battalion.	do	do					do	do	Cmpnt. of 27th Inf. Brig.
42d Machine Gun Battalion.	do	do					do	do	Cmpnt. of 28th Inf. Brig.
43d Machine Gun Battalion.	November 1918	Cp. Logan, Tex.					do	Cp. Logan, Tex.	Cmpnt. of 15th Div.
44th Machine Gun Battalion.	do	do					do	do	Cmpnt. of 29th Inf. Brig.

45th Machine Gun Battalion.	do	do					do	do	Cmpnt. of 30th Inf. Brig.
46th Machine Gun Battalion.									Never orgzd.
47th Machine Gun Battalion.	September 1918	Cp. Kearny, Calif					February 1919	Cp. Kearny, Calif	Cmpnt. of 31st Inf. Brig.
48th Machine Gun Battalion.	do	do					do	do	Cmpnt. of 32d Inf. Brig.
49th Machine Gun Battalion.	do	Cp. Beauregard, La.					January 1919	Cp. Beauregard, La.	Cmpnt. of 17th Div.
50th Machine Gun Battalion.	do	do					do	do	Cmpnt. of 33d Inf. Brig.
51st Machine Gun Battalion.	October 1918	do					do	do	Cmpnt. of 34th Inf. Brig.
52d Machine Gun Battalion.	do	Cp. Travis, Tex					February 1919	Cp. Travis, Tex	Cmpnt. of 18th Div.
53d Machine Gun Battalion.	do	do					do	do	Cmpnt. of 35th Inf. Brig.
54th Machine Gun Battalion.	do	do					do	do	Cmpnt. of 36th Inf. Brig.
55th Machine Gun Battalion.	do	Cp. Dodge, Iowa					January 1919	Cp. Dodge, Iowa	Cmpnt. of 19th Div.
56th Machine Gun Battalion.	do	do					do	do	Cmpnt. of 37th Inf. Brig.
57th Machine Gun Battalion.	do	do					do	do	Cmpnt. of 38th Inf. Brig.
58th Machine Gun Battalion.	do	Cp. Sevier, S. C					do	Cp. Sevier, S. C	Cmpnt. of 20th Div.
59th Machine Gun Battalion.	September 1918	do					February 1919	do	Cmpnt. of 39th Inf. Brig.
60th Machine Gun Battalion.	October 1918	do					January 1919	do	Cmpnt. of 40th Inf. Brig.
61st to 100th Machine Gun Battalions.									Never orgzd.
101st Machine Gun Battalion.	September 1917	Niantic, Conn	October 1917	P. of E., Montreal	October 1917	April 1919	April 1919	Cp. Devens, Mass	Cmpnt. of 26th Div.
102d Machine Gun Battalion.	August 1917	Framingham, Mass.	September 1917	P. of E., Hoboken	September 1917	do	do	do	Cmpnt. of 51st Inf. Brig.
103d Machine Gun Battalion.	do	Westfield, Mass	October 1917	do	October 1917	do	do	do	Cmpnt. of 52d Inf. Brig.

MACHINE GUN BATTALIONS—Continued

Unit designation and redesignation	Organization		Stations in United States		Overseas		Demobilization		Remarks
	Month and year	Place	Month and year	Place	From—	To—	Month and year	Place	
104th Machine Gun Battalion.	October 1917	Cp. Wadsworth, S. C.	May 1918	Cp. Hill, Va					Cmpnt. of 27th Div.
			do	P. of E., Newport News.	May 1918.				
			March 1919	Cp. Mills, N. Y		March 1919	April 1919	Cp. Upton, N. Y.	
105th Machine Gun Battalion.	do	do	May 1918	Cp. Stuart, Va					Cmpnt. of 53d Inf. Brig.
			do	P. of E., Newport News.	May 1918.				
			March 1919	Cp. Mills, N. Y		March 1919	April 1919	Cp. Upton, N. Y.	
106th Machine Gun Battalion.	do	do	May 1918	Cp. Stuart, Va					Cmpnt. of 54th Inf. Brig.
			do	P. of E., Newport News.	May 1918.				
			March 1919	Cp. Merritt, N. J		March 1919	April 1919	Cp. Upton, N. Y.	
107th Machine Gun Battalion.	do	Cp. Hancock, Ga	April 1918	Cp. Upton, N. Y					Cmpnt. of 28th Div.
			May 1918	P. of E., Hoboken	May 1918	May 1919	May 1919	Cp. Dix, N. J.	
108th Machine Gun Battalion.	do	do	April 1918	Cp. Upton, N. Y					Cmpnt. of 55th Inf. Brig.
			May 1918	P. of E., Hoboken	May 1918	May 1919	May 1919	Cp. Dix, N. J.	
109th Machine Gun Battalion.	do	do	May 1918	Cp. Upton, N. Y					Cmpnt. of 56th Inf. Brig.
			do	P. of E., Hoboken	May 1918	April 1919	May 1919	Cp. Dix, N. J.	
110th Machine Gun Battalion.	September 1917	Cp. McClellan, Ala.	June 1918	Cp. Hill, Va					Cmpnt. of 29th Div.
			do	P. of E., Newport News.	June 1918.				
			May 1919	Cp. Merritt, N. J		May 1919	June 1919	Cp. Meade, Md.	
111th Machine Gun Battalion.	do	do	June 1918	Cp. Hill, Va					Cmpnt. of 57th Inf. Brig.
			do	P. of E., Newport News.	June 1918	May 1919	May 1919	Cp. Dix, N. J.	

112th Machine Gun Battalion.	October 1917	do	do	P. of E., Hoboken	do	do	do	Cp. Stuart, Va.	Cmpnt. of 58th Inf. Brig.
113th Machine Gun Battalion.	September 1917	Cp. Sevier, S. C.	May 1918	Cp. Mills, N. Y.					Cmpnt. of 30th Div.
			do	P. of E., Hoboken	May 1918.				
114th Machine Gun Battalion.	do	do	April 1919	Cp. Jackson, S. C.		April 1919	April 1919	Ft. Oglethorpe, Ga.	
			May 1918	Cp. Mills, N. Y.					Cmpnt. of 59th Inf. Brig.
			do	P. of E., Hoboken	May 1918.				
115th Machine Gun Battalion.	do	do	March 1919	Cp. Morrison, Va.		March 1919	April 1919	Ft. Oglethorpe, Ga.	
			May 1918	Cp. Merritt, N. J.					Cmpnt. of 60th Inf. Brig.
			do	P. of E., Philadelphia.	May 1918.				
116th Machine Gun Battalion.	do	Cp. Wheeler, Ga.	March 1919	Cp. Stuart, Va.		March 1919	April 1919	Cp. Jackson, S. C.	
			September 1918	Cp. Mills, N. Y.					Cmpnt. of 31st Div.
			October 1918	P. of E., Hoboken	October 1918				Skeletonized November 1918.
117th Machine Gun Battalion.	do	do	December 1918	Cp. Merritt, N. J.		December 1918	January 1919	Cp. Gordon, Ga.	Record cadre only.
			September 1918	Cp. Mills, N. Y.					Cmpnt. of 61st Inf. Brig.
			October 1918	P. of E., Hoboken	October 1918				Skeletonized November 1918.
118th Machine Gun Battalion.	October 1917	do	December 1918	Cp. Merritt, N. J.		December 1918	January 1919	Cp. Gordon, Ga.	Record cadre only.
			September 1918	Cp. Mills, N. Y.					Cmpnt. of 62d Inf. Brig.
			October 1918	P. of E., Hoboken	October 1918				Skeletonized November 1918.
119th Machine Gun Battalion.	do	Cp. MacArthur, Tex.	December 1918	Cp. Merritt, N. J.		December 1918	January 1919	Cp. Gordon, Ga.	Record cadre only.
			February 1918	do					Cmpnt. of 32d Div.
			do	P. of E., Hoboken	February 1918.				
120th Machine Gun Battalion.	September 1917	do	May 1919	Cp. Mills, N. Y.		May 1919	June 1919	Cp. Grant, Ill.	
			January 1918	Cp. Merritt, N. J.					Cmpnt. of 63d Inf. Brig.
			February 1918	P. of E., Hoboken	February 1918.				
121st Machine Gun Battalion.	do	do	May 1919	Cp. Merritt, N. J.		May 1919	May 1919	Cp. Custer, Mich.	
			January 1918	do					
			February 1918	P. of E., Hoboken	February 1918.				Cmpnt. of 64th Inf. Brig.
			May 1919	Cp. Devens, Mass.		May 1919	May 1919	Cp. Grant, Ill.	

MACHINE GUN BATTALIONS—Continued

Unit designation and redesignation	Organization		Stations in United States		Overseas		Demobilization		Remarks
	Month and year	Place	Month and year	Place	From—	To—	Month and year	Place	
122d Machine Gun Battalion.	October 1917	Cp. Logan, Tex.	May 1918	Cp. Upton, N. Y.					Cmpnt. of 33d Div.
			do	P. of E., Hoboken.	May 1918.				
			May 1919	Cp. Mills, N. Y.		May 1919	May 1919	Cp. Grant, Ill.	
123d Machine Gun Battalion.	do	do	May 1918	Cp. Upton, N. Y.					Cmpnt. of 65th Inf. Brig.
			do	P. of E., Hoboken.	May 1918.				
			May 1919	Cp. Mills, N. Y.		May 1919	May 1919	Cp. Grant, Ill.	
124th Machine Gun Battalion.	do	do	May 1918	Cp. Upton, N. Y.					Cmpnt. of 66th Inf. Brig.
			do	P. of E., Hoboken.	May 1918.				
			May 1919	Cp. Mills, N. Y.		May 1919	May 1919	Cp. Grant, Ill.	
125th Machine Gun Battalion.	do	Cp. Cody, N. Mex.	September 1918	Cp. Dix, N. J.					Cmpnt. of 34th Div.
			do	P. of E., Hoboken.	September 1918				Skeletonized November 1918.
			January 1919	Cp. Merritt, N. J.		January 1919	February 1919	Cp. Grant, Ill.	Record cadre only.
126th Machine Gun Battalion.	do	do	August 1918	Cp. Dix, N. J.					Cmpnt. of 67th Inf. Brig.
			September 1918	P. of E., Hoboken.	September 1918				Skeletonized November 1918.
			January 1919	Cp. Merritt, N. J.		January 1919	February 1919	Cp. Grant, Ill.	Record cadre only.
127th Machine Gun Battalion.	do	do	August 1918	Cp. Dix, N. J.					Cmpnt. of 68th Inf. Brig.
			October 1918	P. of E., Hoboken.	October 1918				Skeletonized November 1918.
			January 1919	Cp. Merritt, N. J.		January 1919	February 1919	Cp. Grant, Ill.	Record cadre only.
128th Machine Gun Battalion.	do	Cp. Doniphan, Okla.	April 1918	Cp. Mills, N. Y.					Cmpnt. of 35th Div.
			do	P. of E., Hoboken.	April 1918.				
			April 1919	Cp. Stuart, Va.		April 1919	May 1919	Cp. Funston, Kans.	

129th Machine Gun Battalion.	do	do	April 1918	Cp. Mills, N. Y.					Cmpnt. of 69th Inf. Brig.
			May 1918	P. of E., Hoboken	May 1918.				
			April 1919	Cp. Stuart, Va.		April 1919	May 1919	Cp. Funston, Kans.	
130th Machine Gun Battalion.	do	do	April 1918	Cp. Mills, N. Y.					Cmpnt. of 70th Inf. Brig.
			May 1918	P. of E., Hoboken	May 1918.				
			April 1919	Cp. Stuart, Va.		April 1919	May 1919	Cp. Funston, Kans.	
131st Machine Gun Battalion.	do	Cp. Bowie, Tex.	July 1918	Cp. Mills, N. Y.					Cmpnt. of 36th Div.
			do	P. of E., Hoboken	July 1918.				
			June 1919	Cp. Mills, N. Y.		June 1919	June 1919	Cp. Bowie, Tex.	
132d Machine Gun Battalion.	do	do	July 1918	do					Cmpnt. of 71st Inf. Brig.
			do	P. of E., Hoboken	July 1918.				
			June 1919	Cp. Mills, N. Y.		June 1919	June 1919	Cp. Bowie, Tex.	
133d Machine Gun Battalion.	do	do	July 1918	do					Cmpnt. of 72d Inf. Brig.
			do	P. of E., Hoboken	July 1918.				
			June 1919	Cp. Mills, N. Y.		June 1919	June 1919	Cp. Bowie, Tex.	
134th Machine Gun Battalion.	September 1917	Cp. Sheridan, Ala.	May 1918	Cp. Lee, Va.					Cmpnt. of 37th Div.
			June 1918	P. of E., Hoboken	June 1918.				
			March 1919	Cp. Mills, N. Y.		March 1919	April 1919	Cp. Sherman, Ohio.	
135th Machine Gun Battalion.	do	do	May 1918	Cp. Lee, Va.					Cmpnt. of 73d Inf Brig.
			June 1918	P. of E., Hoboken	June 1918.				
			March 1919	Cp. Merritt, N. J.		March 1919	April 1919	Cp. Sherman, Ohio.	
136th Machine Gun Battalion.	do	do	May 1918	Cp. Lee, Va.					Cmpnt. of 74th Inf. Brig.
			June 1918	P. of E., Newport News.	June 1918.				
			March 1919	Cp. Merritt, N. J.		March 1919	April 1919	Cp. Sherman, Ohio.	
137th Machine Gun Battalion.	October 1917	Cp. Shelby, Miss.	September 1918	Cp. Mills, N. Y.					Cmpnt. of 38th Div.
			October 1918	P. of E., Hoboken	October 1918				Skeletonized November 1918.
			December 1918	Cp. Hill, Va.		December 1918	January 1919	Cp. Zachary Taylor, Ky.	Record cadre only.

MACHINE GUN BATTALIONS—Continued

Unit designation and redesignation	Organisation		Stations in United States		Overseas		Demobilisation		Remarks
	Month and year	Place	Month and year	Place	From—	To—	Month and year	Place	
138th Machine Gun Battalion.	October 1917	Cp. Shelby, Miss.	September 1918	Cp. Mills, N. Y.					Cmpnt. of 75th Inf. Brig.
			October 1918	P. of E., Hoboken	October 1918				Skeletonized November 1918.
			December 1918	Cp. Hill, Va.		December 1918	January 1919	Cp. Zachary Taylor, Ky.	Record cadre only.
139th Machine Gun Battalion.	do	do	September 1918	Cp. Mills, N. Y.					Cmpnt. of 76th Inf. Brig.
			October 1918	P. of E., Hoboken	October 1918				Skeletonized November 1918.
			December 1918	Cp. Hill, Va.		December 1918	January 1919	Cp. Zachary Taylor, Ky.	Record cadre only.
140th Machine Gun Battalion.	November 1917	Cp. Beauregard, La.	August 1918	Cp. Mills, N. Y.					Cmpnt. of 39th Div.
			do	P. of E., Hoboken	August 1918				Skeletonized November 1918.
			January 1919	Cp. Stuart, Va.		January 1919	January 1919	Cp. Beauregard, La.	Record cadre only.
141st Machine Gun Battalion.	October 1917	do	August 1918	do					Cmpnt. of 77th Inf. Brig.
			do	P. of E., Newport News.	August 1918.				
			January 1919	Cp. Stuart, Va.		January 1919	January 1919	Cp. Beauregard, La.	
142d Machine Gun Battalion.	do	do	August 1918	Cp. Mills, N. Y.					Cmpnt. of 78th Inf. Brig.
			do	P. of E., Hoboken	August 1918				Skeletonized November 1918.
			January 1919	Cp. Stuart, Va.		January 1919	January 1919	Cp. Beauregard, La.	Record cadre only.

143d Machine Gun Battalion.	do	Cp. Kearny, Calif.	August 1918	Cp. Mills, N. Y.					Cmpnt. of 40th Div.
			do	P. of E., Hoboken	August 1918.				
			April 1919	Cp. Mills, N. Y.		April 1919	April 1919	Cp. Grant, Ill.	
144th Machine Gun Battalion.	do	do	August 1918	do					Cmpnt. of 79th Inf. Brig.
			do	P. of E., Hoboken	August 1918.				
			April 1919	Cp. Mills, N. Y.		April 1919	April 1919	Cp. Grant, Ill.	
145th Machine Gun Battalion.	do	do	August 1918	do					Cmpnt. of 80th Inf. Brig.
			do	P. of E., Hoboken	August 1918.				
			May 1919	Cp. Devens, Mass.		May 1919	May 1919	Presidio of San Francisco, Calif.	
146th Machine Gun Battalion.	September 1917	Cp. Greene, N. C.	October 1917	Cp. Mills, N. Y.					Cmpnt. of 41st Div.
			December 1917	Cp. Merritt, N. J.					
			January 1918	P. of E., Hoboken	January 1918.				
			February 1919	Cp. Merritt, N. J.		February 1919	April 1919	Cp. Funston, Kans.	
147th Machine Gun Battalion.	October 1917	do	October 1917	Cp. Mills, N. Y.					Cmpnt. of 81st Inf. Brig.
			December 1917	P. of E., Hoboken	December 1917.				
			February 1919	Cp. Stuart, Va.		February 1919	March 1919	Cp. Upton, N. Y.	
148th Machine Gun Battalion.	do	do	November 1917	Cp. Mills, N. Y.					Cmpnt. of 82d Inf. Brig.
			January 1918	P. of E., Hoboken	January 1918.				
			February 1919	Cp. Merritt, N. J.		February 1919	March 1919	Cp. Dodge, Iowa.	
149th Machine Gun Battalion.	August 1917	Lancaster, Pa.	August 1917	Cp. Mills, N. Y.					Cmpnt. of 42d Div.
			October 1917	Ft. Totten, N. Y.					
			November 1917	P. of E., Hoboken	November 1917.				
			April 1919	Cp. Devens, Mass.		April 1919	May 1919	Cp. Dix, N. J.	
150th Machine Gun Battalion.	do	Cp. Douglas, Wis.	September 1917	Cp. Mills, N. Y.					Cmpnt. of 83d Inf. Brig.
			October 1917	P. of E., Hoboken	October 1917.				
			April 1919	Cp. Devens, Mass.		April 1919	May 1919	Cp. Grant, Ill.	
151st Machine Gun Battalion.	do	Cp. Harris, Ga.	September 1917	Cp. Mills, N. Y.					Cmpnt. of 84th Inf. Brig.
			October 1917	P. of E., Hoboken	October 1917.				
			April 1919	Cp. Merritt, N. J.		April 1919	May 1919	Cp. Gordon, Ga.	

MACHINE GUN BATTALIONS—Continued

Unit designation and redesignation	Organization		Stations in United States		Overseas		Demobilization		Remarks
	Month and year	Place	Month and year	Place	From—	To—	Month and year	Place	
152d to 300th Machine Gun Battalions.									Never orgzd.
301st Machine Gun Battalion.	August 1917	Cp. Devens, Mass.	July 1918	P. of E., Boston	July 1918				Cmpnt. of 76th Div.
			January 1919	Cp. Hill, Va.		January 1919	January 1919	Cp. Devens, Mass.	Skeletonized November 1918. Record cadre only.
302d Machine Gun Battalion.	do	do	July 1918	P. of E., Boston	July 1918				Cmpnt. of 151st Inf. Brig.
			January 1919	Cp. Hill, Va.		January 1919	February 1919	Cp. Devens, Mass.	Skeletonized November 1918. Record cadre only.
303d Machine Gun Battalion.	do	do	July 1918	P. of E., Montreal	do				Cmpnt. of 152d Inf. Brig.
			January 1919	Cp. Hill, Va.		January 1919	February 1919	Cp. Devens, Mass.	Skeletonized November 1918. Record cadre only.
304th Machine Gun Battalion.	September 1917	Cp. Upton, N. Y.	April 1918	P. of E., Hoboken	April 1918				Cmpnt. of 77th Div.
			May 1919	Cp. Mills, N. Y.		May 1919	May 1919	Cp. Upton, N. Y.	
305th Machine Gun Battalion.	do	do	March 1918	P. of E., Portland	March 1918				Cmpnt. of 153d Inf. Brig.
			April 1919	Cp. Mills, N. Y.		April 1919	May 1919	Cp. Upton, N. Y.	
306th Machine Gun Battalion.	do	do	April 1918	P. of E., Boston	April 1918				Cmpnt. of 154th Inf. Brig.
			April 1919	Cp. Mills, N. Y.		April 1919	May 1919	Cp. Upton, N. Y.	
307th Machine Gun Battalion.	do	Cp. Dix, N. J.	May 1918	P. of E., Hoboken	May 1918	May 1919	do	Cp. Dix, N. J.	Cmpnt. of 78th Div.
308th Machine Gun Battalion.	do	do	do	do	do	do	do	do	Cmpnt. of 155th Inf. Brig.
309th Machine Gun Battalion.	do	do	do	do	do	do	do	do	Cmpnt. of 156th Inf. Brig.

310th Machine Gun Battalion.	do	Cp. Meade, Md.	July 1918	do	July 1918	do	do	do	Cmpnt. of 79th Div.
311th Machine Gun Battalion.	do	do	do	do	do				Cmpnt. of 157th Inf. Brig.
			May 1919	Cp. Morrison, Va.		May 1919	June 1919	Cp. Dix, N. J.	
312th Machine Gun Battalion.	do	do	July 1918	P. of E., Hoboken	July 1918	do	May 1919	do	Cmpnt. of 158th Inf. Brig.
313th Machine Gun Battalion.	do	Cp. Lee, Va.	May 1918	P. of E., Newport News.	May 1918				Cmpnt. of 80th Div.
			June 1919	Cp. Devens, Mass.		June 1919	June 1919	Cp. Dix, N. J.	
314th Machine Gun Battalion.	do	do	May 1918	P. of E., Newport News.	May 1918				Cmpnt. of 159th Inf. Brig.
			June 1919	Cp. Devens, Mass.		June 1919	June 1919	Cp. Dix, N. J.	
315th Machine Gun Battalion.	do	do	May 1918	P. of E., Newport News.	May 1918	May 1919	do	do	Cmpnt. of 160th Inf. Brig.
316th Machine Gun Battalion.	do	Cp. Jackson, S. C.	do	Cp. Hancock, Ga.					Cmpnt. of 81st Div.
			July 1918	Cp. Mills, N. Y.					
			do	P. of E., Hoboken	July 1918.				
			June 1919	Cp. Stuart, Va.		June 1919	June 1919	Cp. Upton, N. Y.	
317th Machine Gun Battalion.	do	do	May 1918	Cp. Hancock, Ga.					Cmpnt. of 161st Inf. Brig.
			July 1918	Cp. Mills, N. Y.					
			do	P. of E., Hoboken	July 1918.				
			June 1919	Cp. Merritt, N. J.		June 1919	June 1919	Cp. Upton, N. Y.	
318th Machine Gun Battalion.	do	do	May 1918	Cp. Hancock, Ga.					Cmpnt. of 162d Inf. Inf. Brig.
			July 1918	Cp. Mills, N. Y.					
			do	P. of E., Hoboken	July 1918.				
			June 1919	Cp. Stuart, Va.		June 1919	June 1919	Cp. Upton, N. Y.	
319th Machine Gun Battalion.	do	Cp. Gordon, Ga.	April 1918	Cp. Upton, N. Y.					Cmpnt. of 82d Div.
			May 1918	P. of E., Hoboken	May 1918	May 1919	May 1919	Cp. Dix, N. J.	
320th Machine Gun Battalion.	do	do	April 1918	Cp. Upton, N. Y.					Cmpnt. of 163d Inf. Brig.
			do	P. of E., Hoboken	April 1918	May 1919	May 1919	Cp. Dix, N. J.	
321st Machine Gun Battalion.	do	do	April 1918	Cp. Upton, N. Y.					Cmpnt. of 164th Inf. Brig.
			May 1918	P. of E., Hoboken	May 1918.				
			May 1919	Cp. Morrison, Va.		May 1919	May 1919	Cp. Dix, N. J.	

MACHINE GUN BATTALIONS—Continued

Unit designation and redesignation	Organization		Stations in United States		Overseas		Demobilization		Remarks
	Month and year	Place	Month and year	Place	From—	To—	Month and year	Place	
322d Machine Gun Battalion.	September 1917	Cp. Sherman, Ohio.	June 1918	Cp. Merritt, N. J.					Cmpnt. of 83d Div.
			do	P. of E., Hoboken	June 1918.				
			January 1919	Cp. Mills, N. Y.		January 1919	February 1919	Cp. Sherman, Ohio.	
323d Machine Gun Battalion.	do	do	June 1918	Cp. Merritt, N. J.					Cmpnt. of 165th Inf. Brig.
			do	P. of E., Hoboken	June 1918.				
			January 1919	Cp. Merritt, N. J.		January 1919	March 1919	Cp. Sherman, Ohio.	
324th Machine Gun Battalion.	do	do	May 1918	do					Cmpnt. of 166th Inf. Brig.
			June 1918	P. of E., Hoboken	June 1918.				
			February 1919	Cp. Mills, N. Y.		February 1919	March 1919	Cp. Sherman, Ohio.	
325th Machine Gun Battalion.	August 1917	Cp. Zachary Taylor, Ky.	June 1918	Cp. Sherman, Ohio.					Cmpnt. of 84th Div. Skeletonized November 1918. Record cadre only.
			August 1918	Cp. Mills, N. Y.					
			September 1918	P. of E., Hoboken	September 1918				
			January 1919	Cp. Merritt, N. J.		January 1919	February 1919	Cp. Zachary Taylor, Ky.	
326th Machine Gun Battalion.	September 1917	do	June 1918	Cp. Sherman, Ohio.					Cmpnt. of 167th Inf. Brig. Skeletonized November 1918. Record cadre only.
			August 1918	Cp. Mills, N. Y.					
			September 1918	P. of E., Montreal	September 1918.				
			January 1919	Cp. Merritt, N. J.		January 1919	February 1919	Cp. Zachary Taylor, Ky.	
327th Machine Gun Battalion.	do	do	June 1918	Cp. Sherman, Ohio.					Cmpnt. of 168th Inf. Brig. Skeletonized November 1918. Record cadre only.
			August 1918	Cp. Mills, N. Y.					
			September 1918	P. of E., Montreal	September 1918.				
			January 1919	Cp. Merritt, N. J.		January 1919	February 1919	Cp. Zachary Taylor, Ky.	

328th Machine Gun Battalion.	do	Cp. Custer, Mich.	July 1918	Cp. Mills, N. Y					Cmpnt. of 85th Div.
			do	P. of E., Hoboken	July 1918.				
			April 1919	Cp. Mills, N. Y		April 1919	April 1919	Cp. Custer, Mich.	
329th Machine Gun Battalion.	do	do	July 1918	do					Cmpnt. of 169th Inf. Brig.
			do	P. of E., Hoboken	July 1918.				
			April 1919	Cp. Morrison, Va		April 1919	April 1919	Cp. Custer, Mich.	
330th Machine Gun Battalion.	do	do	July 1918	Cp. Mills, N. Y					Cmpnt. of 170th Inf. Brig.
			do	P. of E. Philadelphia.	July 1918.				
			April 1919	Cp. Stuart, Va		April 1919	April 1919	Cp. Custer, Mich.	
331st Machine Gun Battalion.	do	Cp. Grant, Ill	August 1918	Cp. Mills, N. Y					Cmpnt. of 86th Div.
			September 1918	P. of E., Hoboken	September 1918				Skeletonized November 1918.
			January 1919	Cp. Mills, N. Y		January 1919	January 1919	Cp. Grant, Ill	Record cadre only.
332d Machine Gun Battalion.	do	do	August 1918	Cp. Upton, N. Y					Cmpnt. of 171st Inf. Brig.
			September 1918	P. of E., Hoboken	September 1918.				
			January 1919	Cp. Mills, N. Y		January 1919	January 1919	Cp. Grant, Ill	Record cadre only.
333d Machine Gun Battalion.	do	do	August 1918	do					Cmpnt. of 172d Inf. Brig.
			September 1918	P. of E., Hoboken	September 1918				Skeletonized November 1918.
			January 1919	Cp. Mills, N. Y		January 1919	January 1919	Cp. Grant, Ill	Record cadre only.
334th Machine Gun Battalion.	do	Cp. Pike, Ark	June 1918	Cp. Dix, N. J					Cmpnt. of 87th Div.
			August 1918	P. of E., Hoboken	August 1918.				
			March 1919	Cp. Merritt, N. J		March 1919	March 1919	Cp. Dix, N. J.	
335th Machine Gun Battalion.	do	do	June 1918	Cp. Dix, N. J					Cmpnt. of 173d Inf. Brig.
			August 1918	P. of E., Hoboken	August 1918.				
			March 1919	Cp. Merritt, N. J		March 1919	March 1919	Cp. Dix, N. J.	
336th Machine Gun Battalion.	do	do	June 1918	Cp. Dix, N. J					Cmpnt. of 174th Inf. Brig.
			August 1918	P. of E., Hoboken	August 1918.				
			March 1919	Cp. Merritt, N. J		March 1919	March 1919	Cp. Dix, N. J.	

MACHINE GUN BATTALIONS—Continued

Unit designation and redesignation	Organization		Stations in United States		Overseas		Demobilization		Remarks
	Month and year	Place	Month and year	Place	From—	To—	Month and year	Place	
337th Machine Gun Battalion.	September 1917	Cp. Dodge, Iowa	August 1918	Cp. Mills, N. Y.					Cmpnt. of 88th Div.
337th Machine Gun Battalion.			do	P. of E., Hoboken	August 1918.				
337th Machine Gun Battalion.			May 1919	Cp. Mills, N. Y.		May 1919	June 1919	Cp. Dodge, Iowa.	
338th Machine Gun Battalion.	do	do	August 1918	Cp. Upton, N. Y.					Cmpnt. of 175th Inf. Brig.
338th Machine Gun Battalion.			do	P. of E., Hoboken	August 1918.				
338th Machine Gun Battalion.			June 1919	Cp. Hill, Va.		June 1919	June 1919	Cp. Dodge, Iowa.	
339th Machine Gun Battalion.	do	do	August 1918	Cp. Mills, N. Y.					Cmpnt. of 176th Inf. Brig.
339th Machine Gun Battalion.			do	P. of E., Philadelphia.	August 1918.				
339th Machine Gun Battalion.			May 1919	Cp. Mills, N. Y.		May 1919	June 1919	Cp. Dodge, Iowa.	
340th Machine Gun Battalion.	do	Cp. Funston, Kans.	May 1918	do					Cmpnt. of 89th Div.
340th Machine Gun Battalion.			June 1918	P. of E., Hoboken	June 1918.				
340th Machine Gun Battalion.			May 1919	Cp. Merritt, N. J.		May 1919	June 1919	Cp. Dodge, Iowa.	
341st Machine Gun Battalion.	do	do	May 1918	Cp. Mills, N. Y.					Cmpnt. of 177th Inf. Brig.
341st Machine Gun Battalion.			June 1918	P. of E., Hoboken	June 1918.				
341st Machine Gun Battalion.			May 1919	Cp. Merritt, N. J.		May 1919	June 1919	Cp. Funston, Kans.	
342d Machine Gun Battalion.	do	do	May 1918	Cp. Mills, N. Y.					Cmpnt. of 178th Inf. Brig.
342d Machine Gun Battalion.			June 1918	P. of E., Hoboken	June 1918.				
342d Machine Gun Battalion.			May 1919	Cp. Upton, N. Y.		May 1919	June 1919	Cp. Funston, Kans.	
343d Machine Gun Battalion.	do	Cp. Travis, Tex.	June 1918	Cp. Mills, N. Y.					Cmpnt. of 90th Div.
343d Machine Gun Battalion.			do	P. of E., Hoboken	June 1918.				
343d Machine Gun Battalion.			June 1919	Cp. Mills, N. Y.		June 1919	June 1919	Cp. Bowie, Tex.	
344th Machine Gun Battalion.	do	do	June 1918	do					Cmpnt. of 179th Inf. Brig.
344th Machine Gun Battalion.			do	P. of E., Hoboken	June 1918.				
344th Machine Gun Battalion.			June 1919	Cp. Devens, Mass.		June 1919	June 1919	Cp. Bowie, Tex.	

345th Machine Gun Battalion.	do	do	June 1918	Cp. Mills, N. Y.					Cmpnt. of 180th Inf. Brig.
			do	P. of E. Philadelphia.	June 1918.				
			June 1919	Cp. Merritt, N. J.		June 1919	June 1919	Cp. Bowie, Tex.	
346th Machine Gun Battalion.	do	Cp. Lewis, Wash.	July 1918	do					Cmpnt. of 91st Div.
			do	P. of E., Hoboken	July 1918.				
			April 1919	Cp. Mills, N. Y.		April 1919	April 1919	Ft. D. A. Russell, Wyo.	
347th Machine Gun Battalion.	do	do	June 1918	Cp. Merritt, N. J.					Cmpnt. of 181st Inf. Brig.
			July 1918	P. of E., Hoboken	July 1918.				
			April 1919	Cp. Upton, N. Y.		April 1919	May 1919	Cp. Lewis, Wash.	
348th Machine Gun Battalion.	do	do	June 1918	Cp. Merritt, N. J.					Cmpnt. of 182d Inf. Brig.
			July 1918	P. of E., Hoboken	July 1918.				
			April 1919	Cp. Upton, N. Y.		April 1919	May 1919	Presidio of San Francisco, Calif.	
349th Machine Gun Battalion.	December 1917	Cp. Funston, Kans.	June 1918	do					Cmpnt. of 92d Div.
			do	P. of E., Hoboken	June 1918.				
			March 1919	Cp. Upton, N. Y.		March 1919	April 1919	Cp. Zachary Taylor, Ky.	
350th Machine Gun Battalion.	November 1917	Cp. Grant, Ill.	June 1918	do					Cmpnt. of 183d Inf. Brig.
			do	P. of E., Hoboken	June 1918	March 1919	March 1919	Cp. Upton, N. Y.	
351st Machine Gun Battalion.	do	Cp. Upton, N. Y.	do	do	do				Cmpnt. of 184th Inf. Brig.
			March 1919	Cp. Upton, N. Y.		March 1919	March 1919	Cp. Meade, Md.	
352d to 357th Machine Gun Battalions.									Never orgzd.
358th Machine Gun Battalion.	October 1918	Cp. Sherman, Ohio.					December 1918	Cp. Sherman, Ohio.	Cmpnt. of 95th Div.
359th Machine Gun Battalion.	November 1918	do					do	do	Cmpnt. of 189th Inf. Brig.
360th Machine Gun Battalion.	October 1918	do					do	do	Cmpnt. of 190th Inf. Brig.
361st and 362d Machine Gun Battalions.									Never orgzd.

MACHINE GUN BATTALIONS—Continued

Unit designation and redesignation	Organization		Stations in United States		Overseas		Demobilization		Remarks
	Month and year	Place	Month and year	Place	From—	To—	Month and year	Place	
363d Machine Gun Battalion.	November 1918	Cp. Wadsworth S. C.					January 1919	Cp. Wadsworth S. C.	Cmpnt. of 192d Inf. Brig.
364th and 365th Machine Gun Battalions.									Never orgzd.
366th Machine Gun Battalion.	October 1918	Cp. Cody, N. Mex					December 1918	Cp. Cody, N. Mex.	Cmpnt. of 194th Inf. Brig.

A. A. MACHINE GUN BATTALIONS

Unit designation and redesignation	Organization		Stations in United States		Overseas		Demobilization		Remarks
	Month and year	Place	Month and year	Place	From—	To—	Month and year	Place	
1st Anti-aircraft Machine Gun Battalion.	January 1918	Cp. Wadsworth, S. C.	April 1918 May 1918 May 1919	Cp. Merritt, N. J. P. of E., Hoboken Cp. Mills, N. Y.	May 1918.	May 1919	May 1919	Cp. Sherman, Ohio	Corps troops.
2d Anti-aircraft Machine Gun Battalion.	do	do	June 1918 do	Cp. Hill, Va. P. of E., Newport News.	June 1918	February 1919	February 1919	Cp. Dix, N. J	Do.
3d Anti-aircraft Machine Gun Battalion.	do	do	August 1918 do	Cp. Stuart, Va. P. of E., Newport News.	August 1918	May 1919	May 1919	Cp. Upton, N. Y	Do.
4th Anti-aircraft Machine Gun Battalion.	July 1918	do	August 1918 September 1918 January 1919	Cp. Hill, Va. P. of E., Newport News. Cp. Mills, N. Y	September 1918.	January 1919	January 1919	Cp. Dodge, Iowa	Do.
5th Anti-aircraft Machine Gun Battalion.	do	do	September 1918 October 1918 January 1919	Cp. Merritt, N. J. P. of E., Hoboken Cp. Stuart, Va	October 1918.	do	February 1919	Cp. Wadsworth, S. C.	Do.
6th Anti-aircraft Machine Gun Battalion.	October 1918	do					January 1919	Do.	

AMERICAN RED CROSS CONVALESCENT HOSPITALS

Unit designation and redesignation	Organization		Stations in United States		Overseas		Demobilization		Remarks
	Month and year	Place	Month and year	Place	From—	To—	Month and year	Place	
Convalescent Hospital No. 1.	May 1918	A. E. F.							
a. American Red Cross Convalescent Hospital No. 101.	July 1918	do			July 1918	January 1919			Demblzd. overseas.

AMERICAN RED CROSS HOSPITALS (NON-MILITARY)

Unit designation and redesignation	Organization: Month and year	Organization: Place	Stations in United States: Month and year	Stations in United States: Place	Overseas: From—	Overseas: To—	Demobilization: Month and year	Demobilization: Place	Remarks
American Red Cross Hospital No. 104.[1]					September 1918	November 1918			S.O.S. troops.
American Red Cross Hospital No. 105.[1]					June 1918	August 1918.			
American Red Cross Hospital No. 106.									Never orgzd.
American Red Cross Hospital No. 107.[1]					July 1918	August 1918			S.O.S. troops.
American Red Cross Hospital No. 108.									Never orgzd.
American Red Cross Hospital No. 109.[1]					November 1918	December 1918			S.O.S. troops.
American Red Cross Hospital, Padova, Italy.[1]					October 1918	March 1919.			

AMERICAN RED CROSS MILITARY HOSPITALS

Unit designation and redesignation	Organization: Month and year	Organization: Place	Stations in United States: Month and year	Stations in United States: Place	Overseas: From—	Overseas: To—	Demobilization: Month and year	Demobilization: Place	Remarks
American Red Cross Military Hospital No. 1.[1]	July 1917	A. E. F			July 1917	March 1919			S.O.S. troops.
American Red Cross Military Hospital No. 2.[1]	November 1917	do			November 1917	March 1919			Do.

[1] Orgzd. and demoblzd. overseas.

AMERICAN RED CROSS MILITARY HOSPITALS—Continued

Unit designation and redesignation	Organization		Stations in United States		Overseas		Demobilization		Remarks
	Month and year	Place	Month and year	Place	From—	To—	Month and year	Place	
American Red Cross Military Hospital No. 3.[1]	November 1917	A. E. F			November 1917				S.O.S. troops.
a. Camp Hospital No. 121.[1]	June 1919	do			June 1919	December 1919.			
American Red Cross Military Hospital No. 4.[1]	July 1918	do			July 1918	February 1919			Do.
American Red Cross Military Hospital No. 5.[1]	May 1918	do			May 1918	January 1919			Do.
American Red Cross Military Hospital No. 6.[1]									See Gas Hospital No. 71.
American Red Cross Military Hospital No. 7.[1]	July 1918	A. E. F			July 1918	October 1918.			
American Red Cross Military Hospital No. 8.[1]	August 1918	do			August 1918	December 1918			S.O.S. troops.
American Red Cross Military Hospital No. 9.[1]	July 1918	do			July 1918	January 1919			Do.
American Red Cross Military Hospitals No. 10 to 20.									Never orgzd.
American Red Cross Military Hospital No. 21.[1]	July 1918	A. E. F			July 1918	March 1919			S.O.S. troops.
American Red Cross Military Hospital No. 22.[1]	May 1918	do			May 1918	July 1919			Do.
American Red Cross Military Hospital No. 23.[1]	July 1918	do			July 1918	December 1918			Do.
American Red Cross Military Hospitals No. 24 to 109.									Never orgzd.
American Red Cross Military Hospital No. 110.[1]	September 1918	A. E. F			September 1918	November 1918			S.O.S. troops.
American Red Cross Military Hospital No. 111.[1]	July 1918	do			July 1918	December 1918			Do.

[1] Orgzd. and demblzd. overseas.

BASE HOSPITALS

Base Hospital No. 1	Organized 1916		November 1917	New York City, N. Y.					Mblzd. November 1917.
			February 1918	P. of E., Hoboken	February 1918.				
			April 1919	Cp. Hill, Va.		April 1919	May 1919	Cp. Upton, N. Y.	S.O.S. troops.
Base Hospital No. 2	February 1917	New York City, N. Y.	May 1917	P. of E., Hoboken	May 1917	February 1919	February 1919	Cp. Meade, Md.	Do.
Base Hospital No. 3	Organized 1916		November 1917	New York City, N. Y.					Mblzd. November 1917.
			February 1918	P. of E., Hoboken	February 1918.				
			March 1919	Newport News, Va.		March 1919	March 1919	Cp. Upton, N. Y.	S.O.S. troops.
Base Hospital No. 4	do		May 1917	Cleveland, Ohio					Mblzd. May 1917.
			do	P. of E., Hoboken	May 1917.				
			April 1919	Cp. Devens, Mass.		April 1919	April 1919	Cp. Sherman, Ohio	S.O.S. troops.
Base Hospital No. 5	do		May 1917	Boston, Mass.					Mblzd. May 1917.
			do	P. of E., Hoboken	May 1917.				
			April 1919	Cp. Merritt, N. J.		April 1919	May 1919	Cp. Devens, Mass	S.O.S. troops.
Base Hospital No. 6	do		May 1917	Boston, Mass.					Mblzd. May 1917.
			June 1917	Ft. Strong, Mass.					
			July 1917	P. of E., Hoboken	July 1917.				
			March 1919	Cp. Merritt, N. J.		March 1919	April 1919	Cp. Devens, Mass	S.O.S. troops.
Base Hospital No. 7	do		February 1918	Cp. Devens, Mass					Mblzd. February 1918.
			July 1918	P. of E., Hoboken	July 1918.				
			March 1919	Cp. Merritt, N. J.		March 1919	April 1919	Cp. Devens, Mass	S.O.S. troops.
Base Hospital No. 8	do		July 1917	Ft. Jay, N. Y.					Mblzd. July 1917.
			August 1917	P. of E., Hoboken	August 1917	April 1919	April 1919	Cp. Lee, Va.	S.O.S. troops.
Base Hospital No. 9	do		July 1917	Governors Island, N. Y.					Mblzd. July 1917.
			August 1917	P. of E., Hoboken	August 1917	April 1919	May 1919	Cp. Upton, N. Y.	S.O.S. troops.
Base Hospital No. 10	February 1917	Philadelphia, Pa.	May 1917	do	May 1917	do	April 1919	Cp. Dix, N. J.	Mblzd. May 1917. S.O.S. troops.
Base Hospital No. 11	Organized 1916		March 1918	Chicago, Ill.					Mblzd. March 1918.
			April 1918	Cp. Dodge, Iowa.					
			June 1918	Cp. Mills, N. Y.					
			do	P. of E., Hoboken	June 1918.				
			April 1919	Newport News, Va.		April 1919	April 1919	Cp. Grant, Ill.	S.O.S. troops.
Base Hospital No. 12	do		May 1917	Chicago, Ill.					Mblzd. May 1917.
			do	P. of E., Hoboken	May 1917.				
			April 1919	Cp. Dix, N. J.		April 1919	April 1919	Cp. Grant, Ill.	S.O.S. troops.

BASE HOSPITALS—Continued

Unit designation and redesignation	Organization		Stations in United States		Overseas		Demobilization		Remarks
	Month and year	Place	Month and year	Place	From—	To—	Month and year	Place	
Base Hospital No. 13	Organized 1916		January 1918	Chicago, Ill					Mblzd. January 1918.
			do	Ft. McPherson, Ga.					
			May 1918	Cp. Merritt, N. J.					
			do	P. of E., Hoboken	May 1918.				
			April 1919	Cp. Mills, N. Y.		April 1919	April 1919	Cp. Grant, Ill	S.O.S. troops.
Base Hospital No. 14	do		March 1918	Chicago, Ill					Mblzd. March 1918.
			April 1918	Cp. Custer, Mich					
			July 1918	Cp. Merritt, N. J.					
			do	P. of E., Hoboken	July 1918.				
			April 1919	Cp. Merritt, N. J.		April 1919	May 1919	Cp. Grant, Ill	S.O.S. troops.
Base Hospital No. 15	April 1917	New York City, N. Y.	June 1917	New York City, N. Y.					Mblzd. June 1917.
			July 1917	P. of E., Hoboken	July 1917.				
			April 1919	Cp. Merritt, N. J.		April 1919	July 1919	Cp. Dodge, Iowa	S.O.S. troops.
Base Hospital No. 16	March 1918	do	April 1918	Biltmore, N. C			April 1918	Biltmore, N. C	Absorbed by Gen. Hosp. No. 12.
Base Hospital No. 17	Organized 1916		June 1917	Detroit, Mich					Mblzd. June 1917.
			July 1917	Allentown, Pa.					
			do	P. of E., Hoboken	July 1917.				
			April 1919	Newport News, Va		April 1919	May 1919	Cp. Custer, Mich	S.O.S. troops.
Base Hospital No. 18	do		May 1917	Baltimore, Md					Mblzd. May 1917.
			June 1917	P. of E., Hoboken	June 1917	February 1919	February 1919	Cp. Upton, N. Y.	S.O.S. troops.
Base Hospital No. 19	do		December 1917	Rochester, N. Y					Mblzd. December 1917.
			June 1918	P. of E., Hoboken	June 1918	April 1919	May 1919	Cp. Upton, N. Y.	S.O.S. troops.
Base Hospital No. 20	do		November 1917	Philadelphia, Pa					Mblzd. November 1917.
			April 1918	Cp. Merritt, N. J.					
			do	P. of E., Hoboken	April 1918	April 1919	May 1919	Cp. Dix, N. J	S.O.S. troops.
Base Hospital No. 21	do		April 1917	St. Louis, Mo					Mblsd. April 1917.
			May 1917	P. of E., Hoboken	May 1917.				
			April 1919	Cp. Merritt, N. J.		April 1919	May 1919	Cp. Funston, Kans.	S.O.S. troops.

Base Hospital No. 22	do		January 1918	Milwaukee, Wis.					Mblzd. January 1918.
			May 1918	Cp. Merritt, N. J.					
			June 1918	P. of E., Hoboken	June 1918.				
			March 1919	Cp. Merritt, N. J.		March 1919	March 1919	Cp. Grant, Ill	S.O.S. troops.
Base Hospital No. 23	January 1917	Buffalo, N. Y	August 1917	Ft. Porter, N. Y.					Mobilized August 1917.
			November 1917	P. of E., Hoboken	November 1917	May 1919	May 1919	Cp. Upton, N. Y.	S.O.S. troops.
Base Hospital No. 24	do	New Orleans, La.	August 1917	Jackson Barracks, La.					Mobilized August 1917.
			September 1917	Cp. Greenleaf, Ga.					
			February 1918	P. of E., Hoboken	February 1918.				
			April 1919	Cp. Merritt, N. J.		April 1919	April 1919	Cp. Shelby, Miss.	S.O.S. troops.
Base Hospital No. 25	Organized 1916		March 1918	Cp. Sherman, Ohio.					Mblzd. March 1918.
			June 1918	Cp. Mills, N. Y.					
			do	P. of E., Hoboken	June 1918.				
			April 1919	Cp. Mills, N. Y.		April 1919	May 1919	Cp. Zachary Taylor, Ky.	S.O.S. troops.
Base Hospital No. 26	May 1917	Minneapolis, Minn.	December 1917	Minneapolis, Minn.					Mblzd. December 1917.
			do	Ft. McPherson, Ga.					
			May 1918	Cp. Merritt, N. J.					
			June 1918	P. of E., Hoboken	June 1918.				
			April 1919	Newport News, Va		April 1919	May 1919	Cp. Grant, Ill	S.O.S. troops.
Base Hospital No. 27	Organized 1916		August 1917	Pittsburgh, Pa.					Mblzd. August 1917.
			do	Allentown, Pa.					
			September 1917	P. of E., Hoboken	September 1917	March 1919	March 1919	Cp. Dix, N. J	S.O.S. troops.
Base Hospital No. 28	April 1917	Kansas City, Mo.	January 1918	Kansas City, Mo.					Mblzd. January 1918.
			February 1918	Ft. McPherson, Ga					
			June 1918	Cp. Merritt, N. J.					
			do	P. of E., Hoboken	June 1918	April 1919	May 1919	Cp. Dix, N. J.	S.O.S. troops.
Base Hospital No. 29	do	Denver, Colo.	March 1918	Denver, Colo.					Mblzd. March 1918.
			do	Cp. Cody, N. Mex.					
			June 1918	Cp. Crane, Pa.					
			July 1918	P. of E., Hoboken	July 1918.				
			February 1919	Cp. Merritt, N. J.		February 1919	March 1919	Ft. Logan, Colo.	S.O.S. troops.
Base Hospital No. 30	March 1917	San Francisco, Calif.	November 1917	Ft. Mason, Calif.					Mblzd. November 1917.
			March 1918	Cp. Merritt, N. J.					
			April 1918	P. of E., Hoboken	April 1918.				
			April 1919	Cp. Mills, N. Y.		April 1919	May 1919	Presidio of San Francisco, Calif.	S.O.S. troops.

BASE HOSPITALS—Continued

Unit designation and redesignation	Organization		Stations in United States		Overseas		Demobilization		Remarks
	Month and year	Place	Month and year	Place	From—	To—	Month and year	Place	
Base Hospital No. 31	March 1917	Youngstown, Ohio	September 1917	Youngstown, Ohio					Mblzd. September 1917.
			do	Cp. Crane, Pa.					
			November 1917	Cp. Mills, N. Y.					
			December 1917	P. of E., Hoboken	December 1917	April 1919	May 1919	Cp. Dix, N. J.	S.O.S. troops.
Base Hospital No. 32	February 1917	Indianapolis, Ind.	September 1917	Ft. Benjamin Harrison, Ind.					Mblzd. September 1917.
			December 1917	P. of E., Hoboken	December 1917.	April 1919	May 1919	Cp. Zachary Taylor, Ky.	S.O.S. troops.
			April 1919	Cp. Merritt, N. J.					
Base Hospital No. 33	June 1917	Albany, N. Y.	November 1917	Albany, N. Y.					Mblzd. November 1917.
			April 1918	Cp. Merritt, N. J.					
			May 1918	P. of E., Hoboken	May 1918	February 1919	March 1919	Cp. Upton, N. Y.	S.O.S. troops.
Base Hospital No. 34	April 1917	Philadelphia, Pa.	September 1917	Philadelphia, Pa.					Mblzd. September 1917.
			do	Cp. Crane, Pa.					
			November 1917	Cp. Mills, N. Y.					
			December 1917	P. of E., Hoboken	December 1917	April 1919	April 1919	Cp. Dix, N. J.	S.O.S. troops.
Base Hospital No. 35	do	Los Angeles, Calif.	March 1918	Los Angeles, Calif.					Mblzd. March 1918.
			do	Cp. Kearny, Calif.					
			July 1918	Cp. Merritt, N. J.					
			do	P. of E., Hoboken	July 1918.	April 1919	May 1919	Cp. Kearny, Calif.	S.O.S. troops.
			April 1919	Newport News, Va.					
Base Hospital No. 36	do	Detroit, Mich.	August 1917	Detroit, Mich.					Mblzd. August 1917.
			October 1917	P. of E., Hoboken	October 1917.	April 1919	May 1919	Cp. Custer, Mich.	S.O.S. troops.
			April 1919	Newport News, Va.					
Base Hospital No. 37	July 1917	Brooklyn, N. Y.	January 1918	Brooklyn, N. Y.					Mblzd. January 1918.
			May 1918	P. of E., Hoboken	May 1918	February 1919	March 1919	Cp. Upton, N. Y.	S.O.S. troops.

Base Hospital No. 38	April 1917	Philadelphia, Pa	October 1917	Philadelphia, Pa					Mblzd. October 1917.
			June 1918	P. of E., Hoboken	June 1918	April 1919	May 1919	Cp. Dix, N. J	S.O.S. troops.
Base Hospital No. 39	June 1917	New Haven, Conn.	August 1917	New Haven, Conn.					Mblzd. August 1917.
			do	New York City, N. Y.					
			do	P. of E., Hoboken	August 1917.				
a. Mobile Hospital No. 39.	May 1918	A. E. F	January 1919	Cp. Devens, Mass.		January 1919	January 1919	Cp. Devens, Mass.	S.O.S. troops.
Base Hospital No. 40	June 1917	Lexington, Ky	February 1918	Lexington, Ky					Mblzd. February 1918.
			March 1918	Cp. Zachary Taylor, Ky.					
			June 1918	Cp. Mills, N. Y.					
			July 1918	P. of E., Hoboken	July 1918.				
			March 1919	Cp. Merritt, N. J		March 1919	April 1919	Cp. Zachary Taylor, Ky.	S.O.S. troops.
Base Hospital No. 41	August 1917	Charlottesville, Va.	February 1918	Charlottesville, Va.					Mblzd. February 1918.
			March 1918	Cp. Sevier, S. C.					
			June 1918	Cp. Mills, N. Y.					
			July 1918	P. of E., Hoboken	July 1918	April 1919	April 1919	Cp. Lee, Va	S.O.S. troops.
Base Hospital No. 42	June 1917	Baltimore, Md	April 1918	Cp. Meade, Md					Mblzd. April 1918.
			June 1918	Cp. Mills, N. Y.					
			do	P. of E., Hoboken	June 1918.				
			April 1919	Cp. Merritt, N. J		April 1919	May 1919	Cp. Meade, Md	S.O.S. troops.
Base Hospital No. 43	do	Atlanta, Ga	March 1918	Cp. Gordon, Ga					Mblzd. March 1918.
			June 1918	Cp. Merritt, N. J.					
			do	P. of E., Hoboken	June 1918.				
			March 1919	Newport News, Va.		March 1919	March 1919	Cp. Gordon, Ga	S.O.S. troops.
Base Hospital No. 44	March 1917	Boston, Mass	March 1918	Boston, Mass					Mblzd. March 1918.
			do	Cp. Dix, N. J.					
			July 1918	P. of E., Hoboken	July 1918.				
			April 1919	Cp. Merritt, N. J		April 1919	May 1919	Cp. Devens, Mass.	S.O.S. troops.
Base Hospital No. 45	July 1917	Richmond, Va	March 1918	Cp. Lee, Va					Mblzd. March 1918.
			July 1918	P. of E., Newport News.	July 1918	April 1919	April 1919	Cp. Lee, Va	S.O.S. troops.

BASE HOSPITALS—Continued

Unit designation and redesignation	Organization		Stations in United States		Overseas		Demobilization		Remarks
	Month and year	Place	Month and year	Place	From—	To—	Month and year	Place	
Base Hospital No. 46	May 1917	Portland, Oreg	March 1918	Portland, Oreg					Mblsd. March 1918.
			April 1918	Cp. Lewis, Wash.					
			June 1918	Cp. Merritt, N. J.					
			do	P. of E., Hoboken	June 1918.				
			May 1919	Newport News, Va		May 1919	May 1919	Cp. Lewis, Wash	S.O.S. troops.
Base Hospital No. 47	June 1917	San Francisco, Calif.	December 1917	Cp. Fremont, Calif					Mblsd. December 1917.
			March 1918	Cp. Greenleaf, Ga.					
			June 1918	Cp. Crane, Pa.					
			July 1918	P. of E., Hoboken	July 1918.				
			April 1919	Newport News, Va		April 1919	May 1919	Presidio of San Francisco, Calif.	S.O.S. troops.
Base Hospital No. 48	November 1917	New York City, N. Y.	March 1918	New York City, N. Y.					Mblsd. March 1918.
			do	Ft. McHenry, Md					
			June 1918	Cp. Mills, N. Y.					
			July 1918	P. of E., Hoboken	July 1918	April 1919	May 1919	Cp. Upton, N. Y.	S.O.S. troops.
Base Hospital No. 49	September 1917	Omaha, Nebr	March 1918	Omaha, Nebr					Mblsd. March 1918.
			do	Ft. Des Moines, Iowa.					
			July 1918	Cp. Mills, N. Y.					
			do	P. of E., Hoboken	July 1918				
			April 1919	Cp. Merritt, N. J.		April 1919	May 1919	Cp. Dodge, Iowa	S.O.S. troops.
Base Hospital No. 50	October 1917	Seattle, Wash	March 1918	Ft. Lawton, Wash					Mblsd. March 1918.
			April 1918	Cp. Fremont, Calif					
			July 1918	Cp. Merritt, N. J.					
			do	P. of E., Hoboken	July 1918.				
			April 1919	Hoboken, N. J		April 1919	May 1919	Cp. Lewis, Wash	S.O.S. troops.
Base Hospital No. 51	February 1918	Cp. Greenleaf, Ga.	April 1918	Cp. Wheeler, Ga.					
			July 1918	Cp. Upton, N. Y.					
			August 1918	P. of E., Hoboken	August 1918	June 1919	June 1919	Cp. Dix, N. J	Do.

Base Hospital No. 52	April 1918	do	April 1918	Cp. Gordon, Ga.					
			July 1918	P. of E., Hoboken	July 1918.				
			April 1919	Newport News, Va.		April 1919	May 1919	Cp. Sherman, Ohio.	Do.
Base Hospital No. 53	do	do	April 1918	Cp. Hancock, Ga.					
			July 1918	Cp. Merritt, N. J.					
			do	P. of E., Hoboken	July 1918.				
			June 1919	Cp. Mills, N. Y.		June 1919	July 1919	Cp. Sherman, Ohio.	Do.
Base Hospital No. 54	May 1918	Cp. Greene, N. C.	August 1918	P. of E., Newport News.	August 1918.				
			May 1919	Cp. Mills, N. Y.		May 1919	May 1919	Cp. Grant, Ill.	Do.
Base Hospital No. 55	June 1918	Cp. Greenleaf, Ga.	August 1918	Cp. Merritt, N. J.					
			do	P. of E., Hoboken	August 1918.				
			June 1919	Cp. Merritt, N. J.		June 1919	June 1919	Cp. Pike, Ark.	Do.
Base Hospital No. 56	do	do	June 1918	Cp. Wadsworth, S. C.					
			August 1918	Cp. Merritt, N. J.					
			do	P. of E., Hoboken	August 1918	April 1919	May 1919	Cp. Dix, N. J.	Do.
Base Hospital No. 57	April 1918	do	July 1918	Cp. Merritt, N. J.					
			August 1918	P. of E., Hoboken	August 1918	August 1919			S.O.S. troops. Demobilized overseas.
Base Hospital No. 58	June 1918	Cp. Grant, Ill.	August 1918	Cp. Upton, N. Y.					
			do	P. of E., Hoboken	August 1918.				
			April 1919	Newport News, Va.		April 1919	May 1919	Cp. Dix, N. J.	S.O.S. troops.
Base Hospital No. 59	May 1918	Cp. Greenleaf, Ga.	June 1918	Cp. Shelby, Miss.					
			August 1918	Cp. Stuart, Va.					
			September 1918	P. of E., Newport News.	September 1918.				
			June 1919	Cp. Merritt, N. J.		June 1919	July 1919	do	Do.
Base Hospital No. 60	April 1918	do	April 1918	Cp. Jackson, S. C.					
			August 1918	Cp. Stuart, Va.					
			do	P. of E., Newport News.	August 1918.				
			June 1919	Newport News, Va.		do	July 1919	Cp. Sherman, Ohio.	Do.
Base Hospital No. 61	June 1918	do	June 1918	Cp. Lee, Va.					
			August 1918	P. of E., Newport News.	August 1918	April 1919	April 1919	Cp. Dix, N. J.	Do.
Base Hospital No. 62	do	do	June 1918	Cp. Upton, N. Y.					
			August 1918	P. of E., Hoboken	do				
			May 1919	Newport News, Va.		May 1919	June 1919	do	Do.

BASE HOSPITALS—Continued

Unit designation and redesignation	Organization		Stations in United States		Overseas		Demobilization		Remarks
	Month and year	Place	Month and year	Place	From—	To—	Month and year	Place	
Base Hospital No. 63	June 1918	Cp. Greenleaf, Ga.	June 1918	Cp. McClellan, Ala.					
			August 1918	Cp. Merritt, N. J.					
			do	P. of E., Hoboken	August 1918	April 1919	April 1919	Cp. Merritt, N. J.	S.O.S. troops.
Base Hospital No. 64	do	do	June 1918	Cp. Sevier, S. C.					
			August 1918	Cp. Merritt, N. J.					
			September 1918	P. of E., Hoboken	September 1918.				
			June 1919	Cp. Stuart, Va.		June 1919	June 1919	Cp. Dix, N. J.	Do.
Base Hospital No. 65	March 1918	Ft. McPherson, Ga.	August 1918	Cp. Upton, N. Y.					
			do	P. of E., Hoboken	August 1918	August 1919	August 1919	Cp. Lee, Va.	Do.
Base Hospital No. 66	November 1917	Cp. Merritt, N. J.	December 1917	do	December 1917.				
			February 1919	Newport News, Va.		February 1919	February 1919	Cp. Devens, Mass.	Do.
Base Hospital No. 67	April 1918	Cp. Crane, Pa.	July 1918	P. of E., Hoboken	July 1918.				
			April 1919	Newport News, Va.		April 1919	May 1919	Cp. Dix, N. J., & Cp. Sherman, Ohio.	Do.
Base Hospital No. 68	do	do	July 1918	P. of E., Hoboken	July 1918.				
			April 1919	Newport News, Va.		April 1919	do	do	Do.
Base Hospital No. 69	June 1918	Cp. Greenleaf, Ga.	June 1918	Cp. Meade, Md.					
			August 1918	P. of E., Hoboken	August 1918	July 1919	July 1919	Cp. Grant, Ill.	Do.
Base Hospital No. 70	May 1918	Ft. Riley, Kans.	June 1918	Ft. Ontario, N. Y.					
			September 1918	P. of E., Hoboken	September 1918.				
			April 1919	Cp. Mills, N. Y.		April 1919	May 1919	Cp. Pike, Ark.	Do.
Base Hospital No. 71	July 1918	Cp. Greenleaf, Ga.	August 1918	Cp. Beauregard, La.					
			October 1918	Cp. Upton, N. Y.					
			November 1918	P. of E., Hoboken	November 1918.				
			May 1919	Cp. Merritt, N. J.		May 1919	do	Cp. Shelby, Miss.	Do.
Base Hospital No. 72	do	do	August 1918	Cp. Gordon, Ga.					
			October 1918	P. of E., Hoboken	October 1918	April 1919	April 1919	Cp. Dix, N. J.	Do.

Base Hospital No. 73	September 1918	do					December 1918	Cp. Greenleaf, Ga.	
Base Hospital No. 74	do	do					do	Do.	
Base Hospital No. 75	do	do					do	Do.	
Base Hospital No. 76	June 1918	do	July 1918	Cp. Devens, Mass.					
			September 1918	P. of E., Hoboken	September 1918.				
			April 1919	Cp. Merritt, N. J.		April 1919	May 1919	Cp. Dix, N. J.	Do.
Base Hospital No. 77	do	do	July 1918	Cp. Sherman, Ohio.					
			August 1918	P. of E., Hoboken	August 1918	May 1919	do	Cp. Upton, N. Y.	S. O. S. troops. Skeletonized March 1919.
Base Hospital No. 78	do	do	June 1918	Ft. McHenry, Md.					
			September 1918	P. of E., Hoboken	September 1918	June 1919	June 1919	Cp. Dix, N. J.	S.O.S. troops.
Base Hospital No. 79	do	do	June 1918	Ft. Des Moines, Iowa.					
			September 1918	Cp. Merritt, N. J.					
			do	P. of E., Hoboken	do	do	July 1919	Cp. Upton, N. Y.	Do.
Base Hospital No. 80	do	do	July 1918	Cp. Wheeler, Ga.					
			September 1918	P. of E., Hoboken	do	May 1919	May 1919	do	Do.
Base Hospital No. 81	February 1918	Ft. Riley, Kans.	June 1918	Cp. Travis, Tex.					
			August 1918	Cp. Merritt, N. J.					
			do	P. of E., Hoboken	August 1918.				
			June 1919	Newport News, Va.		June 1919	June 1919	Cp. Dodge, Iowa	Do.
Base Hospital No. 82	April 1918	do	July 1918	Cp. Crane, Pa.					
			August 1918	P. of E., Hoboken	August 1918	do	do	Cp. Devens, Mass.	Do.
Base Hospital No. 83	do	do	June 1918	Cp. Pike, Ark.					
			September 1918	P. of E., Hoboken	September 1918	April 1919	May 1919	Cp. Dix, N. J.	Do.
Base Hospital No. 84	do	do	June 1918	Cp. Bowie, Tex.					
			September 1918	P. of E., Hoboken	Do.				
			May 1919	Cp. Merritt, N. J.		May 1919	July 1919	Cp. Bowie, Tex.	Do.
Base Hospital No. 85	do	do	June 1918	Ft. Sill, Okla.					
			September 1918	P. of E., Hoboken	September 1918	July 1919	do	Cp. Upton, N. Y.	Do.
Base Hospital No. 86	do	do	June 1918	Cp. Logan, Tex.					
			September 1918	P. of E., Hoboken	do	May 1919	May 1919	Cp. Dix, N. J.	Do.
Base Hospital No. 87	do	do	June 1918	Cp. MacArthur, Tex.					
			September 1918	Cp. Mills, N. Y.					
			do	P. of E., Hoboken	do				
			June 1919	Cp. Merritt, N. J.		June 1919	June 1919	Cp. Funston, Kans.	Do.

BASE HOSPITALS—Continued

Unit designation and redesignation	Organization		Stations in United States		Overseas		Demobilization		Remarks
	Month and year	Place	Month and year	Place	From—	To—	Month and year	Place	
Base Hospital No. 88	April 1918	Ft. Riley, Kans.	June 1918	Cp. Dodge, Iowa.					
			September 1918	Cp. Upton, N. Y.					
			do	P. of E., Hoboken	September 1918.				
			July 1919	Cp. Merritt, N. J.		July 1919	July 1919	Cp. Dodge, Iowa	S.O.S. troops.
Base Hospital No. 89	do	do	June 1918	Cp. Sheridan, Ala.					
			September 1918	Cp. Merritt, N. J.					
			do	P. of E., Hoboken	September 1918.				
			May 1919	Cp. Upton, N. Y.		May 1919	do	Cp. Dix, N. J.	Do.
Base Hospital No. 90	May 1918	do	October 1918	Cp. Merritt, N. J.					
			November 1918	P. of E., Hoboken	November 1918.				
			July 1919	Cp. Devens, Mass.		July 1919	do	Cp. Custer, Mich.	Do.
Base Hospital No. 91	June 1918	Cp. Greenleaf, Ga.	August 1918	Cp. Gordon, Ga.					
			November 1918	Cp. Upton, N. Y.					
			do	P. of E., Hoboken	November 1918	August 1919	August 1919	Cp. Upton, N. Y.	Do.
Base Hospital No. 92	do	do	August 1918	Cp. Greene, N. C.					
			October 1918	Cp. Merritt, N. J.					
			November 1918	P. of E., Hoboken	do	March 1919	April 1919	do	S.O.S. troops. Skeletonized February 1919.
Base Hospital No. 93	July 1918	Cp. Lewis, Wash.	October 1918	San Francisco, Calif.					
			do	P. of E., Hoboken	October 1918.				
			June 1919	Cp. Merritt, N. J.		June 1919	June 1919	Cp. Lewis, Wash.	S.O.S. troops.
Base Hospital No. 94	do	Cp. Cody, N. Mex.	October 1918	Cp. Upton, N. Y.					
			do	P. of E., Hoboken	October 1918.				
			April 1919	Cp. Merritt, N. J.		April 1919	April 1919	Cp. Bowie, Tex.	S.O.S. troops. Skeletonized February 1919.
Base Hospital No. 95	August 1918	Cp. Fremont, Calif.	November 1918	Cp. Upton, N. Y.					
			do	P. of E., Hoboken	November 1918.				
			June 1919	Cp. Dix, N. J.		June 1919	July 1919	Ft. D. A. Russell, Wyo.	S.O.S. troops.

Base Hospital No. 96	September 1918	Cp. Kearny, Calif.	October 1918	Cp. Upton, N. Y.					
			do	P. of E., Hoboken	October 1918.				
			May 1919	Cp. Merritt, N. J.		May 1919	May 1919	Presidio of San Francisco, Calif.	S.O.S. troops. Skeletonized December 1918.
Base Hospital No. 97	June 1918	Cp. Newton D. Baker, Tex.	August 1918	Cp. Fort Bliss, Tex.					
			October 1918	P. of E., Hoboken	October 1918	April 1919	April 1919	Cp. Dix, N. J.	S.O.S. troops. Skeletonized February 1919.
Base Hospital No. 98	July 1918	Cp. Greenleaf, Ga.	August 1918	Cp. Hancock, Ga.					
			October 1918	Cp. Merritt, N. J.					
			November 1918	P. of E., Hoboken	November 1918	June 1919	June 1919	do	S.O.S. troops.
Base Hospital No. 99	August 1918	Cp. Custer, Mich.	October 1918	do	October 1918.				
			June 1919	Cp. Mills, N. Y.		do	do	Cp. Custer, Mich.	Do.
Base Hospital No. 100	July 1918	Cp. Greenleaf, Ga.	August 1918	Cp. Custer, Mich.					
			November 1918	Cp. Upton, N. Y.					
			do	P. of E., Hoboken	November 1918	July 1919	July 1919	Cp. Sherman, Ohio.	Do.
Base Hospital No. 101	July 1917	A. E. F.			July 1917	do	do	Cp. Dix, N. J.	Do.
Base Hospital No. 102	February 1918	San Juan, P. R.	June 1918	Cp. Beauregard, La.					
			July 1918	Ft. McHenry, Md.					
			August 1918	P. of E., Baltimore	August 1918.				
			April 1919	Cp. Merritt, N. J.		April 1919	May 1919	Cp. Shelby, Miss.	Do.
Base Hospital No. 103	May 1918	Cp. Greenleaf, Ga.	August 1918	Ft. Sheridan, Ill.					
			October 1918	Cp. Upton, N. Y.					
			do	P. of E., Hoboken	October 1918.				
			July 1919	Cp. Merritt, N. J.		July 1919	July 1919	Cp. Funston, Kans.	Do.
Base Hospital No. 104	July 1918	do	August 1918	Cp. Dodge, Iowa.					
			November 1918	Cp. Upton, N. Y.					
			do	P. of E., Hoboken	November 1918	June 1919	June 1919	Cp. Dix, N. J.	Do.
Base Hospital No. 105	do	do	August 1918	Ft. Benjamin Harrison, Ind.					
			October 1918	P. of E., Hoboken	October 1918	April 1919	April 1919	do	Do.
Base Hospital No. 106	August 1918	do	August 1918	Cp. Jackson, S. C.					
			October 1918	Cp. Merritt, N. J.					
			do	P. of E., Hoboken	do	June 1919	July 1919	do	Do.

BASE HOSPITALS—Continued

Unit designation and redesignation	Organization		Stations in United States		Overseas		Demobilization		Remarks
	Month and year	Place	Month and year	Place	From—	To—	Month and year	Place	
Base Hospital No. 107	July 1918	**Cp. Greenleaf, Ga.**	August 1918	Ft. Snelling, Minn.					
			October 1918	P. of E., Hoboken	**October 1918**	July 1919	**July 1919**	Cp. Pike, Ark	**S.O.S. troops.**
Base Hospital No. 108	August 1918	do	September 1918	Ft. Snelling, Minn.					
			October 1918	P. of E., Hoboken	Do.				
			July 1919	Cp. Merritt, N. J.		do	do	Cp. Dodge, Iowa	Do.
Base Hospital No. 109	do	do	September 1918	Ft. Benjamin Harrison, Ind.					
			October 1918	Cp. Merritt, N. J.					
			do	P. of E., Hoboken	October 1918.				
			May 1919	Cp. Merritt, N. J.		May 1919	May 1919	do	Do.
Base Hospital No. 110	do	do	September 1918	Cp. Sevier, S. C.					
			November 1918	Cp. Upton, N. Y.					
			do	P. of E., Hoboken	November 1918	July 1919	July 1919	Cp. Dix, N. J	**Do.**
Base Hospital No. 111	do	do	September 1918	Cp. Beauregard, **La.**					
			November 1918	Cp. Upton, N. Y.					
			do	P. of E., Hoboken	do	June 1919	June 1919	do	Do.
Base Hospital No. 112	do	do	Spetember 1918	Cp. Sherman, Ohio.					
			October 1918	Cp. Upton, N. Y.					
			November 1918	P. of E., Hoboken	do	April 1919	April 1919	do	Do.
Base Hospital No. 113	do	do	August 1918	Cp. Sherman, Ohio.					
			November 1918	Cp. Upton, N. Y.					
			do	P. of E., Hoboken	do	July 1919	August 1919	do	Do.
Base Hospital No. 114	March 1918	Cp. Crane, Pa	June 1918	do	June 1918	May 1919	May 1919	Cp. Meade, Md	Do.
Base Hospital No. 115	June 1918	Cape May, N. J	August 1918	Cp. Upton, N. Y.					
			do	P. of E., Hoboken	August 1918	April 1919	do	Cp. Dix, N. J	Do.
Base Hospital No. 116	December 1917	New York City, N. Y.	March 1918	do	March 1918	May 1919	do	Cp. Upton, N. Y	Do.
Base Hospital No. 117	March 1918	Cp. Crane, Pa	May 1918	do	May 1918	January 1919			Demblzd. overseas. S.O.S. troops.

Base Hospital No. 118	September 1918	Cp. Zachary Taylor, Ky.	November 1918	Cp. Mills, N. Y.					
			do	P. of E., Hoboken	November 1918	July 1919	July 1919	Cp. Zachary Taylor, Ky.	S.O.S. troops.
Base Hospital No. 119	do	do	October 1918	do	October 1918	do	do	do	Do.
Base Hospital No. 120	August 1918	Cp. Greenleaf, Ga.	September 1918	Cp. Beauregard, La.					
			November 1918	Cp. Upton, N. Y.					
			do	P. of E., Hoboken	November 1918.				
			July 1919	Cp. Merritt, N. J.		do	do	Cp. Dodge, Iowa	Do.
Base Hospital No. 121	do	Cp. Beauregard, La.	November 1918	Cp. Upton, N. Y.					
			do	P. of E., Hoboken	November 1918	do	do	do	**Do.**
Base Hospital No. 122	do	Cp. Greenleaf, Ga.	September 1918	Cp. Greene, N. C.			December 1918	Cp. Greene, N. C.	
Base Hospital No. 123	September 1918	do	do	Do.					
			October 1918	Cp. Mills, N. Y.					
			November 1918	P. of E., Hoboken	November 1918.				
			July 1919	Cp. Merritt, N. J.		July 1919	July 1919	Cp. Pike, Ark	Do.
Base Hospital No. 124	do	do	September 1918	Cp. Hancock, Ga.			January 1919	Cp. Hancock, Ga.	
Base Hospital No. 125	do	do	do	do			do	Do.	
Base Hospital No. 126	do	do	do	Cp. McClellan, Ala.			December 1918	**Cp. McClellan, Ala.**	
Base Hospital No. 127	do	do	do	do			do	Do.	
Base Hospital No. 128	do	do	do	Cp. Sevier, S. C.			do	Cp. Sevier, S. C.	
Base Hospital No. 129	do	do	do	Cp. Shelby, Miss.			do	Cp. Shelby, Miss.	
Base Hospital No. 130	do	do	do	do			do	Do.	
Base Hospital No. 131	July 1918	Jefferson Barracks, Mo.	do	Cp. Upton, N. Y.					
			October 1918	P. of E., Hoboken	October 1918.				
			June 1919	Cp. Upton, N. Y.		June 1919	June 1919	**Cp. Zachary Taylor, Ky.**	S.O.S. troops.
Base Hospital No. 132	September 1918	Cp. Greenleaf, Ga.	September 1918	Cp. Sheridan, Ala.			December 1918	**Cp. Sheridan, Ala.**	
Base Hospital No. 133	do	do	do	do			do	Do.	
Base Hospital No. 134	do	do	do	Cp. Wadsworth, S. C.			January 1919	Cp. Wadsworth, S. C.	
Base Hospital No. 135	do	do	do	do			do	Do.	
Base Hospital No. 136	**do**	**do**	**do**	**Cp. Wheeler, Ga.**					
			October 1918	Cp. Merritt, N. J.					
			do	Cp. Upton, N. Y.					
			November 1918	P. of E., Hoboken	November 1918	July 1919	July 1919	Cp. Upton, N. Y.	Do.

BASE HOSPITALS—Continued

Unit designation and redesignation	Organization		Stations in United States		Overseas		Demobilization		Remarks
	Month and year	Place	Month and year	Place	From—	To—	Month and year	Place	
Base Hospital No. 137	September 1918	Cp. Greenleaf, Ga.	September 1918	Cp. Wheeler, Ga.			December 1918	Cp. Wheeler, Ga.	
Base Hospital No. 138	do	do	do	Ft. Ontario, N. Y.			do	Ft. Ontario, N. Y.	
Base Hospital No. 139	do	do	do	Cape May, N. J.			do	Cape May, N. J.	
Base Hospital No. 140	do	do	do	Cp. Joseph E. Johnston, Fla.			do	Cp. Joseph E. Johnston, Fla.	
Base Hospital No. 141	do	do	do	Ft. Ethan Allen, Vt.			do	Ft. Ethan Allen, Vt.	
Base Hospital No. 142	do	do	do	Ft. Sheridan, Ill.			do	Ft. Sheridan, Ill.	
Base Hospital No. 143	do	do	do	do			do	Do.	
Base Hospital No. 144	do	do	do	Cp. Dodge, Iowa			do	Cp. Dodge, Iowa.	
Base Hospital No. 145	do	do	do	Ft. Benjamin Harrison, Ind.			do	Ft. Benjamin Harrison, Ind.	
Base Hospital No. 146	do	do	do	Cp. Jackson, S. C.			do	Cp. Jackson, S. C.	
Base Hospital No. 147	do	do	do	Cp. Greene, N. C.			do	Cp. Greene, N. C.	
Base Hospital No. 148	do	do	do	Cp. Sevier, S. C.			do	Cp. Sevier, S. C.	
Base Hospital No. 149	do	do	do	Cp. Sherman, Ohio			do	Cp. Sherman, Ohio.	
Base Hospital No. 150	do	Cp. Travis, Tex.					do	Cp. Travis, Tex.	
Base Hospital No. 151	do	Cp. Greenleaf, Ga.					do	Cp. Greenleaf, Ga.	
Base Hospital No. 152	do	do					do	Do.	
Base Hospital No. 153	do	do					do	Do.	
Base Hospital No. 154	do	do					do	Do.	
Base Hospital No. 155	do	do					do	Do.	
Base Hospital No. 156	do	do					do	Do.	
Base Hospital No. 157	October 1918	do					do	Do.	
Base Hospital No. 158	do	do					do	Do.	
Base Hospital No. 159	do	do					do	Do.	
Base Hospital No. 160	do	do					do	Do.	
Base Hospital No. 161	do	do					do	Do.	
Base Hospital No. 162	do	Cp. Lewis, Wash.					do	Cp. Lewis, Wash.	
Base Hospital No. 163	do	Cp. Bowie, Tex.					do	Cp. Bowie, Tex.	
Base Hospital No. 164	do	Cp. Logan, Tex.					January 1919	Cp. Logan, Tex.	

Base Hospital No. 165	November 1918	Cp. MacArthur, Tex.					do	Cp. MacArthur, Tex.	
Base Hospitals Nos. 166 to 201.									Never orgzd.
Base Hospital No. 202	June 1918	A. E. F			June 1918	April 1919	April 1919	Cp. Dix, N. J	S.O.S. troops.
Base Hospital No. 203									Never orgzd.
Base Hospital No. 204					April 1918	January 1919			Orgzd and demblzd. overseas. S.O.S. troops.
Base Hospitals Nos. 205 to 207.									Never orgzd.
Base Hospital No. 208									See Camp Hosp. No. 47.
Base Hospital No. 209									Never orgzd.
Base Hospital No. 210	November 1918	A. E. F	June 1919	Cp. Merritt, N. J	November 1918	June 1919	June 1919	Presidio of San Francisco, Calif.	
Base Hospital Nos. 211 to 213.									Do.
Base Hospital No. 214	November 1918	A. E. F			November 1918	July 1919	July 1919	Cp. Dix, N. J.	
Base Hospital No. 215									Do.
Base Hospital No. 216	November 1918	A. E. F			November 1918	July 1919	July 1919	Cp. Dix, N. J.	
Base Hospital No. 217									Do.
Base Hospital No. 218									See Camp Hosp. No. 61.
Base Hospitals Nos. 219 to 221.									Never orgzd.
Base Hospital No. 222									Orgzd. and demblzd. overseas, November 1918.
Base Hospital No. 223									Never orgzd.
Base Hospital No. 224									Orgzd. and demblzd overseas, November 1918.
Base Hospitals Nos. 225 to 227.									Never orgzd.
Base Hospital No. 228									Orgzd. and demblzd. overseas, December 1918.
Base Hospital No. 229									Never orgzd.

BASE HOSPITALS—Continued

Unit designation and redesignation	Organization		Stations in United States		Overseas		Demobilization		Remarks
	Month and year	Place	Month and year	Place	From—	To—	Month and year	Place	
Base Hospital No. 230									Orgzd. and demblzd. overseas, November 1918.
Base Hospitals No. 231 to 233.									Never orgzd.
Base Hospital No. 234									Orgzd. and demblzd. overseas, November 1918.
Base Hospital No. 235									Never orgzd.
Base Hospital No. 236									See Camp Hosp. No. 92.
Base Hospital No. 237									Never orgzd.
Base Hospital No. 238					November 1918	February 1919			Orgzd. and demblzd. overseas. S.O.S. troops.

CAMP HOSPITALS, A.E.F.

Unit designation and redesignation	Organization		Stations in United States		Overseas		Demobilization		Remarks
	Month and year	Place	Month and year	Place	From—	To—	Month and year	Place	
Camp Hospital No. 1	October 1917	A. E. F			October 1917	June 1919	June 1919	Cp. Dix, N. J	S.O.S. troops.
Camp Hospital No. 2	March 1918	do			March 1918	July 1919	July 1919	Cp. Jackson, S. C	Do.
Camp Hospital No. 3	June 1918	do			June 1918	June 1919	June 1919	Cp. Devens, Mass.	Do.
Camp Hospital No. 4	March 1918	do			March 1918	July 1919	July 1919	Cp. Sherman, Ohio.	Do.
Camp Hospital No. 5	February 1918	do			February 1918	do	do	Cp. Upton, N. Y	Do.
Camp Hospital No. 6	November 1918	do			November 1918	do	do	Cp. Dodge, Iowa	Do.
Camp Hospital No. 7					June 1918	March 1919			Orgzd. and demblzd. overseas. S.O.S. troops.
Camp Hospital No. 8	June 1918	A. E. F			do	June 1919	June 1919	Cp. Sherman, Ohio.	S.O.S. troops.
Camp Hospital No. 9	do	do			do	do	do	do	Do.
Camp Hospital No. 10					April 1918	March 1919			Orgzd. and demblzd. overseas. S.O.S. troops.

Camp Hospital No. 11	March 1918	A. E. F			March 1918	July 1919	July 1919	Cp. Sherman, Ohio.	S.O.S. troops.
Camp Hospital No. 12	October 1917	do			October 1917	do	do	Cp. Gordon, Ga	Do.
Camp Hospital No. 13					November 1917	December 1918			Orgzd. and demblzd. overseas. S.O.S. troops.
Camp Hospital No. 14	October 1917	A. E. F			October 1917	June 1919	June 1919	Cp. Dodge, Iowa	S.O.S. troops.
Camp Hospital No. 15	do	do			do	July 1919	July 1919	do	Do.
Camp Hospitals Nos. 16 and 17.									Never orgzd.
Camp Hospital No. 18					November 1917	August 1918			Orgzd. and demblzd. overseas.
Camp Hospital No. 19	December 1917	A. E. F			December 1917	July 1919	July 1919	Cp. Hill, Va	S.O.S. troops.
Camp Hospital No. 20					do	May 1919			Orgzd. and demblzd. overseas. S.O.S. troops.
Camp Hospital No. 21	February 1918	A. E. F			February 1918	June 1919	June 1919	Cp. Dix, N. J	S.O.S. troops.
Camp Hospital No. 22					January 1918	February 1919			Orgzd. and demblzd. overseas. S.O.S. troops.
Camp Hospital No. 23					February 1918	August 1918			Do.
Camp Hospital No. 24					January 1918	April 1918			Do.
Camp Hospital No. 25	March 1918	A. E. F			March 1918	June 1919	June 1919	Cp. Upton, N. Y.	
Camp Hospital No. 26	April 1918	do			April 1918	do	do	do	S.O.S. troops.
Camp Hospital No. 27	February 1918	do			February 1918	August 1919	August 1919	Cp. Dix, N. J.	Do.
Camp Hospital No. 28	do	do			do	July 1919	July 1919	do	Do.
Camp Hospital No. 29					do	March 1919			Orgzd. and demblzd. overseas. S.O.S. troops.
Camp Hospital No. 30					do	January 1919			Do.
Camp Hospital No. 31					April 1918	April 1919			Do.
Camp Hospital No. 32									Never orgzd.
Camp Hospital No. 33	January 1918	A. E. F							Active through 1919. S.O.S. troops.
Camp Hospital No. 34					March 1918	February 1919			Orgzd. and demblzd. overseas. S.O.S. troops.
Camp Hospital No. 35					January 1918	do			Orgzd. and demblzd. overseas.

CAMP HOSPITALS A.E.F.—Continued

Unit designation and redesignation	Organization		Stations in United States		Overseas		Demobilization		Remarks
	Month and year	Place	Month and year	Place	From—	To—	Month and year	Place	
Camp Hospital No. 36					May 1918	November 1918			Orgzd. and demblzd. overseas. S.O.S. troops.
Camp Hospital No. 37					March 1918	February 1919			Do.
Camp Hospital No. 38					May 1918	April 1919			Do.
Camp Hospital No. 39	July 1918	A. E. F			July 1918	June 1919	June 1919	Cp. Dix, N. J.	S.O.S. troops.
Camp Hospital No. 40	April 1918	do			April 1918	May 1919	May 1919	Cp. Grant, Ill	Do.
Camp Hospital No. 41	March 1918	do			March 1918	July 1919	July 1919	Cp. Devens, Mass	Do.
Camp Hospital No. 42	May 1918	do			May 1918	May 1919	June 1919	Cp. Dodge, Iowa	Do.
Camp Hospital No. 43					April 1918	September 1919			Orgzd. and demblzd. overseas. S.O.S. troops.
Camp Hospital No. 44					do	December 1918			Do.
Camp Hospital No. 45	July 1918	A. E. F			July 1918	July 1919	July 1919	Cp. Grant, Ill	S.O.S. troops.
Camp Hospital No. 46					May 1918	February 1919			Orgzd. and demblzd. overseas. S.O.S. troops.
Camp Hospital No. 47	June 1918	A. E. F.							
a. Base Hospital No. 208.	November 1918	do			November 1918	June 1919	June 1919	Cp. Dix, N. J	S.O.S. troops.
Camp Hospital No. 48	June 1918	do			June 1918	do	July 1919	Cp. Dodge, Iowa	Do.
Camp Hospital No. 49	September 1918	do			September 1918	do	June 1919	Cp. Devens, Mass	Do.
Camp Hospital No. 50	do	do			do	do	July 1919	Cp. Upton, N. Y	S.O.S. troops.
Camp Hospital No. 51					do	December 1918			Orgzd. and demblzd. overseas.
Camp Hospital No. 52	August 1918	A. E. F			August 1918	July 1919	July 1919	Cp. Gordon, Ga	S.O.S. troops.
Camp Hospital No. 53	September 1918	do			September 1918	do	do	Cp. Zachary Taylor, Ky.	Do.
Camp Hospital No. 54	do	Do.							
a. Camp Hospital No. 78.	October 1918	do			October 1918	December 1918			Orgzd. and demblzd. overseas. S.O.S. troops.

Camp Hospital No. 55					January 1918	May 1919			Do.
Camp Hospital No. 56					July 1918	January 1919			Do.
Camp Hospital No. 57					August 1918	do			Do.
Camp Hospital No. 58									Never orgzd.
Camp Hospital No. 59					September 1918	March 1919			Orgzd. and demblzd. overseas. S.O.S. troops.
Camp Hospital No. 60					October 1918	December 1918			Orgzd. and demblzd. overseas.
Camp Hospital No. 61	August 1918	A. E. F			August 1918	July 1919	July 1919	Cp. Upton, N. Y	S.O.S. troops.
Camp Hospital No. 62					do	November 1918			Orgzd. and demblzd. overseas. S.O.S. troops.
Camp Hospital No. 63									Never orgzd.
Camp Hospital No. 64	August 1918	A. E. F			August 1918	June 1919	June 1919	Cp. Dix, N. J	S.O.S. troops.
Camp Hospital No. 65	October 1918	do			October 1918	do	do	Cp. Grant, Ill	Do.
Camp Hospital No. 66	August 1918	do			August 1918	do	July 1919	Cp. Upton, N. Y	Do.
Camp Hospital No. 67					November 1918	April 1919			Orgzd. and demblzd. overseas. S.O.S. troops.
Camp Hospital No. 68	September 1918	A. E. F			September 1918	July 1919	July 1919	Cp. Devens, Mass.	S.O.S. troops.
Camp Hospital No. 69					October 1918	December 1918			Orgzd. and demblzd. overseas. S.O.S. troops.
Camp Hospital No. 70					do	February 1919			Do.
Camp Hospital No. 71					September 1918	October 1918			Do.
Camp Hospital No. 72	September 1918	A. E. F			do	July 1919	July 1919	Cp. Upton, N. Y	S.O.S. troops.
Camp Hospital No. 73					October 1918	January 1919			Orgzd. and demblzd. overseas. S.O.S. troops.
Camp Hospital No. 74									Never orgzd.
Camp Hospital No. 75					October 1918	January 1919			Orgzd. and demblzd. overseas.
Camp Hospital No. 76	March 1918	A. E. F			March 1918	June 1919	July 1919	Cp. Mills, N. Y	S.O.S. troops.
Camp Hospital No. 77					October 1918	November 1918			Orgzd. and demblzd. overseas. S.O.S. troops.
Camp Hospital No. 78									See Cp. Hospital No. 54.

CAMP HOSPITALS A.E.F.—Continued

Unit designation and redesignation	Organization		Stations in United States		Overseas		Demobilization		Remarks
	Month and year	Place	Month and year	Place	From—	To—	Month and year	Place	
Camp Hospital No. 79					October 1918	May 1919			Orgzd. and demblzd. overseas. S.O.S. trroops.
Camp Hospitals Nos. 80 and 81.									Never orgzd.
Camp Hospital No. 82					October 1918	April 1919			Orgzd. and demblzd. overseas. S.O.S. troops.
Camp Hospitals Nos. 83 and 84.									Never orgzd.
Camp Hospital No. 85	November 1918				November 1918	June 1919	July 1919	Cp. Upton, N. Y.	S.O.S. troops.
Camp Hospital No. 86					do				Orgzd. and demblzd. November 1918, overseas.
Camp Hospital No. 87					October 1918	February 1919			Orgzd. and demblzd. overseas. S.O.S. troops.
Camp Hospital No. 88					November 1918	December 1918			Do.
Camp Hospitals Nos. 89 and 90.									Never orgzd.
Camp Hospital No. 91					October 1918	April 1919			Orgzd. and demblzd. overseas. S.O.S. troops.
Camp Hospital No. 92	October 1918	A. E. F.			November 1918	January 1919			Do.
a. Base Hospital No. 236.	November 1918	do							
Camp Hospital No. 93	October 1918	do			October 1918	June 1919	June 1919	Cp. Devens, Mass.	Do.
Camp Hospital No. 94					December 1918	April 1919			Orgzd. and demblzd. overseas.
Camp Hospital No. 95					November 1918	June 1919			
Camp Hospital No. 96					do	January 1919			Do.

Camp Hospital No. 97	December 1918	A. E. F			December 1918	June 1919	July 1919	Cp. Upton, N. Y.	S.O.S. troops.
Camp Hospitals Nos. 98 and 99.									Never orgzd.
Camp Hospital No. 100					November 1918	January 1919			Orgzd. and demblzd. overseas. S.O.S. troops.
Camp Hospital No. 101	November 1918	A. E. F			do	July 1919	July 1919	Cp. Dix, N. J.	
Camp Hospital No. 102					December 1918	May 1919			Orgzd. and demblzd. overseas.
Camp Hospital No. 103	January 1919	A. E. F			January 1919	do	June 1919	Cp. Dix, N. J.	
Camp Hospital No. 104					February 1919	do			Do.
Camp Hospital No. 105					do	do			Do.
Camp Hospital No. 106					do	do			Do.
Camp Hospital No. 107	March 1919	A. E. F			March 1919	July 1919	July 1919	Cp. Upton, N. Y.	
Camp Hospital No. 108	do	do			do	do	do	Cp. Bowie, Tex.	
Camp Hospital No. 109	February 1919	do			February 1919	do	do	Cp. Jackson, S. C.	
Camp Hospital No. 110	do	do			do	do	do	Cp. Gordon, Ga.	
Camp Hospital No. 111	March 1919	do			March 1919	June 1919	June 1919	Cp. Upton, N. Y.	
Camp Hospital No. 112	April 1919	do			April 1919	do	July 1919	Cp. Gordon, Ga.	
Camp Hospital No. 113									Never orgzd.
Camp Hospital No. 114	May 1919	A. E. F			May 1919	July 1919	July 1919	Cp. Upton, N. Y.	
Camp Hospital No. 115	April 1919	do			April 1919	do	do	Cp. Dix, N. J.	
Camp Hospital No. 116									Never orgzd.
Camp Hospital No. 117					April 1919	June 1919			Orgzd. and demblzd. overseas.
Camp Hospital No. 118					do	August 1919			Do.
Camp Hospital No. 119	April 1919	A. E. F			do	July 1919	July 1919	Cp. Devens, Mass.	
Camp Hospital No. 120	do	do			do	do	do	Cp. Gordon, Ga.	
Camp Hospital No. 121									See American Red Cross Military Hospital No. 3.
Camp Hospital No. 122	April 1919	A. E. F			April 1919	August 1919	August 1919	Cp. Devens, Mass.	

EVACUATION HOSPITALS

Evacuation Hospital No. 1.	October 1917	Ft. Riley, Kans.	December 1917	Cp. Merritt, N. J.					
			do	P. of E., Halifax	December 1917.				
			April 1919	Newport News, Va.		April 1919	May 1919	Cp. Funston, Kans.	Army troops.

EVACUATION HOSPITALS—Continued

Unit designation and redesignation	Organization		Stations in United States		Overseas		Demobilization		Remarks
	Month and year	Place	Month and year	Place	From—	To—	Month and year	Place	
Evacuation Hospital No. 2.	July 1917	Ft. Benjamin Harrison, Ind.	December 1917	Cp. Merritt, N. J.					
			January 1918	P. of E., Portland	January 1918.				
			April 1919	Newport News, Va.		**April 1919**	**May 1919**	Cp. Zachary Taylor, Ky.	**Army troops.**
Evacuation Hospital No. 3.	September 1917	Ft. Oglethorpe, Ga.	December 1917	Cp. Merritt, N. J.					
			January 1918	P. of E., Hoboken	January 1918.				
			April 1919	Cp. Dix, N. J.		do	April 1919	Cp. Dix, N. J.	Do.
Evacuation Hospital No. 4.	November 1917	do	March 1918	Cp. Crane, Pa.					
			April 1918	Cp. Mills, N. Y.					
			May 1918	P. of E., Hoboken	May 1918.				
			April 1919	Newport News, Va.		do	May 1919	Cp. Upton, N. Y.	Do.
Evacuation Hospital No. 5.	do	do	March 1918	Cp. Crane, Pa.					
			May 1918	P. of E., Hoboken	May 1918	February 1919	March 1919	Do.	
Evacuation Hospital No. 6.	do	do	April 1918	Cp. Merritt, N. J.					
			do	P. of E., Hoboken	April 1918	April 1919	May 1919	Cp. Dix, N. J.	Do.
Evacuation Hospital No. 7.	do	Ft. Riley, Kans.	do	Cp. Merritt, N. J.					
			May 1918	P. of E., Hoboken	May 1918	do	do	Cp. Devens, Mass.	Do.
Evacuation Hospital No. 8.	January 1918	Ft. Oglethorpe, Ga.	do	Cp. Merritt, N. J.					
			do	P. of E., Hoboken	do	May 1919	June 1919	Cp. Upton, N. Y.	Do.
Evacuation Hospital No. 9.	do	Ft. Riley, Kans.	June 1918	Cp. Merritt, N. J.					
			August 1918	P. of E., Hoboken	August 1918.				
			June 1919	Newport News, Va.		June 1919	July 1919	Cp. Dix, N. J.	Do.

Evacuation Hospital No. 10.	March 1918	do	June 1918	Cp. Dix, N. J.				
			August 1918	P. of E., Hoboken	August 1918.			
			June 1919	Cp. Devens, Mass.		do	June 1919	Cp. Devens, Mass.	Do.
Evacuation Hospital No. 11.	do	do	May 1918	Cp. Crane, Pa.					
			August 1918	P. of E., Hoboken	August 1918.				
			May 1919	Cp. Merritt, N. J.		May 1919	May 1919	Cp. Zachary Taylor, Ky.	Do.
Evacuation Hospital No. 12.	April 1918	do	June 1918	Cp. Dix, N. J.					
			August 1918	P. of E., Hoboken	August 1918.				
			June 1919	Cp. Stuart, Va.		June 1919	July 1919	Cp. Dodge, Iowa	Do.
Evacuation Hospital No. 13.	February 1918	Ft. Oglethorpe, Ga.	June 1918	Cp. Gordon, Ga.					
			August 1918	Cp. Hill, Va.					
			do	P. of E., Newport News.	August 1918.				
			July 1919	Cp. Merritt, N. J.		July 1919	do	Cp. Sherman, Ohio.	Do.
Evacuation Hospital No. 14.	do	Cp. Greenleaf, Ga.	June 1918	Cp. Jackson, S. C.					
			July 1918	P. of E., Newport News.	July 1918.				
			May 1919	Cp. Stuart, Va.		May 1919	May 1919	do	S.O.S. troops.
Evacuation Hospital No. 15.	March 1918	Ft. Riley, Kans.	June 1918	Cp. Lee, Va.					
			August 1918	P. of E., Newport News.	August 1918.				
			June 1919	Cp. Merritt, N. J.		June 1919	June 1919	Cp. Lewis, Wash.	S.O.S. troops. Army troops.
Evacuation Hospital No. 16.	do	do	June 1918	Cp. Meade, Md.					
			August 1918	P. of E., Hoboken	August 1918.				
			August 1919	Cp. Merritt, N. J.		August 1919	August 1919	do	Army troops.
Evacuation Hospital No. 17.	June 1918	do	June 1918	Ft. Sam Houston, Tex.					
			September 1918	P. of E., Presidio of San Francisco.					
			October 1918	Vladivostok, Russia.					Active through 1919.

EVACUATION HOSPITALS—Continued

Unit designation and redesignation	Organization		Stations in United States		Overseas		Demobilization		Remarks
	Month and year	Place	Month and year	Place	From—	To—	Month and year	Place	
Evacuation Hospital No. 18.	June 1918	Ft. Riley, Kans.	June 1918	Cp. Zachary Taylor, Ky.					
			August 1918	Cp. Upton, N. Y.					
			do	P. of E., Hoboken	August 1918.				
			May 1919	Cp. Morrison, Va.		May 1919	May 1919	Cp. Pike, Ark	S.O.S. troops.
Evacuation Hospital No. 19.	do	do	August 1918	Cp. Dix, N. J.					
			September 1918	P. of E., Hoboken	September 1918.				
			August 1919	Cp. Merritt, N. J.		August 1919	August 1919	do	Army troops.
Evacuation Hospital No. 20.	do	do	June 1918	Cp. Grant, Ill.					
			August 1918	Cp. Upton, N. Y.					
			do	P. of E., Hoboken	August 1918.				
			June 1919	Cp. Stuart, Va.		June 1919	June 1919	Cp. Zachary Taylor, Ky.	Do.
Evacuation Hostipal No. 21.	do	do	June 1918	Cp. Custer, Mich.					
			August 1918	Cp. Upton, N. Y.					
			do	P. of E., Hoboken	August 1918.				
			June 1919	Cp. Merritt, N. J.		do	do	Cp. Pike, Ark	S.O.S. troops. Army troops.
Evacuation Hospital No. 22.	do	Cp. Greenleaf, Ga.	June 1918	Cp. Sevier, S. C.					
			August 1918	Cp. Upton, N. Y.					
			do	P. of E., Hoboken	August 1918.				
			June 1919	Cp. Merritt, N. J.		do	do	Cp. Upton, N. Y.	Do.
Evacuation Hospital No. 23.	do	do	June 1918	Ft. McPherson, Ga.					
			August 1918	Cp. Upton, N. Y.					
			September 1918	P. of E., Hoboken	September 1918.				
			June 1919	Cp. Merritt, N. J.		do	do	Cp. Gordon, Ga.	Do.

Evacuation Hospital No. 24.	do	do	June 1918	Cp. Devens, Mass.					
			August 1918	P. of E., Hoboken	August 1918.	May 1919	do	do	Do.
			May 1919	Cp. Upton, N. Y.					
Evacuation Hospital No. 25.	do	do	August 1918	Cp. Dodge, Iowa.					
			October 1918	Cp. Upton, N. Y.					
			November 1918	P. of E., Hoboken	November 1918.	do	May 1919	Cp. Dodge, Iowa	S.O.S. troops.
			May 1919	Cp. Mills, N. Y.					
Evacuation Hospital No. 26.	July 1918	do	September 1918	Cp. Jackson, S. C.					
			October 1918	Cp. Mills, N. Y.					
			do	P. of E., Hoboken	October 1918.	August 1919	August 1919	Cp. Upton, N. Y.	Do.
			August 1919	Cp. Merritt, N. J.					
Evacuation Hospital No. 27.	June 1918	do	September 1918	Cp. Pike, Ark.					
			October 1918	P. of E., Hoboken	October 1918	September 1919	September 1919	Cp. Dix, N. J.	Do.
Evacuation Hospital No. 28	do	do	September 1918	Cp. Sherman, Ohio.					
			October 1918	Cp. Upton, N. Y.					
			do	P. of E., Hoboken	Do.	July 1919	July 1919	Cp. Sherman, Ohio.	Do.
			July 1919	Cp. Mills, N. Y.					
Evacuation Hospital No. 29.	do	do	September 1918	Cp. Beauregard, La.					
			October 1918	Cp. Upton, N. Y.					
			November 1918	P. of E., Hoboken	November 1918.	do	do	Cp. Shelby, Miss.	Do.
			July 1919	Cp. Merritt, N. J.					
Evacuation Hospital No. 30.	do	do	September 1918	Cp. Greene, N. C.					
			October 1918	P. of E., Hoboken	October 1918.	August 1919	August 1919	Cp. Dix, N. J.	Do.
			August 1919	Cp. Merritt, N. J.					
Evacuation Hospital No. 31.	do	do	August 1918	Cp. Hancock, Ga.					
			November 1918	Cp. Mills, N. Y.					
			do	P. of E., Hoboken	November 1918.	July 1919	July 1919	Cp. Pike, Ark.	Do.
			July 1919	Cp. Stuart, Va.					
Evacuation Hospital No. 32.	July 1918	do	September 1918	Cp. McClellan, Ala.					
			November 1918	Cp. Mills, N. Y.					
			do	P. of E., Hoboken	November 1918.	May 1919	June 1919	Cp. Dix, N. J.	Do.
			May 1919	Cp. Merritt, N. J.					

EVACUATION HOSPITALS—Continued

Unit designation and redesignation	Organization		Stations in United States		Overseas		Demobilization		Remarks
	Month and year	Place	Month and year	Place	From—	To—	Month and year	Place	
Evacuation Hospital No. 33.	August 1918	**Cp. Greenleaf, Ga.**	September 1918	Cp. Shelby, Miss.					
			October 1918	Cp. Upton, N. Y.					
			November 1918	P. of E., Hoboken	November 1918.				
			May 1919	Cp. Merritt, N. J.		**May 1919**	May 1919	Cp. Dodge, Iowa	**S.O.S. troops.**
Evacuation Hospital No. 34.	do	do	September 1918	Cp. Sheridan, Ala.					
			November 1918	Cp. Upton, N. Y.					
			do	P. of E., Hoboken	November 1918	do	do	Cp. Dix, N. J	Do.
Evacuation Hospital No. 35.	September 1918	do	September 1918	Cp. Wadsworth, S. C.					
			November 1918	Cp. Upton, N. Y.					
			do	P. of E., Hoboken	do	April 1919	April 1919	Cp. Lee, Va	Do.
Evacuation Hospital No. 36.	August 1918	do	September 1918	Cp. Wheeler, Ga.					
			October 1918	Cp. Upton, N. Y.					
			do	P. of E., Hoboken	October 1918	July 1919	July 1919	Cp. Stuart, Va	Do.
Evacuation Hospital No. 37.	do	do	September 1918	Cp. Grant, Ill.					
			November 1918	Cp. Upton, N. Y.					
			do	P. of E., Hoboken	November 1918	do	do	Cp. Devens, Mass.	Do.
Evacuation Hospital No. 38.	September 1918	do	October 1918	Cp. Meade, Md			December 1918	Cp. Meade, Md.	
Evacuation Hospital No. 39.	**October 1918**	**do**					**do**	**Cp. Greenleaf, Ga.**	
Evacuation Hospital No. 40.	August 1918	do					do	Do.	
Evacuation Hospital No. 41.	September 1918	do					do	Do.	
Evacuation Hospital No. 42.	October 1918	do					do	Do.	
Evacuation Hospital No. 43.	September 1918	do					do	Do.	

Evacuation Hospital No. 44.	do	do					do	Do.	
Evacuation Hospital No. 45.	do	do					do	Do.	
Evacuation Hospital No. 46.	do	do					do	Do.	
Evacuation Hospital No. 47.	do	do					do	Do.	
Evacuation Hospital No. 48.	do	do					do	Do.	
Evacuation Hospital No. 49.	do	do	October 1918 do August 1919	Cp. Merritt, N. J. P. of E., Hoboken Cp. Merritt, N. J.	October 1918.	August 1919	August 1919	Cp. Dix, N. J.	S.O.S. troops.
Evacuation Hospital No. 50.	do	do					December 1918	Cp. Greenleaf, Ga.	
Evacuation Hospital No. 51.	do	do					do	Do.	
Evacuation Hospital No. 52.	do	do					do	Do.	
Evacuation Hospital No. 53.	do	do					do	Do.	
Evacuation Hospital No. 54.	do	do					do	Do.	
Evacuation Hospital No. 55.	October 1918	do					do	Do.	
Evacuation Hospital No. 56.	do	do					do	Do.	
Evacuation Hospital No. 57.	do	do					do	Do.	
Evacuation Hospital No. 58.	do	do					do	Do.	
Evacuation Hospital No. 59.	do	do					do	Do.	
Evacuation Hospital No. 60.	do	do					do	Do.	
Evacuation Hospitals Nos. 61 to 113.									Never orgzd.
Evacuation Hospital No. 114.	November 1918	A. E. F			November 1918	March 1919.			

HOSPITAL CENTERS, A.E.F.

Unit designation and redesignation	Organization		Stations in United States		Overseas		Demobilization		Remarks
	Month and year	Place	Month and year	Place	From—	To—	Month and year	Place	
Hospital Center, Allerey.[1]					June 1918	March 1919.			
Hospital Center, Bazoilles.[1]					July 1918	May 1919.			
Hospital Center, Beau Desert.[1]					do	June 1919.			
Hospital Center, Beaune.[1]					August 1918	March 1919.			
Hospital Center, Clermont-Ferrand.[1]					September 1918	February 1919.			
Hospital Center, Commercy.[1]					November 1918	January 1919.			
Hospital Center, Joue-Les-Tours.[1]					July 1918	June 1919.			
Hospital Center, Kerhuon.[1]					September 1918	July 1919.			
Hospital Center, Langres.[1]					August 1918	January 1919.			
Hospital Center, Limoges.[1]					July 1918	February 1919.			
Hospital Center, Mars-Sur-Allier.[1]					do	May 1919.			
Hospital Center, Mesves.[1]					June 1918	Do.			
Hospital Center, Nantes.[1]					July 1918	Do.			
Hospital Center, Pau.[1]					October 1918	December 1918.			
Hospital Center, Perigueux.[1]					September 1918	May 1919.			
Hospital Center, Rimaucourt.[1]					do	Do.			

Hospital Center, Riviera.[1]					do	June 1919.			
Hospital Center, Savenay.[1]					August 1918	July 1919.			
Hospital Center, Toul[1]					do	May 1919.			
Hospital Center, Vannes.[1]					November 1918	June 1919.			
Hospital Center, Vichy[1]					August 1918	April 1919.			
Hospital Center, Vittel-Contrexeville.[1]					January 1918	January 1919.			

[1] Orgzd. and demblzd. overseas.

SANITARY TRAINS

1st Sanitary Train	August 1917	New York City, N. Y.	August 1917	P. of E., Hoboken	August 1917				Cmpnt. of 1st Div
			September 1919	Cp. Z. Taylor, Ky		September 1919			Active through 1919.
2d Sanitary Train	August 1918	A. E. F			August 1918				Cmpnt. of 2d Div.
			August 1919	Cp. Mills, N. Y		August 1919.			
			do	Cp. Travis, Tex					Active through 1919.
3d Sanitary Train	December 1917	Ft. Clark, Tex	March 1918	Cp. Merritt, N. J					Cmpnt. of 3d Div.
			April 1918	P. of E., Hoboken	April 1918.				
			August 1919	Cp. Pike, Ark		August 1919			Active through 1919.
4th Sanitary Train	March 1918	Cp. Greene, N. C	May 1918	Cp. Merritt, N. J					Cmpnt. of 4th Div.
			do	P. of E., Hoboken	May 1918.				
			August 1919	Cp. Dodge, Iowa		August 1919.			
			do	Cp. Lewis, Wash					Active through 1919.
5th Sanitary Train	December 1917	Cp. Logan, Tex	May 1918	Cp. Upton, N. Y					Cmpnt. of 5th Div.
			June 1918	P. of E., Hoboken	June 1918.				
			July 1919	Cp. Gordon, Ga		July 1919			Active through 1919.
6th Sanitary Train	March 1918	Cp. Wadsworth, S. C.	June 1918	Cp. Mills, N. Y					Cmpnt. of 6th Div.
			July 1918	P. of E., Hoboken	July 1918.				
			June 1919	Cp. Grant, Ill		June 1919			Active through 1919.

SANITARY TRAINS—Continued

Unit designation and redesignation	Organization		Stations in United States		Overseas		Demobilization		Remarks
	Month and year	Place	Month and year	Place	From—	To—	Month and year	Place	
7th Sanitary Train	December 1917	Cp. Greenleaf, Ga.	July 1918	Cp. Merritt, N. J.					Cmpnt. of 7th Div.
			August 1918	P. of E., Hoboken.	August 1918.				
			July 1919	Cp. Funston, Kans.		July 1919			Active through 1919.
8th Sanitary Train	January 1918	Cp. Fremont, Calif.	October 1918	Cp. Mills, N. Y.					Cmpnt. of 8th Div.
			November 1918	Cp. Lee, Va.			February 1919	Cp. Lee, Va.	
9th Sanitary Train	August 1918	Cp. Sheridan, Ala.					do	Cp. Sheridan, Ala.	Cmpnt. of 9th Div.
10th Sanitary Train	do	Cp. Funston, Kans.					do	Cp. Funston, Kans.	Cmpnt. of 10th Div.
11th Sanitary Train	do	Cp. Meade, Md.					do	Cp. Meade, Md.	Cmpnt. of 11th Div.
12th Sanitary Train	July 1918	Cp. Devens, Mass.					January 1919	Cp. Devens, Mass.	Cmpnt. of 12th Div.
13th Sanitary Train	August 1918	Cp. Lewis, Wash.					March 1919	Cp. Lewis, Wash.	Cmpnt. of 13th Div.
14th Sanitary Train	do	Cp. Custer, Mich.					February 1919	Cp. Custer, Mich.	Cmpnt. of 14th Div.
15th Sanitary Train	do	Cp. Logan, Tex.					do	Cp. Logan, Tex.	Cmpnt. of 15th Div.
16th Sanitary Train	September 1918	Cp. Kearny, Calif.					February 1919	Cp. Kearny, Calif.	Cmpnt. of 16th Div.
17th Sanitary Train									Never orgzd.
18th Sanitary Train	September 1918	Cp. Travis, Tex.					February 1919	Cp. Travis, Tex.	Cmpnt. of 18th Div.
19th Sanitary Train	do	Cp. Dodge, Iowa.					January 1919	Cp. Dodge, Iowa.	Cmpnt. of 19th Div.
20th Sanitary Train	do	Cp. Sevier, S. C.					February 1919	Cp. Sevier, S. C.	Cmpnt. of 20th Div.
21st to 100th Sanitary Trains.									Never orgzd.
101st Sanitary Train	August 1917	Framingham, Mass.	October 1917	P. of E., Hoboken.	October 1917	April 1919	April 1919	Cp. Devens, Mass.	Cmpnt. of 26th Div.
102d Sanitary Train	September 1917	Cp. Wadsworth, S. C.	May 1918	Cp. Stuart, Va.					Cmpnt. of 27th Div
			June 1918	P. of E., Newport News.	June 1918.				
			March 1919	Cp. Merritt, N. J.		March 1919	April 1919	Cp. Upton, N. Y.	

103d Sanitary Train	October 1917	Cp. Hancock, Ga.	May 1918	P. of E., Hoboken	May 1918	May 1919	May 1919	Cp. Dix, N. J.	Cmpnt. of 28th Div.
104th Sanitary Train	do	Cp. McClellan, Ala.	June 1918	Cp. Mills, N. Y.					Cmpnt. of 29th Div.
			July 1918	P. of E., Hoboken	July 1918.				
			May 1919	Cp. Merritt, N. J.		May 1919	June 1919	Cp. Meade, Md.	
105th Sanitary Train	do	Cp. Sevier, S. C.	May 1918	Cp. Mills, N. Y.					Cmpnt. of 30th Div.
			June 1918	P. of E., Hoboken	June 1918	April 1919	April 1919	Cp. Jackson, S. C.	
106th Sanitary Train	do	Cp. Wheeler, Ga.	September 1918	Cp. Mills, N. Y.					Cmpnt. of 31st Div.
			October 1918	P. of E., Hoboken	October 1918.				
			May 1919	Cp. Merritt, N. J.		May 1919	June 1919	Cp. Gordon, Ga.	
107th Sanitary Train	do	Cp. MacArthur, Tex.	January 1918	do					Cmpnt. of 32d Div.
			February 1918	P. of E., Hoboken	February 1918.				
			May 1919	Cp. Morrison, Va.		May 1919	May 1919	Cp. Grant, Ill.	
108th Sanitary Train	November 1917	Cp. Logan, Tex.	May 1918	Cp. Merritt, N. J.					Cmpnt. of 33d Div.
			June 1918	P. of E., Hoboken	June 1918.				
			May 1919	Cp. Mills, N. Y.		May 1919	June 1919	Cp. Grant, Ill.	
109th Sanitary Train	October 1917	Cp. Cody, N. Mex.	September 1918	Cp. Dix, N. J.					Cmpnt. of 34th Div.
			October 1918	P. of E., Hoboken	October 1918.				
			January 1919	Cp. Merritt, N. J.		January 1919	February 1919	Cp. Grant, Ill.	
110th Sanitary Train	do	Cp. Doniphan, Okla.	May 1918	P. of E., Hoboken	May 1918				Cmpnt. of 35th Div.
			April 1919	Cp. Stuart, Va.		April 1919	May 1919	Cp. Funston, Kans.	
111th Sanitary Train	do	Cp. Bowie, Tex.	July 1918	Cp. Mills, N. Y.					Cmpnt. of 36th Div.
			do	P. of E., Hoboken	July 1918.				
			June 1919	Cp. Mills, N. Y.		June 1919	June 1919	Cp. Bowie, Tex.	
112th Sanitary Train	September 1917	Cp. Sheridan, Ala.	June 1918	Cp. Upton, N. Y.					Cmpnt. of 37th Div.
			July 1918	P. of E., Hoboken	July 1918.				
			March 1919	Cp. Mills, N. Y.		March 1919	April 1919	Cp. Sherman, Ohio.	
113th Sanitary Train	do	Cp. Shelby, Miss.	September 1918	do					Cmpnt. of 38th Div.
			October 1918	P. of E., Hoboken	October 1918.				
			January 1919	Cp. Merritt, N. J.		January 1919	February 1919	Cp. Zachary Taylor, Ky.	
114th Sanitary Train	October 1917	Cp. Beauregard, La.	August 1918	Cp. Mills, N. Y.					Cmpnt. of 39th Div.
			do	P. of E., Hoboken	August 1918.				
a. VII Corps Sanitary Train.	January 1919	A. E. F.	June 1919	Cp. Devens, Mass.		June 1919	July 1919	Cp. Pike Ark.	
115th Sanitary Train	October 1917	Cp. Kearny, Calif.	August 1918	Cp. Mills, N. Y.					Cmpnt. of 40th Div.
			do	P. of E., Hoboken	August 1918.				
			April 1919	Cp. Merritt, N. J.		April 1919	May 1919	Presidio of San Francisco, Calif.	

SANITARY TRAINS—Continued

Unit designation and redesignation	Organization		Stations in United States		Overseas		Demobilization		Remarks
	Month and year	Place	Month and year	Place	From—	To—	Month and year	Place	
116th Sanitary Train	October 1917	Cp. Greene, N. C.	October 1917	Cp. Mills, N. Y.					Cmpnt. of 41st Div.
			December 1917	P. of E., Hoboken	December 1917	May 1919	May 1919	Cp. Dodge, Iowa	Corps troops.
117th Sanitary Train	September 1917	Cp. Merritt, N. J.	October 1917	do	October 1917				Cmpnt. of 42d Div.
			April 1919	Cp. Merritt, N. J.		April 1919	May 1919	Cp. Custer, Mich.	
118th to 300th Sanitary Trains.									Never orgzd.
301st Sanitary Train	September 1917	Cp. Devens, Mass.	July 1918	P. of E., Montreal	July 1918	June 1919	June 1919	Cp. Devens, Mass.	Cmpnt. of 76th Div.
302d Sanitary Train	do	Cp. Upton, N. Y.	April 1918	P. of E., Hoboken	April 1918	May 1919	May 1919	Cp. Upton, N. Y.	Cmpnt. of 77th Div.
303d Sanitary Train	October 1917	Cp. Dix, N. J.	June 1918	do	June 1918	do	do	Cp. Dix, N. J.	Cmpnt. of 78th Div.
304th Sanitary Train	do	Cp. Meade, Md.	July 1918	do	July 1918	June 1919	June 1919	do	Cmpnt. of 79th Div.
305th Sanitary Train	September 1917	Cp. Lee, Va.	May 1918	P. of E., Newport News.	May 1918	May 1919	do	do	Cmpnt. of 80th Div.
306th Sanitary Train	do	Cp. Jackson, S. C.	do	Cp. Sevier, S. C.					Cmpnt. of 81st Div.
			July 1918	Cp. Mills, N. Y.					
			August 1918	P. of E., Hoboken	August 1918.				
			June 1919	Cp. Stuart, Va.		June 1919	June 1919	Cp. Jackson, S. C.	
307th Sanitary Train	October 1917	Cp. Gordon, Ga.	May 1918	Cp. Mills, N. Y.					Cmpnt. of 82d Div.
			do	P. of E., Hoboken	May 1918	May 1919	May 1919	Cp. Dix, N. J.	
308th Sanitary Train	January 1918	Cp. Sherman, Ohio.	June 1918	Cp. Mills, N. Y.					Cmpnt. of 83d Div.
			do	P. of E., Hoboken	June 1918.				
			February 1919	Cp. Merritt, N. J.		February 1919	February 1919	Cp. Sherman, Ohio.	
309th Sanitary Train	August 1917	Cp. Zachary Taylor, Ky.	June 1918	Cp. Sherman, Ohio.					Cmpnt. of 84th Div.
			August 1918	Cp. Mills, N. Y.					
			September 1918	P. of E., Hoboken	September 1918.				
			January 1919	Cp. Merritt, N. J.		January 1919	January 1919	Cp. Taylor, Ky.	
310th Sanitary Train	January 1918	Cp. Custer, Mich.	July 1918	P. of E., Hoboken	July 1918				Cmpnt. of 85th Div.
			April 1919	Cp. Mills, N. Y.		April 1919	April 1919	Cp. Custer, Mich.	
311th Sanitary Train	August 1917	Cp. Grant, Ill.	August 1918	do					Cmpnt. of 86th Div.
			September 1918	P. of E., Hoboken	September 1918.				
			January 1919	Cp. Merritt, N. J.		January 1919	February 1919	Cp. Grant, Ill.	Skeletonized November 1918.

312th Sanitary Train	September 1917	Cp. Pike, Ark.	June 1918 August 1918 January 1919	Cp. Dix, N. J. P. of E., Hoboken Cp. Merritt, N. J.	 August 1918. 	January 1919	February 1919	Cp. Dix, N. J.	Cmpnt. of 87th Div. Skeletonized December 1918.
313th Sanitary Train	August 1917	Cp. Dodge, Iowa	August 1918 do June 1919	Cp. Mills, N. Y. P. of E., Hoboken Newport News, Va.	 August 1918. 	June 1919	June 1919	Cp. Dodge, Iowa	Cmpnt. of 88th Div.
314th Sanitary Train	September 1917	Cp. Funston, Kans.	June 1918 do May 1919	Cp. Mills, N. Y. P. of E., Hoboken Cp. Upton, N. Y.	 June 1918. 	May 1919	June 1919	Cp. Dodge, Iowa.	Cmpnt. of 89th Div.
315th Sanitary Train	October 1917	Cp. Travis, Tex.	June 1918 do June 1919	Cp. Mills, N. Y. P. of E., Hoboken Newport News, Va.	 June 1918. 	June 1919	June 1919	Cp. Bowie, Tex.	Cmpnt. of 90th Div.
316th Sanitary Train	September 1917	Cp. Lewis, Wash.	June 1918 July 1918 April 1919	Cp. Merritt, N. J. P. of E., Hoboken Cp. Upton, N. Y.	 July 1918. 	April 1919	May 1919	Cp. Lewis, Wash.	Cmpnt. of 91st Div.
317th Sanitary Train	November 1917	Cp. Funston, Kans.	June 1918 February 1919	P. of E., Hoboken Cp. Upton, N. Y.	June 1918 	 February 1919	 March 1919	 Cp. Zachary Taylor, Ky.	Cmpnt. of 92d Div.
318th and 319th Sanitary Trains.									Never orgzd.
320th Sanitary Train	September 1918	Cp. Sherman, Ohio.					December 1918	Cp. Sherman, Ohio.	Cmpnt. of 95th Div.
321st Sanitary Train	November 1918	Cp. Wadsworth, S. C.					January 1919	Cp. Wadsworth, S. C.	Cmpnt. of 96th Div.
322d Sanitary Train	September 1918	Cp. Cody, N. Mex.					December 1918	Cp. Cody, N. Mex.	Cmpnt. of 97th Div.

MEDICAL SPECIAL AND TECHNICAL UNITS

Units	Unit No.	Active service	Unit No.	Active service	Unit No.	Active service	Unit No.	Active service	Unit No.	Active service	Remarks
Ambulance Company (non-Divisional).	1–5	Never orgzd.	6	August 1917–January 1919	7	Never orgzd.	8	1914 through December 1919	9	Never orgzd.	
	10	July 1917 through December 1919	11–13	Never orgzd.	14	June 1917–January 1919	15–17	Never orgzd.	18	June 1917–December 1918	
	19–23	Never orgzd.	24	August 1917–July 1919	25–38	Never orgzd.	39	December 1917–July 1919	40	Never orgzd.	
	41	December 1917–March 1919	42	December 1917–May 1919	43	Never orgzd.	44	July 1918–July 1919	45–62	Never orgzd.	
	63	November 1918–December 1918	64	November 1918–December 1918	65	November 1918–January 1919	66	November 1918–December 1918			
U. S. Army Ambulance Service.	b 501	June 1917–March 1919	b 502	June 1917–May 1919	b 503	June 1917–May 1919	b 504	June 1917–April 1919	b 505	June 1917–May 1919	Originally numbered 1 to 150, renumbered August 1917.
	b 506	June 1917–May 1919	b 507	June 1917–June 1919	b 508	June 1917–June 1919	b 509	June 1917–March 1919	b 510	June 1917–April 1919	a Orgzd. overseas; demobilized in U. S.
	b 511	June 1917–April 1919	b 512	June 1917–April 1919	b 513	June 1917–April 1919	b 514	June 1917–July 1919	b 515	Do.	b S.O.S. Troop .
	b 516	-----do-----------	b 517	June 1917–May 1919	b 518	June 1917–June 1919	519	June 1917–December 1917	b 520	Do.	
	b 521	-----do-----------	b 522	June 1917–June 1919	b 523	June 1917–April 1919	b 524	June 1917–June 1919	b 525	Do.	
	b 526	-----do-----------	b 527	June 1917–April 1919	b 528	June 1917–June 1919	b 529	June 1917–April 1919	b 530	Do.	
	b 531	June 1917–June 1919	b 532	-----do-----------	b 533	June 1917–April 1919	b 534	June 1917–May 1919	b 535	June 1917–May 1919	
	536	June 1917–December 1917	b 537	June 1917–July 1919	538	June 1917–December 1917	b 539	June 1917–April 1919	b 540	June 1917–June 1919	
	b 541	June 1917–July 1919	b 542	June 1917–May 1919	b 543	June 1917–June 1919	b 544	June 1917–June 1919	b 545	June 1917–April 1919	
	b 546	June 1917–March 1919	b 547	June 1917–June 1919	b 548	-----do-----------	549	June 1917–December 1917	b 550	June 1917–June 1919	
	b 551	June 1917–May 1919	b 552	June 1917–April 1919	b 553	June 1917 April 1919	b 554	June 1917–April 1919	b 555	June 1917–April 1919	

b 556	June 1917–June 1919	b 557	do	b 558	June 1917–May 1919	b 559	do	b 560	July 1917–May 1919
561	June 1917–December 1917	b 562	June 1917–June 1919	b 563	July 1917–April 1919	b 564	June 1917–June 1919	b 565	June 1917–April 1919
b 566	June 1917–April 1919	b 567	June 1917–April 1919	b 568	June 1917–May 1919	b 569	July 1917 April 1919	b 570	Do.
b 571	July 1917–May 1919	b 572	July 1917–June 1919	b 573	June 1917–April 1919	b 574	June 1917–May 1919	b 575	July 1917–April 1919
576	July 1917–December 1917	b 577	June 1917–April 1919	b 578	June 1917–May 1919	b 579	June 1917–April 1919	b 580	June 1917–May 1919
b 581	June 1917–April 1919	b 582	July 1917–June 1919	b 583	do	b 584	July 1917–May 1919	b 585	June 1917–April 1919
b 586	July 1917–March 1919	b 587	June 1917–April 1919	b 588	do	b 589	July 1917–July 1919	b 590	July 1917–May 1919
b 591	June 1917–April 1919	b 592	June 1917–May 1919	b 593	July 1917–May 1919	b 594	June 1917–March 1919	b 595	June 1917–June 1919
b 596	do	597	June 1917–December 1917	b 598	June 1917–May 1919	b 599	July 1917–April 1919	b 600	July 1917–April 1919
b 601	July 1917–May 1919	b 602	July 1917–April 1919	b 603	July 1917–May 1919	b 604	do	b 605	July 1917–June 1919
b 606	do	b 607	July 1917–May 1919	b 608	July 1917–June 1919	b 609	July 1917–May 1919	b 610	Do.
b 611	do	b 612	July 1917–June 1919	b 613	do	b 614	July 1917–June 1919	b 615	Do.
b 616	July 1917–June 1919	b 617	August 1917–June 1919	b 618	August 1917–June 1919	b 619	August 1917–June 1919	b 620	September 1917–June 1919
a b 621	September 1917–April 1919	a b 622	October 1917–April 1919	a b 623	October 1917–April 1919	a b 624	November 1917–April 1919	a b 625	November 1917–April 1919
a b 626	November 1917–April 1919	a b 627	November 1917–March 1919	a b 628	November 1917–May 1919	a b 629	November 1917–March 1919	a b 630	November 1917–May 1919
a b 631	November 1917–March 1919	a b 632	November 1917–April 1919	a b 633	November 1917–April 1919	a b 634	November 1917–April 1919	a b 635	November 1917–April 1919
a b 636	November 1917–April 1919	a b 637	do	a b 638	do	a b 639	do	a b 640	Do.
a b 641	November 1917–May 1919	a b 642	November 1917–March 1919	a b 643	do	a b 644	November 1917–May 1919	a b 645	Do.
a b 646	November 1917–April 1919	a b 647	October 1917–May 1919	a b 648	October 1917–April 1919	a b 649	do	a b 650	November 1917–July 1919

MEDICAL SPECIAL AND TECHNICAL UNITS—Continued

Units	Unit No.	Active service	Unit No.	Active service	Unit No.	Active service	Unit No.	Active service	Unit No.	Active service	Remarks
American Red Cross Convalescent Home.	[a] 1	May 1918–January 1919	[a] 2	April 1918–October 1918	[a] 3	May 1918–December 1918	[a] 4	July 1918–December 1918	[a] 5	July 1918–January 1919	a S.O.S. troops.
	[a] 6	July 1918–November 1918	[a] 7	October 1918–April 1919	[a] 8	September 1918–January 1919	9	Never orgzd.	10	Never orgzd.	
	11	January 1919–May 1919									
Convalescent Hospital.	[a] (I) 1	August 1918–November 1918	[d] (II) 1	November 1918–March 1919	[d] 2	October 1918–February 1919	[a d] 3	October 1918–December 1918	[b d] 4	December 1918–June 1919	a Orgzd. and demblzd. overseas. b Orgzd. overseas; demobilized in U. S. c Absorbed by Evac. Hosp. No. 49, December 1918; reconstituted February 1919. d S.O.S. Troops.
	[a c] 5	October 1918–December 1918 February 1919–May 1919									
Debarkation Hospital. [1]	1	August 1918–June 1919	2	See Gen. Hosp. No. 41	3	August 1918–July 1919	4	See Gen. Hosp. No. 39	5	December 1918–June 1919	
	6–50	Never orgzd.	51	See Gen. Hosp. No. 43	52	July 1918–April 1919					
Embarkation Hospital. [2]	1	July 1918–October 1919	2	July 1918–February 1919	3	July 1918–December 1918	4	November 1918–August 1919			
Evacuation Ambulance Company.	[d] 1	December 1917–July 1919	[d] 2	December 1917–May 1919	[d] 3	December 1917–March 1919	[d] 4	December 1917–June 1919	[d] 5	March 1918–July 1919	e Orgzd. in U. S., demblzd. overseas.
	[d] 6	March 1918–May 1919	[d] 7	March 1918–June 1919	[d] 8	March 1918–August 1919	[d] 9	March 1918–July 1919	[d] 10	July 1918–July 1919	
	[d] 11	July 1918–May 1919	[d] 12	July 1918–June 1919	[d] 13	July 1918–July 1919	[d] 14	July 1918–June 1919	[d] 15	Do.	
	[d] 16	July 1918–July 1919	[d] 17	August 1918–August 1919	[d] 18	August 1918–June 1919	[d] 19	August 1918–June 1919	[d] 20	August 1918–June 1919	

	No.	Period	No.	Period	No.	Period	No.	Period	No.	Period
	[d] 21	October 1918–February 1919	[d] 22	October 1918–August 1919	[d] 23	October 1918–February 1919	[d] 24	October 1918–March 1919	[d] 25	October 1918–July 1919
	[e] [d] 26	October 1918–August 1919	[d] 27	October 1918–May 1919	[d] 28	October 1918–August 1919	[d] 29	September 1918–August 1919	[d] 30	September 1918–July 1919
	[d] 31	September 1918–August 1919	[d] 32	September 1918–June 1919	[d] 33	September 1918–July 1919	[d] 34	September 1918–May 1919	[d] 35	September 1918–May 1919
	[d] 36	September 1918–May 1919	[d] 37	November 1918–August 1919	[d] 38	November 1918–August 1919	[e] [d] 39	October 1918–December 1918	[e] [d] 40	November 1918–December 1918
	[d] 41	November 1918–December 1918	42	October 1918–December 1918	43	October 1918–December 1918	44	-----do-----	45	October 1918–December 1918
	46	October 1918–December 1918	47	-----do-----	48	-----do-----	49	-----do-----	[e] [d] 50	November 1918–December 1918
	[e] [d] 51	November 1918–December 1918	[e] [d] 52	November 1918–December 1918	[d] 53	November 1918–June 1919	[e] [d] 54	November 1918–December 1918	[e] [d] 55	Do.
	[e] [d] 56	-----do-----	[e] [d] 57	October 1918–December 1918	[d] 58	October 1918–June 1919	[e] [d] 59	October 1918–December 1918	[e] [d] 60	October 1918–December 1918
	[e] [d] 61	October 1918–December 1918	[d] 62	October 1918–May 1919	[d] 63	October 1918–September 1919	[d] 64	October 1918–May 1919	[d] 65	October 1918–September 1919
	[d] 66	October 1918–July 1919	[d] 67	-----do-----	[d] 68	October 1918–June 1919	[d] 69	October 1918–June 1919	[d] 70	October 1918–July 1919
	[d] 71	October 1918–June 1919	[d] 72	October 1918–June 1919	[e] 73	October 1918–January 1919	74	-----do-----	75	Do.
	76	October 1918–May 1919	77	October 1918–February 1919	78	October 1918–February 1919	[d] 79	October 1918–February 1919	[d] 80	October 1918–March 1919
	[d] 81	October 1918–February 1919								
Field Hospital (non-Divisional).	1–5	Never orgzd.	6	June 1917–January 1919	7–9	Never orgzd.	10	February 1917 through December 1919	11–13	Never orgzd.
	14	June 1917–January 1919	15–17	Never orgzd.	18	July 1917–December 1918	19–23	Never orgzd.	24	August 1917–July 1919
	25–38	Never orgzd.	39	December 1917–July 1919	40	Never orgzd.	41	December 1917–April 1919	42	December 1917–April 1919
	43	-----do-----	44	July 1918–August 1919	45–62	-----do-----	63	August 1918–December 1918	64	November 1918–December 1918
	65	November 1918–December 1918	66	November 1918–December 1918						

[1] **For detailed description of debarkation hospitals, see p. 265, chap. I, sec. 14.**

[2] For detailed description of embarkation hospitals, see p. 265, chap. I, sec. 14.

MEDICAL SPECIAL AND TECHNICAL UNITS—Continued

Units	Unit No.	Active service	Unit No.	Active service	Unit No.	Active service	Unit No.	Active service	Unit No.	Active service	Remarks
Gas Hospital	[a] 1	August 1918–November 1918	[a] 2	September 1918–November 1918	[a] 3	October 1918–November 1918	[a] 4	September 1918–November 1918			a Orgzd. and demblzd. overseas.
General Hospital[3]	1	July 1917–October 1919	2	October 1917–December 1919	3	May 1918–October 1919	4	November 1917–October 1919	5	November 1917–October 1919	
	6	December 1917–December 1919	7	December 1918–December 1919	8	May 1918–December 1919	9	February 1918–May 1919	10	October 1918–June 1919	
	11	February 1918–August 1919	12	April 1918–August 1919	13	March 1918–March 1919	14	March 1918–June 1919	15	April 1918–May 1919	
	16	March 1918–August 1919	17	March 1918–March 1919	18	April 1918–March 1919	19	September 1918–December 1919	20	June 1918–December 1919	
	21	September 1918–December 1919	22	February 1919–June 1919	23	August 1918–March 1919	24	July 1918–July 1919	25	September 1918–August 1919	
	26	September 1918–October 1919	27	September 1918–September 1919	28	September 1918–December 1919	29	September 1918–August 1919	30	September 1918–October 1919	
	31	September 1918–December 1919	32	December 1918–June 1919	33	October 1918–January 1919	34	November 1918–June 1919	35	October 1918–April 1919	
	36	November 1918–July 1919	37	November 1918–March 1919	38	December 1918–July 1919	39	October 1918–March 1919	40	March 1919–June 1919	b Army & Navy Gen. Hosp., Hot Springs, Ark.
	41	June 1918 through December 1919	42	October 1917–September 1919	43	November 1918 through December 1919	([b])	April 1917 through December 1919	([c])	April 1917 through December 1919	c Gen. Hosp. Ft. Bayard, N. Mex.
	([d])	April 1917 through December 1919	([e])	April 1917 through December 1919							d Letterman Gen. Hosp., Pres. of S. F., Calif. e Walter Reed Gen. Hosp., Washington, D. C.
Hospital Train	1	1916–November 1919	2	June 1918 through December 1919	3	May 1918–June 1919	(I) [a] 4	November 1917–July 1919	(II) 4	June 1918–November 1919	a Redes. Hosp. Tn. No. 31, December 1917; No. 61, May 1918.
	5–19	Never orgzd.	[b]u 20	November 1917–June 1919	[c]u 21	November 1917–July 1919	[d]u 22	December 1917–July 1919	[e]u 23	December 1917–July 1919	b Redes. Hosp. Tn. No. 56, February 1918.

No.	Dates	No.	Dates	No.	Dates	No.	Dates	No.	Dates
[bu] 24	November 1917–July 1919	[gu] 25	November 1917–July 1919	[iw] 26	December 1917–September 1919	[jw] 27	do	[kw] 28	do
[uk] 29	December 1917–July 1919	[ul] 30	December 1917–August 1919	[u] 31	See Hosp. Tn. No. 4 (I)	[um] 32	January 1918–July 1919	[nu] 33	January 1918–August 1919
[uo] 34	February 1918–August 1919	[u] 35	January 1918–July 1919	[u] 36	February 1918–July 1919	[up] 37	March 1918–August 1919	[u] 38	March 1918–June 1919
[u] 39	March 1918–May 1919	[u] 40	April 1918–July 1919	[ut] 41	April 1918 through December 1919	[uq] 42	April 1918–August 1919	[u] 43	April 1918–July 1919
[u] 44	March 1918–November 1918	[ur] 45	March 1918–August 1919	[u] 46	August 1918–May 1919	[u] 47	August 1918–May 1919	[u] 48	August 1918–May 1919
[u] 49	September 1918–May 1919	[su] 50	December 1917–March 1919	[su] 51	February 1918–March 1919	52	See Hosp. Tn. No. 21	53	See Hosp. Tn. No. 28
(I) 54	See Hosp. Tn. No. 22	(II) [t] 54	October 1918–January 1919	55	See Hosp. Tn. No. 32	56	See Hosp. Tn. No. 20	57	See Hosp. Tn. No. 24
58	See Hosp. Tn. No. 33	59	See Hosp. Tn. No. 23	60	See Hosp. Tn. No. 25	61	See Hosp. Tn. No. 31	62	See Hosp. Tn. No. 29
63	See Hosp. Tn. No. 27	64	See Hosp. Tn. No. 26	65	See Hosp. Tn. No. 30	66	See Hosp. Tn. No. 34	67	See Hosp. Tn. No. 45
68	See Hosp. Tn. No. 42	69	See Hosp. Tn. No. 37	70	See Hosp. Tn. No. 41				

c Redes. Hosp. Tn. No. 52, February 1918.
d Redes. Hosp. Tn. No. 54 (I), March 1918.
e Redes. Hosp. Tn. No. 59, March 1918.
f Redes. Hosp. Tn. No. 57, June 1918.
g Redes. Hosp. Tn. No. 60, May 1918.
h Redes. Hosp. Tn. No. 64, July 1918.
i Redes. Hosp. Tn. No. 63, April 1918.
j Redes. Hosp. Tn. No. 53, March 1918.
k Redes. Hosp. Tn. No. 62, May 1918.
l Redes. Hosp. Tn. No. 65, July 1918.
m Redes. Hosp. Tn. No. 55, June 1918.
n Redes. Hosp. Tn. No. 58, May 1918.
o Redes. Hosp. Tn. No. 66, May 1918.
p Redes. Hosp. Tn. No. 69, November 1918.
q Redes. Hosp. Tn. No. 68, November 1918.
r Redes. Hosp. Tn. No. 67, November 1918.
s Orgzd. and demblzd. overseas.
t Redes. Hosp. Tn. No. 70, November 1918.
u S.O.S. troops.

[3] For detailed description of Gen. Hosps., see p. 263, Chap. I, Sec. 14.

MEDICAL SPECIAL AND TECHNICAL UNITS—Continued

Units	Unit No.	Active service	Unit No.	Active service	Unit No.	Active service	Unit No.	Active service	Unit No.	Active service	Remarks
Mobile Hospital	[uv] 1	February 1918–May 1919	[wu] 2	May 1918–December 1918	[vw] 3	July 1918–June 1919	[wu] 4	August 1918–January 1919	[wu] 5	August 1918–January 1919	
	[uw] 6	August 1918–January 1919	[vu] 7	September 1918–June 1919	[wu] 8	September 1918–January 1919	[wu] 9	September 1918–April 1919	[vu] 10	September 1918–June 1919	
	[uv] 11	September 1918–June 1919	[w] 12	September 1918–April 1919	13–38	Never orgzd.	39	See Base Hosp. No. 39	40–99	Never orgzd.	
	[u] 100	September 1918–March 1919	[u] 101	September 1918–March 1919	[u] 102	November 1918–March 1919	[u] 103	November 1918–March 1919	[u] 104	November 1918–March 1919	
	[u] 105	November 1918–March 1919	106	November 1918–December 1918	107	November 1918–December 1918	108	November 1918–January 1919	109	November 1918–December 1918	
Mobile Operating Unit.	[u] 1	March 1918–May 1919									u S.O.S. troops. v Orgzd. overseas; demobilized in U. S. w Orgzd. and demblzd. overseas.
Mobile Surgical Unit	[w] 1	May 1918–February 1919	[v] 2	May 1918–September 1919	[w] 3	June 1918–March 1919	4–11	Never orgzd.	[v] 12	September 1918–June 1919	
	13–99	Never orgzd.	100	September 1918–March 1919	101	September 1918–March 1919	102	September 1918–March 1919	103	September 1918–March 1919	
Motor Company	1	May 1918–November 1918	2	May 1918–December 1918	3	May 1918–November 1918	4	May 1918–November 1918	5	May 1918–November 1918	
	6	May 1918–December 1918	7	May 1918–November 1918	8	May 1918–December 1918	9	May 1918–January 1919	10	Do.	
	11	May 1918–January 1919	12	May 1918–October 1918	13	July 1918–January 1919	14	July 1918–November 1918	15	September 1918–January 1919	
	16	September 1918–November 1918	17	September 1918–November 1918							
Neurological Hospital.	[w] 1	September 1918–November 1918	[x] 2	September 1918–October 1918	[w] 3	September 1918–December 1918					x Orgzd. overseas, absorbed by Base Hosp. 87.
Sanitary Company	1	March 1918–March 1919									

Unit	No.	Dates	No.	Dates	No.	Dates	No.	Dates	No.	Dates	Remarks
Sanitary Squad [4]	b 1	January 1918–May 1919	ab 2	January 1918–February 1919	b 3	January 1918–May 1919	b 4	January 1918–June 1919	ab 5	January 1918–February 1919	a Orgzd. in U. S.; demobilized overseas.
	b 6	January 1918–April 1919	b 7	December 1917–May 1919	b 8	December 1917–May 1919	b 9	November 1917–June 1919	b 10	February 1918–July 1919	
	b 11	February 1918–June 1919	b 12	January 1918–July 1919	b 13	January 1918–July 1919	b 14	March 1918–June 1919	b 15	December 1917–July 1919	
	b 16	February 1918–July 1919	b 17	February 1918–June 1919	b 18	February 1918–June 1919	b 19	February 1918–May 1919	b 20	May 1918–July 1919	
	b 21	March 1918–June 1919	b 22	February 1918–July 1918	b 23	February 1918–July 1919	b 24	March 1918–July 1919	b 25	December 1917–July 1919	b S.O.S. troops.
	b 26	December 1917–June 1919	b 27	January 1918–April 1919	b 28	January 1918–April 1919	b 29	January 1918–May 1919	b 30	January 1917–September 1919	
	b 31	May 1918–March 1919	b 32	May 1918–March 1919	b 33	December 1917–June 1919	b 34	December 1917–July 1919	b 35	December 1917–August 1919	
	b 36	December 1917–July 1919	b 37	February 1918–July 1919	b 38	February 1918–June 1919	b 39	March 1918–July 1919	b 40	May 1918–June 1919	
	b 41	do	b 42	December 1917–April 1919	b 43	December 1917–July 1919	b 44	December 1917–June 1919	b 45	May 1918–April 1919	
	b 46	May 1918–April 1919	b 47	January 1917–June 1919	b 48	January 1918–June 1919	b 49	June 1918–July 1919	b 50	June 1918–July 1919	
	b 51	May 1918–June 1919	b 52	May 1918–June 1919	b 53	March 1918–July 1919	b 54	April 1918–June 1919	b 55	March 1918–July 1919	
	b 56	May 1918–July 1919	b 57	December 1917–July 1919	b 58	December 1917–June 1919	b 59	June 1918–July 1919	b 60	June 1918–July 1919	
	b 61	December 1917–May 1919	b 62	January 1918–May 1919	b 63	July 1918–June 1919	b 64	July 1918–July 1919	b 65	December 1917–July 1919	
	ba 66	February 1918–February 1919	b 67	July 1918–June 1919	b 68	July 1918–February 1919	b 69	February 1918–July 1919	b 70	February 1918–September 1919	
	71 & 72	Never orgzd.	ab 73	January 1918–October 1918	ab 74	January 1918–October 1918	ab 75	December 1917–June 1919	b 76	December 1917–June 1919	
	b 77	January 1918–July 1919	b 78	January 1918–July 1919	b 79	April 1918–June 1919	b 80	April 1918–August 1919	ab 81	July 1918–November 1918	
	b 82	July 1918–August 1919	83	February 1918–February 1919	84	February 1918–February 1919	85	August 1918–February 1919	86	September 1918–February 1919	
	87	August 1918–January 1919	88	August 1918–January 1919	89	September 1918–February 1919	90	September 1918–February 1918	91	September 1918–January 1919	
	92	September 1918–January 1919	93	September 1918–March 1919	94	September 1918–March 1919	95	do	96	September 1918–February 1919	

[4] Up to June 1918, Sanitary Squads 1 to 84 were cmpnts. of Divs. Thereafter Divisional units were designated as organizations of the S.O.S.

MEDICAL SPECIAL AND TECHNICAL UNITS—Continued

Units	Unit No.	Active service	Unit No.	Active service	Unit No.	Active service	Unit No.	Active service	Unit No.	Active service	Remarks
Sanitary Squad—Continued	97	October 1918–January 1919	98	October 1918–January 1919	99	October 1918–January 1919	100	October 1918–January 1919	101	January 1918–January 1919	b S.O.S. troops.
	102	Never orgzd.	103	February 1918–February 1919	104	February 1918–February 1919	105	November 1918–January 1919	106–114	Never orgzd.	
	b 115	October 1918–August 1919	b 116	October 1918–August 1919	b 117	November 1918–July 1919	b 118	December 1918–July 1919	b 119	October 1918–June 1919	
	b 120	October 1918–June 1919									

CAMP BASE HOSPITALS

Units	Location and Active Service	Location and Active Service	Location and Active Service	Location and Active Service	Remarks
Camp Base Hospital at -----	Cp. Beauregard, La.: September 1917–February 1919 Cp. Custer, Mich.: September 1917–March 1919 Cp. Eustis, Va.: September 1918–March 1919 Cp. Greene, N. C.: September 1917–March 1919 Cp. Joseph E. Johnston, Fla.: December 1917–February 1919 Cp. Logan, Tex.: September 1917–March 1919 Cp. Pike, Ark.: September 1917–June 1919 Cp. Shelby, Miss.: September 1917–June 1919 Cp. Z. Taylor, Ky.: September 1917–July 1919 Cp. Wheeler, Ga.: September 1917–March 1919	Ft. Bliss, Tex.: April 1917–December 1919 Cp. Devens, Mass.: September 1917–July 1919 Cp. Fremont, Calif.: January 1918–March 1919 Cp. Hancock, Ga.: October 1917–March 1919 Cp. Kearny, Calif.: September 1917–March 1919 Cp. MacArthur, Tex.: September 1917–March 1919 Ft. Riley (Cp. Funston), Kans.: September 1917–June 1919 Cp. Sheridan, Ala.: August 1917–May 1919 Cp. Travis, Tex.: October 1917–March 1919	Cp. Bowie, Tex.: August 1917–July 1919 Cp. Dix, N. J.: October 1917–June 1919 Cp. Gordon, Ga.: December 1917–June 1918 Cp. A. A. Humphreys, Va.: June 1918–February 1919 Cp. Lee, Va.: August 1917–July 1919 Cp. McClellan, Ala.: August 1917–June 1919 Ft. Sam Houston, Tex.: April 1917–December 1919 Cp. Sherman, Ohio: September 1917–July 1919 Cp. Upton, N. Y.: September 1917–July 1919	Cp. Cody, N. Mex.: September 1917–April 1919 Cp. Dodge, Iowa: September 1917–July 1919 Cp. Grant, Ill.: September 1917–July 1919 Cp. Jackson, S. C.: October 1917–July 1919 Cp. Lewis, Wash.: July 1917–July 1919 Cp. Meade, Md.: September 1917–June 1919 Cp. Sevier, S. C.: September 1917–April 1919 Ft. Sill (Cp. Doniphan), Okla.: October 1917–June 1918 Cp. Wadsworth, S. C.: October 1917–October 1919	

MOTOR TRANSPORT CORPS

MOTOR COMMANDS

Unit designation and redesignation	Organization		Stations in United States		Overseas		Demobilization		Remarks
	Month and year	Place	Month and year	Place	From—	To—	Month and year	Place	
1st Motor Command	February 1919	A. E. F	July 1919	Cp. Merritt, N. J.		July 1919	July 1919	Cp. Upton, N. Y.	S.O.S. troops.
2d Motor Command					March 1919	August 1919			Orgzd. and demblzd. overseas. S.O.S. troops.
3d to 5th Motor Commands.									Never orgzd.
6th Motor Command	February 1919	A. E. F	July 1919	Norfolk, Va		August 1919	August 1919	Presidio of San Francisco, Calif.	S.O.S. troops.
7th Motor Command	March 1919	do	June 1919	Cp. Mills, N. Y.		June 1919	June 1919	Cp. Upton, N. Y.	
8th Motor Command	April 1919	do	do	do		do	do	Do.	
9th Motor Command	March 1919	do	do	do		do	do	Do.	
10th and 11th Motor Commands.									Never orgzd.
12th Motor Command	February 1919	A. E. F	June 1919	Cp. Upton, N. Y.		June 1919	June 1919	Cp. Upton, N. Y.	S.O.S. troops.
13th Motor Command	January 1919	do	July 1919	Cp. Devens, Mass.		July 1919	July 1919	Cp. Devens, Mass.	Do.
14th Motor Command									Never orgzd.
15th Motor Command	January 1919	A. E. F	July 1919	Cp. Merritt, N. J.		July 1919	July 1919	Cp. Grant, Ill	Orgzd. fr. 425th Motor Supply Tn. January 1919. S.O.S. troops.
16th Motor Command									Never orgzd.
17th Motor Command					December 1918	September 1919			Orgzd. and demblzd. overseas.
18th Motor Command									Never orgzd.
19th Motor Command	January 1919	A. E. F	August 1919	Cp. Merritt, N. J.		August 1919	August 1919	Cp. Upton, N. Y.	S.O.S. troops.
20th Motor Command	March 1919	do	June 1919	Cp. Upton, N. Y.		June 1919	June 1919	Do.	
21st Motor Command	do	do	do	do		do	do	Do.	
22d Motor Command	do	do	do	Cp. Mills, N. Y.		do	do	Do.	
23d Motor Command	October 1918	Cp. Jesup, Ga	October 1918 August 1919	P. of E., Hoboken Cp. Merritt, N. J.	October 1918.	August 1919	August 1919	Cp. Dix, N. J	Do.

MOTOR COMMANDS—Continued

Unit designation and redesignation	Organization		Stations in United States		Overseas		Demobilization		Remarks
	Month and year	Place	Month and year	Place	From—	To—	Month and year	Place	
24th Motor Command					April 1919	August 1919			Orgzd. and demblzd. overseas. S.O.S. troops.
25th Motor Command	November 1918	Cp. Jesup, Ga							Active through 1919.
26th Motor Command	do	do							Do.
27th Motor Command	do	do							Do.
28th Motor Command	do	do							Do.
29th Motor Command	do	Cp. Joseph E. Johnston, Fla.	December 1918	Cp. Jesup, Ga.					
			January 1919	Cp. Marfa, Tex					Do.
30th Motor Command	do	do	December 1918	Cp. Jesup, Ga.					
			January 1919	Ft. Sam Houston, Tex.					
			September 1919	Ft. Bliss, Tex					Do.
31st and 32d Motor Commands.									Never orgzd.
33d Motor Command	November 1918	Cp. Meigs, D. C	November 1918	Cp. Merritt, N. J.					
			do	Cp. Meigs, D. C.					
			December 1918	Cp. Benning, Ga					Active through 1919.
34th Motor Command	do	do	do	Cp. Holabird, Md			March 1919	Cp. Holabird, Md.	
35th Motor Command	do	do	November 1918	Cp. Merritt, N. J.					
			do	Cp. Meigs, D. C			do	Do.	
36th Motor Command	do	do	do	Cp. Merritt, N. J.					
			do	Cp. Meigs, D. C			do	Do.	
37th to 39th Motor Commands.									Never orgzd.
40th Motor Command	July 1918	Cp. Merritt, N. J							Active through 1919.
41st Motor Command	November 1918	Norfolk, Va					July 1919	Norfolk, Va.	

42d Motor Command	do	Newport News, Va.	December 1918	Cp. Hill, Va			do	Cp. Hill, Va.	
43d Motor Command	do	Cp. Hill, Va					do	Do.	
44th Motor Command	do	Hoboken, N. J							
45th Motor Command	January 1919	Cp. Dix, N. J							Do.
46th Motor Command	November 1918	Cp. Sevier, S. C							Do.
47th to 54th Motor Commands.							April 1919	Cp. Sevier, S. C.	Never orgzd.
55th Motor Command	January 1919	Cp. Sherman, Ohio.							Active through 1919.
56th Motor Command	October 1918	Cp. Upton, N. Y							Do.
57th Motor Command	December 1918	Cp. Mills, N. Y							Do.
58th Motor Command	do	Cp. Gordon, Ga							Do.
59th Motor Command	January 1919	Ft. Sam Houston, Tex.							
a. 19th Motor Company.	December 1919	do							Do.
60th Motor Command	December 1918	Ft. Mason, Calif	December 1919	Ft. Heath, Mass					Do.
61st Motor Command	January 1919	Boston, Mass					June 1919	Boston, Mass.	

MOTOR SUPPLY TRAINS

401st Motor Supply Train.[1] (M.Trk.Cos.301-304)	October 1917	Ft. Strong, Mass	December 1917	P. of E., Hoboken	December 1917				S.O.S. troops.
402d Motor Supply Train.[1] (M.Trk.Cos.305-308)	November 1917	Governors Island, N. Y.	November 1917	do	November 1917				Do.
403d Motor Supply Train.[1] (M.Trk.Cos.309-312)	September 1917	Ft. Benjamin Harrison, Ind.	December 1917	Cp. Merritt, N. J.					
404th Motor Supply Train.[1] (M.Trk.Cos.313-316)	do	do	January 1918 December 1917	P. of E., Portland Cp. Merritt, N. J.	January 1918				Do.
405th Motor Supply Train.[1] (M.Trk.Cos.317-320)	do	do	January 1918 December 1917	P. of E., Portland Cp. Merritt, N. J.	do				Do.
			January 1918	P. of E., Portland	Do.				

[1] Discontinued January 1919; M. Trk. Cos. converted into M. T. Cos.

MOTOR SUPPLY TRAINS—Continued

Unit designation and redesignation	Organization		Stations in United States		Overseas		Demobilization		Remarks
	Month and year	Place	Month and year	Place	From—	To—	Month and year	Place	
406th Motor Supply Train.[1] (M.Trk.Cos.321-324)	September 1917	Presidio of San Francisco, Calif.	December 1917	Cp. Merritt, N. J.					
			January 1918	P. of E., Hoboken	January 1918				
407th Motor Supply Train.[2] (M.Trk.Cos.359-364)	November 1917	Cp. Upton, N. Y.	do	do	do				S.O.S. troops.
408th Motor Supply Train.[2] (M.Trk.Cos.365-370)	do	Cp. Sherman, Ohio.	December 1917	Cp. Merritt, N. J.					
			January 1918	P. of E., Hoboken	do				G.H.Q. troops.
409th Motor Supply Train.[2] (M.Trk.Cos.371-376)	October 1917	Cp. Custer, Mich.	February 1918	Cp. Merritt, N. J.					
			do	P. of E., Hoboken	February 1918				Do.
410th Motor Supply Train.									Never orgzd.
411th Motor Supply Train.	March 1918	Cp. Joseph E. Johnston, Fla.	July 1918	Cp. Hill, Va.					
			do	P. of E., Newport News.	July 1918.				
			July 1919	Cp. Stuart, Va.		July 1919	July 1919	Presidio of San Francisco, Calif.	
412th Motor Supply Train.[1] (M.Trk.Cos.425-430)	April 1918	do	May 1918	P. of E., Newport News.	May 1918				S.O.S. troops.
413th Motor Supply Train.	March 1918	do	July 1918	do	July 1918.				
			July 1919	Cp. Merritt, N. J.		July 1919	July 1919	Cp. Grant, Ill.	Corps troops.
414th Motor Supply Train.	May 1918	do	July 1918	Cp. Hill, Va.					
			do	P. of E., Newport News.	July 1918	do	do	Cp. Upton, N. Y.	Do.

415th Motor Supply Train.	July 1918	do	August 1918	Cp. Stuart, Va.					
			do	P. of E., Newport News.	August 1918.				
			August 1919	Cp. Merritt, N. J.		August 1919	August 1919	do	Do.
416th Motor Supply Train.[1] (M.Trk.Cos.457-462)	do	do	July 1918	P. of E., Hoboken	July 1918				Army troops.
417th Motor Supply Train.	do	do	August 1918	Cp. Stuart, Va.					
			do	P. of E., Newport News.	August 1918.				
			September 1919	Cp. Merritt, N. J.		September 1919	September 1919	Cp. Dix, N. J.	Do.
418th Motor Supply Train.	do	do	August 1918	Cp. Stuart, Va.					
			do	P. of E., Newport News.	August 1918.				
			July 1918	Cp. Merritt, N. J.		July 1919	July 1919	Cp. Upton, N. Y.	Corps troops.
419th Motor Supply Train.[3] (M.Trk.Cos.475-480).	do	do	August 1918	P. of E., Newport News.	August 1918.				
420th Motor Supply train[3] (M.Trk.Cos.489-494).	August 1918	do	September 1918	Cp. Merritt, N. J.					S.O.S. troops.
			do	P. of E., Hoboken	September 1918.				
421st Motor Supply Train.	do	do	do	do	Do.				
			September 1919	Cp. Merritt, N. J.		September 1919	October 1919	Cp. Dix, N. J.	G.H.Q. troops.
422d Motor Supply Train.	do	do	September 1918	P. of E., Hoboken	September 1918.				
			July 1919	Cp. Merritt, N. J.		July 1919	August 1919	Cp. Grant, Ill.	Corps troops.
423d Motor Supply Train.	do	do	September 1918	Cp. Upton, N. Y.					
			do	P. of E., Hoboken	September 1918.				
			September 1919	Cp. Merritt, N. J.		September 1919	September 1919	Do.	

[1] Discontinued January 1919; M.Trk. Cos. converted into M.T. Cos.
[2] Discontinued March 1919; M.Trk. Cos. converted into M.T. Cos.
[3] Discontinued February 1919; M. Trk. Cos. converted into M. T. Cos.

MOTOR SUPPLY TRAINS—Continued

Unit designation and redesignation	Organization		Stations in United States		Overseas		Demobilization		Remarks
	Month and year	Place	Month and year	Place	From—	To—	Month and year	Place	
424th Motor Supply Train.[1] (M.Trk.Cos.521-526).	September 1918	Cp. Joseph E. Johnston, Fla.	September 1918	P. of E., Hoboken	September 1918				S.O.S. troops.
425th Motor Supply Train.[1] (M.Trk.Cos.527-532).	do	do	do	do	do				Do.
426th Motor Supply Train.	do	do	do	Cp. Merritt, N. J.					
			do	P. of E., Hoboken	Do.				
			September 1919	Cp. Merritt, N. J.		September 1919	September 1919	Cp. Dix, N. J.	G.H.Q. troops.
427th Motor Supply Train.	do	do	September 1918	Do.					
			do	P. of E., Hoboken	September 1918	July 1919	July 1919	Cp. Upton, N. Y.	Corps troops.

[1] Discontinued January 1919; M. Trk. Cos. converted into M. T. Cos.

MOTOR REPAIR UNITS

Unit designation and redesignation	Organization: Month and year	Organization: Place	Stations in United States: Month and year	Stations in United States: Place	Overseas: From—	Overseas: To—	Demobilization: Month and year	Demobilization: Place	Remarks
301st Q. M. Mechanical Repair Shop.	October 1917	Cp. Meigs, D. C.	January 1918	P. of E., Hoboken	January 1918				S.O.S. troops.
a. 301st Motor Repair. Unit.	February 1919	A. E. F.	June 1919	Cp. Mills, N. Y.		June 1919	June 1919	Cp. Sherman, Ohio.	
302d Q. M. Mechanical Repair Shop.	November 1917	Cp. Meigs, D. C.	January 1918	P. of E., Hoboken	January 1918.				
a. 302d Motor Repair Unit.	February 1919	A. E. F.	June 1919	Cp. Mills, N. Y.		do	do	do	Do.
303d Q. M. Mechanical Repair Shop.	November 1917	Cp. Meigs, D. C.	January 1918	P. of E., Hoboken	January 1918.				
a. 303d Motor Repair Unit.	February 1919	A. E. F.	June 1919	Cp. Mills, N. Y.		do	do	Cp. Upton, N. Y.	Do.
304th Q. M. Mechanical Repair Shop.	November 1917	Ft. Sam Houston, Tex.							

a. 304th Motor Repair Unit.	September 1918	do	July 1919	Cp. Normoyle, Tex					Active through 1919.
305th Q. M. Mechanical Repair Shop.	October 1917	Ft. Bliss, Tex	May 1918	Cp. Jesup, Ga.					
a. 305th Motor Repair Unit.	September 1918	Cp. Jesup, Ga							Do.
306th Q. M. Mechanical Repair Shop.	December 1917	Newport News, Va	January 1918 March 1918	Cp. Meigs, D. C. Cp. Holabird, Md.					
a. 306th Motor Repair Unit.	September 1918	Cp. Holabird, Md							Do.
307th Motor Repair Unit.	do	do	October 1918 June 1919	P. of E., Hoboken Cp. Mills, N. Y	October 1918.	June 1919	June 1919	Cp. Dix, N. J	S.O.S. troops.
308th Motor Repair Unit.	do	Cp. Jesup, Ga	September 1918 July 1919	P. of E., Hoboken Cp. Merritt, N. J	September 1918.	July 1919	July 1919	Cp. Dodge, Iowa	Do.
309th Motor Repair Unit.	do	Ft. Bliss, Tex	September 1918	P. of E., Hoboken	September 1918	do	do	Norfolk, Va	Do.
310th Motor Repair Unit.	October 1918	Cp. Jesup, Ga	October 1918 September 1919	do Cp. Merritt, N. J	October 1918.	September 1919	September 1919	Cp. Dix, N. J	Do.
311th Motor Repair Unit.	September 1918	Cp. Holabird, Md							Active through 1919.
312th Motor Repair Unit.	October 1918	Ft. Sam Houston, Tex.	November 1918 do July 1919	Cp. Merritt, N. J. P. of E., Hoboken Cp. Mills, N. Y	November 1918.	July 1919	July 1919	Cp. Pike, Ark	S.O.S. troops.
313th and 314th Motor Repair Units.									Never orgzd.
315th Motor Repair Unit.	October 1918	Ft. Bliss, Tex	March 1919	Cp. Boyd, Tex					Active through 1919.
316th (I) Motor Repair Unit.	do	El Paso, Tex					May 1919	Cp. Boyd, Tex.	
316th (II) Motor Repair Unit.	July 1919	Cp. Normoyle, Tex.					November 1919	Cp. Normoyle, Tex.	
317th and 318th Motor Repair Units.									Never orgzd.
319th Motor Repair Unit.	October 1918	Cp. Holabird, Md	June 1919	Cp. Jesup, Ga			December 1919	Cp. Jesup, Ga.	
320th Motor Repair Unit.	November 1918	A. E. F	August 1919	Cp. Merritt, N. J		August 1919	August 1919	Cp. Upton, N. Y.	
321st Motor Repair Unit.	October 1918	Cp. Holabird, Md							Active through 1919.

MOTOR REPAIR UNITS—Continued

Unit designation and redesignation	Organization		Stations in United States		Overseas		Demobilization		Remarks
	Month and year	Place	Month and year	Place	From—	To—	Month and year	Place	
322d Motor Repair Unit.	January 1919	A. E. F.	July 1919	Cp. Merritt, N. J.		July 1919	July 1919	Cp. Dix, N. J.	
323d Motor Repair Unit.									Never orgzd.
324th Motor Repair Unit.	October 1918	Cp. Holabird, Md.					February 1919	Cp. Holabird, Md.	
325th and 326th Motor Repair Units.									Do.
327th Motor Repair Unit.	January 1919	A. E. F.	August 1919	Cp. Merritt, N. J.		August 1919	September 1919	Cp. Dix, N. J.	
328th Motor Repair Unit.	February 1919	do.	July 1919	Cp. Hill, Va.		July 1919	July 1919	Cp. Upton, N. Y.	
329th Motor Repair Unit.	November 1918	Cp. Holabird, Md.							Active through 1919.

M. T. C. SPECIAL AND TECHNICAL UNITS

Units	Unit No.	Active service	Unit No.	Active service	Unit No.	Active service	Unit No.	Active service	Unit No.	Active service	Remarks
Administrative Company.	[a] 1	January 1919–March 1919	[a] 2	January 1919–March 1919	[a] 3	January 1919–March 1919	[a] 4	December 1918–March 1919	[a] 5	December 1918–March 1919	a Orgzd. and demblzd. overseas.
	[a] 6	do.	[a] 7	February 1919–March 1919	8	Never orgzd.	[a] 9	February 1919–March 1919	10	Never orgzd.	
	[a] 11	do.	[a] 12	November 1918–March 1919	[a] 13	February 1919–March 1919					

Motor Car Company.	1	July 1918–December 1918	2–300	Never orgzd.	[1] b 301	January 1918–July 1919	[1] 302	January 1918–August 1919	[1] b 303	January 1918–July 1919	b S.O.S. Troops.
	[1] b 304	January 1918–July 1919	[1] b 305	January 1918–July 1919	[1] b 306	March 1918–July 1919	[1] b 307	June 1918–July 1919	[1] b 308	July 1918–August 1919	
	[1] 309	April 1918 through December 1919	[1] 310	May 1918 through December 1919	[1] 311	June 1918 through December 1919	[1] b 312	August 1918–December 1919	[1] b 313	August 1918–December 1919	
	[1] b 314	August 1918–July 1919									
Motorcycle Company.	c 1	June 1917–March 1918	d 2	August 1917–November 1917	e 3	September 1917–November 1917	4–300	Never orgzd.	301	March 1918–July 1919	c Converted into Mtcl. Co. 301.
	302	November 1917 through December 1919	303	November 1917–September 1919	304	January 1918–August 1919	305	January 1918–September 1919	306	May 1918–December 1919	d Converted into Mtcl. Co. 302.
	307	June 1918–March 1919	308	September 1918–September 1919	309	November 1918-July 1919	310–321	Never orgzd.	f 322	October 1918–August 1919	e Converted into Mtcl. Co. 303. f Orgzd. fr. 462d Engrs. (Mtcl. Co.) October 1918.
	g 323	October 1918–August 1919	324–329	Never orgzd.	330	November 1918 through December 1919	331	December 1918 through December 1919	332	February 1919 through December 1919	g Orgzd. fr. 463d Engrs. (Mtcl. Co.) October 1918.
Motor Truck Company.	[2] b 1	September 1917 through December 1919	[2] b 2	May 1917 through December 1919	[2] b 3	May 1917 through December 1919	[2] (I) 4	May 1917–December 1917	[2] b (II) 4	May 1917 through December 1919	
	[2] b 5	May 1917 through December 1919	6	Never orgzd.	7	October 1917 only	8	October 1917 only	9	October 1917 only	
	10	October 1917 only	11	October 1917 only	12	October 1917 only	(I) 13	October 1917–December 1917	(II) 13	November 1917–December 1917	
	14	November 1917–December 1917	15	July 1917–December 1917	16	November 1917–December 1917	17	November 1917–December 1917	18	November 1917–December 1917	
	(I) 19	1916–December 1917	[2] (II) 19	December 1917 through December 1919	[2] (I) 20	October 1917–December 1917	(II) 20	December 1917–through December 1919	[2] 21	July 1917 through December 1919	

[1] Converted into M. T. Cos. October 1918 and January 1919.
[2] Converted into M. T. Cos. of identical unit designation.

M. T. C. SPECIAL AND TECHNICAL UNITS—Continued

Units	Unit No.	Active service	Unit No.	Active service	Unit No.	Active service	Unit No.	Active service	Unit No.	Active service	Remarks
Motor Truck Company.—Con.	(I) 22	June 1917–December 1917	[a] (II) 22	December 1917 through December 1919	23	1916–December 1917	[a] 24	April 1917–December 1918	[a] 25	April 1918–December 1918	
	[b] 26	June 1917–December 1918	[b] 27	March 1918–December 1918	28	May 1917–December 1917	29	July 1917–October 1917	30	1916–December 1917	
	31	1916–December 1917	32	July 1917–November 1917	33	Never orgzd.	34	June 1917–December 1917	35	July 1917–November 1917	
	36	1916–October 1917	37	Never orgzd.	38	June 1917–September 1917	39	May 1917–October 1917	40	June 1917–November 1917	
	41	Never orgzd.	42	December 1917 only	43	Never orgzd.	44	June 1917–December 1917	45	April 1917–December 1917	
	46	June 1917–October 1917	47	July 1917–December 1917	48	May 1917–November 1917	49	September 1917–October 1917	50	August 1917–October 1917	
	(I) 51	January 1917–October 1917	(II) 51	June 1917–September 1917	52	July 1917–November 1917	53	December 1917–March 1918	54	June 1917–November 1917	
	55	July 1917–October 1917	56	February 1917–November 1917	57	July 1917–October 1917	58	June 1917–October 1917	59	May 1917–October 1917	
	60	1916–December 1917	61	Never orgzd.	62	May 1917–October 1917	63	1916–December 1917	64	-----do-----------	
	65	June 1917–October 1917	66	May 1917–October 1917	67	February 1917–December 1917	68	February 1917–December 1917	69	April 1917–October 1917	
	70	June 1917–December 1917	71	April 1917–December 1917	72	June 1917–October 1917	73	Never orgzd.	74	July 1917–December 1917	
	75	Never orgzd.	76	August 1917–October 1917	77	August 1917–September 1917	78	September 1917–October 1917	79	Never orgzd.	
	80	September 1917–November 1917	81–100	Never orgzd.	(I) 101	(See M. Trk. Co. 2)	(II) 101	June 1917–October 1917	(I) 102	(See M. Trk. Co. 3)	
	(II) 102	June 1917–October 1917	(I) 103	(See M. Trk. Co. 4)	(II) 103	June 1917–December 1917	104	May 1917–October 1917	105–109	Never orgzd.	
	110	July 1917–October 1917	111–119	Never orgzd.	120	July 1917–September 1917	121–123	Never orgzd.	124	July 1917–November 1917	
	125–129	Never orgzd.	130	July 1917–October 1917	131	October 1917–November 1917	132–133	-----do-----------	134	October 1917 only	

135	October 1917 only	136–200	Never orgzd.	(I) 201	June 1917–October 1917	(II) 201	November 1917–March 1918	202	July 1917–September 1917
203	September 1917 only	204–219	do	220	August 1917–October 1917	221–324	Never orgzd.	[2] 325	September 1917 through December 1919
[2] 326	October 1917 through December 1919	[2] 327	September 1917 through December 1919	[2] 328	October 1917–May 1919	[2] 329	October 1917 through December 1919	[2] 330	December 1917–November 1919
[2] 331	November 1917–November 1919	[2] 332	October 1917–December 1919	[2] 333	do	[2] 334	October 1917–April 1919	[2] 335	October 1917–April 1919
[2] 336	October 1917–March 1919	[2] 337	September 1917–July 1919	[2] 338	September 1917–March 1919	[2] 339	October 1917–November 1919	[2] 340	November 1917 through December 1919
[2] 341	October 1917 through December 1919	[2] 342	October 1917 through December 1919	[2] 343	October 1917 through December 1919	[2] 344	October 1917 through December 1919	[2] 345	November 1917–November 1919
[2] 346	October 1917–December 1919	[2] 347	December 1917–November 1919	[2] 348	October 1917–April 1919	[2] 349	November 1917–March 1919	[2] 350	September 1917–January 1919
[2] 351	July 1917–November 1919	[2] 352	October 1917–April 1919	[2] 353	October 1917 through December 1919	[2] 354	February 1918 through December 1919	[2] 355	October 1917–November 1919
[2] 356	September 1917–July 1919	[2] 357	September 1917–July 1919	[2] 358	do	359–376	Never orgzd.	[2] 377	Do.
[2] 378	October 1917 through December 1919	[2] 379	October 1917 through December 1919	[2] 380	October 1917–June 1919	[2] [h] 381	November 1917–June 1919	[2] 382	December 1917–May 1919
[2] 383	December 1917–June 1919	[2] 384	December 1917 through December 1919	[2] 385	December 1917–July 1919	[2] 386	December 1917–December 1919	[2] 387	December 1917–December 1919
[2] 388	December 1917–December 1919	[2] 389	December 1917–December 1919	[2] 390	December 1917–December 1919	[2] 391	do	[2] 392	Do.
[2] 393	January 1918–November 1919	[2] 394	December 1917–June 1919	[2] 395	do	[2] 396	December 1917–March 1919	[2] 397	December 1917 through December 1919
[2] [h] 398	January 1918–May 1919	[2] [h] 399	January 1918–July 1919	[2] 400	January 1918–July 1919	[2] 401	December 1917 through December 1919	[2] 402	December 1917–November 1919

h Army Troops.

[2] Converted into M. T. Cos. of identical unit designation.

M. T. C. SPECIAL AND TECHNICAL UNITS—Continued

Units	Unit No.	Active service	Unit No.	Active service	Unit No.	Active service	Unit No.	Active service	Unit No.	Active service	Remarks
Motor Truck Company.—Con.	[2] 403	January 1918 through December 1919	[2] 404	January 1918 through December 1919	[2] 405	January 1918–July 1919	[2] 406	January 1918 through December 1919	[2] 407	January 1918 through December 1919	h Army Troops.
	[2] 408	January 1918–December 1919	[2] 409	January 1918–July 1919	[2] 410	do	[2] h 411	March 1918–July 1919	h 412	March 1918–July 1919	
	h 413	March 1918–July 1919	h 414	March 1918–July 1919	h 415	March 1918–July 1919	416–421	Never orgzd.	h 422	January 1918–December 1919	
	h 423	January 1918–July 1919	h 424	January 1918–July 1919	425–442	Never orgzd.	h 443	March 1918–August 1919	[2] 444	March 1918–March 1919	
	[2] 445	March 1918–April 1919	h 446	July 1918–July 1919	h 447	July 1918–July 1919	h 448	July 1918–July 1919	h 449	July 1918–August 1919	
	h 450	July 1918–August 1919	451–480	Never orgzd.	[2] 481	April 1918–December 1919	h 482	April 1918 through December 1919	[2] 483	June 1918–March 1919	
	h 484	August 1918–July 1919	h 485	August 1918–December 1919	[2] h 486	August 1918–May 1919	[2] 487	August 1918–June 1919	h 488	August 1918–August 1919	
	489–512	Never orgzd.	513	August 1918 through December 1919	514	July 1918–May 1919	515	July 1918 through December 1919	516	August 1918–April 1919	
	h 517	September 1918–August 1919	h 518	September 1918–August 1919	h 519	September 1918–September 1919	h 520	September 1918–July 1919	521–550	Never orgzd.	
	[2] 551	July 1918–July 1919	[2] 552	August 1918–November 1919	[2] 553	July 1918–March 1919	554	Never orgzd.	[2] 555	November 1918 through December 1919	
	[2] 556	November 1918 through December 1919	557	Never orgzd.	[2] 558	August 1918–May 1919	559–570	Never orgzd.	571	October 1918–June 1919	
	572	September 1918–June 1919	573	September 1918–June 1919	574	September 1918–April 1919	575	September 1918–April 1919	576	September 1918–April 1919	

Motor Transport Company.	1	(See M. Trk. Co. No. 1)	2	(See M. Trk. Cos. No. 2 & 101)	3	(See M. Trk. Cos. No. 3 & 102)	4	(See M. Trk. Cos. No. 4 & 103)	5	(See M. Trk. Cos. No. 5 & 104)	i Orgzd. in U. S., demblzd overseas.
	6–18	Never orgzd.	19	(See M. Trk. Co. No. 19 (II))	20	(See M. Trk. Cos. No. 20 (I) and 392)	21	(See M. Trk. Co. No. 21)	22	(See M. Trk. Co. No. 22)	j G.H.Q. Troops.
	23–300	-----do-----------	[3] 301	September 1917–July 1919	[3] 302	September 1917–July 1919	[3] 303	Never orgzd.	[3] [ij]304	September 1917–July 1919	
	[3] 305	September 1917–July 1919	[3] 306	September 1917–June 1919	[3] 307	-----do-----------	[3] 308	September 1917–July 1919	[3] 309	Do.	
	[3] 310	-----do-----------	[3] 311	September 1917–August 1919	[3] 312	-----do-----------	[3] 313	-----do-----------	[3] 314	Do.	
	[3] 315	-----do-----------	[3] 316	September 1917–July 1919	[3] 317	-----do-----------	[3] 318	-----do-----------	[3] 319	Do.	
	[3] 320	-----do-----------	[3] 321	-----do-----------	[3] 322	September 1917–August 1919	[3] 323	September 1917–June 1919	[3] 324	September 1917–June 1919	
	325	(See M. Trk. Co. No. 325)	326	(See M. Trk. Co. No. 326)	327	(See M. Trk. Co. No. 327)	328	(See M. Trk. Co. No. 328)	329	(See M. Trk. Co. No. 329)	
	330	(See M. Trk. Co. No. 330)	331	(See M. Trk. Co. No. 331)	332	(See M. Trk. Co. No. 332)	333	(See M. Trk. Co. No. 333)	334	(See M. Trk. Co. No. 334)	
	335	(See M. Trk. Co. No. 335)	336	(See M. Trk. Co. No. 336)	337	(See M. Trk. Co. No. 337)	338	(See M. Trk. Co. No. 338)	339	(See M. Trk. Co. No. 339)	
	340	(See M. Trk. Co. No. 340)	341	(See M. Trk. Co. No. 341)	342	(See M. Trk. Co. No. 342)	343	(See M. Trk. Co. No. 343)	344	(See M. Trk. Co. No. 344)	
	345	(See M. Trk. Co. No. 345)	346	(See M. Trk. Co. No. 346)	347	(See M. Trk. Co. No. 347)	348	(See M. Trk. Co. No. 348)	349	(See M. Trk. Co. No. 349)	
	350	(See M. Trk. Co. No. 350)	351	(See M. Trk. Co. No. 351)	352	(See M. Trk. Co. No. 352)	353	(See M. Trk. Co. No. 353)	354	(See M. Trk. Co. No. 354)	
	355	(See M. Trk. Co. No. 355)	356	(See M. Trk. Co. No. 356)	357	(See M. Trk. Co. No. 357)	358	(See M. Trk. Co. No. 358)	[4] 359	November 1917–June 1919	
	[4] 360	November 1917–June 1919	[4] 361	November 1917–June 1919	[4] 362	November 1917–June 1919	[4] 363	November 1917–June 1919	[4] 364	Do.	
	[4] 365	-----do-----------	[4] 366	-----do-----------	[4] 367	-----do-----------	[4] 368	-----do-----------	[4] 369	Do.	
	[4] 370	-----do-----------	[4] 371	November 1917–July 1919	[4] 372	-----do-----------	[4] 373	-----do-----------	[4] 374	Do.	
	[4] 375	November 1917–July 1919	[4] 376	-----do-----------	377	(See M. Trk. Co. No. 377)	378	(See M. Trk. Co. No. 378)	379	(See M. Trk. Co. No. 379)	

[2] Converted into M. T. Cos. of identical unit designation.
[3] Originally a component of one of M. Sup. Tns. 401–406, till January 1919, under designation of M. Trk. Co.
[4] Originally a component of one of M. Sup. Tns. 407–409, till March 1919, under designation of M. Trk. Co.

M. T. C. SPECIAL AND TECHNICAL UNITS—Continued

Units	Unit No.	Active service	Unit No.	Active service	Unit No.	Active service	Unit No.	Active service	Unit No.	Active service	Remarks
Motor Transport Company—Con.	380	(See M. Trk. Co. No. 380)	381	(See M. Trk. Co. No. 381)	382	(See M. Trk. Co. No. 382)	383	(See M. Trk. Co. No. 383)	384	(See M. Trk. Co. No. 384)	
	385	(See M. Trk. Co. No. 385)	386	(See M. Trk. Co. No. 386)	387	(See M. Trk. Co. No. 387)	388	(See M. Trk. Co. No. 388)	389	(See M. Trk. Co. No. 389)	
	390	(See M. Trk. Co. No. 390)	391	(See M. Trk. Co. No. 391)	392	(See M. Trk. Co. No. 392)	393	(See M. Trk. Co. No. 393)	394	(See M. Trk. Co. No. 394)	
	395	(See M. Trk. Co. No. 395)	396	(See M. Trk. Co. No. 396)	397	(See M. Trk. Co. No. 397)	398	(See M. Trk. Co. No. 398)	399	(See M. Trk. Co. No. 399)	
	400	(See M. Trk. Co. No. 400)	401	(See M. Trk. Co. No. 401)	402	(See M. Trk. Co. No. 402)	403	(See M. Trk. Co. No. 403)	404	(See M. Trk. Co. No. 404)	
	405	(See M. Trk. Co. No. 405)	406	(See M. Trk. Co. No. 406)	407	(See M. Trk. Co. No. 407)	408	(See M. Trk. Co. No. 408)	409	(See M. Trk. Co. No. 409)	
	410	(See M. Trk. Co. No. 410)	411	(See M. Trk. Co. No. 411)	412–424	Never orgzd.	[5] 425	April 1918–August 1919	[5] 426	April 1918–July 1919	
	[5] 427	April 1918–July 1919	[5] 428	April 1918–September 1919	[5] 429	April 1918–August 1919	[5] 430	April 1918–September 1919	431–443	Never orgzd.	
	444	(See M. Trk. Co. No. 444)	445	(See M. Trk. Co. No. 445)	446–456	Never orgzd.	[6] 457	July 1918–August 1919	[6] 458	July 1918–August 1919	
	[6] 459	July 1918–July 1919	[6] 460	July 1918–July 1919	[6] 461	July 1918–July 1919	[6] 462	do	463–474	Never orgzd.	
	[6] 475	July 1918–June 1919	[6] 476	do	[6] 477	July 1918–August 1919	[6] 478	July 1918–July 1919	[6] 479	July 1918–July 1919	
	[6] 480	July 1918–September 1919	481	(See M. Trk. Co. No. 481)	482	(See M. Trk. Co. No. 482)	483	(See M. Trk. Co. No. 483)	484–485	Never orgzd.	
	486	(See M. Trk. Co. No. 486)	487	(See M. Trk. Co. No. 487)	488	Never orgzd.	[6] 489	August 1918–July 1919	[6] 490	August 1918–August 1919	
	[6] 491	August 1918–July 1919	[6] 492	August 1918–September 1919	[6] 493	August 1918–September 1919	[6] 494	do	495–520	Never orgzd.	
	[7] 521	September 1918–July 1919	[7] 522	September 1918–July 1919	[7] 523	September 1918–July 1919	[7] 524	September 1918–July 1919	[7] 525	September 1918–July 1919	i Orgzd. in U. S., demobilized overseas.
	[7] 526	do	[7] 527	do	[7] 528	do	[7] 529	September 1918–August 1919	[7] 530	Do.	

[7] 531	do	[7] 532	do	533–544	Never orgzd.	[7] 545	September 1918–November 1919	[7] 546	September 1918 through December 1919
[7] 547	September 1918–December 1919	[7] 548	September 1918–November 1919	[7][i] 549	September 1918–October 1919	[7][i] 550	September 1918–October 1919	551	(See M. Trk. Co. No. 551)
552	(See M. Trk. Co. No. 552)	553	(See M. Trk. Co. No. 553)	554	October 1918 through December 1919	555	(See M. Trk. Co. No. 555)	556	(See M. Trk. Co. No. 556)
557	July 1918–July 1919	558	(See M. Trk. Co. No. 558)	559–576	Never orgzd.	577	November 1918–June 1919	578	November 1918–June 1919
579–587	Never orgzd.	588	October 1918–March 1919	589	October 1918 through December 1919	590	October 1918 through December 1919	591	October 1918–December 1919
592	October 1918–through December 1919	593	October 1918–July 1919	594	November 1918–January 1919	595	November 1918–December 1918	596	November 1918 through December 1919
597	Never orgzd.	598	October 1918–August 1919	599–602	Never orgzd.	603	October 1918–May 1919	604	October 1918–November 1919
605	do	606	(See M. C. Co. 301)	607	(See M. C. Co. 302)	608	(See M. C. Co. 303)	609	(See M. C. Co. 304)
610	(See M. C. Co. 305)	611	(See M. C. Co. 306)	612	(See M. C. Co. 307)	613	(See M. C. Co. 308)	614	(See M. C. Co. 309)
615	(See M. C. Co. 310)	616	(See M. C. Co. 311)	617	(See M. C. Co. 312)	618	(See M. C. Co. 313)	619	(See M. C. Co. 314)
620–630	Never orgzd.	631	January 1919–December 1919	632–656	Never orgzd.	657	December 1918 through December 1919	658	December 1918 through December 1919
659	November 1918–November 1919	660	March 1919–December 1919	661–662	do	663	October 1918–May 1919	664	October 1918 through December 1919
665	December 1918 through December 1919	666	January 1919–May 1919	667	November 1918–March 1919	668	January 1919 through December 1919	669	January 1919 through December 1919
670	January 1919–June 1919	671	October 1918 through December 1919	672	February 1919–November 1919	673–674	Never orgzd.	675	February 1919–December 1919
676	December 1918–March 1919	677–679	Never orgzd.	[k] 680	February 1919–July 1919	[8] 681	December 1918–August 1919	[8] 682	December 1918–August 1919

k Orgzd. overseas, demobilized in U. S.

[5] Originally component of M. Sup. Tn. 412, till December 1918, under designation of M. Trk. Co.
[6] Originally a component of one of the M. Sup. Tns. 416, 419, 420, till December 1918, under designation of M. Trk. Co.
[7] Originally a component of one of the M. Sup. Tns. 424, 425, 428, till December 1918, under designation of M. Trk. Co.

M. T. C. SPECIAL AND TECHNICAL UNITS—Continued

Units	Unit No.	Active service	Unit No.	Active service	Unit No.	Active service	Unit No.	Active service	Unit No.	Active service	Remarks
Motor Transport Company—Con.	[8] 683	December 1918–November 1919	[8] 684	December 1918–July 1919	[8] 685	December 1918–July 1919	[8] 686	December 1918–July 1919	[8] 687	January 1919–August 1919	
	(I) 688	(See M. T. Co. 617)	[8](II)688	do	[8] 689	November 1918–August 1919	[8] 690	do	[8] 691	December 1918–July 1919	
	[8] 692	December 1918–July 1919	[8] 693	November 1918–July 1919	[8] 694	December 1918–June 1919	[8] 695	do	[8] 696	November 1918–July 1919	
	[k] 697	November 1918–June 1919	[8] 698	November 1918–October 1919	[8] 699	December 1918–November 1919	[8] 700	December 1918–December 1919	[k] 701	January 1919–May 1919	
	[k] 702	January 1919–May 1919	[k] 703	January 1919–May 1919	[k] 704	January 1919–May 1919	[k] 705	December 1918–August 1919	[k] 706	December 1918–August 1919	
	[k] 707	December 1918–June 1919	[8] 708	December 1918–June 1919	[8] 709	December 1918–June 1919	[8] 710	December 1918–July 1919	[8] 711	December 1918–July 1919	
	712	March 1919 through December 1919	713	December 1918 through December 1919	714	(See M. T. Co. 698)	715	(See M. T. Co. 699)	716	(See M. T. Co. 700)	
	717	January 1919 through December 1919	718	January 1919 through December 1919	719	Never orgzd.	720	January 1919 through December 1919	721	December 1918–July 1919	
	722	November 1918–July 1919	723	December 1918–March 1919	724	December 1918–July 1919	725	December 1918–July 1919	726–727	Never orgzd.	
	728	December 1918 through December 1919	729	December 1918–July 1919	730	December 1918–July 1919	731	December 1918–July 1919	732 & 733	Never orgzd.	
	734	December 1918–July 1919	735	October 1918–April 1919	736	October 1918 through December 1919	737	November 1918 through December 1919	738	November 1918–May 1919	
	739	January 1919 through December 1919	740	December 1918–July 1919	741 & 742	Never orgzd.	743	December 1918 through December 1919	744	December 1918–April 1919	
	745	January 1919–June 1919	746	January 1919–June 1919	747	January 1919–through December 1919	748–782	Never orgzd.	783	December 1918–May 1919	

	No.	Dates	No.	Dates	No.	Dates	No.	Dates	No.	Dates	
	784	December 1918–May 1919	785	January 1919–March 1919	786	December 1918 through December 1919	787	November 1918–June 1919	788	November 1918 through December 1919	
	789	November 1918–November 1919	790	January 1919 through December 1919	791	January 1919 through December 1919	792	January 1919–March 1919	793	January 1919–June 1919	
	794	January 1919–July 1919	795	December 1918 through December 1919	796	do	797	December 1918 through December 1919	798	February 1919 through December 1919	
	799	January 1919 through December 1919	800	do	801	do	802	January 1919–August 1919	803	January 1919–March 1919	
	804	January 1919–March 1919	805	January 1919 through December 1919	806	January 1919–June 1919	807	January 1919 through December 1919	808	January 1919 through December 1919	
	809	January 1919 through December 1919	810	do	811	January 1919 through December 1919	812	do	813	February 1919 through December 1919	
	814	November 1918–August 1919	815	November 1918–August 1919	816	February 1919–August 1919	817	November 1918–August 1919	818	December 1918–August 1919	
	819	December 1918–August 1919	820	January 1919–July 1919	821	December 1918–August 1919	822	December 1918–August 1919	823	January 1919–July 1919	
	824	January 1919–July 1919	825	do	826	February 1919–July 1919	827	February 1919–July 1919	828	do	k Orgzd. overseas, demobilized in U. S.
	829	February 1919–July 1919	800	February 1919–July 1919	831	January 1919–August 1919	832	do	833	February 1919–July 1919	
	834	do	835	do	836	February 1919–August 1919	k 837	March 1918–June 1919	k 838	November 1917–June 1919	
	k 839	November 1917–June 1919	k 840	November 1917–June 1919	k 841	March 1918–June 1919	k 842	April 1918–June 1919	k 843	June 1918–June 1919	
	k 844	June 1918–June 1919									
Service Park Unit [9]	1–300	Never orgzd.	b 301	December 1917–September 1919	b 302	December 1917–July 1919	b 303	December 1917–August 1919	b 304	December 1917–July 1919	a Orgzd. and demblzd. overseas.
	b 305	December 1917–August 1919	b 306	do	b 307	December 1917–August 1919	bh 308	January 1918–July 1919	bij 309	do	

[8] Converted into M. T. Cos. fr. Engr. M. Trk. Serv., December 1918.

[9] Originally orgzd. as Machine Shop Truck Units; redesignated during 1918–19.

M. T. C. SPECIAL AND TECHNICAL UNITS—Continued

Units	Unit No.	Active service	Unit No.	Active service	Unit No.	Active service	Unit No.	Active service	Unit No.	Active service	Remarks
Service Park Unit—Continued.	b 310	January 1918–July 1919	b 311	November 1917–July 1919	b 312	December 1917–June 1919	b 313	December 1917–June 1919	b 314	December 1917–May 1919	b S.O.S. troops.
	b 315	December 1917–May 1919	b 316	December 1917–June 1919	b 317	December 1917–July 1919	b 318	February 1918–August 1919	319	February 1918–March 1919	h Army troops.
	b 320	February 1918–July 1919	321	February 1918–May 1919	b 322	February 1918–July 1919	323	February 1918–April 1919	324	January 1918–April 1919	i Orgzd. in U. S., demobilized overseas.
	b 325	January 1918–August 1919	326	February 1918–April 1919	327	January 1918–November 1919	328	January 1918–April 1919	329	December 1917–August 1919	j G.H.Q. troops.
	330	February 1918 through December 1919	331	January 1918–March 1919	332	February 1918 through December 1919	333	February 1918 through December 1919	334	February 1918 through December 1919	k Orgzd. overseas, demobilized in U. S.
	b 335	February 1918–July 1919	b 336	February 1918–September 1919	337	February 1918–May 1919	b 338	February 1918–August 1919	339	Do.	l Orgzd. overseas.
	b 340	do	341	February 1918 through December 1919	342	February 1918 through December 1919	343	February 1918–June 1919	344	January 1918 through December 1919	
	345	January 1918 through December 1919	346	do	347	January 1918–May 1919	348	January 1918 through December 1919	349	Do.	
	b 350	February 1918–October 1919	351	January 1918–July 1919	b 352	February 1918–July 1919	353	February 1918–January 1919	354	February 1918 through December 1919	
	b 355	February 1918–July 1919	356	March 1918–June 1919	357	March 1918 through December 1919	358	March 1918 through December 1919	359	March 1918–June 1919	
	b 360	January 1918–August 1919	b 361	January 1918–July 1919	b 362	March 1918–July 1919	b 363	March 1918–August 1919	b 364	April 1918–August 1919	
	b 365	April 1918–June 1919	b 366	April 1918–September 1919	b 367	April 1918–July 1919	bh 368	April 1918–July 1919	bh 369	April 1918–June 1919	
	370	June 1918–March 1919	371	June 1918 through December 1919	372	June 1918–March 1919	373	June 1918–June 1919	374	June 1918 through December 1919	
	b 375	June 1918–August 1919	b 376	June 1918–August 1919	b 377	June 1918–August 1919	b 378	June 1918–September 1919	b 379	June 1918–August 1919	

380	June 1918–November 1919	381	June 1918 through December 1919	382	June 1918 through December 1919	383	June 1918 through December 1919	384	June 1918–July 1919
385	June 1918–March 1919	386	June 1918–July 1919	[b] 387	June 1918–July 1919	[b] 388	June 1918–August 1919	[b] 389	June 1918–July 1919
[b] 390	June 1918–August 1919	[b] 391	June 1918–June 1919	[b] 392	do	[b] 393	June 1918–July 1919	[b] 394	June 1918–August 1919
[b] 395	June 1918–July 1919	[b h] 396	June 1918–October 1919	[b] 397	June 1918–September 1919	[b] 398	June 1918–June 1919	[b] 399	June 1918–October 1919
[b] 400	June 1918–August 1919	[b] 401	June 1918–August 1919	[b] 402	June 1918–July 1919	[b] 403	June 1918–August 1919	[b] 404	June 1918–July 1919
[h] 405	June 1918–July 1919	[b] 406	do	[b] 407	July 1918–July 1919	[b] 408	July 1918–June 1919	[b] 409	July 1918–August 1919
[h] 410	July 1918–September 1919	[h] 411	June 1918–July 1919	[h] 412	do	[h] 413	October 1918–July 1919	[h] 414	September 1918–July 1919
[h] 415	September 1918–July 1919	[h] 416	September 1918–July 1919	[h] 417	September 1918–July 1919	[h] 418	October 1918–August 1919	[h] 419	October 1918–September 1919
[h] 420	October 1918–December 1919	[h] 421	October 1918–September 1919	[h] 422	October 1918–July 1919	423	October 1918–March 1919	424	October 1918–March 1919
425	October 1918–March 1919	426	October 1918–June 1919	427	November 1918–March 1919	428	November 1918–February 1919	429	November 1918–February 1919
430	November 1918–February 1919	431	November 1918–February 1919	432	November 1918–February 1919	433	do	434	Do.
435	do	436	do	437	do	438	do	439	Do.
440	do	441	do	442	do	443	do	444	Do.
445	do	446	do	447	Never orgzd.	[h i] 448	October 1918–September 1919	449	December 1918–March 1919
450	December 1918 through December 1919	451	December 1918–May 1919	452	November 1918–March 1919	453	November 1918–March 1919	454	November 1918–March 1919
455	November 1918–March 1919	456	November 1918–March 1919	457	do	458	do	459	Do.
460	do	461	do	462	do	463	do	464	Do.
465	do	466	do	467	do	468	November 1918 through December 1919	469–477	Never orgzd.
478	July 1918 through December 1919	479	October 1918 through December 1919	480	October 1918–June 1919	481	October 1918–May 1919	482	October 1918 through December 1919

M. T. C. SPECIAL AND TECHNICAL UNITS—Continued

Units	Unit No.	Active service	Unit No.	Active service	Unit No.	Active service	Unit No.	Active service	Unit No.	Active service	Remarks
Service Park Unit—Continued.	483	November 1918–March 1919	484	November 1918–December 1919	485	November 1918 through December 1919	486	November 1918–May 1919	487	November 1918–November 1919	
	488	do	489	November 1918–November 1919	490	November 1918–November 1919	491	November 1918–November 1919	492	November 1918–May 1919	
	493	November 1918 through December 1919	494	November 1918–July 1919	495	November 1918–May 1919	496	November 1918–May 1919	497	November 1918–July 1919	
	498	November 1918–March 1919	499	November 1918 through December 1919	500	do	501	November 1918–October 1919	502	November 1918–May 1919	
	503	November 1918 through December 1919	504	November 1918–May 1919	505	do	506	November 1918–November 1919	507	Do.	
	508	November 1918–November 1919	509–512	Never orgzd.	513	November 1918–November 1919	514	November 1918–May 1919	515	November 1918 through December 1919	
	516	do	517	November 1918–November 1919	518–527	Never orgzd.	h 528	October 1918–July 1919	h 529	October 1918–July 1919	
	h 530	October 1918–July 1919	b 531	October 1918–September 1919	b 532	October 1918–September 1919	b 533	October 1918–September 1919	b 534	October 1918–September 1919	
	b 535	October 1918–October 1919	b 536	October 1918–October 1919	b 537	do	538	October 1918–December 1919	539	October 1918–April 1919	
	540	do	541	October 1918–April 1919	542	October 1918–November 1919	543	October 1918 through December 1919	544	Do.	
	545	October 1918–April 1919	546	do	547	October 1918–April 1919	548–594	Never orgzd.	595	October 1918 through December 1919	
	596–677	Never orgzd.	678	November 1918–December 1919	679	November 1918 through December 1919	680–691	do	692	November 1918–December 1919	

Units	Unit No.	Active service	Unit No.	Active service	Unit No.	Active service	Unit No.	Active service	Unit No.	Active service	Remarks
	[k] 693	January 1918–July 1919	[b] 694	May 1917–December 1919	[b] [l] 695	September 1917 through December 1919	[b] [k] 696	March 1919–August 1919	697–702	Never orgzd.	
	[k] 703	December 1918–July 1919	[k] 704	January 1919–August 1919	[a] 705	January 1919–July 1919	[k] 706	January 1919–July 1919	[k] 707	February 1919–July 1919	
	[k] 708	February 1919–July 1919	709–711	Never orgzd.	[k] 712	March 1919–September 1919	713	January 1919–July 1919	[k] 714	December 1918–December 1919	
	715	December 1918–July 1919	716	November 1918–July 1919	717	November 1918–December 1919	718–725	Never orgzd.	726	June 1918–May 1919	
	727–811	Never orgzd.	812	January 1919 through December 1919	813 & 814	Never orgzd.	815	December 1918 through December 1919	816	Never orgzd.	
	817	February 1919 through December 1919	818	December 1918 through December 1919	819	December 1918–March 1919	820	September 1918–March 1919			

ORDNANCE DEPARTMENT

ORDNANCE SPECIAL AND TECHNICAL UNITS

Units	Unit No.	Active service	Unit No.	Active service	Unit No.	Active service	Unit No.	Active service	Unit No.	Active service	Remarks
Mobile Ordnance Repair Shop.	[a] 1	January 1918–September 1919	2	October 1917 through December 1919	3	February 1918–December 1919	4	February 1918–December 1919	5	January 1918–August 1919	a Orgzd. and demblzd. overseas.
	6	April 1918–June 1919	7	March 1918–July 1919	8	April 1918–February 1919	9	September 1918–December 1918	10	August 1918–February 1919	b Orgzd. in U. S.; demobilized overseas.
	11	November 1918–December 1918	12 & 13	Never orgzd.	14	October 1918–February 1919	15–100	Never orgzd.	[a] 101	January 1918–April 1919	c Orgzd. overseas; demobilized in U. S.
	102	December 1917–April 1919	103	November 1917–May 1919	104	December 1917–May 1919	105	December 1917–April 1919	106	October 1917–May 1919	d Corps troops.
	107	December 1917–May 1919	108	December 1917–May 1919	109	October 1917–June 1919	110	January 1918–May 1919	111	November 1917–June 1919	e Army troops. f G.H.Q. troops.
	112	October 1917–April 1919	113	December 1917–July 1919	114	December 1917–May 1919	115	November 1917–May 1919	[b] (I) 116	See Heavy MORS No. 2	116th MORS redes. 2d Heavy MORS.
	[a] (II) 116	June 1918–November 1918	[c] 117	February 1918–May 1919	118–300	Never orgzd.	[b] 301	January 1918–July 1919	302	December 1917–May 1919	

ORDNANCE SPECIAL AND TECHNICAL UNITS—Continued

Units	Unit No.	Active service	Unit No.	Active service	Unit No.	Active service	Unit No.	Active service	Unit No.	Active service	Remarks
Mobile Ordnance Repair Shop—Con.	303	April 1918–May 1919	304	March 1918–May 1919	305	December 1917–May 1919	306	November 1917–June 1919	307	October 1917–May 1919	
	[b] 308	November 1917–January 1919	309	November 1917–May 1919	310	November 1917–May 1919	311	November 1917–February 1919	312	September 1917–May 1919	
	313	December 1917–June 1919	314	November 1917–June 1919	315	December 1917–June 1919	316	November 1917–May 1919	317	December 1917–March 1919	
	318–500	Never orgzd.	[d] 501	March 1918–September 1919	[d] 502–505	Records incomplete	506–600	Never orgzd.	[e] 601	March 1918–May 1919	
Heavy Mobile Ordnance Repair Shop.	[e] 1	February 1918–September 1919	[e] 2	February 1918–January 1919	[e] 3	May 1918–May 1919	[e] 4	May 1918–July 1919	[b] [e](I) 5	May 1918–January 1919	
	[c] [e](II) 5	April 1919 through December 1919	[e] 6	May 1918–March 1919	[e] 7	August 1918–February 1919	[e] 8	August 1918–April 1919			
Railway Artillery Ordnance Repair Shop.	[f] 1	April 1918–February 1919	[f] 2	June 1918–February 1919	3	Record incomplete	[f] 4	October 1918–December 1918	5	October 1918–January 1919	
	6	November 1918–January 1919									
Ordnance Depot Company.	1–100	Records incomplete	101	September 1917 through December 1919	102	August 1917 through December 1919	103	August 1917 through December 1919	104	September 1917–September 1919	
	105	September 1917 through December 1919	106	-----do----------	107	October 1917 through December 1919	108	September 1917 through December 1919	109	October 1917 through December 1919	
	110	March 1918 through December 1919	111	October 1917 through December 1919	112	-----do----------	113	October 1917 through December 1919	114	September 1917 through December 1919	
	115	September 1917 through December 1919	116	September 1917 through December 1919	117	August 1917–March 1919	118	August 1917–March 1918	119	August 1917–March 1919	

	120	August 1917–July 1919	121	October 1917–March 1919	122	August 1917–April 1919	123	August 1917–March 1919	124	Do.
	125	August 1917–January 1919	126	October 1917 through December 1919	127	August 1917–November 1919	128	August 1917–April 1919	129	August 1917 through December 1919
	130	September 1917–March 1919	131	August 1917 through December 1919	132	July 1917–February 1919	133	October 1917–December 1919	134	August 1918–February 1919
	135	October 1917–February 1919	136	April 1918–January 1919	137	February 1918 through December 1919	138	June 1918–January 1919	139	June 1918–July 1919
	140	December 1918 through December 1919	141	February 1919 through December 1919	142	November 1918 through December 1919	143 & 144	Never orgzd.	145	June 1918–February 1919
	146	September 1918 through December 1919								
Ordnance Guard Company.	1	August 1918–March 1919	2	August 1918–March 1919	3	August 1918–March 1919	4	August 1918–November 1918	5	August 1918–March 1919
	6	-----do-----------	7	-----do-----------	8	August 1918–December 1918	9	August 1918–March 1919	10	Do.
	11	September 1918–March 1919	12	December 1918–March 1919	13	Never orgzd.	14	December 1918–March 1919	15	December 1918–March 1919
	16	December 1918–March 1919	17	-----do-----------	18	December 1918–March 1919	19	-----do-----------	20	See Ord. Gd. Co. No. 16
	21	See Ord. Gd. Co. No. 17	22	January 1919–March 1919	23	January 1919–March 1919				
Ordnance Supply Company.	1	August 1918–March 1919	2	August 1918–March 1919	3	August 1918–March 1919	4	August 1918–March 1919	5	August 1918–March 1919
	6	-----do-----------	7	August 1918–January 1919	8	August 1918–January 1919	9	August 1918–February 1919	10–15	Never orgzd.
	16	October 1918–March 1919	17	October 1918–March 1919	18	October 1918–March 1919	19	October 1918–March 1919	20	October 1918–March 1919
	21	-----do-----------	22	October 1918–December 1918	23	October 1918–December 1918	24	October 1918–December 1918		

QUARTERMASTER CORPS

AUXILIARY REMOUNT DEPOTS

Unit designation and redesignation	Organization		Stations in United States		Overseas		Demobilization		Remarks
	Month and year	Place	Month and year	Place	From—	To—	Month and year	Place	
Auxiliary Remount Depot No. 301.	August 1917	Cp. Devens, Mass.							Active through 1919.
Auxiliary Remount Depot No. 302.	do	Cp. Upton, N. Y.							Do.
Auxiliary Remount Depot No. 303.	September 1917	Cp. Dix, N. J.							Do.
Auxiliary Remount Depot No. 304.	August 1917	Cp. Meade, Md.							Do.
Auxiliary Remount Depot No. 305.	September 1917	Cp. Lee, Va.							Do.
Auxiliary Remount Depot No. 306.	do	Cp. Greene, N. C.					April 1919	Cp. Greene, N. C.	
Auxiliary Remount Depot No. 307.	do	Cp. Wadsworth, S. C.					May 1919	Cp. Wadsworth, S. C.	
Auxiliary Remount Depot No. 308.	do	Cp. Hancock, Ga.					do	Cp. Hancock, Ga.	
Auxiliary Remount Depot No. 309.	do	Cp. McClellan, Ala.					July 1919	Cp. McClellan, Ala.	
Auxiliary Remount Depot No. 310.	August 1917	Cp. Sevier, S. C.					May 1919	Cp. Sevier, S. C.	
Auxiliary Remount Depot No. 311.	September 1917	Cp. Wheeler, Ga.					June 1919	Cp. Wheeler, Ga.	
Auxiliary Remount Depot No. 312.	do	Cp. Sheridan, Ala.					May 1919	Cp. Sheridan, Ala.	
Auxiliary Remount Depot No. 313.	do	Cp. Shelby, Miss.					do	Cp. Shelby, Miss.	
Auxiliary Remount Depot No. 314.	do	Cp. Beauregard, Ala.					March 1919	Cp. Beauregard, Ala.	
Auxiliary Remount Depot No. 315.	do	Cp. Jackson, S. C.					December 1919	Cp. Jackson, S. C.	

Auxiliary Remount Depot No. 316.	August 1917	Cp. Gordon, Ga.							Do.
Auxiliary Remount Depot No. 317	September 1917	Cp. Pike, Ark.							Do.
Auxiliary Remount Depot No. 318.	do	Cp. Sherman, Ohio.					December 1919	Cp. Sherman, Ohio.	
Auxiliary Remount Depot No. 319.	October 1917	Cp. Z. Taylor, Ky.					May 1919	Cp. Z. Taylor, Ky.	
Auxiliary Remount Depot No. 320.	September 1917	Cp. Custer, Mich.							Do.
Auxiliary Remount Depot No. 321.	August 1917	Cp. Grant, Ill.							Do.
Auxiliary Remount Depot No. 322.	September 1917	Cp. Dodge, Iowa.							Do.
Auxiliary Remount Depot No. 323.	October 1917	Cp. Funston, Kans.					December 1919	Cp. Funston, Kans.	
Auxiliary Remount Depot No. 324.	August 1917	Cp. MacArthur, Tex.					May 1919	Cp. MacArthur, Tex.	
Auxiliary Remount Depot No. 325.	September 1917	Cp. Logan, Tex.					March 1919	Cp. Logan, Tex.	
Auxiliary Remount Depot No. 326.	do	Cp. Cody, N. Mex.					May 1919	Cp. Cody, N. Mex.	
Auxiliary Remount Depot No. 327.	August 1917	Ft. Sill, Okla.					August 1919	Ft. Sill, Okla.	
Auxiliary Remount Depot No. 328.	do	Cp. Bowie, Tex.					June 1919	Cp. Bowie, Tex.	
Auxiliary Remount Depot No. 329.	September 1917	Cp. Travis, Tex.					May 1919	Cp. Travis, Tex.	
Auxiliary Remount Depot No. 330.	do	Cp. Kearny, Calif.							Do.
Auxiliary Remount Depot No. 331.	do	Cp. Lewis, Wash.							Do.
Auxiliary Remount Depot No. 332.	do	Cp. Fremont, Calif.					April 1919	Cp. Fremont, Calif.	
Auxiliary Remount Depot No. 333.	January 1918	Cp. Joseph E. Johnston, Fla.					March 1919	Cp. Joseph E. Johnston, Fla.	

FIELD REMOUNT SQUADRONS

Unit designation and redesignation	Organization		Stations in United States		Overseas		Demobilization		Remarks
	Month and year	Place	Month and year	Place	From—	To—	Month and year	Place	
Field Remount Squadron, Nos. 1 to 300.									Never orgzd.
Field Remount Squadron No. 301.	February 1918	Cp. Joseph E. Johnston, Fla.	April 1918	Cp. Merritt, N. J.					
			do	P. of E., Hoboken	April 1918.				
			October 1919	Cp. Merritt, N. J.		October 1919	October 1919	Cp. Dix, N. J	Corps troops.
Field Remount Squadron No. 302.	do	do	April 1918	Do.					
			do	P. of E., Hoboken	April 1918.				
			October 1919	Cp. Merritt, N. J.		do	do	do	Do.
Field Remount Squadron No. 303.	do	do	April 1918	Do.					
			do	P. of E., Hoboken	April 1918.				
			September 1919	Cp. Merritt, N. J.		September 1919	do	do	Army troops.
Field Remount Squadron No. 304.	do	do	April 1918	Do.					
			do	P. of E., Hoboken	April 1918.				
			September 1919	Cp. Merritt, N. J.		do	September 1919	do	Corps troops.
Field Remount Squadron No. 305.	April 1918	do	June 1918	P. of E., Newport News.	June 1918.				
			June 1919	Cp. Jackson, S. C.		June 1919	July 1919	do	Army troops.
Field Remount Squadron No. 306.	do	do	June 1918	P. of E., Newport News.	June 1918.				
			October 1919	Cp. Merritt, N. J.		October 1919	October 1919	Cp. Pike, Ark	Corps troops.
Field Remount Squadron No. 307.	do	do	June 1918	P. of E., Newport News.	June 1918	July 1919	July 1919	Cp. Devens, Mass.	Do.
Field Remount Squadron No. 308.	do	do	do	do	do				
			June 1919	Cp. Merritt, N. J.		June 1919	June 1919	Cp. Grant, Ill	Do.
Field Remount Squadron No. 309.	June 1918	do	July 1918	P. of E., Newport News.	July 1918.				
			July 1919	Cp. Mills, N. Y		July 1919	July 1919	Cp. Upton, N. Y	Do.

Field Remount Squadron No. 310.	do	do	July 1918	P. of E., Newport News.	July 1918.				
			October 1919	Cp. Merritt, N. J.		October 1919	October 1919	Cp. Dix, N. J.	Do.
Field Remount Squadron No. 311.	do	do	July 1918	Cp. Hill, Va.					
			August 1918	P. of E., Newport News.	August 1918	November 1919	November 1919	do	Army troops.
Field Remount Squadron No. 312.	do	do	July 1918	Cp. Hill, Va.					
			August 1918	P. of E., Newport News.	Do.				
			October 1919	Cp. Merritt, N. J.		October 1919	October 1919	do	Do.
Field Remount Squadron No. 313.	July 1918	do	August 1918	Cp. Hill, Va.					
			do	P. of E., Newport News.	August 1918	July 1919	July 1919	Cp. Devens, Mass.	Do.
Field Remount Squadron No. 314.	do	do	July 1918	Cp. Hill, Va.					
			August 1918	P. of E., Newport News.	August 1918	November 1919	November 1919	Cp. Dix, N. J.	Army troops.
Field Remount Squadron No. 315.	do	do	do	Cp. Hill, Va.					
			do	P. of E., Newport News.	Do.				
			July 1919	Cp. Mills, N. Y.		July 1919	July 1919	Cp. Upton, N. Y.	Corps troops.
Field Remount Squadron No. 316.	do	do	August 1918	Cp. Hill, Va.					
			do	P. of E., Newport News.	August 1918	June 1919	June 1919	Cp. Dix, N. J.	Army troops.
Field Remount Squadron No. 317.	do	do	do	Cp. Hill, Va.					
			do	P. of E., Newport News.	do	do	do	do	Do.
Field Remount Squadron No. 318.	do	do	do	Cp. Hill, Va.					
			do	P. of E., Newport News.	do	July 1919	July 1919	Cp. Devens, Mass.	S.O.S. troops.
Field Remount Squadron No. 319.	do	do	do	Cp. Hill, Va.					
			September 1918	P. of E., Newport News.	September 1918	June 1919	June 1919	Cp. Dix, N. J.	Do.

FIELD REMOUNT SQUADRONS—Continued

Unit designation and redesignation	Organization		Stations in United States		Overseas		Demobilization		Remarks
	Month and year	Place	Month and year	Place	From—	To—	Month and year	Place	
Field Remount Squadron No. 320.	July 1918	Cp. Joseph E. Johnston, Fla.	September 1918	P. of E., Newport News.	September 1918.				
			June 1919	Cp. Merritt, N. J.		June 1919	July 1919	Cp. Funston, Kans.	S.O.S. troops
Field Remount Squadron No. 321.	do	do	September 1918	P. of E., Newport News.	September 1918	July 1919	do	Cp. Devens, Mass.	Do.
Field Remount Squadron No. 322.	do	do	do	do	do	November 1919	November 1919	Cp. Dix, N. J	Do.
Field Remount Squadron No. 323.	do	do	do	do	Do.				
			June 1919	Cp. Merritt, N. J.		June 1919	July 1919	Cp. Bowie, Tex	Do.
Field Remount Squadron No. 324.	do	do	September 1918	P. of E., Newport News.	September 1918	July 1919	do	Cp. Devens, Mass.	Do.
Field Remount Squadron No. 325.	August 1918	do	do	do	Do.				
			June 1919	Cp. Hill, Va		June 1919	do	Cp. Upton, N. Y.	Do.
Field Remount Squadron No. 326.	do	do	September 1918	P. of E., Newport News.	September 1918	do*	June 1919	Cp. Dix, N. J	Do.
Field Remount Squadron No. 327.	do	do	do	do	do	July 1919	July 1919	Cp. Jackson, S. C.	Do.
Field Remount Squadron No. 328.	do	do	do	do	Do.				
			June 1919	Cp. Merritt, N. J.		June 1919	do	Cp. Bowie, Tex	Do.
Field Remount Squadron No. 329.	do	do	September 1918	Cp. Stuart, Va.					
			do	P. of E., Newport News.	September 1918				
			July 1919	Cp. Mills, N. Y.		July 1919	do	Cp. Upton, N. Y.	Do.
Field Remount Squadron No. 330.	do	do	September 1918	P. of E., Newport News.	September 1918.				
			July 1919	Cp. Mills, N. Y.		do	do	do	Do.

Field Remount Squadron No. 331.	do	do	September 1918	Cp. Hill, Va.					
			October 1918	P. of E., Newport News.	October 1918.				
			July 1919	Cp. Merritt, N. J.		do	do	Cp. Sherman, Ohio.	Do.
Field Remount Squadron No. 332.	do	do	September 1918	Cp. Hill, Va.					
			October 1918	P. of E., Newport News.	October 1918.				
			July 1919	Cp. Merritt, N. J.		do	do	Cp. Pike, Ark	Do.
Field Remount Squadron No. 333.	do	do	September 1918	Cp. Hill, Va.					
			October 1918	P. of E., Newport News.	October 1918.				
			July 1919	Cp. Merritt, N. J.		do	do	do	Do.
Field Remount Squadron No. 334.	do	do	September 1918	Cp. Hill, Va.					
			October 1918	P. of E., Newport News.	October 1918.				
			July 1919	Cp. Stuart, Va		do	do	do	Do.
Field Remount Squadron No. 335.	do	do	September 1918	Cp. Hill, Va.					
			October 1918	P. of E., Newport News.					
			June 1919	Cp. Mills, N. Y.		June 1919	do	Cp. Upton, N. Y.	Do.
Field Remount Squadron No. 336.	do	do	September 1918	Cp. Hill, Va.					
			October 1918	P. of E., Newport News.	October 1918.				
			June 1919	Cp. Jackson, S. C.		do	do	Cp. Bowie, Tex	Do.
Field Remount Squadron No. 337.	do	do	September 1918	Cp. Hill, Va.					
			October 1918	P. of E., Newport News.	October 1918.				
			July 1919	Cp. Mills, N. Y.		July 1919	do	Cp. Pike, Ark	Do.
Field Remount Squadron No. 338.	do	do	September 1918	Cp. Hill, Va.					
			October 1918	P. of E., Newport News.	October 1918.				
			July 1919	Cp. Hill, Va		do	do	Cp. Bowie, Tex	Do.

FIELD REMOUNT SQUADRONS—Continued

Unit designation and redesignation	Organization		Stations in United State		Overseas		Demobilization		Remarks
	Month and year	Place	Month and year	Place	From—	To—	Month and year	Place	
Field Remount Squadron, No. 339.	September 1918	Cp. Joseph E. Johnston, Fla.	October 1918	Cp. Upton, N. Y.					
			do	P. of E., Hoboken	October 1918.				
			June 1919	Cp. Merritt, N. J.		June 1919	July 1919	Cp. Bowie, Tex	S.O.S. troops.
Field Remount Squadron No. 340.	do	do	October 1918	P. of E., Hoboken	October 1918.				
			July 1919	Cp. Merritt, N. J.		July 1919	do	Cp. Dodge, Iowa	Do.
Field Remount Squadron No. 341.	do	do	October 1918	P. of E., Hoboken	October 1918.				
			July 1919	Cp. Jackson, S. C.		do	do	do	Do.
Field Remount Squadron No. 342.	do	do	October 1918	P. of E., Hoboken	October 1918.				
			July 1919	Cp. Mills, N. Y.		do	do	do	Do.
Field Remount Squadron No. 343.	do	do	October 1918	P. of E., Hoboken	October 1918	do	do	Cp. Jackson, S. C.	Do.
Field Remount Squadron No. 344.	do	do	do	do	do	November 1919	November 1919	Cp. Dix, N. J.	Do.
Field Remount Squadron No. 345.	do	do	do	do	do	July 1919	July 1919	Cp. Devens, Mass.	Do.
Field Remount Squadron No. 346.	October 1918	do	do	do	Do.				
			July 1919	Cp. Stuart, Va.		do	do	Cp. Grant, Ill.	Do.
Field Remount Squadron No. 347.	do	do	November 1918	Cp. Hill, Va.			February 1919	Cp. Lee, Va.	
Field Remount Squadron No. 348.	do	do	do	do			January 1919	Do.	
Field Remount Squadron No. 349.	do	do	December 1918	Cp. Jackson, S. C.			May 1919	Cp. Jackson, S. C.	
Field Remount Squadron No. 350.	November 1918	do	January 1919	Cp. Sherman, Ohio			do	Cp. Sherman, Ohio	
Field Remount Squadron No. 351.	do	do	February 1919	Cp. McClellan, Ala.			do	Cp. McClellan, Ala.	

Field Remount Squadron No. 352.	do	do	January 1919	Cp. Bowie, Tex.			do	Cp. Bowie, Tex.	
Field Remount Squadron No. 353.	do	do	do	Cp. Wadsworth, S. C.			do	Cp. Wadsworth, S. C.	
Field Remount Squadron No. 354.	do	do	February 1919	Cp. McClellan, Ala.			June 1919	Cp. McClellan, Ala.	
Field Remount Squadron No. 355.	do	do					December 1918	Cp. Joseph E. Johnston, Fla.	
Field Remount Squadron No. 356.	do	do					do	Do.	
Field Remount Squadron No. 357.	do	do					do	Do.	
Field Remount Squadron No. 358.	do	do					do	Do.	
Field Remount Squadron No. 359.	do	do					do	Do.	
Field Remount Squadron No. 360.	do	do					do	Do.	
Field Remount Squadron No. 361.	do	do					do	Do.	
Field Remount Squadron No. 362.	do	do					do	Do.	
Field Remount Squadron No. 363.	do	do					do	Do.	
Field Remount Squadron No. 364.	do	do					do	Do.	
Field Remount Squadron No. 365.	do	do					do	Do.	
Field Remount Squadron No. 366.	do	do					do	Do.	

SERVICE BATTALIONS [1]

Service Battalions Nos. 1 to 303.									Never orgzd.
Service Battalion No. 304.	June 1918	A. E. F.	June 1919	Cp. Lee, Va.		June 1919	June 1919	Cp. Lee, Va.	

[1] Originally orgzd. as Labor Bns.; redes. May 1919.

SERVICE BATTALIONS—Continued

Unit designation and redesignation	Organization: Month and year	Organization: Place	Stations in United States: Month and year	Stations in United States: Place	Overseas: From—	Overseas: To—	Demobilization: Month and year	Demobilization: Place	Remarks
Service Battalion No. 305.	June 1918	A. E. F	July 1919	Cp. Mills, N. Y		July 1919	July 1919	Cp. Jackson, S. C.	S.O.S. troops.
Service Battalion No. 306.	do	do	do	Cp. Hill, Va		do	do	Cp. Hill, Va	Do.
Service Battalion No. 307.	do	do	May 1919	Cp. Upton, N. Y		May 1919	June 1919	Cp. Upton, N. Y	Do.
Service Battalion No. 308.	March 1918	Cp. Hill, Va	March 1918	P. of E., Newport News.	March 1918.				
			July 1919	Cp. Mills, N. Y		July 1919	July 1919	Cp. Gordon, Ga	Do.
Service Battalion No. 309.	do	do	April 1918	P. of E., Newport News.	April 1918				Orgsd. fr. 4th Prov. Labor. Bn. March 1918. S.O.S. troops.
			June 1919	Cp. Jackson, S. C.		June 1919	July 1919	Cp. Pike, Ark.	
Service Battalion No. 310.	do	do	April 1918	P. of E., Newport News.	April 1918				Orgsd. fr. 5th Prov. Labor Bn. March 1918. S.O.S. troops.
			August 1919	Cp. Merritt, N. J.		August 1919	September 1919	Cp. Shelby, Miss.	
Service Battalion No. 311.	do	do	June 1918	P. of E., Newport News.	June 1918	July 1918	July 1918	A. E. F	Orgsd. fr. 6th Prov. Labor Bn. March 1918.
Service Battalion No. 312.	do	do	March 1918	P. of E., Hoboken	March 1918				Orgsd. fr. 1st Prov. Labor Bn. March 1918.
			June 1919	Cp. Upton, N. Y		June 1919	June 1919	Cp. Gordon, Ga.	S.O.S. troops.
Service Battalion No. 313.	do	do	March 1918	P. of E., Newport News.	March 1918				Orgsd. fr. 2d Prov. Labor Bn. March 1918.
			June 1919	Cp. Alexander, Va.		June 1919	July 1919	Cp. Gordon, Ga.	S.O.S. troops.

Service Battalion No. 314.	July 1918	Cp. Gordon, Ga.	July 1918	P. of E., Newport News.	July 1918.				
			July 1919	Cp. Stuart, Va.		July 1919	do	do	S.O.S. troops.
Service Battalion No. 315.	August 1918	do	September 1918	P. of E., Hoboken.	September 1918.				
			July 1919	Cp. Hill, Va.		do	do	do	Do.
Service Battalion (I) No. 316.	May 1918	Cp. Joseph E. Johnston, Fla.	June 1918	Cp. Mills, N. Y.					
a. 427th Reserve Labor Battalion.	September 1918	Cp. Mills, N. Y.					September 1919	Cp. Mills, N. Y.	
Service Battalion (II) No. 316.	do	Cp. Alexander, Va.	September 1918	P. of E., Newport News.	September 1918.				Do.
			July 1919	Norfolk, Va.		July 1919	August 1919	Cp. Gordon, Ga.	
Service Battalion No. 317.	May 1918	Cp. Zachary Taylor, Ky.	June 1918	P. of E., Newport News.	June 1918.				
			June 1919	Cp. Alexander, Va.		June 1919	July 1919	Cp. Zachary Taylor, Ky.	Do.
Service Battalion No. 318.	June 1918	Cp. Hill, Va.	June 1918	P. of E., Newport News.	June 1918.				
			June 1919	Cp. Merritt, N. J.		do	do	Cp. Shelby, Miss.	Do.
Service Battalion No. 319.	do	do	July 1918	P. of E., Newport News.	July 1918.				
			July 1919	Cp. Alexander, Va.		July 1919	do	do	Do.
Service Battalion No. 320.	do	Cp. Lee, Va.	July 1918	P. of E., Newport News.	July 1918.				
			July 1919	Cp. Alexander, Va.		do	do	Cp. Lee, Va.	Do.
Service Battalion No. 321.	May 1918	Cp. Jackson, S. C.	May 1918	Cp. Sevier, S. C.					
			July 1918	Cp. Upton, N. Y.					
			do	P. of E., Hoboken.	July 1918.				
			August 1919	Cp. Merritt, N. J.		August 1919	August 1919	do	Do.
Service Battalion No. 322.	July 1918	Cp. Travis, Tex.	July 1918	Cp. Hill, Va.					
			August 1918	P. of E., Newport News.	August 1918.				
			July 1919	Cp. Mills, N. Y.		July 1919	July 1919	Cp. Travis, Tex.	Do.
Service Battalion No. 323.	May 1918	Cp. Grant, Ill.	July 1918	Cp. Upton, N. Y.					
			do	P. of E., Hoboken	July 1918.				
			July 1919	Cp. Mills, N. Y.		do	do	Cp. Lee, Va.	Do.

SERVICE BATTALIONS—Continued

Unit designation and redesignation	Organization		Stations in United States		Overseas		Demobilization		Remarks
	Month and year	Place	Month and year	Place	From—	To—	Month and year	Place	
Service Battalion No. 324.	July 1918	Cp. Custer, Mich.	July 1918	Cp. Upton, N. Y.					
			do	P. of E., Hoboken.	July 1918.				
			July 1919	Cp. Mills, N. Y.		July 1919	July 1919	Cp. Gordon, Ga.	S.O.S. troops.
Service Battalion No. 325.	May 1918	Cp. Funston, Kans	August 1918	Cp. Upton, N. Y.					
			do	P. of E., Hoboken.	August 1918.				
			July 1919	Cp. Alexander, Va.		do	do	Cp. Shelby, Miss.	Do.
Service Battalion No. 326.	September 1918	Cp. McClellan, Ala	October 1918	Cp. Merritt, N. J.					
			do	P. of E., Hoboken.	October 1918.				
			June 1919	Cp. Merritt, N. J.		June 1919	do	do	Do.
Service Battalion No. 327.	June 1918	Cp. Wheeler, Ga.	June 1918	Cp. Hill, Va.					
			July 1918	P. of E., Newport News.	July 1918.				
			July 1919	Cp. Mills, N. Y.		July 1919	do	Cp. Gordon, Ga.	Do.
Service Battalion (I) No. 328.	March 1918	Cp. Jackson, S. C.	June 1918	Pisgah Forest, N.C					
a. 444th Reserve Labor Battalion	October 1918	Pisgah Forest, N. C.	December 1918	Cp. Sevier, S. C.			January 1919	Cp. Sevier, S. C.	
Service Battalion, (II) No. 328.	September 1918	Cp. Alexander, Va	October 1918	P. of E., Newport News.	October 1918.				
			August 1919	Cp. Merritt, N. J.		August 1919	August 1919	Cp. Gordon, Ga.	Do.
Service Battalion No. 329.	May 1918	Cp. Grant, Ill.	August 1918	Cp. Upton, N. Y.					
			do	P. of E., Hoboken.	August 1918.				
			June 1919	Cp. Jackson, S. C.		June 1919	July 1919	Cp. Shelby, Miss.	Do.
Service Battalion No. 330.	June 1918	Cp. Jackson, S. C.	June 1918	Cp. Wadsworth, S. C.					
			August 1918	Cp. Merritt, N. J.					
			September 1918	P. of E., Hoboken.	September 1918.				
			September 1919	Cp. Merritt, N. J.		September 1919	September 1919	Cp. Lee, Va.	Do.

Service Battalion No. 331.	May 1918	Cp. Travis, Tex.	May 1918	Cp. MacArthur, Tex.					
			July 1918	Cp. Hill, Va.					
			do	P. of E., Newport News.	July 1918.				
Service Battalion No. 332.	July 1918	do	July 1919	Cp. Jackson, S. C.		July 1919	July 1919	Cp. Travis, Tex.	Do.
			July 1918	Cp. Hill, Va.					
			do	P. of E., Newport News.	July 1918.				
Service Battalion No. 333.	do	Cp. Meade, Md.	July 1919	Cp. Mills, N. Y.		do	do	Cp. Pike, Ark.	Do.
			August 1918	P. of E., Hoboken.	August 1918.				
Service Battalion No. 334.	May 1918	Cp. Shelby, Miss.	June 1919	Cp. Upton, N. Y.		June 1919	do	Cp. Meade, Md.	Do.
			July 1918	Cp. Hill, Va.					
			do	P. of E., Newport News.	July 1918.				
Service Battalion No. 335.	June 1918	Cp. Pike, Ark.	July 1919	Cp. Mills, N. Y.		July 1919	do	Cp. Pike, Ark.	Do.
			July 1918	Cp. Stuart, Va.					
			do	P. of E., Newport News.	July 1918.				
Service Battalion No. 336.	May 1918	Cp. Hill, Va.	July 1919	Cp. Jackson, S. C.		do	do	Cp. Shelby, Miss.	Do.
			June 1918	P. of E., Newport News.	June 1918	August 1918			Absorbed by 301st Steve. Bn. August 1918.
Service Battalion No. 337.	do	do	do	do	do	July 1918			Absorbed by 301st Steve. Bn. July 1918.
Service Battalion No. 338.	August 1918	Cp. Lee, Va.	August 1918	Cp. Hill, Va.					
			do	P. of E., Newport News.	August 1918.				
Service Battalion No. 339.	do	Cp. Alexander, Va.	July 1919	Cp. Mills, N. Y.		July 1919	July 1919	Cp. Dix, N. J.	S.O.S. troops.
			August 1918	Cp. Stuart, Va.					
			September 1918	P. of E., Newport News.	September 1918.				
			August 1919	Cp. Merritt, N. J.		August 1919	August 1919	Cp. Lee, Va.	Do.

SERVICE BATTALIONS—Continued

Unit designation and redesignation	Organization		Stations in United States		Overseas		Demobilization		Remarks
	Month and year	Place	Month and year	Place	From—	To—	Month and year	Place	
Service Battalion No. 340.	August 1918	Cp. Alexander, Va.	September 1918	P. of E., Newport News.	September 1918.				
			July 1919	Cp. Alexander, Va		July 1919	July 1919	Cp. Shelby, Miss.	S.O.S. troops.
Service Battalion No. 341.	do	do	September 1918	P. of E., Newport News.	September 1918	do	do	Cp. Mills, N. Y.	Do.
Service Battalion No. 342.	September 1918	do	do	do	Do.				
			July 1919	Norfolk, Va.		do	do	Cp. Gordon, Ga.	Do.
Service Battalion No. 343.	do	do	October 1918	P. of E., Newport News.	October 1918	do	do	Cp. Hill, Va.	Do.
Service Battalion No. 344.	do	Cp. Greene, N. C.	September 1918	Cp. Upton, N. Y.					
			do	P. of E., Hoboken	September 1918	June 1919	do	Cp. Lee, Va.	Do.
Service Battalion No. 345.	do	do	do	Cp. Upton, N. Y.					
			do	P. of E., Hoboken	Do.				
			July 1919	Cp. Mills, N. Y.		July 1919	do	Cp. Gordon, Ga.	Do.
Service Battalion No. 346.	do	do	September 1918	Cp. Merritt, N. J.					
			do	P. of E., Hoboken	September 1918.				
			July 1919	Cp. Alexander, Va.		do	do	Cp. Jackson, S. C.	Do.
Service Battalion No. 347.	do	do	October 1918	Cp. Stuart, Va.					
			do	P. of E., Newport News.	October 1918.				
			June 1919	Cp. Alexander, Va		June 1919	do	Cp. Lee, Va.	Do.
Service Battalion No. 348.	do	do	October 1918	Cp. Mills, N. Y.					
			do	P. of E., Hoboken	October 1918.				
			August 1919	Cp. Mills, N. Y.		August 1919	August 1919	do	Do.
Service Battalion No. 349.	do	do	November 1918	Charleston, S. C.			April 1919	Charleston, S. C.	

Service Battalion No. 350.	October 1918	do					March 1919	Cp. Greene, N. C.	
Service Battalion No. 351.	do	do					January 1919	Do.	
Service Battalion No. 352.	do	do					do	Do.	
Service Battalion No. 353.	do	do					do	Do.	
Service Battalion No. 354.	do	do					do	Do.	
Service Battalion No. 355.	do	Cp. Alexander, Va.	December 1918	New Cumberland, Pa.			April 1919	New Cumberland, Pa.	
Service Battalions No. 356 to 400.									Never orgzd.
Service Battalion No. 401 (Reserve)	September 1918	Cp. Eustis, Va					April 1919	Cp. Eustis, Va.	
Service Battalion No. 402 (Reserve)	June 1918	Cp. Hancock, Ga					March 1919	Cp. Hancock, Ga.	
Service Battalion No. 403 (Reserve)	do	Cp. Wheeler, Ga					do	Cp. Wheeler, Ga.	
Service Battalion No. 404 (Reserve).	July 1918	Cp. Hill, Va					August 1919	Cp. Hill, Va.	
Service Battalion No. 405 (Reserve).	May 1918	Newport News, Va.					do	Do.	
Service Battalion No. 406 (Reserve).	July 1918	Cp. Gordon, Ga					September 1919	Cp. Gordon, Ga.	
Service Battalion No. 407 (Reserve).	August 1918	Cp. Lee, Va					do	Cp. Lee, Va.	
Service Battalion No. 408 (Reserve).	July 1918	Cp. Jackson, S. C					July 1919	Cp. Jackson, S. C.	
Service Battalion No. 409 (Reserve).	September 1918	Cp. Pike, Ark					June 1919	Cp. Pike, Ark.	
Service Battalion No. 410 (Reserve).	August 1918	Cp. MacArthur, Tex.					March 1919	Cp. MacArthur, Tex.	
Service Battalion No. 411 (Reserve).	do	Cp. Z. Taylor, Ky					September 1919	Cp. Z. Taylor, Ky.	
Service Battalion No. 412 (Reserve).	September 1918	Cp. Travis, Tex					April 1919	Cp. Travis, Tex.	
Service Battalion No 413 (Reserve).	August 1918	Cp. Dix, N. J					July 1919	Cp. Dix, N. J.	

SERVICE BATTALIONS—Continued

Unit designation and redesignation	Organization		Stations in United States		Overseas		Demobilization		Remarks
	Month and year	Place	Month and year	Place	From—	To—	Month and year	Place	
Service Battalion No. 414 (Reserve).	August 1918	Cp. Dodge, Iowa					July 1919	Cp. Dodge, Iowa.	
Service Battalion No. 415 (Reserve).	do	Cp. Funston, Kans.					September 1919	Cp. Funston, Kans.	
Service Battalion No. 416 (Reserve).	July 1918	Cp. Grant, Ill					May 1919	Cp. Grant, Ill.	
Service Battalion No. 417 (Reserve).	September 1918	Cp. Meade, Md					June 1919	Cp. Meade, Md.	
Service Battalion No. 418 (Reserve).	August 1918	Cp. Sherman, Ohio.							
a. 418th Service Company.	June 1919	do					September 1919	Cp. Sherman, Ohio.	
Service Battalion No. 419 (Reserve).	August 1918	Cp. Beauregard, La.					March 1919	Cp. Beauregard, La.	
Service Battalion No. 420 (Reserve).	July 1918	Cp. Shelby, Miss					September 1919	Cp. Shelby, Miss.	
Service Battalion No. 421 (Reserve).	October 1918	Cp. Sheridan, Ala					March 1919	Cp. Sheridan, Ala.	
Service Battalion No. 422 (Reserve).	August 1918	Cp. Wadsworth, S. C.					do	Cp. Wadsworth, S. C.	
Service Battalion No. 423 (Reserve).	do	Cp. Greene, N. C					do	Cp. Greene, N. C.	
Service Battalion No. 424 (Reserve).	do	Governors Island, N. Y.					May 1919	Governors Island, N. Y.	
Service Battalion No. 425 (Reserve).	September 1918	Ft. Riley, Kans					April 1919	Ft. Riley, Kans.	
Service Battalion No. 426 (Reserve).	August 1918	Cp. Sevier, S. C					March 1919	Cp. Sevier, S. C.	
Service Battalion No. 427 (Reserve).									See Serv. Bn. 316.

Service Battalion No. 428 (Reserve).	August 1918	Port Newark, N. J.					March 1919	Cp. Merritt, N. J.	
Service Battalion No. 429 (Reserve).	September 1918	Cp. Alexander, Va.					January 1919	Cp. Alexander, Va.	
Service Battalion No. 430 (Reserve).	do	do					March 1919	Do.	
Service Battalion No. 431 (Reserve).	August 1918	Cp. Eustis, Va.	January 1919	Cp. Upton, N. Y.			October 1919	Cp. Upton, N. Y.	
Service Battalion No. 432 (Reserve).	September 1918	Cp. Holabird, Md.					March 1919	Cp. Holabird, Md.	
Service Battalion No. 433 (Reserve).	do	Cp. Hancock, Ga.					January 1919	Cp. Hancock, Ga.	
Service Battalion No. 434 (Reserve).	October 1918	Cp. Logan, Tex.					March 1919	Cp. Logan, Tex.	
Service Battalion No. 435 (Reserve).	December 1918	Cp. Bowie, Tex.					May 1919	Cp. Bowie, Tex.	
Service Battalion No. 436 (Reserve).									Never orgzd.
Service Battalion No. 437 (Reserve).	September 1918	Cp. McClellan, Ala.					March 1919	Cp. McClellan, Ala.	
Service Battalion No. 438 (Reserve).	October 1918	Cp. Joseph E. Johnston, Fla.					January 1919	Cp. Joseph E. Johnston, Fla.	
Service Battalion No. 439 (Reserve).	do	Ft. Sill, Okla.					August 1919	Ft. Sill, Okla.	
Service Battalion No. 440 (Reserve).									Never orgzd.
Service Battalion No. 441 (Reserve).	October 1918	Cp. Polk, N. C.					April 1919	Cp. Polk, N. C.	
Service Battalion No. 442 (Reserve).	do	Cp. Knox, Ky.					May 1919	Cp. Knox, Ky.	
Service Battalion No. 443 (Reserve).	November 1918	Cp. Devens, Mass.					June 1919	Cp. Devens, Mass.	
Service Battalion No. 444 (Reserve).									See Serv. Bn. 328.
Service Battalion No. 445 (Reserve).	October 1918	Cp. Stanley, Tex.					May 1919	Cp. Stanley, Tex.	
Service Battalion No. 446 (Reserve).	do	Cp. Mills, N. Y.					June 1919	Cp. Mills, N. Y.	
Service Battalion No. 447 (Reserve).	November 1918	Cp. A. A. Humphreys, Va.					April 1919	Cp. A. A. Humphreys, Va.	

SERVICE BATTALIONS—Continued

Unit designation and redesignation	Organization		Stations in United States		Overseas		Demobilization		Remarks
	Month and year	Place	Month and year	Place	From—	To—	Month and year	Place	
Service Battalion No. 448 (Reserve).	October 1918	Cp. Custer, Mich					July 1919	Cp. Custer, Mich.	
Service Battalion No. 449 (Reserve).	do	Cp. Alexander, Va					January 1919	Cp. Alexander, Va.	
Service Battalion No. 450 (Reserve).									Never orgzd.

SUPPLY TRAINS

Unit designation and redesignation	Organization		Stations in United States		Overseas		Demobilization		Remarks
	Month and year	Place	Month and year	Place	From—	To—	Month and year	Place	
1st Supply Train	February 1918	A. E. F	September 1919	Cp. Mills, N. Y		September 1919			Cmpnt. of 1st Div.
			do	Cp. Meade, Md.					
			October 1919	Cp. Z. Taylor, Ky.					Active through 1919.
2d Supply Train	October 1917	Ft. Sam Houston, Tex.	October 1917	Ft. Oglethorpe, Ga.					Cmpnt. of 2d Div.
			December 1917	Cp. Merritt, N. J.					
			January 1918	P. of E., Hoboken	January 1918.				
			August 1919	Cp. Merritt, N. J		August 1919.			
			do	Cp. Travis, Tex					Active through 1919.
3d Supply Train	November 1917	do	December 1917	Chickamauga Park, Ga.					Cmpnt. of 3d Div.
			March 1918	Detroit, Mich.					
			do	Cp. Merritt, N. J.					
			April 1918	P. of E., Hoboken	April 1918.				
			August 1919	Cp. Merritt, N. J		August 1919.			
			do	Cp. Pike, Ark					Active through 1919.
4th Supply Train	December 1917	Cp. Greene, N. C	May 1918	Cp. Merritt, N. J					Cmpnt. of 4th Div.
			do	P. of E., Hoboken	May 1918.				
			July 1919	Cp. Merritt, N. J		July 1919.			
			August 1919	Cp. Dodge, Iowa					Active through 1919.

5th Supply Train	do	Cp. Joseph E. Johnston, Fla.	May 1918	Cp. Upton, N. Y.					Cmpnt. of 5th Div.
			June 1918	P. of E., Hoboken	June 1918.				
			July 1919	Cp. Merritt, N. J.		July 1919.			
			do	Cp. Gordon, Ga.					Active through 1919.
6th Supply Train	February 1918	Cp. McClellan, Ala.	March 1918	Cp. Forrest, Ga.					Cmpnt. of 6th Div.
			May 1918	Cp. Wadsworth, S. C.					
			July 1918	Cp. Mills, N. Y.					
			do	P. of E., Hoboken	July 1918.				
			June 1919	Cp. Stuart, Va.		June 1919.			
			do	Cp. Grant, Ill.					Active through 1919.
7th Supply Train	May 1918	Cp. MacArthur, Tex.	July 1918	Cp. Merritt, N. J.					Cmpnt. of 7th Div.
			August 1918	P. of E., Hoboken	August 1918.				
			June 1919	Cp. Stuart, Va.		June 1919.			
			July 1919	Cp. Funston, Kans.					Active through 1919.
8th Supply Train	January 1918	Cp. Joseph E. Johnston, Fla.	March 1918	Detroit, Mich.					Cmpnt. of 8th Div.
			do	Cp. Holabird, Md.					
			October 1918	Cp. Mills, N. Y.					
			November 1918	Cp. Lee, Va.			February 1919	Cp. Lee, Va.	
9th Supply Train	September 1918	Cp. Sheridan, Ala.	October 1918	Detroit, Mich.					Cmpnt. of 9th Div.
			January 1919	Cp. Sheridan, Ala.			February 1919	Cp. Sheridan, Ala.	
10th Supply Train	August 1918	Cp. Funston, Kans.	October 1918	Detroit, Mich.					Cmpnt. of 10th Div.
			do	Cp. Holabird, Md.			February 1919	Cp. Funston, Kans.	
11th Supply Train	September 1918	Cp. Meade, Md.					do	Cp. Meade, Md.	Cmpnt. of 11th Div.
12th Supply Train	July 1918	Cp. Devens, Mass.					January 1919	Cp. Devens, Mass.	Cmpnt. of 12th Div.
13th Supply Train	September 1918	Cp. Lewis, Wash.					March 1919	Cp. Lewis, Wash.	Cmpnt. of 13th Div.
14th Supply Train	do	Cp. Custer, Mich.					February 1919	Cp. Custer, Mich.	Cmpnt. of 14th Div.
15th Supply Train	October 1918	Cp. Logan, Tex.					do	Cp. Logan, Tex.	Cmpnt. of 15th Div.
16th Supply Train	September 1918	Cp. Kearny, Calif.					do	Cp. Kearny, Calif.	Cmpnt. of 16th Div.
17th Supply Train	October 1918	Cp. Beauregard, La.					January 1919	Cp. Beauregard, La.	Cmpnt. of 17th Div.
18th Supply Train	September 1918	Cp. Travis, Tex.					February 1919	Cp. Travis, Tex.	Cmpnt. of 18th Div.
19th Supply Train	October 1918	Cp. Dodge, Iowa					do	Cp. Dodge, Iowa	Cmpnt. of 19th Div.
20th Supply Train	September 1918	Cp. Sevier, S. C.					do	Cp. Sevier, S. C.	Cmpnt. of 20th Div.

SUPPLY TRAINS—Continued

Unit designation and redesignation	Organization		Stations in United States		Overseas		Demobilization		Remarks
	Month and year	Place	Month and year	Place	From—	To—	Month and year	Place	
21st to 100th Supply Trains.									Never orgzd.
101st Supply Train	August 1917	Cp. Bartlett, Mass.	September 1917	P. of E., Hoboken	September 1917	April 1919	April 1919	Cp. Devens, Mass.	Cmpnt. of 26th Div.
102d Supply Train	July 1917	New York City, N. Y.	do	Cp. Wadsworth, S. C.					Cmpnt. of 27th Div.
			May 1918	Cp. Stuart, Va.					
			June 1918	P. of E., Newport News	June 1918.				
			March 1919	Cp. Merritt, N. J.		March 1919	April 1919	Cp. Upton, N. Y.	
103d Supply Train	do	Mt. Gretna, Pa.	August 1917	Cp. Hancock, Ga.					Cmpnt. of 28th Div.
			March 1918	Detroit, Mich.					
			April 1918	Cp. Holabird, Md.					
			May 1918	Cp. Mills, N. Y.					
			do	P. of E., Hoboken	May 1918	May 1919	May 1919	Cp. Dix, N. J.	
104th Supply Train	November 1917	Cp. McClellan, Ala.	June 1918	do	June 1918				Cmpnt. of 29th Div.
			May 1919	Cp. Merritt, N. J.		May 1919	May 1919	Cp. Meade, Md.	
105th Supply Train	September 1917	Cp. Sevier, S. C.	April 1918	Chicago, Ill					Cmpnt. of 30th Div.
			May 1918	Cp. Mills, N. Y.					
			June 1918	P. of E., Hoboken	June 1918	April 1919	April 1919	Cp. Jackson, S. C.	
106th Supply Train	October 1917	Cp. Wheeler, Ga.	April 1918	Buffalo, N. Y.					Cmpnt. of 31st Div.
			June 1918	Cp. Wheeler, Ga.					
			July 1918	Buffalo, N. Y.					
			September 1918	Cp. Mills, N. Y.					
			October 1918	P. of E., Hoboken	October 1918.				
			July 1919	Cp. Jackson, S. C.		July 1919	July 1919	Cp. Gordon, Ga.	
107th Supply Train	do	Cp. MacArthur, Tex.	January 1918	Cp. Merritt, N. J.					Cmpnt. of 32d Div.
			do	P. of E., Hoboken	January 1918.				
			May 1919	Cp. Morrison, Va.		May 1919	May 1919	Cp. Grant, Ill.	
108th Supply Train	do	Cp. Logan, Tex.	May 1918	Cp. Merritt, N. J.					Cmpnt. of 33d Div.
			do	P. of E., Hoboken	May 1918.				
			May 1919	Cp. Mills, N. Y.		May 1919	June 1919	Cp. Grant, Ill.	

109th Supply Train	do	Cp. Cody, N. Mex.	July 1918 September 1918 October 1918 June 1919	Detroit, Mich. Cp. Dix, N. J. P. of E., Hoboken Cp. Morrison, Va.	October 1918.	June 1919	June 1919	Cp. Dodge, Iowa	Cmpnt. of 34th Div. Corps troops.
110th Supply Train	do	Cp. Doniphan, Okla.	May 1918 do April 1919	Cp. Mills, N. Y. P. of E., Hoboken Cp. Stuart, Va.	May 1918.	April 1919	May 1919	Cp. Funston, Kans.	Cmpnt. of 35th Div.
111th Supply Train	do	Cp. Bowie, Tex.	July 1918 do June 1919	Cp. Mills, N. Y. P. of E., Hoboken Cp. Mills, N. Y.	July 1918.	June 1919	June 1919	Cp. Bowie, Tex.	Cmpnt. of 36th Div.
112th Supply Train	July 1917	Columbus, Ohio	August 1917 June 1918 do March 1919	Cp. Sheridan, Ala. Cp. Upton, N. Y. P. of E., Hoboken Cp. Mills, N. Y.	June 1918.	March 1919	April 1919	Cp. Sherman, Ohio.	Cmpnt. of 37th Div.
113th Supply Train	October 1917	Cp. Shelby, Miss.	August 1918 September 1918 October 1918 June 1919	Buffalo, N. Y. Cp. Mills, N. Y. P. of E., Hoboken Cp. Mills, N. Y.	October 1918.	June 1919	July 1919	Cp. Z. Taylor, Ky.	Cmpnt. of 38th Div. Corps troops.
114th Supply Train	November 1917	Cp. Beauregard, La.	June 1918 August 1918 do January 1919	Detroit, Mich. Cp. Mills, N. Y. P. of E., Hoboken Cp. Stuart, Va.	August 1918.	January 1919	January 1919	Cp. Beauregard, La.	Cmpnt. of 39th Div.
115th Supply Train	October 1917	Cp. Kearny, Calif.	August 1918 do April 1919	Cp. Mills, N. Y. P. of E., Hoboken Cp. Mills, N. Y.	August 1918.	April 1919	May 1919	Cp. Kearny, Calif.	Cmpnt. of 40th Div.
116th Supply Train	do	Cp. Greene, N. C.	November 1917 December 1917	do P. of E., Hoboken	December 1917	February 1919	February 1919	Cp. Dix, N. J.	Cmpnt. of 41st Div.
117th Supply Train	August 1917	Cp. Bowie, Tex.	September 1917 October 1917 April 1919	Cp. Mills, N. Y. P. of E., Hoboken Cp. Morrison, Va.	October 1917.	April 1919	September 1919	Cp. Bowie, Tex.	Cmpnt. of 42d Div.
118th to 300th Supply Trains.									Never orgzd.
301st Supply Train	August 1917	Cp. Devens, Mass.	July 1918 June 1919	P. of E., Boston Cp. Mills, N. Y.	July 1918	June 1919	June 1919	Cp. Upton, N. Y.	Cmpnt. of 76th Div.
302d Supply Train	September 1917	Cp. Upton, N. Y.	April 1918 May 1919	P. of E., Hoboken Cp. Mills, N. Y.	April 1918	May 1919	May 1919	Cp. Upton, N. Y.	Cmpnt. of 77th Div.
303d Supply Train	December 1917	Cp. Dix, N. J.	May 1918	P. of E., Philadelphia.	May 1918	June 1919	June 1919	Cp. Dix, N. J.	Cmpnt. of 78th Div.

SUPPLY TRAINS—Continued

Unit designation and redesignation	Organization		Stations in United States		Overseas		Demobilization		Remarks
	Month and year	Place	Month and year	Place	From—	To—	Month and year	Place	
304th Supply Train	September 1917	Cp. Meade, Md	July 1918	P. of E., Phila	July 1918	May 1919	May 1919	Cp. Dix, N. J	Cmpnt. of 79th Div.
305th Supply Train	January 1918	Cp. Lee, Va	May 1918	P. of E., Newport News.	May 1918	do	June 1919	do	Cmpnt. of 80th Div.
306th Supply Train	October 1917	Cp. Jackson, S. C	do	Cp. Sevier, S. C					Cmpnt. of 81st Div.
			July 1918	Cp. Mills, N. Y.					
			August 1918	P. of E., Hoboken	August 1918.				
			June 1919	Cp. Stuart, Va		June 1919	June 1919	Cp. Lee, Va.	
307th Supply Train	do	Cp. Gordon, Ga	March 1918	Detroit, Mich					Cmpnt. of 82d Div.
			May 1918	Cp. Holabird, Md.					
			June 1918	Cp. Mills, N. Y.					
			do	P. of E., Hoboken	June 1918	May 1919	May 1919	Cp. Dix, N. J.	
308th Supply Train	September 1917	Cp. Sherman, Ohio.	do	Cp. Mills, N. Y					Cmpnt. of 83d Div.
			do	P. of E., Hoboken	June 1918.				
			January 1919	Cp. Merritt, N. J		January 1919	February 1919	Cp. Sherman, Ohio.	
309th Supply Train	do	Cp. Z. Taylor, Ky.	May 1918	Buffalo, N. Y					Cmpnt. of 84th Div.
			July 1918	Cp. Holabird, Md.					
			August 1918	Cp. Sherman, Ohio.					
			September 1918	Cp. Mills, N. Y.					
			do	P. of E., Hoboken	September 1918.				
			June 1919	Cp. Merritt, N. J		June 1919	July 1919	Cp. Sherman, Ohio.	
310th Supply Train	do	Cp. Custer, Mich	June 1918	Detroit, Mich					Cmpnt. of 85th Div.
			July 1918	Cp. Holabird, Md.					
			do	Cp. Mills, N. Y.					
			do	P. of E., Hoboken	July 1918.				
			April 1919	Cp. Mills, N. Y		April 1919	April 1919	Cp. Custer, Mich.	
311th Supply Train	do	Cp. Grant, Ill	June 1918	Chicago, Ill					Cmpnt. of 86th Div.
			September 1918	Cp. Mills, N. Y.					
			October 1918	P. of E., Hoboken	October 1918.				
			July 1919	Cp. Stuart, Va		July 1919	July 1919	Cp. Grant, Ill.	

312th Supply Train	do	Cp. Pike, Ark.	June 1918	Cp. Dix, N. J.					Cmpnt. of 87th Div.
			August 1918	P. of E., Montreal	August 1918.				
			July 1919	Cp. Stuart, Va.		July 1919	July 1919	Cp. Grant, Ill.	
313th Supply Train	October 1917	Cp. Dodge, Iowa	June 1918	Chicago, Ill.					Cmpnt. of 88th Div.
			August 1918	Cp. Mills, N. Y.					
			do	P. of E., Hoboken	August 1918.				
			June 1919	Cp. Morrison, Va.		June 1919	June 1919	Cp. Dodge, Iowa.	
314th Supply Train	September 1917	Cp. Funston, Kans.	June 1918	Cp. Mills, N. Y.					Cmpnt. of 89th Div.
			do	P. of E., Hoboken	June 1918.				
			May 1919	Cp. Upton, N. Y.		May 1919	June 1919	Cp. Dodge, Iowa.	
315th Supply Train	do	Cp. Travis, Tex.	June 1918	Cp. Mills, N. Y.					Cmpnt. of 90th Div.
			do	P. of E., Hoboken	June 1918.				
			June 1919	Cp. Morrison, Va.		June 1919	June 1919	Cp. Bowie, Tex.	
316th Supply Train	do	Cp. Lewis, Wash.	June 1918	Cp. Mills, N. Y.					Cmpnt. of 91st Div.
			July 1918	P. of E., Hoboken	July 1918.				
			April 1919	Cp. Upton, N. Y.		April 1919	May 1919	Presidio of San Francisco, Calif.	
317th Supply Train	December 1917	Cp. Funston, Kans.	June 1918	do					Cmpnt. of 92d Div.
			do	P. of E., Hoboken	June 1918.				
			February 1919	Cp. Upton, N. Y.		February 1919	March 1919	Cp. Z. Taylor, Ky.	
318th and 319th Supply Trains.									Never orgzd.
320th Supply Train	September 1918	Cp. Sherman, Ohio.					December 1918	Cp. Sherman, Ohio.	Cmpnt. of 95th Div.
321st Supply Train									Never orgzd.
322d Supply Train	October 1918	Cp. Cody, N. Mex.					December 1918	Cp. Cody, N. Mex.	Cmpnt. of 97th Div.

PROVISIONAL GUARD AND FIRE BATTALIONS

1st Provisional Guard and Fire Battalion.	July 1918	P. of E., Hoboken					May 1919	P. of E., Hoboken	
2d Provisional Guard and Fire Battalion.	October 1918	Brooklyn, N. Y.					February 1919	Brooklyn, N. Y.	
3d Provisional Guard and Fire Battalion.	July 1918	Port Newark, N. J.					April 1919	Port Newark, N. J.	
4th Provisional Guard and Fire Battalion.	August 1918	Cp. Mills, N. Y.					January 1919	Cp. Mills, N. Y.	
5th Provisional Guard and Fire Battalion.	do	Syracuse, N. Y.					December 1918	Cp. Merritt, N. J.	

STEVEDORE REGIMENTS

Unit designation and redesignation	Organization		Stations in United States		Overseas		Demobilization		Remarks
	Month and year	Place	Month and year	Place	From—	To—	Month and year	Place	
301st Stevedore Regiment.	September 1917	Cp. Hill, Va	October 1917	P. of E., Hoboken					Trfd. to T.C. September 1918.
302d Stevedore Regiment.	October 1917	do	December 1917	do					Do.
303d Stevedore Regiment.	do	do	do	do					Do.
304th Stevedore Regiment.	do	do					February 1918	Cp. Hill, Va.	

WATER TANK TRAINS

Unit designation and redesignation	Organization: Month and year	Organization: Place	Stations in United States: Month and year	Stations in United States: Place	Overseas: From—	Overseas: To—	Demobilization: Month and year	Demobilization: Place	Remarks
Water Tank Train No. 301.	May 1918	Cp. Holabird, Md	September 1918. July 1919	P. of E., Hoboken Cp. Mills, N. Y	September 1918.	July 1919	July 1919	Cp. Dix, N. J	G.H.Q. troops.
Water Tank Train No. 302.	August 1918	do	September 1918 July 1919	P. of E., Hoboken Cp. Merritt, N. J	September 1918.	do	August 1919	Cp. Grant, Ill	Do.

Q. M. C. SPECIAL AND TECHNICAL UNITS

Units	Unit No.	Active service	Unit No.	Active service	Unit No.	Active service	Unit No.	Active service	Unit No.	Active service	Remarks
Advance Animal Transport Depot.	b 301 b 306	March 1918–July 1919 September 1918–July 1919	b a 302	May 1918–July 1919	b 303	July 1918–July 1919	b 304	August 1918–July 1919	b 305	September 1918–July 1919	a Orgzd. overseas; demobilized in U. S. b S.O.S. troops.

	No.	Period	No.	Period	No.	Period	No.	Period	No.	Period
Base Animal Transport Depot.	[a][b] 301	December 1918–July 1919	[b] 302	July 1918–July 1919						
Bakery Company	[b] 1	April 1917 through December 1919	[b] 2	April 1917 through December 1919	[b] 3	1916 through December 1919	4	1916 through December 1919	5	October 1917 through December 1919
	6	1915 through December 1919	[b] 7	1916 through December 1919	8	do	[b] 9	do	[b] 10	1916 through December 1919
	[b] 11	1916 through December 1919	12	1917 through December 1919	[1] 13–50		51–100	Never orgzd.	[b] 101	August 1917–June 1919
	[b] 102	August 1917–July 1919	103–300	Never orgzd.	[b] 301	August 1917–June 1919	[b] 302	August 1917–August 1919	[b] 303	Do.
	[b] 304	August 1917–April 1919	[b] 305	November 1917–May 1919	[b] 306	August 1917–May 1919	[b] 307	September 1917–June 1919	[b] 308	August 1917–August 1919
	[b] 309	August 1917–July 1919	[b] 310	August 1917–August 1919	[b] 311	June 1917–July 1919	[b] 312	August 1917–July 1919	[b] 313	August 1917–June 1919
	[b] 314	do	[b] 315	August 1917–June 1919	[b] 316	August 1917–July 1919	[b] 317	do	[b] 318	Do.
	[b] 319	August 1917–June 1919	[b] 320	do	[b] 321	August 1917–August 1919	[b] 322	August 1917–August 1919	[b] 323	August 1917–May 1919
	[b] 324	August 1917–May 1919	[b] 325	August 1917–May 1919	[b] 326	October 1917–May 1919	[b] 327	December 1917–May 1919	[b] 328	July 1917–March 1919
	[b] 329	August 1917–July 1919	[b] 330	August 1917–June 1919	[b] 331	September 1917–July 1919	[b] 332	August 1917–June 1919	[b] 333	August 1917–March 1919
	[b] 334	September 1917–August 1919	[b] 335	October 1917–June 1919	[b] 336	do	[b] 337	September 1917–June 1919	338	September 1917–January 1919
	[b] 339	October 1917–July 1919	[b] 340	February 1918–July 1919	[b] 341	November 1917–August 1919	342	November 1917–March 1919	[b] 343	November 1917–June 1919
	[b] 344	November 1917–June 1919	[b] 345	February 1918–June 1919	[b] 346	February 1918–August 1919	[b] 347	February 1918–June 1919	[b] 348	February 1918–September 1919
	[b] 349	February 1918–July 1919	[b] 350	February 1918–April 1919	[b] 351	February 1918–September 1919	352	February 1918–January 1919	[b] 353	February 1918–July 1919
	[b] 354	do	[b] 355	February 1918–June 1919	356	do	357	February 1918–February 1919	358	August 1917–March 1919
	359	March 1918–January 1919	360	April 1918–January 1919	[b] 361	March 1918–July 1919	362	April 1918–February 1919	363	August 1917–January 1919
	364	April 1918–February 1919	[b] 365	April 1918–July 1919	[b] 366	April 1918–January 1919	367	April 1918–May 1919	368	April 1918–December 1918

[1] Renumbered Bkry. Cos. 301–338 incl., August 1917.

Q. M. C. SPECIAL AND TECHNICAL UNITS—Continued

Units	Unit No.	Active service	Unit No.	Active service	Unit No.	Active service	Unit No.	Active service	Unit No.	Active service	Remarks
Bakery Company—Continued	[b] 369	May 1918–August 1919	[b] 370	April 1918–August 1919	371	April 1918–December 1918	372	May 1918–December 1919	373	May 1918–July 1919	
	374	May 1918–January 1919	375	May 1918–February 1919	376	May 1918–December 1918	377	May 1918–March 1919	378	May 1918–January 1919	
	379	-----do-----------	380	May 1918–March 1919	381	May 1918–February 1919	382	May 1918–December 1919	[b] 383	May 1918–March 1919	
	384	July 1918–January 1919	385	June 1918–December 1918	386	June 1918–February 1919	387	June 1918–March 1919	[b] 388	June 1918–May 1919	
	389	July 1918–December 1918	390	July 1918–March 1919	391	July 1918–January 1919	392	July 1918–January 1919	393	August 1918–January 1919	
	[b] 394	August 1918–April 1919	395	September 1918–January 1919	396	August 1918–December 1918	[b] 397	August 1918–April 1919	[b] 398	September 1918–April 1919	
	399	October 1918–January 1919	400	August 1918–December 1918	401	-----do-----------	402	October 1918–December 1918	403	October 1918–December 1918	
	404	November 1918–December 1918	405	September 1918–December 1918	406	September 1918–January 1919	407	October 1918–July 1919	408	October 1918–January 1919	
	409	October 1918–May 1919	410	November 1918–May 1919	411	November 1918–December 1918	412	November 1918–December 1918	413	Do.	
	414	October 1918–January 1919	415	October 1918–December 1918	416	October 1918–December 1918	417	-----do-----------	418 & 419	Never orgzd.	
	420	October 1918–December 1918	421	November 1918–December 1918	422	September 1918–October 1919	423	November 1918–April 1919	424	November 1918–December 1918	
	425	Never orgzd.	426	Do.							
Bathing and Delousing Unit.	1–15	See Mobile Bath Units.	[a] 16	January 1919–June 1919	[c] 17	January 1919–July 1919	[c] 18	February 1919–September 1919	[a] 19	March 1919–July 1919	a Orgzd. overseas; demobilized in U. S.
	20	March 1919–July 1919	21 & 22	Never orgzd.	[a] 23	April 1919–September 1919					b S.O.S. troops. c Orgzd. and demblzd. overseas.
Butchery Company	1–300	Never orgzd.	301	February 1918–July 1919	302	February 1918–July 1919	303	February 1918–June 1919	304	February 1918–August 1919	d Orgzd. in U. S.; demobilized overseas.
	305	February 1918–July 1919	306	February 1917–August 1919	307	March 1918–July 1919	308	May 1918–July 1919	[d] 309	April 1918–August 1919	

Unit	No.	Period	No.	Period	No.	Period	No.	Period	No.	Period
	310	April 1918–June 1919	311	April 1918–July 1919	312	April 1918–July 1919	313	June 1918–June 1919	314	June 1918–July 1919
	[d] 315	June 1918–December 1918	316	June 1918–September 1919	317	June 1918–June 1919	318	June 1918–July 1919	319	July 1918–June 1919
	320	July 1918–August 1919	321	July 1918–September 1919	322	July 1918–August 1919	323	July 1918–July 1919	324	July 1918–August 1919
	325	July 1918–July 1919	326	July 1918–August 1919	327	July 1918–July 1919	328	July 1918–September 1919	329	July 1918–July 1919
	330	July 1918–August 1919	331	July 1918–July 1919	332	do	333	July 1918–July 1919	334	Do.
	335	July 1918–September 1919	336	July 1918–April 1919	337	July 1918–April 1919	338	do	339	Do.
	340	July 1918–July 1919	341	July 1918–June 1919	342	July 1918–June 1919	343	August 1918–August 1919	344	August 1918–July 1919
	345	August 1918–July 1919	346	August 1918–July 1919	347	August 1918–July 1919	348	August 1918–July 1919	349	September 1918–July 1919
	350	September 1918–January 1919	351	September 1918–April 1919	352	September 1918–July 1919	353	September 1918–August 1919	354	September 1918–August 1919
	355	September 1918–July 1919	356	September 1918–August 1919	357	September 1918–August 1919				
Clothing Unit	1–300	Never orgzd	[b] 301	July 1918–April 1919	[b,d] 302	July 1918–November 1918	[b] 303	July 1918–June 1919	[b] 304	July 1918–July 1919
	[b] 305	July 1918–May 1919	[b] 306	July 1918–July 1919	[b,d] 307	July 1918–February 1919	[b] 308	do	[b] 309	July 1918–June 1919
	[b,d] 310	July 1918–January 1919	[b] 311	July 1918–June 1919	[b] 312	July 1918–May 1919	[b,d] 313	July 1918–December 1919	[b] 314	July 1918–July 1919
	[b] 315	July 1918–June 1919	[b,d] 316	August 1918–June 1919	[b,d] 317	August 1918–February 1919	[b] 318	August 1918–June 1919		
Clothing and Bath Unit.	1–318	Never orgzd.	[b] 319	November 1918–September 1919	[b] 320	November 1918–August 1919	[b] 321	November 1918–August 1919	[a,b] 322	November 1918–July 1919
	[b] 323	November 1918–July 1919	[b] 324	do	[b] 325	November 1918–July 1919	[b] 326	November 1918–June 1919	[b,a] 327	do
	[b,a] 328	February 1919–June 1919	329	Never orgzd.	[b,a] 330	February 1919–May 1919	331	Never orgzd.	[b] 332	February 1919–June 1919
	[b] 333	do	[b,a] 334	January 1919–May 1919	[b,a] 335	February 1919–June 1919	[b,a] 336	February 1919–June 1919		

Q. M. C. SPECIAL AND TECHNICAL UNITS—Continued

Units	Unit No.	Active service	Unit No.	Active service	Unit No.	Active service	Unit No.	Active service	Unit No.	Active service	Remarks
Clothing Squad	[b,c] 1	September 1918–May 1919	[a,b] 2	September 1918–June 1919	[a,b] 3	November 1918–June 1919	4	Never orgzd.	[b,c] 5	June 1918–January 1919	a Orgzd. overseas; demobilized in U. S. b S.O.S. troops. c Orgzd. and demblzd. overseas.
	[b,c] 6	June 1918–January 1919	[b,c] 7	December 1918–April 1919	[b,c] 8	January 1919	[b,c] 9	June 1918–January 1919	[a,b] 10	March 1919–July 1919	
	[b,c] 11	September 1918–March 1919	[a,b] 12	March 1919–July 1919	[b,c] 13	October 1918–January 1919	[b,c] 14	September 1918–February 1919	[a,b] 15	March 1919–July 1919	
Delousing Unit	1–500	Never orgzd.	[c] 501	February 1919–June 1919	502	Never orgzd.	[c] 503	January 1919–June 1919	[c] 504	January 1919–June 1919	
	[c] 505	December 1918–June 1919	506–508	Never orgzd.	[c] 509	January 1919–May 1919	[c] 5010	do	[c] 5011	Do.	
	5012–5015	Never orgzd.	[c] 5016	March 1919–June 1919	[c] 5017	March 1919–May 1919	[c] 5018	Do.			
Fire Truck and Hose Company.	1–300	Never orgzd.	301	December 1917–October 1919	302	September 1917–December 1918	303	October 1917–October 1919	304	October 1917–May 1919	a S.O.S. troops.
	305	October 1917–May 1919	306	February 1918–April 1919	307	September 1917–April 1919	308	December 1917–October 1919	309	November 1917–May 1919	
	310	October 1917–October 1919	311	October 1917–December 1919	312	May 1918–December 1919	313	August 1918–October 1919	314	August 1918–October 1919	
	315	September 1917–August 1919	316	October 1917 through December 1919	[a] 317	January 1918–July 1919	[a] 318	January 1918–September 1919	[a] 319	January 1918–September 1919	
	[a] 320	January 1918–July 1919	[a] 321	March 1918–July 1919	[a] 322	March 1918–October 1919	323	March 1918–March 1919	324	March 1918–April 1919	
	325	March 1918–April 1919	326	June 1918–April 1919	327	April 1918–April 1919	328	April 1918–April 1919	329	May 1918–April 1919	
	330	February 1918–March 1919	331	October 1918–March 1919	332	February 1918–December 1919	333	June 1918–October 1919	334	June 1918–March 1919	
	335	June 1918–May 1919	336	September 1918–April 1919	337	February 1918–December 1919	338	February 1918–April 1919	339	March 1918–December 1919	
	340	April 1918–December 1919	341	September 1918–May 1919	342	April 1918–May 1919	343	May 1918–July 1919	[a] 344	April 1918–September 1919	

	[a] 345	April 1918–July 1919	346	May 1918–July 1919	347	August 1918 through December 1919	348	January 1919–July 1919	349	September 1918–December 1918	
	350–353	Never orgzd.	354	November 1918–December 1919	355 & 356	Never orgzd.	357	November 1918–August 1919			
Graves Registration Service Unit.	Hq. Det.	December 1918–July 1919	[b] A	June 1918–July 1919	[b] B	July 1918–July 1919	[b] C	September 1918–July 1919	[b] D	October 1918–July 1919	b Orgzd. and demobilized overseas.
	[c] E	November 1918–August 1919	1–300	Never orgzd.	[a] 301	October 1917–July 1919	[a] 302	October 1917–July 1919	[a] 303	October 1917–July 1919	c Orgzd. overseas; demobilized in U. S.
	[a] 304	October 1917–August 1919	[a] 305	August 1918–July 1919	[a] 306	August 1918–July 1919	[a] 307	August 1918–July 1919	[a] 308	August 1918–July 1919	
	[a] 309	August 1918–August 1919	[a] 310	do	[a] 311	do	[a] 312	October 1918–July 1919	[a] 313	October 1918–July 1919	
	314	October 1918–December 1918	315	October 1918–December 1918	316	October 1918–December 1918					
Guard and Fire Company.	1	Never orgzd.	2	March 1919 through December 1919	3 to 300	Never orgzd.	301	April 1918–April 1919	302	April 1918–December 1918	
	303	April 1918–February 1919	304	April 1918–April 1919	305	April 1918–February 1919	306	April 1918–February 1919	307	Do.	
	308	April 1918–March 1919	309	March 1918–May 1919	310	April 1918–January 1919	311	May 1918–December 1918	312	May 1918–December 1918	
	313	May 1918–December 1918	314	August 1918–December 1918	315	August 1918–January 1919	316	August 1918–January 1919	317	August 1918–December 1918	
	318	August 1918–December 1918	319	do	320	August 1918–December 1918	321	May 1918–June 1919	322	September 1918–December 1918	
	323	September 1918–November 1919	324	September 1918–December 1918	325	September 1918–December 1918	326	September 1918–November 1919	327	September 1918–March 1919	
	328	September 1918–December 1918	329	August 1918–January 1919	330	August 1918–January 1919	331	August 1918–January 1919	332	August 1918–January 1919	
	333	August 1918–January 1919	334	do	335	August 1918–December 1918	336	August 1918–December 1918	337	August 1918–December 1918	
	338	August 1918–December 1918	339	August 1918–December 1919	340	August 1918–December 1919	341	August 1918–May 1919	342	August 1918–May 1919	
	343	August 1918–May 1919									

Q. M. C. SPECIAL AND TECHNICAL UNITS—Continued

Units	Unit No.	Active service	Unit No.	Active service	Unit No.	Active service	Unit No.	Active service	Unit No.	Active service	Remarks
Ice Plant Company	1–300	Never orgzd.	[a] 301	December 1917–June 1919							[a] S.O.S. troops.
Labor Company	[a] (I) 301	October 1917–May 1918	(II) 301	March 1918–July 1919	[b] (I) 302	October 1917–May 1918	(II) 302	March 1918–July 1919	[c] (I) 303	October 1917–May 1918	a, b, g, i—Redes. Cos. A, B, C, D, 304th Serv. Bn. d, e, h, j—Redes. Cos. A, B, C, D, 305th Serv. Bn. c, f, o, p—Redes. Cos. A, B, C, D, 306th Serv. Bn. k, l, m, n—Redes. Cos. A, B, C, D, 307th Serv. Bn.
	(II) 303	June 1918–June 1919	[d] (I) 304	October 1917–May 1918	(II) 304	June 1918–August 1918	[e] (I) 305	October 1917–May 1918	(II) 305	June 1918–August 1918	
	[f] (I) 306	November 1917–May 1918	(II) 306	July 1918–June 1919	[g] (I) 307	November 1917–May 1918	(II) 307	July 1918–May 1919	[h] 308	November 1917–May 1918	
	[i] 309	do	[j] 310	November 1917–May 1918	[k] 311	do	[l] 312	October 1917–May 1918	[m] 313	October 1917–May 1918	
	[n] 314	do	[o] 315	do	[p] 316	Do.					
Laundry Company [1]	501	February 1918–July 1919	502	February 1918–July 1919	503	February 1918–August 1919	504	February 1918–June 1919	505	February 1918–June 1919	a Orgzd. in U. S.; demobilized overseas. b Orgzd. overseas; demobilized in U. S. c Orgzd. and demblzd. overseas.
	506	do	[a] 507	February 1918–August 1919	508	February 1918–June 1919	509	February 1918–July 1919	510	February 1918–July 1919	
	[a] 511	February 1918–August 1919	512	February 1918–June 1919	[a] 513	February 1918–July 1919	514	do	[a] 515	do	
	516	February 1918–July 1919	[a] 517	do	[a] 518	March 1918–July 1919	[a] 519	March 1918–June 1919	520	April 1918–July 1919	
	521	April 1918–July 1919	[a] 522	April 1918–July 1919	523	July 1918–August 1919	[a] 524	July 1918–July 1919	525	August 1918–August 1919	
	526	August 1918–July 1919	527	September 1918–July 1919	528	September 1918–June 1919	[c] 529	January 1919–June 1919	[b] 530	February 1919–July 1919	
Provisional Laundry Company.	[c] A	March 1918–May 1919	[a] B	March 1918–June 1919							
Mobile Bath Unit [2]	1 & 2	Never orgzd.	[c] 3	December 1918–June 1919	[a] 4	December 1918–June 1919	[c] 5	December 1918–June 1919	[a] 6	December 1918–June 1919	
	[a] 7	December 1918–June 1919	[c] 8	do	[c] 9	do	[b] 10	January 1919–August 1919	[b] 11	January 1919–June 1919	

	b 12	January 1919– July 1919	b 13	January 1919– June 1919	b 14	January 1919– June 1919	b 15	January 1919– June 1919			
Mobile Laundry Company.	1–300	Never orgzd.	b 301	June 1918– August 1919	b 302	June 1918– July 1919	b 303	June 1918– June 1919	b 304	June 1918– June 1919	a Orgzd. in U. S.; demobilized overseas. b S.O.S. troops.
	b 305	June 1918– July 1919	b 306	June 1918– July 1919	b 307	do	b 308	do	b 309	July 1918– June 1919	
	b 310	July 1918– July 1919	b 311	July 1918– July 1919	b 312	July 1918– September 1919	b 313	July 1918– August 1919	b 314	July 1918– September 1919	
	b 315	July 1918– August 1919	b 316	July 1918– August 1919	b 317	July 1918– August 1919	a b 318	July 1918– July 1919	b 319	August 1918– July 1919	
	b 320	August 1918– July 1919	b 321	August 1918– July 1919	b 322	August 1918– July 1919	b 323	August 1918– August 1919	a b 324	Do.	
	b 325	September 1918– July 1919	b 326	September 1918– August 1919	b 327	September 1918– August 1919	b 328	September 1918– August 1919	b 329	September 1918– August 1919	
	330	September 1918– June 1919	331	September 1918– July 1919	332	September 1918– June 1919	333	do	334	September 1918– September 1919	
	335	September 1918– July 1919	336	September 1918– March 1919	337	September 1918– March 1919	338	September 1918– March 1919	339	September 1918– March 1919	
	340	September 1918 October 1919	341	September 1918– October 1919	342	September 1918– January 1919	343	do	344	September 1918– October 1919	
	345	October 1918– March 1919	346	October 1918– March 1919	347	October 1918– March 1919	348	October 1918– March 1919	349	October 1918– May 1919	
	350	October 1918– May 1919	351	October 1918– December 1918	352	October 1918– December 1918	b 353	October 1918– July 1919	b 354	October 1918– July 1919	
	355	do	b 356	October 1918– June 1919							
Pack Train	1	1917 through December 1919	2	1917 through December 1919	3	1917 through December 1919	4	1917 through December 1919	5	1917 through December 1918	Pack Trains 1–31 orgzd. prior to April 1917. a Orgzd. in U. S.; demblzd. overseas. b S.O.S. Troops.
	6	do	7	do	8	do	9	do	a b 10	1917– August 1919	
	11	do	12	do	13	do	14	do	15	1917 through December 1919	
	16	do	17	do	18	do	19	do	20	Do.	
	21	do	22	do	23	do	24	do	25	Do.	
	26	do	27	do	28	do	29	do	30	Do.	

[3] Originally orgzd. as Bathing and Delousing Units.
[1] Originally orgzd. as Cos. 301 to 326; redes. August 1918. S.O.S. troops.

Q. M. C. SPECIAL AND TECHNICAL UNITS—Continued

Units	Unit No.	Active service	Unit No.	Active service	Unit No.	Active service	Unit No.	Active service	Unit No.	Active service	Remarks
Pack Train—Con.	31	1917 through December 1919	32–300	Never orgzd.	b 301	February 1918–July 1919	b 302	April 1918–July 1919	b 303	April 1918–July 1919	Pack Trains 1–31 orgzd. prior to April 1917. a Orgzd. in U. S.; demblzd. overseas. b S.O.S. Troops.
	b 304	April 1918–July 1919	b 305	April 1918–July 1919	a b 306	April 1918 July 1919	a b 307	do	b 308	Do.	
	a b 309	do	b 310	do	b 311	June 1918–July 1919	b 312	June 1918–July 1919	b 313	June 1918–July 1919	
	b 314	June 1918–July 1919	b 315	June 1918–July 1919	b 316	do	b 317	do	b 318	April 1918–July 1919	
	b 319	April 1918–July 1919	b 320	April 1918–July 1919	b 321	April 1918–July 1919	b 322	July 1918–July 1919	b 323	July 1918–July 1919	
	b 324	July 1918–July 1919	b 325	July 1918–July 1919	b 326	July 1918–July 1919	b 327	do	b 328	Do.	
	b 329	August 1918–July 1919	b 330	August 1918–July 1919							
Railhead Supply Detachment.	1–300	Never orgzd.	301	September 1918–July 1919	302	September 1918–August 1919	303	September 1918–August 1919	304	September 1918–July 1919	
	305	September 1918–August 1919	306	September 1918–December 1918	307	September 1918–December 1918	308	September 1918–December 1918	309	November 1918–December 1918	
	310	November 1918–December 1918									
Refrigerating Plant Company.	501	July 1918–July 1919	502	July 1918–July 1919							Originally orgzd. as Cos. 301 and 302; redes. November 1918. S. O. S. troops.
Sales Commissary Unit.	a c 1	April 1918–August 1919	b c 2	April 1918–July 1919	a c 3	April 1918–June 1919	a c 4	April 1918–August 1919	a c 5	April 1918–May 1919	a Orgzd. overseas; demobilized in U. S. b Orgzd. and demblzd. overseas. c S.O.S. troops.
	a c 6	June 1918–August 1919	a c 7	June 1918–August 1919	a c 8	June 1918–May 1919	a c 9	June 1918–June 1919	a c 10	June 1918–June 1919	
	a c 11	July 1918–June 1919	a 12	August 1918–August 1919	a c 13	July 1918–June 1919	c 14	Never orgzd.	a c 15	January 1919–April 1919	
	a c 16	July 1918–July 1919	a c 17	July 1918–June 1919	b c 18	August 1918–May 1919	a c 19	July 1918–May 1919	a c 20	July 1918–August 1919	

	a c 21	August 1918–June 1919	a c 22	April 1918–June 1919	a c 23	July 1918–June 1919	b c 24	June 1918–August 1919	a c 25	September 1918–July 1919	
	a c 26	March 1918–July 1919	a c 27	August 1918–June 1919	a c 28	June 1918–July 1919	b c 29	October 1918–March 1919	a c 30	August 1918–July 1919	
	a c 31	August 1918–June 1919	a c 32	August 1918–May 1919	a c 33	August 1918–August 1919	a c 34	July 1918–July 1919	a c 35	October 1918–July 1919	
	a c 36	October 1918–July 1919	a c 37	August 1918–June 1919	a c 38	October 1918–June 1919	a c 39	October 1918–August 1919	a c 40	October 1918–July 1919	
	a c 41	November 1918–January 1919	a c 42	October 1918–July 1919	a c 43	September 1918–June 1919	a c 44	October 1918–July 1919	a c 45	November 1918–June 1919	
	a c 46	September 1918–June 1919	a c 47	November 1918–August 1919	a c 48	August 1918–July 1919	a 49	November 1918–August 1919	a 50	Do.	
	a 51	December 1918–June 1919	b 52	December 1918–July 1919	53 & 54	Never orgzd.	a 55	October 1918–July 1919	a 56	January 1919–August 1919	
	a 57	December 1918–August 1919	a 58	January 1919–June 1919	a 59	December 1918–July 1919	b 60	May 1919–July 1919	a 61	February 1919–June 1919	
	62	Never orgzd.	b 63	May 1919–June 1919	b 64	May 1919–June 1919	b 65	May 1919–June 1919	b 66	May 1919–June 1919	
	b 67	May 1919–June 1919	68–300	Never orgzd.	c 301	July 1918–June 1919	c 302	July 1918–August 1919	c 303	July 1918–June 1919	
	c 304	July 1918–June 1919	c 305	July 1918–June 1919	c 306	July 1918–July 1919	c 307	July 1918–May 1919	c 308	Do.	
	c 309	July 1918–September 1919	c 310	July 1918–July 1919	c 311	July 1918–May 1919	c 312	July 1918–August 1919	c 313	Do.	
	c 314	July 1918–July 1919	c 315	July 1918–May 1919	c 316	July 1918–June 1919	c 317	do	c 318	July 1918–July 1919	
Salvage Squad	b 1	April 1918–August 1919	b 2	April 1918–August 1919	b 3	April 1918–August 1919	b 4	April 1918–June 1919	b 5	April 1918–May 1919	b Orgzd. overseas; demobilized in U. S.
	b 6	April 1918–July 1919	b 7	April 1918–July 1919	b 8	May 1918–July 1919	b 9	May 1918–July 1919	b 10	June 1918–August 1919	c Orgzd. and demblzd. overseas.
	b 11	June 1918–July 1919	b 12	July 1918–September 1919	b 13	August 1918–July 1919	b 14	July 1918–July 1919	b 15	July 1918–June 1919	All units S.O.S. troops
	b 16	June 1918–September 1919	b 17	July 1918–July 1919	b 18	July 1918–May 1919	b 19	August 1918–June 1919	b 20	September 1918–April 1919	
	b 21	October 1918–August 1919	b 22	September 1918–September 1919	b 23	August 1918–August 1919	c 24	October 1918–May 1919	b 25	October 1918–May 1919	
	b 26	September 1918–July 1919									

Q. M. C. SPECIAL AND TECHNICAL UNITS—Continued

Units	Unit No.	Active service	Unit No.	Active service	Unit No.	Active service	Unit No.	Active service	Unit No.	Active service	Remarks
Salvage Unit	1–300	Never orgzd.	[a] 301	July 1918–August 1918	[a] 302	July 1918–June 1919	[a] 303	July 1918–July 1919	[a] 304	July 1918–July 1919	a S.O.S. troops.
	[a] 305	July 1918–July 1919	[a] 306	July 1918–September 1919	[a] 307	July 1918–July 1919	[a] 308	do.	[a] 309	July 1918–August 1919	
	[a] 310	do.	[a] 311	July 1918–June 1919	[a] 312	July 1918–June 1919	[a] 313	do.	[a] 314	July 1918–July 1919	
	[a] 315	do.	[a] 316	July 1918–July 1919	[a] 317	July 1918–July 1919	[a] 318	August 1918–July 1919	[a] 319	September 1918–July 1919	
	320	September 1918–December 1918	321	September 1918–December 1918	322	September 1918–December 1918					
Ship Repair Shop Unit.	301	May 1918–April 1919									
Supply Company	1–300	Never orgzd.	[b] 301	September 1917–July 1919	[b] 302	September 1917–June 1919	[b] 303	September 1917–June 1919	[b] 304	September 1917–August 1919	a Orgzd. in U. S.; demobilized overseas. b S.O.S. troops.
	[b] 305	September 1917–July 1919	[b] 306	October 1917–July 1919	[b] 307	October 1917–July 1919	[b] 308	October 1917–July 1919	[b] 309	March 1918–July 1919	
	[b] 310	March 1918–July 1919	[b] 311	March 1918–July 1919	[b] 312	March 1918–July 1919	[b] 313	March 1918–July 1919	[b] 314	Do.	
	[b] 315	December 1918–July 1919	[b] 316	July 1918–June 1919	[b] 317	July 1918–July 1919	[b] 318	July 1918–July 1919	[b] 319	July 1918–July 1919	
	[b] 320	July 1918–July 1919	[a] [b] 321	July 1918–September 1919	[a] [b] 322	July 1918–September 1919	[b] 323	July 1918–August 1919	[b] 324	Do.	
	[b] 325	do.	[b] 326	August 1918–June 1919	[b] 327	August 1918–September 1919	[b] 328	August 1918–July 1919	[b] 329	Do.	
	[b] 330	July 1918–August 1919	[b] 331	September 1918–July 1919	[b] 332	September 1918–July 1919	[b] 333	September 1918–July 1919	[b] 334	September 1918–August 1919	
	[b] 335	September 1918–September 1919	[b] 336	September 1918–August 1919	337	September 1918–December 1918	338	September 1918–December 1918	339	September 1918–December 1918	
	340	September 1918–December 1918	341	September 1918–December 1918	342	do.	343	Do.			

Wagon Company	[a] (I) 1	1915–July 1917	[b] [e] (II) 1	June 1917 through December 1919	[d] [e] 2	1915 through December 1919	[e] (I) 3	1916–January 1918	(II) 3	November 1917 through December 1919	a Absorbed by Aux. Remount Depot No. 317. b Orgsd. originally as Co. No. 100.
	4	1916–through December 1919	5	March 1918–May 1919	6–30	Never orgzd.	31	September 1917–March 1919	32–300	Never orgzd.	c Absorbed by Aux. Remount Depot No. 319.
	301	February 1918–May 1919	[e] 302	February 1918–September 1919	[e] 303	April 1918–August 1919	[e] 304	July 1918–August 1919			d Known as 101 in A.E.F. e S.O.S. troops.

SIGNAL CORPS

DEPOT BATTALIONS

Unit designation and redesignation	Organization		Stations in United States		Overseas		Demobilization		Remarks
	Month and year	Place	Month and year	Place	From—	To—	Month and year	Place	
1st Depot Battalion	November 1917	New York, N. Y.	December 1917	P. of E., Hoboken	December 1917	February 1918			S.O.S. troops.
2d Depot Battalion	January 1918	Ft. Leavenworth, Kans.	May 1918	Cp. Mills, N. Y.					1st to 11th Depot Bns. demblzd. overseas.
			June 1918	P. of E., Hoboken	June 1918	July 1918			S.O.S. troops.
3d Depot Battalion	February 1918	do	May 1918	Cp. Mills, N. Y.					
			June 1918	P. of E., Hoboken	do	do			Do.
4th Depot Battalion	April 1918	do	July 1918	Cp. Upton, N. Y.					
			do	P. of E., Hoboken	July 1918	February 1919			Do.
5th Depot Battalion	do	do	do	Cp. Upton, N. Y.					
			do	P. of E., Hoboken	do	August 1918			Do.
6th Depot Battalion	do	do	do	Cp. Upton, N. Y.					
			do	P. of E., Hoboken	July 1918	September 1918			Do.
7th Depot Battalion	May 1918	do	do	Cp. Alfred Vail, N. J.					
			August 1918	P. of E., Hoboken	August 1918	do			Do.
8th Depot Battalion	June 1918	do	do	Cp. Upton, N. Y.					
			do	P. of E., Hoboken	do	do			Do.
9th Depot Battalion	July 1918	do	do	Cp. Merritt, N. J.					
			September 1918	P. of E., Hoboken	September 1918	do			Do.

DEPOT BATTALIONS—Continued

Unit designation and redesignation	Organization		Stations in United States		Overseas		Demobilization		Remarks
	Month and year	Place	Month and year	Place	From—	To—	Month and year	Place	
10th Depot Battalion	July 1918	Ft. Leavenworth, Kans.	September 1918	Cp. Merritt, N. J.					
			do	P. of E., Hoboken	September 1918	October 1918			S.O.S. troops.
11th Depot Battalion	September 1918	do	November 1918	do	November 1918	November 1918			Do.
12th Depot Battalion	November 1918	Cp. Alfred Vail, N. J.					January 1919	Cp. Alfred Vail, N. J.	
13th Depot Battalion	do	Cp. Meade, Md.					do	Cp. Meade, Md.	

FIELD SIGNAL BATTALIONS

Unit designation and redesignation	Organization		Stations in United States		Overseas		Demobilization		Remarks
	Month and year	Place	Month and year	Place	From—	To—	Month and year	Place	
1st Field Signal Battalion.	1916	Cp. Fort Bliss, Tex.	September 1917	Cp. Alfred Vail, N. J.					Cmpnt. of 2d Div
			December 1917	P. of E., Hoboken	December 1917				Overseas through December 1919.
2d Field Signal Battalion	do	Ft. Sam Houston, Tex.	October 1916	Brownsville, Tex.					Cmpnt. of 1st Div.
			July 1917	P. of E., Hoboken	July 1917.				
			September 1919	Cp. Mills, N. Y.		September 1919.			
			do	Cp. Meade, Md.					
			October 1919	Cp. Z. Taylor, Ky.					Active through 1919.
3d Field Signal Battalion	do	Ft. McKinley, P. I.	July 1917	Ft. Kamehameha, T. H.					Do.
4th Field Signal Battalion.	February 1917	Ft. Leavenworth, Kans.	April 1917	Corozal, C. Z.					Do.
5th Field Signal Battalion.	April 1917	do	February 1918	P. of E., Hoboken	February 1918				Cmpnt. of 3d Div.
			August 1919	Cp. Merritt, N. J.		August 1919.			
			do	Cp. Pike, Ark.					Active through 1919.
6th Field Signal Battalion.	June 1917	do	May 1918	Cp. Wadsworth, S. C.					Cmpnt. of 6th Div.

			July 1918	P. of E., Hoboken	July 1918.				
			June 1919	Cp. Mills, N. Y.		June 1919.			
			do	Cp. Grant, Ill.					Active through 1919.
7th Field Signal Battalion.	do	Ft. Oglethorpe, Ga	December 1917	Cp. Owen Beirne, Tex.					
			April 1918	Cp. Fort Bliss, Tex					Do.
8th Field Signal Battalion.	July 1917	Presidio of Monterey, Calif.	January 1918	Cp. Greene, N. C.					Cmpnt. of 4th Div.
			May 1918	Cp. Merritt, N. J.					
			do	P. of E., Hoboken	May 1918.				
			July 1919	Newport News, Va		July 1919.			
			August 1919	Cp. Dodge, Iowa					Active through 1919.
9th Field Signal Battalion.	do	Leon Springs, Tex	April 1918	Cp. Merritt, N. J.					Cmpnt. of 5th Div.
			do	P. of E., Hoboken	April 1918.				
			July 1919	Cp. Mills, N. Y.		July 1919.			
			August 1919	Cp. Gordon, Ga.					Active through 1919.
10th Field Signal Battalion.	do	Cp. Alfred Vail, N. J.	August 1918	P. of E., Hoboken	August 1918				Cmpnt. of 7th Div.
			June 1919	Cp. Mills, N. Y.		June 1919.			
			July 1919	Cp. Funston, Kans					
			August 1919	Ft. Leavenworth, Kans.					Active through 1919.
11th to 100th Field Signal Battalions.									Never orgzd.
101st Field Signal Battalion.	July 1917	Allston, Mass.	September 1917	P. of E., Hoboken	September 1917				Cmpnt. of 26th Div.
			April 1919	Cp. Devens, Mass.		April 1919	April 1919	Cp. Devens, Mass	
102d Field Signal Battalion.	August 1917	New York, N. Y.	September 1917	Cp. Wadsworth, S. C.					Cmpnt. of 27th Div.
			May 1918	P. of E., Newport News.	May 1918.				
			March 1919	Cp. Merritt, N. J.		March 1919	March 1919	Cp. Upton, N. Y.	
103d Field Signal Battalion.	do	Pittsburgh, Pa.	September 1917	Cp. Hancock, Ga.					Cmpnt. of 28th Div.
			May 1918	Cp. Mills, N. Y.					
			do	P. of E., Hoboken	May 1918.				
			May 1919	Cp. Dix, N. J.		May 1919	May 1919	Cp. Dix, N. J.	

FIELD SIGNAL BATTALIONS—Continued

Unit designation and redesignation	Organization		Stations in United States		Overseas		Demobilization		Remarks
	Month and year	Place	Month and year	Place	From—	To—	Month and year	Place	
104th Field Signal Battalion.	July 1917	Jersey City, N. J.	July 1917	Cp. Edge, N. J.					Cmpnt. of 29th Div.
			September 1917	Cp. McClellan, Ala.					
			June 1918	P. of E., Hoboken	June 1918.				
			May 1919	Cp. Merritt, N. J.		May 1919	May 1919	Cp. Dix, N. J.	
105th Field Signal Battalion.	do	Sylva, N. C.	August 1917	Cp. Sevier, S. C.					Cmpnt. of 30th Div.
			May 1918	P. of E., Hoboken	May 1918.				
			April 1919	Cp. Jackson, S. C.		April 1919	April 1919	Ft. Oglethorpe, Ga	
106th Field Signal Battalion.	October 1917	Cp. Wheeler, Ga.	September 1918	Cp. Mills, N. Y.					Cmpnt. of 31st Div.
			October 1918	P. of E., Hoboken	October 1918.				
			April 1919	Cp. Upton, N. Y.		April 1919	May 1919	Cp. Jackson, S. C.	
107th Field Signal Battalion.	August 1917	Cp. Douglas, Wis.	September 1917	Cp. MacArthur, Tex.					Cmpnt. of 32d Div.
			January 1918	Cp. Merritt, N. J.					
			do	P. of E., Hoboken	January 1918.				
			May 1919	Cp. Devens, Mass.		May 1919	May 1919	Cp. Grant, Ill.	
108th Field Signal Battalion.	do	Chicago, Ill.	May 1918	Cp. Merritt, N. J.					Cmpnt. of 33d Div.
			do	P. of E., Hoboken	May 1918.				
			May 1919	Cp. Mills, N. Y.		May 1919	May 1919	Cp. Grant, Ill.	
109th Field Signal Battalion.	October 1917	Cp. Cody, N. Mex.	September 1918	Cp. Dix, N. J.					Cmpnt. of 34th Div.
			October 1918	P. of E., Hoboken	October 1918.				
			April 1919	Cp. Upton, N. Y.		April 1919	May 1919	Cp. Dodge, Iowa	
110th Field Signal Battalion.	August 1917	Topeka, Kans.	September 1917	Cp. Doniphan, Okla.					Cmpnt. of 35th Div.
			May 1918	Cp. Mills, N. Y.					
			do	P. of E., Hoboken	May 1918.				
			April 1919	Cp. Stuart, Va.		April 1919	May 1919	Cp. Funston, Kans.	

111th Field Signal Battalion.	do	Houston, Tex	September 1917	Cp. Bowie, Tex					Cmpnt. of 36th Div.
			July 1918	P. of E., Hoboken	July 1918.				
			June 1919	Cp. Mills, N. Y		June 1919	June 1919	Cp. Bowie, Tex.	
112th Field Signal Battalion.	do	Cp. Perry, Ohio	September 1917	Cp. Sheridan, Ala					Cmpnt. of 37th Div.
			May 1918	Cp. Lee, Va.					
			June 1918	P. of E., Newport News.	June 1918.				
			March 1919	Cp. Merritt, N. J		March 1919	April 1919	Cp. Sherman, Ohio.	
113th Field Signal Battalion.	do	Indianapolis, Ind	September 1917	Cp. Shelby, Miss					Cmpnt. of 38th Div.
			September 1918	Cp. Mills, N. Y.					
			October 1918	P. of E., Hoboken	October 1918.				
			May 1919	Cp. Mills, N. Y		May 1919	May 1919	Cp. Sherman, Ohio.	
114th Field Signal Battalion.	November 1917	Cp. Beauregard, La.	August 1918	do					Cmpnt. of 39th Div.
			do	P. of E., Hoboken	August 1918.				
			April 1919	Cp. Merritt, N. J		April 1919	May 1919	Cp. Shelby, Miss.	Corps troops.
115th Field Signal Battalion.	August 1917	Cp. Baldwin, Colo.	September 1917	Cp. Kearny, Calif					Cmpnt. of 40th Div.
			July 1918	Cp. Mills, N. Y.					
			August 1918	P. of E., Montreal	August 1918.				
			July 1919	Cp. Mills, N. Y		July 1919	July 1919	Presidio of San Francisco, Calif.	Army troops.
116th Field Signal Battalion.	do	Cp. Murray, Wash.	September 1917	Cp. Greene, N. C					Cmpnt. of 41st Div.
			October 1917	Cp. Mills, N. Y.					
			November 1917	P. of E., Hoboken	November 1917	February 1919	February 1919	Cp. Dix, N. J.	
117th Field Signal Battalion.	do	Kansas City, Mo	August 1917	Cp. Clark, Mo					Cmpnt. of 42d Div.
			September 1917	Cp. Mills, N. Y.					
			November 1917	P. of E., Hoboken	November 1917.				
			April 1919	Cp. Morrison, Va		April 1919	May 1919	Cp. Funston, Kans.	
118th to 208th Field Signal Battalions.									Never orgzd.
209th Field Signal Battalion.	July 1918	Cp. Sheridan, Ala					February 1919	Cp. Sheridan, Ala	Cmpnt. of 9th Div.
210th Field Signal Battalion.	do	Cp. Funston, Kans					do	Cp. Funston, Kans	Cmpnt. of 10th Div.

FIELD SIGNAL BATTALIONS—Continued

Unit designation and redesignation	Organization		Stations in United States		Overseas		Demobilization		Remarks
	Month and year	Place	Month and year	Place	From—	To—	Month and year	Place	
211th Field Signal Battalion.	July 1918	Cp. Meade, Md					February 1919	Cp. Meade, Md	Cmpnt. of 11th Div.
212th Field Signal Battalion.	do	Cp. Devens, Mass					January 1919	Cp. Devens, Mass	Cmpnt. of 12th Div.
213th Field Signal Battalion.	do	Cp. Lewis, Wash					February 1919	Cp. Lewis, Wash	Cmpnt. of 13th Div.
214th Field Signal Battalion.	do	Cp. Custer, Mich					do	Cp. Custer, Mich	Cmpnt. of 14th Div.
215th Field Signal Battalion.	September 1918	Cp. Logan, Tex					do	Cp. Logan, Tex	Cmpnt. of 15th Div.
216th Field Signal Battalion.	August 1918	Cp. Kearny, Calif					do	Cp. Kearny, Calif	Cmpnt. of 16th Div.
217th Field Signal Battalion.	do	Cp. Beauregard, La					January 1919	Cp. Beauregard, La	Cmpnt. of 17th Div.
218th Field Signal Battalion.	September 1918	Cp. Travis, Tex					February 1919	Cp. Travis, Tex	Cmpnt. of 18th Div.
219th Field Signal Battalion.	August 1918	Cp. Dodge, Iowa					January 1919	Cp. Dodge, Iowa	Cmpnt. of 19th Div.
220th Field Signal Battalion.	do	Cp. Sevier, S. C					do	Cp. Sevier, S. C	Cmpnt. of 20th Div.
221st Field Singal Battalion.	October 1918	Cp. Alfred Vail, N. J.					do	Cp. Alfred Vail, N. J.	
222d Field Signal Battalion.	November 1918	Cp. Meade, Md					do	Cp. Meade, Md.	
223d Field Signal Battalion.	do	do					do	Do.	
224th to 300th Field Signal Battalions.									Never orgzd.
301st Field Signal Battalion.	October 1917	Cp. Devens, Mass	July 1918	P. of E., Montreal.	July 1918	May 1919	May 1919	Cp. Devens, Mass	Cmpnt. of 76th Div. Corps troops.

302d Field Signal Battalion.	do	Cp. Upton, N. Y.	March 1918	P. of E., Hoboken	March 1918	do	do	Cp. Upton, N. Y.	Cmpnt. of 77th Div.
303d Field Signal Battalion.	do	Cp. Dix, N. J.	May 1918	do	May 1918	June 1919	June 1919	Cp. Dix, N. J.	Cmpnt. of 78th Div.
304th Field Signal Battalion.	do	Cp. Meade, Md.	July 1918	do	July 1918	May 1919	May 1919	do	Cmpnt. of 79th Div.
305th Field Signal Battalion.	do	Cp. Lee, Va.	May 1918	P. of E., Newport News	May 1918	do	June 1919	do	Cmpnt. of 80th Div.
306th Field Signal Battalion.	do	Cp. Jackson, S. C.	do	Cp. Sevier, S. C.					Cmpnt. of 81st Div.
			July 1918	Cp. Mills, N. Y.					
			do	P. of E., Hoboken	July 1918	June 1919	June 1919	Cp. Jackson, S. C.	
307th Field Signal Battalion.	September 1917	Cp. Gordon, Ga.	May 1918	Cp. Mills N. Y.					Cmpnt. of 82d Div.
			do	P. of E., Hoboken	May 1918	May 1919	May 1919	Cp. Morrison, Va.	
308th Field Signal Battalion.	October 1917	Cp. Sherman, Ohio	May 1918	Cp. Merritt, N. J.					Cmpnt. of 83d Div.
			June 1918	P. of E., Hoboken	June 1918.				
			August 1919	Cp. Merritt, N. J.		August 1919	August 1919	Cp. Sherman, Ohio	Corps troops.
309th Field Signal Battalion.	August 1917	Cp. Z. Taylor, Ky	June 1918	Cp. Sherman, Ohio					Cmpnt. of 84th Div.
			August 1918	Cp. Mills, N. Y.					
			September 1918	P. of E., Hoboken	September 1918				
			May 1919	Cp. Mills, N. Y.		May 1919	May 1919	Cp. Grant, Ill.	
310th Field Signal Battalion.	September 1917	Cp. Custer, Mich.	July 1918	do					Cmpnt. of 85th Div.
			do	P. of E., Hoboken	July 1918.				
			June 1919	Cp. Merritt, N. J.		June 1919	June 1919	Cp. Custer, Mich.	Corps troops.
311th Field Signal Battalion.	do	Cp. Grant, Ill.	August 1918	Cp. Mills, N. Y.					Cmpnt. of 86th Div.
			September 1918	P. of E., Hoboken	September 1918.				
			January 1919	Cp. Stuart, Va.		January 1919	February 1919	Cp. Grant, Ill.	
312th Field Signal Battalion.	do	Cp. Pike, Ark.	June 1918	Cp. Dix, N. J.					Cmpnt. of 87th Div.
			August 1918	P. of E., Hoboken	August 1918.				
			March 1919	Cp. Merritt, N. J.		March 1919	March 1919	Cp. Dix, N. J.	
313th Field Signal Battalion.	October 1917	Cp. Dodge, Iowa	August 1918	P. of E., Hoboken	August 1918				Cmpnt. of 88th Div.
			May 1919	Cp. Mills, N. Y.		May 1919	June 1919	Cp. Dodge, Iowa	

FIELD SIGNAL BATTALIONS—Continued

Unit designation and redesignation	Organization		Stations in United States		Overseas		Demobilization		Remarks
	Month and year	Place	Month and year	Place	From—	To—	Month and year	Place	
314th Field Signal Battalion.	October 1917	Cp. Funston, Kans.	May 1918	Cp. Mills, N. Y.					Cmpnt. of 89th Div.
			June 1918	P. of E., Hoboken	June 1918.				
			May 1919	Cp. Upton, N. Y.		May 1919	June 1919	Cp. Funston, Kans.	
315th Field Signal Battalion.	do	Cp. Travis, Tex.	June 1918	Cp. Mills, N. Y.					Cmpnt. of 90th Div.
			do	P. of E., Hoboken	June 1918.				
			June 1919	Cp. Morrison, Va.		June 1919	June 1919	Cp. Bowie, Tex.	
316th Field Signal Battalion.	do	Cp. Lewis, Wash.	June 1918	Cp. Merritt, N. J.					Cmpnt. of 91st Div.
			July 1918	P. of E., Hoboken	July 1918.				
			April 1919	Cp. Mills, N. Y.		April 1919	May 1919	Cp. Kearny, Calif.	
317th Field Signal Battalion.	November 1917	Cp. Devens, Mass.	July 1918	P. of E., Hoboken	July 1918.				
			June 1919	Cp. Mills, N. Y.		June 1919	June 1919	Cp. Devens, Mass	Corps troops.
318th Field Signal Battalion.	do	Cp. Jackson, S. C.	May 1918	Cp. Wadsworth, S. C.					
			July 1918	P. of E., Hoboken	July 1918	March 1919	March 1919	Cp. Dix, N. J.	Do.
319th Field Signal Battalion.	do	Cp. Sherman, Ohio.	May 1918	P. of E., Hoboken	May 1918.				
			May 1919	Cp. Upton, N. Y.		May 1919	June 1919	Cp. Sherman, Ohio.	Army troops.
320th Field Signal Battalion.	do	Cp. Dodge, Iowa	January 1918	Cp. Fremont, Calif.					Cmpnt. of 8th Div.
			October 1918	Cp. Mills, N. Y.					
			November 1918	Cp. Lee, Va			February 1919	Cp. Lee, Va	
321st Field Signal Battalion.	do	Cp. Upton, N. Y.	May 1918	Plattsburg Bks., N. Y.					
			September 1918	P. of E., Hoboken	September 1918.				
			April 1919	Cp. Mills, N. Y.		April 1919	April 1919	Cp. Upton, N. Y.	Corps troops.
322d Field Signal Battalion.	do	Cp. Lewis, Wash.	April 1918	Cp. Merritt, N. J.					

			May 1918	P. of E., Hoboken	May 1918.				
			August 1919	Cp. Merritt, N. J.		August 1919	August 1919	Presidio of San Francisco, Calif.	Army troops.
323d Field Signal Battalion.	do	Cp. Funston, Kans.	April 1918	Cp. Samuel F. B. Morse, Tex.					
			September 1918	P. of E., Hoboken	September 1918.				
			May 1919	Cp. Mills, N. Y.		May 1919	May 1919	Cp. Sherman, Ohio.	Corps troops.
324th Field Signal Battalion.	do	Cp. Meade, Md.	August 1918	Cp. Alfred Vail, N. J.					
			November 1918	Cp. Mills, N. Y.					
			do	Cp. Merritt, N. J.					
			do	Cp. Meade, Md.			January 1919	Cp. Meade, Md.	
325th Field Signal Battalion.	December 1917	Cp. Sherman, Ohio.	May 1918	Cp. Upton, N. Y.					Cmpnt. of 92d Div.
			June 1918	P. of E., Hoboken.	June 1918.				
			February 1919	Cp. Merritt, N. J.		February 1919	March 1919	Cp. Meade, Md.	
326th Field Signal Battalion.	January 1918	Cp. Wadsworth, S. C.	August 1918	P. of E., Newport News.	August 1918.				
			June 1919	Cp. Merritt, N. J.		June 1919	July 1919	Cp. Upton, N. Y.	Corps troops.
327th to 619th Field Signal Battalions.									Never orgzd.
620th Field Signal Battalion.	September 1918	Cp. Sherman, Ohio.					December 1918	Cp. Sherman, Ohio.	Cmpnt. of 95th Div.
621st Field Signal Battalion.	October 1918	Cp. Wadsworth, S. C.					January 1919	Cp. Wadsworth, S. C.	Cmpnt. of 96th Div.
622d Field Signal Battalion.	September 1918	Ft. Leavenworth, Kans.					December 1918	Cp. Cody, N. Mex.	Cmpnt. of 97th Div.

TELEGRAPH BATTALIONS

1st (I) Telegraph Battalion.									See 51st Telegraph Battalion.
1st (II) Telegraph Battalion, Reserve.									See 406th Telegraph Battalion.
2d (I) Telegraph Battalion.									See 52d Telegraph Battalion.
2d (II) Telegraph Battalion.									See 407th Telegraph Battalion.
3d Telegraph Battalion									See 53d Telegraph Battalion.

TELEGRAPH BATTALIONS—Continued

Unit designation and redesignation	Organization		Stations in United States		Overseas		Demobilization		Remarks
	Month and year	Place	Month and year	Place	From—	To—	Month and year	Place	
4th Telegraph Battalion									See 54th Telegraph Battalion.
5th Telegraph Battalion									See 55th Telegraph Battalion.
6th Telegraph Battalion, Reserve.									See 410th Telegraph Battalion.
7th Telegraph Battalion, Reserve.									See 408th Telegraph Battalion.
8th Telegraph Battalion, Reserve.									See 411th Telegraph Battalion.
9th Telegraph Battalion, Reserve.									See 402d Telegraph Battalion.
10th Telegraph Battalion, Reserve.									See 412th Telegraph Battalion.
11th Telegraph Battalion, Reserve.									See 409th Telegraph Battalion.
12th Telegraph Battalion, Reserve.									See 405th Telegraph Battalion.
13th to 50th Telegraph Battalions.									Never orgzd.
51st Telegraph Battalion.	1916	Ft. Sam Houston, Tex.	August 1918	Cp. Upton, N. Y.					Orgzd. fr. 1st Tg. Bn., October 1917.
			do	P. of E., Hoboken	August 1918.				
			August 1919	Cp. Merritt, N. J.		August 1919.			
			do	Ft. Sam Houston, Tex.					Corps troops. Active through 1919.
52d Telegraph Battalion	do	Columbus, N. Mex	March 1917	Cp. Newton D. Baker, Tex.					Orgzd. fr. 2d Tg. Bn., October 1917.

			September 1917	Cp. Alfred Vail, N. J.					
			December 1917	P. of E., Hoboken	December 1917.				
			August 1919	Cp. Dix, N. J.		August 1919.			
			do	Ft. Sam Houston, Tex.					Active through 1919. Corps troops.
53d Telegraph Battalion									Orgzd. fr. 3d Tg. Bn., October 1917.
Company "D"	1916	Manila, P. I.	September 1917	Ft. McKinley, P. I.					
			September 1918	Vladivostok, Russia.					Active through 1919.
Company "E"	do	Ft. Shafter, T. H.	July 1918	Schofield Bks., T. H.					Do.
54th Telegraph Battalion.	do	Corozal, C. Z.							Orgzd. fr. 4th Tg. Bn., October 1917. Active through 1919.
55th Telegraph Battalion.	July 1917	Cp. Alfred Vail, N. J.	April 1918	P. of E., Hoboken	April 1918				Orgzd. fr. 5th Tg. Bn., October 1917.
			June 1919	Cp. Mills, N. J.		June 1919.			
			July 1919	Cp. Alfred Vail, N. J.					Corps troops. Active through 1919.
56th to 400th Telegraph Battalions.									Never orgzd.
401st Telegraph Battalion.	October 1917	Cp. Devens, Mass.	February 1918	Cp. Merritt, N. J.					Orgzd. fr. 5th Tg. Bn., October 1917.
			March 1918	P. of E., Hoboken	March 1918.				
			May 1919	Cp. Merritt, N. J.		May 1919	May 1919	Cp. Devens, Mass.	Army troops.
402d Telegraph Battalion.	do	Cp. Jackson, S. C.	May 1918	Cp. Hill, Va.					Orgzd. fr. 9th Tg. Bn., October 1917.
			June 1918	P. of E., Newport News.	June 1918.				
			June 1919	Cp. Mills, N. Y.		June 1919	July 1919	Cp. Sherman, Ohio	S.O.S. troops.

TELEGRAPH BATTALIONS—Continued

Unit designation and redesignation	Organization		Stations in United States		Overseas		Demobilization		Remarks
	Month and year	Place	Month and year	Place	From—	To—	Month and year	Place	
403d Telegraph Battalion.	October 1917	Cp. Sherman, Ohio.	May 1918	Cp. Mills, N. Y.					
			June 1918	P. of E., Hoboken.	June 1918.				
			June 1919	Cp. Mills, N. Y.		June 1919	July 1919	Cp. Sherman, Ohio.	S.O.S. troops.
404th Telegraph Battalion.	do	Cp. Dodge, Iowa	July 1918	Do.					
			do	P. of E., Hoboken.	July 1918.				
			June 1919	Cp. Mills, N. Y.		June 1919	July 1919	Cp. Dix, N. J.	Do.
405th Telegraph Battalion.	do	Cp. Lewis, Wash.	April 1918	Cp. Merritt, N. J.					Orgzd. fr. 12th Tg. Bn., October 1917.
			do	P. of E., Hoboken.	April 1918.				
			June 1919	Cp. Merritt, N. J.		June 1919	June 1919	Ft. D. A. Russell, Wyo.	Corps troops.
406th Telegraph Battalion.	June 1917	Pittsburgh, Pa.	June 1917	Monmouth Park, N. J.					Orgzd. fr. 1st Tg. Bn. Res., October 1917.
			August 1917	P. of E., Hoboken.	August 1917.				
			April 1919	Cp. Upton, N. Y.		April 1919	April 1919	Cp. Dix, N. J.	Corps troops.
407th Telegraph Battalion.	do	New York, N. Y.	June 1917	Monmouth Park, N. J.					Orgzd. fr. 2d Tg. Bn. Res., October 1917.
			August 1917	P. of E., Hoboken.	August 1917.				
			April 1919	Cp. Upton, N. Y.		April 1919	May 1919	Cp. Upton, N. Y.	Corps troops.
408th Telegraph Battalion.	September 1917	Chicago, Ill.	September 1917	Cp. Alfred Vail, N. J.					Orgzd. fr. 7th Tg. Bn., October 1917.
			November 1917	P. of E., Hoboken.	November 1917.				
			May 1919	Cp. Mills, N. Y.		May 1919	May 1919	Cp. Dodge, Iowa.	S.O.S. troops.
409th Telegraph Battalion.	August 1917	do	August 1917	Cp. Alfred Vail, N. J.					Orgzd. fr. 11th Tg. Bn., October 1917.
			October 1917	P. of E., Hoboken.	October 1917.				
			April 1919	Cp. Mills, N. Y.		April 1919	April 1919	Cp. Grant, Ill.	Army troops.

410th Telegraph Battalion.	July 1917	do	July 1917	Ft. Leavenworth, Kans.					Orgzd. fr. 6th Tg. Bn., October 1917.
			December 1917	Cp. Samuel F. B. Morse, Tex.					
			July 1918	Cp. Mills, N. Y.					
			do	P. of E., Hoboken	July 1918.				
			July 1919	Cp. Mills, N. Y.		July 1919	July 1919	Cp. Grant, Ill	S.O.S. troops.
411th Telegraph Battalion.	June 1917	Presidio of Monterey, Calif.	February 1918	Cp. Merritt, N. J.					Orgzd. fr. 8th Tg. Bn., October 1917.
			do	P. of E., Hoboken	February 1918.				
			April 1919	Cp. Mills, N. Y.		April 1919	May 1919	Presidio of San Francisco, Calif.	Army troops.
412th Telegraph Battalion.	July 1917	Cp. Funston, Tex.	December 1917	Cp. Merritt, N. J.					Orgzd. fr. 10th Tg. Bn. October 1917.
			January 1918	P. of E., Hoboken	January 1918.				
			March 1919	Cp. Morrison, Va.		March 1919	March 1919	Cp. Zachary Taylor, Ky.	Corps troops.
413th Telegraph Battalion.	November 1917	Jersey City, N. J.	January 1918	P. of E., Hoboken	January 1918	April 1919	April 1919	Cp. Dix, N. J.	S.O.S. troops.
414th Telegraph Battalion.	December 1917	New York, N. Y.	February 1918	do	February 1918.				
			June 1919	Cp. Mills, N. Y.		June 1919	July 1919	Cp. Upton, N. Y.	Do.
415th Telegraph Battalion.	January 1918	Chicago, Ill	March 1918	P. of E., Hoboken	March 1918.				
			May 1919	Cp. Merritt, N. J.		May 1919	May 1919	Cp. Grant, Ill	Do.
416th Telegraph Battalion.	do	do	February 1918	Do.					
			March 1918	P. of E., Hoboken	March 1918	July 1919			S.O.S. troops. Demblzd. overseas.
417th Telegraph Battalion.	April 1918	Cp. Alfred Vail, N. J.	August 1918	do	August 1918.				
			August 1919	Norfolk, Va.		August 1919	August 1919	Cp. Upton, N. Y.	Corps troops.
418th Telegraph Battalion.	May 1918	do	September 1918	P. of E., Hoboken	September 1918.				
			July 1919	Newport News, Va.		July 1919	July 1919	Cp. Grant, Ill	S.O.S. troops.
419th Telegraph Battalion.	April 1918	Cp. Samuel F. B. Morse, Tex.	September 1918	Cp. Mills, N. Y.					
			do	P. of E., Hoboken	September 1918.				
			July 1919	Cp. Merritt, N. J.		do	do	Cp. Travis, Tex.	Army troops.
420th Telegraph Battalion.	September 1918	Cp. Alfred Vail, N. J.	October 1918	P. of E., Hoboken	October 1918.				
			March 1919	Cp. Merritt, N. J.		March 1919	March 1919	Cp. Dix, N. J.	Corps troops.

TELEGRAPH BATTALIONS—Continued

Unit designation and redesignation	Organization		Stations in United States		Overseas		Demobilization		Remarks
	Month and year	Place	Month and year	Place	From—	To—	Month and year	Place	
421st Telegraph Battalion.	September 1918	Ft. Leavenworth, Kans.	October 1918	P. of E., Hoboken	October 1918.				
			January 1919	Cp. Stuart, Va		January 1919	February 1919	Cp. Meade, Md	S.O.S. troops.
422d Telegraph Battalion.	do	Cp. Alfred Vail, N. J.	October 1918	P. of E., Hoboken	October 1918.				
			January 1919	Cp. Stuart, Va		do	do	do	Do.
423rd Telegraph Battalion.	do	Ft. Leavenworth, Kans.	October 1918	P. of E., Hoboken	October 1918.				
			March 1919	Cp. Stuart, Va		March 1919	March 1919	Cp. Zachary Taylor, Ky.	Do.
424th Telegraph Battalion.	do	do	November 1918	Cp. Upton, N. Y.					
			do	Cp. Meade, Md			January 1919	Cp. Meade, Md.	
425th Telegraph Battalion.	October 1918	Cp. Alfred Vail, N. J.					do	Cp. Alfred Vail, N. J.	
426th Telegraph Battalion.	November 1918	Cp. Meade, Md					do	Cp. Meade, Md.	
427th Telegraph Battalion.	do	do					do	Do.	
428th Telegraph Battalion.	do	do					do	Do.	
429th Telegraph Battalion.	do	do					do	Do.	

TRAINING BATTALIONS

Unit designation and redesignation	Organization Month and year	Organization Place	Stations Month and year	Stations Place	Overseas From—	Overseas To—	Demobilization Month and year	Demobilization Place	Remarks
1st Training Battalion	August 1918	Ft. Leavenworth, Kans.	November 1918	Cp. Meade, Md			November 1918	Cp. Meade, Md.	
2nd Training Battalion	do	do	do	do			do	Do.	
3rd Training Battalion	do	do	September 1918	do			January 1919	Do.	
4th Training Battalion	do	do	November 1918	do			do	Do.	
5th Training Battalion	do	do	do	do			do	Do.	
6th Training Battalion	do	do	do	do			do	Do.	

S. C. SPECIAL AND TECHNICAL UNITS

Units	Unit No.	Active service	Unit No.	Active service	Unit No.	Active service	Unit No.	Active service	Unit No.	Active service	Remarks
Service Company	1	1916 through December 1919	2	1916 through December 1919	3	September 1917 through December 1919	4	June 1917 through December 1919	5	July 1917 through December 1919	1. Orgzd. fr. Depot Co. F, Alaska. 2. Orgzd. fr. Depot Co. G, Alaska.
	6	July 1917 through December 1919	7	do	8	1916 through December 1919	9	April 1918 through December 1919	10	April 1918 through December 1919	3. Orgzd. fr. Depot Co. F, Burlington, Va. 4. Orgzd. fr. Depot Co. H, New York.
	11	April 1918 through December 1919	[d] 12	February 1918–July 1919	13	April 1918–November 1919	14	March 1918–March 1919	15	1899 through December 1919	5. Orgzd. fr. Depot Co. G, Cp. Wadsworth, S. C. 6. Orgzd. fr. Depot Co. I, Chicago.
	16	1916–October 1919	17	March 1918 through December 1919	18	March 1918–January 1919	19	February 1918–December 1918	20	April 1918–January 1919	7. Orgzd. fr. Depot Co. K, Ft. Sam Houston, Tex.
	21	February 1918–January 1919	22	April 1918–January 1919	23	Never orgzd.	24	March 1918–December 1918	25	February 1918–January 1919	8. Orgzd. fr. Depot Co. L, San Francisco, Calif.
	26	Never orgzd.	27	April 1918 through December 1919	28	February 1918–January 1919	29	June 1918–May 1919	[d] 30	June 1918–February 1919	b Orgzd. overseas; demobilized in U. S.
	31	June 1918–March 1919	32	June 1918–January 1919	[c, d] 33	do	[b, d] 34	February 1918–September 1919	[c, d] 35	February 1918–July 1919	c Orgzd. and demobilized overseas.
	[c, d] 36	July 1918–September 1918	[c, d] 37	July 1918–August 1919	[c, d] 38	July 1918–August 1919	[c, d] 39	July 1918–April 1919	[c, d] 40	July 1918–September 1919	
	[c, d] 41	July 1918–June 1919	[c, d] 42	July 1918–April 1919	[c, d] 43	July 1918–May 1919	[c, d] 44	July 1918–August 1919	[c, d] 45	November 1918–February 1919	d S.O.S. troops.
	[d] 46	July 1918–December 1918	47	July 1918–January 1919	48	August 1918–December 1918	49–53	Never orgzd.	[c] 54	January 1919–June 1919	
	[c, d] 55	October 1918–June 1919	[c] 56	January 1919–June 1919	[c] 57	February 1919–June 1919	[c] 58	February 1919–August 1919			

TANK CORPS

TANK CENTERS

Unit designation and redesignation	Organization		Stations in United States		Overseas		Demobilization		Remarks
	Month and year	Place	Month and year	Place	From—	To—	Month and year	Place	
1st Light Tank Center	February 1918	A. E. F.							
a. 311th Center	June 1918	Do.							
b. 302d (II) Center	September 1918	do	April 1919	Cp. Merritt, N. J.		April 1919.			
			do	Cp. Meade, Md.					Active through 1919. G.H.Q. troops.
2d Heavy Tank Center	March 1918	Do.							
a. 302d (I) Center	do	Do.							
b. 301st Center	June 1918	do	March 1919	Cp. Mills, N. Y.		March 1919	April 1919	Cp. Meade, Md.	G.H.Q. troops.
3d to 300th Tank Centers.									Never orgzd.
301st Tank Center									See 2d Hv. Tk. Center.
302d Tank Center									See 1st L. Tk. and 2d Hv. Tk. Centers.
303 Tank Center									See 304th and 314th Tank Centers.
304th Tank Center	September 1918	Cp. Colt, Pa.	October 1918	Cp. Mills, N. Y.					
			do	P. of E., Hoboken	October 1918.				
a. 303d (II) Center	November 1918	A. E. F.	May 1919	Cp. Stuart, Va.		May 1919	May 1919	Cp. Meade, Md.	G.H.Q. troops.
305th to 308th Tank Centers.									Never orgzd.
309th Tank Center	October 1918	Cp. Colt, Pa.					December 1918	Cp. Dix, N. J.	
310th Tank Center	do	do					do	Do.	
311th Tank Center									See 1st L. Tk. Center.
312th and 313th Tank Centers.									Never orgzd.

314th Tank Center	June 1918	Cp. Colt, Pa.							
a. 303d (I) Center	July 1918	do	September 1918	Cp. Tobyhanna, Pa.					
			do	P. of E., Hoboken	September 1918.				
b. 303d Center Hq. Company.	October 1918	A. E. F.							Redes. Hq. Co. 307th Brig. November 6, 1918.

TANK BRIGADES

1st Provisional Tank Brigade.	August 1918	A. E. F.							
a. 304th Tank Brigade.	November 1918	do	March 1919	Cp. Mills, N. Y.		March 1919.			
			do	Cp. Meade, Md.					Active through 1919. G. H. Q. troops.
2d Provisional Tank Brigade.	October 1918	Do.							
a. 305th Tank Brigade.	November 1918	do	do	Cp. Mills, N. Y.		March 1919.			
			do	Cp. Meade, Md.					Active through 1919.
3d Provisional Tank Brigade.	October 1918	Do.							
a. 306th Tank Brigade.	November 1918	do	do	Cp. Upton, N. Y.		March 1919.			
			do	Cp. Meade, Md.			September 1919	Cp. Meade, Md.	
4th Provisional Tank Brigade.	October 1918	Do.							
a. 307th Tank Brigade.	November 1918	do	May 1919	Cp. Stuart, Va.		May 1919	May 1919	do	G.H.Q. troops.

TANK BATTALIONS

1st Separate Battalion, Heavy Tank Service, 65th Engineers.	February 1918	Cp. Upton, N. Y.							
a. 1st Heavy Battalion, Tank Service.	March 1918	do	March 1918	Cp. Merritt, N. J.					
			do	P. of E., Hoboken	March 1918.				
b. 301st Battalion, Tank Corps.	April 1918	A. E. F.	March 1919	Cp. Mills, N. Y.		March 1919.			
			do	Cp. Meade, Md.					G.H.Q. troops Active through 1919.

TANK BATTALIONS—Continued

Unit designation and redesignation	Organization		Stations in United States		Overseas		Demobilization		Remarks
	Month and year	Place	Month and year	Place	From—	To—	Month and year	Place	
1st Battalion, Light Tanl Service, 65th Engineers.	February 1918	Cp. Upton, N. Y.							
a. 1st Light Battalion, Tank Service.	March 1918	do	March 1918	Cp. Colt, Pa.					
b. 326th (I) Battalion, Tank Corps.	April 1918	Cp. Colt, Pa	July 1918	Cp. Summerall, Pa					
			September 1918	P. of E., Hoboken	September 1918				
			May 1919	Cp. Stuart, Va		May 1919	May 1919	Cp. Meade, Md	G.H.Q. troops.
2d Battalion, Light Tank Service, 65th Engineers.	February 1918	Cp. Upton, N. Y.							
a. 2d Light Battalion, Tank Service.	March 1918	do	March 1918	Cp. Colt, Pa.					
b. 327th (I) Battalion, Tank Corps.	April 1918	Cp. Colt, Pa	September 1918	Cp. Summerall, Pa					
			do	P. of E., Hoboken	September 1918				
			May 1919	Cp. Stuart, Va		do	do	do	Do.
Co. D, 2d Battalion, Heavy Tank Service, 65th Engineers.	February 1918	Cp. Meade, Md.							
a. 2d Heavy Battalion, Tank Service.	March 1918	do	March 1918	Cp. Colt, Pa.					
b. 302d (I) Tank Battalion.	April 1918	Cp. Colt, Pa	July 1918	Cp. Summerall, Pa					
			September 1918	P. of E., Hoboken	September 1918				
			May 1919	Cp. Stuart, Va		do	do	do	Do.

3d to 300th Tank Battalions.									Never orgzd.
301st Tank Battalion									See 1st Sep. Bn., Hv. Tk. Serv., 65th Engrs.
302d (I) Tank Battalion									See 2d Bn., Hv. Tk. Serv., 65th Engrs.
302d (II) Tank Battalion	June 1918	A. E. F.							
a. 302d Provisional Battalion.	September 1918	do							Redes. 306th Tk. Bn. October 1918.
303d Tank Battalion	May 1918	Cp. Colt, Pa.	August 1918	P. of E., Hoboken	August 1918.				
			March 1919	Cp. Mills, N. Y.		March 1919.			
			do	Cp. Meade, Md.					Active through 1919. G. H. Q. troops.
304th Tank Battalion	do	do	October 1918	P. of E., Hoboken	October 1918.				
			May 1919	Cp. Mills, N. Y.		May 1919	May 1919	Cp. Meade, Md.	G.H.Q. troops.
305th Tank Battalion	June 1918	do	September 1918	Method, N. C.					
			do	Cp. Polk, N. C.			December 1918	Cp. Greene, N. C.	
306th Tank Battalion	October 1918	A. E. F.	March 1919	Cp. Upton, N. Y.		March 1919.			
			do	Cp. Meade, Md.			October 1919	Cp. Meade, Md.	Do.
307th Tank Battalion	do	Cp. Polk, N. C.					December 1918	Cp. Greene, N. C.	
308th Tank Battalion	November 1918	do					do	Do.	
309th to 325th Tank Battalions.									Never orgzd.
326th (I) Tank Battalion									See 1st Bn. L. Tk. Serv., 65th Engrs.
326th (II) Tank Battalion.	June 1918	A. E. F.							
a. 344th Tank Battalion.	September 1918	do	March 1919	Cp. Mills, N. Y.		March 1919.			
			do	Cp. Meade, Md.					Active through 1919. G. H. Q. troops.
327th (I) Tank Battalion									See 2d Bn. L. Tk. Serv., 65th Engrs.
327th (II) Tank Battalion.	June 1918	A. E. F.							
a. 345th Tank Battalion.	September 1918	do	March 1919	Cp. Upton, N. Y.		March 1919.			
			do	Cp. Meade, Md.					Active through 1919.

TANK BATTALIONS—Continued

Unit designation and redesignation	Organization		Stations in United States		Overseas		Demobilization		Remarks
	Month and year	Place	Month and year	Place	From—	To—	Month and year	Place	
328th Tank Battalion	April 1918	Cp. Colt, Pa	August 1918	P. of E., Hoboken	August 1918.				
			March 1919	Cp. Mills, N. Y		March 1919.			
			do	Cp. Meade, Md					Active through 1919. G. H. Q. troops.
329th Tank Battalion	May 1918	do	August 1918	P. of E., Hoboken	August 1918.				
			March 1919	Cp. Mills, N. Y		March 1919.			
			do	Cp. Meade, Md					Do.
330th Tank Battalion	do	do	August 1918	P. of E., Hoboken	August 1918.				
			March 1919	Cp. Mills, N. Y		March 1919.			
			do	Cp. Meade, Md			October 1919	Cp. Meade, Md	G.H.Q. troops.
331st Tank Battalion	June 1918	do	August 1918	P. of E., Hoboken	September 1918.				
			March 1919	Cp. Upton, N. Y		March 1919.			
			do	Cp. Meade, Md			do	Do.	
332d Tank Battalion	do	do	September 1918	Cp. Summerall, Pa.					
			do	P. of E., Hoboken	September 1918.				
			May 1919	Cp. Mills, N. Y		May 1919	May 1919	do	Do.
333d Tank Battalion	do	do					December 1918	Cp. Dix, N. J.	
334th Tank Battalion	August 1918	do					do	Do.	
335th Tank Battalion	September 1918	do	October 1918	P. of E., Hoboken	October 1918.				
			May 1919	Cp. Mills, N. Y		May 1919	May 1919	Cp. Meade, Md	Do.
336th Tank Battalion	do	do	October 1918	P. of E., Hoboken	October 1918.				
			May 1919	Cp. Mills, N. Y		do	do	do	Do.
337th Tank Battalion	do	do	October 1918	P. of E., Hoboken	October 1918.				
			May 1919	Cp. Mills, N. Y		do	do	do	Do.
338th Tank Battalion	do	do					December 1918	Cp. Dix, N. J.	
339th Tank Battalion	October 1918	do					do	Do.	
340th Tank Battalion	November 1918	Cp. Polk, N. C					do	Cp. Greene, N. C.	
341st Tank Battalion	do	do					do	Do.	
342d Tank Battalion	do	do					do	Do.	

343d Tank Battalion	do	do					do	Do.	
344th Tank Battalion									See 326th (II) T.Bn
345th Tank Battalion									See 327th (II) T.Bn.
346th Tank Battalion	October 1918	Cp. Colt, Pa					December 1918	Cp. Dix, N. J.	

TK. C. SPECIAL AND TECHNICAL UNITS

Units	Unit No.	Active service	Unit No.	Active service	Unit No.	Active service	Unit No.	Active service	Unit No.	Active service	Remarks
Provisional Depot Company.	[a] 1	November 1918–October 1919									a Orgzd. overseas; demobilized in U. S.
Depot Company	301	July 1918–December 1918									
Repair & Salvage Company.	1–305	Never orgzd.	306	July 1918 through December 1919	[b] 307	September 1918–May 1919	308–315	Never orgzd.	(I) 316	See Rep. & Salv. Co. 321.	b G.H.Q. troops.
	(II) 316	July 1918–September 1919	[b] 317	August 1918–November 1919	[b] 318	do	319	October 1918–December 1918	320	October 1918–December 1918	
	[b] 321	June 1918 through December 1919	322–350	Never orgzd.	351	October 1918–December 1918					321st redes. fr. 316th September 1918.
Training & Replacement Company.	1–375	Never orgzd.	[b] 376	July 1918–May 1919	[b] 377	July 1918–May 1919	[b] 378	July 1918–May 1919	[b] 379	July 1918–May 1919	b G.H.Q. troops.
	[b] 380	September 1918–May 1919	[b] 381	September 1918–May 1919	382	October 1918–December 1918	383	October 1918–December 1918			

TRANSPORTATION CORPS

T. C. GRAND DIVISIONS

Unit designation and redesignation	Organization		Stations in United States		Overseas		Demobilization		Remarks
	Month and year	Place	Month and year	Place	From—	To—	Month and year	Place	
1st Grand Division [1]					November 1918	October 1919.			
2d Grand Division [1]					do	September 1919.			
3d Grand Division [1]					do	October 1919.			
4th Grand Division [1]					do	April 1919.			
5th Grand Division	November 1918	A. E. F							A. E. F. through 1919.
6th Grand Division [1]					November 1918	April 1919.			
7th Grand Division	January 1919	A. E. F	July 1919	Cp. Merritt, N. J.		July 1919	July 1919	Cp. Merritt, N. J.	
8th Grand Division									Never orgzd.
9th Grand Division [1]					May 1919	Sometime in 1919.			
10th Grand Division									Do.
11th Grand Division [1]					November 1918	April 1919.			
12th Grand Division [1]					do	June 1919.			
13th Grand Division [1]					December 1918	August 1919.			
14th Grand Division [1]					November 1918	Do.			
15th Grand Division [1]					December 1918	Do.			
16th Grand Division [1]					do	Do.			
17th Grand Division [1]					November 1918	June 1919.			
18th Grand Division [1]					do	Do.			
19th Grand Division [1]					do	Do.			
20th Grand Division [1]					do	April 1919.			
21st Grand Division [1]					December 1918	Do.			
22d Grand Division [1]					November 1918	Do.			
23d Grand Division [1]					January 1919	May 1919.			
24th Grand Division [1]					March 1919	July 1919.			

T. C. REGIMENTS

Unit designation and redesignation	Organization Month and year	Organization Place	Stations Month and year	Stations Place	Overseas From—	Overseas To—	Demobilization Month and year	Demobilization Place	Remarks
1st to 18th Regiments									Never orgzd.
19th Regiment [1]					September 1918	December 1918			Orgzd. fr. 19th Engrs. S.O.S. troops.

20th to 30th Regiments									Never orgzd.
31st Regiment [1]					September 1918	December 1918			Orgzd. fr. 31st Engrs. S.O.S. troops.
32d to 34th Regiments									Never orgzd.
35th Regiments [1]					September 1918	December 1918			Orgzd. fr. 35th Engrs. S.O.S. troops.
36th Regiment [1]					do	do			Orgzd. fr. 36th Engrs. S.O.S. troops.
37th Regiment									Never orgzd.
38th Regiment [1]					September 1918	November 1918			Orgzd. fr. 38th Engrs.
39th Regiment [1]					do	December 1918			Orgzd. fr. 39th Engrs. S.O.S troops.
40th to 43d Regiments									Never orgzd.
44th Regiment [1]					September 1918	December 1918			Orgzd. fr. 44th Engrs. S.O.S. troops.
45th Regiment [1]					do	do			Orgzd. fr. 45th Engrs. S.O.S. troops.
46th Regiment [1]					do	do			Orgzd. fr. 46th Engrs. S.O.S. troops.
47th Regiment [1]					do	do			Orgzd. fr. 47th Engrs. S.O.S. troops.
48th Regiment [1]					do	do			Orgzd. fr. 48th Engrs. S.O.S. troops.
49th Regiment [1]					do	do			Orgzd. fr. 49th Engrs. S.O.S. troops.
50th Regiment [1]					do	do			Orgzd. fr. 50th Engrs. S.O.S. troops.

[1] Organized and demobilized overseas.

T. C. REGIMENTS—Continued

Unit designation and redesignation	Organization		Stations in United States		Overseas		Demobilization		Remarks
	Month and year	Place	Month and year	Place	From—	To—	Month and year	Place	
51st Regiment [1]					September 1918	December 1918			Orgsd. fr. 51st Engrs. troops.
52d Regiment [1]					do	do			Orgsd. fr. 52d Engrs. S.O.S. troops.
53d Regiment [1]					do	do			Orgsd. fr. 53d Engrs. S.O.S. troops.
54th Regiment [1]					do	do			Orgzd. fr. 54th Engrs. S.O.S. troops.
55th to 56th Regiments									Never orgzd.
57th Regiment [1]					September 1918	December 1918			Orgsd. fr. 57th Engrs.
58th Regiment [1]					do	do			Orgsd. fr. 58th Engrs. S.O.S. troops.
59th Regiment [1]					do	do			Orgzd. fr. 59th Engrs. S.O.S. troops.
60th Regiment [1]					do	do			Orgsd. fr. 60th Engrs. S.O.S. troops.
61st Regiment [1]					do	do			Orgsd. fr. 61st Engrs. S.O.S. troops.
62d Regiment [1]					do	November 1918			Orgsd. fr. 62d Engrs. S.O.S. troops.
63d Regiment [1]					do	do			Orgsd. fr. 63d Engrs. S.O.S. troops.

64th Regiment [1]					do	December 1918			Orgzd. fr. 64th Engrs. S.O.S. troops.
65th Regiment [1]					do	do			Orgzd. fr. 65th Engrs. S.O.S. troops.
66th Regiment [1]					do	November 1918			Orgzd. fr. 66th Engrs. S.O.S. troops.
67th Regiment [1]					do	December 1918			Orgzd. fr. 67th Engrs. S.O.S. troops.
68th to 445th Regiments									Never orgzd.
446th Regiment [1]					September 1918	November 1918			Orgzd. fr. 446th Engrs.
447th to 468th Regiments.									Never orgzd.
469th Regiment [1]					September 1918	November 1918			Orgzd. fr. 469th Engrs.

STEVEDORE BATTALIONS

1st to 800th Stevedore Battalions.									Never orgzd.
801st Stevedore Battalion.[1]					October 1918	November 1918			Orgzd. fr. 301st Stevedore Regt., Q.M.C. S.O.S. troops.
802d Stevedore Battalion.[1]					do	do			Do.
803d Stevedore Battalion.[1]					do	do			Do.
804th Stevedore Battalion.[1]					do	do			Do.
805th Stevedore Battalion.[1]					do	do			Do.
806th Stevedore Battalion.[1]					do	do			Do.

[1] Organised and demobilised overseas.

STEVEDORE BATTALIONS—Continued

Unit designation and redesignation	Organization		Stations in United States		Overseas		Demobilization		Remarks
	Month and year	Place	Month and year	Place	From—	To—	Month and year	Place	
807th Stevedore Battalion.[1]					October 1918	November 1918			Orgzd. fr. 302d Stevedore Regt., Q.M.C. S.O.S. troops.
808th Stevedore Battalion.[1]					do	do			Do.
809th Stevedore Battalion.[1]					do	do			Do.
810th Stevedore Battalion.[1]					do	do			Do.
811th Stevedore Battalion.[1]					do	do			Do.
812th Stevedore Battalion.[1]					do	do			Do.
813th Stevedore Battalion.[1]					do	do			Orgzd. fr. 303d Stevedore Regt., Q.M.C. S.O.S. troops.
814th Stevedore Battalion.[1]					do	do			Do.
815th Stevedore Battalion.[1]					do	do			Do.

T. C. COMPANIES

Unit designation and redesignation	Organization: Month and year	Organization: Place	Stations in United States: Month and year	Stations in United States: Place	Overseas: From—	Overseas: To—	Demobilization: Month and year	Demobilization: Place	Remarks
1st Company	December 1918	A. E. F	August 1919	Cp. Merritt, N. J.		August 1919	August 1919	Cp. Dodge, Iowa	Orgzd. fr. Co. A' 31st Regt., T.C'
2d Company	do	do	do	do		do	do	do	Orgzd. fr. Co. B' 31st Regt., T.C'
3d Company	do	do	July 1919	Cp. Dix, N. J.		July 1919	July 1919	Cp. Dix, N. J.	Orgzd. fr. Co. C' 31st Regt., T.C'

4th Company	do	do	do	Cp. Merritt, N. J.		do	August 1919	Cp. Dodge, Iowa	Orgzd. fr. Co. D, 31st Regt., T.C.
5th Company	do	do	do	do		do	do	do	Orgzd. fr. Co. E, 31st Regt., T.C.
6th Company	do	do	do	do		do	July 1919	do	Orgzd. fr. Co. F, 31st Regt., T.C.
7th Company	do	do	do	Cp. Mills, N. Y.		do	do	Cp. Dix, N. J.	Orgzd. fr. Co. A, 45th Regt., T.C.
8th Company	do	do	do	do		do	do	do	Orgzd. fr. Co. B, 45th Regt., T.C.
9th Company	do	do	do	do		do	do	do	Orgzd. fr. Co. C, 45th Regt., T.C.
10th Company	do	do	June 1919	Cp. Jackson, S. C.		June 1919	do	Cp. Grant, Ill.	Orgzd. fr. Co. A, 67th Regt., T.C.
11th Company	do	do	July 1919	Cp. Mills, N. Y.		July 1919	do	Cp. Dix, N. J.	Orgzd. fr. Co. B, 67th Regt., T.C.
12th Company	do	do	do	do		do	do	Cp. Grant, Ill.	Orgzd. fr. Co. C, 67th Regt., T.C.
13th Company	January 1919	do	do	do		do	August 1919	Cp. Zachary Taylor, Ky.	Orgzd. fr. Pl. of 67th Regt., T.C.
14th Company	**December 1918**	**do**	**do**	**Cp. Merritt, N. J.**		**do**	**July 1919**	**do**	**Orgzd. fr. Co. A, 44th Regt., T.C.**
15th Company	December 1918	do	do	do		do	do	Ft. D. A. Russell, Wyo.	Orgzd. fr. Co. B, 44th Regt., T.C.
16th Company	do	do	do	do		do	August 1919	Cp. Dix, N. J.	Orgzd. fr. 5th Co., Aug. A.R.D.
17th Company	do	do	do	Norfolk, Va.		do	do	do	Orgzd. fr. 6th Co., Aug. A.R.D.
18th Company	do	do	August 1919	do		August 1919	do	do	Orgzd. fr. 7th Co., Aug. A.R.D.
19th Company					December 1918	April 1919			Orgzd. fr. Co. L, 19th Regt., T.C. Orgzd. and demobilized overseas.
20th Company	November 1918	A. E. F.	April 1919	Cp. Dix, N. J.		do	April 1919	Cp. Dix, N. J.	Orgzd. fr. Co. K, 35th Regt., T.C.
21st Company	December 1918	do	July 1919	Norfolk, Va.		July 1919	August 1919	Cp. Pike, Ark.	Pl. fr. 66th Engrs.

[1] Orgzd. and demblzd. overseas.

T. C. COMPANIES—Continued

Unit designation and redesignation	Organization		Stations in United States		Overseas		Demobilization		Remarks
	Month and year	Place	Month and year	Place	From—	To—	Month and year	Place	
22d Company	December 1918	A. E. F	September 1919	Cp. Merritt, N. J		September 1919	October 1919	Cp. Dix, N. J.	
23d Company	do	do	July 1919	Cp. Devens, Mass		July 1919	July 1919	Cp. Devens, Mass	Orgzd. fr. Co. A, 36th Regt., T.C.
24th Company	do	do	do	do		do	do	do	Orgzd. fr. Co. B, 36th Regt., T.C.
25th Company	do	do	September 1919	Cp. Merritt, N. J		September 1919	September 1919	Cp. Dix, N. J	Orgzd. fr. Co. C, 36th Regt., T.C.
26th Company	do	do	July 1919	Cp. Jackson, S. C		July 1919	July 1919	Cp. Jackson, S. C	Orgzd. fr. Co. A, 39th Regt., T.C.
27th Company	do	do	do	Cp. Merritt, N. J		do	do	Cp. Dodge, Iowa	Orgzd. fr. Co. B, 39th Regt., T.C.
28th Company	do	do	do	do		do	do	do	Orgzd. fr. Co. C, 39th Regt., T.C.
29th Company	do	do	do	Cp. Devens, Mass		do	do	Cp. Devens, Mass	Orgzd. fr. Co. A, 46th Regt., T.C.
30th Company	do	do	June 1919	Cp. Merritt, N. J.		June 1919	do	Cp. Gordon, Ga	Orgzd. fr. Co. B, 46th Regt., T.C.
31st Company	do	do	July 1919	Cp. Hill, Va		July 1919	do	do	Orgzd. fr. Co. C, 46th Regt., T.C.
32d Company	do	do	do	Cp. Merritt, N. J		do	do	Cp. Sherman, Ohio	Orgzd. fr. Co. A, 53d Regt., T.C.
33d Company	do	do	do	Cp. Hill, Va		do	do	Cp. Grant, Ill	Orgzd. fr. Co. B, 53d Regt., T.C.
34th Company	do	do	do	do		do	do	do	Orgzd. fr. Co. C, 53d Regt., T.C.
35th Company	do	do	do	Cp. Merritt, N. J		do	August 1919	Cp. Sherman, Ohio	Orgzd. fr. 64th Regt., T.C.
36th Company	do	do	September 1919	do		September 1919	September 1919	Cp. Dix, N. J	Do.
37th Company	do	do	July 1919	Cp. Devens, Mass		July 1919	July 1919	Cp. Devens, Mass	Do.
38th Company	do	do	do	Cp. Mills, N. Y		do	do	Cp. Grant, Ill	Do.
39th Company	do	do	May 1919	Cp. Upton, N. Y		May 1919	May 1919	Cp. Upton, N. Y	Do.

40th Company	March 1919	do	July 1919	Cp. Mills, N. Y		July 1919	July 1919	Cp. Dix, N. J	Do.
41st Company	December 1918	do	June 1919	do		June 1919	June 1919	do	Orgzd. fr. Co. A, 47th Regt., T.C.
42d Company	do	do	do	do		do	do	do	Orgzd. fr. Co. B, 47th Regt., T.C.
43d Company	do	do	do	do		do	do	do	Orgzd. fr. Co. C, 47th Regt., T.C.
44th Company	do	do	July 1919	Newport News, Va.		July 1919	July 1919	do	Orgzd. fr. Co. A, 52d Regt., T.C.
45th Company [1]					December 1918	June 1919			Orgzd. fr. Co. B, 52d Regt., T.C.
46th Company [1]					do	do			Orgzd. fr. Co. C, 52d Regt., T.C.
47th Company	December 1918	A. E. F	July 1919	Cp. Stuart, Va		July 1919	July 1919	Cp. Grant, Ill	Orgzd. fr. Co. A, 54th Regt., T.C.
48th Company	do	do	do	Cp. Hill, Va		do	do	Cp. Dodge, Iowa	Orgzd. fr. Co. B, 54th Regt., T.C.
49th Company [1]					December 1918	June 1919			Orgzd. fr. Co. C, 54th Regt., T.C.
50th Company	December 1918	A. E. F	August 1919	Norfolk, Va		August 1919	September 1919	Cp. Dix, N. J	Orgzd. fr. Co. A, 65th Regt., T.C.
51st Company	do	do	July 1919	Cp. Hill, Va		July 1919	July 1919	Cp. Grant, Ill	Orgzd. fr. Co. B, 65th Regt., T.C.
52d Company	do	do	do	do		do	do	do	Orgzd. fr. Co. C, 65th Regt., T.C.
53d Company	do	do	March 1919	Cp. Merritt, N. J		March 1919	March 1919	Cp. Dix, N. J	Orgzd. fr. 65th Regt., T.C.
54th Company	do	do	June 1919	Cp. Hill, Va		June 1919	June 1919	Cp. Grant, Ill	Orgzd. fr. Co. A, 68th Regt., T.C. S.O.S. troops.
55th Company	do	do	July 1919	Cp. Mills, N. Y		July 1919	July 1919	Cp. Upton, N. Y	Orgzd. fr. Co. B, 68th Regt., T.C. S.O.S. troops.
56th Company	do	do	do	Cp. Devens, Mass		do	do	Cp. Grant, Ill	Orgzd. fr. Co. C, 68th Regt., T.C. S.O.S. troops.
57th Company	do	do	September 1919	Cp. Merritt, N. J		September 1919	September 1919	Cp. Dodge, Iowa	Orgzd. fr. Co. A 81st Regt., T.C.

[1] Orgzd. and demblzd. overseas.

T. C. COMPANIES—Continued

Unit designation and redesignation	Organization		Stations in United States		Overseas		Demobilization		Remarks
	Month and year	Place	Month and year	Place	From—	To—	Month and year	Place	
58th Company	December 1918	A. E. F.	September 1919	Cp. Merritt, N. J.		September 1919	September 1919	Cp. Dix, N. J.	Orgzd. fr. Co. B, 61st Regt., T.C.
59th Company	do	do	do	do		do	do	Cp. Dodge, Iowa	Orgzd. fr. Co. C, 61st Regt., T.C.
60th Company	do	do	March 1919	Cp. Mills, N. Y.		March 1919	April 1919	Cp. Zachary Taylor, Ky.	Orgzd. fr. Co. M, 19th Regt., T.C.
61st Company	do	do	July 1919	Cp. Merritt, N. J.		July 1919	July 1919	Ft. D. A. Russell, Wyo.	Orgzd. fr. Co. C, 44th Regt., T.C.
62d Company	do	do	do	Norfolk, Va.		do	August 1919	Cp. Dix, N. J.	Orgzd. fr. Co. I, 19th Regt., T.C.
63d Company	do	do	do	Cp. Merritt, N. J.		do	July 1919	do	Orgzd. fr. Co. A, 58th Regt., T.C.
64th Company	do	do	do	do		do	do	do	Orgzd. fr. Co. B, 58th Regt., T.C.
65th Company	do	do	do	do		do	do	do	Orgzd. fr. Co. C, 65th Regt., T.C.
66th Company	do	do	May 1919	Cp. Mills, N. Y.		May 1919	May 1919	Cp. Mills, N. Y.	Orgzd. fr. Co. D, 66th Regt., T.C.
67th Company	do	do	June 1919	do		June 1919	June 1919	Cp. Sherman, Ohio	Orgzd. fr. Co. A, 60th Regt., T.C.
68th Company	do	do	do	do		do	do	Cp. Dix, N. J.	Orgzd. fr. Co. B, 60th Regt., T.C.
69th Company	do	do	July 1919	Cp. Merritt, N. J.		July 1919	July 1919	Cp. Dodge, Iowa	Orgzd. fr. Co. C, 60th Regt., T.C.
70th Company	do	do	do	do		do	do	Cp. Dix, N. J.	Orgzd. fr. Co. A, 63d Regt., T.C.
71st Company	do	do	June 1919	Cp. Mills, N. Y.		June 1919	June 1919	do	Orgzd. fr. Co. B, 63d Regt., T.C.
72d Company	do	do	do	Cp. Merritt, N. J.		do	July 1919	Cp. Meade, Md.	Orgzd. fr. Co. C, 63d Regt., T.C.

73d Company	do	do	July 1919	Cp. Mills, N. Y		July 1919	do	Cp. Dix, N. J	Orgzd. fr. Co. A, 66th Regt., T.C.
74th Company	do	do	do	Cp. Merritt, N. J		do	do	Cp. Bowie, Tex	Orgzd. fr. 66th Regt., T.C.
75th Company	do	do	do	Cp. Mills, N. Y		do	do	Cp. Dix, N. J	Orgzd. fr. Co. D, 66th Regt., T.C.
76th Company [1]					December 1918	April 1919			Orgzd. fr. Co. F, 66th Regt., T.C.
77th Company	December 1918	A. E. F	August 1919	Cp. Merritt, N. J		August 1919	August 1919	Cp. Dix, N. J	Pl. fr. 66th Regt., T.C.
78th Company	do	do	June 1919	do		June 1919	July 1919	Cp. Zachary Taylor, Ky.	Orgzd. fr. Co. A, 48th Regt., T.C.
79th Company	do	do	do	do		do	do	Ft. D. A. Russell, Wyo.	Orgzd. fr. Co. B, 48th Regt., T.C.
80th Company	do	do	do	Cp. Mills, N. Y		do	June 1919	do	Orgzd. fr. Co. C, 48th Regt., T.C.
81st Company	do	do	March 1919	do		March 1919	April 1919	Cp. Dix, N. J	Orgzd. fr. Co. K, 19th Regt., T.C.
82d Company	do	do	do	do		do	March 1919	Cp. Lee, Va	Orgzd. fr. Co. H, 19th Regt., T.C.
83d Company	do	do	July 1919	Cp. Merritt, N. J		July 1919	July 1919	Cp. Dix, N. J	Orgzd. fr. Co. A, 51st Regt., T.C.
84th Company	do	do	April 1919	Cp. Upton, N. Y		April 1919	May 1919	do	Orgzd. fr. Co. B, 51st Regt., T.C.
85th Company	do	do	July 1919	Cp. Merritt, N. J		July 1919	July 1919	Cp. Sherman, Ohio	Orgzd. fr. Co. C, 51st Regt., T.C.
86th Company	do	do	June 1919	do		June 1919	do	do	Orgzd. fr. Co. A, 62d Regt., T.C.
87th Company	do	do	do	do		do	do	Cp. Dodge, Iowa	Orgzd. fr. Co. B, 62d Regt., T.C.
88th Company	do	do	do	do		do	do	Cp. Sherman, Ohio	Orgzd. fr. Co. C, 62d Regt., T.C.
89th Company	do	do	July 1919	do		July 1919	do	Cp. Grant, Ill	Orgzd. fr. Co. A, 59th Regt., T.C.
90th Company	do	do	do	do		do	do	Cp. Dix, N. J	Orgzd. fr. Co. B, 59th Regt., T.C.
91st Company	do	do	do	do		do	do	do	Orgzd. fr. Co. C, 59th Regt., T.C.

[1] Orgzd. and demblzd. overseas.

T. C. COMPANIES—Continued

Unit designation and redesignation	Organization		Stations in United States		Overseas		Demobilization		Remarks
	Month and year	Place	Month and year	Place	From—	To—	Month and year	Place	
92d Company	December 1918	A. E. F	April 1919	Cp. Mills, N. Y		April 1919	April 1919	Cp. Dix, N. J	Orgzd. fr. Co. A, 35th Regt., T.C.
93d Company	do	do	do	do		do	do	do	Orgzd. fr. Co. B, 35th Regt., T.C.
94th Company	do	do	do	do		do	do	do	Orgzd. fr. Co. C, 35th Regt., T.C.
95th Company	do	do	May 1919	Cp. Merritt, N. J		May 1919	May 1919	do	Orgzd. fr. Co. D, 35th Regt., T.C.
96th Company	do	do	do	do		do	do	Cp. Grant, Ill	Orgzd. fr. Co. E, 35th Regt., T.C.
97th Company [1]					December 1918	January 1919			Orgzd. fr. Co. F, 35th Regt., T.C.
98th Company	December 1918	A. E. F	April 1919	Cp. Upton, N. Y		April 1919	May 1919	Cp. Sherman, Ohio	Orgzd. fr. Co. G, 35th Regt., T.C.
99th Company	do	do	June 1919	Cp. Merritt, N. J		June 1919	June 1919	Cp. Dix, N. J	Orgzd. fr. Co. H, 35th Regt., T.C.
100th Company	do	do	do	do		do	do	do	Orgzd. fr. Co. I, 35th Regt., T.C.
101st Company [1]					December 1918	February 1919			Orgzd. fr. Co. L, 35th Regt., T.C.
102d Company	December 1918	A. E. F	April 1919	Cp. Upton, N. Y		April 1919	May 1919	Cp. Upton, N. Y	Orgzd. fr. Co. M, 35th Regt., T.C.
103d Company	do	do	June 1919	Cp. Merritt, N. J		June 1919	July 1919	Cp. Sherman, Ohio	Orgzd. fr. Co. N, 35th Regt., T.C.
104th Company	do	do	March 1919	Cp. Mills, N. Y		March 1919	April 1919	Cp. Dix, N. J	Orgzd. fr. Co. O, 35th Regt., T.C.
105th Company [1]					December 1918	January 1919			Orgzd. fr. Co. P, 35th Regt., T.C.
106th Company	December 1918	A. E. F	March 1919	Cp. Mills, N. Y		March 1919	March 1919	Cp. Meade, Md	Orgzd. fr. Co. D, 19th Regt., T.C.

107th Company	do	do	do	do		do	April 1919	Cp. Sherman, Ohio	Orgzd. fr. Co. E, 19th Regt., T.C.
108th Company	do	do	April 1919	Cp. Dix, N. J		April 1919	do	Cp. Dix, N. J	Orgzd. fr. Co. F, 19th Regt., T.C.
109th Company	do	do	July 1919	Cp. Merritt, N. J		July 1919	July 1919	do	Orgzd. fr. Co. N, 19th Regt., T.C.
110th Company	do	do	do	Cp. Mills, N. Y		do	do	Cp. Upton, N. Y	Orgzd. fr. Co. O, 19th Regt., T.C.
111th Company	do	do	April 1919	do		April 1919	April 1919	Cp. Dix, N. J	Orgzd. fr. Co. A, 19th Regt., T.C.
112th Company [1]					December 1918	January 1919			Orgzd. fr. Co. B, 19th Regt., T.C.
113th Company	December 1918	A. E. F	April 1919	Cp. Upton, N. Y		April 1919	May 1919	Cp. Sherman, Ohio	Orgzd. fr. Co. C, 19th Regt., T.C.
114th Company	do	do	do	Cp. Jackson, S. C		do	April 1919	Cp. Jackson, S. C	Orgzd. fr. Co. P, 19th Regt., T.C.
115th Company	do	do	March 1919	Cp. Mills, N. Y		March 1919	do	Cp. Dix, N. J	Orgzd. fr. Co. G, 19th Regt., T.C.
116th Company	do	do	July 1919	Cp. Merritt, N. J		July 1919	July 1919	do	Orgzd. fr. Co. A, 50th Regt., T.C.
117th Company	do	do	do	Cp. Mills, N. Y		do	do	Cp. Upton, N. Y	Orgzd. fr. Co. B, 50th Regt., T.C.
118th Company	do	do	do	Cp. Merritt, N. J		do	do	Cp. Dix, N. J	Orgzd. fr. Co. C, 50th Regt., T.C.
119th Company	do	do	do	Cp. Mills, N. Y		do	do	do	Orgzd. fr. Co. A, 49th Regt., T.C.
120th Company	do	do	June 1919	Cp. Merritt, N. J		June 1919	do	do	Orgzd. fr. Co. C, 49th Regt., T.C.
121st Company	do	do	July 1919	Cp. Mills, N. Y		July 1919	do	do	Orgzd. fr. Co. B, 49th Regt., T.C.
122d Company	do	do	do	Norfolk, Va		do	August 1919	Cp. Lee, Va	Orgzd. fr. Co. A, 49th Regt., T.C.
123d Company	do	do	August 1919	Cp. Dix, N. J		August 1919	do	Cp. Dix, N. J	Orgzd. fr. Co. B, 57th Regt., T.C.
124th Company	do	do	July 1919	Cp. Devens, Mass		July 1919	July 1919	Cp. Devens, Mass	Orgzd. fr. Co. C, 57th Regt., T.C.
125th Company	do	do	do	Cp. Merritt, N. J		do	do	Cp. Dix, N. J	Orgzd. fr. Co. D, 57th Regt., T.C.

[1] Orgzd. and demblzd. overseas.

T. C. COMPANIES—Continued

Unit designation and redesignation	Organization		Stations in United States		Overseas		Demobilization		Remarks
	Month and year	Place	Month and year	Place	From—	To—	Month and year	Place	
126th Company	December 1918	A. E. F	June 1919	Cp. Dix, N. J		June 1919	June 1919	Cp. Dix, N. J	Orgzd. fr. Co. A, 38th Regt., T.C.
127th Company	do	do	do	Cp. Merritt, N. J		do	do	do	Orgzd. fr. Co. B, 38th Regt., T.C.
128th Company	do	do	do	Newport News, Va		do	do	do	Pl. fr. 66th Regt., T.C.
129th Company	do	do	April 1919	Cp. Dix, N. J		April 1919	April 1919	do	Orgzd. fr. Co. R, 35th Regt., T.C.
130th Company									Never orgzd.
131st Company	December 1918	A. E. F	June 1919	Cp. Hill, Va		June 1919	June 1919	Cp. Dix, N. J.	
132d Company	January 1919	do	July 1919	Cp. Merritt, N. J		July 1919	August 1919	Cp. Dodge, Iowa.	
133d Company	February 1919	do	do	Cp. Stuart, Va		do	July 1919	Cp. Dix, N. J.	
134th Company	December 1918	do	do	Cp. Merritt, N. J		do	do	do	Orgzd. fr. Co. A, 69th Engrs. S.O.S. troops.
135th Company	do	do	do	do		do	do	do	Orgzd. fr. Co. C, 69th Engrs. S.O.S. troops.
136th Company	do	do	do	do		do	do	do	Do.
137th Company	do	do	March 1919	Cp. Mills, N. Y		March 1919	April 1919	Cp. Grant, Ill	Orgzd. fr. Co. A, 81st Engrs. S.O.S. troops.
138th Company	do	do	July 1919	Cp. Devens, Mass		July 1919	July 1919	Cp. Devens, Mass	Orgzd. fr. Co. A, 93d Engrs. S.O.S. troops.
139th Company					December 1918	March 1919			Orgzd. and demobilized overseas.
140th Company	January 1919	A. E. F	July 1919	Cp. Mills, N. Y		July 1919	July 1919	Cp. Dix, N. J	Orgzd. fr. Co. B, 118th Engrs. S.O.S. troops.

141st Company	December 1918	do	August 1919	Norfolk, Va.		August 1919	September 1919	Cp. Grant, Ill.	Orgzd. fr. Co. C, 118th Engrs. S.O.S. troops.
142d Company	do	do	July 1919	Cp. Merritt, N. J.		July 1919	July 1919	Cp. Dix, N. J.	Orgzd. fr. Co. D, 118th Engrs. S.O.S. troops.
143d Company	do	do	June 1919	Cp. Mills, N. Y.		June 1919	June 1919	Cp. Dodge, Iowa.	Orgzd. fr. Co. E, 118th Engrs. S.O.S. troops.
144th Company	do	do	September 1919	Cp. Merritt, N. J.		September 1919	September 1919	Cp. Dix, N. J.	Orgzd. fr. Co. F, 118th Engrs. S.O.S. troops.
145th Company	do	do	July 1919	Cp. Mills, N. Y.		July 1919	July 1919	do	Orgzd. fr. Co. G, 118th Engrs. S.O.S. troops.
146th Company	do	do	do	do		do	do	do	Orgzd. fr. Co. H, 118th Engrs. S.O.S. troops.
147th Company	January 1919	do	September 1919	Cp. Merritt, N. J.		September 1919	September 1919	do	Orgzd. fr. Co. I, 118th Engrs. S.O.S. troops.
148th Company [1]					December 1918	February 1919			Orgzd. fr. Co. K, 118th Engrs. S.O.S. troops.
149th Company	December 1918	A. E. F.	September 1919	Cp. Merritt, N. J.		September 1919	September 1919	Cp. Dix, N. J.	Orgzd. fr. Co. L, 118th Engrs. S.O.S. troops.
150th Company	do	do	August 1919	do		August 1919	August 1919	do	Orgzd. fr. Co. M, 118th Engrs. S.O.S. troops.
151st Company	January 1919	do	September 1919	do		September 1919	October 1919	Do.	
152d Company	do	do	do	do		do	September 1919	Do.	
153d Company	April 1919	do	July 1919	do		July 1919	August 1919	Cp. Upton, N. Y.	
154th Company	January 1919	do	September 1919	do		September 1919	September 1919	Cp. Dix, N. J.	
155th Company	February 1919	do	July 1919	Cp. Jackson, S. C.		July 1919	July 1919	Do.	
156th Company	do	do	do	Norfolk, Va.		do	do	Cp. Upton, N. Y.	
157th Company	do	do	do	Cp. Devens, Mass.		do	do	Cp. Devens, Mass.	
158th Company	do	do	do	Cp. Merritt, N. J.		do	do	Cp. Dix, N. J.	

[1] Orgzd. and demblzd. overseas.

T. C. COMPANIES—Continued

Unit designation and redesignation	Organisation		Stations in United States		Overseas		Demobilisation		Remarks
	Month and year	Place	Month and year	Place	From—	To—	Month and year	Place	
159th Company	February 1919	A. E. F	June 1919	Cp. Dix, N. J		June 1919	June 1919	Cp. Dix, N. J.	
160th Company	do	do	July 1919	Cp. Merritt, N. J		July 1919	July 1919	Cp. Devens, Mass.	
161st Company	do	do	do	Cp. Devens, Mass		do	do	Do.	
162d Company	March 1919	do	do	Cp. Merritt, N. J		do	do	Cp. Dix, N. J.	
163d Company	do	do	do	Cp. Jackson, S. C		do	do	Cp. Grant, Ill.	
164th Company	February 1919	do	do	Cp. Upton, N. Y		do	do	Cp. Upton, N. Y.	
165th Company	March 1919	do	do	Cp. Mills, N. Y		do	do	Do.	
166th Company	February 1919	do	do	Cp. Hill, Va		do	do	Cp. Devens, Mass.	
167th Company	March 1919	do	August 1919	Cp. Merritt, N. J		August 1919	August 1919	Cp. Dix, N. J.	
168th Company	March 1919	A. E. F	August 1919	Cp. Merritt, N. J		August 1919	August 1919	Cp. Dix, N. J.	
169th Company					April 1919	September 1919			Orgzd. and demobilized overseas.
170th to 800th Companies.									Never orgzd.
801st Company	November 1918	A. E. F	April 1919	Cp. Jackson, S. C		April 1919	April 1919	Cp. Jackson, S. C	Orgzd. fr. cmpnt. of 801st Stevedore Bn.
802d Company	do	do	do	do		do	do	do	Do.
803d Company	do	do	May 1919	Cp. Alexander, Va		May 1919	May 1919	Cp. Gordon, Ga	Do.
804th Company	do	do	June 1919	do		June 1919	June 1919	do	Do.
805th Company	do	do	do	do		do	July 1919	Cp. Jackson, S. C	Orgzd. fr. cmpnt. of 802d Stevedore Bn.
806th Company	do	do	July 1919	Cp. Jackson, S. C		July 1919	do	Cp. Gordon, Ga	Do.
807th Company	do	do	do	do		do	do	Cp. Jackson, S. C	Do.
808th Company	do	do	do	Cp. Alexander, Va		do	do	Cp. Lee, Va	Do.
809th Company	do	do	do	Cp. Jackson, S. C		do	do	Cp. Shelby, Miss	Orgzd. fr. cmpnt. of 803d Stevedore Bn.
810th Company	do	do	do	Cp. Mills, N. Y		do	do	Cp. Gordon, Ga	Do.
811th Company	do	do	do	Cp. Alexander, Va		do	do	do	Do.
812th Company	do	do	do	Cp. Stuart, Va		do	do	Cp. Stuart, Va	Do.

813th Company	do	do	do	Cp. Alexander, Va.		do	do	Cp. Shelby, Miss.	Orgzd. fr. empnt. of 804th Stevedore Bn.
814th Company	do	do	do	do		do	do	Cp. Lee, Va.	Do.
815th Company	do	do	do	Cp. Mills, N. Y.		do	do	Cp. Gordon, Ga.	Do.
816th Company	do	do	do	Cp. Stuart, Va.		do	do	Cp. Pike, Ark.	Do.
817th Company	do	do	do	Cp. Mills, N. Y.		do	do	Cp. Travis, Tex.	Orgzd. fr. empnt. of 805th Stevedore Bn.
818th Company	do	do	do	Cp. Hill, Va.		do	do	do	Do
819th Company	do	do	do	Cp. Mills, N. Y.		do	do	Cp. Gordon, Ga.	Do.
820th Company	do	do	do	Norfolk, Va.		do	do	Cp. Pike, Ark.	Do.
821st Company	do	do	do	Cp. Mills, N. Y.		do	do	do	Orgzd. fr. empnt. of 806th Stevedore Bn.
822d Company	do	do	do	Cp. Hill, Va.		do	do	Cp. Gordon, Ga.	Do.
823d Company	do	do	do	do		do	do	do	Do.
824th Company	do	do	do	Cp. Mills, N. Y.		do	do	do	Do.
825th Company	do	do	May 1919	Cp. Jackson, S. C.		May 1919	May 1919	Cp. Jackson, S. C.	Orgzd. fr. empnt. of 807th Stevedore Bn.
826th Company	do	do	July 1919	do		July 1919	July 1919	Cp. Gordon, Ga.	Do.
827th Company	do	do	May 1919	do		May 1919	May 1919	Cp. Jackson, S. C.	Do.
828th Company	do	do	July 1919	do		July 1919	July 1919	Cp. Shelby, Miss.	Do.
829th Company	do	do	June 1919	Cp. Alexander, Va.		June 1919	June 1919	do	Orgzd. fr. empnt. of 808th Stevedore Bn.
830th Company	do	do	July 1919	Cp. Jackson, S. C.		July 1919	July 1919	Cp. Gordon, Ga.	Do.
831st Company	do	do	do	do		do	do	Cp. Jackson, S. C.	Do.
832d Company	do	do	June 1919	Cp. Alexander, Va.		June 1919	June 1919	Cp. Lee, Va.	Do.
833d Company	do	do	May 1919	Cp. Jackson, S. C.		May 1919	May 1919	Cp. Jackson, S. C.	Orgzd. fr. empnt. of 809th Stevedore Bn.
834th Company	do	do	June 1919	Cp. Upton, N. Y.		June 1919	July 1919	Cp. Upton, N. Y.	Do.
835th Company	do	do	February 1919	Cp. Alexander, Va.		February 1919	March 1919	Cp. Jackson, S. C.	Do.
836th Company	do	do	July 1919	Cp. Jackson, S. C.		July 1919	July 1919	do	Do.
837th Company	do	do	do	do		do	do	do	Orgzd. fr. empnt. of 810th Stevedore Bn.

T. C. COMPANIES—Continued

Unit designation and redesignation	Organization		Stations in United States		Overseas		Demobilization		Remarks
	Month and year	Place	Month and year	Place	From—	To—	Month and year	Place	
838th Company	November 1918	A. E. F	July 1919	Cp. Alexander, Va.		July 1919	July 1919	Cp. Shelby, Miss	Orgzd. fr. cmpnt. of 810th Stevedore, Bn.
839th Company	do	do	do	do		do	do	do	Do.
840th Company	do	do	do	do		do	do	Cp. Meade, Md	Do.
841st Company	do	do	do	do		do	do	Cp. Lee, Va	Orgzd. fr. cmpnt. of 811th Stevedore Bn.
842d Company	do	do	do	do		do	do	do	Do.
843d Company	do	do	do	Cp. Stuart, Va		do	do	Cp. Grant, Ill	Do.
844th Company	do	do	do	Cp. Alexander, Va.		do	do	Cp. Lee, Va	Do.
845th Company	do	do	do	Cp. Jackson, S. C		do	do	Cp. Shelby, Miss	Orgzd. fr. cmpnt. of 812th Stevedore Bn.
846th Company	December 1918	do	do	Norfolk, Va		do	August 1919	Cp. Gordon, Ga	Orgzd. fr. Co. A, 518th Engrs.
847th Company	do	do	do	Cp. Alexander, Va.		do	July 1919	do	Orgzd. fr. Co. B, 518th Engrs.
848th Company	do	do	August 1919	Cp. Merritt, N. J		August 1919	August 1919	do	Orgzd. fr. Co. C 518th Engrs.
849th Company	November 1918	do	July 1919	Cp. Mills, N. Y		July 1919	July 1919	Cp. Dix, N. J	Orgzd. fr. cmpnt. of 813th Stevedore Bn.
850th Company	do	do	do	do		do	do	Cp. Gordon, Ga	Do.
851st Company	do	do	April 1919	Cp. Upton, N. Y		April 1919	April 1919	Cp. Upton, N. Y	Do.
852d Company	do	do	July 1919	Cp. Mills, N. Y		July 1919	July 1919	Cp. Dix, N. J	Do.
853d Company	do	do	April 1919	Cp. Upton, N. Y		April 1919	April 1919	Cp. Upton, N. Y	Orgzd. fr. cmpnt. of 814th Stevedore Bn.
854th Company	do	do	February 1919	do		February 1919	February 1919	Cp. Meade, Md	Do.

855th Company	January 1919	do	June 1919	do		June 1919	July 1919	Cp. Gordon, Ga	Orgzd. fr. Co. D, 518th Engrs.
856th Company	do	do	July 1919	Norfolk, Va		July 1919	do	Cp. Lee, Va	Orgzd. fr. Co. A, 538th Engrs.
857th Company	November 1918	do	do	Cp. Mills, N. Y		do	August 1919	Cp. Dix, N. J	Pl. fr. 815th Stevedore Bn.
858th Company	January 1919	do	do	Norfolk, Va		do	July 1919	Cp. Lee, Va	Orgzd. fr. Co. B, 538th Engrs.
859th Company	do	do	do	do		do	August 1919	do	Orgzd. fr. Co. C, 538th Engrs.
860th Company	do	do	do	Cp. Mills, N. Y		do	July 1919	Cp. Dix, N. J	Orgzd. fr. Co. D, 538th Engrs.
861st Company	do	do	June 1919	Cp. Upton, N. Y		June 1919	do	Cp. Meade, Md	Orgzd. fr. 701st Engrs. S.O.S. troops.
862d Company	do	do	do	do		do	do	do	Do.
863d Company	do	do	October 1919	Cp. Merritt, N. J		October 1919	October 1919	Cp. Dix, N. J	Do.
864th Company	do	do	September 1919	do		September 1919	do	do	Do.
865th Company	December 1918	do	July 1919	Cp. Mills, N. Y		July 1919	August 1919	do	Orgzd. fr. 702d Engrs. S.O.S. troops.
866th Company	do	do	do	Cp. Alexander, Va		do	July 1919	Cp. Alexander, Va	Do.
867th Company	do	do	June 1919	Cp. Upton, N. Y		June 1919	do	Cp. Upton, N. Y	Do.
868th Company	do	do	August 1919	Cp. Merritt, N. J		August 1919	August 1919	Cp. Dix, N. J	Do.
869th Company	January 1919	do	July 1919	Cp. Mills, N. Y		July 1919	July 1919	Do.	
870th Company	do	do	do	Cp. Hill, Va		do	do	Cp. Upton, N. Y.	
871st Company	do	do	do	Cp. Merritt, N. J		do	August 1919	Cp. Shelby, Miss.	
872d Company	do	do	do	do		do	do	Do.	
873d Company	February 1919	do	do	Cp. Alexander, Va		do	July 1919	Cp. Lee, Va.	
874th Company	do	do	June 1919	Cp. Dix, N. J		June 1919	June 1919	Cp. Dix, N. J.	
875th Company	do	do	July 1919	Cp. Stuart, Va		Ju'y 1919	Ju'y 1919	Cp. Upton, N. Y.	

UNITED STATES GUARDS

BATTALIONS

Unit designation and redesignation	Organization		Stations in United States		Overseas		Demobilization		Remarks
	Month and year	Place	Month and year	Place	From—	To—	Month and year	Place	
1st Battalion (less Cos. B and C).	February 1918	Plattsburg Bks., N. Y.	May 1918	Jersey City, N. J.			January 1919	Cp. Dix, N. J.	
Company B	January 1918	do	April 1918	Do.					
			July 1918	Brooklyn, N. Y.			do	Do.	
Company C	March 1918	do	April 1918	do			December 1918	Do.	
2d Battalion (less Co. B)	January 1918	Ft. Sam Houston, Tex.	July 1918	Galveston, Tex.			January 1919	Cp. Logan, Tex.	
Company B	do	do	June 1918	Freeport, Tex.			do	Do.	
3d Battalion	May 1918	Boston, Mass.	do	Allston, Mass.			December 1918	Cp. Devens, Mass.	
4th Battalion (Hq. only)	June 1918	Cp. Nicholls, La.	July 1918	New Orleans, La.					
			September 1918	Mobile, Ala.			do	Cp. Beauregard, La.	
Company A	February 1918	do	March 1918	do			do	Do.	
Company B	June 1918	do	October 1918	Baton Rouge, La.			do	Do.	
Company C	do	do	do	Westwego, La.			do	Do.	
Company D	do	do	September 1918	Pensacola, Fla.			do	Do.	
5th Battalion (less Co. A).	May 1918	Ft. Robinson, Nebr.	August 1918	Rock Island Arsenal, Ill.			January 1919	Cp. Funston, Kans.	
Company A	January 1918	Ft. Sheridan, Ill.	January 1918	Ft. Leavenworth, Kans.			do	Do.	
6th Battalion (less Cos. A, B, and C).	do	Presidio of San Francisco, Calif.	September 1918	Ft. Lawton, Wash.			December 1918	Cp. Lewis, Wash.	
Company A	December 1917	do	March 1918	Bremerton, Wash.			do	Do.	
Company B	June 1918	do	September 1918	Seattle, Wash.			do	Do.	
Company C	do	do	do	Tacoma, Wash.			do	Do.	
7th Battalion (less Cos. B and C).	do	Ft. Adams, R. I.	October 1918	Watertown Arsenal, Mass.			do	Cp. Devens, Mass.	
Company B	do	do	do	Groton, Conn.			do	Do.	
Company C	do	do	do	Allston, Mass.			do	Do.	
8th Battalion	do	Springfield, Mass.					do	Do.	

9th Battalion (Hq. only)	May 1918	Ft. Niagara, N. Y.					January 1919	Cp. Dix, N. J.
Company A	do	do	July 1918	Dover, N. J.				
			September 1918	Baltimore, Md.			do	Do.
Company B	do	do	July 1918	Dover, N. J.				
			September 1918	Curtis Bay, Md.			do	Do.
Company C	do	do	August 1918	New York, N. Y.			do	Do.
Company D	do	do	do	do			do	Do.
10th Battalion (less Cos. A, B, and D).	do	do	July 1918	Port Newark, N. J.			do	Do.
Company A	do	do	do	New York, N. Y.				
			October 1918	Cp. Morgan, N. J.				
			November 1918	Metuchen, N. J.			do	Do.
Company B	do	do	July 1918	Kearny Meadows, N. J.			do	Do.
Company D	do	do	do	Newark, N. J.				
			November 1918	Metuchen, N. J.			do	Do.
11th Battalion	June 1918	do	July 1918	do			do	Do.
12th Battalion (less Cos. A, C, and D).	do	do	do	Wilmington, Del.			February 1919	Do.
Company A	do	do	do	Philadelphia, Pa.			January 1919	Do.
Company C	do	do	do	Bristol, Pa.			February 1919	Do.
Company D	do	do	do	Pigeon Point, Del.			do	Do.
13th Battalion (less Cos. A, B, and D).	July 1918	do	October 1918	Chester, Pa.			do	Do.
Company A	do	do	July 1918	Gloucester, N. Y.			January 1919	Do.
Company B	do	do	October 1918	Elizabethport, N. J.			February 1919	Do.
Company D	do	do	July 1918	Cp. Holabird, Md.			do	Do.
14th Battalion	do	do	August 1918	Curtis Bay, Md.			January 1919	Cp. Meade, Md.
15th Battalion (less Cos. B and C).	do	do	September 1918	Sandy Hook, N. J.			do	Cp. Dix, N. J.
Company B	do	do	August 1918	South Amboy, N. J.			do	Do.
Company C	do	do	do	Newburgh, N. Y.			do	Do.
16th Battalion (less Co. D).	do	do	November 1918	Philadelphia, Pa.			do	Do.
Company D	do	do	October 1918	Sellers Point, Md.			do	Do.
17th Battalion (less Cos. A, B, and D).	June 1918	Ft. McPherson, Ga.	July 1918	Charleston, S. C.			do	Cp. Greene, N. C.
Company A	do	do	August 1918	Tampa, Fla.			do	Do.
Company B	do	do	do	Wilmington, N. C.			do	Do.
Company D	do	do	do	Savannah, Ga.			do	Do.

BATTALIONS—Continued

Unit designation and redesignation	Organization		Stations in United States		Overseas		Demobilization		Remarks
	Month and year	Place	Month and year	Place	From—	To—	Month and year	Place	
18th Battalion	July 1918	Ft. Snelling, Minn.	August 1918	Ft. Brady, Mich.			January 1919	Cp. Grant, Ill.	
19th Battalion (less Cos. A and D).	June 1918	Cp. Stanley, Tex.	July 1918	Beaumont, Tex.			February 1919	Cp. Logan, Tex.	
Company A	do	do	do	Orange, Tex.			January 1919	Do.	
Company D	do	do	do	Port Arthur, Tex.			do	Do.	
20th Battalion	May 1918	do	June 1918	Ft. Sam Houston, Tex.			do	Cp. Travis, Tex.	
21st Battalion (less Co. A).	June 1918	do	July 1918	Ft. Bliss, Tex.					
			October 1918	Cp. Cotton, Tex.			do	Do.	
Company A	do	do	July 1918	Ft. Bliss, Tex.					
			August 1918	Marfa, Tex.			do	Do.	
22d Battalion (less Cos. A and C).	do	do	do	Globe, Ariz.			do	Do.	
Company A	do	do	do	Lowell, Ariz.			do	Do.	
Company C	do	do	do	Houston, Tex.			do	Do.	
23d Battalion (less Cos. A, B, and C).	do	Presidio of San Francisco, Calif.	do	Ft. Douglas, Utah					
			September 1918	Ft. Geo. Wright, Wash.			do	Cp. Lewis, Wash.	
Company A	do	do	do	Portland, Oreg.			do	Do.	
Company B	do	do	June 1918	Ft. Douglas, Utah.					
			September 1918	Butte, Montana			do	Do.	
Company C	do	do	August 1918	Ft. D. A. Russell, Wyo.			do	Do.	
24th Battalion	do	do					do	Presidio of San Francisco, Calif.	
25th Battalion (less Co. B).	do	do	August 1918	Cp. Taliaferro, Calif.			do	Cp. Kearny, Calif.	
Company B	do	do	do	Long Beach, Calif.			do	Do.	

26th Battalion (less Cos. A and B).	do	Ft. Crook, Nebr	do	Nitro, W. Va			do	**Cp. Sherman, Ohio.**
Company A	do	do	**September 1918**	**Ft. Riley, Kans**			**do**	**Do.**
Company B	do	do	**August 1918**	**Point Pleasant, W. Va.**			**do**	**Do.**
27th Battalion (Hq. only).	**do**	Ft. Ethan Allen, Vt.	September 1918	Watertown Arsenal, Mass.				
			October 1918	Ft. Preble, Me			**December 1918**	Cp. Devens, Mass.
Company A	do	do	September 1918	Bath, Me			do	Do.
Company B	July 1918	do	do	**East Deering, Me**			do	Do.
Company C	do	do	**do**	**Portsmouth, N. H**			do	Do.
Company D	do	do	do	**Watertown Arsenal Mass.**				
			October 1918	Portland, Me			do	Do.
28th Battalion (less Cos. B and C).	do	Ft. McPherson, Ga.					**January 1919**	Cp. Gordon, Ga.
Company B	do	do	**September 1918**	**Jacksonville, Fla**			do	Do.
Company C	do	do	**August 1918**	**Brunswick, Ga**			**do**	Do.
29th Battalion	do	Ft. Snelling, Minn	do	**Chicago, Ill**			do	Cp. Grant, Ill.
30th Battalion (less Cos. B, C and D).	do	Ft. Wm. H. Seward, Alaska.					**June 1919**	Cp. Lewis, Wash.
Company B	do	Ft. Liscum, Alaska					**August 1919**	Do.
Company C	do	Ft. St. Michael, Alaska.					**September 1919**	**Ft. St. Michael, Alaska.**
Company D	do	Ft. Gibbons, Alaska.					November 1919	Presidio of San Francisco, Calif.
31st Battalion	August 1918	Ft. Ethan Allen, Vt.					December 1918	Cp. Devens, Mass.
32d Battalion	do	Ft. Niagara, N. Y					January 1919	Cp. Dix, N. J.
33d Battalion	September 1918	do					**do**	Do.
34th Battalion (less Co. C).	do	do					**do**	Do.
Company C	do	do					**October 1918**	Ft. Niagara, N. Y.
35th Battalion (less Co. C).	August 1918	New Orleans, La					**December 1918**	Cp. Beauregard, La.
Company C	do	do	September 1918	Little Rock, Ark			do	Do.
36th Battalion	do	Ft. Sheridan, Ill					**February 1919**	Cp. Grant, Ill.
37th Battalion (less Co. A).	do	Presidio of San Francisco, Calif.					**January 1919**	Presidio of San Francisco, Calif.
Company A	do	do	September 1918	Astoria, Oreg			do	Do.

BATTALIONS—Continued

Unit designation and redesignation	Organization		Stations in United States		Overseas		Demobilization		Remarks
	Month and year	Place	Month and year	Place	From—	To—	Month and year	Place	
38th Battalion	August 1918	Presidio of San Francisco, Calif.					December 1918	Presidio of San Francisco, Calif.	
39th Battalion	do	Ft. Sam Houston, Tex.					do	Cp. Travis, Tex.	
40th Battalion	do	Ft. Bliss, Tex					do	Ft. Bliss, Tex.	
41st Battalion	September 1918	Cp. Greene, N. C					January 1919	Cp. Greene, N. C.	
42d Battalion	do	Cp. Shelby, Miss	November 1918	Waco, Ga			do	Cp. Gordon, Ga.	
43d Battalion	do	Presidio of San Francisco, Calif.					do	Cp. Fremont, Calif.	
44th Battalion	do	Cp. Taliaferro, Calif.					December 1918	Ft. Douglas, Utah	
45th Battalion (less Co. C).	do	Ft. Niagara, N. Y	November 1918	Hampton, Va			January 1919	Cp. Dix, N. J.	
Company C	do	do	do	Sparrows Point, Md.			do	Do.	
46th Battalion	October 1918	Ft. Riley Kans					December 1918	Cp. Funston, Kans	
47th Battalion (less Co. A).	do	Ft. Niagara, N. Y					January 1919	Cp. Dix, N. J.	
Company A	do	do	October 1918	Bayonne, N. J			do	Do.	
48th Battalion	November 1918	do	November 1918	Cp. Morgan, N. J			do	Do.	

VETERINARY CORPS

VETERINARY HOSPITALS

Unit designation and redesignation	Organization		Stations in United States		Overseas		Demobilization		Remarks
	Month and year	Place	Month and year	Place	From—	To—	Month and year	Place	
Veterinary Hospital No. 1.	February 1918	Cp. Devens, Mass.	April 1918	P. of E., Hoboken.	April 1918	June 1919	June 1919	Cp. Devens, Mass.	S.O.S. troops.
Veterinary Hospital No. 2.	January 1918	Cp. Upton, N. Y.	March 1918	do	March 1918		October 1918	A. E. F	Do.
1. Advance Veterinary Hospital, No. 2-A.	October 1918	A. E. F				June 1919	June 1919	Cp. Upton, N. Y.	Orgzd. fr. Co. A, Vet. Hosp. No. 2.
2. Advance Veterinary Hospital, No. 2-B.	do	do				do	do	do	Orgzd. fr. Co. B, Vet. Hosp. No. 2.
Veterinary Hospital No. 3.	January 1918	Cp. Lee, Va	May 1918	P. of E., Newport News.	May 1918	do	do	Cp. Lee, Va	S.O.S. troops.
Veterinary Hospital No. 4.	do	do	April 1918 do	Cp. Hill, Va. P. of E., Newport News.	April 1918	do	do	Cp. Upton, N. Y.	Do.
Veterinary Hospital No. 5.	do	do	do May 1918	Cp. Hill, Va. P. of E., Newport News.	May 1918	do	do	Cp. Lee, Va	Do.
Veterinary Hospital No. 6.	February 1918	Cp. Upton, N. Y.	March 1918	P. of E., Hoboken.	March 1918	do	do	Cp. Upton, N. Y.	Do.
Veterinary Hospital No. 7.	June 1918	Cp. Lee, Va	July 1918	P. of E., Newport News.	July 1918	do	do	Cp. Stuart, Va.	Do.
Veterinary Hospital No. 8.	do	do	do	do	do	do	do	Cp. Upton, N. Y.	Do.
Veterinary Hospital No. 9.	do	do	do June 1919	Do. Cp. Jackson, S. C.		do	July 1919	Cp. Grant, Ill	Do.
Veterinary Hospital No. 10.	do	do	July 1918 June 1919	P. of E., Newport News. Cp. Morrison, Va.	July 1918.	do	June 1919	do	Do.

VETERINARY HOSPITALS—Continued

Unit designation and redesignation	Organization		Stations in United States		Overseas		Demobilization		Remarks
	Month and year	Place	Month and year	Place	From—	To—	Month and year	Place	
Veterinary Hospital No. 11.	June 1918	Cp. Lee, Va.	July 1918	P. of E., Newport News.	July 1918	June 1919	June 1919	Cp. Devens, Mass.	S.O.S. troops.
Veterinary Hospital No. 12.	August 1918	do	October 1918	do	October 1918	July 1919	July 1919	Cp. Grant, Ill.	Do.
Veterinary Hospital No. 13.	do	do	do	Cp. Upton, N. Y.					
			do	P. of E., Hoboken.	November 1918	June 1919	do	Cp. Dix, N. J.	Do.
Veterinary Hospital No. 14.	do	do	do	P. of E., Newport News.	October 1918	do	do	Cp. Grant, Ill.	Do.
Veterinary Hospital No. 15.	do	do	do	do	Do.				
			July 1919	Cp. Merritt, N. J.		July 1919	do	Cp. Pike, Ark.	Do.
Veterinary Hospital No. 16.	do	do	October 1918	Cp. Upton, N. Y.					
			do	P. of E., Hoboken.	October 1918	June 1919	June 1919	Cp. Dix, N. J.	Do.
Veterinary Hospital No. 17.	September 1918	do	do	P. of E., Newport News.	do	July 1919	July 1919	Cp. Devens, Mass.	Do.
Veterinary Hospital No. 18.	do	do	do	Cp. Mills, N. Y.					
			November 1918	P. of E., Hoboken.	November 1918	do	do	Cp. Dodge, Iowa	Do.
Veterinary Hospital No. 19.	do	do	October 1918	P. of E., Newport News.	October 1918	June 1919	June 1919	Cp. Lee, Va.	Do.
Veterinary Hospital No. 20.	do	do	do	do	do	do	do	do	Do.
Veterinary Hospital No. 21.	do	do	do	do	do	do	July 1919	Cp. Gordon, Ga.	Do.
Veterinary Hospital No. 22.	November 1918	do					January 1919	Cp. Lee, Va.	
Veterinary Hospital No. 23.	do	do					do	Do.	
Veterinary Hospital No. 24.	December 1918	do					do	Do.	
Veterinary Hospital No. 25.	November 1918	do					February 1919	Do.	

V. C. SPECIAL AND TECHNICAL UNITS

Units	Unit No.	Active service	Unit No.	Active service	Unit No.	Active service	Unit No.	Active service	Unit No.	Active service	Remarks
Army Mobile Veterinary Hospital.	1	June 1918–September 1919	[a] 1–B	September 1918–December 1918	2	November 1918–December 1918					a Orgzd. in U. S.; demobilized overseas.
Base Veterinary Hospital.	[b] 1	January 1918–June 1919	[b] 2	August 1918–July 1919	3	November 1918–January 1919					b S.O.S. troops.
Corps Mobile Veterinary Hospital.	1	February 1918–September 1919	2	June 1918–July 1919	3	August 1918–December 1918	4	July 1918–December 1918	5	November 1918–December 1918	
	[c] 6	Never orgzd.	7	November 1918–August 1919	8	November 1918–June 1919	9	November 1918–July 1919	[c] IV Corps	September 1918–June 1919	c Orgzd. overseas; demobilized in U. S.
Mobile Veterinary Section.	1	May 1918 through December 1919	2	January 1918 through December 1919	3	March 1918 through December 1919	4	March 1918–August 1919	5	March 1918–August 1919	d Redes. Sec. 15–3 August 1918.
	6	July 1918–July 1919	7	April 1918 through December 1919	8	March 1918–February 1919	9	September 1918–February 1919	10	August 1918–February 1919	
	[d] 11	See Sec. 15–3	12	August 1918–January 1919	13	May 1918–February 1919	14	August 1918–February 1919	15–1	August 1918–March 1919	
	15–2	March 1918–March 1919	15–3	March 1918–March 1919	16	October 1918–February 1919	17	October 1918–February 1919	18	October 1918–January 1919	
	19	October 1918–February 1919	20	October 1918–January 1919	21–100	Never orgzd.	101	January 1918–June 1919	102	February 1918–June 1919	
	103	March 1918–June 1919	104	June 1918–May 1919	105	April 1918–February 1919	106	March 1918–February 1919	107	March 1918–May 1919	
	[c] 108	March 1918–February 1919	109	December 1917–June 1919	110	December 1917–May 1919	111	December 1917–November 1918	112	March 1918–June 1919	
	113	May 1918–June 1919	114	February 1918–January 1919	115	January 1918–November 1918	116	February 1918–June 1919	117	December 1917–May 1919	
	118–300	Never orgzd.	301	April 1918–June 1919	302	January 1918–May 1919	303	March 1918–June 1919	304	April 1918–May 1919	
	305	March 1918–June 1919	306	do	307	February 1918–May 1919	308	January 1918–October 1919	309	October 1918–November 1918	

V. C. SPECIAL AND TECHNICAL UNITS—Continued

Units	Unit No.	Active service	Unit No.	Active service	Unit No.	Active service	Unit No.	Active service	Unit No.	Active service	Remarks
Mobile Veterinary Section—Con.	310	January 1918–February 1919	311	June 1918–June 1919	312	December 1917–June 1919	313	February 1918–June 1919	314	February 1918–June 1919	c Orgzd. overseas; demobilized in U. S.
	315	May 1918–June 1919	316	February 1918–May 1919	317	April 1918–March 1919					
Veterinary Evacuation Section.	c 1	December 1918–September 1919	c 2	November 1918–August 1919	c 3	December 1918–August 1919	4–6	Never orgzd.	c 7	November 1918–June 1919	
	c 8	November 1918–June 1919									

ABBREVIATIONS

A.A.	Antiaircraft
A.A.A.	Antiaircraft Artillery
A.A.F.	Army Air Forces
Adm.	Administrative
Adv. Vet. Hosp.	Advance Veterinary Hospital
A.E.F.	American Expeditionary Forces
Aer. Sq.	Aero Squadron
A.G.D.	Adjutant General's Department
Am.	Ammunition
Amb.	Ambulance
A.P.C.	Air Production Center
A.R.D.	Automatic Replacement Draft
Arty.	Artillery
A.S.	Air Service
A.S.C.	Army Service Corps
A.S.P.	Air Service, Aircraft Production
A.S. Sig. C.	Aviation Section, Signal Corps
A.S. Sig. O.R.C.	Aviation Section Signal Organized Reserve Corps
Asst.	Assistant
Aux. Hosp.	Auxiliary Hospital
Aux. Rmt. Dep.	Auxiliary Remount Depot
Avn.	Aviation
Avn. Sch. Sq.	Aviation School Squadron
Bkrs. & Cks. Sch.	Bakers and Cooks School
Bkry. Co.	Bakery Company
Bks.	Barracks
Bln.	Balloon
Bn.	Battalion
Brig.	Brigade
Btry.	Battery
Bul.	Bulletin
Butch. Co.	Butchery Company
Bvt.	Brevet
C.	Chart
C.A.	Coast Artillery
C.A.C.	Coast Artillery Corps
Carto. R. Div.	Cartographic Records Division
Cav.	Cavalry
C.D.	Coast Defense(s)
C.D.C.	Coast Defense Command
C. Dept.	Central Department
Ck.	Cook
Cmpnt.	Component
cm.	Centimeter
Co.	Company
Cons.	Construction
Corresp.	Correspondence
Cp. Hosp.	Camp Hospital
C.W.S.	Chemical Warfare Service
C.Z.	Canal Zone
Demblzd.	Demobilized
Dep.	Depot
Dept.	Department
Det.	Detachment
Devlpt.	Development
DHQ.	Division Headquarters
Div.	Division
D.M.A.	Department of Military Aeronautics
D.W.	Deadweight
E. Dept.	Eastern Department
E.M.	Enlisted Men

Engr.	Engineer
E.N.Y.	Eastern New York
Evac. Hosp.	Evacuation Hospital
F.A.	Field Artillery
F. Hosp.	Field Hospital
F. Trk. & H. Co.	Fire Truck and Hose Company
Flng. Sch. Det.	Flying School Detachment
fr.	from
F. Rmt. Sq.	Field Remount Squadron
F. Sig. Bn.	Field Signal Battalion
F.W.D.	Four-Wheel Drive
Gen.	General
Gp.	Group
G.P.F.	High Power (grande puissance) Filloux Rifle
G.S.	General Staff
G.S.O.D.	General Supply Ordnance Depot
H. Dept.	Hawaiian Department
Hist. Sec., A.W.C.	Historical Section, Army War College
Hq.	Headquarters
H.R.	House of Representatives
Hv.	Heavy
Hv. Mob. Ord. Rep. Sh.	Heavy Mobile Ordnance Repair Shop
H.T.A.	Heavier-than-air
Inf.	Infantry
L.	Light
L. Mob. Ord. Rep. Sh.	Light Mobile Ordnance Repair Shop
L.T.A.	Lighter-than-air
M.	Map
Mblzd.	Mobilized
M. Comd.	Motor Command
Mec.	Mechanic (al)
Med.	Medical
M. G. Bn.	Machine Gun Battalion
mm.	Millimeter
M.P.	Military Police
M.R.S.U.	Mechanical Repair Shop Unit
M. Sh. Trk. U.	Machine Shop Truck Unit
M. Sup. Tn.	Motor Supply Train
M.T.C.	Motor Transport Corps
Mtcl. Co.	Motorcycle Company
M. T. Co.	Motor Transport Company
Mtd.	Mounted
Mtn.	Mountain
M. Trk. Co.	Motor Truck Company
N.A.	National Army
Nat. Arch.	National Archives
N.E. Dept.	Northeastern Department
N.G.	National Guard
N. W. C. Libr.	National War College Library
O., Off.	Officer
Obsn.	Observation
O.R.C.	Officers' Reserve Corps
Ord.	Ordnance
Orgzd.	Organized
p. (pp.)	Page(s)
P. C. Dept.	Panama Canal Department
P. D. C. A. Trs.	Provisional Depot, Corps, and Army Troops
P. Dept.	Philippine Department

P.I.	Philippine Islands
Pion. Inf.	Pioneer Infantry
P.N.G.	Philippine National Guard
Pnl.	Personnel
P. of E.	Port of Embarkation
P.R.	Puerto Rico
Prov.	Provisional
Provost Gd. Co.	Provost Guard Company
P.S.	Philippine Scouts
P. S. & T.	Purchase, Storage, and Traffic
Pur.	Pursuit
QMC	Quartermaster Corps
Rec. Ref.	Record Reference
Redes.	Redesignated
Regt.	Regiment
Reorgzd.	Reorganized
Repl. U.	Replacement Unit
Rep. U.	Repair Unit
Res.	Reserve
R. Gp.	Records Group
Salv.	Salvage
S.A.T.C.	Student Army Training Corps
S. Dept.	Southern Department
Sec.	Section
S.E. Dept.	Southeastern Department
Sep.	Separate
Serv.	Service
Sig. C.	Signal Corps
Sig. Serv. Co.	Signal Service Company
Sn.	Sanitary
S.N.Y.	Southern New York
Sq.	Squadron
Stat. Br.	Statistics Branch
Stev.	Stevedore
Sup.	Supply
T. Co.	Transportation Company
Tg.	Telegraph
T.H.	Territory of Hawaii
Tk.	Tank
T.M.	Trench Mortar
Tn.	Train
Tr.	Troop
Transp.	Transportation
U.	Unit
Univ.	University
U.S.A.	United States Army
U. S. Gd.	United States Guards
U.S.M.C.	United States Marine Corps
Util.	Utilities
Wag. Co.	Wagon Company
Water Tk. Tn.	Water-Tank Train
W.D.	War Department
W. Dept.	Western Department
W.P.D.	War Plans Division
W.R.O., Nat. Arch.	War Records Office, National Archives
W.W. I Gp., Hist. Div., S.S. U.S.A.	World War I Group, Historical Division, Special Staff United States Army

LIST OF SOURCE MATERIAL

(Numbers on right margin represent designation of sources as referred to in manuscript; the latter is on file in Historical Division, Special Staff, United States Army, The Pentagon, Washington 25, D. C.)

Source No.

AIR SERVICE:

Aircraft Inquiry, report of—by Charles E. Hughes, October 28, 1918 (N.W.C. Libr.) 162

Air Service, summary of work of—to July 20, 1918; special reports (W.R.O., Nat. Arch., rec. ref. Hist. 319.1, folder 23) 188

Air Service Stations, report of activities at—according to supervisory districts, November 18, 1918 (A.A.F. Rec. Sec., 703 Columbia Pike, rec. ref. 323.6) 257

Air Service Stations, directory of—April 19, 1919; July 10, 1919; October 10, 1919 (W.R.O., Nat. Arch. rec. ref. 323.7, box 491) 253

Bureau of Aircraft Production, report of—May 24, 1917, to June 30, 1918 (N.W.C. Libr.) 164

Idem, information folder of (W.W.I. Gp. Hist. Div., S.S.U.S.A.). 164½

Director of Air Service, annual report of the—July 1, 1918, to June 30, 1919 (N.W.C. Libr.) 165

Industrial Demobilization (W.R.O., Nat. Arch. rec. ref. 7-12.7) 168½

Signal Corps and Air Service, the—monograph No. 16, Hist. Sec. A.W.C. (N.W.C. Libr.) 168

Spruce Division, U.S. Army, history of the—by Brig. Gen. Brice P. Disque (N.W.C. Libr.) 167

Spruce Production Division, report of the (W.R.O., Nat. Arch., rec. ref. 166-11.4) 188½

Supply Section, Division of Military Aeronautics, history of the—to April 5, 1918 (N.W.C. Libr.) 166

ADJUTANT GENERAL'S DEPARTMENT:

Adjutant General's Department, a brief history of the—by Maj. Livingston Watrous (N.W.C. Libr.) 176

Adjutant General's Office, information folder of—containing extracts from official documents (W.W. I Gp., Hist. Div., S.S. U.S.A.) 177

Central Officers' Training Schools, memorandum of information on (W.W. I Gp., Hist. Div. S.S.U.S.A.) 241

Central Officers' Training Schools, final reports of (W.R.O., Nat. Arch., rec. ref. A.G. 354.102—1919). 254

Line Officers' Training Schools and Camps, report on—by Col. Henry Cabell (W.R.O., Nat. Arch., rec. ref. 7—52.8). 246

Officers' Training Camps and Schools, miscellaneous data on (W.R.O., Nat. Arch., rec. ref. A.G. 354.1—1918). 255

Officers' Training Camps, third series of (W.R.O., Nat. Arch., rec. ref. A.G. 354.1). 252

ARMY WAR COLLEGE:

Historical Section, history of (W.W. I Gp., Hist. Div., corresp. file 3336). 103

CHEMICAL WARFARE SERVICE:

Annual Report, extracts from—September 26, 1918; folder (W.W. I Gp. Hist. Div., S.S.U.S.A.). 316

Industrial Demobilization of the Chemical Warfare Service (W.R.O., Nat. Arch., rec. ref. 154—17, A.G.O.). 172

CHIEF OF COAST ARTILLERY:

Coast Artillery Units in France and in the United States, at date of armistice; prepared in office of C. of C.A.C. (W.R.O., Nat. Arch.). 194

Coast Artillery Districts, including command lists, coast defenses, posts, and other data; information folder of (W.W. I Gp. Hist. Div., S.S.U.S.A.). 428

CHIEF OF FIELD ARTILLERY:

Field Artillery Organization and Activities During World War I, summary of—prepared by C. of F.A. (W.R.O., Nat. Arch., rec. ref. 7-60.11; 7-60.534; 7-53.4). 314C

Source No.

Sign Posts of Experience, World War memoirs of Maj. Gen. Snow, 1941 (N.W.C. Libr.). ---------- 201

CONSTRUCTION DIVISION:

History of the Construction Division (W.R.O., Nat. Arch., rec. ref. 306.1 Hist. Br.). ---------- 114

Project Map, showing locations of camps, army posts, coast defenses, quartermaster and ordnance depots, hospitals, aviation fields, etc., as of April 1, 1919 (Cartogr. R. Div., R. Gp. 77, Nat. Arch.). ---------- 329

CORPS OF ENGINEERS:

America's Demobilization, Engineers (W.R.O., Nat. Arch., rec. ref. 154.13, 7—42.12). ---------- 148E

Chief of Engineers, American Expeditionary Forces, historical report of the—1917 to 1919 (N.W.C. Libr., W.D. Doc. 907). ---------- 171

Chief of Engineers, annual reports of the—for 1917, 1918, 1919, 1920; part of W.D. annual reports (N.W.C. Libr.). ---------- 149, 150, 151, 151½, 155

Chief of Engineers, history of the office of—September 10, 1919 (Engr. Libr., Ft. Belvoir, Va., rec. ref. 218-2). ---------- 148

Chief of Engineers, office of—organization chart of April 1918 (W.R.O., Nat. Arch.). ---------- 146

Director General of Military Railways, history of the office of the —with appendixes (W.R.O., Nat. Arch., rec. ref. 190.1, A.G.O.). ---------- 156

Engineer Depots and Ports of Embarkation, general data on—1919, vols. I, II, IV, V, by Captain Kingdon (Engr. Libr., Ft. Belvoir, Va.). ---------- 148B

Engineer Motor Transport Service, history of the—by Captain Howard J. Cole (Engr. Libr., Ft. Belvoir, Va.). ---------- 148D

Engineers in the War of 1917-19, the (W.R.O., Nat. Arch., rec. ref. 218, A.G.O.). ---------- 154

Engineer Officers, on active duty 1917-18 (W.R.O., Nat. Arch.). ---------- 153

General Engineer Depot, historical data of Depot Department (Engr. Libr., Ft. Belvoir, Va.). ---------- 157

General Engineer Depot, history of the—1917 to 1919, vols. I and II (Engr. Libr., Ft. Belvoir, Va., rec. ref. 314). ---------- 148A

Official Bulletins, covering expansion of Corps of Engineers, 1917 to 1918 (W.R.O., Nat. Arch.). ---------- 152

Supply System of the Corps of Engineers, organization and operation of the—July 15, 1918 (W.R.O., Nat. Arch.). ---------- 147

Twentieth Engineers (Forestry), reorganization of the—by Captain Arno Kolbe (Engr. Libr., Ft. Belvoir, Va.). ---------- 148C

DIRECTORY OF TROOPS:

Depot Brigades, command lists of—51st to 64th, and 151st to 166th Brigs. (W.W. I Gp., Hist. Div., S.S.U.S.A., rec. ref. book 13). ---------- 313

Organization Directory, showing stations and post office addresses of organizations of the Army, January 11 to November 22, 1919; compiled in Adjutant General's Office (N.W.C. Libr.). ---------- 186

Organizations in the Army, numerical designations of—special report September 15, 1918, Statist. Br., G.S. (W.R.O., Nat. Arch., rec. ref. 107-D). ---------- 197

Organizations which composed the Regular Army during the World War (1917-18), list of (W.R.O., Nat. Arch., rec. ref. 1294). ---------- 198

Returns and Rosters, World War I (W.R.O., Nat. Arch.). ---------- 247A

Returns and Rosters, World War I, index to—(W.R.O., Nat. Arch.). ---------- 247

Unit History Cards, World War I, form 491, A.G.O. (W.R.O., Nat. Arch.). ---------- 161

JUDGE ADVOCATE GENERAL'S DEPARTMENT:

Information Folder, containing extracts from official documents (W.W. I Gp., Hist. Div., S.S.U.S.A.). ---------- 180

MEDICAL DEPARTMENT:

Demobilization, medical history of (W.R.O., Nat. Arch., rec. ref. 7-12.7). ---------- 144

Source No.

Economic Agencies, handbook of—Surgeon General, manuscript (W.R.O., Nat. Arch.). 145
Medical Department of the United States Army in World War, the —prepared under the direction of Maj. Gen. M. W. Ireland, M.D., Surgeon General of the Army, volume V (N.W.C. Libr.). 123
Idem—volumes I, II, III, IV, VI, VII, VIII, IX, X, XI, XII, XIII, XIV, XV (N.W.C. Libr.) 142
Report of Surgeon General for 1919, part of W.D. annual reports, Vol. 1, parts 2 and 3 (N.W.C. Libr.). 143

MILITIA BUREAU:
National Guard Divisions, composition of (W.R.O., Nat. Arch., rec. ref. misc. 320). 199
National Guard Units, former, disposition of (W.R.O., Nat. Arch., rec. ref. misc. 320). 199

MISCELLANEOUS:
American Expeditionary Forces, general orders and bulletins of G.H.Q. (W.W. I Group, Hist. Div., S.S.U.S.A.). 190
Congressional Directories, sixty-fifth and sixty-sixth Congresses, 1917-20 (N.W.C. Libr.). 99
Control of Industry in the United States during the World War, agencies for the—extracts from hearings, Committee on Military Affairs, March 11, 13, and 20, 1924, H. R. (N.W.C. libr.). 95
Demobilization of Manpower in the United States, 1918-19, monograph by Col. Henry Hossfeld and Capt. Charles H. Collins, 1942 (W.W. I Gp., Hist. Div., S.S.U.S.A.). 159
Federal World War Agencies and their Records, handbook of—1917 to 1921. The National Archives, 1943 (N.W.C. Libr.). 158
How America Went to War: The Giant Hand, the Road to France, the Armies of Industry, Demobilization; by Benj. F. Crowell and Robert F. Wilson, 1921 (N.W.C. Libr.). 160, 160A, 160B, 160C, 160D, 140
National Defense Act, the—approved June 3, 1916, as amended to include March 4, 1927; with related acts, decisions, and opinions (N.W.C. Libr.). 23, 191
Services of Supply, some accomplishments of the—by Statistics Branch, General Staff, Hq. S.O.S., A.E.F.; revised to May 1, 1919, by Col. W. E. Haseltine, Engr. Res. (W.W. I Gp., Hist. Div., S.S.U.S.A.). 175
Universal Mobilization for War Purposes, hearings, sixty-eighth Congress, First Session, 1924-25, House Committee on Military Affairs (N.W.C. Libr.). 97

ORDNANCE DEPARTMENT:
Chief of Ordnance, office of the—office memorandums, series 1917 to 1919 (W.R.O., Nat. Arch.). 139½
Idem—office orders (W.R.O., Nat. Arch.). 130
Idem—office orders No. 104 and organization chart of January 14, 1918 (W.R.O., Nat. Arch.). 137
Idem—outline of organization, February and August 1918 (W.R.O., Nat. Arch.). 133
Field Establishments, directory of (W.R.O., Nat. Arch.). 136
Handbook Material 1917-18, organization (W.R.O., Nat. Arch.) 131
Handbook Material 1918, organization (W.R.O., Nat. Arch.). 132
Industrial Demobilization of the Ordnance Department, volumes 1 and 2 (W.R.O., Nat. Arch.). 135A, B, C
Organization and Functional Charts of the Ordnance Department (Libr. C. of Ord., chart file UF 23, X019). 138
Organization Chart of August 10, 1918 (W.R.O., Nat. Arch.). 129
Organization Records (W.R.O., Nat. Arch.). 139
Outline of Organization, April 6, 1917, to November 11, 1918 (W.R.O., Nat. Arch.). 133½

POSTS, CAMPS, AND STATIONS:
Army Posts and Towns, by Charles J. Sullivan (N.W.C. Libr.). 245
Army Posts, Camps, Cantonments, Depots, etc. in the United States, November 15, 1918 (N.W.C. Libr., rec. ref. doc. 871). 229
Army Station List for the United States, November 11, 1918 (W.R.O., Nat. Arch., rec. ref. Stat. Br., G.S., report No. 129). 256

Source No.

Camps, command lists of—1917 to 1919, Camp Alexander to Camp Funston (W.W. I Gp., Hist. Div., S.S.U.S.A., rec. ref. book 1). 301
Idem—1917 to 1919, Camp Gordon to Camp Lewis (W.W. I Gp., Hist. Div., S.S.U.S.A., rec. ref. book 2). 302
Idem—1917 to 1919, Camp Logan to Camp Wheeler (W.W. I Gp., Hist. Div., S.S.U.S.A., rec. ref. book 3). 303
Camp Alexander, Va., information folder of[1] 346B
Camp Bartlett, Westfield, Mass., information folder of[1] 409
Camp Beauregard, La., information folder of[1] 331
Camp Benning, Ga., information folder of[1] 400
Camp Bowie, Tex., information folder of[1] 332
Camp Bragg, N. C., information folder of[1] 363
Camp Cody, N. Mex., information folder of[1] 333
Camp Colt, Pa., information folder of[1] 378
Camp Crane, Pa., information folder of[1] 371
Camp Custer, Mich., information folder of[1] 347
Camp Del Rio, Tex., information folder of [1] 393
Camp Devens, Mass., information folder of[1] 348
Camp Dix, N. J., information folder of[1] 350
Camp Dodge, Iowa, information folder of[1] 349
Camp Doniphan, Okla., information folder of[1] 334
Camp Eustis, Abraham, Va., information folder of[1] 380
Camp Forrest, Ga., information folder of[1] 369
Camp Fremont, Calif., information folder of[1] 335
Camp Funston, Kans., information folder of[1] 351
Camp Gaillard, C.Z., information folder of[1] 408
Camp Glenburnie, Md., information folder of[1] 388
Camp Gordon, Ga., information folder of[1] 352
Camp Grant, Ill., information folder of[1] 353
Camp Greene, N. C., information folder of[1] 336
Camp Greenleaf, Ga., information folder of[1] 372
Camp Hancock, Ga., information folder of[1] 337
Camp Hill, Va., information folder of[1] 365
Camp Holabird, Md., information folder of[1] 373
Camp Humphreys, A.A., Va., information folder of[1] 370
Camp Jackson, S. C., information folder of[1] 354
Camp Jesup, Ga., information folder of[1] 374
Camp Johnston, Joseph E., Fla., information folder of[1] 376
Idem—completion report (W.R.O., Nat. Arch., rec. ref. Hist. 306.1) 193
Camp Jones, Harry J., Douglas, Ariz., information folder of[1] 394
Camp Kearny, Calif., information folder of[1] 338
Camp Kendrick, N. J., information folder of[1] 411
Camp Knox, Ky., information folder of[1] 364
Camp Las Casas, P.R., information folder of[1] 404
Camp Laurel, Md., information folder of[1] 387
Camp Leach, D. C., information folder of[1] 402
Camp Lee, Va., information folder of[1] 355
Camp Lewis, Wash., information folder of[1] 356
Camp Logan, Tex., information folder of[1] 339
Camp MacArthur, Tex., information folder of[1] 340
Camp McClellan, Ala., information folder of[1] 341
Camp Meade, Md., information folder of[1] 357
Camp Meigs, D. C., information folder of[1] 376A
Camp Merritt, N. J., annual report of commanding general of—to commanding general, Port of Embarkation, Hoboken, N. J., from establishment to July 31, 1918 (W.R.O., Nat. Arch.). 359
Idem—To commanding general, Port of Embarkation, Hoboken, N. J., for fiscal year 1919 (W.R.O., Nat. Arch.). 260
Camp Merritt, N. J., information folder of[1] 366
Camp Mills, Albert L., N. Y., information folder of[1] 367
Camp Morrison, Va., information folder of[1] 401
Camp Normoyle, Tex., information folder of[1] 375
Camp Pike, Ark., information folder of[1] 358
Camp Polk, N. C., information folder of[1] 379

[1] (W.W. I Gp. Hist. Div., S.S.U.S.A.)

[1] (W.W.IGp. Hist. Div., S.S. U.S.A.)

Source No.

Source No.

Command Lists, 1917 to 1919, of 94th, 95th, 96th, 97th, 98th, 99th, 100th, 101st, 102d Divs.; 15th Cav. Div.; 1st Phil. Div. (W.W. I Gp. Hist. Div., S.S.U.S.A., rec. ref. book 5). ______ 305

Returns and Rosters, World War I (W.R.O., Nat. Arch.). ______ 247A

TANK CORPS:

Tank Corps, creation of the (W.R.O., Nat. Arch., rec. ref. 10226-A27; 15,698-1). ______ 192B

Tank Corps, report on the (W.R.O., Nat. Arch.). ______ 96

Tank Corps, information folder of—containing extracts from documents on file in N.W.C. Libr. (W.W. I Gp., Hist. Div., S.S.-U.S.A.). ______ 174

Tank Corps Organization, November 24, 1917, and March 6, 1918 (W.R.O., Nat. Arch., rec. ref. 7-61.13). ______ 192D

Tank Corps Units, organized in the United States, as of November 30, 1918 (W.R.O., Nat. Arch., rec. ref. 7-61.13). ______ 192C

Tanks, Armored Automobiles, and Cars (W.R.O., Nat. Arch., rec. ref. G.S. No. 8479, 1-91). ______ 192, 192A

TERRITORIAL DEPARTMENTS:

Annual Reports, extracts from—folder containing information regarding all nine departments for period 1917 to 1919 (W.W. I Gp., Hist. Div., S.S.U.S.A.). ______ 330

Border Patrol Districts, command lists of—1917 to 1919 (W.W. I Gp., Hist. Div., S.S.U.S.A., rec. ref. book 10). ______ 310

Border Patrol Districts, information folder of—containing extracts from official documents (W.W. I Gp., Hist. Div., S.S.U.S.A.). 206

Central Department, annual reports of—for the fiscal years 1917, 1918, 1919, 1920 (W.D. Rec. Br., A.G.O., Staff Rec. Sec. No. 1, 703 Columbia Pike, Rec. Ref. A.G. 319.12). ______ 219

Central Department, command list and National Guard data of—prepared in Hist. Sec., A.W.C. (W.W. I Gp., Hist. Div., S.S.U.S.A.). ______ 232

Central Department, monthly returns of—for period 1917 to 1919 (W.R.O., Nat. Arch.). ______ 250A

Central Department, station list of—folder forming part of study on Military Activities in the U.S. During World War I, by Lt. Col. Marcel F. J. Brunow, A.G.D. (W.W. I Gp., Hist. Div., S.S.U.S.A.). ______ 231

Central Department, troop list of—prepared in Hist Sec., A.W.C. (W.W. I Gp., Hist. Div., S.S.U.S.A.). ______ 233

Coast Artillery Districts, command lists of—for period 1917 to 1919 (W.W. I Gp., Hist. Div., S.S.U.S.A., rec. ref. book 11). __ 311

Colleges in Wartime and After, the—by Parke Rexford Kolbe (N.W.C. Libr.). ______ 244

Eastern Department, annual reports of—for the fiscal years 1917, 1918, 1920 (W.D. Rec. Br., A.G.O., Staff Rec. Sec. No. 1, 703 Columbia Pike, rec. ref. A.G. 319.12). ______ 220

Eastern Department, command list and National Guard data of—prepared in Hist. Sec., A.W.C. (W.W. I Gp., Hist. Div., S.S.U.S.A.). ______ 225A

Eastern Department, monthly returns of—for period 1917 to 1919 (W.R.O., Nat. Arch.). ______ 226

Eastern Department, station list of—folder forming part of Study on Military Activities in the U.S. during World War I, by Lt. Col. Marcel F. J. Brunow, A.G.D. (W.W. I Gp., Hist. Div., S.S.U.S.A.). ______ 225

Educational Institutions imparting military training, Reserve Officers' Training Corps units at—information folder containing extracts from official documents (W.W. I Gp., Hist. Div., S.S.U.S.A.). ______ 208-I

Educational Institutions imparting military training, training detachments and Students' Army Training Corps units at—information folder containing extracts from official documents (W.W. I Gp., Hist. Div., S.S.U.S.A.). ______ 208-II

Hawaiian Department, annual reports of—for the fiscal years 1917, 1918, 1919, 1920 (W.D. Rec. Br., A.G.O., Staff Rec. Sec. No 1, 703 Columbia Pike, rec. ref. A.G. 319.12). ______ 222

Source No.

Southern Department, station list of—folder forming part of Study on Military Activities in the U. S. during World War I, by Lt. Col. Marcel F. J. Brunow, A.G.D. (W.W. I Gp., Hist. Div., S.S.U.S.A.). 209
Southern Department, troops in—as of Apr. 30, 1917 (W.R.O., Nat. Arch., G.H.Q. station returns). 195
Students' Army Training Corps, the—discipline circular, Oct. 14, 1918 (W.R.O., Nat. Arch.). 228
Students' Army Training Corps, vocational section of—report data contained in vols. I, II, III, IV, (W.R.O., Nat. Arch.). 243
Territorial Departments and Coast Artillery Districts, data on (W.W. I Gp., Hist. Div., S.S.U.S.A.). 427
Territorial Departments, command lists of—for period 1917 to 1919 (W.W. I Gp., Hist. Div., S.S.U.S.A., rec. ref. book 6). 306
Universities, Colleges, and Professional Schools, 1917–18, statistics of (N.W.C. Libr.). 227
Western Department, annual reports of—for the fiscal years 1917, 1918, 1919, 1920 (W.D. Rec. Br., A.G.O., Staff Rec. Sec. No. 1, 703 Columbia Pike, rec. ref. A.G. 319.12). 223
Western Department, command list and National Guard data of—prepared in Hist. Sec., A.W.C. (W.W. I Gp., Hist. Div., S.S. U.S.A.). 236
Western Department, monthly returns of—for period 1917 to 1919 (W.R.O., Nat. Arch.). 207
Western Department, Southern California Border Patrol District, station list and troop list of—prepared in Hist. Sec., A.W.C. (W.W. I Gp., Hist. Div., S.S.U.S.A.). 234
Western Department, station list of—folder forming part of Study on Military Activities in the U. S. during World War I, by Lt. Col. Marcel F. J. Brunow, A.G.D. (W.W. I Gp., Hist. Div., S.S.U.S.A.). 235
Western Department, troops list of—prepared in Hist. Sec., A.W.C. (W.W. I Gp., Hist. Div., S.S.U.S.A.). 237

TRANSPORTATION SERVICE:

Port and Zone Transportation Officer, Transportation Service, New York City, historical report of office of (W.R.O., Nat. Arch.). 124
Port of Embarkation, Army Supply Base, Norfolk, Va., history of (W.R.O., Nat. Arch., rec. ref. 18-11.4). 116
Port of Embarkation Hoboken, N. J., annual report of—for the fiscal year 1918 (W.R.O., Nat. Arch.). 120
Idem—for the fiscal year 1919 (W.R.O., Nat. Arch.). 121
Idem—for the fiscal year 1920 (W.R.O., Nat. Arch.). 121½
Port of Embarkation Hoboken, N. J., historical narrative of (W.R.O., Nat. Arch.). 117
Port of Embarkation Hoboken, N. J., information folder of—containing extracts from official documents (W.W. I Gp., Hist. Div., S.S.U.S.A.). 178
Port of Embarkation Newport News, Va., general report on—September 1, 1918 (W.R.O., Nat. Arch.). 118
Port of Embarkation Newport News, Va., history of—chapters III, IV, V, VI, VII (W.R.O., Nat. Arch.). 119
Port of Embarkation Newport News, Va., information folder of—containing extracts from official documents (W.W. I Gp., Hist. Div., S.S.U.S.A.). 179
Transport Service, a history of the—by Vice Admiral Albert Gleaves, U. S. Navy (N.W.C. Libr.). 127

WAR DEPARTMENT:

America's Munitions, 1917–18, report of Benedict Crowell, the Assistant Secretary of War, Director of Munitions (N.W.C. Libr.). 1
Annual Reports, for the fiscal years 1916, 1917, 1918, 1919, 1920 (N.W.C. Libr.). 2-5½
Army List and Directory, April 20, 1917 (N.W.C. Libr.). 98

Source No.

Idem, for period February 1, 1919, to December 1, 1919 (N.W.C. Libr.). 214
Army of the United States, the—by Theo. F. Rodenbough, Bvt. Brig. Gen. U.S.A., and William L. Haskin, Maj. 1st Arty., 1896 (N.W.C. Libr.). 182
Army of the United States, dictionary of the—by Charles K. Gardner (N.W.C. Libr.). 183
Army Regulations 1913, corrected to April 15, 1917 (N.W.C. Libr.). 185
Economic Agencies of the War of 1917, a handbook of—monograph No. 3, Hist. Br., W.P. Div., G.S., 1919 (N.W.C. Libr.). 8
Economic and Industrial Support of Our National Effort in War, methods of securing and controlling the (N.W.C. Libr., rec. ref. 345-3). 7
Economic and Industrial Support of War (N.W.C. Libr., rec. ref. 384-6). 6
Economic Mobilization in the United States, chart of—July 16, 1917, showing structure of Government (W.R.O., Nat. Arch.). 10
Idem—October 3, 1917, showing activities of the several Government agencies (W.R.O., Nat. Arch.). 11
Economic Mobilization in the United States for the War of 1917, Monograph No. 2, Hist. Br., W.P. Div., G.S., 1918 (N.W.C. Libr.). 9
Final Report of Gen. John J. Pershing, September 1, 1919 (N.W.C. Libr.). 189
General Orders, Bulletins, and Circulars for period 1916–20 (N.W.C. Libr). 12-14
Official Army Register, December 1, 1918 (N.W.C. Libr.). 100
Secretary of the Treasury, annual report of the—on the state of the finances for the fiscal year 1930 (W.W. I Gp., Hist. Div., S.S.U.S.A.). 264
Secretary of War, report of the—to the President, 1921 (N.W.C. Libr.). 173
War Department, general history of the—by Hamersley (N.W.C. Libr.). 184½
War Department, history of the—by L. D. Ingersoll, 1879 (N.W.C. Libr.). 184
War Department Organization, by Benedict Crowell, February 2, 1920 (N.W.C. Libr., rec. ref. 6-4, No. 19). 15
War Department, organization chart of the—April 6, 1917 (W.R.O., Nat. Arch., rec. ref. 7-13.5, A.G.O.). 17, 18, 94
Idem—November 11, 1918 (W.R.O., Nat. Arch., rec. ref. R-200-0.1, A.G.O.). 19
War Department, report of Committee No. 1 (N.W.C. Libr., rec. ref. 3-1940-1). 20
War Department, subject index of the general orders of the—volume I, 1809 to 1860; volume II, 1861 to 1880; volume III, 1881 to 1900 (N.W.C. Libr.). 203
War Department and the General Staff, reorganization of the—charts showing principal stages from April 6, 1917 to August 12, 1919 (N.W.C. Libr., rec. ref. 114). 16
War Department General Staff and Bureaus, command lists of—1917 to 1919 (W.W. I Gp., Hist. Div., S.S.U.S.A., rec. ref. book 7). 169, 307
War Department Telephone Directories, issues of—April 27, 1918; July 22, 1918; November 15, 1918; January 18, 1919; March 22, 1919; July 19, 1919 (N.W.C. Libr.). 92

WAR DEPARTMENT GENERAL STAFF:

Army, authorized strength of the—January 28, 1919 (W.R.O., Nat. Arch., W.P. Div., G.S.). 196
Army Supply Problem, by Maj. Gen. George W. Burr, Assistant Chief of Staff, Director of Purchase and Storage (N.W.C. Libr., rec. ref. G-4, No. 9, 1919–20). 72
Army Supply System, reorganization of the—memorandum for the Chief of Staff, July 18, 1918 (W.R.O., Nat. Arch., rec. ref. 7-46.1, A.G.O.). 58

Source No.

Chief of Staff, United States Army, report of—for period April 6, 1917, to June 30, 1919 (W.R.O., Nat. Arch.). 200
Composition of the Army, as of November 11, 1918; statistical data, War Department expenditures, prepared by Stat. Br., W.D.G.S., June 28, 1919 (W.R.O., Nat. Arch.). 187
Demobilization 1918–19, description of War Department's system of demobilization (N.W.C. Libr., rec. ref. 160-9). 42
Duties and Responsibilities of the War Department General Staff and Its Relations to the Office of the Assistant Secretary of War (N.W.C. Libr., rec. ref. 114-32). 21
Equipment Branch, War Department General Staff, by Col. R. E. Wyllie, G. S. (N.W.C. Libr., rec. ref. G-1-16, 1920). 34
General Staff Corps Personnel, consolidated lists for November 1918, December 1918, February 1919, March 1919, April 1919, May 1919 (N.W.C. Libr.). 29
General Staff Functions, organization and methods (N.W.C. Libr., rec. ref. 343-1). 22
General Staff of the Army of the United States, legislative history of the—from 1775 to 1901 (N.W.C. Libr.). 202
Historical Branch, War Plans Division, historical data of (W.W. I Gp., Hist. Div., S.S.U.S.A., correspondence file 3336). 104
History of the General Staff, summary of—with supporting exhibits (N.W.C. Libr.). 33
Industrial Demobilization (W.R.O., Nat. Arch., rec. ref. 7-46.1, A.G.O.). 53
Military Intelligence Division, the—by Brig. Gen. M. Churchill, G.S., September 4, 1919 (N.W.C. Libr., rec. ref. G-2, No. 35, 1919–20). 43
Military Intelligence Division, functions of the—with brief history, October 1, 1918 (N.W.C. Libr., rec. ref. 117-3A). 44
Military Intelligence Division, organization data of (W.R.O., Nat. Arch., rec. ref. 7-46.1, A.G.O.). 90
Military Intelligence Division, work and activities of the—October 1, 1918 (N.W.C. Libr., rec. ref. 117-3B). 101
Military Intelligence Section, War College Division, organization of the (N.W.C. Libr., rec. ref. 639-145). 45
Mobilization of the Emergency Army, by Maj. Gen. Henry Jervey, Chief of Operations Division, General Staff (N.W.C. Libr., rec. ref. G-1, No. 15, 1920). 41
Officers to be Detailed in General Staff, September 19, 1917 (N.W.C. Libr., rec. ref. 8261-187). 30
Operations Branch, Operations Division, General Staff, report of—for period of the war, 1917–19; mobilization, training, movement overseas, and demobilization (N.W.C. Libr., rec. ref. No. 18, 1919–20). 35
Operations Branch, Operations Division, General Staff, résumé of activities of—for period July 1, 1918 to June 30, 1919 (N.W.C. Libr., rec. ref. 174-5). 108
Operations Branch, report of activities of the—for the fiscal year ending June 30, 1919 (W.R.O., Nat. Arch.). 49A
Operations Division, General Staff, history of organization of (W.R.O., Nat. Arch., rec. ref. 7-13.5, A.G.O.). 88, 105
Operations Division, General Staff, organization of the—October 31, 1918, and August 31, 1919 (W.R.O., Nat. Arch., rec. ref. 7-13.5, A.G.O.). 93
Organization and Duties of General Staff (N.W.C. Libr., rec. ref. 131-180). 25
Idem (N.W.C. Libr., rec. ref. 181-220). 26
Organization Charts of the War Department General Staff, from November 1903 to May 1, 1929 (N.W.C. Libr., rec. ref. 114-39-C). 24
Organization of General Staff, from 1903 to 1929, showing chiefs of divisions, branches, or other subdivisions by name (N.W.C. Libr., rec. ref. 114-39-D). 27

CALENDAR 1917

JANUARY

Sun	M	Tu	W	Th	F	Sat
	1	2	3	4	5	6
7	8	9	10	11	12	13
14	15	16	17	18	19	20
21	22	23	24	25	26	27
28	29	30	31			

FEBRUARY

Sun	M	Tu	W	Th	F	Sat
				1	2	3
4	5	6	7	8	9	10
11	12	13	14	15	16	17
18	19	20	21	22	23	24
25	26	27	28			

MARCH

Sun	M	Tu	W	Th	F	Sat
				1	2	3
4	5	6	7	8	9	10
11	12	13	14	15	16	17
18	19	20	21	22	23	24
25	26	27	28	29	30	31

APRIL

Sun	M	Tu	W	Th	F	Sat
1	2	3	4	5	6	7
8	9	10	11	12	13	14
15	16	17	18	19	20	21
22	23	24	25	26	27	28
29	30					

MAY

Sun	M	Tu	W	Th	F	Sat
		1	2	3	4	5
6	7	8	9	10	11	12
13	14	15	16	17	18	19
20	21	22	23	24	25	26
27	28	29	30	31		

JUNE

Sun	M	Tu	W	Th	F	Sat
					1	2
3	4	5	6	7	8	9
10	11	12	13	14	15	16
17	18	19	20	21	22	23
24	25	26	27	28	29	30

JULY

Sun	M	Tu	W	Th	F	Sat
1	2	3	4	5	6	7
8	9	10	11	12	13	14
15	16	17	18	19	20	21
22	23	24	25	26	27	28
29	30	31				

AUGUST

Sun	M	Tu	W	Th	F	Sat
			1	2	3	4
5	6	7	8	9	10	11
12	13	14	15	16	17	18
19	20	21	22	23	24	25
26	27	28	29	30	31	

SEPTEMBER

Sun	M	Tu	W	Th	F	Sat
						1
2	3	4	5	6	7	8
9	10	11	12	13	14	15
16	17	18	19	20	21	22
23	24	25	26	27	28	29
30						

OCTOBER

Sun	M	Tu	W	Th	F	Sat
	1	2	3	4	5	6
7	8	9	10	11	12	13
14	15	16	17	18	19	20
21	22	23	24	25	26	27
28	29	30	31			

NOVEMBER

Sun	M	Tu	W	Th	F	Sat
				1	2	3
4	5	6	7	8	9	10
11	12	13	14	15	16	17
18	19	20	21	22	23	24
25	26	27	28	29	30	

DECEMBER

Sun	M	Tu	W	Th	F	Sat
						1
2	3	4	5	6	7	8
9	10	11	12	13	14	15
16	17	18	19	20	21	22
23	24	25	26	27	28	29
30	31					

CALENDAR 1918

JANUARY

Sun	M	Tu	W	Th	F	Sat
		1	2	3	4	5
6	7	8	9	10	11	12
13	14	15	16	17	18	19
20	21	22	23	24	25	26
27	28	29	30	31		

FEBRUARY

Sun	M	Tu	W	Th	F	Sat
					1	2
3	4	5	6	7	8	9
10	11	12	13	14	15	16
17	18	19	20	21	22	23
24	25	26	27	28		

MARCH

Sun	M	Tu	W	Th	F	Sat
					1	2
3	4	5	6	7	8	9
10	11	12	13	14	15	16
17	18	19	20	21	22	23
24	25	26	27	28	29	30
31						

APRIL

Sun	M	Tu	W	Th	F	Sat
	1	2	3	4	5	6
7	8	9	10	11	12	13
14	15	16	17	18	19	20
21	22	23	24	25	26	27
28	29	30				

MAY

Sun	M	Tu	W	Th	F	Sat
			1	2	3	4
5	6	7	8	9	10	11
12	13	14	15	16	17	18
19	20	21	22	23	24	25
26	27	28	29	30	31	

JUNE

Sun	M	Tu	W	Th	F	Sat
						1
2	3	4	5	6	7	8
9	10	11	12	13	14	15
16	17	18	19	20	21	22
23	24	25	26	27	28	29
30						

JULY

Sun	M	Tu	W	Th	F	Sat
	1	2	3	4	5	6
7	8	9	10	11	12	13
14	15	16	17	18	19	20
21	22	23	24	25	26	27
28	29	30	31			

AUGUST

Sun	M	Tu	W	Th	F	Sat
				1	2	3
4	5	6	7	8	9	10
11	12	13	14	15	16	17
18	19	20	21	22	23	24
25	26	27	28	29	30	31

SEPTEMBER

Sun	M	Tu	W	Th	F	Sat
1	2	3	4	5	6	7
8	9	10	11	12	13	14
15	16	17	18	19	20	21
22	23	24	25	26	27	28
29	30					

OCTOBER

Sun	M	Tu	W	Th	F	Sat
		1	2	3	4	5
6	7	8	9	10	11	12
13	14	15	16	17	18	19
20	21	22	23	24	25	26
27	28	29	30	31		

NOVEMBER

Sun	M	Tu	W	Th	F	Sat
					1	2
3	4	5	6	7	8	9
10	11	12	13	14	15	16
17	18	19	20	21	22	23
24	25	26	27	28	29	30

DECEMBER

Sun	M	Tu	W	Th	F	Sat
1	2	3	4	5	6	7
8	9	10	11	12	13	14
15	16	17	18	19	20	21
22	23	24	25	26	27	28
29	30	31				

CALENDAR 1919

JANUARY

Sun	M	Tu	W	Th	F	Sat
			1	2	3	4
5	6	7	8	9	10	11
12	13	14	15	16	17	18
19	20	21	22	23	24	25
26	27	28	29	30	31	

FEBRUARY

Sun	M	Tu	W	Th	F	Sat
						1
2	3	4	5	6	7	8
9	10	11	12	13	14	15
16	17	18	19	20	21	22
23	24	25	26	27	28	

MARCH

Sun	M	Tu	W	Th	F	Sat
						1
2	3	4	5	6	7	8
9	10	11	12	13	14	15
16	17	18	19	20	21	22
23	24	25	26	27	28	29
30	31					

APRIL

Sun	M	Tu	W	Th	F	Sat
		1	2	3	4	5
6	7	8	9	10	11	12
13	14	15	16	17	18	19
20	21	22	23	24	25	26
27	28	29	30			

MAY

Sun	M	Tu	W	Th	F	Sat
				1	2	3
4	5	6	7	8	9	10
11	12	13	14	15	16	17
18	19	20	21	22	23	24
25	26	27	28	29	30	31

JUNE

Sun	M	Tu	W	Th	F	Sat
1	2	3	4	5	6	7
8	9	10	11	12	13	14
15	16	17	18	19	20	21
22	23	24	25	26	27	28
29	30					

JULY

Sun	M	Tu	W	Th	F	Sat
		1	2	3	4	5
6	7	8	9	10	11	12
13	14	15	16	17	18	19
20	21	22	23	24	25	26
27	28	29	30	31		

AUGUST

Sun	M	Tu	W	Th	F	Sat
					1	2
3	4	5	6	7	8	9
10	11	12	13	14	15	16
17	18	19	20	21	22	23
24	25	26	27	28	29	30
31						

SEPTEMBER

Sun	M	Tu	W	Th	F	Sat
	1	2	3	4	5	6
7	8	9	10	11	12	13
14	15	16	17	18	19	20
21	22	23	24	25	26	27
28	29	30				

OCTOBER

Sun	M	Tu	W	Th	F	Sat
			1	2	3	4
5	6	7	8	9	10	11
12	13	14	15	16	17	18
19	20	21	22	23	24	25
26	27	28	29	30	31	

NOVEMBER

Sun	M	Tu	W	Th	F	Sat
						1
2	3	4	5	6	7	8
9	10	11	12	13	14	15
16	17	18	19	20	21	22
23	24	25	26	27	28	29
30						

DECEMBER

Sun	M	Tu	W	Th	F	Sat
	1	2	3	4	5	6
7	8	9	10	11	12	13
14	15	16	17	18	19	20
21	22	23	24	25	26	27
28	29	30	31			

PIN: 062756-000